Object-Oriented Client/Server Internet Environments

The Modern IT Infrastructure

Amjad Umar, Ph.D.
Bell Communications Research (Bellcore)
Piscataway, New Jersey

To join a Prentice Hall PTR internet mailing list,
point to: **http://www.prenhall.com/register**

Prentice Hall PTR
Upper Saddle River, NJ 07458
http://www.prenhall.com

Library of Congress Cataloging-in-Publication Data

Umar, Amjad.
   Object-oriented client/server Internet environments / Amjad Umar.
      p.   cm.
   Includes bibliographical references and index.
   ISBN 0-13-375544-4
   1. Client/server computing. 2. Object-oriented methods (Computer
science) 3. Internet (Computer network) I. Title.
QA76.9.C55U53   1997
004'.36--dc21   96-38139
                                CIP

Editorial/production supervision: *Eileen Clark*
Cover design director: *Jerry Votta*
Cover design: *Design Source*
Manufacturing manager: *Alexis Heyd*t
Acquisitions editor: *Paul Becker*
Editorial Assistant: *Maureen Diana*
Marketing Manager: *Dan Rush*

© 1997 by Prentice Hall PTR
Prentice-Hall, Inc.
A Simon & Schuster Company
Upper Saddle River, New Jersey 07458

The publisher offers discounts on this book when ordered in bulk quantities.
For more information, contact:

        Corporate Sales Department
        Prentice Hall PTR
        One Lake Street
        Upper Saddle River, NJ 07458
        Phone: 800-382-3419 Fax: 201-536-7141
        E-mail: corpsales@prenhall.com

Printed in the United States of America
10 9 8 7 6 5 4 3

ISBN 0-13-375544-4

Prentice-Hall International (UK) Limited, *London*
Prentice-Hall of Australia Pty. Limited, *Sydney*
Prentice-Hall Canada Inc., *Toronto*
Prentice-Hall Hispanoamericana, S.A., *Mexico*
Prentice-Hall of India Private Limited, *New Delhi*
Prentice-Hall of Japan, Inc., *Tokyo*
Simon & Schuster Asia Pte. Ltd., *Singapore*
Editora Prentice-Hall do Brasil, Ltda., *Rio de Janeiro*

The Book at a Glance

Trademark Acknowledgments

The following list recognizes the commercial and intellectual property of the trademark holders whose products are mentioned in this book. Omission from this list is inadvertent:

ActiveX is a trademark of Microsoft Corporation

Adapt/X Harness is a trademark of Bellcore

Adapt/X Traxway is a trademark of Bellcore

AIX is a trademark of IBM Corporation

CORBA is a trademark of Object Management Group

DB2 is a trademark of IBM Corporation

DCE is a trademark of Open Software Foundation

DSOM is a trademark of IBM Corporation

EDA/SQL is a trademark of Information Builders, Inc.

Encina is a trademark of IBM Corporation

Flowmark is a trademark of IBM Corporation

HotJava is a trademark of Sun Microsystems

IPX/SPX is a trademark of Novell Corporation

Java is a trademark of Sun Microsystems

Lotus Notes is a trademark of IBM Corporation

NetBIOS is a trademark of IBM Corporation

NetWare is a trademark of Novell Corporation

ODBC is a trademark of Microsoft Corporation

OLE is a trademark of Microsoft Corporation

OpenMail is a trademark of Hewlett Packard

Orbix is a trademark of Iona Technologies

UNIX is a registered trademark licensed exclusively through X/Open Company, Ltd.

WebObjects is a trademark of NeXT Corporation

Windows is a trademark of Microsoft Corporation

Disclaimer

This book presents a broad picture of information technologies as they relate to distributed systems. The material has been compiled and prepared as a textbook for computer and information-systems students and as a reference for information technology practitioners and managers. The views and opinions presented in this book are solely those of the author and do not represent the views of Bell Communications Research, Inc. (Bellcore). The names of the vendor products mentioned should not be construed as a recommendation from Bellcore. Bellcore does not provide comparative analysis or evaluation of products or suppliers. Any mention of products or suppliers in this book is done where necessary for the sake of scientific accuracy and precision, or for background information to a point-of-technology discussion, or to provide an example of a technology for illustrative purposes, and should not be viewed or construed as either positive or negative commentary on that product or supplier, neither should the inclusion of a product or a supplier in this book, nor the omission of a product or supplier on the part of the author.

Dedicated to my family:

my loving wife Dolorese, fond memories of my parents, and the rest of the gang.

About the Author

Dr. Amjad Umar is a Senior Scientist at Bell Communications Research, Inc. (Bellcore) and an Adjunct Professor at Rutgers University, Stevens Institute of Technology, and Fordham Graduate School of Business. At Bellcore, he specializes in distributed systems and consults/leads projects in middleware for advanced data networks, data reconciliation, Web access to corporate resources, distributed databases, and legacy system reengineering. As an Adjunct Professor, he teaches graduate-level courses in distributed systems, networks, and object-oriented technologies. He has also developed and taught numerous industrial seminars in client/server systems, distributed computing, networks, and databases for the telecommunications industry, the Society of Manufacturing Engineers, U.S. Department of Navy, and Frost and Sullivan (England). He is the author of two other books: *Distributed Computing and Client-Server Systems* (Prentice Hall, 1993) and *Application (Re)Engineering: Building Web-based Applications and Dealing with Legacies* (Prentice Hall 1997). Before joining Bellcore, he was on the faculty at the University of Michigan (Dearborn and Ann Arbor campuses), where he received the Distinguished Faculty award. His prior work experience includes management of a statewide computing network and development/consulting assignments with manufacturing organizations, educational institutions, and organizations in England, Singapore, China, and Canada. He has an M.S. in Computer, Information, and Control Engineering and a Ph.D. in Industrial and Operations Engineering (major in Information Systems Engineering) from the University of Michigan.

TABLE OF CONTENTS

PART II: UNDERSTANDING THE MIDDLEWARE

Chapter 3: Basic C/S Middleware and OSF DCE

Chapter 5: Distributed-Data Management and Remote SQL Middleware

Chapter 6: Client/Server Transaction Processing

Chapter 7: Distributed Objects (CORBA and OLE/ActiveX)

Chapter 8: Mobile Computing, Groupware, Multimedia, and Legacy Data Access Middleware

Chapter 9: Putting the Pieces Together—A Synthesis

PART III: TUTORIALS ON SPECIAL TOPICS

Chapter 10: Object-Oriented Concepts and Technologies—A Tutorial

Chapter 11: Network Technologies and Architecture—A Tutorial

Preface

Book Objectives and Highlights

The basic premise of this book is that the applications of today and tomorrow will be increasingly based on three fundamental technologies: object orientation, client/server, and Internet (especially World Wide Web). The focus of this book is on the infrastructure (environment) that supports these applications (we call this, for a lack of better term, the object-oriented client/server Internet environment). In particular, we concentrate on the complex and crucial enabling technologies known as "middleware." These technologies provide business-unaware services to enable the modern distributed applications and services. There is no "one size fits all" solution at present; thus the modern environments will continue to consist of numerous middleware components such as Web browsers, SQL servers, client/server transaction processors, OSF/DCE, CORBA, OLE, mobile computing middleware, distributed-multimedia middleware, Lotus Notes, workflow software, and mediators ("surround technologies") for access/integration of legacy systems. Therefore, it is extremely important to concentrate on interrelationships instead of detailed discussion of one topic.

The objective of this book is to discuss the key enabling technologies, their characteristics, and their interrelationships. Our particular focus is on middleware, owing to its importance and complexity. We will define middleware, establish its role, discuss the key players in the middleware field, and show how the middleware components interrelate with other building blocks such as network services and applications. The book is intended as a guide and a tutorial for the IT managers and practitioners who are involved in IT engineering and reengineering. It has been, and can be, used as a text or a reference book in university courses. The topics discussed are shown in the sidebar "Book Outline."

This book has the following key features:

- A framework for discussion is introduced early to serve as a roadmap for study and to guide the analysis and synthesis of the existing and evolving technologies.

- Tutorials on network technologies and object-oriented concepts are included so that the book can be used by experienced professionals as well as novices.

- A single case study is introduced in the first chapter and developed throughout the book to illustrate the topics discussed. Hints and outline solutions are suggested for the case study. In addition, several other examples and case studies are included in each chapter.

- Each chapter highlights key points and includes several sidebars for quick study.

- Each chapter concludes with a discussion of state of the market (e.g., available products), state of the practice (e.g., case studies and examples), and state of the art (e.g., standards and continuing research).

- Each chapter is written as a self-contained tutorial with numerous references for additional studies.

Book Outline

PART I: GETTING STARTED

Chapter 1: The Big Picture

Chapter 2: Information-Technology Building Blocks

PART II: UNDERSTANDING THE MIDDLEWARE

Chapter 3: Basic C/S Middleware and OSF DCE

Chapter 4: Internet and World Wide Web

Chapter 5: Distributed-Data Management and SQL Middleware

Chapter 6: Client/Server Transaction Processing

Chapter 7: Distributed Objects (CORBA and OLE/ActiveX)

Chapter 8: Mobile Computing, Groupware, Multimedia, and Legacy Access Middleware

Chapter 9: Putting the Pieces Together—A Synthesis

APPENDICES: TUTORIALS ON SPECIAL TOPICS

Chapter 10: Object-Oriented Concepts and Technologies—A Tutorial

Chapter 11: Network Technologies and Network Architectures—A Tutorial

---

The readers of this book should be able to develop an understanding of the key components of the object-oriented client/server Internet environments, the interrelationships between its components, and their role in enabling the modern distributed enterprises.

This book can be used as a guide to modern distributed computing platforms. However, discussion of application issues is beyond its scope. A companion book *Application (Re)Engineering: Building Web-based Applications and Dealing with Legacies,* Prentice Hall concentrates on application issues and covers topics such as methodology for application engineering/reengineering, Web-based application development considerations, enterprise data architectures, software application architectures, strategies to deal with legacy applications, Web access and integration of legacy systems, data warehouses, and application migration/transition issues. These two are intended as complimentary books.

Intended Audience and Recommended Usage

This book is based on a synthesis of experience gained from three different sources. First, extensive project-management, consulting, and system-integration assignments in the recent years in client/server systems, object-oriented technologies, Web-based applications, middleware evaluation, legacy data access, data warehousing, and data migration. Second, development and teaching of industrial training courses on client/server technologies and distributed systems that have been taught several times in the telecommunications industry and general IT community. Finally, teaching of graduate-level special- topics courses in distributed systems for IT majors and computer-science students. This experience indicates that this book should be useful as a reference for most IT managers and practitioners and also as a textbook for university courses and industrial training seminars. Specifically, this book should be of value to:

- Architects and designers of information services (application designers, database designers, network designers)
- Analysts and consultants of information technologies
- Planners of IT infrastructure and platforms
- Technical-support personnel
- Managers of information technologies (CIO, MIS managers, database administrators, application- development managers).
- System integrators who combine databases, networks, and application among platforms.
- Teachers of university courses in information technologies
- Technical trainers for professional-development courses in information technologies
- Researchers in information technologies who need a broad coverage of the subject matter
- Students for an introduction to the subject matter with numerous references for additional studies

Depending on the reader's background and interest, the book can be used in a variety of ways. Perhaps the best way is to go through it sequentially and read the tutorials in Part III on an as-needed basis.

Two suggested outlines follow: one for a university course and one for a two-day professional training course. These outlines are based on experience of teaching several university courses and industrial seminars in the recent years (topics have naturally evolved over time). To assure a clear understanding, these courses are very case-study/ project intensive.

University Course Outline: Modern Distributed Computing Platforms

Week	Topic	Reading
1	Introduction	Chapter 1
2	Network Technologies	Chapter 11
3	Network Architectures	Chapter 11
4	IT Building Blocks	Chapter 2
5	Basic Client/Server and OSF DCE	Chapter 3
6	Internet and World Wide Web	Chapter 4
7	Distributed-Data Management	Chapter 5
8	Midterm Examination (or Project 1 Due)	
9	Client/Server Transaction Processing	Chapter 6
10	Object-Oriented Concepts	Chapter 10
11	Distributed Object Technologies	Chapter 7
12	Emerging Technologies (Mobile Computing, Groupware, Distributed Multimedia)	Chapter 8
13	Synthesis	Chapter 9
14	Conclusions and Wrapup	
15	Final Examination (or Project 2 Due)	

Professional Training Course: Emerging Distributed Computing Technologies

Session	Topic	Duration	Reading
1	Introduction	1 Hour	Chapter 1
2	Network Technologies and Architectures	2 Hours	Chapter 11
3	IT Building Blocks	1.5 Hour	Chapter 2
4	Basic Client/Server and OSF DCE	1.5 Hour	Chapter 3
5	Internet and World Wide Web	1.5 Hour	Chapter 4
6	Distributed-Data Management	1 Hour	Chapter 5
7	Client/Server Transaction Processing	1 Hour	Chapter 6
8	Object-Oriented Concepts and Distributed Object Technologies	2 Hours	Chapter 10 & Chapter 7
9	Emerging Technologies (Mobile Computing, Groupware, Distributed Multimedia)	1 Hour	Chapter 8
10	Synthesis	0.5 Hour	Chapter 9
11	Case Studies and Wrapup	1 Hour	

Conventions Used

We will use the following conventions in this book. **_Bold italics_** are used to indicate definition of new terms, _italics_ are used for emphasis and **bold letters** are used for subject headings.

Acknowledgments

Many of my colleagues and friends at Bellcore graciously agreed to review specific chapters for content and/or style. Here is an alphabetical list of the reviewers who commented on at least one chapter (some reviewed four to five): Paul Ballman, Prasad Ganti, Joe Ghetie, Dr. Bruce Horowitz, Dr. George Karabatis, Frank Marchese, Malesh Mariswamy, Mike Meiner, Dr. Sharad Singhal, and Dr. Gomer Thomas. I really feel fortunate to have access to so many experts who are also very nice folks.

Dr. Andrew Herbert, Technical Director of the ANSA Consortium, patiently read through the entire manuscript and gave me extremely useful feedback. Very few have braved through this much material and survived.

In addition, many of my university friends read early drafts and made numerous suggestions. Professor Nabil Adams of Rutgers Graduate School of Business, Professor Ahmed Elmagarmid of Purdue University, Professor Peter Jurkat of the Stevens Institute of Technology, and Professor Irina Neuman of Fordham Graduate School of Business gave valuable suggestions about different topics.

I should not forget the contribution of many university students at Stevens Institute of Technology, Rutgers, and Fordham who "suffered" through very rough drafts of many chapters. In addition, many attendees of professional training seminars volunteered to review different chapters. The list of topics included in this book is based on extensive discussions with the university students and seminar attendees.

I want to express my gratitude toward my management (Dr. Satish Thatte, Rich Jacowleff, Jerry Surak, and Jack Simensen) for their understanding and support.

I should mention that I have really enjoyed working with Paul Becker as an editor and Eileen Clark as the production editor for this book. Paul, Eileen and I have become friends through numerous emails, letters, phone calls, and face to face meetings.

Finally, I want to thank Dolorese, my best friend, who also happens to be my wife. She has patiently seen me struggle through all of this and has advised and helped me at numerous occasions. It is simply impossible for me to engage in writing of this nature while working on a demanding full time job at Bellcore without her constant understanding and support.

Amjad Umar
Piscataway, New Jersey
umar@ctt.bellcore.com

P A R T   I

GETTING STARTED

1

The Big Picture

1.1   Introduction

Enterprises of the 1990s and beyond are typically characterized by flatter organizational structures, increased demands for flexibility, pressures to respond quickly to market conditions, intense local and global competition, and continued business-process reengineering and improvements for enterprise efficiency. To meet these and other competitive challenges, enterprises are increasingly relying on information technologies. We live in times where businesses are being fundamentally transformed through information technologies (ITs) [Davenport 1995, Henderson 1993, Keene 1991, Charan 1991]. Common examples can be found in almost all sectors ranging from small businesses (e.g., flower shops advertising over the Internet) to large international organizations (e.g., auto manufacturers, financial institutions, and the airlines relying exclusively on IT for the majority of their business).

So how will the IT landscape look in the next few years? The visions, even from different perspectives, seem to have the following key common characteristics [Bernstein 1996, Brodie 1995, Caldwell 1996, Javenpaa 1994, Kador 1996]:

- Increased use of distributed systems, especially client/server architectures
- Adoption of object-oriented technologies
- Widespread use of World Wide Web over Internet

In essence, the object-oriented, client/server, Internet-based (OCSI) applications are expected to support the enterprises of the 1990s and beyond. In fact, most of the applications being developed at present and in the near future will be based to some extent on the OCSI paradigm. According to this paradigm, the knowledge workers have desktop computers that are interconnected over fast digital networks. The information resources of corporations around the globe appear as objects on the workstation that can be created, viewed, modified, and deleted on an as-needed basis through Web browsers or other graphical user interfaces (GUI). For example, a worker can perform the following operations from his/her desktop or mobile computer:

- Review "inbox" that displays email, voice mail, magazines received (i.e., simulate a real mail box).
- Respond to urgent matters (these may appear as red flashing icons).
- Query the status of his/her projects, browse through a variety of information, and interact with multiple applications that may be dispersed around the globe (many of these applications and resources are "encapsulated" as objects).
- Participate in conference calls and video conferences.

This book concentrates on the infrastructure needed to support these applications. We will call this infrastructure, for lack of a better term, the ***object-oriented, client/server, Internet (OCSI) environment.*** What does an OCSI environment consist of? Well, obviously, we need computers and we need networks to interconnect the computers. But is that enough? What is the glue that ties all computers over networks together and gives the user an impression of a seamless pool of resources that may be physically distributed at different sites anywhere in the world? This glue, called the *middleware*, is the primary focus of this book. Middleware is the crucial enabling technology for the modern distributed enterprises that are increasingly relying on the combined power of Web, object orientation, and client/server to deliver business value. Without proper middleware, the visions of global information systems may qualify as hallucinations (after all, "there is a thin line between vision and hallucination" [Charan 1991]). In fact, the main reason we are as far along as we are in achieving this vision is the availability of off-the-shelf middleware from a variety of vendors.

An understanding of the environment and, in particular, the middleware is essential for modern organizations to fully realize the potential of emerging information technologies. Unfortunately, this environment itself is quite complex for several reasons: (a) it is not well defined (b) it consists of numerous components that are interrelated in a complex manner (c) it is typically "glued together" with different components from different suppliers because there is no "one size fits all" solution and (d) it is surrounded by a very confusing set of jargon and terms. For example, consider the IT "jungle" shown in Figure 1.1 (if you understand most of the terms and the interrelationships shown in this figure, then you probably do not need to read the rest of this book).

Figure 1.1 The IT Environment Jungle

Distributed Objects (CORBA, OLE/ActiveX, OpenDoc)

World Wide Web (Web browsers, Web servers, Web gateways)

Middleware for Mobile Computing, Multimedia, Groupware, and Legacy Access

Client/Server Transaction-Processing Middleware, Replication Servers

Distributed-Data Middleware (SQL Gateways, ODBC, DRDA)

Open Software Foundation's Distributed Computing Environment (OSF DCE)

Remote-Procedure Calls (RPC's), Remote SQL, Message-Oriented Middleware

Network Services (LU6.2, TCP/IP Sockets, NetBIOS)

? ? ? ? ?

The objective of this book is to explain the components and the interrelationships between the components of OCSI environments. In particular, we will focus on middleware and attempt to answer the following questions:

- What is middleware and why is it important?
- What are the different categories of middleware and what do they do?
- How do the different middleware components interrelate with each other, with the applications, and with other components of the infrastructure (e.g., networks)?
- Where can additional information be found?

This chapter gives a broad overview of the subject matter and is expected to set the tone for the rest of this book. We first start by establishing a framework for discussion that identifies the major components of information systems of today and tomorrow (Section 1.2). This framework will be refined and expanded as we proceed. Sections 1.3 and 1.4 explain the two essential compounds of the framework: applications and middleware. Section 1.5 describes the goals of this book in more detail and sketches out the overall approach. The chapter concludes by making general observations about middleware state of the art (research and development trends), state of the market (industrial products), and state of the practice (industrial examples).

Key Points

- *Object-oriented, client/server, Internet (OCSI) environment* provides the infrastructure needed to support modern distributed applications.

- OCSI environments combine three powerful technologies to deliver business value: Web is a natural technology for human-to-program interactions, OO is a natural technology for program-to-program interactions, and client/server will stay with us for a long time for distributing work among multiple machines.

- *Middleware* is a set of common business-unaware services that enable applications and end users to interact with each other across a network. In essence, middleware is the software that resides above the network and below the business-aware application software.

- The best-known example of middleware is email. Other examples are Web browsers, Lotus Notes, database gateways, DCE (Distributed Computing Environment), CORBA (Common Object Request Broker Architecture), OLE (Object Linking and Embedding), X.500 Directory Server, FTP (File Transfer Protocol), Telnet, NFS (Network File System), Novell's Netware, Information Builder's EDA/SQL, and screen scrapers.

- Middleware is a key enabler for information systems of today and tomorrow because it provides the services needed by modern applications. If you do not buy middleware for these services, then you have to write your own code (it is usually better to buy than to develop your own).

1.2   A Framework for Discussion

Figure 1.2 shows a simple framework that illustrates the role of IT in the enterprises of the 1990s and beyond. The framework consists of three high-level components and their role as drivers and enablers:

- Business processes
- Applications
- IT infrastructure (also known as IT platforms)

Figure 1.2 Interrelationships among Key Components

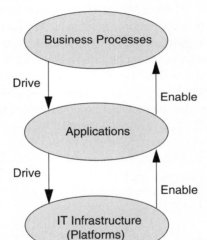

Business processes represent the day-to-day business-related activities of an enterprise (e.g., operating a cable TV company, manufacturing a car, publishing books, operating an airline, running a bank, providing mail delivery, teaching students, etc.). For example, if you want to open a training business, then business processes need to be established for advertising, enrolling students, scheduling classrooms, etc. Business processes support corporate goals and thus establish the requirements and the business drivers for the lower-level technology utilization. Business processes may be centralized or distributed. Business processes of most organizations are distributed among multiple sites (e.g., cars are designed in one place, assembled in many places, and shipped to dealers at several places).

Applications provide automated support to the business processes. Applications, also known as application systems, are *business aware* for the purpose of this book. For example, an airline reservation system contains business logic and data that is not the same as a hotel reservation system (business awareness). Applications also *provide business value to an enterprise*. Obviously, an airline reservation system provides business value to the airline business. Applications use information technologies to support the enterprise and thus enable the business processes. Modern enterprises use applications such as marketing support systems, order-processing and tracking systems, financial planning systems, electronic commerce systems, telecommunications provisioning systems, and real-time manufacturing control systems to gain/retain competitive edge, reduce costs, and improve management decision making. Applications consist of user data, a set of programs to access and manipulate the data, and user interfaces to invoke appropriate programs. An application may also be centralized or distributed. A *distributed application* consists of user interface, user data, and programs residing at different computers on a network.

Information-technology (IT) infrastructure is used to build, deploy, and operate the applications. IT infrastructure, also known as *IT platform,* consists of technologies such as computers, networks, databases, and transaction managers (we will discuss IT infrastructure in the next chapter). IT infrastructure enables the applications and is *business unaware*. For example, the same types of networks and computers are used in both airline reservation systems and hotel reservation systems. The focus of this book is on *middleware*, an increasingly important and, at the same time, bewildering component of the contemporary IT infrastructure. Middleware is needed to interconnect and support applications across a network (see the sidebar "Key Points"). Middleware services typically include directories, facilities to call remotely located procedures, and software to access and manipulate remotely located databases. Middleware services are commonly provided by specialized software packages (for example, Lotus Notes is a middleware package that supports groupware applications). However, middleware services may reside in a combination of database managers, computer operating systems, and transaction managers.

The simple framework presented in Figure 1.2 is refined in Figure 1.3. This framework highlights the following key points that are essential for IT managers and practitioners:

- The business processes provide the requirements and the business drivers that should drive the applications and the IT infrastructure.

- Applications enable the business processes, and IT infrastructure enables the applications. This must be kept in mind while making IT infrastructure choices.

- IT infrastructure (this includes middleware) does not add any direct business value. For example, installing a fast network may not help a company unless the network is used effectively to meet business needs.

- IT infrastructure enables applications and, if not handled properly, can disable applications and business processes. For example, owing to computer and network congestion, New York Stock Exchange trading traffic topped out at 608 million shares instead of reaching the daily maximum of 1.4 billion shares on October 20, 1987.[1]

---

1. M. Hayes, "The Tale of Two Cities," *Information Week,* December 1995, pp. 58–64.

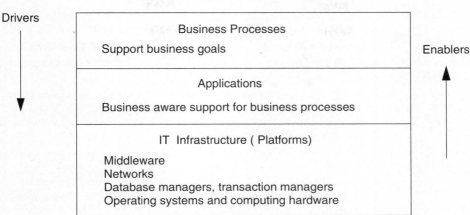

Figure 1.3 A Framework for IT's Role

- A key role of the IT infrastructure in the 1990s and beyond is to enable enterprisewide distributed applications to support the distributed business processes. For example, business processes are typically distributed to support a dispersed business topology (e.g., different branch and local offices). However, many applications that support these distributed business processes are still centralized, owing to lack of adequate IT infrastructure (e.g., slow/congested networks and lack of tools to manage and support distributed applications).

- Availability of off-the-shelf middleware will serve as a catalyst to enable enterprisewide distributed applications. For example, although the concepts of client/server- based distributed applications is not new, the availability of vendor-provided middleware packages fueled the client/server revolution.

We will refine this framework throughout this book and use it as a roadmap.

1.3   Applications in the 1990s and Beyond

Applications, as stated previously, provide automated support to the business processes and are *business aware*. Applications in contemporary enterprises are multidimensional and complex. This section presents a taxonomy of modern applications, the key technologies being used in modern applications (i.e., object orientation, client/server, and Internet), and the promises/pitfalls associated with these new technologies. The focus of this discussion is on enterprisewide applications and not on small home-entertainment type applications (many principles are applicable in different domains, but our emphasis is on enterprisewide applications).

Figure 1.4 A Classification of Applications

TYPE SPAN	Decision Support Applications	Operational Support Applications	Real Time Applications
Group/Depart-mental	Example: Regional marketing information system	Example: Regional inventory control system	Example: Video conferencing within a group
Enterprise wide	Example: Corporate data warehouse for product planning	Example: Enterprise wide cash management system	Example: Enterprise-wide network management
Inter-enterprise	Example: Web browsing over the Internet	Example: Electronic commerce over the Internet	Example: - Distributed multimedia over the Internet

1.3.1   Classification of Applications

For our purpose, we focus on two dimensions of applications: **type** and **span** (see Figure 1.4). Application types, for the purpose of our discussion, are subdivided into operational support, decision-support/retrieval, and real-time applications. The span indicates the level of usage (e.g., departmental applications, enterprisewide applications, and interenterprise applications).

Operational support applications support the day-to-day operational activities of an organization. A well-known example is the classical business data-processing applications, known as OLTP (on-line transaction processing). As the name implies, these applications support on-line users and require robust transaction-processing facilities such as logging, integrity control, and backup/recovery [Leff 1991]. OLTP applications are typically involved in the day-to-day operational activities such as order processing, purchasing, shipping, and inventory control. As a result, they tend to update data frequently and require immediate response.

Decision-support (retrieval) applications are primarily intended for a class of users known as "knowledge" workers and managers. A large body of management literature on decision-support systems has accumulated since the mid-1980s (see, for example, Turban's textbook [Turban 1995]). Decision-support applications focus on informational data to drive the business and not on operational data to help in day-to-day operations. Examples of decision-support applications are data warehouses, marketing-information systems, executive-information systems, and business planning systems.

Real-time applications are embedded in real-life activities such as manufacturing processing and telecommunications switching systems. While the operational support and decision-support applications provide information to users, the real-time applications *are part of* a real-life process. For this reason, these applications impose stringent requirements for performance (subsecond response time) and availability (continuous and often fault tolerant). Examples of real-time applications are video conferencing systems, interactive TV, manufacturing control systems, real-time market-data monitoring systems, command and control systems, and telecommunications network managers.

These applications can be used at different organizational levels (spans): **group/departmental level, enterprisewide,** and **interenterprise**. The group/departmental applications are developed and used within a workgroup or a department of an enterprise. These applications are typically developed around LANs and have used C/S technology effectively. The enterprisewide applications are used throughout an enterprise. These applications are typically heterogeneous, because they span a diverse array of computers (desktop PCs, PC servers, Apple Macintoshes, UNIX workstations and midrange computers, mainframes), networks (LANs, WANs), and database managers (Informix, Oracle, DB2). Utilization of C/S applications for large-enterprise networks is sparse at the time of this writing (corporate "Intranets" could change this). Interenterprise applications are used between organizations. A very common example of these applications is Internet-based applications using the Web browsers. Many of the Internet applications at the time of this writing are for decision support (e.g., browsing documents). It is expected that operational support applications over the Internet will become popular over the next few years.

1.3.2 Object-Oriented Client/Server Internet Applications

Currently, most of the new applications are being developed by combining three powerful concepts:

- Client/server,
- Object orientation, and increasingly
- Internet based (in particular, Web based)[2]

The client/server concept is used to describe communications between computing processes that are classified as service consumers (*clients*) and service providers (*servers*). For example, a spreadsheet on a desktop, acting as a client, can access a remotely located database, acting as a server, to analyze marketing information located on the remote database. Figure 1.5 presents a simple C/S model. The basic features of a C/S model are displayed in the sidebar "Features of a Client/Server Model" (we will discuss these features in detail in Chapter 2).

---

2. It is important to separate Internet from World Wide Web (WWW). Technically, WWW runs on top of the Internet.

Figure 1.5 Conceptual View of Client/Server

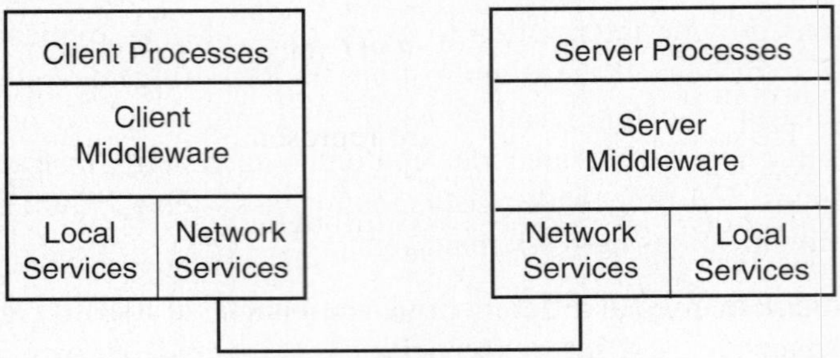

Client Processes		
Client Middleware		
Local Services	Network Services	

Server Processes		
Server Middleware		
Network Services	Local Services	

Simply stated, client/server environments allow application processes (business-aware programs and subroutines) at different sites to interactively exchange information (e.g., transfer funds, monitor the status of a robot, and query a database). Before C/S environments, application processes at different sites communicated through terminal emulation or file transfer. For example, consider a spreadsheet residing on a workstation which needs data from three different databases at three different computers. The steps in the "old days" were as follows:

1. Log on to computer 1.
2. Extract needed information from the database by using an extract program.
3. Download the data to the workstation by using a file-transfer package.
4. Repeat steps 1 through 3 for the other two computers.
5. Aggregate and consolidate data for use by the spreadsheet.
6. Now (finally) run the spreadsheet on the workstation.

In a C/S environment, the spreadsheet uses a client software package (e.g., Lotus Data Lens) which accesses the three remote databases *in real time* during the execution of the spreadsheet. The aforementioned steps 1 to 5 are bypassed.

Key Client/Server Features

The following features represent the core attributes of client/server:

1. Clients and servers are functional modules that represent a consumer/provider relationship.

2. For a given service , clients and servers do not reverse roles (i.e., a client stays a client and a server stays a server).

3. All information exchange between clients and servers is through messages (no global variables).

The following features are not required, but are typical:

4. Message exchange between clients and servers is typically interactive.

5. Clients and servers reside on different machines connected through a network.

Object orientation is being used widely to develop reusable software. The key concepts of the object-oriented paradigm are object, class, inheritance, encapsulation, abstraction, and polymorphism (see the sidebar "Object-Oriented Concepts" for definitions). The basic idea is to view information in software systems in terms of "natural" objects such as customers and sales regions. These "natural" objects are represented by "software" objects that can be easily created, viewed, used, modified, reused, and deleted over time. The goal is that the users view applications in terms of objects through graphical user interfaces, programmers develop codes that perform operations on objects, and database managers store, retrieve, and manipulate objects. Chapter 10 gives a short tutorial on object-oriented concepts and technologies.

Key Object-Oriented Concepts

Software Object: A piece of data surrounded by code (i.e., the data can only be accessed through code). This code is known as *methods* of an object. The data has certain *attributes* (e.g., name, address, age), and the methods are used to operate on these attributes.

Classes: A collection of like objects. A class acts as a template for similar objects (e.g., a class representing all Chevrolets). An object is an instance of a class.

Inheritance: Obtaining of properties by objects from other objects. Technically, inheritance allows you to create subclasses from parent classes. Subclasses inherit properties from parent classes. Subclasses can inherit multiple properties from multiple parent classes.

Encapsulation: The restriction of access to the object state via a well-defined interface (the operations). This involves a combination of two aspects: the grouping of object state and operation, and data hiding.

Abstraction: The ability to group associated entities according to common properties—for example, the set of instances belonging to a class.

Polymorphism: The ability of abstractions to overlap and intersect. A popular form of polymorphism is inclusion polymorphism, in which operations on a given type are also applicable to its subtype (for example, "start a printer" will start all types of printers). Inclusion polymorphism is often implemented via an inheritance mechanism.

We adopt the following definition of object oriented [Nicol 1993]:

Object oriented = encapsulation + abstraction + polymorphism

Nicol, J., et al., "Object Orientation in Heterogeneous Distributed Computing Systems," *IEEE Computer,* June 1993. pp. 57–67.

Internet-based applications have gained popularity owing to the tremendous growth of the World Wide Web, which allows GUI access to "resources" (i.e., data and programs) located in different sites. See the sidebar "Internet, Intranet, and World Wide Web." Technically, Internet is just a large TCP/IP network that interconnects a very large number of computers located around the globe. The *World Wide Web,* also known as the *Web*, runs on top of the Internet. The Web provides a GUI interface, known as a Web browser, that gives point-and-click access to information through hypertext links highlighted on the browser screen. Most of the Internet work at present is document-centric (i.e., you can retrieve and browse through articles, vendor announcements, stock quotes, etc.). However, Web gateways are being developed rapidly for providing access to corporate databases and applications through Web browsers.

The main appeal of Web for enterprisewide applications is that organizations can standardize on Web browsers for the end-user access. In other words, Web browsers can be used for user interfaces of applications in marketing, human resources, or engineering of an enterprise. In addition, the same Web interface can be used for applications that cross the company, industry, and country boundaries. We will discuss Web developments in Chapter 4.

An *object-oriented, client/server, Internet-based (OCSI)* application architecture combines these powerful technologies to deliver business functionality. Figure 1.6 shows an idealized view of these applications. *This view illustrates the key idea that the Web is a natural technology for human-to-program interactions, OO is a natural technology for program-to-program interactions, and SQL will stay with us for a long time for program-to-database interactions.* In particular, we make the following observations:

- The Web is used to access programs that may be located anywhere in the network. Although Web technology is being used heavily for document browsing, it will be used increasingly for corporate applications.

- The application programs are becoming increasingly OO with the popularity of OO programming languages such as C++, Smalltalk, and Java.These programs appear as objects that communicate with each other by using OO paradigm.

- The databases are largely non-OO. Existing databases are accessed typically through SQL or other data access technologies.

Figure 1.6 Ideal View of Contemporary Applications

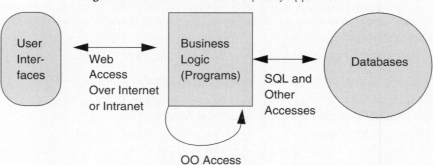

Internet, Intranets, and World Wide Web

- **Internet** is a collection of TCP/IP networks that are interconnected to give the appearance of a large global network.

- **Intranet** is a private Internet used by a corporation for its internal use (i.e., an internal TCP/IP network). Intranets are used to provide corporate services and they use the Web technologies, in addition to others (e.g., email, database access).

- **World Wide Web (WWW)**, also known as **Web**, operates on top of the Internet to support users and applications.

- World Wide Web is based on the following concepts and technologies:
    - Web servers house the resources (data, application programs).
    - Uniform Resource Locator (URL) is an address used by the Web to locate resources.
    - Hypertext Transfer Protocol (HTTP) is a protocol used by the Web browsers and Web servers to exchange information.
    - Hypertext Markup Language (HTML) is a language used to create hypertext documents that can be displayed on the browsers.
    - Web browsers are ubiquitous GUI tools that exploit HTTP, URL and HTML to access the Internet resources in a generic fashion.
    - Web navigation and search tools are used to "surf" the Internet.
    - Web gateways to non-Web resources are used to allow Web users to access non-Web resources (e.g., corporate databases).

- WWW's unique feature is that it makes hypermedia available on the Internet in what has evolved into a global information system.

- The same Web interface can be used for applications that cross the company, industry, and country boundaries.

- Java is a programming language designed to work on the Web. The main thing is that small Java applications (known as Java **applets)** can run on the Web browsers (i.e., the user desktops). This allows Web browsers to run applications at the user desktops instead of relying on remote operations at Web servers.

- Web access to relational databases is provided through "relational gateways" that serve as translators and mediators between Web browsers and relational database managers.

The OCSI applications are a transition stage between the "first-generation" C/S applications (these applications basically replaced local SQL calls with remote SQL calls) and the fully distributed object computing applications with Web interfaces (see Figure 1.7). Fully distributed Web object architectures view, through Web browsers, all application components, including databases, as objects that are dispersed over a network. These architectures offer many potential benefits to contemporary enterprises (see the next section), but it may be a while before we see them widely deployed in businesses. We can make the following additional observations from Figure 1.7:

- Most of the OO concepts at present are being used more on the client side of business logic because OO technology is very useful for GUI programming. There is no reason why OO technology cannot be equally useful on the server side, owing to the advances in distributed-object computing and OO databases.

- Object orientation is used in at least one component of the application architecture. At present, most of the OO concepts are utilized in developing graphical user interfaces.

- Client/server paradigm is used in at least one component of the application. In other words, user interfaces, application programs, and databases of an application are split across at least two machines.

- Web is fast becoming the primary user interface that will be used to access all information, including corporate databases.

- Object orientation, client/server, and Web technologies will coexist and evolve with time.

Figure 1.7 Evolution of Applications

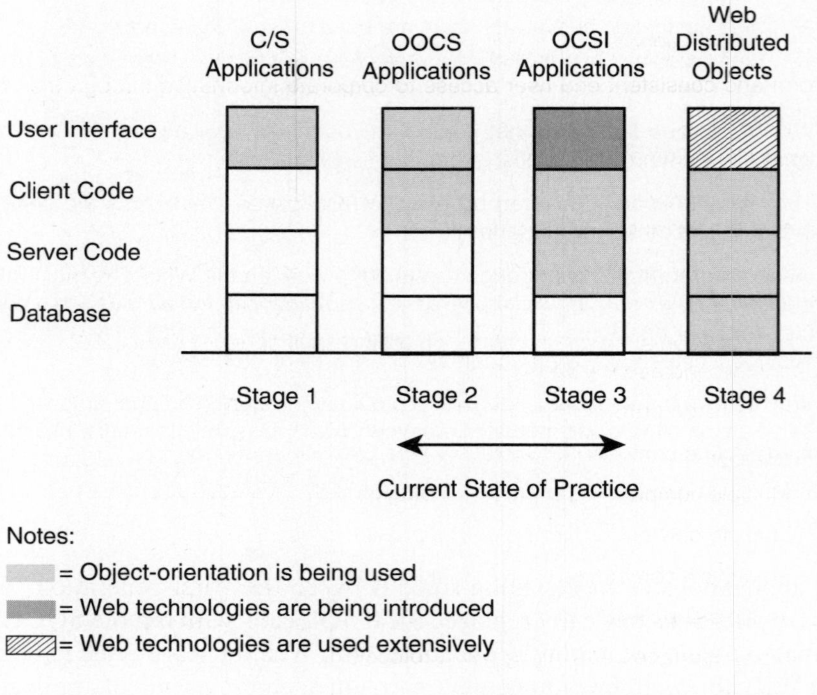

Notes:

▨ = Object-orientation is being used

▨ = Web technologies are being introduced

▨ = Web technologies are used extensively

1.3.3   Promises and Pitfalls

Applications that effectively combine the object-oriented, client/server, and Internet technologies provide many benefits to businesses. The key benefit is that they respond to the business pressures of maximum flexibility and availability. Given a suitable IT infrastructure, IT planners and architects can configure the applications by using mixtures of mainframes, midrange computers, and desktops/laptops to meet different business requirements and to respond to competitive pressures quickly. However, these applications introduce many challenges in management, performance, and security, among others. In other words, while there are many promises of using new technologies, they do have some potential pitfalls. Consequently, migration to new technologies should be evaluated very carefully (this issue is discussed in Umar [1997]).

A summary of key promises and pitfalls associated with this new breed of applications follows.

The key promises are:

- Flexibility, scalability, and evolutionary growth in supporting growing and ever-changing enterprises by seamlessly combining

    Desktop processing

    Departmental services

    Corporate services

- Uniform and consistent end-user access to corporate information through the ubiquitous Web technologies

- Increased end-user control by allowing users to have specialized clients

- Potential for improved availability and performance through functional specialization of servers, shared resources and configuration options

- More suitable for modern applications with sophisticated GUI user interfaces and multimedia presentations

- Industrial attention and interest leading to off-the-shelf servers, clients, tools, and a multitude of new services and applications

The main pitfalls to be considered are:

- More underlying complexity (hidden from the end users) due to:

    Multiple computing-platform technologies

    Multiple network technologies and architectures

    Many new components (e.g., "middleware")

    Multiple suppliers

    Many interfaces, standards, and protocols

- Many difficult management challenges (how to smoothly manage the aforementioned complexity)

- Increased interdependencies and points of failure creating many intricate error scenarios that are extremely difficult to detect and correct

- Higher software and staffing costs due to many hidden costs, multiple licenses and environments [DePompa 1995, Caldwell 1996]

- Security, performance, and interoperability issues

- A need for more coordination of discipline (databases, networks, operating systems)

Most of the trade and vendor literature is filled with the promises of the new technology, with very few mentions of the pitfalls. This seems to be changing somewhat, especially for the much-touted client/server systems. For example, see DePompa [1995]; Caldwell [1996]; "Dirty Downsizing," *Computerworld,* Special Report, August 10, 1992; the Standish Group conference on client/server failures; and "Where Do Client/Server Apps Go Wrong," *Datamation,* January 21, 1994, p. 30. We will discuss these issues in more detail in Umar [1997].

So what should be done? The best approach is to clearly specify the business drivers and application requirements. Based on this, a judgment needs to be made about how well the new technologies enable these drivers and requirements. If new technologies are chosen, then the potential pitfalls need to be clearly understood and managed as risks. For example, HP initiated an effort to move its terminal-host legacy information systems to client/server applications when C/S was in its infancy [Ross 1994]. This move was driven by the following key business drivers:

- The rapidly changing business requirements required flexibility and end-user control which was not possible using the terminal-host information systems.

- The HP management needed real-time access to operational data (e.g., information about the status of business). This data was embedded in "vertical" applications which made it very difficult to access cross-application data.

- The global customers expected HP to act and look the same anywhere in the world, while the local customers in different countries needed different "local" views to support local legal and competition requirements.

The C/S technologies were adopted because they conformed to these business drivers. Based on this, a careful pilot project was initiated to clarify the risks and pitfalls and to develop an approach that maximized the chances for success. This case study has been used as an illustration for successful projects.

In addition to sound management approaches, are there technical approaches to reduce the pitfalls? A crucial approach is to improve the infrastructure, especially the middleware, so that many of the potential pitfalls (e.g., complexity, interfaces, failure points) are minimized. Thus middleware, the focus of this book, is a key enabler for the new breed of applications that are needed to meet the business challenges of today and tomorrow.

1.4 Object-Oriented Client/Server Internet Environments

1.4.1 Concepts

An object-oriented client/server Internet (OCSI) environment is an IT infrastructure that supports applications with the following characteristics:

- **Client/server** to allow application components to behave as service consumers (**clients**) and service providers (**servers**)

- **Object orientation** to allow applications to be viewed in terms of "natural" objects that can be easily created, viewed, used, modified, reused, and deleted over time

- **Internet** to support World Wide Web for accessing "resources" (e.g., databases) located around the world from Web browsers

It should be emphasized that not all applications in OCSI environments need to have all these characteristics. The key point is that an *OCSI environment provides an infrastructure that allows applications to use any of these concepts if needed.* In these environments, terminal host-based "legacy applications" coexist with the newer breed of Web-based distributed-object applications.

What does an OCSI environment consist of? The two key components are middleware and networks. We are primarily focusing on the mysterious world of middleware (networks are discussed in Chapter 11).

1.4.2 What Is Middleware?

Although middleware is difficult to define precisely, it basically is the connectivity software that allows applications and users to interact with each other across a network (see Figure 1.8). We will use the following definition in this book:

> **Definition**: Middleware is a set of common business-unaware services that enable applications and end users to interact with each other across a network. In essence, middleware is the software that resides above the network and below the business-aware application software.

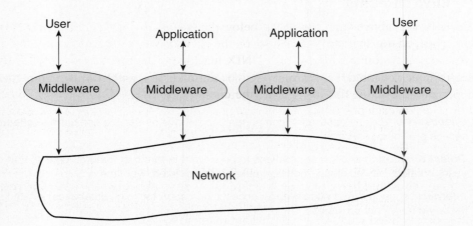

Figure 1.8 Middleware—An End User View

According to this definition, the key ingredients of middleware are:

- It provides common business-unaware services.
- It enables applications and end users to interact with each other across a network.
- It resides above the network and below the business-aware application software.

Middleware is business unaware (i.e., it does not have any business logic) and is available as a common set of routines. The services provided by these routines are available to the applications through *application programming interfaces (APIs)* and to the human users through commands and/or graphical user interfaces (GUIs). The commonality implies that these routines are available to multiple applications and users. Ideally, middleware should be transparent to end users but necessary— the end users should be unaware when it is there and aware only when it is not.

Middleware is enabling software for applications and end users to exchange information across networks. Ideally, midddleware should make the networks irrelevant to the applications and end users. In other words, the users and applications should be able to perform the same operations across a network that they can perform locally. This implies that middleware should also hide the details of computing hardware, operating systems, and other software components (e.g., databases) across networks. Thus SQL middleware can allow users and applications residing on PCs under Windows to access an Oracle database residing on a Sun UNIX computer and a DB2 database on a mainframe MVS computer. We should also point out the significance of end users and applications as the users of middleware (many definitions restrict middleware usage to applications). According to our definition middleware can support interactions from users to users (e.g., email), users to applications (e.g., Web browsers), and application to application (e.g., electronic fund-transfer).

Middleware resides above the network and below the *business-aware* application software to provide the needed transparency—it resides on the client as well as server sides[3]. For example, if you want a customer database on a UNIX machine to be remotely accessed from 100 PCs, then one copy of middleware will need to be purchased/installed for the UNIX machine (e.g., SQL database server) and a copy of the client-side middleware will need to be purchased/installed on each one of the 100 PCs. In general, middleware can be decomposed into client middleware that resides on every client machine and server middleware that resides on the server machines. There are cost as well as management implications of this.

These three ingredients of our definition can be used to determine if a particular software package qualifies as middleware or not. According to our definition, the following software qualifies as middleware (if you do not know about these software packages, do not worry; the rest of the book is filled with information about many of them):

- Terminal emulators, file-transfer packages and email. (They provide very primitive "thin" middleware services.)

- Web browsers. (They are business unaware and support user access to resources on the Internet. As a matter of fact, as we will see in Chapter 4, the World Wide Web is a collection of middleware services.)

- Database drivers and gateways such as ODBC drivers and Sybase Omni Server. (They provide access to remotely located databases.)

- Open Software Foundation's DCE (Distributed Computing Environment) because it provides remote-procedure calls, directory, and security services for distributed applications.

- Object Management Group's CORBA (Common Object Request Broker Architecture) because it provides services for distributed-object applications.

Here is a list of software packages that do not qualify as middleware, according to our definition:

- Database management software such as IMS DB (it operates only on local databases)

- Airline reservation system (it is business aware)

- Network routers (they do not reside above the network—they are part of network services)

Many definitions of middleware have been reported in the literature (see the sidebars "Middleware: Views and Definitions" and "Middleware: Sources of Views and Definitions"). Most of these definitions are very close to ours.

---

3. As we develop better support for cooperative and multimedia applications, we'll find some middleware functions in the network devices (i.e., done by switches/routers). This sould cause no confusion.

Middleware: Views and Definitions

A glib definition of middleware is that it is the slash ("/") in the term "client/server" [Eckerson 1995, Orfali 1994]. In the same vein, Richard Soley, Vice President of Object Management Group, defines middleware as "software that no one wants to pay for" [Soley 1996]. Here is a sampling of some definitions:

- "Middleware is software that allows elements of applications to interoperate across network links, despite differences in underlying communication protocols, systems architectures, OSes, databases, and other application services" [Rymer 1996].

- "Vendors are offering distributed system services that have standard programming interfaces and protocols. These services are called middleware services, because they sit 'in the middle,' in a layer above the OS and networking software and below industry-specific applications" [Bernstein 1996].

- "Middleware is composed of higher-level functions that are used in common by a number of applications. These functions . . . permit applications to be constructed as a set of building blocks" [NRENAISSANCE 1994].

- "Middleware succeeds . . . by providing five main services: hardware independence, interchangeability of key software components (e.g., DBMSs), network independence, operational savings (i.e., some middleware facilitates manual load balancing), and administrative savings (e.g., if you need to redeploy a server piece to a different box, you can simply change its location in the middleware component)" [Delesus 1996].

- "Middleware . . . covers database connectivity, remote procedure calls, messaging mechanisms, and other key elements of the enterprise information architecture" [Hackathorn 1994].

- "Middleware should do several things. First, it provides a way to get data from one place (..) to another (..). Second, it should mask the differences between OSes, platforms, and network protocols. Third, it should conceal the complexity of the network transport process from the application developer" [Salamone 1996].

- "It (middleware) starts with the API set on the client side that is used to invoke a service, and it covers the transmission of the request over the network and the resulting response" [Orfali 1994, p. 18].

- "Middleware is simply connectivity software that consists of a set of enabling services that allow multiple processes running on one or more machines to interact across a network" [Eckerson 1995].

Middleware: Sources of Views and Definitions

Bernstein, P., "Middleware: A Model for Distributed Systems Services," *Communications of ACM,* February 1996, pp. 86–98.

Delesus, E., "The Middleware Riddle," *Byte Magazine,* April 1996, p. 65.

Eckerson, W., "Searching for the Middleground," *Business Communications Review,* April 1995, pp. 46–50.

Francett, B., "Middleware on the March," *Data Management/DBMS Software Magazine,* April 1996, pp. 71–79.

Hackathorn, R., and Schlack, M., "How to Pick Client/server Middleware," *Datamation,* July 15, 1994, pp. 52–56.

NRENAISSANCE Committee, *Realizing the Information Future: The Internet and Beyond,* National Academy Press, 1994.

Orfali, R., Harkey, D., and Edwards, J., *Essential Client/Server Guide,* Wiley 1994, pp. 18–19.

Rymer, J., "The Muddle in the Middle," *Byte Magazine,* April 1996, pp. 67–70.

Salamone, S., "Middle(ware) Management," *Byte Magazine,* April 1996, pp. 71–78.

Soley, R., "Discussion Session," ICDP96, Dresden, March 1996.

1.4.3   Functional View of Middleware

Middleware provides a wide range of functionality, such as establishment of sessions between client processes and server processes, security, compression/decompression, and failure handling. Its main functions can be cast into the following broad categories (see Figure 1.9):

- Information-exchange services
- Application-specific services
- Management and support services

Information-exchange services send the needed information across a network in response to a request. In particular, these services may be needed to transfer data, issue commands, receive responses, check status, resolve deadlocks, and establish/break connections between remotely located application processes and end users. These services typically include *synchronous* calls (i.e. client sends a request and waits for a response). In many cases, it is desirable to provide *asynchronous* communication (i.e., keep sending requests without waiting for responses) between remote programs so that the execution of a program is not suspended while waiting for responses. Information-exchange must include facility for the servers to handle many concurrent and asynchronous requests simultaneously from many clients. Information-exchange services are supported by the middleware through primitive services (e.g., file transfer, terminal emulation, email) and client/server information-exchange services (e.g., remote-procedure calls).

Figure 1.9 Middleware: A Functional View

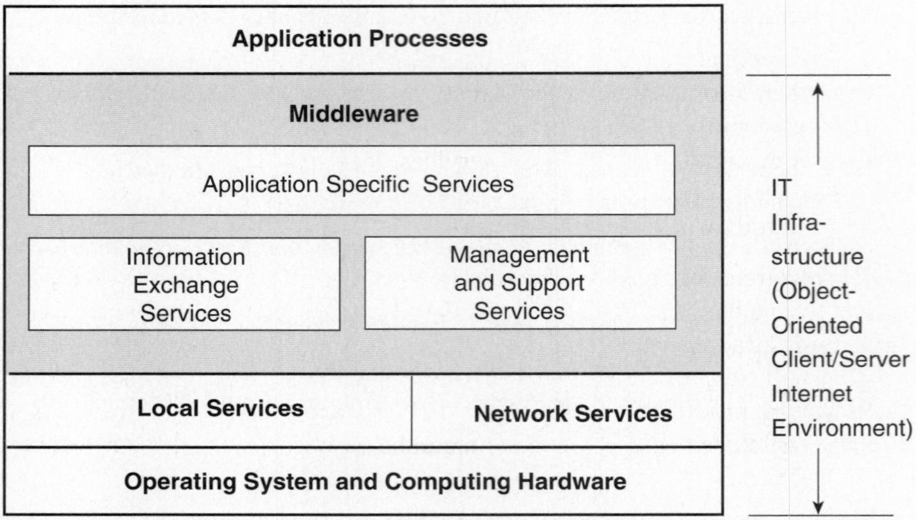

Application-specific services provide the services needed by different classes of applications. For example, these services access and manipulate distributed databases that are located at multiple sites. Another example is the distributed transaction-processing service that maintains integrity of single or multiple copies of data for transaction processing. Other examples of these services are data-replication services, groupware services for collaborative processing, workflow services, distributed-object services to shuffle messages between distributed objects, and specialized services needed for mobile computing and distributed multimedia applications. As new classes of applications emerge (we discussed a few in Section 1.3.1), more application-specific middleware services will emerge. Keep in mind that the middleware for a class of applications itself is not business aware (e.g., middleware for distributed transaction processing is business unaware, but a distributed transaction-processing application such as electronic funds transfer is business aware).

Management and support services are needed to locate distributed resources and administer these resources across networks. Examples of these services include directory (naming), security, fault, and performance services. In particular, these services include the following:

● Facility for the clients to locate a server (which server to invoke), send the request to a server, receive response from a server, and parse and interpret the response.

- Ability to handle security (authentication and journaling).

- Facility to handle failure (timeouts, deadlocks, hardware/software) at the distributed sites (clients as well as servers).

- Ability to monitor and improve the run-time performance of the distributed programs. This should allow measurement of communication traffic, program wait states, deadlocks, etc.

Figure 1.9 shows a refinement of the framework presented in Figure 1.2 and highlights the major functions performed by the middleware. We will further refine this framework in the next section. The application processes are business-aware software and databases that interact with each other through the IT infrastructure. The IT infrastructure (i.e., platform) is needed to develop, deploy, support, and manage the applications. At a high level, the IT infrastructure consists of middleware, network services, local services (e.g., database managers, transaction managers), operating systems, and computing hardware. Our main interest at present is on the middleware (the shaded area).

Example. To illustrate the middleware functions, consider, for example, that you need to transfer funds from a bank in Chicago to a bank in New York. To accomplish this, you need at least three things: (a) a network to connect the two banks, (b) application processes on the two banks that will transfer the funds, and (c) the middleware that will support the funds-transfer application processes. Specifically, the middleware will reside on the Chicago machine (client middleware) and New York machine (server middleware) to provide the following major services:

- Information-exchange services that will first establish a connection between the client program (Chicago) and the server program (New York) and then transfer the funds between the two remotely located programs (the program in Chicago will debit one account and the program in New York will credit the other account).

- Application-specific services that will make sure the transaction is completed successfully. These services will ensure that the money is transferred either completely or not at all.

- Management and support services such as directory, security, and administrative support to help locate the resources from authorized users (i.e., make sure no one else starts transferring your funds to Switzerland!).

The services provided by the middleware have evolved, and continue to evolve. This evolution has been driven to satisfy the following objectives:

- Support of newer applications (e.g.,World Wide Web applications, mobile computing applications, distributed multimedia applications, and computer-supported collaborative work).

- Increased transparency for the users (i.e., the user is not aware of what activities are taking place where in the network), developers (i.e., the application developers should be shielded from the details of different systems while developing applications), and managers (i.e., the managers should be able to manage distributed systems as a single system).

- Improved portability and interoperability of applications across computer systems.

- Consistency and repeatability of services.

- Improved response time and availability of services.

- Better management tools and infrastructures.

This evolution of middleware is intended to minimize the risks and costs of developing new applications. If continued, this evolution will shape the nature of applications and business practices in the future. We will describe in the next section how the middleware has evolved to meet these goals.

1.4.4 Middleware Logical Components (Layers) and Examples

In practice, middleware services can be viewed in terms of a combination of logical components (layers) such as the following (see Figure 1.10):

- Primitive services software such as terminal emulators, email, and file-transfer packages. These services are not the focus of this book and are briefly reviewed in Chapter 3.

- Basic C/S middleware, which includes Remote-Procedure Call (RPC), Remote-Data Access (RDA), and Message-Oriented Middleware (MOM). This middleware is typically built on top of the network transport services. These services also include management services such as security and directory. We will discuss this middleware in Chapter 3.

- World Wide Web middleware to support the dramatically evolving applications over the Internet and Intranets.This includes Web browsers, Web servers, search engines, Hypertext Transfer Protocol (HTTP), Hypertext Markup Language (HTML), Java, and Web gateways to access non-Web applications. We will discuss this middleware in Chapter 4.

- Distributed-data and transaction management middleware that is responsible for access, manipulation, and update of distributed as well as replicated data. This middleware includes protocols such as two-phase commit, transactional RPCs, and XA. Many of these protocols utilize the basic C/S middleware (e.g., transactional RPCs use the basic RPCs). We group this middleware in the following two broad categories:

  - Distributed-data access middleware that allows users to primarily retrieve data dispersed around a network. We will discuss this middleware, commonly known as SQL middleware, in Chapter 5.

  - Client/server transaction-processing middleware that handles the knotty issue of updating related data in distributed environments. Distributed-transaction processing, also known as "TP-heavy," is one option. However, a popular choice at present includes "TP-lite," in which stored procedures are used to update master databases and "replication servers" are used to synchronize duplicate data. We will discuss different approaches to C/S transaction processing in Chapter 6.

- Distributed-object services that send messages to objects in the network. Examples of these services and standards are the Object Management Group's Common Object Request Broker Architecture (OMG CORBA), Microsoft's Object Linking and Embedding (OLE), ActiveX and OpenDoc. Some of these services are built on top of the Basic C/S middleware (e.g., many CORBA implementations are developed on top of RPCs). We will discuss this middleware in Chapter 7.

Figure 1.10 IT Building Blocks—A Layered View

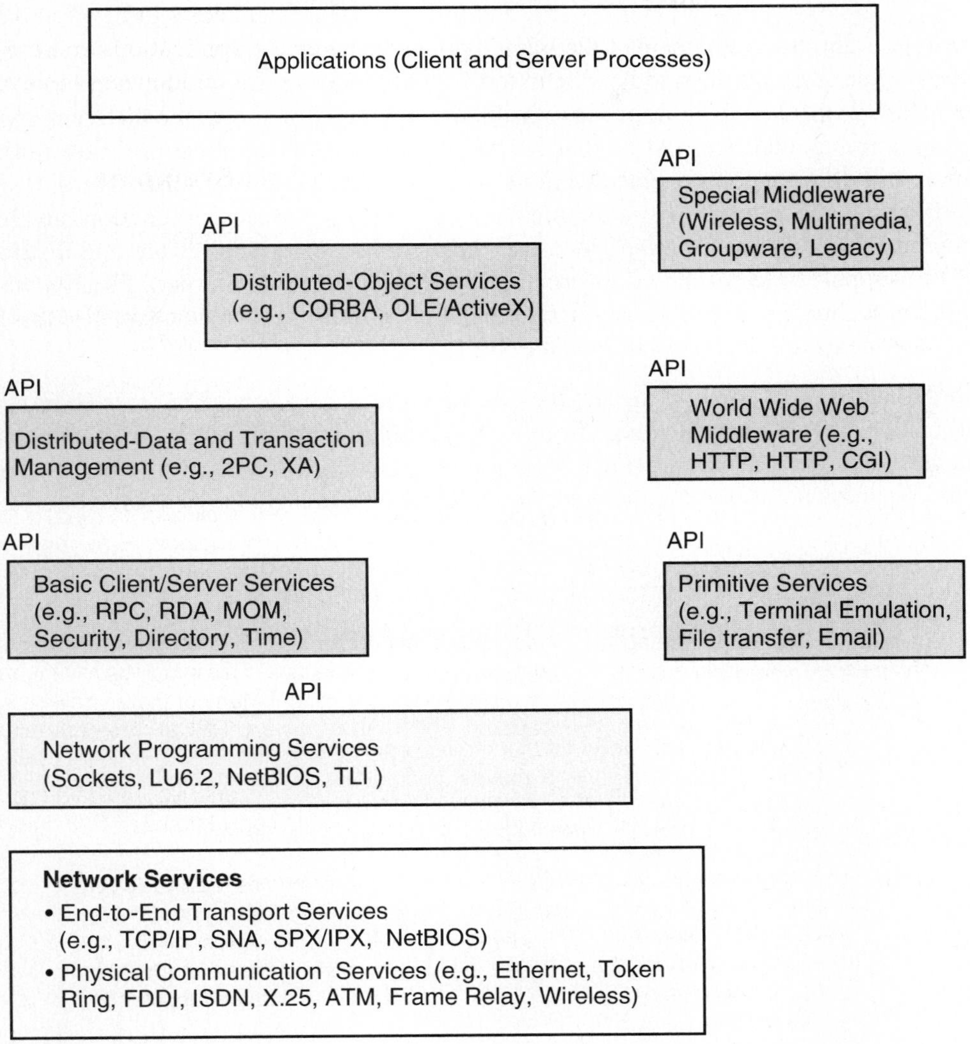

```
┌──────────────────────────────────────────────────────────┐
│                                                          │
│         Applications (Client and Server Processes)       │
│                                                          │
└──────────────────────────────────────────────────────────┘

                                              API
                                    ┌─────────────────────────┐
                                    │ Special Middleware      │
                    API             │ (Wireless, Multimedia,  │
            ┌─────────────────────┐ │ Groupware, Legacy)      │
            │ Distributed-Object  │ └─────────────────────────┘
            │ Services            │
            │ (e.g., CORBA,       │
            │ OLE/ActiveX)        │
            └─────────────────────┘
                                              API
   API                                ┌─────────────────────────┐
┌────────────────────────────┐        │ World Wide Web          │
│ Distributed-Data and       │        │ Middleware (e.g.,       │
│ Transaction                │        │ HTTP, HTTP, CGI)        │
│ Management (e.g., 2PC, XA) │        └─────────────────────────┘
└────────────────────────────┘
   API                                   API
┌────────────────────────────┐        ┌─────────────────────────┐
│ Basic Client/Server        │        │ Primitive Services      │
│ Services                   │        │ (e.g., Terminal         │
│ (e.g., RPC, RDA, MOM,      │        │ Emulation,              │
│ Security, Directory, Time) │        │ File transfer, Email)   │
└────────────────────────────┘        └─────────────────────────┘
                    API
┌──────────────────────────────────────────┐
│ Network Programming Services             │
│ (Sockets, LU6.2, NetBIOS, TLI )          │
└──────────────────────────────────────────┘

┌──────────────────────────────────────────────┐
│ Network Services                             │
│ • End-to-End Transport Services              │
│   (e.g., TCP/IP, SNA, SPX/IPX, NetBIOS)      │
│ • Physical Communication Services (e.g.,     │
│   Ethernet, Token Ring, FDDI, ISDN, X.25,    │
│   ATM, Frame Relay, Wireless)                │
└──────────────────────────────────────────────┘
```

Legend used in layers:
      Dark shaded area = middleware
      Light shaded area = not usually considered as middleware
      Unshaded area = not middleware

- Special-purpose middleware that is being developed for emerging applications. Examples are the wireless middleware for mobile computing applications, middleware for distributed multimedia applications, middleware for groupware (e.g., Lotus Notes), and middleware legacy system access/integration. We will discuss this middleware in Chapter 8.

Figure 1.10 is another refinement of the framework presented in Figure 1.2 and serves several purposes. First, it shows the middleware in terms of the components that are commonly used in the industry (this will help in product evaluation). Second, it shows the different application programming interfaces (APIs) that can be invoked from the applications (this illustrates that more middleware components can increase complexity of applications). Third, it shows how different components can be combined together to support different functions and to satisfy the business drivers (for example, a user may choose Web middleware and distributed objects to support object-oriented information exchange over the Internet). Finally, we will use this figure throughout this book as a roadmap (i.e., it tells us in which chapter of this book these components are discussed in more detail).

We should clarify that some of the services we describe as middleware (e.g., Web browsers, email) can be viewed as applications from a computing point of view. However, we classify all business-unaware services that reside on top of networks as middleware, because from a user and business point of view these services add no business value.

Categories of Commercial Middleware

The commercially available middleware generally falls into three broad categories:

- **Middleware components** that provide only one service. For example, HTTP is used to retrieve remote documents, X.400 supports only email, ODBC drivers allow access to remote databases, Sun RPC supports only RPC, and IBM's MQSeries supports only MOM.

- **Middleware environments** that combine many services from one or more layers to provide integrated middleware services. For example, OSF DCE integrates RPC, security, directory, time, and file services into a single package. Similarly, Encina provides distributed-transaction processing over DCE, and CORBA 2.0 is defining many services over ORB.

- **Compound middleware environments** that combine many middleware environments into a single framework. For example, IBM's Open Distributed Computing (ODC) Blueprint combines OSF DCE, MQSeries, CORBA, distributed data management, and distributed-transaction management into a single framework.

1.5   Why This Book?

The focus of this book is on the IT infrastructure that will support the enterprises of the 1990s and beyond. In particular, we zero in on middleware needed to support the object-oriented client/server Internet-based applications. Why? Here are some reasons.

Middleware enables new applications. The new applications being developed at present, and in the near future, will rely increasingly on middleware to provide the underlying services needed for distributed applications. These applications have several attractive features (e.g., flexibility, scalability) that are crucial to the enterprises of 1990 and beyond.

Middleware can reduce time, effort, and money needed to develop and deploy new applications. There is a trade-off between the complexity of application and the complexity of the middleware. If the services provided by the middleware are simple and do not meet the application requirements, then this complexity shifts to the application developers. New applications need services that are expensive and time consuming to build. If you do not use middleware, then you have to invest in developing these services—a very expensive undertaking.

Middleware can, if managed carefully, reduce the risk of failure. By spending some effort in understanding and carefully planning the middleware components that will be needed to support your applications, you can minimize unpleasant surprises.

Middleware is big business and is growing rapidly. Both the number of vendors and the revenues in the middleware market are growing. For example, according to an International Data Corporation (IDC) report, the total 1995 revenues for middleware exceeded $1 billion [Levin 1996].

Middleware is needed to deal with legacy applications. Dealing with legacy applications is a crucial issue facing modern enterprises. Middleware products help in interfacing new applications with existing and re-architecture of legacy applications.

Middleware offers many, almost too many, options that must be carefully examined. Each middleware package comes with its own set of APIs (application programming interfaces) that can be used to develop applications. Most middleware packages have hundreds of APIs (for example, Microsoft's OLE has almost 700 APIs). If you have seven middleware packages, with several hundred APIs, this could cause discomfort (to say the least).

Middleware is complex. Middleware is growing rapidly and many of the issues and trade-offs are not well understood, thus increasing the risk of failures. A particular problem with this "riddle in the middle" is that a plethora of jargon, interrelationships, models, frameworks, products, and techniques have been introduced. Information-technology practitioners and managers need to understand the various aspects of middleware.

Middleware facilitates portability and interoperability. Middleware products are becoming available from different vendors that do not interoperate with other vendor products. However, some middleware products do allow you to build applications that can be ported to different environments and do interoperate with each other. A systematic approach is needed to categorize and understand the different families of middleware products.

Middleware does not add direct business value and can be expensive. Middleware is business unaware but it adds to the hidden IT costs. For example, many SQL gateway middleware products for mainframes can range from $200 K to $300 K, and the cost per desktop for the middleware can range from $200 to $400. This cost must be taken into account.

Investment on middleware must be carefully watched and justified. An example will illustrate this problem. The IT department of a large organization was funded very heavily by the business partners to support new business initiatives. The IT department spent a great deal of time and money in studying, evaluating, and establishing IT infrastructure and especially the middleware. However, the middleware effort did not add business value after a great deal of expense. This created an embarrassing situation for the management when the IT department was reviewed and audited.

Organizational issues are not well understood. Each middleware component has to be properly installed, supported, and managed. Especially, the technical and customer support staff needs to be trained. Some middleware components such as Open Software Foundation's Distributed Computing Environment (OSF DCE) are large and complex systems that need special attention. From an organizational-structure point of view, most middleware products at present are supported by a mixture of network support, database support, or operating-systems groups (in many cases, middleware is "grabbed" by someone who may not have other interesting work.

As stated previously, the objective of this book is to explain the components and the interrelationships among the various components of middleware. In particular, we will attempt to answer the following questions:

- What is middleware and why is it important?
- What are the different categories of middleware and what do they do?
- How do the different middleware components interrelate with each other?
- What are the issues and trade-offs associated with middleware?
- What are the sources of additional information?

This book is intended to serve as a tutorial on technical as well as management aspects of middleware. The topics discussed should be useful in establishing middleware architectures that support development of new applications and facilitate strategies to deal with legacy applications. This book is a companion and a prerequisite to a second book that describes how the middleware can be used to engineer new applications and to reengineer existing (legacy) applications [Umar 1997]. Owing to the widespread industrial applications and continuing research efforts in middleware-related topics, our discussion will include (see Figure 1.11):

- *State-of-the-Art* approaches, which are prototypes and/or research and development reports and papers
- *State-of-the-Market* information to show commercial availability of the approaches as products
- *State-of-the-Practice* information to show that the approaches/products are being actually used by organizations

A coverage of all three aspects will give the reader a more realistic view of the subject matter. This is especially important because, owing to the delays and filters built into the industry,

Figure 1.11 Different States of Technologies

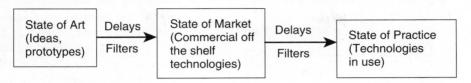

only a few of the state-of-the-art ideas become state of the market and even fewer become state of the practice. Focus on one area only (e.g., state of the art) may give the reader the wrong impression about the potential impact of the topics discussed. The emphasis is on synthesis and interrelationships and not on detailed technical coverage of one topic. The book will intentionally cover a great deal of ground, so that different views, perspectives, and interrelationships can be understood. The approach used in this book is shown in Figure 1.12 (i.e., a coverage of the terms, concepts, building blocks, and interrelationships instead of detailed discussion of one topic or a broad-brush discussion).

Figure 1.13 shows the book roadmap. The network technologies are discussed in Chapter 11. The main discussion of middleware is in Part II of this book. The topics discussed proceed from lower-level middleware services to higher-level application-specific services in Chapters 3 through 9. Each chapter is written as a self-contained tutorial on the subject matter. Different levels of discussion are included in each chapter (conceptual overviews, technical details, analysis) to support different audiences. Each chapter concludes with a brief discussion of state of the practice (examples and case studies), state of the market (vendor products and relevant standards), and state of the art (research notes). Numerous references for additional study are provided.

Figure 1.12 Coverage of Middleware

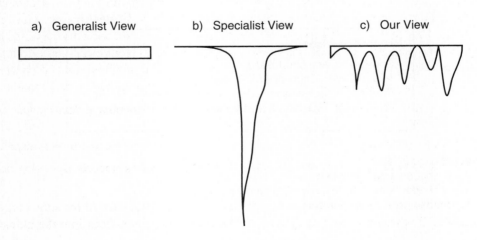

Figure 1.13 Book Roadmap

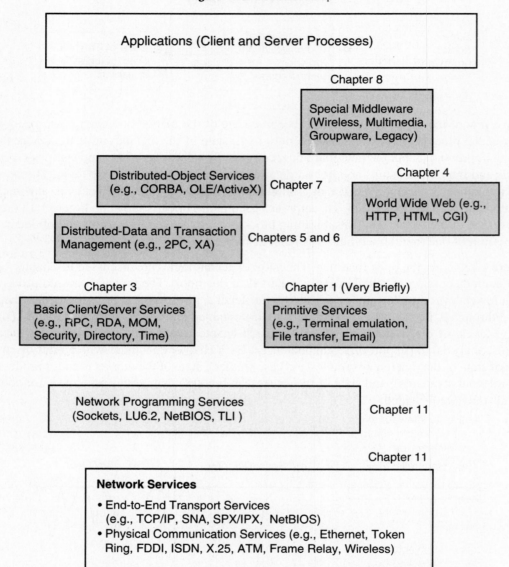

Legend used in layers:
Dark shaded area = middleware
Light shaded area = not usually considered as middleware
Unshaded area = not middleware

1.6   State of the Practice: General Observations

Many new applications currently being implemented are either using or planning to use the object-oriented client/server Internet architectures to some extent. Many success stories and future plans are published in the trade literature (e.g., *Datamation, Client/Server Today, Database Programming and Design, Information Week*), are advertised over the Internet, and appear in the vendor literature. Failures are rarely reported, for obvious reasons (who will allow their employees to advertise that their corporate effort failed?). However, a few moments of truth do trickle through. In particular, the initial euphoria about client/server seems to be somewhat moderated. Some cautions about C/S systems have been mentioned in the past (see "Dirty Downsizing," *Computerworld,* Special Report, August 10, 1992, and "Where Do Client/Server Apps Go Wrong?" *Datamation,* January 21, 1994). More attention is being paid now [Caldwell 1996, Kador 1966, DePompa 1995]. We will review different case studies in each chapter as we go along.

What do the typical contemporary information-system environments look like? Figure 1.14 shows a high-level view of a "modern" environment in a typical medium-sized organization. The corporate office houses one or more mainframes to support corporate databases that are accessed from a diverse array of remotely located users and programs. The remotely located sites typically house minicomputers that serve PC Windows users in a regional office of the organization, database servers that support some regional offices with many UNIX workstations, and some remote PCs, minicomputers, UNIX workstations, and minicomputers connected to the mainframe from business partners. In addition, several Web servers are proliferating to store information that is accessed from Web browsers.

The following middleware is used in this environment:

- Primitive middleware such as terminal emulation and file transfer are used between the mainframe and remote computers. For example, the business-partner computers access the mainframe systems by using terminal emulators, and the data from the corporate databases is extracted and transferred to the regional minicomputer by using file transfer.

- Basic client/server (C/S) middleware is typically used within regional networks and only rarely at corporate level. For example, the PCs and workstations access the database servers and minicomputers via the C/S middleware by using RPC (remote-procedure call) and remote-SQL middleware.

- Distributed objects are relatively new at this time (are being "investigated") and may be used within regions and between regions (CORBA and Microsoft's OLE/ActiveX are contenders in this area).

- Many corporations are exploring the use of Intranets (i.e., private Internets) and World Wide Web (i.e., Web browsers, Web servers, Web gateways) to access enterprisewide information. Many companies are exploring Web browsers as a standard user interface for all applications.

- An enterprisewide information architecture that supports users-to-computers interactions through Web and computers-to-computers interactions through object-oriented technologies is being explored.

It should be noted that while new middleware is being acquired by many organizations, the old middleware is not dying out. You still need terminal emulations and file transfers. The main challenge is to develop an IT architecture that allows different middleware technologies to coexist for maximum business benefits.

Figure 1.14 A High-Level View of a Typical Environment

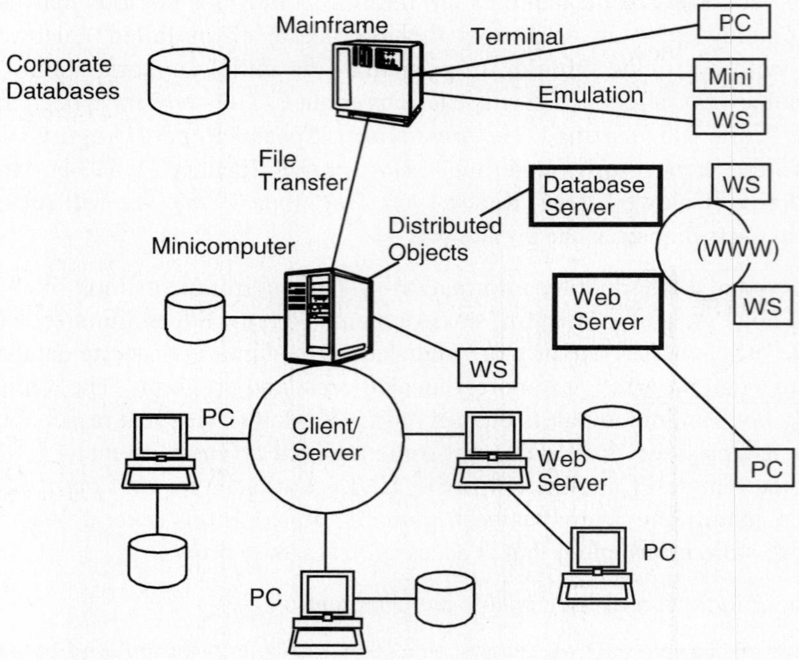

PC = Personal Computer

WS = UNIX Work Station

1.7   State of the Market: General Observations

Off-the-shelf middleware software is currently available from a very large number of providers. For example, the Basic C/S middleware such as Open Software Foundation's Distributed Computing Environment (DCE) is currently available from vendors such as IBM, HP, and Digital. The distributed data-management middleware such as remote-SQL gateways, is available, naturally, from database vendors such as Oracle, Sybase, Informix, and IBM. Distributed transaction-processing middleware is available from companies such as IBM (IBM bought Transarc—a company that builds and markets a distributed transaction-management system called Encina). A handful of vendors are beginning to provide distributed-object middleware such as CORBA (IBM, Hewlett Packard, Sun, and Iona are examples), and OLE/ActiveX (being marketed by Microsoft). Middleware for Web is being announced by a bevy of companies, ranging from small new firms such as Netscape to large established organizations such as IBM and Microsoft (as a matter of fact, it is difficult to find a computer software company that does not want to get into the Web market). We will review state of the market for different middleware in each chapter.

The two-dimensional view of applications introduced in Section 1.3.1 can be used to understand the overall state of the middleware market at present. Table 1.1 shows the type of middleware that is available and being used for different classes of applications. This picture may change with time.

TABLE 1.1 USAGE OF MIDDLEWARE—A SUMMARY

SIZE / TYPE	Decision Support/ Retrieval	Operational Support/ OLTP	Real Time
Group/Departmental	Basic C/S middleware (RPC, RDA) very mature OO is emerging Groupware is mature	C/S transaction processing is still evolving	Multimedia technology is maturing
Enterprisewide	C/S is possible, but not mature Groupware is maturing Web over Intranets is becoming popular	C/S not mature at present Web technology mastering	Middleware not commercially available
Interenterprise	Web technology for document centric work	C/S not mature Web technology maturing	Middleware not available

1.8   State of the Art: General Trends

The need for IT infrastructure and, in particular, the middleware to quickly enable interoperable and portable applications will continue to grow to meet the business pressures of flexibility, rapid development, and efficiency. We will discuss trends for each middleware component in the relevant chapters. At present, let us note the following interrelated trends:

- Continuing application trends
  - Pressure to provide business value
  - Pressure to conform to business topology (i.e., businesses are distributed thus applications should be distributed, too)
  - Increased use of object-oriented C/S systems over the Internet
- Continuing IT platform (infrastructure) trends
  - Networks getting faster
  - Computing hardware becoming faster, cheaper, more reliable (in particular the desktops/ laptops)
  - Operating systems more efficient
  - Relational database managers becoming more efficient (object-oriented databases are still looming around)
  - Transaction managers (TMs) becoming portable and interoperable (e.g., TM from one vendor interoperating with database managers from different vendors)
  - Many off-the-shelf tools for decision support (4GL, spreadsheets, data browsers, etc.) are growing
  - Computers being personal and not shared
  - Increased integration of multimedia (e.g., text, voice, video) in user presentations

So what does this mean for middleware? Middleware will continue to become more sophisticated by extending the scope of local services to distributed environments. This will allow users and applications to perform same actions across networks that are typically performed on local machines. In particular, middleware will provide increased end-user transparency and increased support for World Wide Web and distributed objects. Standards will play an important role, because without standards each new middleware component will add more complexity (see Figure 1.15).

A promising future scenario is the three-tiered architecture shown in Figure 1.16. This scenario separates the computing resources (databases and programs) into Web (directly accessible from the Web browser) and non-Web (not directly accessible from the Web browser) resources. As the capabilities of Web browsers increase, many of the databases and applications will be directly accessible from Web browsers, thus strengthening the middle tier. The middle tier will house Web resources and also serve as a gateway to the back-end non-Web resources. The non-Web resources (usually legacy systems) are accessed from the middle tier by using gateways that invoke the traditional middleware such as terminal emulations, remote SQL, and file transfers. Object orientation can play a key role at all tiers (using OO calls from Web browsers, making Web resources more OO, and wrapping the legacy back-end systems with OO wrappers). This marriage of object orientation with Web is being recognized in the industry and convergence was initiated at a combined World Wide Web Consortium and the Object Management Group (OMG) meeting held in Boston (June, 1996).

Figure 1.15 The Role of Standards

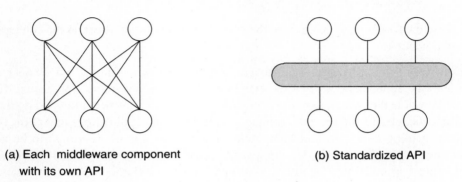

(a) Each middleware component
    with its own API

(b) Standardized API

Figure 1.16 A Potential Future Scenario

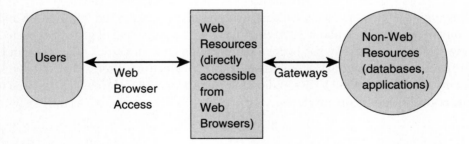

1.9   Summary

Middleware is a major enabling technology for the applications that require flexibility and end-user control. In particular, middleware is needed to support the emerging object-oriented, client/server, Internet-based applications. Effective IT solutions require an understanding of the interrelationships between business drivers, careful assessment of the middleware options, and cost/benefit analysis of various options. The central idea is that middleware should be chosen based on business drivers. In particular, the type of current and future applications to be supported by the enterprise must be the key determining factor. Owing to the complexity of middleware, goals must be clearly defined and adhered to. The chapters in this book serve as tutorials on the various middleware components. This information should be useful in establishing middleware architectures that support development of new applications and facilitate strategies to deal with legacy applications.

1.10   A Case Study

We will use the following case study at the end of each chapter to illustrate the concepts introduced in this book.

XYZCorp was formed by Ms. Jones to provide technology solutions to a diverse array of industries. Ms. Jones believes that the latest OO, Web-based products that utilize C/S concepts will provide the company with a competitive edge in a relatively crowded market. Here is her basic idea: build and test interconnection products and applications that allow different databases residing over different computers (mainframes, minis, desktops) to be accessed through the World Wide Web. The long-range focus of the company is on Web-based distributed-object applications (for internal use and external marketing). The company will also develop/acquire and market a variety of desktop tools. The company wants to "field test" most of its services by trying them in-house. If needed, the company could also start offering consultation and training services.

The company headquarters are in Chicago with branch offices in the US, Europe and Asia. The company has currently about 3000 employees with a great deal of growth expected in the next few years. The company has formed partnerships with numerous other computer hardware/software vendors and has acquired several retail electronic stores that sell and service microcomputers, televisions, VCRs, radios and calculators. These stores will be used to market and service the company products.

The company operates many regional offices (HQs are given in parentheses): Southern (Atlanta), Western (San Francisco), Eastern (New York), Midwestern (Detroit), North Western (Seattle), European (Paris), and Asian (Tokyo). Each region supports 10 local offices (some of these offices are stores, the others are marketing, training, consulting, and support centers), with an average of 200 staff members per region.

Ms. Jones has been thinking a lot lately. A corporate planning committee has been formed to establish an IT infrastructure that will allow development and support of the variety of applications and services the company needs that could also be marketed externally. In particular, the planning committee will initiate and supervise the completion of the following projects (we will discuss these projects in the chapters indicated):

- Develop a high-level IT architecture that shows the various building blocks and how they interrelate with each other. (Chapter 2)

- Identify the core C/S middleware services and a network operating system such as OSF/DCE (Chapter 3).

- Develop an Intranet and select the Web technologies that will be used in XYZCorp (Chapter 4).

- Establish an approach to access the corporate databases (mostly relational) from Web and select appropriate SQL middleware to enable this access (Chapter 5).

- Develop a strategy for client/server transaction processing and choose appropriate middleware to support this strategy (Chapter 6).

- Investigate the use of distributed-object technologies and select the appropriate middleware to support this strategy (Chapter 7).

- Explore how the latest developments in mobile computing, distributed multimedia, groupware, and legacy data access can be used in this company (Chapter 8).

- Synthesize the different pieces into a cohesive information-technology architecture (Chapter 9).

- Investigate and select specific OO technologies to be used in XYZCorp (Chapter 10).

- Develop an enterprise network architecture to support the exchange of information between all business players such as the corporate office, regional offices, local offices, and business offices (Chapter 11).

We will discuss these projects at the end of each chapter and give hints and guidelines about how they could be completed.

1.11 Problems and Exercises

1. In your view, what is the main strength of combining OO, C/S, and Web under the same umbrella? What is the main weakness (risk)?

2. Illustrate the three-level framework (business processes, applications, IT platforms) through five examples.

3. Find another definition of middleware and compare/contrast it with the definitions introduced in this chapter.

4. Suppose that you have been asked to develop a two-day management training program in modern IT infrastructure. What topics would you cover in this program?

1.12 Additional Information

Literature on middleware that is enabling distributed enterprises is growing steadily. The sidebars that follow point you to books, technical journals, and trade magazines where you can find additional information. We will present numerous other sources of additional information as we go along.

1.13   References

Andrews, G., "Paradigms for Interprocess Interactions in Distributed Programs," *ACM Computing Surveys,* March 1991, pp. 49–90.

Bernstein, P., "Middleware: A Model for Distributed Systems Services," *Communications of ACM,* February 1996, pp. 86–98.

Brodie, M.L., and Stonebroker, M., *Migrating Legacy Systems: Gateways, Interfaces & Incremental Approach,* Morgan Kauffman, 1995.

Caldwell, B., "Client-Server: Can It Be Saved?" *Information Week,* April 8, 1996, pp. 36–44.

Charan, R., "How Networks Reshape Organizations—For Results," *Harvard Business Review,* September–October 1991, pp.104–115.

Davenport, T., "Cultivating an Information Culture," *CIO Magazine,* January 1995.

DePompa, B., "Corporate Migration: Harder Than It Looks," *Information Week,* December 4, 1995, pp. 60–68.

Eckerson, W., "Searching for the Middleground," *Business Communications Review,* April 1995, pp. 46–50.

Hackathorn, R., and Schlack, M., "How to Pick Client/server Middleware," *Datamation,* July 15, 1994, pp. 52–56.

Henderson, J., and Venkatraman, "Strategic Alignment: Leveraging Information Technology for Transforming Organizations," *IBM Systems Journal,* Vol. 32, No. 1 (1993), pp. 4–16.

Javenpaa, S., and Ives, B., "The Global Network Organization of the Future: Information Management Opportunities and Challenges," *Journal of Management Information Systems,* Spring 1994, pp. 25–57.

Kador, J., "The Ultimate Middleware," *Byte Magazine,* April 1996, pp. 81–83.

Keen, P., "Shaping the Future," *Harvard Business School Press,* Boston, 1991.

Leff, A., and Pu, C., "A Classification of Transaction Processing Systems," *IEEE Computer,* June 1991, pp. 63–65.

Levin, R., "A Sea of Change for Middleware," *Information Week,* May 13, 1996, pp. 92–93.

Ozsu, M., and Valduriez, P., *Distributed Database Systems,* Prentice Hall, 1991.

Richter, J., "Distributing Data," *Byte,* June 1994, pp, 139–145.

Ross, W., "Hewlett-Packard's Migration to Client/Server Architectures," published in *Distributed Computing,* ed. by R. Kanna, Prentice Hall, 1994.

Salamone, S., "Middle(ware) Management," *Byte Magazine,* April 1996, pp. 71–78.

Soley, R., "Distributed Platforms: Impacts on the Infobahn," Panel discussion, International Conference on Distributed Computing Platforms, Dresden, Germany, February 1996.

Turban, E., *Decision Support and Expert Systems,* 4th ed., MacMillan, 1995.

Umar, A., *Application Engineering/Reengineering Building Web-based Object-Oriented Applications and Dealing with Legacies,* Prentice Hall, 1997.

Umar, A., *Distributed Computing and Client/Server Systems,* Prentice Hall, 1993

State-of-the-Market/Practice Magazines and Periodicals

The following trade magazines publish case studies and new products:

- *Client/Server Today*
- *Client/Server Computing*
- *Datamation* (Cahners Publication)
- *Data Communications Magazine* (McGraw-Hill)
- *Distributed Computing Monitor,* Patricia Seybold Group Publications
- *Gartner Group Reports on Client/Server*
- *Network Computing* (CMP Publication)
- *Business Communications Review*
- *Database Programming and Design*
- *Enterprise Systems Journal*
- *Information Week*
- *Computerworld, Weekly* (section on networks and standards)
- *Infoworld, Weekly* (section on networks)
- *LAN Technology* (M&T Publication)
- *UNIX World*
- *Byte Magazine*
- *PC Magazine*
- *PC Computing*
- *Software Industry Report* (Computer Age Publication)
- *Web Week*
- *Web Developer*

Relevant Books

At present, no single book covers the different aspects of middleware needed for the contemporary organizations (why do you think this book was written!). The following books discuss several topics that are currently being clustered under the general umbrella of "middleware."

- Berson, A., *Client/Server Architectures*, McGraw-Hill, 1993.

- Bukhres, O., and Elmagarmid, A., *Object-Oriented Multidatabase Systems,* Prentice Hall, 1996.

- Deffler, F., *Guide To Connectivity,* 3d ed., Ziff-Davis Press, 1995.

- Khanna, R., *Distributed Computing: Implementation and Management Strategies*, Prentice Hall, 1993.

- Martin, J., and Leben, J., *Client/Server Databases,* Prentice Hall, 1995.

- Mowbray, T., and Zahavi, R., *The Essential CORBA,* Wiley, 1995.

- Mullender, S., ed., *Distributed Systems*, ACM Press, Addison-Wesley, 2d ed., 1993.

- NRENAISSANCE Committee, *Realizing the Information Future: The Internet and Beyond,* National Academy Press, 1994.

- Orfali, R., Harkey, D., and Edwards, J., *Essential Client/server survival Guide,* Wiley, 1994.

- Orfali, R., Harkey, D., and Edwards, J., *The Essential Distributed Objects Survival Guide,* Wiley, 1996.

- Peterson, M., *DCE: A Guide to Developing Portable Applications,* McGraw-Hill, 1995.

- Ryan, T., *Distributed Object Technology,* Prentice Hall, 1996

- Schill, A., et al., "Distributed Computing Platforms," *Proceedings of International Conference on Distributed Computing Platforms,* Dresden, Germany, February 1996.

- Umar, A., *Distributed Computing and Client/Server Systems,* Prentice Hall, rev. ed., 1993.

- Vaskevitz, D., *Client/Server Strategies: A Survival Guide for Corporate Reengineers*, IDG Books, 1993.

State-of-the-Art Periodicals and Conference Proceedings

The following conference proceedings and technical periodicals publish articles on technical and research issues related to middleware.

- International Conference on Distributed Platforms (held once a year; the 1996 conference was held in Dresden, Germany, February 1996).

- The International Conference on Distributed Computing Systems (held every year).

- *IEEE Computer Magazine.*

- *IEEE Software Magazine.*

- *IEEE Transactions on Software Engineering.*

- *ACM Computing Surveys.*

- *Communications of ACM.*

- *ACM Standard View.*

2

Information—Technology Building Blocks

2.1   Introduction

This chapter identifies the core IT building blocks, reviews the interrelationships among them, and establishes their roles. Figure 2.1 shows the core building blocks and serves as a general framework for discussion. This framework, introduced in Chapter 1, emphasizes the role of middleware as a glue between application processes and other infrastructure components such as network services, local software services, operating systems, and computing hardware. Our objective is to quickly scan the key players in the IT infrastructure before digging deeply into the middleware details in Part II of this book.

Throughout, we will concentrate on multivendor environments that are becoming common to support enterprisewide distributed-application architectures. These architectures may employ object-oriented, client/server, and Internet technologies. In fact, the core of these architectures is the client/server paradigm that is currently being combined with object orientation and Internet. Consequently, we focus on the C/S concepts in this chapter (object-oriented concepts and technologies are discussed in Chapter 10, distributed objects in Chapter 7, and Internet in Chapter 4).

The discussion in this chapter is motivated by the following questions:

- What are the key client/server concepts and what are the interrelationships between client/server and distributed computing environments? (Section 2.2)

- What are the main IT building blocks, what are the functions performed by these building blocks, and how do they interrelate with each other? (Section 2.3)

- How can the applications be architected, and what are the trade-offs between two-tiered and three-tiered application architectures? (Section 2.4)

- What are the different layers of middleware, and how can it be used to develop applications? (Section 2.5)

- What type of general observations can be made about the state of the art, state of the market, and state of the practice in IT environments? (Sections 2.6, 2.7, 2.8)

Figure 2.1 Information-Technology (IT) Building Blocks

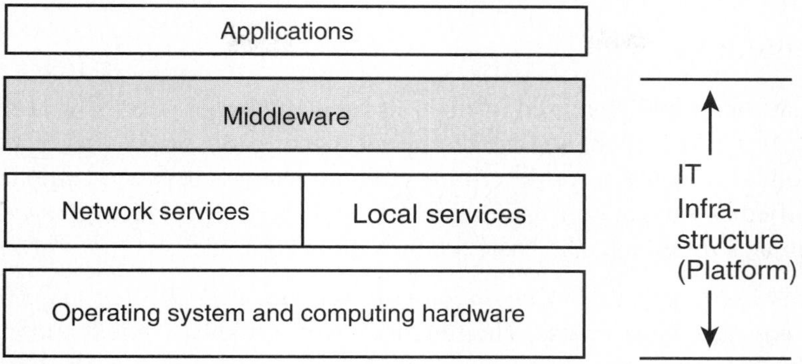

Applications

Middleware

Network services	Local services

Operating system and computing hardware

IT
Infra-
structure
(Platform)

Key Points

- IT building blocks are the applications, the middleware, network services, local services, operating systems, and computing hardware.

- C/S model is a special case of distributed computing model.

- C/S model can be *implemented* at the following two broad levels: (a) to provide business-unaware (i.e., computing-platform) services, and (b) to provide business-aware (i.e., application) services.

- Client/server applications utilize the C/S model to split business-aware functionality across machines.

- There is a trade-off between the complexity of C/S application and the complexity of the C/S middleware. If the services provided by the C/S middleware are simple and do not meet the application requirements, then this complexity shifts to the C/S application developers.

- Client/server applications can be architected as two or three physical tiers.

- C/S middleware can itself be viewed as layers, where each layer performs a unique set of services.

- A given application system can choose any layer of middleware needed.

- C/S application architects must be aware of the interplays between C/S middleware and C/S applications. In particular, the following key ideas must be kept in mind:
  - *Application Programming Interfaces (APIs) provided by the middleware impact the portability of C/S applications.*
  - *Exchange protocols used between the C/S middleware impact the interoperability of C/S applications.*

- Middleware stacks (layers) impact the performance as well as cost of a C/S application. Higher-level middleware makes it easier and cheaper to develop complex C/S applications, but too many stacks can obviously impede the performance of a C/S application.

2.2   Client/Server Fundamentals

2.2.1   Definitions

The term client/server has been used in business for a number of years. For example, in a restaurant the customer is a client and the restaurant owner is the server. In computing, the *client/server model* is a concept for describing communications between computing processes that are classified as service consumers (*clients*) and service providers (*servers*). Figure 2.2 presents a simple C/S model. The basic features of a C/S model are:

1. *Clients and servers are functional modules with well-defined interfaces (i.e., they hide internal information).* The functions performed by a client and a server can be implemented by a set of software modules, hardware components, or a combination thereof. Clients and/or servers may run on dedicated machines, if needed. It is unfortunate that some machines are called "servers." This causes confusion (try explaining to an already bewildered user that a client software is running on a machine called "the server"). We will avoid this usage as much as possible.

2. *Each client/server relationship is established between two functional modules when one module (**client**) initiates a service request and the other (**server**) chooses to respond to the service request.* Examples of service requests (SRs) are "retrieve customer name," "produce net income in last year," etc. For a given service request, clients and servers do not reverse roles (i.e., a client stays a client and a server stays a server). However, a server for SR R1 may become a client for SR R2 when it issues requests to another server (see Figure 2.2). For example, a client may issue an SR which may generate other SRs.

3. *Information exchange between clients and servers is strictly through messages (i.e., no information is exchanged through global variables).* The service request and additional information are placed into a message that is sent to the server. The server's response, similarly, is another message that is sent back to the client.

4. *Messages exchanged between clients and servers are typically interactive.* In other words, the C/S model does not normally represent an off-line process.

Conceptually, clients and servers may run on the same machine or on separate machines. In this book, however, our primary interest is in *distributed client/server systems* where clients and servers reside on separate machines (were it not for distributed C/S systems, this book would be only ten pages long!). Thus, we introduce the following additional feature of a client/server model:

5. *Clients and servers reside on separate machines connected through a network.* Thus, all C/S service requests are real-time messages that are exchanged through network services. This restriction introduces several technical issues, such as portability, interoperability, security, and performance (see Chapter 3).

Figure 2.2 Conceptual Client/Server Model

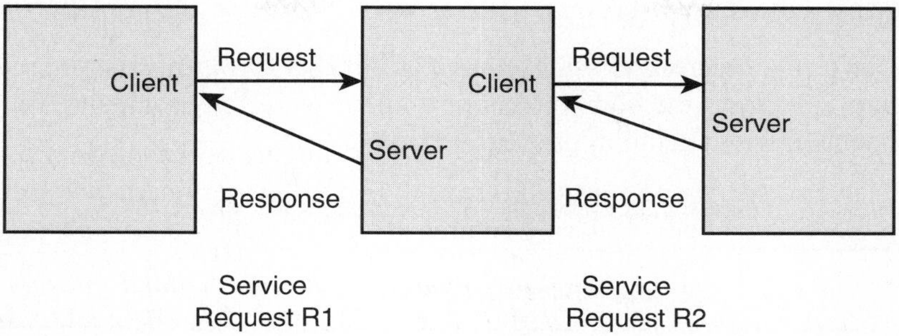

Client/server model with the aforementioned properties can be *implemented* at the following two broad levels:

- To provide business-unaware (i.e., computing-platform) services
- To provide business-aware (i.e., application) services

Our main interest is in using the C/S model to deliver business-aware functionality. Business awareness here means knowledge of business processes (e.g., the activities needed to support business goals). Implementations of the C/S model to deliver business-unaware (i.e., infra-structure) services such as print services, mail services, and file services, have been around since the early 1980s. For example, LAN "network operating systems" such as Novell Net-Ware and Banyan Vines have been providing print and file services by using the C/S model since the early 1980s.

Client/server applications, an area of vital importance to us, employ the C/S model to deliver business-aware functionalities. C/S applications provide a powerful and flexible mechanism for organizations to design applications to fit business needs. For example, an order-process-ing application can be implemented, using the C/S model, by keeping the order-processing databases (e.g., customers, products) at the corporate office and developing/customizing the order-processing logic and user interfaces for different stores that initiate orders. In this case, order-processing clients may reside on store computers to perform initial checking and pre-processing; and the order-processing servers may exist at the corporate mainframe to perform final approval and shipping. In addition, C/S applications improve the resource management and hardware economy. Thus C/S applications are critical to business enterprises of the 1990s and beyond.

Client/server platforms provide the infrastructure needed to develop, deploy, support, and manage client/server applications. In this book, we will attempt to distinguish between C/S applications and C/S platforms (also known as the C/S infrastructure). An *infrastructure* pro-vides generally useful, business-independent functions. For C/S applications, the infrastructure provides functionality such as operating-system services, local data and transaction management, network services, C/S middleware, and associated services such as directory/naming services, and security services. See Section 2.3 for additional details.

We will use the term ***client/server environment*** to indicate C/S infrastructure plus C/S applications. Figure 2.3 shows the components of a client/server environment. We will review these components in more detail in the next section.

Figure 2.3 Components of a Client/Server Environment

Application Processes				
Client/Server Middleware				
Local Services			Network Services	
Database Managers	Transaction Managers	Print & File Services		
Operating and Computing Hardware				

Client/Server Platform (Infrastructure)

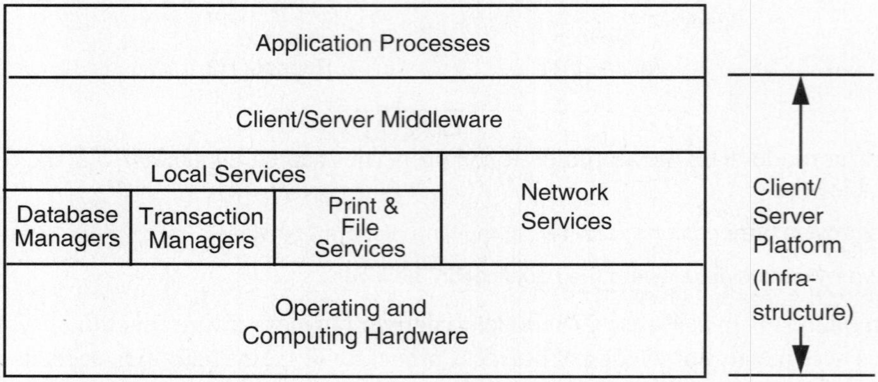

In summary, we have defined the basic properties of the client/server model and emphasized the use of this model to deliver distributed business-aware functionality. Table 2.1 summarizes the fundamental C/S properties. We will use these properties as a litmus test to differentiate between C/S and non-C/S systems.

TABLE 2.1 FUNDAMENTAL CLIENT/SERVER PROPERTIES

1. Clients and servers are functional modules that represent a consumer/provider relationship.

2. For a given service, a client initiates a service request and a server chooses to respond to this service request.

3. All information exchange between clients and servers is through messages (no global variables).

4. Message exchange between clients and servers is typically interactive.

5. Clients and servers reside on different machines connected through a network. (This is not required but is a feature of main interest.)

2.2.2   Client/Server as a Special Case of Distributed Computing

Is client/server the same as a distributed computing? If not, how do they interrelate? Figure 2.4 shows the interrelationships between distributed computing and client/server models. Conceptually, the client/server model is a special case of the distributed computing model. Let us illustrate these interrelationships in more detail.

Figure 2.4 Interrelationships Between Computing Models

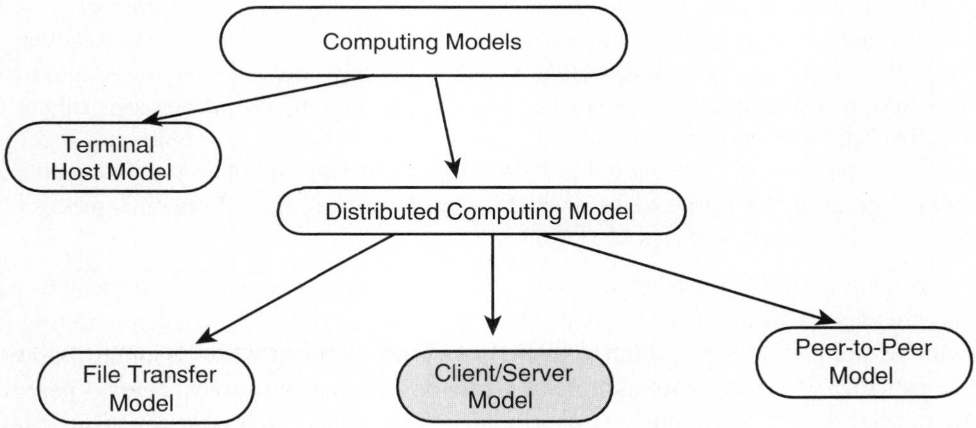

A *distributed computing system (DCS)* is a collection of autonomous computers interconnected through a communication network to achieve business functions. Technically, the computers do not share main memory so that the information cannot be transferred through global variables. The information (knowledge) between the computers is exchanged only through messages over a network.

The restriction of no shared memory and information exchange through messages is of key importance because it distinguishes between DCS and shared memory multiprocessor computing systems. This definition requires that the DCS computers are connected through a network which is responsible for the information exchange between computers. The definition also requires that the computers have to work together and cooperate with each other to satisfy enterprise needs (see [Umar 1993, Chapter 1] for more discussion of DCS).

Distributed computing can be achieved through one or more of the following:

- File-transfer model
- Client/server model
- Peer-to-peer model

The *file-transfer model* is one of the oldest models to achieve distributed computing at a very minimal level. Basically, programs at different computers communicate with each other by using file transfer. In fact, email is a special case of file transfer. Although this is a very old and extremely limited model of distributed computing, it is still used to support loosely coupled distributed computers. For example, media clips, news items, and portions of corporate databases are typically exchanged between remote computers through file transfers.

The *C/S model*, discussed earlier in this chapter, is state-of-the-market and state-of-the-practice for distributed computing at the time of this writing. The C/S model, as stated previously, allows application processes at different sites to interactively exchange messages and is thus more interactive and transactional than the file-transfer model. Initial versions of the C/S model utilized the remote-procedure call paradigm, which extends the scope of a local procedure call. At present, the C/S model is increasingly utilizing the distributed-objects paradigm, which extends the scope of local object paradigm (i.e., the application processes at different sites are viewed as distributed objects).

The *peer-to-peer model* allows the processes at different sites to invoke each other. The basic difference between C/S and peer to peer is that in a peer-to-peer model the interacting processes can be a client, server, or both, while in a C/S model one process assumes the role of a service provider while the other assumes the role of a service consumer. Peer-to-peer middleware is used to build peer-to-peer distributed applications. A few applications use the peer-to-peer model.

In this book, we will primarily concentrate on the C/S model. The file-transfer model is older and does not need additional discussion. We will also not dwell on the peer-to-peer model because peer-to-peer applications are not state-of-the-market and state-of-the-practice at the time of this writing.

2.3   IT Building Blocks—The C/S View

Figure 2.5 shows a conceptual view of the main IT building blocks:

- Client and server processes (applications)
- Middleware
- Network services
- Local services (e.g., database managers and transaction managers)
- Operating systems
- Computing hardware

Before describing these components, let us use an example to illustrate the interactions between them. Let us assume that a report writer (client process) on a desktop needs to list the best customers, where the customer information is located in a relational database (server process) on a remote machine. The client process will issue the appropriate SQL statement and submit it in a format that conforms to the application programming interface (API) of the client middleware. The client middleware will accept this SQL statement, establish a connection with the remote-database server process, package SQL statement into a particular format, and submit the request to network services. The network services will send the SQL statement as a message over the network to the network services on the remote machine. On the remote (server) machine, the SQL statement will be received by the network services and passed up to the server middleware. The server middleware must be able to understand the format in which SQL statement was sent by the client middleware. This exchange protocol between the client/server middleware plays a key role in C/S interoperability (in many cases this exchange protocol is proprietary and thus requires clients from vendor X to interoperate with servers from vendor X only). The server middleware will schedule this request for execution by sending it to the customer database manager. After the SQL statement has been processed, the results are passed back by the server middleware to the client middleware in a mutually understandable exchange protocol.

Figure 2.5 Conceptual View of a Client/Server Environment

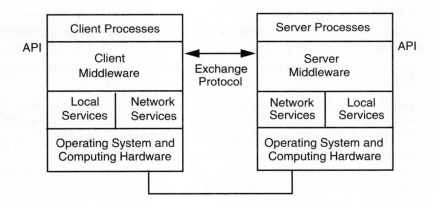

2.3.1 Client/Server Processes—The Applications

Client processes perform the application functions on the client side. Client processes can range from simple user interfaces and spreadsheets to complete application systems. Increasingly, the client processes are becoming Internet based (i.e., they utilize Web browsers to interact with end users). A client process, commonly referred to as a client, has the following characteristics:

- It interacts with a user through a user interface. User interfaces are typically graphical user interfaces (GUIs) or object-oriented user interfaces (OOUIs) which allow users to invoke services through icons. GUIs and OOUIs attempt to hide the location of the services by representing them through icons, which a user can invoke through a pointing device (e.g., a mouse) without having to explicitly log on to different systems.

- It performs some application functions, if needed. Examples of the application functions include user interface processing, spreadsheets, report generation, and object manipulation.

- It interacts with the client middleware by forming queries and/or commands in an application-programming-interface (API) format understandable by the client middleware. This API is important, because if a client middleware changes, then the client application will have to change (different client middlewares support different APIs). Ideally, these APIs should be independent of networks, operating systems, and platforms.

- It receives the responses from the server middleware and displays them, if needed, on the user interface.

Server processes perform the application functions on the server side. A server process, commonly referred to as a server, has the following characteristics:

- It provides a service to the client. Server processes can be very simple functions such as time of day (TOD), or sophisticated applications such as order processing, electronic funds transfer, or CAD/CAM services. Other examples of server processes are print services, database services, and mail services.

- Ideally, it hides internal information (e.g., the type of data being accessed) so that the clients do not have to know these details.

- It is invoked by the server middleware (described later) and returns the results back to the server middleware.

- It may provide some scheduling services so that multiple clients can be provided the service concurrently. Although scheduling a service process is generally the responsibility of server middleware (discussed later), some large server processes may schedule activities within each service.

- It provides error-recovery and failure-handling services. In the case of transactions, the server must provide typical transaction-processing capabilities (see Chapter 6).

Over the years, the sophistication of the client as well as server processes has increased. For the purpose of analysis, we can group these improvements into three generations:

First generation (mostly 1980s): The client as well as server processes had to be developed from scratch. Off-the-shelf processes, if available, supported very simple functionalities. For example, server processes in this generation were simple file and print servers, and virtually no off-the-shelf processes were available (the client processes were developed around API commands to print files on the print servers and to read and manipulate the files on the file servers).

Second generation (early 1990s). More sophisticated client and server processes became commercially available. For example, server processes included a diverse array of off-the-shelf SQL servers from a variety of DBMS vendors. Similarly, client processes included a large number of desktop decision-support tools such as spreadsheets, data browsers, report writers, and object viewers.

Third generation (mid 1990s). The capabilities of off-the-shelf client and server processes increased dramatically. For example, server processes have started providing transaction-management capabilities, and the client processes have been extended to include off-the-shelf C/S applications (e.g., the Human Resource applications from PeopleSoft), and CASE tools (e.g., PowerBuilder from PowerSoft). In particular, the widespread off-the-shelf avail-ability of very powerful client processes has led to considerable activity in C/S computing.

2.3.2   Middleware

Middleware, as discussed in the previous chapter, provides a wide range of functionality, such as establishment of sessions between client processes and server processes, security, compression/decompression, and failure handling. The C/S middleware itself can be viewed in terms of client middleware that resides on every client machine and server middleware that resides on the server platforms. Let us look at the client and server sides of middleware.

Client middleware provides the interfaces between client processes and remote server pro-cesses. *Client middleware is essentially a set of software modules which can be invoked by the client processes through an application programming interface (API).* For example, many SQL servers provide API/SQL software which a client process can use to send SQL statements to the SQL servers. Examples of client middleware are SQLNet from Oracle, Open Database Connect (ODBC) from Microsoft, DCE RPC client stubs, etc. (We will exam-ine some of these middleware products in Section 2.5). Client middleware routines perform the following functions:[1]

- Provide an API that can be used by client processes. It is desirable that the client middleware provide a standardized API so that client processes are portable across different client/server environments. Examples of de facto API standards are Open Software Foundation's Remote Procedure Call (OSF DCE) and Microsoft's Open Database Connect (ODBC). See Section 2.5.

- Establish connection with server processes by issuing commands through the network interface and the server middleware. For example, if a "database connect" command is issued by a client process, then the client middleware is responsible for sending this command to the appropriate database server by interfacing with the network services.

- Send request to the server middleware by using an exchange protocol understandable to the server. For example, the request is sent in a Sybase exchange format if a Sybase server is used on the other side. At present, different C/S middleware vendors use different exchange proto-cols, and this leads to interoperability problems. In general, client processes that use client mid-

---

1. We have discussed most of these functions in general terms previously.

dleware from vendor X cannot interoperate with server processes that use server middleware from vendor Y (unless an exchange protocol has been agreed upon between vendors X and Y). Standards in remote-procedure calls (e.g., OSF DCE RPC) and remote-data access (e.g., ISO RDA) are intended to address this problem.

- Receive response from the server middleware, and parse and interpret the response. Once again, the client middleware must understand the format in which the server is sending the results.

- Handle failure and synchronization of activity if needed. For example, if the server disappears during communications, then the client middleware is responsible for detecting this failure and initiating proper actions.

- Handle access control (e.g., by passing the client ID and password to the server so that a user does not have to log on to different systems explicitly).

Server middleware monitors the client requests and invokes appropriate server processes. Server middleware performs the following functions:

- It receives a client request from the network services and parses the request. In order to parse, the server middleware must be able to understand the format in which SQL statement was sent by the client middleware. This exchange protocol between the client/server middleware is a key to C/S interoperability (in many cases this exchange protocol is proprietary and thus requires clients from vendor X to interoperate with servers from vendor X only). C/S middleware can provide open services to receive requests from any clients that understand the server interface, or closed services which do not publicize the server interface specifications.

- It checks for security by authenticating the client. For example, server middleware on MVS uses Resource Access Control Facility (RACF) for verification.

- It schedules a server process to satisfy the client request. The request may be for a single-step service performed by a single process (e.g., a time-of-day service). Most requests require multistep, multithreaded services, in which the middleware may include sophisticated scheduling. This scheduling may be done exclusively by server middleware or in cooperation with existing transaction monitors. For example, many server middleware products on MVS use IMS and/or CICS scheduling services.

- It receives response from a server process and sends the response back to the clients.

- It is responsible for handling locks and attempts to recover from failures in clients, servers, networks, and any other components.

Client middleware is typically simple because it usually handles few client requests from desktop users (this situation is changing rapidly as more sophisticated client processes become common). At the time of this writing, the cost for typical client middleware ranges from $300 to $500 per client machine. The server middleware, on the other hand, can be quite complex and expensive, depending on the type of services needed. Design of a multistep server scheduler is a complicated task which requires attention to scheduling, network protocols, error handling, performance, and security. Typical multistep servers for mainframes range from $100,000 to $200,000. Open services need to include extensive security and reliability code because anyone can invoke them. In addition, server schedulers in large systems

What Does Middleware Do? Some Details

The following middleware facilities are needed to support OCSI applications [Adler 1995, Andrews 1991, Nehmer 1992, Shatz 1987]:

Initiation. Ability to initiate several programs at different computers. The programs may be created dynamically during the execution of the software or may be created statically at compile time and then invoked later.

Session Management. Ability to provide communication between remotely located programs. The communications may be needed to transfer data, issue commands, check status, resolve deadlocks, etc. It is desirable to provide asynchronous communication between remote programs so that the execution of a program is not suspended while waiting for responses from another program. This may be accomplished through "native" communication protocols, such as TCP/IP Sockets and LU6.2, or a suitable remote-procedure-call (RPC) software package.

Directory. Facility for the clients to locate a server (which server to invoke), send the request to a server, receive response from a server, and parse and interpret the response.

Remote-Data Access. Provision to access and manipulate remotely located data. The data may be stored in flat files or databases under the control of hierarchical, network, relational, or object-oriented DBMS.

Concurrency Control. Facility for the servers to handle many concurrent and asynchronous requests simultaneously from many clients. The servers may need the facility to invoke (fork) new processes to handle the complex client requests. For example, if a server has to just supply time of day, this can be done by the server. However, if the server needs to query a database, it is better to create a separate process which queries the database.

Security and Integrity. Ability to handle security (authentication and journaling) and handle failure (timeouts, distributed updates, two-phase commit) at the distributed sites (clients as well as servers).

Monitoring. Ability to monitor and improve the run-time performance of the distributed programs. This should allow measurement of communication traffic, program wait states, deadlocks, etc.

Termination. Ability to terminate remote sessions and remotely located programs. The programs of a distributed application system may be terminated when the main program is terminated, through explicit terminate commands or owing to other conditions that may prohibit a program from continuing. For example, a program may terminate when none of the events it is waiting for can occur. Another condition for program termination may be a deadlock resolution by forcing a timeout, which occurs when a program p1 has to wait for an event beyond a certain specified time limit (this typically indicates that the other program might have died).

must be able to handle thousands of client requests. Workstation-based systems need to be able to handle the thousands of requests typically found on mainframe systems. Server scheduling is also dependent on operating systems.

In general, there is a trade-off between the complexity of application and the complexity of the middleware. If the services provided by the middleware are simple and do not meet the application requirements, then this complexity shifts to the application developers.

2.3.3   Network Services

Communication networks, or just networks, provide the lowest level of service (i.e., information transport) in distributed computing and C/S environments. In this context, a communication network is a collection of equipment, software modules, and physical media, viewed as one autonomous whole, that interconnects two or more computers. A wide variety of network configurations exist in enterprises. For example, a network may consist of three desktops connected through a cable, or it may serve an international airlines reservation system which employs global communication satellites, large processors, and thousands of terminals and workstations.

A network can be configured as a wide-area network (WAN), which utilizes common carrier facilities for communications; a local-area network (LAN), which utilizes vendor-supplied cables for connecting computers within a building; a metropolitan-area network (MAN) within a region, which may use the communication facilities of Cable TV, or a combination of LANs, MANs, and WANs. In addition, the communication between computing devices on a network can use analog or digital data-transmission facilities over copper, wireless, or fiber optic communication media. The state-of-the-art advancement in network transmission technologies is the development of high-speed local- and wide-area transmissions, typically in the range of 100 million bits per second (Mbps) or higher. Another area of advancement is the integration of voice, data, and video images for multimedia applications such as teleconferencing and group problem solving, among others. Examples of the evolving network communication technologies are Asynchronous Transfer Mode (ATM), Frame Relay, Fiber Distributed Data Interface (FDDI), and wireless networks. In general, networks are becoming faster, ubiquitous, and more reliable.

A *network architecture* describes the physical components, the functions performed by the components, and the interfaces between the components of a network. Network architecture standards are needed to interconnect different networks from different vendors with different capabilities. For example, a Chicago bank which uses a Sun-supported network needs to communicate with a New York bank which uses an IBM-supplied network. The ***Open System Interconnection (OSI) Reference Model*** specifies standards for networks from different vendors to exchange information freely. The OSI Model casts the functions needed to exchange information between interconnected computers in terms of seven layers (see Figure 2.6). Many network architectures have evolved in the last 20 years. Examples of the state-of-the-market/practice network architectures are the ***Transmission Control Protocol/Internet***

Protocol (TCP/IP) stack, IBM's *System Network Architecture (SNA)*, Novell's *NetWare LAN,* and the Open System Interconnection (OSI) Model. See Chapter 11 for a brief overview of these network architectures.

Network services provide the basic addressing and transport mechanisms across a network. These services communicate with the server and client middleware. Network services are provided typically by TCP/IP, SNA, and LAN protocols such as NetBIOS and Novell NetWare SPX/IPX. *Network interconnectivity* is the key issue addressed by network services in enterprisewide networks to provide interfaces and transport of messages between remotely located client and server processes.The principal network interconnectivity devices are:

- **Bridges** connect two LANs to form a larger LAN. Bridges are simple devices which do not deal with the issues of routing and session control needed in enterprisewide networks.

- **Routers** find a path for a message in larger networks and then send the message over the selected path. A router is more sophisticated than a bridge because it knows alternate routes for a message and uses the alternate routes if needed. In most cases, enterprises have replaced bridges with routers. Over the years, routers have accumulated additional functionality such as security checking ("the fire walls").[2]

Figure 2.6 The OSI Reference Model

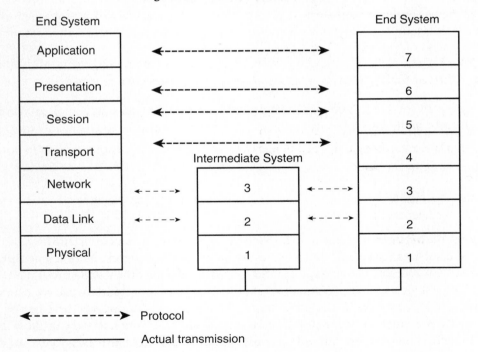

---

2. Some commercially available routers also convert lower-level protocol (e.g., Ethernet to Token Ring).

- **Gateways** translate one type of protocol to another. In most large networks, protocols of some subnetworks need to be converted to protocols of other subnetworks for end-to-end communications. A gateway connects two dissimilar network architectures and is essentially a protocol converter. A gateway may be a special-purpose computer, a workstation with associated software (e.g., a PS2 with gateway software), or a software module which runs as a task in a mainframe. Examples of gateways for network interconnectivity are TCP/IP-to-SNA gateway and Novell NetWare-to-mainframe gateway.

Routers and gateways are used commonly in enterprisewide networks. For example, if a client spreadsheet on a PC TCP/IP network in Chicago needs to access a database server on an MVS SNA network in New York, then a series of routers will be needed to find the path between the client and server process. In addition, a TCP/IP-to-SNA gateway will be needed for translating messages from TCP/IP to SNA protocols.

Figure 2.7 shows a realistic enterprise network that uses TCP/IP very heavily, except the SNA network at the mainframe. The routers are used between all TCP/IP network segments, and a gateway is used to convert TCP/IP messages to SNA.

Detailed discussion of network issues is beyond the scope of this book. The tutorial in Chapter 11 gives a quick overview of the most important networking issues for C/S systems (e.g., emerging network technologies, network architectures, and network interconnectivity devices such as routers and gateways). A more thorough discussion of this topic can be found in Umar [1993]. Bell [1996] gives a good survey of the topic. Additional sources of information are listed in Chapter 11.

2.3.4   Local Software

The local software in a C/S environment provides access and manipulation of data and processes located on the machines in a C/S environment. Examples of the local software are:

- Database managers
- Transaction managers
- File managers
- Print managers

Database managers, also known as database management systems (DBMSs), provide access to databases for on-line and batch users. In a typical database environment, different users can view, access, and manipulate the data in a database. A DBMS is designed to (a) manage logical views of data so that different users can access and manipulate the data without having to know its physical representation (b) manage concurrent access to data by multiple users, enforcing logical isolation of transactions, and (c) enforce security to allow access to authorized users only, and provide integrity controls and backup/recovery of a database. Relational database managers such as DB2, Oracle, Sybase, and/or Informix are typically used in many contemporary applications. Older systems use hierarchical database managers such as IMS. Object-oriented databases are still in their infancy (see Chapter 10). The key issue in C/S environments is to access remotely located databases from a variety of client processes. We will discuss this issue in detail in Chapter 5.

Figure 2.7 Network Interconnectivity in Client/Server Environment

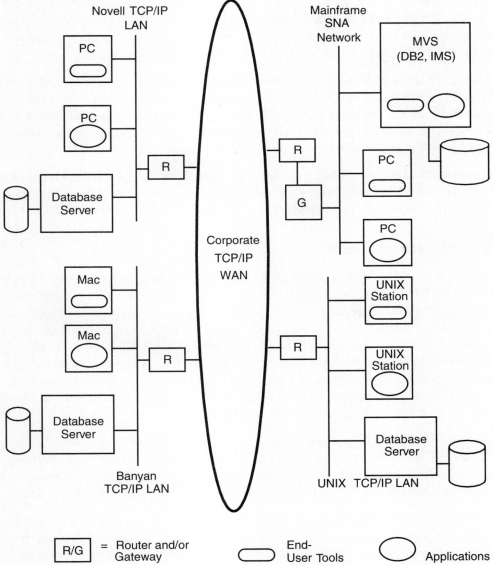

Transaction managers (TMs), also known as transaction-processing monitors (TP monitors), monitor the execution of transactions (sequence of statements that must be executed as a unit). TMs specialize in managing transactions from their point of origin to their termination (planned or unplanned). Some TM facilities are integrated with the DBMS facilities to allow database queries from different transactions to access/update one or several data items (IBM's IMS DB/DC is an example). However, some TMs specialize in handling transactions only (CICS, Tuxedo, and Encina are examples). The key issue in C/S environments is how to extend the scope of local transaction management to managing the execution of transactions across multiple sites. See Chapter 6 for a detailed discussion of this topic.

File managers are responsible for providing access and manipulation of text documents, diagrams, charts, images, and indexed files. A very wide range of file managers have been developed since the 1960s. An important issue in C/S environments is to provide access to files that are dispersed around a network. This issue has been addressed by middleware such as the SUN Network File Server (NFS).

Print managers are responsible for printing operations. Obviously, different types of print managers are available for different types of print devices. Almost all LANs at present provide access to print managers on the LAN.

2.3.5   Operating Systems

Simply stated, operating systems schedule and allocate the computer-system resources (e.g., main memory, CPU, disks) to the programs and interactive users. To allow multiple users to access multiple resources simultaneously, operating systems provide a set of services such as task scheduling, interprocess communications, security, and resource protection. Examples of existing operating systems are (a) IBM's MVS (Multitasking Virtual System) that operates the IBM mainframes (b) various UNIX operating systems for a wide range of midrange computers (e.g., HP-UX for Hewlett Packard and AIX for IBM's RS6000 machines (c) Microsoft's Windows, Windows NT, and Windows 95 for IBM PCs (d) IBM's OS/2 for IBM PCs, and (e) Mac OS for Apple Macintosh computers.

Let us briefly discuss the type of operating-system services that are needed by a C/S environment. Examples are multitasking, multiprocessing, synchronization (semaphores), intertask protection mechanisms, efficient memory management, and dynamically linked run-time libraries. These services, needed to build servers, are provided by most available operating systems.

From a C/S perspective, the main role of operating systems is to schedule server processes that need access to resources such as main memory, files, databases, and printers. In some operating systems, such as UNIX, it is relatively easy to schedule new requests by using forking and daemons. However, in the MVS operating system, scheduling is done by transaction managers such as IMS and CICS, which are oriented toward a terminal-mainframe model.[3] To build a server on MVS, some effort is needed to use IMS and/or CICS as server schedulers. In some cases, several instances of a server are installed on the same or different machines for performance or availability reasons. A server manager may be needed to create servers on demand and route requests to a duplicate server if one server fails. Generalized server schedulers for MVS as well as UNIX environments are commercially available. Examples are the INETD server scheduler for UNIX and the IBM/370 Server Task Manager for MVS. On PCs, operating systems such as OS/2, Windows, and Windows NT all provide capabilities for developing client as well as server software (this is commonly accomplished through Dynamic Link Libraries).

Two additional services (threads and interprocess communications) are of particular importance in C/S environments.

Threads provide units of concurrency within programs. Threads are used to create concurrent, event-driven server programs. Threads are available in some operating systems (e.g., UNIX). In other cases, C/S middleware such as OSF DCE provides thread support (see Chapter 3).

Interprocess communications (IPC) services are needed for independent processes to exchange information. Different operating systems provide different types of IPCs. For example, UNIX provides a wide range of IPC services such as pipes, streams, sockets, and TLI [Stevens 1990]. Currently available operating systems such as OS/2, Windows NT, Novell NetWare, UNIX, and MVS provide these capabilities with varying degrees of sophistication.

Microkernel Operating Systems. Owing to the differences between different operating systems and the operating-system-dependent code that has to be developed for basic C/S middleware, a trend toward ***microkernel operating systems*** has emerged. For example, the IBM Workplace OS is a microkernel that will run OS/2, DOS, Windows, UNIX, OS/400, and Taligent applications. Basically a microkernel OS is a minimal operating system that provides basic resources (device drivers, processors, address spaces; everything else, e.g., files are at a higher level). The bulk of the operating-system functions are provided through a set of modular components that plug and play on top of the microkernel. Examples of these "personality-neutral" components are device drivers, security servers, memory managers, and file systems. The services of these components are invoked by clients through the microkernel. Thus the microkernels provide an operating-system-independent environment for clients to access services, albeit in a single-machine environment. See Goulde [1993] for detailed analysis of microkernel operating systems.

---

3. As we will see in Chapter 9, IBM has announced C/S strategies for IMS as well as CICS. However, the origin of these products is terminal host.

Many textbooks describe operating systems in detail (see, for example, Tannenbaum [1992], Nutt [1992]). Discussion of distributed operating systems can be found in Umar [1993, chap. 7].

2.3.6 Computing Hardware

In a C/S environment, client and server processes can reside on computing-hardware personal computers (PCs), powerful workstations, midrange computers, and mainframes. As we all know, computer hardware is becoming faster, cheaper, smaller, and more reliable. For C/S environments, the growth of multiprocessing machines (unfortunately known as "servers"[4]) is of significance. Multiprocessors utilize many CPUs in the same machine to maximize parallel operations. Multiprocessors typically used to house server processes such as database servers for fast access, come in two flavors:

- Asymmetric multiprocessors (AMPs)
- Symmetric multiprocessors (SMPs)

Asymmetric multiprocessing (AMP) dedicates processors to different (asymmetric) tasks such as network I/O, disk I/O, and compute processes. The operating system runs in a dedicated processor and monitors the activities of other processors.

Symmetric multiprocessing (SMP) configurations treat all processors equally (symmetrically). Any processor can perform I/O, network I/O, or compute processes just like any other processor. In essence, there is a "processor pool" that is used by applications on an as-needed basis. SMPs are in general more efficient than AMPs. Applications for SMP are organized as threads that can run on any processor. Thus the application designers must design applications in terms of parallel threads to fully exploit SMP hardware. This is the main reason why SMP hardware is used by database managers, because many RDBMS vendors such as Oracle and Informix at present design their DBMSs as threaded applications. In addition, most operating systems, such as UNIX, OS/2, and Windows NT, support SMP machines.

It is far beyond the scope of this book to get into technical details of computing hardware. We just need to keep in mind that the availability of fast and cheap hardware devices is a key enabler of C/S environments, because client and server processes can be assigned to dedicated machines. From a C/S point of view, scalability, performance, and availability of computing hardware are of key importance. Quick surveys of computing hardware can be found in Comerford [1996], Gillooly [1996], and Foley [1996].

erver is a function and should not be used to represent hardware.

2.4   Application Architectures and Sample Configurations

2.4.1   Overview

We will use the following definition of *application software architecture* that was developed in a software architecture discussion at the Software Engineering Institute [Garlan 1995]:

> The structure of the components of a program/system, their interrelationships, and principles and guidelines governing their design and evolution over time.

In C/S environments, application architectures raise fundamental questions such as the following:

- How can the application be decomposed into clients and servers to provide maximum flexibility and suitability?

- What are the most appropriate infrastructure services needed by the application to provide maximum portability and interoperability? In particular, how can the application take advantage of existing and evolving open standards and architectures?

- Where will the application components (e.g., databases, programs, user interfaces) be allocated to maximize performance and availability?

These issues are of fundamental importance and are discussed in detail in the companion book Umar [1997]. Let us briefly review the main issues and highlight the key trade-offs.

A major step in establishing application architectures is to identify *application layers* and specify the abstract messages between these layers. The three logical layers of an application (user interface layer, the processing layer, and the data layer) are also known as *logical tiers*. The next step is to structure and cast these layers into a physical client/server configuration, i.e., allocate these layers to computers[5]. For example, the application layers can be allocated to a single machine (*single physical tier*), to a client machine and a server machine (*two physical tiers*), or to a middle machine in addition to a client and a server machine (*three physical tiers*). Figure 2.8 illustrates this mapping—the logical model represented in terms of user, processing and data layers is cast into *physical tiers.* Note that our view of tiers is a generalization of the common industrial views [Dickman 1995, Dhumne 1996, Schulte 1995]. Let us discuss the configurations shown in Figure 2.8. Determination of an appropriate level of distribution (physical tiers) is of fundamental importance in C/S architectures. This decision impacts the choice of infrastructure, especially middleware, performance results, and implementation considerations.

---

5. In reality, the layers are organized into processes that can run on different computers.

2.4.2 Single-Physical-Tiered Architectures

The single-tiered (terminal-host) architectures at present are getting no respect because they represent "old mainframe model." However, this model is still quite suitable for mission-critical OLTP applications. Since the early 1970s, the CICS- and IMS-based OLTP systems have gradually improved in performance, reliability, and administrative control features. By way of contrast, the C/S transaction-processing middleware is still evolving (see Chapter 6). Availability of industrial-strength C/S transaction processors is a crucial issue for enterprisewide C/S applications [Johnson 1995]. In the meantime, single-tiered architectures may still be a viable choice for enterprisewide mission-critical applications that require strong central control and high transactions per second for thousands of users. The modern "network computers" potentially make the single-tiered model more popular because these computers are little more than programmable terminals that need significant server backup.

Figure 2.8 Logical to Physical Tiers (Typical Configurations)

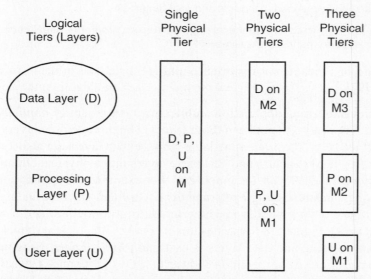

Legend: M, M1, M2, and M3 are machines (computers) on which objects can reside

2.4.3 Two-Physical-Tiered Architecture Overview

The architectures shown in Figure 2.9 (a) through (e) show the two-tiered architectures (these architectural configurations are known as the "Gartner Group" configurations [Schulte 1995]). The first two architectures, Figure 2.9 (a) and (b), are used in many presentation-intensive applications to provide a "face lift" to legacy applications by building a GUI/OOUI interface that invokes the older text-based user interfaces. Figure 2.9 (c) represents the distributed-application-program architecture, in which the application programs are split between the client and server machines and they communicate with each other through the remote-procedure-call (RPC) middleware. Figure 2.9 (d) represents the remote data architecture in which the remote data is typically stored in an "SQL server" and is accessed through ad hoc SQL statements sent over the network. Figure 2.9 (e) represents the case where the data exists at client as well as server machines (distributed-data architecture).

Although a given C/S application can be architected in any of these configurations, the remote-data and distributed-program configurations are quite popular at present. The remote-data configuration at present is very popular for departmental applications and is heavily supported by tools such as PowerBuilder and Gupta SQL Windows (as a matter of fact this configuration is used to represent typical two-tiered architectures that rely on data passing, e.g., ad hoc SQL). However, the distributed-programs configuration is very useful for enterprise-wide applications, because the application programs on both sides can exchange information through messages. The distributed data approach, discussed in detail in Chapter 5, introduces several technical and administrative issues, and should be approached carefully.

Figure 2.9 Two-Tiered Client/Server Architectures

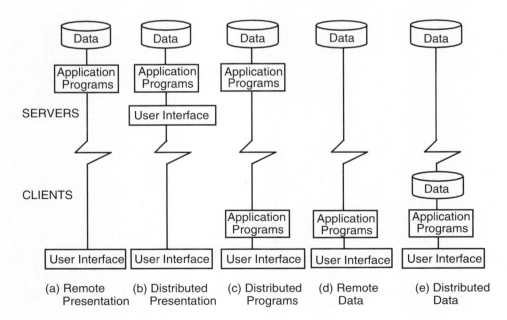

2.4.4   Three-Physical-Tiered Architecture Overview

The configurations in Figure 2.10 show sample three-tiered C/S architectures. In a three-tiered C/S model, the C/S application objects are split across three types of machines: a front-end machine (usually a desktop), a middle machine (usually a LAN server or a minicomputer), and a back-end machine (usually a mainframe). It is important that the interactions in every tier use a C/S model (several real-life systems use file transfer between back-end and middle machine, thus implementing *hybrid* architectures instead of three-tiered C/S architectures). In addition, some business-aware functionality must exist at each of the tiers for a three-tiered C/S application. In many cases, the middle machines serve as gateways that essentially convert one type of protocol to another (e.g., network gateways that convert one type of network protocol to another and database gateways that convert one type of database call to another). More importantly, middle machines can merge/integrate results from different data sources and can serve as gateways between the desktop applications and the back-end legacy applications by mediating between the two worlds (see Chapter 8 for a discussion of legacy access gateways).

Figure 2.10 Sample Three-Tiered C/S Architectures

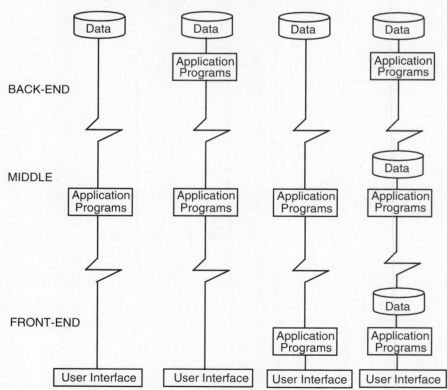

2.4.5   Sample Configuration

In most enterprisewide distributed-computing environments, a combination of single-tiered, two-tiered, three-tiered, and hybrid architectures exists. For example, the configuration in Figure 2.5 showed a combination of terminal emulation, file transfer, and C/S in a typical enterprise distributed-computing environment.

Figure 2.11 shows a real-life configuration which consists of an IBM SNA mainframe, and many Ethernet LANs (UNIX TCP/IP LANs, a Novell LAN, and an Appleshare LAN), all interconnected through a TCP/IP corporatewide backbone. The routers are used to find the appropriate paths between various computers in this network. A gateway is used to convert the TCP/IP network protocols to Token Ring and SNA. All computers on this network can access other computer resources through terminal emulation and file transfer. The Novell and Appleshare servers are used in this network for file and print services.

Let us concentrate on how the two databases (MVS DB2 and UNIX Oracle) are accessed by the client processes (e.g., spreadsheets) on various PCs in Figure 2.11. These client processes can access the DB2 and UNIX databases by using a two-tiered architecture. However, some specialized application processes (e.g., forecasting applications) reside on the UNIX application server that also need the data located in the UNIX database server. In this case, the PC

Figure 2.11 A Sample C/S Configuration

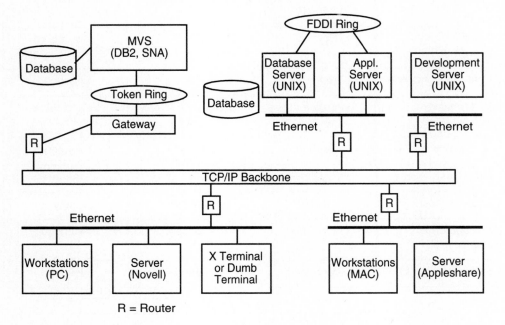

client processes access the application server, which in turn issues the SQL statements against the UNIX database server by using a three-tiered architecture. The FDDI ring is used to provide fast access to the UNIX database server (FDDI is a 100-million-bits-per-second LAN, as compared to the old Ethernet LANs that operate at 10 million bits per second).

2.4.6   Choosing Number of Tiers

An application can be configured as a single-, two-, three-, or mixed-tiered architecture. Table 2.2 shows trade-offs between the different tiered configurations in terms of application types, flexibility, end-user independence, performance, availability, initial cost, upgrade cost, manageability, and security. We have chosen a few factors for illustration. Other factors can be added, based on application requirements. We also recognize that different configurations within two- and three-tiered architectures can exist. However, our objective here is to give a broad discussion of trade-offs.

TABLE 2.2 TRADE-OFFS BETWEEN DIFFERENT TIERS

	Single Physical Tiered (Terminal Host)	Two Physical Tiered	Three Physical Tiered
Typical Application Type	Enterprisewide mission-critical OLTP	Departmental decision support	Enterprisewide applications
Flexibility and Growth	Not good	Good	Very good
User Independence	Not good	Good	Very good
Performance	Congestion at host	Congestion at network	Many choices
Availability	Not good	Good	Very good
Initial Cost	Low	Medium	High
Upgrade Cost	High	Medium	Low
Manageability and Control	Very good	Good	Not good
Security	Very good	Good	Not good

The fundamental question in analyzing these trade-offs is: *what are the key business drivers?* If flexibility and end-user independence are the key drivers, then more tiers are better (the other factors have to be considered as business risks). Another important question is: what type of application is being developed? The three-tiered model is very flexible and is a natural fit for enterprisewide applications because it fits the "three-tiered business topologies" (i.e., headquarters, regional offices, local offices). However, it lacks, at the time of this writing, the extensive transaction-processing capabilities of mainframe-based systems. More tiers can introduce several unnecessary points of failure, performance bottlenecks, and security exposures (most of these issues can be mitigated through careful design).

2.5 IT Building Blocks—A Second Look

Figure 2.12 shows the layered view that we introduced in Chapter 1 and that will be used as a roadmap for discussion in Part II of this book. For the sake of simplicity, this view does not show the operating systems and local support services. Let us revisit it based on the information introduced in this chapter.

The applications are at the highest layer, the network services at the lowest layers. The middleware layers are shown within the context of the OSI 7-layered Reference Model (network transport services encompass layers 1 to 4, and C/S middleware and C/S applications encompass layers 5 to 7). The reader may want to preview Chapter 11 for a short discussion of the OSI Reference Model layers.

We should reemphasize that some of the services we describe as middleware (e.g., Web browsers, email) are viewed as applications from a computing point of view. However, according to our definition, all business-unaware services that reside above networks are viewed as middleware, because from a user and business point of view, they add no business value.

2.5.1 Network Services

Network services are responsible for transporting messages between different machines. These services can be broadly viewed in terms of (a) physical communication services, and (b) end-to-end transport services (see Chapter 11 for details).

Physical communication services are provided by the lower layers (layers 1 to 3 of ISO/OSI Model). These services focus on the communication media used (coaxial cables, twisted pair, optical fiber, wireless), transmission techniques employed (broadband, baseband, carrierband), transmission data rates allowed for each standard, and data-link protocols such as Token Ring, Ethernet, FDDI, SDLC, X.25 packet-switching standard, the ISDN standard, and standards for ATM and Frame Relay networks.

End-to-end transport services are needed to assure that a message can transmit from one end system to another, even if the two end systems are connected over several intermediate

Figure 2.12 Layered View of IT Building Blocks

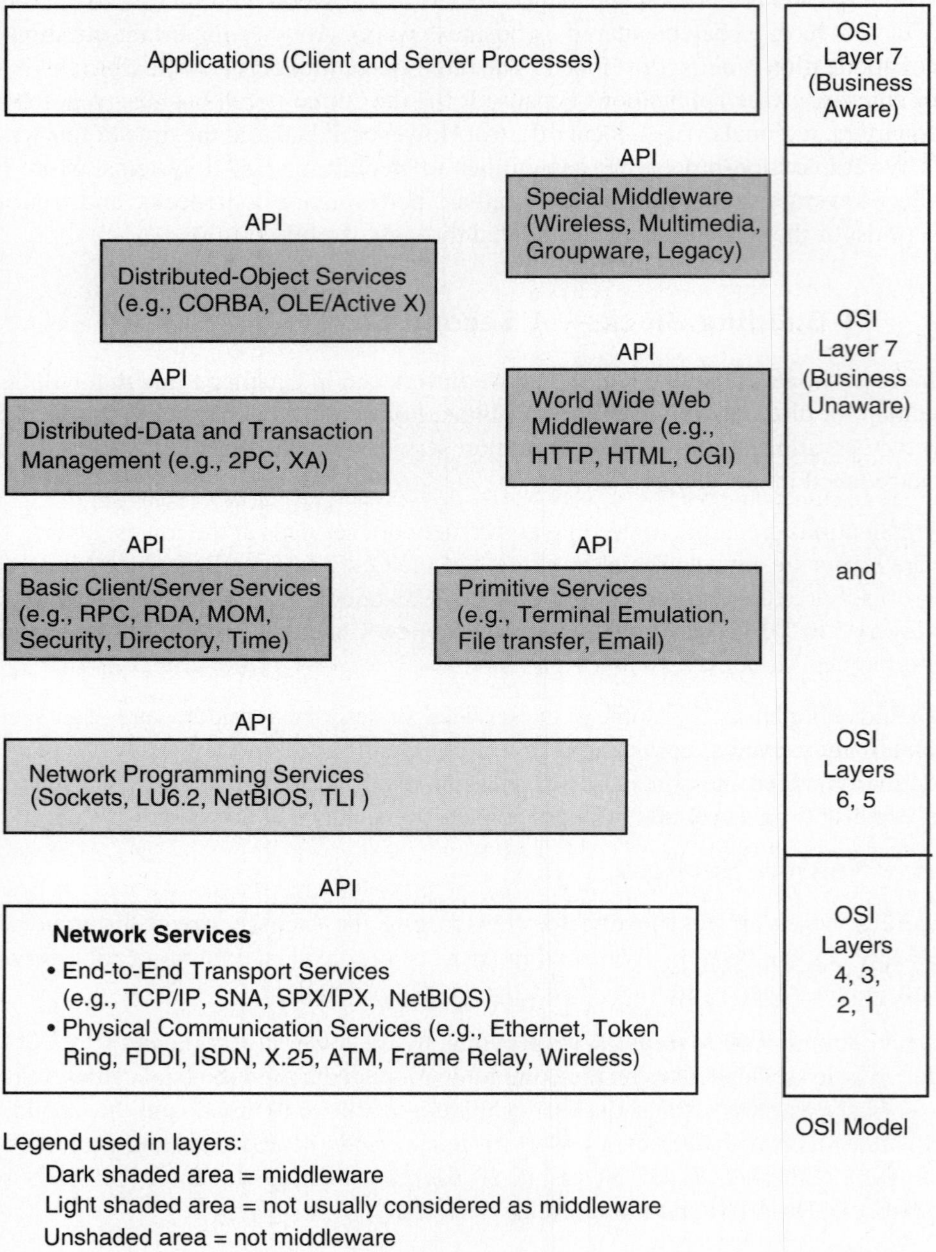

Legend used in layers:

    Dark shaded area = middleware

    Light shaded area = not usually considered as middleware

    Unshaded area = not middleware

network segments (e.g., LANs interconnected over a WAN). End-to-end transport is typically provided by the middle layers of the OSI model (layers 4 and 3). Transmission Control Protocol (TCP), one of the best-known layer-4 protocols, runs on top of IP (Internet Protocol), a layer-3 protocol (TCP/IP is used to support Internet). Other popular end-to-end transport services are the IBM Network Control Program (NCP) and Novell NetWare SPX/IPX.

2.5.2   Middleware Layers—A Closer Look

The middleware services have evolved, and continue to evolve, since the mid-1980s. Each layer has added more functionality and made it easier to develop and deploy distributed applications.The services provided by each layer are made available to the application programs through APIs. Examples of middleware layers are:

- Network programming services such as TCP/IP sockets
- Primitive services software such as terminal emulators and file-transfer packages
- Basic client-server software for information exchange
- Distributed data-management software to access remotely located databases
- Distributed transaction-management software to guarantee transactions across systems
- Distributed-object software to allow access and invocation of objects across systems
- World Wide Web middleware to support the applications over the Internet
- Specialized software for emerging areas such as mobile computing, distributed multimedia, groupware, and legacy system integration

Network programming services that are used to invoke network services through APIs.[6] Examples of this low-level middleware are TCP/IP sockets, SNA Logical Unit 6.2 (LU6.2), IBM's NetBIOS for LANs, and AT&T's Transport Layer Interface (TLI). This middleware, also known as first-generation C/S middleware, is difficult to use (it is similar to writing assembly-language code). This middleware is beyond the scope of this book. A brief overview is given in Chapter 11 (see Umar [1993] for additional details).

Primitive services middleware includes "thin" middleware services such as terminal emulation, file transfer, and email. Terminal emulators make a computer look like a terminal which is connected to another computer. Through terminal emulation, a user sitting in Chicago can log on to a Los Angeles computer and access the account information. Terminal emulators have been around since the 1970s; many of them operate on multiple computer systems (e.g., Kermit, Telnet). A file-transfer package allows a file to be transferred between different computers (e.g., transfer a customer's credit history from one computer to another). Terminal emulators as well as file-transfer packages are location sensitive: The user must know the location and the syntax used at each computer system. Thus, if a teller needs to access the

---

6. It can be argued that these services are too low level to be included in middleware.

accounts of a customer from 10 different banks, he or she will have to explicitly log on to 10 different computers with 10 different passwords (this may take some time). Email software allows users to send mail electronically, reply to mail, save it, etc. We will not discuss these primitive services in this book (why bother!).

Basic client/server middleware extends the scope of local information exchanges between local programs to networks. It allows application processes at different sites to interactively exchange messages with each other by using the C/S paradigm. Typically, a user workstation acts as a client, issuing service requests to applications and databases which may be located at many remote sites. Basic C/S middleware was the foundation of the "client/server computing revolution" in the early 1990s. The main appeal of C/S computing is that it goes beyond the terminal-emulation/file-transfer paradigm that has been the foundation of the terminal-host computing model.

Basic C/S middleware includes information-exchange services such as remote-procedure call (RPC), remote-data access (RDA), and message-oriented middleware (MOM). In addition, basic C/S middleware may include management and support facilities such as security and directory. Basic C/S middleware is typically built on top of the network programming services (for example, RPC is built on top of TCP/IP sockets). Many vendors provide the Basic C/S middleware. For example, Sun and Netwise provide RPCs, database vendors support RDA, and Peerlogic supplies a MOM package. Although basic middleware can be "assembled" from different suppliers, some ***network operating systems (NOSs)*** assemble the different pieces of basic C/S middleware for us. Examples of NOSs for local-area networks are Novell and Windows NT. A better example of an NOS for enterprisewide C/S systems is the Open Software Foundation's DCE (distributed computing environment). We discuss the basic C/S middleware and OSF DCE in Chapter 3.

World Wide Web (WWW) middleware is evolving to meet the explosive demand for Internet applications that use the WWW graphical user interface to access Internet "resources." At present, this middleware consists of Web browsers, Web servers, search engines, Hypertext Markup Language (HTML), Hypertext Transfer Protocol (HTTP), and gateways to access corporate databases and applications.[7] In addition, Sun Microsystems has introduced an interpretive language, called **Java**, that is becoming very popular for developing Web applications. An area of particular interest is ***Intranets***—the private Internets that support corporate computing and use the WWW technology within an organization. It is being contended that Intranets and Web will provide the ultimate middleware for enterprisewide information systems [Caldwell 1996, Kador 1996]. We discuss this middleware in Chapter 4.

Distributed-data management middleware extends the scope of a local-data manager to a distributed-data manager. Local-data managers, especially database managers, allow users to

---

7. From a computing point of view, these Web services are viewed as applications. From a user and business point of view, these are middleware services. We take the second view.

access and manipulate data without having to know on what physical disk the data is located (for example, you *never* have to say on what disk a customer database is located to issue SQL queries). In a similar manner, users of distributed-data management middleware should not have to know *on what computer* the customer database is located. Distributed-data management middleware adds a layer (i.e., sophistication) on top of the basic client/server middleware. This middleware allows a user to store, access, and manipulate data transparently from multiple computers (i.e., SQL joins across computers). For example, a customer's profile information (age, address, credit rating) located on one computer could be joined with the purchases made by the customer from a supplier stored on another computer for promotional advertising. The following levels of transparency may be provided by a distributed-data management middleware:

- *Read transparency from multiple sites:* The user can read and join data from any site without knowing the site where the data is located.

- *Vendor transparency:* The user can read and join information across database vendors (e.g., joins between Informix and Oracle databases).

At present, middleware for distributed-data management with varying degrees of capabilities is state-of-the-market and state-of-the-practice. Most of the available products, also known as *remote SQL gateways*, are available from many database vendors. See Chapter 5 for more details.

Distributed-transaction-processing middleware extends the scope of local-transaction processing (LTP) to distributed-transaction processing (DTP). A transaction is a unit of consistency that must be done entirely or not at all. For example, money transfer between two banks is a transaction (either the entire amount is transferred or nothing is transferred). Transaction processors allow users to update data concurrently while maintaining the integrity of transactions during system failures (these systems keep extensive logs and employ algorithms to undo transactions in case of failures). DTP is an order of magnitude more complex than LTP (it is extremely difficult to keep interrelated and duplicated data synchronized between different sites that are connected over an enterprise network). For example, if a failure occurred while money was being transferred between two banks, then a DTP middleware would attempt to roll back the changes made by the failing transaction. DTP middleware is also much more sophisticated than the retrieval-oriented distributed data-management middleware (e.g., the remote SQL gateways). The following levels of transparency may be provided by a DTP middleware:

- *Update transparency:* The user can update data that may be duplicated at many sites. This implies that data updated at one site is synchronized with other copies to maintain database consistency and integrity.

- *Transaction execution transparency:* A transaction may be decomposed into many subtransactions which may execute at many sites to access distributed data.

- *Failure transparency:* The user is isolated from site and network failures so that he or she access the desired data through alternate routes at alternate sites.

Design and deployment of DTP middleware to support these capabilities involves many issues in update-synchronization algorithms, deadlock detection, and failure handling in distributed systems. Such DTP middleware is referred to as *TP heavy*. In many C/S applications that operate in PC LAN environments, a TP-heavy approach incurs too much overhead. For this reason a *TP-lite* approach is adopted in many C/S applications, where the updates are synchronized periodically by using commercially available replication servers. At present, DTP middleware to support varying degrees of TP-lite as well as TP-heavy capabilities is state-of-the-market and state-of-the-practice. We will discuss DTP middleware in Chapter 6.

Distributed-object middleware extends the scope of local object-oriented (OO) software to objects that are dispersed over a network. Most of the commonly available OO software environments, such as C++ and Smalltalk run-time environments, allow an object to send messages to other objects in the same machine. Distributed-object middleware allows objects on machine A to send messages to objects on machine B. This middleware is of crucial importance for OCSI architectures and is the backbone of the emerging distributed-object computing. The foundation of this middleware is:

- A broker, an *object request broker (ORB)*, that transfers requests and responses between object clients and object servers.
- A repository that keeps track of the distributed objects and helps the ORB to locate needed objects across a network.

Distributed-object middleware provides a very powerful tool for development of new applications. This is an area of considerable industrial and standards activity. Examples of key services and standards are the Object Management Group's Common Object Request Broker Architecture (OMG CORBA), Microsoft's Object Link Embedding (OLE/ActiveX), and OpenDoc. Distributed-object middleware is just becoming state-of-the-market and is not fully state of the practice at the time of this writing. Many distributed-object middleware products are built on top of network programming services such as TCP/IP sockets, while a few are built on top of the Basic C/S middleware (e.g., some CORBA implementations are developed on top of RPCs). We will discuss the principles of distributed-object middleware and describe CORBA, OLE/ActiveX, and OpenDoc in Chapter 7.

Emerging special-purpose middleware is being developed to enable emerging applications. As new areas of applications and new network technologies emerge, the need for middleware to support them is growing. Examples of main emerging middleware are as follows:

- *Groupware middleware,* such as Lotus Notes, to support group activities on a network
- *Mobile computing middleware* to support the special features needed by wireless applications mobile users)
- *middleware* to enable the development of distributed, multimedia applications
- *integration middleware* to allow integration and coexistence of legacy systems applications.

emerging middleware in Chapter 8.

It can be seen that middleware has grown gradually as layers of services that reside over the network transport services. It has grown from simple terminal-emulator/file-transfer packages to sophisticated transaction processors and distributed-object managers. The ultimate in middleware is the ***distributed operating system (DISOS)*** that extends the scope of local operating systems to networks. A DISOS synthesizes and extends all middleware services, so that a user request arriving at computer C1 may use *any* of the resources located anywhere in the network *without* knowledge of their location. Examples of the resources are remote data, CPU, main memory, and a variety of print, file, security, database, and directory services. The functionalities of a distributed operating system include:

- Total transparency to the end user, so that the entire network appears as one large computing system with all processing, memory units, devices, and services available to the authorized users.

- Automatic selection of an appropriate computer system or a server for execution of a request. The selection may be based on criteria such as fastest or cheapest execution.

- Automatic rerouting of a request to an appropriate computing system or a server when failures or congestions occur in the network.

Most DISOSs at present are in the state-of-the-art stage; there are many active university projects. Discussion of DISOS is beyond the scope of this book. Interested readers can find information about DISOS in Umar [1993, chap. 7].

In addition to the layers discussed so far, the middleware also provides a variety of management and support services, such as security, directory, time, and management services. Although these services can span several layers, it is best to view them as part of the basic C/S middleware layer. We will review these services in Chapter 3.

It should be noted that while middleware functionality can be viewed in terms of middleware layers, the implementations do not need to; indeed, it is often inefficient to do so. To improve efficiency, there is a general trend towards dropping middleware layers so that the top level API is as close to the operating system (even inside it) as possible.[8]

2.5.3 Applications

Applications represent the business-aware functionality that is split between different machines. Basically, a C/S application is an application that has been split into two parts: client and server. Distributed C/S programs (C/S processes) communicate with each other through messages which travel over communication networks. The basic difference between parallel and distributed programs is that parallel programs can use shared memory to transfer information through global variables while distributed programs cannot. For this reason only some of the algorithms and techniques developed for efficient parallel programs are applicable to distributed programming [Andrews 1983], [Andrews 1991], and [Blelloch 1996]. This situation

---

8. This was pointed out by Dr. Andrew Herbert, Technical Director of the ANSA Consortium during the book review process.

could change as research progresses in developing shared-memory distributed computer systems progress (see Nitzberg [1991]) for a survey of issues and approaches in shared memory for distributed computing).

A given application system can choose any layer of middleware needed. For example, consider an application that needs to update duplicated data at two different sites. The application developers have the following choices: (a) use the distributed data-management services (b) use the basic services such as RPCs and do update synchronization yourself, or (c) use the network-dependent services and do whatever programming needs to be done to access and update duplicated data. Naturally, it is desirable to use off-the-shelf C/S middleware services to reduce application development costs. The application programs utilize the APIs provided by the chosen services. For example, if RPC is chosen by the application developers, then the APIs provided by the specific RPC middleware (e.g., DCE RPC) are used to issue RPCs.

C/S application architects must be aware of the interplays between C/S middleware and C/S applications. In particular, the following key ideas must be kept in mind:

- Application programming interfaces (APIs) provided by the middleware impact the portability of C/S applications. For example, a client program that uses an RDA API cannot be ported to an RPC environment without some reengineering.

- Exchange protocols used between the C/S middleware impact the interoperability of C/S applications. For example, if a server uses RPCs, then the clients must adhere to the specific RPC implementation used by the server.

- Middleware stacks (layers) impact the performance as well as cost of a C/S application. Higher-level middleware makes it easier and cheaper to develop complex C/S applications, but too many stacks can impede C/S application performance.

2.6   State of the Practice: Typical Examples

2.6.1   Overview

C/S systems are deeply state-of-the-practice at the time of this writing. Most new applications being developed at present and in the near future will employ the C/S architectures. Numerous case studies appear regularly in the literature to highlight different aspects of current architectures. Examples of success stories can be found in *Computerworld Client/Server Journal*, Special Issue, June 1995, "In Pursuit of Client/Server Excellence"; *Datamation*, March 1, 1994, highlighted section on "The Best in Client/Server Computing"; and vendor-provided case studies (e.g., the "Rightsizing/Downsizing Case Studies" published by Sun Microsystems).[9] Examples of failures, although less frequently reported, can be found in

---

9. Many of the vendor-provided case studies obviously glorify the vendor products, but you can still see many interesting approaches to architect client/server systems.

"Dirty Downsizing," *Computerworld*, Special Report, August 10, 1992; the Standish Group Conference on Client/Server Failures, and "Where Do Client/Server Apps Go Wrong?" *Datamation,* January 21, 1994, p. 30.

Let us discuss some typical examples.

Figure 2.13 shows a high-level view of a typical IT environment in a typical organization. This environment is very similar to the one shown in Chapter 1. Let us look into more details of this configuration. The information exchanged between various computer systems is through terminal emulation, file-transfer packages, or client-server messages. Note that this environment shows a combination of single-tiered (i.e., terminal emulation with business partners), two-tiered C/S (i.e., clients running on PCs and UNIX workstations accessing the minicomputer and database server resources, respectively, in real time), three-tiered C/S (i.e., the UNIX LAN communicating with mainframe in C/S), and hybrid (minicomputer receives data from mainframe through nightly file transfers but delivers the information to PC users through C/S). In addition, different C/S paradigms can be employed at different parts of this organization. For example, the database server supports the RDA paradigm for its clients but uses RPCs to access mainframe data.

Figure 2.13 A High-Level View of a C/S Environment

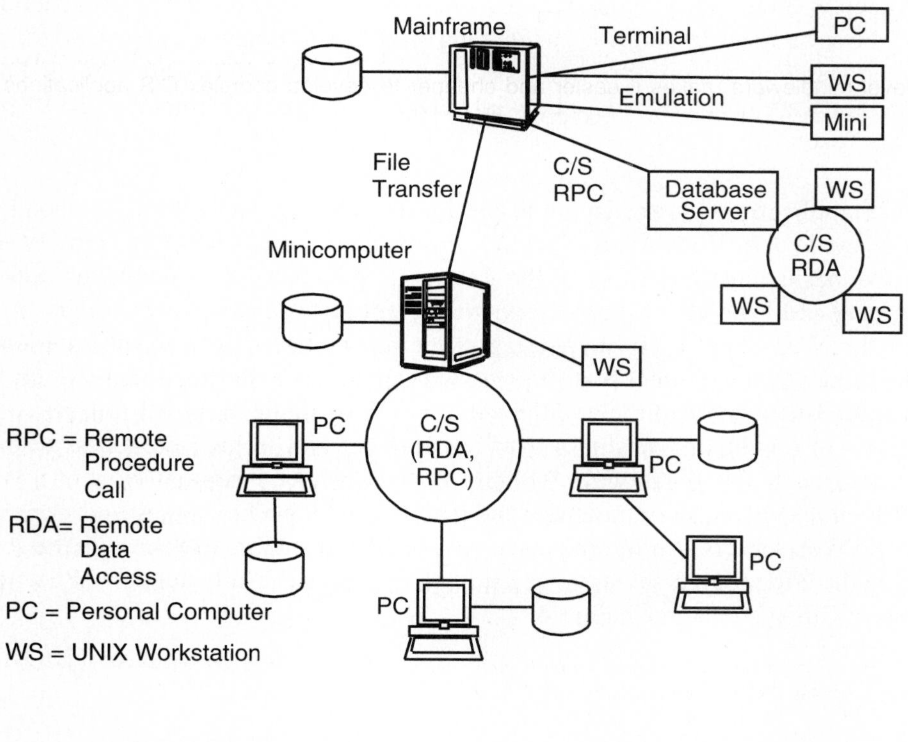

In the environment shown in Figure 2.13, some application systems can be centralized, some can be decentralized, and others can be distributed by using a combination of terminal emulation, file transfer, and C/S middleware. For example, a payroll application system can be centralized so that all the payroll data, the programs, and the user-interface processing resides at the corporate mainframe. A material-requirement-planning (MRP) system can be distributed between the mainframe and the regional minicomputers so that portions of MRP data may be at the mainframe and other at the minicomputer. All word-processing systems can operate as standalone (decentralized) systems in the regional offices. A common user interface at the PCs and UNIX workstations can provide an integrated view of the applications, even though the individual application components reside at different computers.

The configuration shown in Figure 2.13 represents a "kinder, gentler" view of C/S environments in an enterprise. This diagram does not show many details of network layout and design on which the C/S middleware and applications reside. Figure 2.14 shows a more detailed view of a typical C/S environment. This figure shows the various routers and network gateways needed to interconnect the various UNIX, Novell, Appleshare, and PC LANs to a mainframe over a corporate TCP/IP backbone. It also shows how Apple computers and PCs can be connected to the mainframe over an SNA WAN. It is beyond the scope of this book to delve deeply into the networking issues (interested readers should review Chapter 11 for a short tutorial on network interconnectivity). However, the reader should keep in mind that a sound network interconnectivity architecture is a foundation of any C/S environment. In addition, while choosing C/S middleware products, the analysts must understand on what type of networks a particular C/S middleware resides. For example, RPC software is heavily biased toward TCP/IP networks, while many RDA packages reside on Token Ring LANs.

Many C/S applications at present are becoming Web based, owing to the tremendous popularity of the **World Wide Web (WWW).** From an end user's point of view, WWW provides two basic capabilities over the Internet: Web sites to operate as information repositories, and Web clients (browsers) with graphical user interfaces (GUIs) to wander through the Web sites. Web browsers provide an intuitive view of information, where hypertext links (links to other text information) appear as underlined items or highlighted text/images. The purpose of the middleware for WWW applications is to support the growing interest in conducting business over the Internet and to provide access to corporate databases through "Web gateways." Figure 2.15 shows a conceptual view of a Web. The Web content providers, say a company and a magazine publisher, create and store information on the Web servers. An Internet user can connect to and browse through the servers by supplying the URL (universal resource locator) for the needed information. We will discuss Web-based C/S systems in Chapter 4.

Figure 2.14 Physical View of a C/S Environment

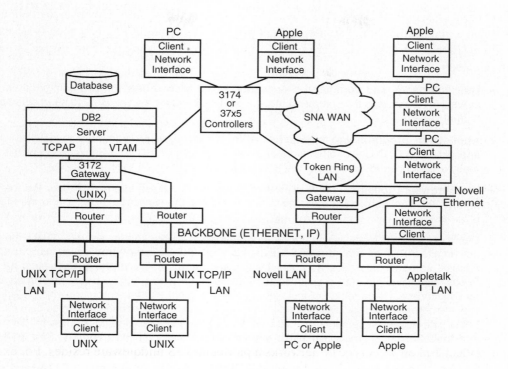

Figure 2.15 World Wide Web Concepual View

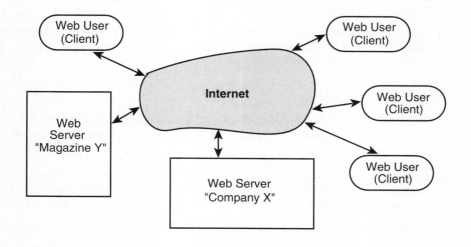

2.6.2   Client Examples

Client processes, or just clients, typically reside on desktop computers. However, a client may reside on a mainframe. For example, a client program on a mainframe may need to access a database server on a LAN. Here are some examples of clients, ranging from simple to more complicated:

- **User interfaces and command processors**, which allow a user to send commands to the server. An example is the command processor in LANs which allows users to send commands to print servers.

- **Application programming interfaces (APIs)**, which allow programmers to develop client applications in C, Cobol, or other languages. An example is the TCP/IP Socket API which is currently available on PCs, Macs, UNIX, and MVS computers.

- **Web browsers (clients)**, which allow Internet users to access information over the Internet through GUIs. Common Web browsers at present are the Netscape browser and the Mosaic browser.

- **Decision-support tools**, which are preprogrammed to access remote servers. These tools do not require API-level programming. Examples are the SQL query processors such as Clear Access, spreadsheets such as Lotus Data Lens, fourth-generation languages such as PC/Focus, executive-information systems such as Lightship, and graphical query generators such as ObjectView. These tools are installed on top of a client interface program which interfaces with the network software. For example, Lotus Data Lens is a client interface which converts the Lotus data-access statements to SQL calls for database servers. In addition, many "data-mining" tools are becoming available for sophisticated decision-support queries. See Edelstein [1996], Finkelstein [1992], and Zuck [1992] for a review of decision-support tools.

- **Purchased and/or developed client applications**, which access remote data when needed. For example, an order-processing application on a workstation may behave as a client and access customer information from a remotely located database server. Some off-the-shelf client applications are beginning to appear in the market. See, for example, Trllica [1996], and Ricciuti [1992] for a review of off-the-shelf client applications.

- **Client-application development tools**, which allow development of client applications on workstations. For example, PowerBuilder from PowerSoft is a popular C/S application development environment. See Hines [1996], and Gallagher [1996] .

2.6.3   Server Examples

In a C/S environment, a variety of servers, dispersed across a network, can be accessed from clients which may reside at different computers. Examples of some of the commonly known servers are as follows:

- **LAN servers** (e.g., Novell NetWare), which are used in LANs so that many users (clients) can share the same printers and files. See Johnson [1995] for a review of the various LAN "network operating systems (NOSs)."

- **Terminal servers** (e.g., DEC terminal servers) which allow many terminals to share the same line (see Hirsch [1990], and Nesset [1990] for details).

- **Window servers** (e.g., XWindow) which manage user windows (screens) on a workstation (see Johnson [1990], and Scheife [1990]).

- **Web servers,** which receive requests from Web clients to provide Internet services. Examples of Web servers are advertising databases and commercially available Web servers such as the Publishing and Commerce server from Netscape.

- **Name/directory servers** which show the location of a named object (e.g., file, program).

- **Authentication servers** which check to see if a particular user is authorized to access particular resources.

- **Distributed file servers,** which provide transparent access to files allocated to different computers. Network File System (NFS) and Andrew File Server (AFS) are examples.

- **Database servers** (e.g., SQL servers) which take a SQL query and return the desired information (note that the SQL server may in fact access a nonrelational database).

- **Transaction servers,** which receive a transaction (e.g., update a bank account) and respond appropriately. A transaction server is responsible for assuring that the transaction either completes successfully ("commits") or is completely rolled out.

- **Application servers,** which provide a complete application (e.g., credit checking) in response to a request from a client.

- **Groupware servers** (e.g., Lotus Notes), that manage semistructured information such as text, image, mail, bulletin boards, and workflow.

These functional servers can run on a variety of hardware boxes ranging from laptops to mainframes. These hardware boxes, which unfortunately are also called "servers," must have the hardware capability and the associated operating-system support to schedule and execute multiple tasks. We briefly reviewed the hardware boxes in Section 2.3.6. However, we will discuss many of the functional servers listed above in Part II of this book.

2.7   State of the Market: Commercial Products

The market for the C/S building blocks (e.g., C/S applications, C/S middleware, networks, database managers, transaction managers, operating systems, and computing hardware) is cluttered with hundreds of off-the-shelf products that are discussed regularly in trade magazines such as *Client/Server Today, Client/Server Computing, Datamation, Database Programming and Design,* and *Data Communications.* In addition, analyses of products are published regularly in the reports by Gartner Group, Forrester Research, Seybold Group, and the Yankee Group. Let us focus on the C/S middleware products and the C/S application products. We will quickly scan the state of the market for these key building blocks.

C/S Middleware Products. The C/S middleware services have evolved, and continue to evolve, as layers since the early 1990s. Each layer has added more functionality and made it easier to develop and deploy C/S applications. Highlights of C/S middleware products for each layer are given below (we will discuss details in later chapters):

- Primitive services such as terminal emulation, file transfer, and distributed file/print servers are completely supported by almost all LAN vendors and are currently available over TCP/IP and SNA WANs.

- Basic C/S services with remote-procedure call (RPC) are fully supported through Open Software Foundation's Distributed Computing Environment (OSF DCE). OSF DCE is currently available from Hewlett Packard, IBM, SUN, Prime, and several other vendors.

- Distributed-data management services for access of distributed as well as replicated data are available through a variety of "remote SQL middleware" products, such as the database gateways from Oracle, Sybase, Ingres, and Information Builders, Inc.

- Distributed-transaction management services for update of distributed as well as replicated data are available through distributed transaction processors such as Tuxedo, CICS, and Encina. The state of the market in this area needs to mature somewhat.

- Distributed-object services are becoming available through Object Management Group's Common Object Request Broker Architecture (OMG's CORBA) and Microsoft's Object Linking and Embedding (OLE) and ActiveX. CORBA-based products are currently available from IBM, Sun, Hewlett Packard, Digital Equipment, among others.

- Middleware for Internet and mobile computing is evolving very rapidly at the time of this writing. However, middleware for groupware is widely available through Lotus Notes.

The growing number of commercially available middleware products should be seriously considered before undertaking in-house development. In most cases, it is better to develop C/S applications which utilize the commercially available C/S middleware. It is generally better to use the high-level client/server protocols and services, if available, because they reduce the application complexity.

C/S Application Products. Many C/S applications are also becoming commercially available. Examples are the Human Resource Applications by PeopleSoft and the integrated applications by SAP. The need to develop client/server software should be evaluated against the off-the-shelf available products. Over the years, the sophistication of the C/S applications for client as well as server processes has increased (see Figure 2.16). For example, in the first generation of C/S applications, the client as well as server processes had to be developed from scratch. Off-the-shelf processes, if available, supported very simple functionalities. In the second generation, the server processes included a diverse array of off-the-shelf SQL Servers from a variety of DBMS vendors. The client processes also included a large number of desktop decision-support tools such as spreadsheets, data browsers, report writers, and object viewers. The capabilities of off-the-shelf client and server processes have increased dramatically in the current (third) generation. Complete off-the-shelf C/S applications from vendors such as SAP, Oracle, PeopleSoft, and others are becoming available. In addition, CASE tools to develop C/S applications are commercially available.

Figure 2.16 Generations of C/S Applications

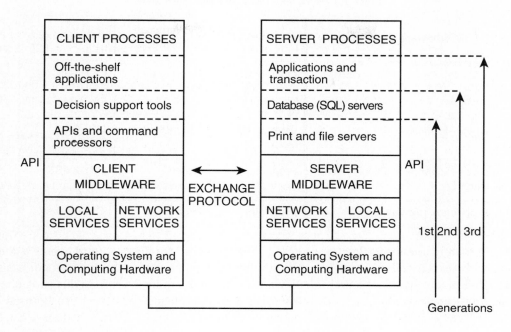

2.8   State of the Art: Standards and Trends

Standards for middleware are needed for portability and interoperability of C/S applications. In particular:

- Application programming interfaces (APIs) provided by the middleware impact the portability of C/S applications.For example, a client application that uses the Sybase API to issue remote SQL calls has to be reprogrammed if the middleware changes from (say) Sybase to Informix.

- Exchange protocols used between the C/S middleware impact the interoperability of C/S applications. For example, Oracle client middleware encodes the remote SQL in a proprietary format so that only an Oracle server can decode it. Thus an Oracle client cannot interoperate with an Informix server, and vice versa, without "gateways" that convert the exchange protocols.

Each middleware comes with its own APIs and exchange protocols. Ideally, the APIs as well as exchange protocols should be open and based on standards. Unfortunately, many APIs as well as the exchange protocols are proprietary. Figure 2.17 shows a few sample middleware configurations that can be used to analyze middleware standards, and Table 2.3 shows some sample standards.

TABLE 2.3 CATEGORIES OF MIDDLEWARE STANDARDS

Middleware Categories	API	Exchange Protocols	Examples
Completely open middleware	Open or de facto	Open or de facto	DCE RPC, CORBA, OpenDoc
Open API middleware	Open or de facto	Proprietary	ODBC
Open exchange protocol middleware	Proprietary	Open	DRDA, ISO RDA
Proprietary middleware	Proprietary	Proprietary	OLE/ActiveX

The **completely open middleware** represents the "nirvana" for the end users, where a common API is used by all client middleware vendors and a common exchange protocol is also used between the client and server middleware as shown in Figure 2.17(a). In this case, client applications are *portable* across vendors (e.g., the same client application can be used to access Informix or Oracle databases) and also *interoperable* (e.g., an Oracle database can be accessed from Informix and Sybase clients *without* translation). Basically, this middleware, if available, would allow any-client-to-any-server communication without any gateways that translate exchange protocols. We are not yet so lucky. The closest approaches at present are the Open Software Foundation's DCE and Object Management Group's CORBA.

The **open API middleware** configuration, shown in Figure 2.17(b), allows clients from vendor A to be portable to vendor B, because the same API is used; however, different drivers are needed to access different servers, because the exchange protocols are not common. This situation is quite common at the time of this writing, owing to the widespread availability of the ODBC drivers. Thus the ODBC API-based SQL middleware to access multiple databases is becoming a de facto standard (see Chapter 5 for a discussion of ODBC).

The **open exchange protocol middleware** configuration, shown in Figure 2.17(c), allows clients from different vendors to use a common exchange protocol. However, the clients use proprietary APIs. This situation is currently being achieved by the IBM Distributed Relational Database Architecture (DRDA) gateways, which translate the proprietary protocols to IBM's DRDA to access DB2 data. For example, Informix and Oracle clients use their own proprietary APIs and drivers but use the DRDA gateways to convert the proprietary exchange protocol to a DB2 accepted exchange protocol (see Chapter 5 for a discussion of DRDA).

Figure 2.17 Configurations for Middleware

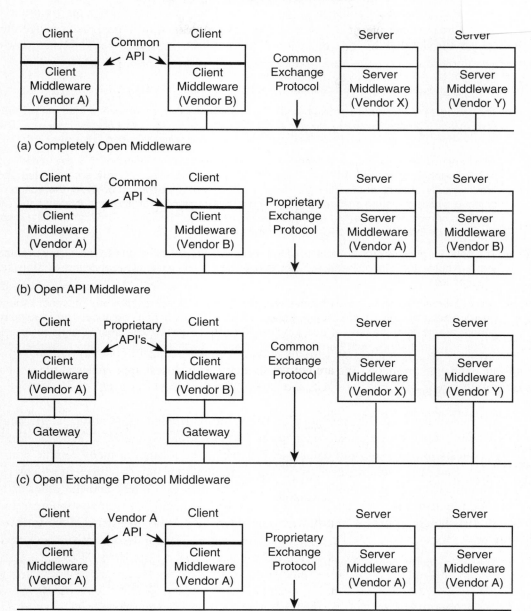

(a) Completely Open Middleware

(b) Open API Middleware

(c) Open Exchange Protocol Middleware

(d) Completely Proprietary Middleware

The **completely proprietary middleware**, shown in Figure 2.17(d), shows the most common middleware at present. In this case, the APIs as well as exchange protocols are proprietary. Clients are portable among the same vendor environments (one hopes!) and can operate only with servers supplied by the same vendor. Many remote data access middleware products are examples.

The following general trends in client/server systems are worth noting:

- The notion of client/server paradigm could be outdated by the emergence of many new situations in which processes cooperate with each other as peers without any clients or servers. The peer-to-peer OSI application layer protocols could play a significant role in this.

- The trend toward higher-level services and protocols which are independent of the underlying network architectures will continue. The RPC facilities have become more sophisticated and have virtually eliminated the need for network-dependent protocols. In addition, the notion of object-oriented message systems is becoming increasingly popular. In these systems, the clients and servers will be treated as objects which exchange messages. The format of the messages will be independent of the location of the objects.

- The need for multiple protocols will continue. For example, even though RPCs are very popular, they are not suitable for bulk data transfer, continuous stream multimedia, and store and forward applications.

- More off-the-shelf software will become available for client/server middleware. At present, many decision-support applications which access remotely located SQL databases from spreadsheets are state-of-the-market and practice. Other off-the-shelf client/server applications in manufacturing, finance, and human-resource management are also becoming available from database vendors. This trend will continue.

2.9   Summary

The client/server model is the most popular model for distributed applications, at the time of this writing. This allows a user program at a workstation, typically, to act as a client issuing requests to programs and databases which may be located at many remote computing sites. Basically, a client/server model assumes that there are two types of processes that communicate with each other in real time—one acts as a client and the other as a server. We identified the key characteristics of the C/S model (consumer/supplier relationship, distributed processes, real-time exchange of messages). We defined the following key concepts:

- The C/S model is a conceptual framework that can be applied to many computing situations.
- C/S computing utilizes the C/S model to provide computing (business-unaware) services.
- C/S applications utilize the C/S model to provide business-aware functionality.
- C/S computing environments provide the infrastructure needed to develop, deploy, support, and manage client/server applications.
- C/S middleware provides the software that interconnects client and server modules located on different machines.

Development of client/server applications is not trivial and requires detailed architectural analysis (e.g., how to split the application code between client and server machines, two-versus three-tiered architectures). In addition, a good understanding of the middleware is essential. The middleware services have evolved, and continue to evolve, as layers since the mid 1990s. Each layer has added more functionality and made it easier to develop and deploy C/S applications. Examples of these layers are primitive services such as terminal emulation and file transfer, basic C/S services which include popular protocols such as Remote Procedure Call (RPC), distributed-data and transaction management services for retrieval and update of distributed data, distributed-object services such as CORBA and OLE, and services for emerging technologies such as Internet, mobile computing, and groupware. We will discuss these layers in Part II of this book.

Development of C/S architectures involves a variety of issues of security, performance, network independence, and failure management. Issues of particular importance to management are the interoperability and portability of client-side software with server-side software supplied by different vendors. At present, many vendors use proprietary protocols between their clients and servers. This may lead to the situation where 10 client applications from 10 vendors may require 10 different servers to access the same database. Middleware standards for APIs and exchange protocols are needed for "open" C/S environments.

2.10 Case Study: IT Building Blocks for XYZCorp

XYZCorp has initiated a project to develop a high-level information-technology architecture and its building blocks which will allow different applications and users at different sites to communicate with each other ("any data from any application anywhere in the company"). The current platforms consist of a variety of computers. The regional offices house minicomputers (mainly UNIX) which are connected to the corporate mainframe (MVS). The regional computers maintain regional inventory, customer information, and prices of items sold in the region. Some regions (e.g., Atlanta and San Francisco) are very UNIX oriented. Other regions have Novell LANs. The corporate headquarters is IBM mainframe oriented (MVS, DB2, IMS, SNA, Token Ring). PCs are used commonly throughout the organization. Many applications are operational. Examples of some of the applications are:

- IMS-based inventory control system
- DB2-based financial system
- Many UNIX-Oracle-based regional systems
- Novell-based human-resource system at PC LANs

As a first step toward the new architecture, the management is concentrating on the corporate-inventory system, the financial-information system, and a decision-support system which allows spreadsheets at the user sites to interactively access the marketing information located on a UNIX-Oracle server. This architecture should address the following issues:

- Levels of interconnectivity for each application area
- Identification and discussion of the key building blocks needed
- Interrelationships between the building blocks

Hints about the Case Study

A high-level view of the XYZCorp architecture is shown in Figure 2.18 (this is similar to the one shown in Figure 2.13). There are two broad levels of interconnectivity:

- Network-to-network interconnectivity (i.e., bridges, routers)
- Application-to-application interconnectivity (i.e., middleware)

The network-interconnectivity issues are covered in Chapter 11. We have given enough information on middleware in this chapter to discuss the application to application interconnectivity.

The main building blocks are discussed in Section 2.3. Additional details are given in Section 2.5. This information should suffice to identify the building blocks.

Figure 2.18 XYZCorp Overall Environment

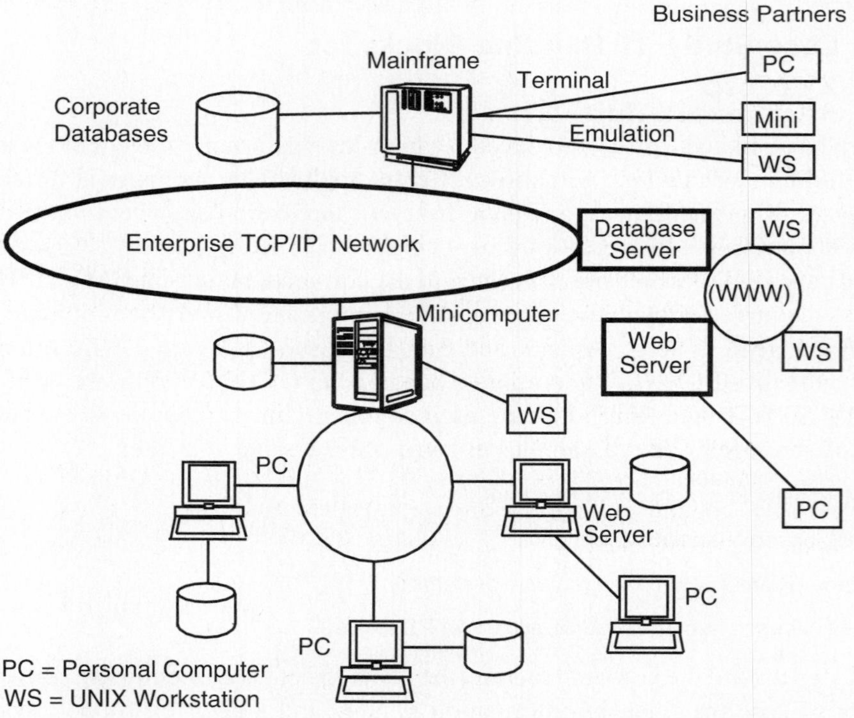

2.11   Problems and Exercises

1. Compare and contrast client/server systems with distributed computing systems.

2. What are the trade-offs between client/server, terminal emulation and file transfer? Explain through an example.

3. Give an example of a distributed application that does not use the client/server model.

4. Suppose financial information from a corporate mainframe is needed by the branch offices for spreadsheet analysis. List the options available and explain the trade-offs between them.

5. Draw a conceptual diagram of client/server computing in an environment of your choice (e.g., business, finance, engineering, manufacturing).

6. Describe a client/server system of your choice.

7. Use Table 2.2 to show the trade-offs between two- and three-tiered C/S architectures.

8. Figure 2.12 shows a layered view of C/S middleware. Expand this diagram to show additional protocols not included in Figure 2.12.

9. List the factors you will use to evaluate off-the-shelf client/server middleware.

2.12   Additional Information

Literature on C/S computing is growing steadily. A number of books [Berson 1993, Khanna 1993, Orfali 1974, Stevens 1990, Umar 1993, Vaskevitz 1993] discuss different aspects of C/S. State-of-the-market and state-of-the-practice articles on client/server computing appear regularly in trade journals such as *Client/Server Today, Datamation, Database Programming and Design,* and *Data Communications.* Many C/S middleware products are being announced regularly in the industrial literature (see, for example, the *Database Design and Programming Magazine*'s Buyer's Guide Issue, December 1994). Analysis of client/server directions can be found in the reports published by the Gartner Group, Forrester Research, and the Yankee Group. For example, the Gartner Group Briefing "Enterprise Client/Server: Can We Get There From Here?" July/August 1994, contains an interesting analysis of the C/S issues and approaches. Some articles about C/S are also beginning to appear in the computer science literature (see, for example, the *IEEE Computer* April 1995 issue).

2.13   References

Adler, R., "Distributed Coordination Models for Client/Server Computing," *IEEE Computer Magazine,* April 1995, pp. 14–22.

Amaru, C., "Building Distributed Applications with MOM," *Client/Server Today,* November 1994, pp. 83–93.

Andrews, G. R., "Paradigms for Process Interaction in Distributed Programs," *ACM Computing Surveys,* March 1991, pp. 49–90.

Andrews, G., and Schneider, F., "Concepts and Notations for Concurrent Programming," *ACM Computing Survey,* Vol. 15, No. 1 (March 1983), pp.3–44.

Bell, T., Adam, J., and Lowe, S., "Communications," *IEEE Spectrum 1996,* January 1996, pp. 30–41.

Berson, A., *Client/Server Architectures,* McGraw-Hill, 1993.

Birrel, A. D. and Nelson, B. J., "Implementing Remote Procedure Call," *ACM Transactions on Computer Systems,* Vol. 2, pp. 39–59.

Blelloch, G., "Programming Parallel Algorithms," *Communications of ACM,* March 1996, pp. 85–97.

Caldwell, B., "Client-Server: Can It Be Save?" *Information Week,* April 8, 1996, pp. 36–44.

Comeau, Greg, "Networking with UNIX," *Byte,* February 1989, pp. 265–267.

Comerford, R., "Computers," *IEEE Software,* January 1996, pp. 42–25.

Comport, J., "Packaged Applications: Buy an Application, Inherit an Architecture," Gartner Group Briefing, San Diego, February 1995.

Corbin, J. R., *The Art of Distributed Applications: Programming Techniques for Remote Procedure Calls,* Springer-Verlag, 1991.

Coulouris, G., and Dollimore, J., *Distributed Systems: Concepts and Design,* Addison Wesley, 1988.

Davis, Ralph, "A Logical Choice," *Byte,* January 1989, pp. 309–315.

Dhumne, A., "Multitier Application Benefits," *Application Development Trends,* June 1996, pp. 52–56.

Dickman, A., "Two-Tier Versus Three-Tier Apps," *Information Week,* November 13, 1995, pp. 74–80.

Eckerson, W., "Searching for the Middleground," *Business Communications Review,* September 1995, pp. 46–50.

Edelstein, H., "Mining Data Warehouses," *Information Week,* January 8, 1996, pp. 48–51.

Finkelstein, R., "A Client for Your Server," *Database Programming and Design,* March 1992, pp. 31–45.

Foley, J., "High Speed Processors," *Information Week,* January 1, 1996, pp. 39–41.

Gallagher, S., "Constructing Better Visual," *Information Week,* January 1, 1996, pp. 50–53.

Gantz, J., "Cooperative Processing and the Enterprise Network," *Networking Management,* January 1991, pp. 25–40.

Garlan, D., and Perry, D., "Introduction to the Special Issue on Software Architecture: Guest Editorial," *IEEE Transactions on Software Engineering,* April 1995, pp. 269–274.

Gillooly, B., "Multiprocessor Systems," *Information Week,* January 1, 1996, pp. 35–37.

Glass, B., "Relying on NetWare NLMs," *Infoworld,* October 12, 1992, pp. S80.

Goulde, M., "Tomorrow's Microkernel-Based UNIX Operating Systems," in Patricia Seybold's Group Report, "Open Information Systems," August 1993.

Griswold, Charles, "LU6.2: A View from the Database," *Database Programming and Design,* May 1988, pp 34–39.

Hackathorn, R. and Schlack, M., "How to Pick Client/Server Middleware," *Datamation,* July 15, 1994, pp. 52–56.

Hines, J., "Software Engineering," *IEEE Spectrum,* January 1996, pp. 60–64.

Hirsch, D., "Terminal Servers: Here to Stay," *Data Communications,* April 1990, pp. 105–114.

Hurwicz, Michael, "Connectivity Pathways: APPC or NETBIOS," *PC Tech Journal,* Vol. 5, No. 11, November 1987, pp. 156–170.

IBM (International Business Machines), "Advanced Program-to-Program Communication for the IBM Personal Computer, Programming Guide," February 1986.

ISO/DP 9072/1 report, "Remote Operations Model—Notation and Service Definition," Geneva, Switzerland, October 1986.

Johnson and Reichard, *Advanced XWindow Applications Programming,* MIT Press, 1990.

Johnson, J., "Enterprise NOSs: Now Is the Time," *Data Communications,* May 15, 1995.

Kador, J., "The Ultimate Middleware," *Byte Magazine,* April 1996, pp. 81-83.

Kernighan, B. W. and Pike, R., *The UNIX Programming Environment,* Prentice Hall, 1984.

Khanaa, R., *Distributed Computing: Implementation and Management Strategies,* Prentice Hall, 1993.

Lewis, T., "Where Is Client/Server Software Headed?" *IEEE Computer Magazine,* April 1995, pp. 49–55.

Livingston, D., "Software Links Multivendor Networks," *Micro-Mini Systems,* March 1988.

Moad, J., "Double Impact," *Datamation,* August 1, 1992, pp. 28–33.

Naylor, A., and Volz, R., "Design of Integrated Manufacturing System Control Software," *IEEE Transactions on Systems, Man and Cybernetics,* Vol. SMC-17, No. 6, November/December 1987.

Nehmer, J., and Mattern, F., "Framework for the Organization of Cooperative Services in Distributed Client/Server Systems," *Computer Communications,* Vol. 15, No. 4 (May 1992), pp. 261–269.

Nesset, D., and Lee, G., "Terminal Services in Heterogeneous Distributed Systems," *Journal of Computer Networks and ISDN Systems,* Vol. 19 (1990), pp. 105–128.

Nitzberg, B., and Lo, V., "Distributed Shared Memory: A Survey of Issues and Approaches," *IEEE Computer,* August 1991, pp. 52–60.

Neuman, B., and Ts'o, T., "Kerberosi: An Authentication Service for Computer Networks," *IEEE Communications Magazine,* pp. 33–37.

Nutt, G., *Centralized and Distributed Operating Systems,* Prentice Hall, 1992.

Orfali, R., Harkey, D., and Edwards, J., *Client/Server Survival Guide,* Van Nostrand Reinholt, 1994.

Ozsu, M., and Valdurez, P., "Distributed Database Systems: Where Are We Now?" *IEEE Computer,* August 1991, pp. 68–78.

Pountain, D., "The X Window System," *Byte,* January 1989, pp.353–360.

Ricciuti, M., "Universal Data Access," *Datamation,* November 1, 1991.

Ricciuti, M., "Here Come The HR Client/Server Systems," *Datamation,* July 1, 1992.

Schiller, J., "Secure Distributed Computing," *Scientific American,* November 1994, pp. 72–76.

Scheife, R., *X Protocol Reference Manual,* O'Reilly and Associates, 1990

Schlack, M., "The Key to Client/Server OLTP," *Datamation,* April 1, 1995, pp. 53–56.

Schulte, R., "Distributed Software Architecture in Full Bloom," Gartner Group Briefing, San Diego, February 1995

Sechrest, S., "An Introductory 4.3BSD Interprocess Communications Tutorial," Computer Science Research Division, Department of Electrical Engineering and Computer Science, University of California, Berkeley, 1986.

Shatz, S. M, and J. P. Wang, "Introduction to Distributed Software Engineering," *IEEE Computer,* October 1987.

Sinha, A., "Client/Server Computing: Current Technology Review," *Communications of ACM,* July 1992, pp. 77–96.

Snell, N., "The New MVS: Tuned to Serve?" *Datamation,* July 15, 1992, pp.76–77.

Stevens, W., *UNIX Network Programming,* Prentice Hall, 1990.

Svobodova, L., "File Servers for Network-Based Distributed Systems," *ACM Computing Surveys,* December 1984, pp. 353–398.

Tannenbaum, A., *Computer Networks,* 2d ed., Prentice Hall, 1988.

Tannenbaum, A., *Modern Operating Systems,* Prentice Hall, 1992.

Trllica, C. "Software Applications," *IEEE Spectrum,* January 1996, pp. 56–59.

Umar, A., *Application (Re) Engineering: Building Web-Based Object Oriented Applications and Dealing with Legacies*, Prentice Hall, 1997.

Umar, A., *Distributed Computing and Client/Server Systems,* Prentice Hall, rev. ed., 1993.

Vaskevitz, D., *Client/Server Strategies: A Survival Guide for Corporate Reengineers,* IDG Books, 1993.

Vinzant, D., "SQL Database Servers," *Data Communications,* January 1990, pp.72–86.

White, D., "SQL Database Servers: Networking Meets Data Management," *Data Communications,* September 1990, pp. 31–39.

Whiting, R. (a), "Getting on the Middleware Express," *Client/Server Today,* November 1994, pp. 70–75.

Whiting, R. (b), "Turning to MOM for the Answers," *Client/Server Today,* November 1994, pp. 76–81.

Wilbur, S., and Bacarisse, B., "Building Distributed Systems with Remote Procedure Calls," *Software Engineering Journal,* Sept. 1987, pp. 148–159.

Wood, A., "Predicting Client/Server Availability," *IEEE Computer Magazine,* April 1995, pp. 41–48.

Zuck, J., "Front-end Tools," *PC Magazine,* September 1992, pp. 295–332.

P A R T II

UNDERSTANDING THE MIDDLEWARE

Chapter 3: Basic C/S Middleware and OSF DCE

Chapter 4: Internet and World Wide Web

Chapter 5: Distributed-Data Management and SQL Middleware

Chapter 6: Client/Server Transaction Processing

Chapter 7: Distributed Objects (CORBA and OLE/ActiveX)

Chapter 8: Mobile Computing, Multimedia, Groupware, and Legacy Access Middleware

Chapter 9: Putting the Pieces Together—A Synthesis

Applications (Client and Server Processes)	OSI Layer 7 (Business Aware)

Chapter 8

Special Middleware (Wireless, Multimedia, Groupware, Legacy)

Chapter 7

Distributed Object Services (e.g., CORBA, OLE/ActiveX)

Chapter 4

World Wide Web Middleware (e.g., HTTP, HTML, CGI)

Chapters 5 and 6

Distributed Data and Transaction Management (e.g., 2PC, XA)

Chapter 3

Basic Client/Server Services (e.g., RPC, RDA, MOM, Security, Directory, Time)

Chapter 1 (Very Briefly)

Primitive Services (e.g., Terminal emulation, File transfer, Email)

OSI Layer 7 (Business Unaware)

and

Chapter 11

Network Programming Services (Sockets, LU6.2, NetBIOS, TLI)

OSI Layers 6, 5

Chapter 11

Network Services
- End-to-End Transport Services (e.g., TCP/IP, SNA, SPX/IPX, NetBIOS)
- Physical Communication Services (e.g., Ethernet, Token Ring, FDDI, ISDN, X.25, ATM, Frame Relay, Wireless)

OSI Layers 4, 3, 2, 1

OSI Model

Legend used in layers:
    Dark shaded area = middleware
    Light shaded area = not usually considered as middleware
    Unshaded area = not middleware

3

Basic C/S Middleware and OSF DCE

3.1   Introduction

This chapter deals with the basic C/S (client/server) middleware that is responsible for providing transparent and interactive access to resources (programs, databases) located across the network. The basic C/S middleware provides information-exchange services such as remote file/database access and real-time message exchanges between remote programs supported by directory, security, and failure-handling services. This middleware is the foundation of the "client/server computing revolution" in the early 1990s. An understanding of this middleware is essential for developing any contemporary distributed application, because many higher- level middleware services rely on it. This chapter explains the basic C/S middleware and answers questions such as the following:

- What are the main services provided by the basic C/S middleware, and who provides these services?

- What type of information-exchange services are provided by this middleware (e.g., remote-procedure call, remote data access, and message-oriented middleware)?

- What type of management and support services are provided by this middleware?

- What is OSF DCE and how does it provide the basic C/S middleware services?

Who exactly is responsible for providing these services? The answer can range from extensions to operating systems, *network operating systems (NOSs),* and special-purpose C/S middleware that sits on top of operating systems and NOSs. Many commercially available middleware products provide subsets of these services. For example, many NOSs such as Novell Netware, Windows NT, Banyan Vines, and IBM's LAN Manager provide several capabilities for accessing remote files, printers, and programs. In addition, these NOSs provide email, directory, and backup/recovery services (see Johnson [1995]). We will briefly discuss the role of NOSs in providing basic C/S middleware in Section 3.2.

C/S programs (clients and servers) require the basic C/S middleware to support one or more of the following well-known paradigms to exchange information. (According to Webster, a *paradigm* is an example used as a model. Thus the terms paradigm and model are used interchangeably.)

- Remote-procedure call (Section 3.3)
- Remote-data access (Section 3.4)
- Message-oriented access (Section 3.5)

In addition, enterprisewide C/S applications need basic management and support services such as security, directory, and recovery (Section 3.7).

We will discuss Open Software Foundation's Distributed Computing Environment (OSF DCE) as an illustration of basic C/S middleware. OSF DCE integrates remote-procedure call (RPC) with security, directory, time, file, and print services. OSF DCE is a good candidate for providing an open C/S environment where clients and servers from different vendors can interoperate with each other. Consequently, OSF DCE has been termed the "NOS of the future" [Johnson 1995, Orfali 1994].

Key Points

- Basic C/S middleware services include:
  - Remote communication interface paradigms such as remote-procedure call (RPC), remote-data access (RDA), and message-oriented middleware (MOM)
  - Management and support services such as security, directories, time, and failure management
  - Distributed print and file services
- Many network operating systems for LANs provide the basic C/S middleware services.
- OSF DCE is a good example of an open, standards-based, basic C/S middleware.
- Many other middleware services are built on top of basic C/S middleware.
- Each paradigm has its own weaknesses and strengths. Ideally, C/S middleware needs to support RDA, RPC, and MOM paradigms to provide C/S application developers maximum flexibility.

3.2   Basic C/S Middleware and Network Operating Systems

Figure 3.1 shows a conceptual view of basic C/S middleware and depicts how a client application interacts with a server application through the C/S middleware. The basic C/S middleware provides the following:

- Remote communication interfaces (RCIs) for sending/receiving information across a network. RCI may use the basic C/S protocols such as remote-procedure call (RPC), remote-data access, and message-oriented middleware (MOM).

- Global directories that show the location of resources (servers, databases, files, printers) in the network. For example, Figure 3.1 shows a global directory indicating that data table d is located on computer C2.

- Print and file services.

Figure 3.1 The Basic Client/Server Model

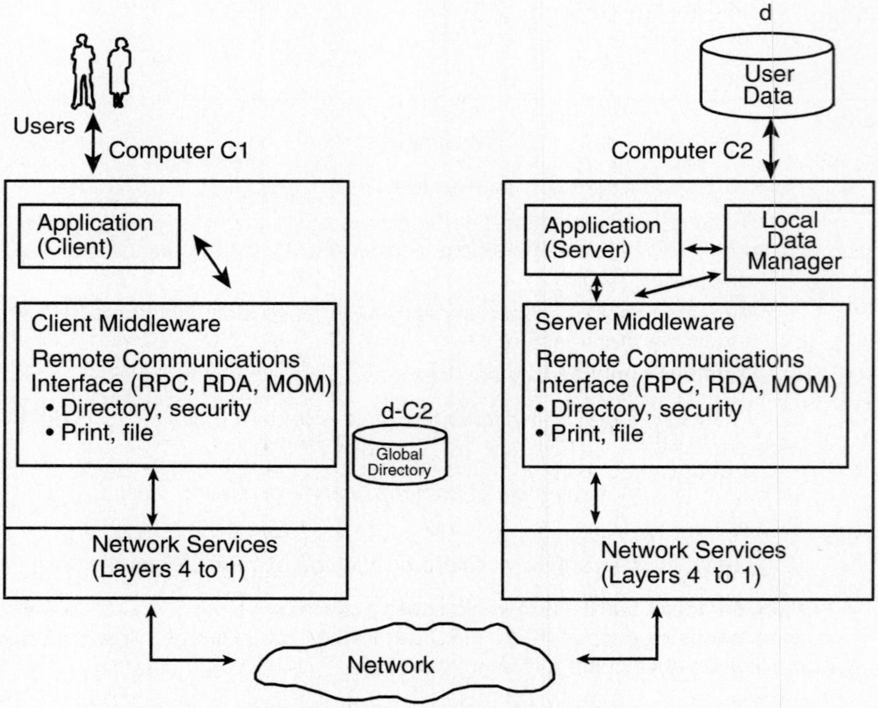

Note: The global directory is part of the middleware services.

The client side of the middleware is typically lightweight (it usually just routes the requests to the servers), but the server side is quite sophisticated because it needs to schedule and manage numerous client requests. For example, several client applications or users could request access to the applications, databases, printers, and files located at the same server. The C/S middleware relies on network services to transport the messages between sites. The network services may include, if needed, network gateways to convert network protocols (e.g., TCP/IP to SNA).

Network operating systems (NOSs) have traditionally provided some, if not all, of the basic C/S middleware services. A NOS is essentially an operating system that provides the capabilities for transparent access to resources such as printers and files across a network. Historically, NOSs have originated from LANs and have concentrated on directing the user's request to appropriate print and file servers. Novell Netware is one of the best-known NOSs. Other examples are Windows NT, Banyan Vines, IBM's LAN Manager, Apple's Local Talk, and AT&T's StarLAN. However, with time, NOSs have started providing other services needed for distributed C/S applications, such as the following:

- Remote communications to access remotely located programs and databases (e.g., RDA and RPC)
- Directory services
- Security
- Time services
- Failure handling
- Task scheduling

Most of the currently available NOSs provide these services within a single LAN. See Johnson [1995] for a comparison and analysis of four leading NOSs: Novell Netware, Windows NT, Banyan Vines, and IBM's LAN Manager. For enterprisewide C/S computing, available NOSs are glued together through "gateways" that convert protocols from one NOS to another. For mission-critical enterprisewide C/S applications, enterprisewide directory, security, and failure-handling capabilities are crucial. In addition, facilities for accessing remotely located programs and databases are essential. Many C/S middleware products provide some of these services on top of the available NOSs. For example, database servers from many vendors are available on Netware and Windows NT. Open Software Foundation's Distributed Computing Environment (OSF DCE) provides most of the basic middleware services and is frequently referred to as the NOS of the next generation. We will first discuss the generic concepts of the basic C/S services needed for enterprisewide C/S applications and then show how OSF DCE provides some of these facilities.

3.3   Remote-Procedure Call (RPC)

3.3.1   The RPC Paradigm

In this paradigm, the client process invokes a remotely located procedure (in a server process), the remote procedure executes and sends the response back to the client process. The remote procedure can be simple (e.g., retrieve time of day) or complex (e.g., retrieve all customers from Chicago who have a good credit rating). Each request/response of an RPC is treated as a separate unit of work, thus each request must carry enough information needed by the server process to generate and send back a response.

A remote-procedure-call (RPC) facility allows a language-level (local) procedure call by the client to be turned into a language-level call at the server. In a remote- procedure call, a local process invokes a remote process. RPCs have the main advantage that a programmer issues a call to a remote process in a manner that is very similar to the local calls. The RPC software attempts to hide all the network-related details from the client-server developers. The client call is referred to as *request* and the server results being returned are *responses*.

RPC uses a type-checking mechanism similar to a local-procedure-call mechanism. RPC calls may be implemented in a compiler by using the same syntax as the local- procedure calls. In many RPC facilities the synchronization of the client and server is constrained because the client is blocked until the server has responded. In addition, binding between servers and clients is usually one-to-one to reflect the language-procedure-call primitives (see the discussion on binding later).

Figure 3.2 shows the steps that take place in a remote-procedure call. The client and server routines are in two separate processes, usually on two different machines. RPC software creates a dummy procedure with the same name as the server and places it in the client process. This dummy procedure, called a ***stub***, takes the calling parameters and packages them into suitable network transmission messages. Another stub is generated for the server side to perform the reverse processing. Client and server stubs are instances of the client and server middleware we have discussed earlier (RPC introduces new terms, not new concepts). Stubs are generated through an interface definition language (IDL) facility (see the sidebar "Interface Definition Languages"). The following steps shown in Figure 3.2 are executed in order:

1. The client issues a call to a local procedure, called a client stub. The client stub appears to the caller as if it were a local procedure. This stub mainly translates the remote-procedure call into appropriate network messages in the proper Network Interface Services format (usually TCP/IP Sockets). The stub also determines the actual network address of the server and "binds" to it (sometimes this is done by the run-time libraries associated with the stubs).

Interface Definition Language (IDL)

The concept of interface definition languages (IDLs) is used commonly in building C/S applications. Examples of the C/S applications that use IDL are RPC applications, CORBA applications and OLE/ActiveX applications.

Simply stated, an **interface** specifies the API that the clients can use to invoke remote operations. In particular, an interface describes: (a) the set of operations that can be performed on an object, and (b) the parameters needed to perform the operations. For C/S applications, interface definitions are used to advertise the set of operations that a server can provide to prospective clients.

The interfaces are defined by using an **interface definition language (IDL)**. IDLs are basically declarative languages—they do not specify any executable code. IDL declarations (e.g., syntax, character types allowed, argument coding, etc.) must conform to the vendor provided IDL compilers. After you create the interface definition using IDL, you compile the IDL file to create header files and "stubs" that are used in building clients and servers.

RPC application development involves the following major activities:

1. **Create interface definitions.** These definitions are used to advertise the external interfaces (services) that are available to prospective clients.

2. **Compile IDL.** The vendor provided IDL compilers create headers and generate client stubs and server stubs.

3. **Build server programs**. The server programs that provide the advertised services are coded and compiled along with the server stub and the headers generated by the IDL compiler.

4. **Build client programs**. The client programs that invoke the servers are coded and compiled along with the client stub and the headers generated by the IDL compiler.

This process is used for CORBA and other C/S applications also. The main difference is in the IDL syntax—it varies between different C/S middleware. We will see examples of DCE, Encina, and CORBA IDL later in this book (Section 3.8, Chapter 6, and Chapter 7, respectively).

---

2. The network messages are prepared and sent to the remote site through network transport services.

3. The messages are sent over the communication media and are received by the network transport services of the server machine. If the network architecture of the client machine is different from that server machine, then a network gateway may be needed (e.g., TCP/IP-to-SNA gateway).

4. The server network system informs the server stub that a request has arrived for it.

5. The server stub gets the network message, translates it into a local procedure call format, and executes this call to the server process.

6. The server executes the call and develops a response which is sent to the server stub.

7. The server stub translates the response into one or more network messages which are sent to the network system.

8. The server network system sends the response back to the client network system. Once again, a gateway may be needed if the client and server network architectures are dissimilar.

9. The client network system sends the response messages to the client stub.

10. The client stub receives the response message, translates this message into call responses, and sends the response back to the client.

Figure 3.2 Remote-Procedure Call

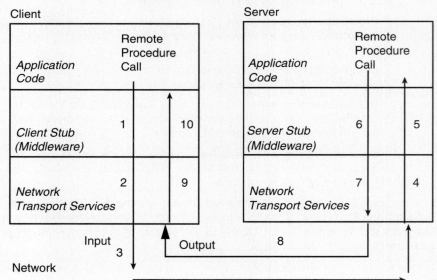

3.3.2   RPC Analysis

Many decisions are made in various steps of the remote-procedure call. Examples of some of these decisions are stub generation, parameter passing, binding, server management, error handling, transport protocols, data representation, performance, and security. These issues are briefly discussed next. For a detailed discussion, the reader is referred to Wilbur [1987] and the book on distributed systems by Coulouris and Dollimore [Coulouris 1994]. The book *The Art of Distributed Applications: Programming Techniques for Remote Procedure Calls* by J.R. Corbin [Corbin 1991] gives many technical details.

Stub Generation. Stubs can be generated automatically or by a programmer. For a programmer-generated stub, the RPC system provides a set of functions which can be used to construct a stub. This mechanism has been used by the SUN microsystem RPC. For automated stub generation, an interface definition language (IDL) is provided which is compiled by a stub generator to construct client and server stubs. See the sidebar "Interface Definition Language (IDL)".

Parameter Passing. The passing of parameters between remote procedures creates special problems. For example, if the client passes parameters by value, then these values can be copied by the client stub into the network transmission messages. But if a parameter is passed by address, then it is difficult to pass, because memory address on one system does not mean much on another system. For this reason, parameter by address in remote-procedure calls is not always allowed. Programming details about passing parameters can be found in Shirley [1993].

Binding. Binding refers to establishing a contact between a client and a server. When a call to a server is received by the client stub, it tries to bind the client with an appropriate server on a remote site. Binding requires two major decisions:

- How to find an appropriate host for a service
- How to find the appropriate server on the chosen host

This is a typical problem in networks. Where should the directory of hosts and servers be located? Some RPC systems use centralized directories to which the servers register when they are started. In other systems, each client system knows the address of the servers. For example, Open Software Foundation's Distributed Computing Environment (OSF DCE) solves this problem by using a distributed directory.

Server Management. In some implementations of RPCs, several instances of a server are installed on the same or different machines for performance or availability reasons. In some implementations there is a server manager which can create servers on demand and route requests to a duplicate server if one server fails. (This is more typical of transaction-processing systems.)

Data Representation. The data format of the client and server may be different, especially when the client and server reside on different computing systems. Data translation may be done at the client or the server site. A common approach used in many RPCs is an intermediate data format which is used by all clients and server stubs in an RPC system. (This approach is used in the OSI RPC and the SUN RPC.)

Type Consistency. It is important that the number and type of parameters sent by the client are consistent with the server parameters, especially if the clients and servers are implemented in different programming languages supporting different data types. This issue is important in server design because a server must be able to handle corrupt requests.

Call Execution and Call Semantics. In a distributed system, the client and server can fail independently and then be restarted. In such situations, it is not clear how many times a call to a server has been executed. For example, if a server or the transport network failed before the server had a chance to execute the request, then the call was not processed. However, if the server crashed after completing the request, then the request has been executed once. Some procedures do not harm anything if they are executed several times (e.g., time of day, reading a specific record from a file). The call semantics determine how often the remote service might be performed under fault conditions. The following semantics are possible.

- *Exactly once* means that the server procedure was executed once. This semantics requires extensive checking and is suitable for very reliable distributed systems.

- *At most once* means that the server procedure is performed once or not at all. The client and the server use sequenced protocol, where a sequence number is attached to each request. This semantics is checked by the server process to make sure that the server process does not execute more than once.

- *At least once* means that the server process can be executed several times. This semantics allows the client to send the same request a few times if the server does not respond. This semantics is suitable for read-only servers.

Transport Protocols. Most RPC systems have been built on top of TCP/IP Protocol Suite. Either TCP or UDP is used to transmit the messages across the network. If an RPC system allows UDP[1] as well as TCP protocol, then a parameter may be used in the RPC call for a choice. At present, other than TCP/IP, very few transport protocols are supported by the existing RPC systems. For example, the ISO RPC standard that uses OSI stack has not resulted in a viable product. It is expected that RPC facilities will be available on other stacks such as OSI and SNA (IBM has announced an "AnyNet" feature that supports RPCs over SNA networks; however, the practical use of RPCs over SNA is very sparse).

Error Handling. Many error and exceptional situations can arise in client-server systems. For example, a server may crash or may go into a loop. In this case, the client may need to recover from the error by using timeouts or may need to stop the server. Similarly, a client may crash before getting response from the server. In this case, the server may hang around and may need to be stopped somehow. In addition, the transport network may fail while the requests and/or responses are being transmitted. Error handling becomes especially difficult when the server communicates with other servers to provide a service (e.g., a server responsible for managing distributed data may need to communicate with other sites where the cop-

---

1. UDP (User Datagram Protocol) is an alternative to TCP (UDP and TCP run on top of IP). UDP is an unreliable (connectionless) protocol, while TCP is a reliable (connection-based) protocol.

ies of data exist). A variety of techniques, such as two-phase commit, are used in such cases (see Chapter 6).

Performance and Security. Implementation of RPCs introduces many performance and security concerns. For example, the network delays need to be taken into account when designing distributed applications. It has been reported that remote- procedure calls incur two to three times more overhead than the local calls [Wilbur 1987]. Some performance studies have highlighted the performance impact of number of parameters and the parameter sizes [Birrel 1984]. This is especially serious when parameter data needs to be converted. A common technique in performance improvement is to use an object-oriented approach, where the server is called to perform operations instead of sending data structures back and forth. In addition, the impact of starting up a new server process for every client request (perhaps through UNIX forking) needs to be examined. It might be better to keep one reentrant server which is called repetitively every time a client needs the service. It is also important to verify the security of the client before sending the response to it. Multithreaded server environments help this. The Open Software Foundation supports a secure RPC to address the security issues.

3.3.3 Strengths and Weaknesses of RPC

RPCs are well understood, are widely supported, and can provide an easy transition from centralized to distributed programs. For example, a centralized program which consists of many procedures to perform specialized tasks can be distributed by simply replacing the procedure calls with the RPC calls to remotely located programs. However, RPC is not a panacea. In many cases RPCs are awkward, especially because the parameter passing can be only through value and not by references.

The currently available RPCs do not support asynchronous queries (most RPCs block the client calls). Another limitation is that RPCs are not well suited for ad hoc query processing. For example, an ad hoc SQL query can return many rows with many columns. It is very difficult to set RPC parameters between senders and receivers in this situation. For this reason, a separate data-access standard, called Remote-Data Access (RDA), is used heavily by the DBMS community (see next section). In a generalized client-server environment, RPC as well as RDA is needed.

In this section we have primarily discussed the generic RPC paradigm. Many extensions to RPCs have been suggested (see Coulouris [1994]). Of particular interest to us is the extension of RPCs to handle transaction processing. These "transactional" RPCs become a unit of consistency (i.e., the transactional RPC is either committed in total or rolled back). We will review transactional RPCs in Chapter 6.

3.4   Remote-Data Access (RDA)

3.4.1   RDA Paradigm

This paradigm allows client programs and/or end-user tools to issue ad hoc[2] queries, usually SQL, against remotely located databases. The key technical difference between RDA and RPC is that in an RDA the size of the result is not known in advance. For example, consider the following SQL statement that is sent to a remotely located database server:

        SELECT * FROM CUSTOMER;

The result of this query could be one row or thousands of rows, depending on the number of customers in the customer table. In addition, we do not know how many columns will be returned in each row. In contrast, each parameter for the RPC must be clearly specified. Owing to this difference, the RDA paradigm supports a dialog between clients and servers so that a client can retrieve one row at a time (through SQL FETCH verb) and process it. Thus each C/S interaction is not a self-contained and independent unit of work. Instead, just like human conversations, the interactions depend on the context of the conversation (this implies that some context related information is kept and used during the conversation). Conversational processing requires both parties to be alive during the conversation. In addition, the exchanges are usually synchronous. The client interface in RDA paradigm is row by row, typically the server middleware transports blocks of rows for efficiency.

Figure 3.3 shows the steps that take place in a remote-data access. The client and server routines are in two separate processes, usually on two different machines. RDA software basically gives an impression to the RDA client that SQL calls are being issued to a local database. The following steps are executed in order:

1. The client issues an SQL call in an API made available by the client middleware (we will discuss the two API formats later). The client API calls can be issued from end-user tools or application programs. The client middleware mainly encodes the SQL call into appropriate network messages. As we will see later, the client middleware may support "database procedure" calls in addition to remote SQL calls. The middleware also determines the actual network address of the server and "binds" to it.

2. The network message, containing the SQL statement, is prepared and sent to the remote site through network transport services.

3. The message is sent over the communication media and is received by the network transport services of the server machine. If the network architecture of the client machine is different from that of the server machine, then a network gateway may be needed (e.g., TCP/IP-to-SNA gateway).

---

2. The term ad hoc for most of our purposes indicates improvised, spur-of-the-moment activity.

4. The server network system informs the server middleware that a request has arrived for it.

5. The server middleware gets the network message and schedules execution of this call by the database server. As we will discuss later, the middleware may invoke a database procedure consisting of several SQL calls, instead of one SQL call.

6. The database server processes the SQL call and develops a response (selected table rows and columns), which is sent to the server middleware.

7. The server middleware translates the response into one or more network messages, which are sent to the network system. The middleware may cache many messages before an appropriate response to the client can be developed. For example, the server middleware may not send the entire selected table back to client as a single response; instead it may send large tables as several blocks (e.g., 4 megabytes) of data.

8. The server network system sends the response back to the client network system. Once again, a gateway may be needed if the client and server network architectures are dissimilar.

9. The client network system sends the response messages to the client middleware.

10. The client middleware receives the response message, translates this message into call responses, and sends the response back to the client. The middleware may supply the response to the client one row at a time, based on "FETCH" statements issued by the client process.

Figure 3.3 Remote-Data Access

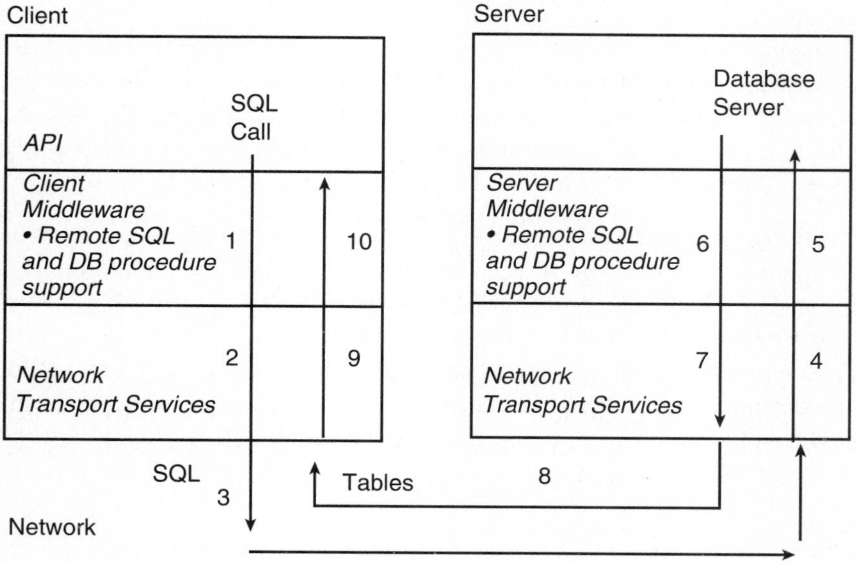

3.4.2 RDA Analysis

Many decisions are made in various steps of the remote-data-access paradigm. Examples of some of these decisions are discussed here.

Call Level versus Embedded API. Call-level interface (CLI) and embedded SQL are the two generally accepted application programming interfaces (APIs) for RDA. In CLI, an SQL statement is passed as a character-string parameter to the SQL server. For example, the client process may issue the following call to run an SQL statement:

```
CALL SQLRUN ("SELECT * FROM CUSTOMERS", RESULTS, RC)
```

After this call, the client process may issue additional calls to fetch rows. A CLI may provide additional calls for connecting to a particular server, breaking the connection, etc. Open Database Connect (ODBC) is an example of a CLI. The embedded SQL API allows client processes to include SQL statements in program code. The embedded SQL statements are distinguished from the other program code through special indicators (e.g., a $ in the first column). For example, an embedded SQL query may appear as

```
$ SELECT * FROM CUSTOMERS
```

Typically, vendors provide a preprocessor that converts the embedded SQL statements to calls that are sent across the network.

Static versus Dynamic SQL. Static SQL statements are known and explicitly coded into a program before it is compiled. In contrast, dynamic SQL statements are generated at run time, typically through desktop tools.

Static SQL statements can be optimized and prepared for execution at the time the program is compiled and linked. An "execution plan" can be generated at compile time to efficiently run the SQL statements when invoked. Static SQL, although efficient for local database calls, is not generally suitable for RDA because the data in a network can move around several times between the time the program is compiled and the time it is run. For this reason, most RDA middleware products only support dynamic SQL or support dynamic preparation (plan generation) at run time.

Stored (Database) Procedures. Most RDBMS vendors at present support database procedures which contain a collection of SQL statements that can be invoked through a single call (see Figure 3.4). Database procedures, also known as *stored procedures*, are typically implemented by extending SQL to include programming constructs (e.g., branching and looping). These procedures are compiled and stored for later invocation by authorized programs. For example, a database update that requires modification of several tables can be implemented as a stored procedure and invoked by authorized application programs. The mechanism for invoking these procedures is usually a special call. Stored procedures offer several potential benefits:

- They can enforce data integrity and extra security by requiring updates to be performed only through stored procedures. As a matter of fact, there is currently a debate in the C/S community whether distributed transaction managers can be replaced with stored procedures.

- They can improve performance by issuing one message that can generate multiple SQL statements at the SQL server (see Figure 3.4).

- They can introduce a degree of "object orientation" to a relational database by providing a set of "methods" that can be invoked through messages without requiring knowledge of the internal table structure.

Many RDA middleware products provide support for remote SQL as well as database procedures. Database procedures allow applications to intermix SQL calls and database-procedure calls (e.g., an application can issue an SQL call, invoke a database procedure, and again issue a series of SQL calls). Although database procedures somewhat resemble the RPCs, they differ primarily in that a database procedure returns a table which can be navigated by the application through subsequent fetches; RPCs typically return a fixed number of parameters with virtually no capability for navigating through variable-length objects.

Distributed-Query Processing and Distributed-Transaction Management. Some applications may need to access data on multiple database servers concurrently. There are two basic approaches to support this:

- Allow programs to explicitly connect with each database server and then issue a remote SQL or database procedure against the database. In this case, a single SQL statement operates on a single database server.

- Employ a distributed-query processor which presents a virtual database consisting of data at multiple sites. The distributed-query processor receives an SQL statement from client programs against this virtual database and sends requests to multiple servers to access remotely located data. Typically, distributed-query processors allow joins between remotely located tables.

Figure 3.4 Remote SQL versus Database Procedure

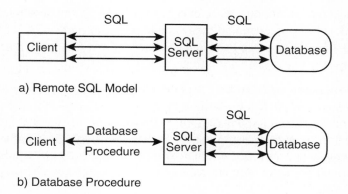

a) Remote SQL Model

b) Database Procedure

A distributed-transaction manager is needed if the data at multiple sites needs to be updated by the client programs. The distinction is that query processing is read only, whereas transaction processing supports data writes/updates that require additional capabilities. We will discuss the issues of distributed-query processing and distributed-transaction management in Chapters 5 and 6.

3.4.3   Strengths and Weaknesses of RDA

RDAs are widely supported by DBMS vendors, and an almost unlimited number of RDA-based desktop tools are commercially available. The main strength of RDA (especially remote SQL) is that no server software needs to be developed (the database server *is* the procedure invoked by remote SQL). In addition, the large number of RDA-based desktop tools facilitate "plug-and-play" C/S capabilities. In contrast, users of RPC must code a client as well as a server process. However, RDA needs to be carefully evaluated. In many cases, remote SQL can generate a great deal of traffic on the network, owing to large tables being shipped across the network. At a minimum, this can cause "minor discomfort" to the user community at large. In general, remote SQL is a good paradigm for ad hoc queries, while RPCs (and database procedures) work well for database updates.

3.5   Message-Oriented Middleware (MOM)

3.5.1   Queued-Message-Processing (QMP) Paradigm

In the queued-message-processing (QMP) paradigm, the client message is stored in a queue and the server works on it when free (Figure 3.5). The server stores ("puts") the response in another queue, and the client actively retrieves ("gets") the responses from this queue. This model, used in many transaction-processing systems, allows the clients to asynchronously send requests to the server. Once a request is queued, the request is processed, even if the sender is disconnected (intentionally or due to a failure). In queued-message processing, arriving messages are first queued and then scheduled for execution. After storing the message in the queue, the client can go back and continue its work. In particular, once execution of a request begins, the client does not interact with the execution process.

MOM (message-oriented middleware) supports the message-queuing paradigm in a C/S environment.[3] It provides APIs for getting and putting messages into and out of the queues and supports the queued-messaging paradigm. MOM has recently gained industrial attention, owing to its appeal to "nomadic" computing (e.g., wireless-based detachable computers) that favors the type of asynchronous processing provided by MOM (the detachable computers are not always connected for RPC- and RDA-type message exchanges). Case studies of MOM

---

3. MOM also supports message passing between end processes, but our focus is on queued messaging.

applications can be found in Camara [1996], Stahl [1995], Whiting [1994b], and the experiences of building distributed applications with MOM can be found in Dolgicer [1996] and Amaru [1994].

Figure 3.5 Conceptual Views of Queued Message Processing

(a) One Queue for Sending Messages, the Other for Receiving

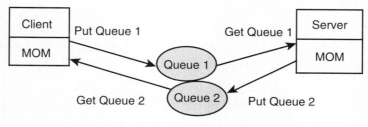

MOM = Message-Oriented Middleware

(b) A Client-Side Queue and a Server-Side Queue

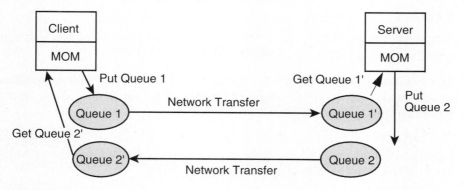

Each logical queue may be physically implemented as two queues—one on the client side and the other on the server side. The client queue gets the message; a network transfer package transfers this message to the server queue, where it is processed. This approach provides extra recoverability.

Figure 3.6 shows the steps that take place in queued-message processing. The client and server routines are in two separate processes, usually on two different machines. We are showing two logical queues for the purpose of discussion; Q1 is the input queue, in which the clients store their messages, and Q2 is the output queue from which the clients receive their results. Designers and implementers of QMP can choose different queue numbers for performance and availability purposes. For conceptual discussion, we will also assume that the queues are located "somewhere" on the network. In practice, the queues may exist at the server machine, at client machines, in a middle machine (e.g., a gateway), or a combination thereof. The following steps are executed in order:

1. The client issues a "Put message on Q1" call in an API made available by the client middleware. The client API calls can be issued from end-user tools or application programs. The client middleware mainly encodes the call into appropriate network messages.

2. The network message, containing the put message, is prepared and sent to the remote site through network transport services.

3. The message is sent over the communication media and is stored in the input queue (Q1). If the network architecture of the client machine is different from that of the server machine, then a network gateway may be needed (e.g., TCP/IP-to-SNA gateway). Q1 may be allocated to this gateway.

4. The message is stored in Q1. The server middleware is notified that a request has arrived for it (in some cases, the server middleware scans the queue for any new messages).

5. The server middleware retrieves the message by issuing a "Get Q1" and schedules execution of this call by the database server.

6. The database server processes the message and develops a response message which is sent to the server middleware. The message is sent to the output queue (Q2) through a "put Q2" message.

7. The server middleware translates the response message into one or more network messages. For example, if a very large response is generated, the server middleware may not send the entire message to the output queue.

8. The server network sends the response back to the client network system and stores the message(s) in Q2. Once again, recall our assumption that the queues are located somewhere on the network.

9. The client middleware is notified of any responses in Q2.

10. The client middleware sends the response to the client process whenever it receives a "get Q2" statement from the client process.

This model can be easily extended to include client-side and server-side queues.

Figure 3.6 Queued-Message Processing

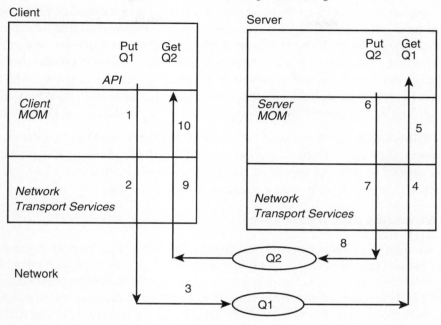

3.5.2 QMP Analysis

Many decisions are made in various steps of the queued-message paradigm. Examples of some of these decisions are discussed here.

Asynchronous ("nonblocked") paradigm. The clients can put a message on the queue and then continue processing. Another segment of client code can continue to monitor the output queue for any responses and process the outputs received. Asynchronous processing has the following benefits:

- It is suitable for detachable (e.g., wireless) computers that need to access data asynchronously without having to be in constant session with the hosts.

- Failure of server does not stop the clients from continuing to process as much as possible.

- Clients can be more efficient and responsive because they do not have to wait for the server to respond.

- Clients and servers can use "deferred-message" or callback features if a response is not available.

However, it must be kept in mind that developing good asynchronous code is non-triv⸱ Why? Because of the need to match up returned messages to requests, clients must keⱸ of outstanding "transactions."

Queue Considerations. The message queues can be stored on disk (persistent) or in main memory (nonpersistent). In most cases, queues are stored on disks for failure recovery. The queues can be at client machines, at server machines, in a middle machine, or replicated on client and server machines. If the queues are replicated, then "data movers" are provided as part of MOM that move queues from one machine to another. A major consideration in QMP is handling of very large messages in the queue. If queries generate large tables with millions of rows as responses to be stored in queues, then very large queue sizes need to be allocated. Queue overflows can be quite dangerous to the health of QMP-based C/S environments.

Handling Different-Speed Processors. A major advantage of QMP is that the queues can be written into and retrieved from a diverse array of client and server processes. These processes can operate at different speeds on different machines and not cause any interference and/or delays. (You still have to worry about queues overflowing.)

3.5.3   Strengths and Weaknesses

The main strength of message-oriented middleware (MOM) is asynchronous processing; i.e., the clients and servers are not blocked while waiting for responses from each other. This feature of MOM also allows development of peer-to-peer distributed applications. Another strength of MOM is recoverability from failures, because the message queues on disks can be used to recover the system after failures. For example, once a message has been received and queued by MOM, these messages are not lost (the queues are used to restart applications, if needed). MOM also gives you network independence because you are interacting with queues.

Yet another strength of MOM is that it can be used to link existing legacy applications very easily without modifying any code at either side (i.e., redirect the output of application A to a disk queue and redirect the input of application B from the same disk queue). This approach does not require additional software development on either side (you do not need a client that issues an RPC and a server that receives, parses, and dispatches processes). MOM also provides an appealing solution for distributed-transaction processing, because the queue messaging can be transactional (i.e., MOM can make sure that only one message is transferred and that automated rollback recovery is available). This is very familiar territory for mainframe-based transaction managers such as IMS (IMS has been using queued messages ~   1970s). We will discuss the MOM approach to distributed-transaction
                      r 6.

                  f MOM is that the overhead of writing/reading from disk queues can
                  ation. In addition, queuing of unpredictably large responses can result
                  ijor limitation of MOM is that it introduces some unique end-to-end
                  use many security packages at present assume a direct connection
                  ing parties ("no middle man"). MOMs also do not support IDLs and
                  tions can be less interactive and require low-level programming.

In balance, MOM provides a very powerful approach for providing reliable and asynchronous communication between very heterogeneous applications. Due to this, "Message Broker" architectures are being investigated Bort [1996]. A detailed discussion of message queuing with analysis of various trade-offs can be found in Dolgicer [1996].

Ideally, C/S middleware needs to support RDA, RPC, and QMP paradigms to provide C/S application developers maximum flexibility.

3.6   Other Paradigms

Programs at different machines can interact with each other by using a wide variety of paradigms. The paradigms discussed so far are very popular interactive message exchanges and are supported by many suppliers. However, several other paradigms have been presented in the literature. Here are some examples (a detailed discussion of these and other paradigms with numerous examples for algorithm analysis can be found in Andrews [1991]).

- *Peer-to-peer model,* in which either remotely located process can initiate an interaction. The basic distinguishing feature of the C/S model is that a client initiates an interaction with a server by sending a message or by invoking an operation. In contrast, either process of a peer-to-peer model can initiate an interaction. A C/S model can be implemented over peer-to-peer protocols. C/S computing systems at present are based on the C/S model. "Distributed cooperative processing systems" use peer-to-peer or C/S model for processes at different computers to interactively exchange information with each other (C/S computing is a subcategory of distributed cooperative processing).

- *One-way data flow from one process to another (named "pipelines").* This can be used when no response is expected and is natural for the type of programs which receive streams of input and produce streams of output. This technique minimizes control (handshaking) messages between distributed programs and is simplex (one- way traffic). For example, this technique can be used in file transfers and invocation of remotely located text formatters (e.g., UNIX Troff). Another example is a speech-recognition system that constantly monitors an audio port for sound (the sound is transferred one-way) and processes speech whenever it arrives.[4]

- *Broadcasting.* In this paradigm, one program needs to send the same data to several other programs. Broadcasting is a commonly used technique in network technologies and is often implemented as a low-level primitive (e.g., in Ethernet). In order to implement broadcasting between application programs (e.g., to notify loss of a critical data file), the application programs have to choose and implement search criteria such as spanning trees.

- *Token passing between distributed programs.* This technique, also borrowed from lower-level network protocols, can be used between application programs to circulate messages.

- *Heartbeat and probe/echo processing.* The processes send messages to neighbor processes and forward requests to successor processes, respectively. These algorithms are used in many cooperative processing situations where none of the servers have complete information. In

---

4. This example was suggested by my colleague Dr. Sharad Singhal.

these cases, the servers coordinate their work with each other by sending/receiving messages to neighbors and successors.

- *Replicated server processing.* This is used when many servers at different sites perform the same activities. For example, many name servers may be replicated in a network. The replicated servers can either choose one server to perform the task or split a task among many replicated servers for load balancing.

In addition, remote programs can interact with each other by using the paradigms and associated protocols that we will discuss in later chapters (e.g., the distributed-object interactions, Web access to remote resources through HTTP, mobile code applications such as Java applets)[5].

Which paradigm should be used when? We have discussed the trade-offs between RPCs, RDA, and MOM. The main consideration is minimization of the communication message traffic and reliability of the protocols. However, we need to keep the following factors in mind:

- *Application requirements:* which paradigm best meets the application needs?
- *Time and money constraints:* how much time and money is allowed for this project?
- *Availability of off-the-shelf middleware:* what is commercially available to satisfy application needs within the time and money constraints?

3.7   Basic Management and Support Services

3.7.1   Security

Client/server systems introduce many security exposures. For example, it is the responsibility of the C/S middleware to assure that unauthorized clients do not get access to servers. The clients and servers may use encryption routines and authentication protocols for information access. Here is one possible scenario:

- Client middleware authenticates if the client can request the service.
- Client middleware encrypts the data if needed.
- Server middleware authenticates the client request.
- Server middleware decrypts the message, performs additional security checking, and builds audit trails.

This is dramatically different from the traditional mainframe model, in which all users of the mainframe resources were under the control of a centralized security manager such as IBM's Resource Access Control Facility (RACF). In general, security in distributed systems, includ-

---

5. As we will see, HTTP uses RPC and Java applets use TCP/IP sockets or Remote Method Invocation (an RPC).

ing C/S systems, is a major challenge, because more points of contact (files and programs are accessible from network) exist, and each host cannot know all its potential users. Conceptually, security needs to be enforced at several levels:

- *Authentication:* verify a user is who he/she claims to be
- *Authorization:* give access to rightful user (implemented through access control lists)
- *Audit:* keep track (trails) of access
- *Confidentiality:* keeping messages private
- *Integrity:* insure that only correct messages are honored
- *Non-repudiation:* preventing denial of messages

This discussion assumes that the server is secure. In large systems, each server also needs to be authenticated.

Different C/S environments have implemented different aspects of security differently. Kerberos, developed at MIT for Project Athena, is currently the de facto standard for security in distributed computing and C/S environments. The basic theory of Kerberos is that instead of the traditional two-tiered security system (i.e., security information is exchanged between a host and users), a three-tiered security system is needed (clients, servers, and security servers). The security server keeps track of passwords, IDs, and other relevant information and enforces security in a C/S environment. In particular, the Kerberos three-tiered security system employs the following process:

- User presents a password to the client process
- The password is converted to a secret key and is sent to a Kerberos security server
- The Kerberos security server creates a ticket and sends it back to the client process
- The client process sends the ticket to the server
- The server checks the ticket and starts communications

Kerberos is being included in many C/S environments and provides the security foundation for the Open Software Foundation's Distributed Computing Environment (OSF DCE). We will discuss OSF DCE in Section 3.8 and will discuss Kerberos in more detail at that point.

The reader should not forget that security within one C/S vendor environment is easier to deal with than security between systems that cross many vendor environments (e.g., MVS, UNIX, OSF DCE, Novell). Additional information about C/S security can be found in Schiller [1994], and Neuman [1994].

3.7.2   Fault (Failure) Management

Fault management is concerned with detecting, isolating, and correcting faults in the application systems. The basic goal of fault-management services is to provide smooth and fault-free operations. Since downtime is intolerable in most applications, the fault management must be proactive (i.e., it should forecast faults and provide support to prevent fault occurrence). The basic fault-management functions are as follows:

- *Fault detection,* which includes detecting faults in the individual components or the paths between the components, providing notification of the detected faults, and predicting faults before they occur.

- *Fault isolation,* which includes determining the failing component and/or components which are causing the problem.

- *Fault resolution,* which includes determining the corrective actions and then executing them if possible.

Fault management in C/S systems is nontrivial. A client and server can fail independently and then be restarted. For example, a server or the transport network may fail before the server had a chance to execute the request, or a server may crash after completing a request. For some services (e.g., read only), no harm is done if a service is requested several times whenever an error occurs. However, if the service performed updates, then some sequencing control is needed to assure that the same service is not executed more than once. Error handling becomes especially difficult when the server communicates with other servers to provide a service (e.g., a server responsible for managing distributed data may need to communicate with other sites where the copies of data exist). A variety of techniques, such as two-phase-commit protocols, are used in such cases. We will discuss failure handling of transactions in Chapter 6.

3.7.3   Naming and Directory Services

A client-server system needs to know the names and locations of the objects being managed. For example, a client needing access to a file should be able to access the file by its symbolic name without having to know its network address. A directory service provides a lookup service which translates an object name into a physical- network address. For example, in the TCP/IP networks, the Domain Name Services are used to translate a UNIX computer name such as BIRD to a physical network hardware address such as 18.32.1.22. In addition, naming and directory services can be used to enforce security by denying network addresses to unauthorized users. The ANSI/OSI Directory Standard (X.500) is a standard for global naming and directory services.

Name servers involve the following steps:

- An appropriate name server is found. This is accomplished through global directories.

- The names of the objects to be used globally are registered in a name table. Each registered name has an external component, which is known to the users, and an internal component, which is used by the distributed operating systems to locate the objects physically.

- A process needing a service or a set of objects consults the name table to determine where the needed objects and services are located. The name server may translate the external object name into an internal physical address.

It is possible to have two-level name servers: one global name server and many local name servers. The global name server is consulted to determine the computer on which the object is located. The local name server at each computer shows the particular device within a computer (e.g., a disk) on which the object is located. This is in essence similar to the distributed (global) data directory in which the global directory points to a local database directory for exact data location and format. In large networks it is possible to have the following three levels of name services:

- A universal name server, which shows what objects are located in what subnets (network domains). The total network is assumed to be partitioned into several subnets (domains). For example, each LAN can be a subnet.

- A subnet name server, one per subnet, which shows the computer within the subnet where the resource is located.

- A local name server, one per computer, which shows where within the computer system the resource is located.

The main problem with this paradigm is that the universal name service can become a performance and availability bottleneck. To circumvent this problem, duplicate copies of universal names can be maintained, and/or naming conventions, similar to the telephone number systems, can be employed to identify subnets without an explicit table lookup. For example, the telephone area code indicates a region without an explicit table lookup. For distributed operating systems in small networks, such as LANs, it is possible to use a broadcast naming service in which the request for an object is broadcasted to the entire network. Each computer checks its local name table to find a match. If a match is found, it responds with a physical address; otherwise it ignores the request. The ANSI/OSI Directory Standard (X.500) is being developed for global naming and directory services.

3.7.4   Performance

The performance of a C/S system must be carefully evaluated. For example, the network delays as well as the node processing must be taken into account when designing distributed C/S applications. For node processing, we need to examine the trade-off between firing up a new server for every client request versus a single reentrant server which is called repetitively. The main network-performance consideration is minimization of the communication messages between clients and servers. The network-performance problems are aggravated for several reasons.

- The network traffic patterns are not predictable, primarily owing to the message traffic and remote joins between distributed databases. This presents challenges in estimating the bandwidth and the best/worst cases for a given network.

- The network response time is hard to predict, because a given message can be routed through several potential delay points.

- The need for enterprise network management becomes more acute because all networks, LAN as well as WAN, provide transport services from clients to servers located anywhere in the network. In heterogeneous networks, the need for cooperation between network-management applications will increase, leading to an enterprisewide network management. In fact, an enterprisewide network manager is itself a distributed cooperating processing application.

- The problems of scaling are not well understood. It is not clear, for example, how the current protocols and algorithms will perform on very large networks that may span many countries [Ozsu 1991]. We should keep in mind that the emerging high-speed broadband networks discussed in Chapter 11 will change the emphasis of many of the networking issues considered important at present.

3.8   Distributed Computing Environment (DCE)

3.8.1   Overview

The Open Software Foundation (OSF) was formed by UNIX (non-AT&T) vendors to standardize a version of UNIX that could run on many computers. Many vendors, including IBM, DEC, and Hewlett-Packard, are participating in OSF. A nonprofit company, OSF has gone through many changes in the past few years. While its initial focus has been on standardizing UNIX, it realized that a standardized UNIX is not enough to provide transportable distributed applications across computers. OSF is especially concentrating on interoperability between multiple products from multiple vendors. For example, parts of applications may reside at mainframes, at UNIX minicomputers, or OS/2 workstations. The main focus is on distributed cooperative processing and on standards to help connections at many levels.

OSF Distributed Computing Environment (DCE) packages and implements an "open" and de facto standard into an environment for distributed computing. OSF DCE, also commonly known as DCE, enjoys very heavy vendor participation and is available on a wide range of computing platforms such as UNIX, OS/2, and IBM MVS, with many other vendors announcing support. Figure 3.7 shows the main components of OSF DCE. The applications are at the highest level and the transport services are at the lowest level in DCE (at present, DCE uses the TCP/IP transport services). The security and management functions are built at various levels and are applicable to all components. The distributed file access to access remotely located data, naming services for accessing objects across the network, remote-procedure calls (RPCs), and presentation services are at the core of DCE. DCE allows for growth of future services, which will be enabled as future technologies become available. DCE services, reviewed in the following sections, are portable to many computers.

Figure 3.7 OSF DCE

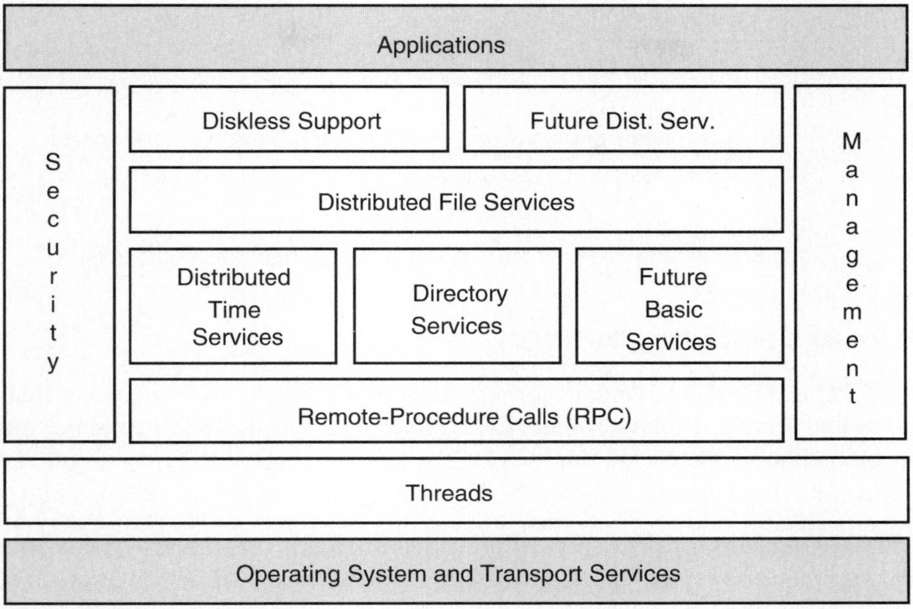

```
┌─────────────────────────────────────────────────────────────────┐
│                          Applications                             │
├───┬─────────────────────────────────────────────────────────┬───┤
│ S │ ┌──────────────────────┐ ┌──────────────────────────┐   │ M │
│ e │ │   Diskless Support    │ │    Future Dist. Serv.    │   │ a │
│ c │ └──────────────────────┘ └──────────────────────────┘   │ n │
│ u │ ┌───────────────────────────────────────────────────┐   │ a │
│ r │ │          Distributed File Services                │   │ g │
│ i │ └───────────────────────────────────────────────────┘   │ e │
│ t │ ┌────────────┐ ┌────────────┐ ┌────────────┐           │ m │
│ y │ │ Distributed│ │            │ │  Future    │           │ e │
│   │ │   Time     │ │ Directory  │ │  Basic     │           │ n │
│   │ │  Services  │ │ Services   │ │  Services  │           │ t │
│   │ └────────────┘ └────────────┘ └────────────┘           │   │
│   │ ┌───────────────────────────────────────────────────┐ │   │
│   │ │       Remote-Procedure Calls (RPC)                │ │   │
│   │ └───────────────────────────────────────────────────┘ │   │
├───┴─────────────────────────────────────────────────────────┴───┤
│                           Threads                                 │
├───────────────────────────────────────────────────────────────────┤
│          Operating System and Transport Services                  │
└───────────────────────────────────────────────────────────────────┘
```

3.8.2 OSF DCE Services

3.8.2.1 Threads Service

The OSF threads service allows application programs to perform many services simultaneously. For example, one thread can be used to issue a remote procedure call while the other can be used to receive input. Each thread is essentially an independent path in a program, thus allowing one client program to simultaneously interact with several servers and vice versa (see Figure 3.8). Threads can be used to perform asynchronous RPC processing even though each thread performs a synchronous RPC. For example, the client shown in Figure 3.8 can initiate three RPCs on the three threads one after another and then wait for the responses in the same order.

The threads service includes operations to create and control multiple threads in a single process and to synchronize global data access. The threads service is used by a number of DCE components such as RPCs, directory, security and time services, and the distributed-file system. The main features of the threads service are as follows:

- A simple programming method for building concurrent applications. For example, one client can open five threads to simultaneously communicate with five servers.
- Support for C and other high-level languages.
- Ability to build threads in an operating system or on top of an operating system.

Figure 3.8 DCE Threads

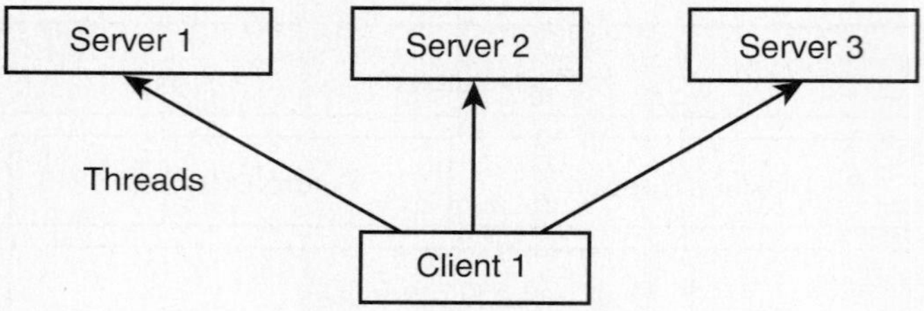

Note: Each thread does not have to invoke a separate remote process.

3.8.2.2 Remote-Procedure Call (RPC)

The DCE RPC is a de facto standard for remote-procedure calls—it provides portability of DCE clients and servers from one vendor DCE to another, and also interoperability of a DCE client developed on vendor X DCE with a DCE server on vendor Y. For example, DCE clients on Sun and HP machines can interoperate with a DCE server on MVS machine.

OSF's RPC supports direct calls to remote procedures, usually on remote systems (see Figure 3.9). RPC presentation services mask the differences between data representation on different computers. This facilitates programs to interact with each other across heterogeneous computers. OSF's RPC provides a compiler that converts high-level interface descriptions of the remote procedures into C source code. The calls to remote procedures behave the same way as local-procedure calls. Main features of the OSF RPC are as follows:

- Network and protocol independence by shielding the network transport services from the application programs. Connectionless as well as connection-oriented services are supported.

- Secure RPC communication between clients and servers. Authenticity, integrity, and privacy of communications is guaranteed through integration with DCE security service.

- Multiplicity of clients and servers for mutual interactions and location of servers by name. These features are supported by the threads service and the directory service, respectively, of the DCE.

- Support for large data-processing applications by permitting unlimited argument size and handling of bulk data.

- Support of international character sets (e.g., Japanese, Arabic, and Chinese) as specified by the ISO standards.

Interface Definition Language (IDL). DCE provides an Interface Definition Language (IDL) for defining parameters used in an RPC. An *interface* represents the information that is shared between client and server applications. A typical interface definition has a unique interface identifier, and it shows all the procedures offered by the server and the parameters being passed for each procedure. For example, the following IDL describes the interface known as "simple" that shows two remote procedures: "simple_sum" that returns the sum of first three parameters in the fourth parameter, and "simple_product" that multiplies the first three parameters and returns the product in the fourth parameter (DCE IDL resembles C syntax):

```
uuid (C38950-0000-2122) /* unique universal identifier */
 interface simple /* interface name is simple */
 void simple_sum ( /*The procedure name is simple_sum */
 [in] integer in1; /* input parameter 1*/
 [in] integer in2; /* input parameter 2*/
 [in] integer in3; /* input parameter 3*/
 [out] integer sum;) /* output parameter */
 void simple_product ( /*The procedure is simple_product */
 [in] integer in1; /* input parameter 1*/
 [in] integer in2; /* input parameter 2*/
 [in] integer in3; /* input parameter 3*/
 [out] integer product;) /* output parameter */
```

Figure 3.9 Remote-Procedure Call

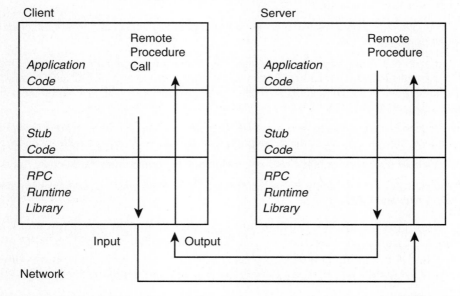

After developing the IDL, the code for the client that issues the RPC is developed and the code for the server procedures is developed. For example, a DCE client to invoke the simple_sum procedure and print the resulting sum may look like the following pseudocode:

```
a = 10; b= 20; c=35; /* initialize the parameters */
simple_sum (a, b, c, d ); /* invoke the remote procedure */
printf (d);    /* print the sum returned */
```

After developing the IDL and the client and server codes, the IDL and the client and server codes are compiled by using the DCE-provided compilers. **Stubs** are generated by the DCE compilers to hide network details. Stubs are created for client as well as server processes (see Figure 3.10). For example, the client stub receives input parameters from client application, finds ("binds with") the server, constructs a request to be sent over the network, sends a request to the server, and receives the response. The server stub code receives the request from client applications, checks security, invokes server application processes, and sends response and status back to the client code. In addition, client and server stubs perform argument **Marshalling/Unmarshalling**, i.e., convert the arguments passed and place them into buffers for use. Note that the DCE compilers automatically include security and directory information in RPCs.

3.8.2.3 Distributed Directory and Name Service

The OSF Directory Service allows users to name resources such as servers, files, disks, or print queues, and gain access to them without having to know where they are located in the network. Thus the resource names can stay the same even if their location in the network changes. This also allows scaling of services from small networks to large and vice versa. The main features of this service are:

- Access of each computer in DCE environment to directory services. These directories are tied together through X.500.

- Integration of X.500 global naming system with a replicated local naming system. This allows programmers to move transparently from environments supporting full ISO functionality to those supporting only the local naming service. The X/Open Directory Service API (application programming interface) of the directory service offers full X.500 functionality.

- Replication of critical data to increase availability and caching of recent lookups to improve performance. Update synchronization mechanisms are provided to ensure data consistency.

- Secure communication and authority control through integration with the Security Service.

- Network transport independence by utilizing the OSF RPCs which operate transparently over many LANs and MANs.

These services provide location information (address, attributes) about resources located throughout a network. The directory services are automatically utilized by RPC to locate resources. The DCE naming and directory services provide a consistent naming convention (tree), i.e., /.:/service/server1. The support exists in terms of DCE cells:[6]

- Within a cell (stored in cell directory)

- Between cells (X.500 and domain name services)

---

6. A DCE cell is a collection of DCE clients and servers that typically belong to an organizational unit (e.g., a department) and interact frequently with each other.

Figure 3.10 Compiling DCE Programs

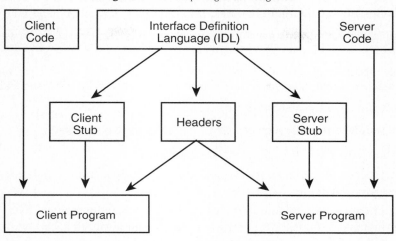

Replicated directories are synchronized through update propagation of master directory (immediate) and "skulking": periodic distribution of updates.

3.8.2.4 Time Service

DCE provides fault-tolerant clock synchronization for computers tied together in WANs, MANs, and LANs. The time service supplies time with a plus/minus range so that close times can be matched. This service is also integrated with other DCE facilities such as RPCs, security service to issue time stamp, and directory service to locate time servers.

3.8.2.5 Security Service

DCE security services are provided through a security server instead of each host. It should be noted that DCE security features are automatically included in RPCs, i.e., DCE security is transparent to the application developers. DCE uses Kerberos security and provides security at three levels:

- *Authentication:* verify a user is who he/she claims
- *Authorization:* give access to rightful user (implemented through access control lists)
- *Audit:* keep track (trails) of access

The DCE security service provides authentication, authorization, and user account management in different manners. The basic authentication and authorization is provided by the message-corruption detection facility of OSF RPC. In addition, the Kerberos system is used by the security service for authentication. The OSF authorization tools are well integrated with the Kerberos authentication system. OSF's user registry addresses the user account-management problems in DCE by maintaining a logical database which contains user IDs, passwords, etc. Following are the main features of this service:

- The authenticity of requests made across a network is trusted by multiple hosts and operating systems.
- A single repository of user accounts is maintained to avoid conflicts in logins and passwords. This database is replicated across the network for high availability and response.
- Different privileges and authorities are supported.
- Data privacy is ensured through encryption/decryption across networks.

Figure 3.11 shows the basic steps in using DCE security:

1. A DCE security administrator registers each principal (user, computer or server) in the registry database.
2. An application administrator creates ACLs (authorization control lists) which show the principals, groups, or organizations and the authority to access various objects.
3. When a user logs in to DCE, the login process acquires the "tickets" and privilege attributes needed to access resources.
4. When a user starts an application client, the client inherits the privilege attributes and uses them in first RPC. The application server determines the privileges needed before executing the RPC.

Figure 3.11 DCE Security Flow

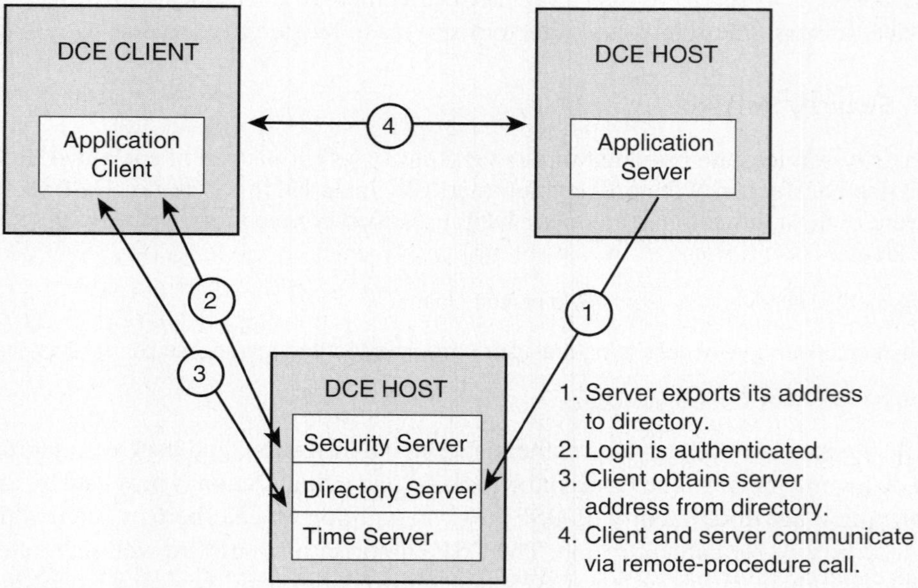

1. Server exports its address to directory.
2. Login is authenticated.
3. Client obtains server address from directory.
4. Client and server communicate via remote-procedure call.

3.8.2.6 Distributed-File System (DFS)

OSF DFS makes global file access easy by providing a consistent interface to file systems at individual computers. OSF DFS uses a client-server model to access remotely located files. The main features of OSF DFS are as follows:

- It is based on the Andrew File System but is intended to interoperate with the SUN Network File System (NFS) and other file servers.
- It includes high-performance and availability features through file replication and caching of recently used files.
- It is scalable from small users on a LAN to large number of users across multiple networks.
- It uses OSF's secure RPC and utilizes access control lists for allowing access to appropriate files.

3.8.2.7 Diskless Support

This support is provided for low-cost diskless workstations which need to access disks located on servers. OSF Diskless Support provides well-defined and general- purpose protocols for diskless operations.

3.8.2.8 Management

A set of management capabilities are included in DCE. These capabilities are bundled with the individual technologies included in DCE. OSF is expanding and integrating these capabilities by working with different standardization bodies. The progress on this front is somewhat slow.

3.8.3 A DCE Example

Figure 3.12 shows example of an actual operational DCE environment in which the DCE clients and servers reside on MVS, Hewlett-Packard, and RS6000 machines. In particular, server A resides on the MVS machine and server B resides on the HP machine. A client (client X) was developed first on an HP workstation and tested for connection with the HP resident Server B. This client was moved to the IBM RS6000 machine by simply recompiling the same code at this site. Owing to the multivendor support provided by DCE, this client could communicate with Server B on HP from the new platforms without any changes to the client or server code (DCE established the binding between clients and servers by looking at the directory). More clients and servers (e.g., Server B and Client X) were developed and moved around from one type of platform to another and still were able to establish connections with changes in the application code (the MVS server code has to be modified slightly if it moves from MVS to non-MVS environments).

The main observation made from this test example is that DCE clients and servers can interoperate and are portable in multivendor environments.

3.8.4   DCE Summary and Trends

DCE is an *implementation* (OSF ships DCE code to the vendors, and the vendors customize this code to run on their machines) and not a specification. Thus DCE is intended to provide portability and interoperability between vendor environments (a big plus). For example, a DCE client developed on a SUN DCE is portable to an HP DCE environment and can interoperate with an HP DCE server. Owing to its emphasis on multivendor environments, DCE is very popular in large-scale computing environments where interoperability and portability of clients and servers is a crucial issue. In addition, DCE RPC has become a favorite "transport" mechanism which carries other higher-level protocols as RPC parameters (we will see examples of this in Encina, CORBA, and ActiveX).

The main limitation of DCE at the time of this writing is that it does not provide direct database support. In other words, ad hoc SQL support is not available in DCE—a user must develop a client that passes SQL statements as parameters and provide his/her own parsing/interpretation of results. This effectively means that each user is forced to develop his/her own remote-data access (RDA) protocol. However, many database vendors such as IBM, Informix, Oracle and Sybase have announced integration of DCE services with their database managers. Some other vendors have started providing special "add-ons" to DCE for database support. For example, Open Horizon has developed a "Connection/DCE" product that issues ODBC calls over DCE RPC (a Connection/DCE Client accepts ODBC calls and builds an RPC, while a Connection/DCE Server receives this RPC and routes it to an appropriate database manager). It is expected that DCE support for ad hoc database access will become state-of-the-market.

Figure 3.12 A DCE Example

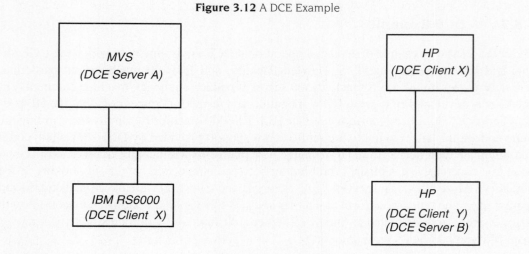

At the time of this writing, development tools for DCE applications are scarce. As a result, developers have to confront and use the vast number of DCE API functions, details of which are spread over several thick manuals. In particular, writing DCE applications by using threads is a particularly bitter task for programmers who are trained to write Cobol programs. In short, writing DCE applications is a nontrivial task. For details about writing DCE applications, see Shirley [1993].

At present, DCE is being developed by active participation of many organizations. It has been deployed on many computing environments (for example, the Hewlett-Packard 700 Series, IBM RS6000, SUNs, PCs, MVS). Adoption of OSF DCE as an important part of IBM's Open Distributed Computing strategy has raised considerable industrial interest (see Chapter 9). OSF is planning a very wide deployment on additional platforms. A process called the Request For Technology (RFT) has been established to introduce new technologies and standards. OSF supports ISO and Internet Standards and is a member of X/Open. In addition, many industrial organizations are active members of OSF.

Owing to the potential difficulties of achieving agreement among diverse participants on a large range of issues, the main challenge facing OSF is to balance proprietary versus open systems. Another challenge is to be accepted for corporatewide critical applications. The competition between CORBA and OSF DCE for the growing distributed-objects model is also worth noting. DCE is becoming more object oriented, but CORBA is gaining popularity steadily. Initially, DCE RPC was considered as the natural transport mechanism to carry CORBA messages. But CORBA 2.0 has allowed CORBA over TCP/IP Sockets as an alternative to CORBA over DCE RPC. Thus, DCE becomes an option for CORBA users, not a prerequisite. We will have to see the implications of this in the next few years. Interestingly, Microsoft's Distributed OLE/ActiveX is based on DCE RPC. We will visit these issues in Chapter 6.

3.9   State of the Practice: Short Case Studies

The basic C/S middleware is heavily state-of-the-practice in the LAN environments because many C/S applications have been developed on LAN NOSs, such as Novell Netware, Windows NT, IBM LAN Manager, and Banyan Vines. In particular, RPC is very commonly used because many existing products use RPCs (see the discussion in next section). Moreover, RPC is at the heart of OSF DCE—thus any user of DCE is automatically using RPCs. RDA is also very popular because it is the basic mechanism used for remote SQL. Most of the "two-tiered" applications in LAN environments that rely on SQL servers use RDA (i.e., issue remote SQL calls to SQL servers). Thus the applications using the Gupta SQL Server, Microsoft SQL Server, or any other SQL server heavily use the RDA paradigm. In addition, many C/S CASE tools, such as PowerBuilder from PowerSoft, use remote SQL. Off-the-shelf applications such as PeopleSoft's Human Resource Application also use RDA. The use of QMP is somewhat slow but is expected to increase due to increased vendor attention, especially in the mobile computing area. An interesting example of using message-oriented middleware (MOM), given by Kramer [1995], shows how MOM is used to support a managed-care solution by SMS, Inc.

Let us briefly review a few short case studies to highlight the state of the practice. We will concentrate on OSF DCE mainly because it utilizes RPC as well as many other basic middleware services such as security, directory, and time. Here are some short OSF DCE case studies (the main sources for these case studies are the *Computerworld Client/Server Journal* (February 1995, June 1995), *Datamation* (March 1, 1994), and International Conference on Distributed Computing Platforms (ICDP95, ICDP96):

- Charles Schwab, a San Francisco discount brokerage firm, initiated a move away from mainframe-centric to distributed C/S computing in 1992. The move involved tens of millions of dollars and more than 200 people. OSF DCE has been at the heart of the migration strategy, owing to its ability to coordinate among mixed computing environments. The basic premise of the project was to develop applications that were developed on top of DCE, which itself resided on mixed machines with different operating systems. However, the project has slowed down for several reasons. First, lack of off-the-shelf development tools made it very difficult for the 150 programmers, previously trained in Cobol, to develop DCE-based applications (DCE applications are exclusively written in C or C++). Second, the DCE application code was extremely complex and hard to understand. Finally, concerns were raised about the scalability of DCE applications to handle millions of transactions per day (RPC was found to be a major bottleneck). Charles Schwab is proceeding with the project very cautiously.

- The University of Michigan, Ann Arbor, Michigan, has launched the Institutional File System (IFS) project to support a heterogeneous network of 30,000 desktop machines. The University is moving away from its homegrown mainframe-based operating system—MTS (Michigan Terminal System). OSF DCE is a key part of this project. A key technology expected from DCE is the DCE Distributed-File System (DFS) that will be used to store and retrieve data from file servers across the campus. Additional applications are also expected to be constructed around DCE. The IFS project has encountered several difficulties. For example, the lack of development and debugging tools on DCE is a major impediment. In addition, tools for remote diagnostics are missing. The main appeal of DCE, however, is that the DCE servers can be installed on IBM RS/6000, SUN, and HP workstations as well as on MVS/ESA machines, and accessed from Macs and PCs in a transparent manner (DCE hides all the operating systems and machine details).

- The US Naval Space Command in Dahlgren, Va., uses DCE applications to track 8,000 space objects. The current DCE configuration supports 250 concurrent users. The computation time on DCE based on the IBM RS/6000 is reportedly six times faster than on the mainframe.

- Connecticut Mutual Life Insurance, a Hartford, Connecticut, insurance firm, is trying to eliminate paper shuffling with an image/workflow system and enterprisewide E-mail and electronic forms system. The system currently employs Sybase SQL Server and a database gateway to MVS DB2 databases. However, the system is being transitioned to DCE.

- The University of Massachusetts at Amherst adopted DCE as a foundation for providing an advanced computing environment called Project Pilgrim. Project Pilgrim is completing its own distributed printing, mail, and event-notification on top of DCE.

- Many large organizations such as Boeing, Citicorp, and US WEST Communications are piloting and/or using DCE in production.

Basically, OSF DCE has been piloted in several organizations. However, use of OSF DCE for large-scale, mission-critical, enterprisewide applications is rare. The main question is: can DCE deliver? The response is mixed. The main success stories center around small applications or large-scale distributed print and file services projects (universities fit this picture). However, database-intensive business applications on top of DCE are few and far between at the time of this writing. See Bozman [1995] for additional discussion.

3.10 State of the Market: Products

C/S middleware to support RPC, RDA, and QMP is commercially available at the time of this writing. In addition, many management and support services are also being included in off-the-shelf products. Here is a brief synopsis of the state of the market.

Remote-procedure call (RPC)-based middleware is widely available in UNIX environments and is gaining popularity on MVS and PC environments. Here are some examples of RPC products:

- Open Software Foundation's RPC (this is included in OSF DCE)
- SUN RPC system
- Netwise RPC (this is merging with SUN RPC)
- Novell Netware RPC
- Information Builder's EDA/SQL RPC
- IBM TCP/IP RPC

RDA products are currently heavily supported by the "database server industry." Simply stated, a database server houses a database and controls user access to the database. As stated previously, a large number of vendors are developing SQL database servers which basically handle SQL calls from clients and respond with results. Most of the database servers were originally developed for LANs (e.g., the Gupta SQL Server for IBM Token Ring LANs). Database servers in mainframe WAN environments are now available from database vendors such as Sybase, Oracle, and Ingres. IBM's DRDA (Distributed Relational Database Architecture) has emerged as a popular approach for accessing mainframe DB2 databases from clients operating in UNIX and PC environments.

QMP is supported by MOM (message-oriented middleware). MOM products have been getting serious vendor attention since 1993. Interest in MOM is fueled by the dramatic increase of detachable computers and the application requirements that require asynchronous behavior. The trade-offs between MOM and other C/S paradigms, industrial product announcements, and case studies where MOM has been of value are appearing in the industrial press (see, for example, the *Client/Server Today* magazine special issue on MOM, November 1994). A partial list of MOM products in the industry is:

- MQ Series of products from IBM that include a variety of services ranging from database replication to downsizing of mainframe applications
- DEC Message Q from Digital Equipment Corporation
- Message-oriented middleware used in Tuxedo and Encina
- Enterprise Messaging Services (EMS) from Sybase for Sybase Open Client/Open Server
- MOM-based workflow systems from Momentum, Inc.
- Communications Integrator from Covia Technologies
- X_IPC middleware for MOM
- Pipes Platform from Peer Logics

The management and support features such as security, directory services, and time services are included in many network operating systems such as Windows NT, Novell Netware, and Banyan Vines. OSF DCE is the best example of integrating standards-based services that include RPC, directory, security, distributed-time, and distributed file services. OSF DCE is commercially available from many vendors such as IBM, HP, and Sun. We have discussed OSF DCE previously in this chapter.

3.11   State of the Art: Standards

Standards for the basic middleware are important for application portability as well as interoperability. This is because each middleware introduces its own API and exchange protocols. Standards for RPCs, RDA, QMP, directory, security, time, and other services are maturing quickly at the time of this writing. Let us quickly review these standards.

RPC standards are needed because each RPC middleware introduces its own API and exchange protocols. Thus applications based on SUN RPC and Netwise RPC do not interoperate. Fortunately, the OSF DCE RPC has emerged as a de facto standard, leading to portability and interoperability of DCE-based applications across many computing environments.

Another issue in RPC interoperability is the underlying network on which RPC is implemented. Theoretically, RPCs can be built on top of any network protocols and services such as LU6.2 and TCP/IP Sockets. In practice, most of the available RPCs are built on top of TCP/IP Sockets. Fortunately however, TCP/IP is extremely popular once again and continues to gain ground (TCP/IP is used to support the Internet and is obviously widespread). DCE is built on top of TCP/IP; thus DCE RPC-based applications are portable and interoperable across many computing and networking environments.

Many RDA middleware products in the market use proprietary APIs and exchange protocols. Thus a database server from vendor A can be used only by client tools from vendor A or from vendors who are "business partners" of vendor A. Standardizing bodies such as X/Open and ISO have been trying to define standards in this area. In addition, several de facto standards have emerged and are widely practiced. Examples of the key standards are:

- *SQL API standards.* These standards include the ANSI/ISO standards for embedded SQL API and the X/Open and SQL Access Group (SAG) SQL standards for Command Level Interface API.

- *RDA standards.* The ISO and X/Open RDA standards specify the exchange protocols for interoperability. We will review ISO RDA in Chapter 5.

- *ODBC and DRDA de facto industry standards.* IBM's DRDA (Distributed Relational Database Architecture) was introduced by IBM to provide an "open" exchange protocol for other DBMS clients to access DB2 data. At present, more than 30 DBMS vendors provide DRDA gateways that translate different vendor DBMS calls to DRDA format for DB2 access. Microsoft's ODBC (Open Database Connect) is an API standard based on X/Open and SAG Command Level Interface API. Users of ODBC issue the same API calls to access databases from different vendors. ODBC relies on "drivers" which convert ODBC calls to appropriate database calls. At present, a large number of ODBC drivers for accessing Informix, Oracle, Sybase, and other databases are commercially available. We will discuss DRDA and ODBC in Chapter 5.

Standards for MOM are needed for APIs to store and retrieve information from the queues. IBM has submitted MQI, the API set for its MQSeries to X/Open for standardization. Novell Inc. also submitted the message-queuing interface from its Tuxedo transaction-processing system to X/Open. Some interest has been expressed to integrate RPCs with MOMs, and prototypes have shown that RPCs can use MOM as a transport mechanism [Whiting 1994]. Generally accepted standards for MOM are not available at the time of this writing. However, a Message Oriented Middleware Association (MOMA) has been formed to establish MOM standards.

For directory services, X.500 is a widely accepted standard. X.500 supports replicated directories (i.e., the same directory can exist at different sites). Programs can access the X.500 directory services by using the X/Open Directory Service (XDS) API. The XDS APIs support typical directory operations (e.g., read, compare, update, add and delete directory entries). In addition, they support operations such as list directories and entries based on attributes. The X.500 standard also specifies an API for defining object classes (the X/Open Management API—the XOM API) and protocols to be used between directory clients and directory servers (the Directory Access Protocol—DAP) and between directory servers to synchronize information (the Directory System Protocol—DSP).

For security standards, we need to look at C2—a government-specified security standard. C2 requires that users and applications be authenticated before gaining access to any operating-system resource. C2 security in a distributed environment is complicated because all clients must provide an authenticated user ID, all resources must be protected by access control lists

(ACLs), access rights must not be transferred between users, and audit trails must be provided. OSF DCE comes quite close to C2 level security in a distributed environment.

3.12   Summary

Basic C/S middleware services include popular services such as remote-procedure call (RPC), remote-data access (RDA), and message-oriented middleware (MOM). In addition, the management and support services of security, directories, time, and failure management are included in the basic services. OSF DCE is a very good example of an open, standards-based, basic C/S middleware.

3.13   Case Study: XYZCorp Chooses a Network Operating System

XYZCorp needs to identify a network operating system (NOS) that provides the core C/S middleware services throughout its organization. The NOS will provide the services for remote communications between programs and databases, file services, print services, security services, and directory services. Specifically, the management is seeking answers to the following questions:

- Can Novell Netware, Windows NT, or any other LAN operating system do the job?

- How does OSF DCE fare as the corporate NOS?

- Which one of the three remote communication protocols (RPC, RDA, MOM) should be used as the primary remote communication protocol and why? Which type of protocols are suited for which type of applications?

- How can multiple clients and servers that support different protocols exist in the XYZCorp environment?

Hints about the Case Study

The typical LAN operating systems are not very well suited for enterprisewide systems that span several regions of the United States and overseas. The article by Johnson [1995] should be consulted for a detailed analysis of main LAN OSs.

OSF DCE, in principle, is very well suited as an enterprisewide NOS because it has well integrated security, directory services, file services, print services, and remote communications. However, the state of the market for OSF DCE needs to be carefully evaluated.

The following table can be used to compare and contrast RPC, RDA, and MOM. The information discussed in Sections 3.3 through 3.5 can be used to complete this table.

	Strengths	Weakness	Sample Applications
RPC			
RDA			
MOM			

The following diagram shows a conceptual view of middleware to be installed at clients and servers to support an environment in which DCE coexists with other servers.

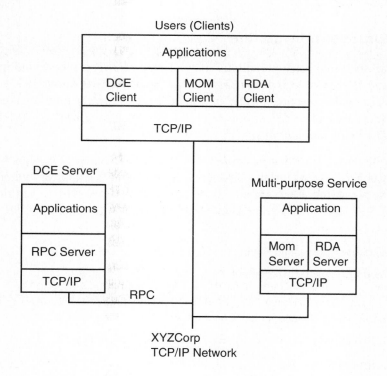

3.14   Problems and Exercises

1. Compare and contrast the RDA, RPC, and MOM paradigms. Explain what type of applications can best utilize RPC, RDA, or MOM.

2. Develop a pseudocode for a Lotus 123 client which accesses an SQL server on a remote site. You may choose any of the protocols and facilities to develop the pseudocode.

3. Describe the peer-to-peer protocol by using the framework used to describe the RPC, RDA, and MOM paradigms.

4. List the factors you will use to evaluate off-the-shelf basic client/server middleware products.

5. Compare and contrast OSF DCE with a NOS of your choice (e.g., Novell Netware, Windows NT).

3.15   Additional Information

Descriptions of the three basic paradigms (RPC, RDA, MOM) can be found in a number of sources [Berson 1993, Couloris 1994, Orfali 1974, Stevens 1990, Umar 1993]. State-of-the-market and state-of-the-practice articles on the basic client/server middleware appear regularly in trade journals such as *Client/Server Today, Datamation, Database Programming and Design,* and *Data Communications.*

Owing to its popularity, information about DCE is readily available. The book by Rosenberry [1993] is very popular. Many articles on different aspects of DCE appear regularly in the popular computing press (see, for example, *Object Magazine,* May 1996). In addition, DCE OSF publishes the following documents and white papers which explain OSF services and approaches:

*   OSF Distributed Computing Environment Rationale, OSF Document
*   Distributed Computing Environment, An Overview, OSF Document
*   Remote Procedure Call in a Distributed Computing Environment, OSF White Paper
*   The OSF Distributed Management Environment, OSF White Paper
*   Security in a Distributed Computing Environment, OSF White Paper

These and additional documents can be obtained from:

Open Software Foundation
11 Cambridge Center
Cambridge, MA 02142
Web home page (*http://www.osf.org*)

3.16 References

Amaru, C., "Building Distributed Applications with MOM," *Client/Server Today,* November 1994, pp. 83–93.

Andrews, G. R., "Paradigms for Process Interaction in Distributed Programs," *ACM Computing Surveys,* March 1991, pp. 49–90.

Berson, A., *Client/Server Architectures,* McGraw-Hill, 1993.

Birrel, A. D., and Nelson, B. J., "Implementing Remote Procedure Call," *ACM Transactions on Computer Systems,* Vol. 2, 1984, pp. 39–59.

Bort, J., "Can Message Brokers Deliver?" *Applications Software Magazine,* June 1996, pp. 70–76.

Bozman, J., "Can DCE Deliver?" *Computerworld Client/Server Journal,* February 1995, pp. 28–32.

Camara, J., et al., "A Message-Oriented Communication Service for the Portuguese Energy Market," ICDP96, Dresden, February 1996.

Comeau, Greg, "Networking with UNIX," *BYTE,* February 1989, pp. 265–267.

Corbin, J. R., *The Art of Distributed Applications: Programming Techniques for Remote Procedure Calls,* Springer-Verlag, 1991.

Coulouris, G., and Dollimore, J., *Distributed Systems: Concepts and Design,* Addison Wesley, 2d ed., 1994.

Davis, Ralph, "A Logical Choice," *BYTE,* January 1989, pp. 309–315.

Dolgicer, M., "Unmasking the Mysteries of Message Queuing," *Application Development Trends,* June 1996, pp. 57–67.

Gantz, J., "Cooperative Processing and the Enterprise Network," *Networking Management,* January. 1991, pp. 25–40.

Glass, B., "Relying on Netware NLMs," *Infoworld,* October 12, 1992, p. S80.

Griswold, Charles, "LU6.2: A View from the Database," *Database Programming and Design,* May 1988, pp 34–39.

Hurwicz, Michael, "Connectivity Pathways: APPC or NETBIOS," *PC Tech Journal,* Vol. 5, No. 11, November 1987, pp. 156–170.

IBM (International Business Machines), "Advanced Program-to-Program Communication for the IBM Personal Computer, Programming Guide," February 1986.

ISO/DP 9072/1 report, "Remote Operations Model—Notation and Service Definition," Geneva, Switzerland, October 1986.

Johnson, J., "Enterprise NOSs: Now Is the Time," *Data Communications,* May 15, 1995.

Kernighan, B. W. and Pike, R., *The UNIX Programming Environment,* Prentice Hall, Englewood Cliffs, N.J., 1984.

Khanaa, R., *Distributed Computing: Implementation and Management Strategies,* Prentice Hall, 1993.

Kramer, M., "How Message-Oriented Middleware Supports a Managed Care Solution," *Distributed Computing Monitor, Patricia Seybold Group,* Vol. 10, No. 5 (1995), pp. 23–28.

Lewis, T., "Where Is Client/Server Software Headed?" *IEEE Computer Magazine,* April 1995, pp. 49–55.

Livingston, D., "Software Links Multivendor Networks," *Micro-Mini Systems,* March 1988.

Neuman, B. ,and Ts'o, T., "Kerberos: An Authentication Service for Computer Networks," *IEEE Communications Magazine,* 1994, pp. 33–37.

Orfali, R., Harkey, D., and Edwards, J., *Client/Server Survival Guide,* Van Nostrand Reinholt, 1994.

Ozsu, M., and Valdurez, P., "Distributed Database Systems: Where Are We Now?" *IEEE Computer,* August 1991, pp. 68–78.

Ricciuti, M., "Universal Data Access," *Datamation,* November 1, 1991.

Rosenberry, W., et al., *Understanding DCE,* O'Reily & Associates, 1993.

Schiller, J., "Secure Distributed Computing," *Scientific American,* November 1994, pp. 72–76.

Sechrest, S., "An Introductory 4.3BSD Interprocess Communications Tutorial," Computer Science Research Division, Department of Electrical Engineering and Computer Science, University of California, Berkeley, 1986.

Shirley, J., *Guide to Writing DCE Applications,* O'Reily & Associates, 1993.

Sinha, A., "Client/Server Computing: Current Technology Review," *Comm. of ACM,* July 1992, pp. 77–96.

Stahl, S., "Peer Logic Helps Insurer Access Data," *Information Week,* January 9, 1995.

Stevens, W., *UNIX Network Programming,* Prentice Hall, 1990.

Umar, A., *Distributed Computing and Client/server Systems,* Prentice Hall, rev. ed., 1993.

Vaskevitz, D., *Client/Server Strategies: A Survival Guide for Corporate Reengineers,* IDG Books, 1993.

Vinzant, D., "SQL Database Servers," *Data Communications,* January 1990, pp. 72–86.

White, D., "SQL Database Servers: Networking Meets Data Management," *Data Communications,* September 1990, pp. 31–39.

Whiting, R. (a), "Getting on the Middleware Express," *Client/Server Today,* November 1994, pp. 70–75.

Whiting, R. (b), "Turning to MOM for the Answers," *Client/Server Today,* November 1994, pp. 76–81.

Wilbur, S., and Bacarisse, B., "Building Distributed Systems with Remote Procedure Calls," *Software Engineering Journal,* September 1987, pp. 148–159.

Wood, A., "Predicting Client/Server Availability," *IEEE Computer Magazine,* April 1995, pp. 41–48.

Zuck, J., "Front-end Tools," *PC Magazine,* September 1992, pp. 295–332.

4

Internet and World Wide Web

145

4.1   Introduction

The growth in the use of Internet is astounding.[1] The origin of Internet is the ARPANET
(Advanced Research Projects Agency Network) that was initiated in 1969 to support
researchers on DOD (Department of Defense) projects. For many years, Internet was used
mainly by scientists and programmers to transfer files and send/receive electronic mail. The
users of Internet relied on text-based user interfaces and an incoherent set of different commands to access remote computing resources. In 1989, this changed with the introduction of
World Wide Web (WWW), commonly referred to as the Web. The Web has been a major
contributor in turning the Internet, once an obscure tool, into a household word. The Web
allows users to access, navigate, and share information around the globe through GUI clients
("Web browsers") that are available on almost all computing platforms. The Web browsers
allow users to access information that is linked through hypermedia links. Thus a user transparently browses around, or "surfs" around, different pieces of information located on different computers in different cities and even in different countries.

The Web is quickly becoming the primary means of accessing the majority of information
needed by hobbyists, students, researchers, consumers, and corporations. For example, many
businesses are beginning to use their Web site as their main source of advertising. In addition,
the Web is being used for a myriad of new applications (e.g., publishing, advertising, and
electronic commerce) and is being integrated with traditional business applications to solve
business problems. For example, many C/S applications being developed at present are
increasingly using Web browsers for end-user access. In addition, *Intranet* (a private Internet
used by an enterprise internally) is becoming a favorite vehicle for enterprisewide information systems. Some industry observers are predicting that the Web will eliminate the need for
much of the existing middleware [Kador 1996] and that it will become the first tier of multitiered application architectures [Bickell 1996].

---

1. It is difficult to estimate the exact number of users being supported on the Internet. However, most estimates hover around
   100 million users.

The interest and potential use of the Web is creating new requirements for middleware. The purpose of this chapter is to review the core concepts and technologies that comprise World Wide Web middleware and attempt to answer the following questions:

- What is Internet and how does it relate to Intranets and the World Wide Web (Section 4.2)?

- What are the key concepts and components of World Wide Web (Section 4.3)?

- What do terms such as HTML, HTTP, Web browsers, and Web servers mean (Sections 4.4, 4.5, 4.6, and 4.8)?

- What is Java and why is it so hot (Section 4.7)?

- What type of gateways are needed to integrate Web with existing applications and how can corporate information be accessed through the Web (Section 4.9)?

- What is the state of the practice, market, and art in World Wide Web (Sections 4.10, 4.11, and 4.12)?

- What are the sources of additional information (Section 4.16)?

4.2 Internet and Intranets: A Quick Overview

Technically speaking, Internet is a network based on the TCP/IP protocol stack (see Chapter 11 for an overview of TCP/IP). At present, the term Internet is used to refer to a large collection of TCP/IP networks that are tied together through network interconnectivity devices such as routers and gateways (see Chapter 11 for a discussion of interconnectivity devices).[2] The term *cyberspace*, first introduced through a science-fiction book by Gibson [1984], has been permanently transferred to our vocabulary. It represents thousands of computers and computer resources around the globe interconnected through the Internet. At present, the term Internet is used to symbolize the following two situations:

- *Public Internet*, or just the Internet, that is not owned by any single entity—it consists of many independent TCP/IP networks that are tied together loosely. Initially, the public Internet was used to tie different university networks together. With time, several commercial and private networks have joined the public Internet. The computers on the public Internet have publicly known Internet Protocol (IP) addresses that are used to exchange information over the public Internet (see discussion on addressing that follows). The public Internet at present consists of thousands of networks.

- Private Internets, or *Intranets*, are the TCP/IP networks that are used by corporations for their own business, especially by exploiting Web technologies. Technically, an Intranet uses the same technology as the public Internet—it is only smaller and privately owned and thus hopefully better controlled and more secure. Thus any applications and services that are available on the public Internet are also available on the Intranets. This is an important point for WWW, because many companies are using WWW technologies on their Intranets for internal applications (e.g., employee information systems).

---

2. Some people use internet (with small i) for any TCP/IP network and Internet (with capital i) for *the* public TCP/IP network.

Key Points

- The World Wide Web is essentially middleware that operates on top of the Internet to support a community of users and applications.

- Web users can access corporate information by using Web gateways.

- *Intranet* is a private Internet used by a corporation internally. Intranets use Web technology for corporate services and applications.

- The main appeal of Web for enterprisewide applications is that organizations can standardize on Web browsers for the end-user access to all applications (e.g., marketing, human resources, or engineering). In addition, the same Web interface can be used for applications that cross company, industry, and country boundaries.

- Middleware for Web is based on the following concepts and technologies:
  - Web servers
  - Web browsers
  - Uniform Resource Locator (URL)
  - Hypertext Transfer Protocol (HTTP)
  - Hypertext Markup Language (HTML)
  - Web navigation and search tools
  - Gateways to non-Web resources

- WWW is unique in that it makes hypermedia available on the Internet in what has evolved into a global information system.

- Java is a programming language designed to work on the Web. The main thing is that Java application components (known as Java applets) can run on the Web browser site. Thus Java applets can be used to execute business logic at the Web browser sites, thereby implementing the first tier of C/S applications.

- Web access to non-Web resources is provided through Web gateways. For example, Web access to relational databases is provided through "relational gateways" that serve as translators and mediators between Web browsers and relational database managers.

Unless otherwise indicated, the discussion in this chapter is oriented toward the public Internet, although most concepts also apply to the Intranets.

Domain naming services (DNSs) are used in the Internet to locate different resources. This protocol defines hierarchical naming structures which are much easier to remember than the IP addresses. For example, the machine with an IP address of 135.25.7.82 may have a domain name of shoeshop.com. A user "mills" may have an email address mills@shoeshop.com. The

DNS naming structures define the organization type, organization name, etc. The last word in the domain name identifies an organization type or a country. Consider, for example, the following domain names:

```
bellcore.com = commercial company Bellcore
ibm.com = commercial company IBM
um.edu = educational institution University of Michigan
omg.org = organization OMG (Object Management Group)
waterloo.ca = Waterloo University in Canada
lancs.ac.uk = Lancaster University in the UK
ansa.co.uk = ANSA consortium in the UK
iona.ie = Iona Corporation in Ireland
```

The Internet uses a large number of domain name servers that translate domain names to IP addresses (the IP routers only understand IP addresses). Domain names are used in the Internet as well as the Web.

Figure 4.1 shows a conceptual and partial view of Internet. This Internet shows three networks (a university network with two computers, a commercial company network, and a network in the UK). Each computer ("host") on this network has an IP address and also has been assigned a domain name. Internet is very heterogeneous (i.e., different computers, different physical networks.) However, to the users of this network, it provides a set of uniform TCP/IP services (TCP/IP hides many details). We will use this simple Internet to illustrate the key Internet capabilities.

Figure 4.1 Partial View of Internet

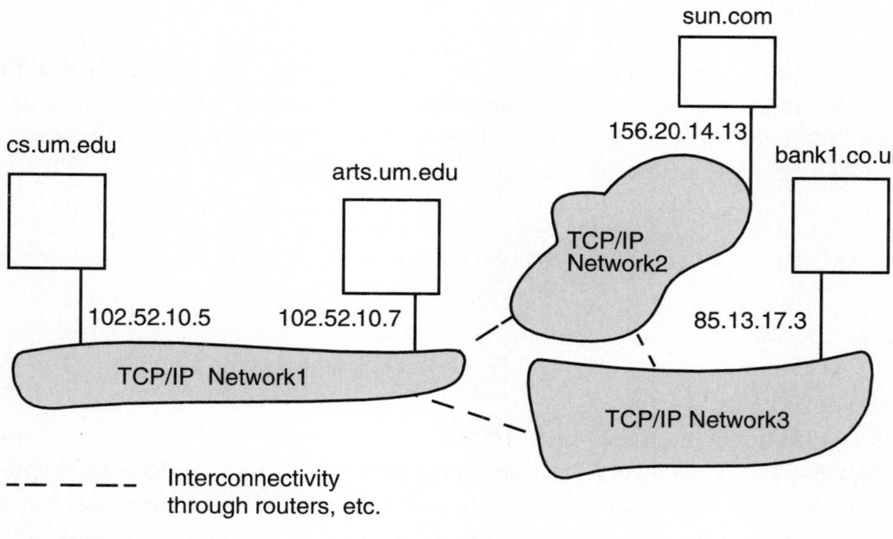

Since the Internet is based on TCP/IP, the applications and services provided by TCP are also available on the Internet. From an end-user point of view, the following services have been, and still are, used very heavily on the Internet:

- Email
- Telnet
- FTP
- Gopher
- WAIS (Wide Area Information Servers)

Electronic mail on the Internet is based on the **Simple Mail Transfer Protocol (SMTP)**. This TCP-based protocol is the Internet electronic mail-exchange mechanism. Email is still one of the most heavily used services on the Internet. Users on the Internet have email addresses such as johnm@cs.um.edu, hevner@sun.com, and howard@bank1.co.uk.

Terminal emulation is used to remotely log on to other machines. **Telnet** is used to provide terminal access to hosts and runs on top of TCP. Let us assume that a user "joe" on cs.um.edu needs to remotely log on to the bank1.co.uk machine to run a program "directory." The user would use the following steps (the steps are explained through comments in /* */):

```
>telnet bank1.co.uk    /* invoke Telnet. Could have typed " telnet 85.13.17.3".*/
bank1>enter logon: joe/* prompt from bank1 for logon ID. joe is ID */
bank1>password: xxxx  /* prompt from bank1 for password */
bank1>directory       /* run the program "directory"  */
bank1>exit            /* quit telnet */
```

File transfer is used for bulk of data transfer over the Internet. The **File Transfer Protocol (FTP)** provides a way to transfer files between hosts on the Internet. Let us assume that a user "garner" on "sun.com" needs to transfer a file from the host arts.um.edu. The following steps would be used (the steps are explained through comments in /* */):

```
>ftp arts.um.edu         /* invoke FTP. Could have typed " ftp 102.52..10.7"*/
arts>enter logon: garner/* prompt from arts.um for logon ID. garner is ID */
arts>password: xxxx      /* prompt from arts.um for password */
arts>get file1 file2     /* FTP file transfer command */
arts>exit (or quit)      /* quit FTP */
```

Gopher is a well-known interface for the Internet. Developed at the University of Minnesota, Gopher predates WWW because it provides a friendly face to tools such as FTP and Telnet, among others. However, Gopher does not support hypertext. Gopher provides a numbered list or, in some cases, icons to represent different files that you can transfer and access over the Internet.

WAIS (Wide Area Information Servers) generates and allows you to search a huge range of databases stored on the Internet based on search keys. These databases contain pointers to locations on the Internet that hold documents containing the search keys. WAIS rates its search results (e.g., a rating of 1000 means direct hit and 100 means marginal hit). WAIS allows you to keep narrowing the search until you find exactly what you are looking for. It is used in WWW for full-keyword searching (in most cases, you do not know that the Web is using WAIS internally).

For many years, Internet had been used mainly by researchers, teachers, scientists, students, and programmers to transfer files and send/receive electronic mail. These users relied on text-based commands to do their job. WWW is a set of services that run on top of the Internet. The two main features of WWW are use of GUI and of hypertext to make the life of Internet users easy and fun. We will discuss WWW in the next section in more detail.

We should mention that the users access the Internet either directly or indirectly. *Direct Internet users* reside on the machines that have IP addresses, while *indirect Internet users* remotely log on to the machines with IP addresses. For example, America Online is an Internet Access Provider that actually has machines with IP addresses (direct access). If you subscribe to America Online, then you dial into an America Online machine (i.e., you are indirectly accessing the Internet).

We have covered the Internet very briefly. Many books describe the Internet in great detail. For example, several books [Comer 1988, Comer 1991, Stevens 1990] discuss the networking and programming aspects of the Internet by describing TCP/IP in great technical details. Several other books, such as Barron [1995], and Hahn [1996], present an end user's view of the Internet (i.e., what resources are available on the Internet and how you can access/use these resources).

4.3 Overview of World Wide Web

4.3.1 Brief History

World Wide Web (WWW) is a wide-area information-retrieval project which was started in 1989 by Tim Berners-Lee at the Geneva European Laboratory for Particle Physics (known as CERN, based on the laboratory's French name) [Berners-Lee 1993]. The initial proposal suggested development of a "hypertext system" to enable efficient and easy information sharing among geographically separated teams of researchers in the high-energy physics community. The initial proposal had three basic components:

- A common and consistent user interface
- Incorporation of a wide range of technologies and document types
- A "universal readership" to allow anyone sitting anywhere on the network, on a wide variety of computers, to easily read the same document as anyone else

Internet Role Players

Different individuals, groups and organizations play different roles in the Internet. To illustrate these roles, let us envision the Internet as an electronic shopping mall. Then we can discuss the following roles:

- **Internet users** are the people who visit the shopping mall (i.e., log on to the Internet). The Internet users are essentially the consumers of the services provided by the Internet.

- **Content providers** are the merchants (individuals, groups, or organizations) that provide the products in the shopping mall (i.e., resources available on the Internet). You can think of these content providers as the merchants in the shopping mall.

- **Internet access providers (IAPs)** are the organizations that facilitate your access to the shopping mall (i.e., give you a communication line and an access port on the Internet). You can think of IAPs as the local authorities that provide you with roads and signs to get you to the shopping malls.

- **Internet service providers (ISPs)** are the individuals and organizations that help the content providers set up their shops in the shopping mall (i.e., help in building Web sites). Many small content providers seek the help of ISPs to set up Web servers with appropriate security and backup/recovery.

By the end of 1990, a line browser (called www) had been developed which implemented the principles of hypertext access and the reading of different document types. In 1991, the line browser was made available to the CERN community, and a gateway for Wide Area Information Servers (WAIS) searches was developed. In 1992, a few more browsers were developed and around 50 Web sites (the machines which house Web documents) were implemented. In 1993, an extremely important event took place, i.e., the Mosaic browser for GUI access was developed at NCSA (National Center for Supercomputing Applications at University of Illinois). Ignited by the ease of use provided by the Mosaic GUI browser, the Web took off during 1993—the number of Web sites increased to 500, and the Web network traffic grew from 0.1 percent of Internet traffic to 1 percent (a 10-fold increase). Since 1994, the Web has been gaining popularity dramatically, with astounding increases in the number of browsers, search engines, Web servers, and usage.

4.3.2   World Wide Web Middleware

Technically speaking, *WWW is a collection of middleware that operates on top of TCP/IP networks (i.e., the Internet).* Figure 4.2 shows this layered view. The purpose of the WWW middleware is to support the growing number of users and applications ranging from enter-

Figure 4.2 Technical View of World Wide Web

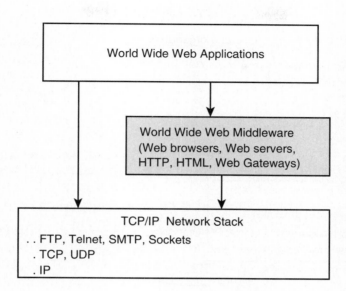

tainment to corporate information systems. Like many other (successful) Internet technologies, the WWW middleware is based on a few simple concepts and technologies such as the following (see Figure 4.3):

- Web servers and sites

- Web browsers

- Uniform Resource Locator (URL)

- Hypertext Transfer Protocol (HTTP)

- Hypertext Markup Language (HTML)

- Web navigation and search tools

- Gateways to non-Web resources

Let us briefly review these components and show how they tie with each other through an example. We will discuss these components in more detail later on in this chapter.

Web sites provide the content that is accessed by Web users. Web sites are populated and in many cases managed by the ***content providers***. For example, Web sites provide the commercial presence for each of the content providers doing business over the Internet. Con-

Figure 4.3 Conceptual View of World Wide Web

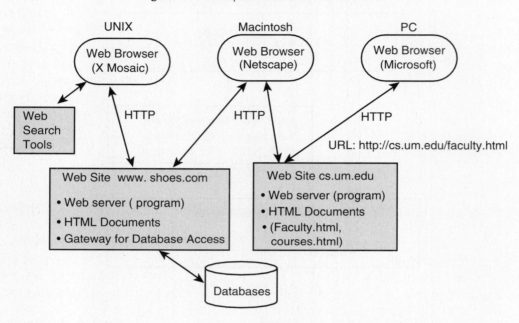

ceptually, a Web site is a catalog of information for each content provider over the Web. In reality, a Web site consists of three types of components: a Web server (a program), content files ("Web pages"), and/or gateways (programs that access non-Web content). A ***Web server*** is a program (technically a server process) that receives calls from Web clients and retrieves Web pages and/or receives information from gateways (we will discuss gateways later). Once again, a Web user views a Web site as a collection of files on a computer, usually a UNIX or Windows NT machine. In many cases, a machine is dedicated/designated as a Web site on which Web-accessible contents are stored. As a matter of convention, the entry point to a Web site is a "home page" which advertises the company business. Very much like storefront signs in a shopping mall, the home pages include company logo, fancy artwork for attention, special deals, overviews, pointers to additional information, etc. The large number of Web sites containing a wide range of information that can be navigated and searched transparently by Web users is the main strength of WWW. Figure 4.3 shows two Web sites—one for a shoe shop (www.shoes.com) and the other for a computer science department for a university (cs.um.edu). Web sites and Web servers are explained in Section 4.8.

Web browsers are the clients that typically use graphical user interfaces to wander through the Web sites. The first GUI browser, Mosaic, was developed at the National Center for Supercomputer Applications at the University of Illinois. Mosaic runs on PC Windows, Macintosh, UNIX, and Xterminals. At present, Web browsers are commercially available from Netscape, Microsoft, and many other software/freeware providers. These Web browsers provide an intuitive view of information where *hyperlinks* (links to other text information) appear as underlined items or highlighted text/images. If a user points and clicks on the highlighted text/images, then the Web browser uses HTTP to fetch the requested document from an appropriate Web site. Web browsers are designed to display information prepared in a markup language, known as HTML. We will discuss HTTP and HTML later. Three different browsers are shown in Figure 4.3. Even though these are different browsers residing on different machines, they all use the same protocol (HTTP) to communicate with the Web servers (HTTP compliance is a basic requirement for Web browsers). The Web browsers are reviewed in Section 4.6.

Most browsers at present are relatively dumb (i.e., they just pass user requests to Web servers and display the results). However, this is changing very quickly because of Java, a programming language developed by Sun Microsystems. Java programs, known as *Java applets,* can run on Java-compatible browsers. This is creating many interesting possibilities where Java applets are downloaded to the Java-enabled browsers where they run, producing graphs/charts, invoking multimedia applications, and accessing remote databases. We will discuss Java and Java applets in Section 4.7.

Uniform Resource Locator (URL) is the basis for locating resources in WWW. A URL consists of a string of characters that uniquely identifies a resource. A user can connect to resources by typing the URL in a browser window or by clicking on a hyperlink that implicitly invokes a URL. Perhaps the best way to explain URLs is through an example. Let us look at the URL "http://cs.um.edu/faculty.html" shown in Figure 4.3. The "http" in the URL tells the server that an HTTP request is being initiated (if you replace http with ftp, then an FTP session is initiated). The "cs.um.edu" is the name of the machine running the Web server (this is actually the domain name used by the Internet to locate machines on the Internet). The "faculty.html" is the name of a file on the machine cs.um.edu. The "html" suffix indicates that this is an HTML file. When this URL is clicked or typed, the browser initiates a connection to "cs.um.edu" machine and initiates a "Get" request for the "faculty.html" file. Depending on the type of browser you are using, you can see these requests flying around in an appropriate window spot. Eventually, this document is fetched, transferred to and displayed at the Web browser. You can access any information through the Web by specifying a URL (directly or indirectly). As we will see later, the

Web search tools basically return a bunch of URLs in response to a search query. The general format of URL is:

protocol://host:port/path

where

protocol represents the protocol to retrieve or send information. Examples of valid protocols are HTTP, FTP, Telnet, Gopher, and NNTP (Network News Transfer Protocol).

host is the computer host on which the resource resides.

port is an optional port number (this is not needed unless you want to override the HTTP default port, port 80).

path is an identification, typically a file name, on the computer host.

Hypertext Markup Language (HTML) is an easy-to-use language that tags the text files for display at Web browsers. HTML also helps in creation of **hypertext link**s, usually called hyperlinks, that provide a path from one document to another. The hyperlinks contain URLs for the needed resources. The main purpose of HTML is to allow users to flip through Web documents in a manner similar to flipping through a book, magazine, or catalog. The Web site "cs.um.edu" shown in Figure 4.3 contains two HTML documents: "faculty.html" and "courses.html." HTML documents can embed text, images, audio, and video. We will discuss HTML in more detail in Section 4.4.

Hypertext Transfer Protocol (HTTP) is an application-level protocol designed for Web users. It is intended for collaborative, distributed, hypermedia information systems. HTTP uses an extremely simple request/response model that establishes connection with the Web server specified in the URL, retrieves the needed document, and closes the connection. Once the document has been transferred to your Web browser, then the browser takes over. Keep in mind that every time you click on a hyperlink, you are initiating an HTTP session to transfer the needed information to your browser. The Web users shown in Figure 4.3 access the information stored in the two servers by using the HTTP protocol. We will discuss more details of HTTP in Section 4.5.

Web navigation and search services are used to search and surf the vast resources available over the "cyberspace." The term cyberspace, as stated previously, was first introduced through a science-fiction book [Gibson 1984] but currently refers to the computer-mediated experiences for visualization, communication, and browse/decision support. The general search paradigm used is that each search service contains an index of information available on Web sites. This index is almost always created and updated by **spiders** that crawl around the Web sites chasing hyperlinks for different pieces of information. Search engines support key-word and/or subject-oriented browsing through the index. The result of this browsing is a "hit list" of hyperlinks (URLs) that the user can click on to access the needed information. For example, the Web users in Figure 4.3 can issue a keyword search, say by using a search service for shoe stores in Chicago. This will return a hit list of potential shoe stores that are Web content providers. You then point and click till you find a shoe store of your choice.

Many search services are currently available on the Web. Examples are Yahoo, Lycos, and Alta Vista. At present, many of these tools are being integrated with Web pages and Web browsers. For example, the Netscape Browser automatically invokes the Netscape home page, which displays search tools that you can invoke by just pointing and clicking. It is beyond the scope of this book to describe the various Web navigation and search tools. Many books on Internet describe these search tools quite well. For example, the book by December [1995] has an extensive discussion of Web search and navigation tools with information about how to locate and use them.

Gateways to non-Web resources are used to bridge the gap between Web browsers and the corporate applications and databases. Web gateways are used for accessing information from heterogeneous data sources (e.g., relational databases, indexed files, and legacy information sources) and can be used to handle almost anything that is not designed with an HTML interface. The basic issue is that the Web browsers can display HTML information. These gateways are used to access non-HTML information and convert it to HTML format for display at a Web browser. The gateway programs typically run on Web sites and are invoked by the Web servers. At present, Common Gateway Interface (CGI) is used frequently. We will discuss CGI gateways and other types of Web gateways in Section 4.9. "Relational gateways" that provide access to relational databases from Web browsers are an area of active work. We will discuss relational gateways in Section 4.10.

4.3.3   A Simple Example

Figure 4.4 illustrates how the Web components can be used for a department store "Clothes-XYZ." This store wants to advertise its products on the Web (i.e., wants to be a Web content provider). The store first designates a machine, or buys services on a machine, called "clothes.com" as a Web site. It then creates an overview document "overview.html" that tells the potential customers of the product highlights (think of this as the first few pages of a catalog). In addition, several HTML documents on the Web site for different types of clothes (men.html, women. html, kids.html) are created with pictures of clothes, size information etc. (once again think of this as a catalog). We can assume that the overview page has hyperlinks to the other documents (as a matter of fact, it could have hyperlinks to other branches of Clothes-XYZ). In reality, design of the Web pages would require a richer, deeper tree structure design as well as sequential links for alphabetical and keyword searches needed to support the "flipping through the catalog" behavior.

Once HTML documents have been created on the Web server, then an Internet user can browse through them as if he/she were flipping through a catalog. The customers typically supply the URL, directly or indirectly, for the overview (http://clothes.com/overview.html) and then use the hyperlinks to look at different types of clothes. Experienced customers may directly go to the type of clothes needed (e.g., men may directly go to "men.html" document). As shown in Figure 4.4, the URL consists of three components: the protocol (http), the Web server name (clothes.com), and the needed document (overview.html). HTTP provides the transfer of information between the Web users (the clients) and the Web servers.

At first, Clothes-XYZ is using Web only to store an electronic catalog. After a customer has browsed through the catalog and has selected an item, he/she calls the store and places an order. Let us say that Clothes-XYZ wants to be more forward looking and wants the customers to purchase the items over the Internet. In this case, a "purchasing gateway" software is developed and installed at the Web site. This gateway program gets into action when a user clicks on the "purchase" button on his screen. It prompts the user with a form (HTML supports forms) that the user fills out. The gateway program uses this form information to interact with a purchasing system that processes the purchase (see Figure 4.4). The purchasing system can be an existing system that is used for traditional purchasing. The role of the gateway is to provide a Web interface to the purchasing system. We will discuss gateways later in this chapter (Sections 4.8 and 4.9).

Figure 4.4 World Wide Web Conceptual View

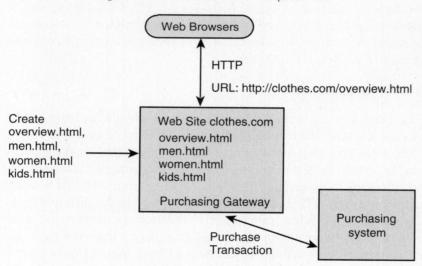

4.4   Hypertext Markup Language (HTML)

HTML prepares the media type that the Web browsers understand. HTML is a cross-platform documentation language—any computer equipped with a Web browser can read and display your document. HTML is based on the Standard Generalized Markup Language (SGML) that was developed at IBM to make documents readable across a variety of computing platforms.[3]

---

3. Technically, SGML is a "document schema" definition language and HTML is a particular schema defined by SGML.

HTML documents are not WYSIWYG (what you see is what you get). You create an HTML document as an ASCII text file by using HTML markup tags (see the sidebar giving an HTML example). HTML tags are used to indicate headings, italics, bolds, ordered lists, and places where graphics, sound bites, and other pieces of information can be located in the document.

A Simple HTML Example

Suppose you wanted to create a simple home page that looks like the following:

Consulting Group1

Welcome to our consulting group. By using this home page, you can do the following:
- Read about our services
- Access home pages of the technologies we work with (OMG and OSF)

Now choose the connections by pointing and clicking to the following hotlinks.

Our services
CORBA Information
OSF DCE Information

The following HTML statements can be used to design this home page (we have inserted appropriate URLs for the hot links):

```
<TITLE>Consulting Group1 </TITLE>
<H1>Consulting Group1 </H1>
<P> Welcome to our consulting group. By using this home
page, you can do the following:
<UL>
<LI> Read about our services .
<LI> Access home pages of the technologies we work
with (OMG and OSF)
</UL>
<P> Now choose the connections by pointing and clicking
to the following hotlinks.
<a href="http://www.myserver.com/services.html"> Our
services</a>
<a href="http://www.omg.org"> CORBA Information </a>
<a href="http://www.osf.org"> OSF DCE Information </a>
```

Hypertext and hypermedia are at the core of HTML and WWW. A *hypertext* is a series of documents, each of which displays at least one visible link on the screen, called a *hypertext link*, to another document in the set. *Hypermedia* extends hypertext in two ways: it incorporates multimedia into hypertext documents, and it allows graphic, audio, and video elements to become links to other documents or multimedia elements. In other words, hypermedia allows you to link multimedia elements by providing multimedia links (i.e., you can click on a graphic instead of just a text link).

What makes HTML and WWW unique is that they make hypermedia, as defined by the Dexter Model [Halasz 1994], available on the Internet in what has evolved into a powerful global information system. The *Dexter Model* for multimedia is a result of a multimedia designers' workshop held at the Dexter Inn in Sunapee, New Hampshire, in October 1988. Over subsequent meetings, the "Dexter Group" developed a data and process model that could act as a reference standard against which new hypertext systems could be analyzed, evaluated, and compared. The Dexter Model has been discussed extensively in the literature (for example, the *Communications of ACM,* February 1994, is a special issue on hypermedia with many articles on the Dexter Model).

For our purpose we need to concentrate on the *hotlinks* that are the main distinguishing feature of hypertext, hypermedia, and HTML. These hotlinks[4] are hyperlinks (i.e., hypertext or hypermedia links) that provide a path from one document to another. HTML provides tags so that you can create these hyperlinks anywhere in your document. The hyperlinks are highlighted (usually in color and underlined) when displayed by the Web browsers. Use of HTML allows you to browse through Web documents in a manner similar to, but more powerful than, browsing through a library—you click on the hotlink and get access to the needed page/document that may be located anywhere on the Web. For example, suppose that you are browsing an "HTML-ized" article that describes various communications products, where each product reviewed has a hyperlink to the vendor page. Then, you can directly access additional information about chosen products by simply pointing and clicking. By using hyperlinks, you can start with a home page in Chicago and read next a page from New York City and then a page from England. The hyperlinks use the URL to locate information. Each click to a hyperlink initiates an HTTP session.

HTML capabilities include basic features as well as "fill-in forms" for sending search arguments, comments, and other pieces of information (e.g., credit card numbers, telephone numbers, and addresses) to the Web servers. The basic features describe how to use the HTML tags to define titles, lists, paragraphs, image placements, and the like. The simple HTML example shown in the sidebar illustrates many of these features. The fill-in form capabilities are provided by the FORM statement. FORM is an HTML construct that has been used for developing Web gateways to corporate information systems and relational databases. Basically a FORM contains some fields where the user enters data in a structured way, a button to submit the form (which simulates submitting a similar form to the real world), and a button to clear the user's input so that the form can be used again. The browser uses the FORM state-

---

4. In this book, we will use the term hyperlink to indicate the family of hotlinks such as hypertext link and hypermedia links.

ment to construct a URL and data that is sent to the Web server. The Web server passes this information to a script that performs the needed operations and returns the results back to the client.

A FORM is implemented as follows in HTML:

```
<FORM ACTION="URL"METHOD=GET | POST >
<INPUT TYPE="TEXT"NAME ="Keyword1" SIZE = "length" <P>
<INPUT TYPE="TEXT"NAME ="Keyword2" SIZE = "length" <P>
     .....
     .....

<INPUT TYPE="SUBMIT" VALUE="Submit your form"> <P>
<INPUT TYPE="RESET" VALUE="Reset your form"> <P>
</FORM>
```

The METHOD keyword specifies the HTTP method to be used to submit the form information to the server. METHOD uses two arguments, GET (this sends the form data as part of URL) and POST (this sends the form data as a separate message to the Web server). Most browsers at present use POST because it is more efficient. The ACTION keyword specifies the URL to which the form data will be sent. This URL is typically a link to an executable script or binary file that can be used as a gateway program. The INPUT statements are used to receive different types of inputs such as text (TYPE = "TEXT"), pressing of submit button (TYPE = "SUBMIT"), and clearing of typed inputs (TYPE = "RESET"). Typically a series of TYPE = "TEXT" statements are used to receive customer inputs and assign names to the form input fields (these fields are used by the processing scripts). The following HTML page illustrates a simple form that allows a user to type in a 30-byte-long query and push a submit button after typing the statement (the statements are processed by a gateway process "/cgi.bin/userquery"):

```
<TITLE> User Query </TITLE>
<HI> User Query </HI>
Please enter your query:
<FORM METHOD=POST ACTION="/cgi.bin/userquery"
Enter your query: <INPUT TYPE = 'TEXT' NAME="query" SIZE "30" <P>
<INPUT TYPE="SUBMIT"   VALUE="Submit your form"> <P>
</FORM>
```

Many browsers at present use HTML 2.0, with HTML 3.0 becoming more popular. Owing to the popularity of the Web and the proliferation of browsers, many new tags and parameters keep appearing in HTML. Like many other active areas in computing, HTML standards lag implementations. There are differences between approved standards, proposed standards and vendor extensions. It seems that every vendor browser introduces a few new twists to HTML. Although browsers usually skip the unrecognized tags, this creates problems for content developers because they have to test their Web pages against a bevy of browsers to make sure that the material developed looks acceptable on different browsers. To address this issue, IETF (Internet Engineering Task Force) introduced an HTML standard in November 1995 [Berners-Lee 1995]. However, many HTML pages at present are already using supersets of this standard.

Although HTML documents can be developed by using any ASCII text editor, special-purpose "HTML editors" are commercially available to assist users in building HTML documents. These editors automatically place HTML tags in the document; the user simply points and clicks icons from the toolbars. Examples of such editors are the Microsoft Internet Assistant for Word, Quarterdeck's Webauthor, HTML Assistant, HTML Editor, etc. In addition, *filters* are commercially available that convert documents created in popular word processors (e.g., Frame Maker, Microsoft Word, Word Perfect, Latex) to HTML.

It is not our purpose here to give a complete tutorial on HTML. Many books do this quite well [Graham 1996, Tittel 1995, Chandler 1995, December 1995]. Detailed information about HTML can be obtained from (*http://info.cern.ch/hypertext/WWW/MarkUp/HTML.html*). HTML standards and proposals are being promulgated by the World Wide Web Consortium (*http://w3.org/*), and independent extensions are being proposed by companies such as Netscape Corporation (*http://www.netscape.com/*).

4.5   Hypertext Transfer Protocol (HTTP)

The Hypertext Transfer Protocol (HTTP) is at the core of the middleware for WWW. HTTP is an application-level protocol designed to give interactive users the lightness and speed necessary for collaborative hypermedia work. Hence it must accomplish its tasks reasonably fast. HTTP accomplishes this mainly by using an extremely simple model that consists of the following four steps (see Figure 4.5):

- **Connection**—The client establishes a connection with the server.
- **Request**—The client sends a request message to the server.
- **Response**—The server responds to the client with an answer.
- **Close**—The client or server closes the connection.

Figure 4.5 A Typical HTTP Session

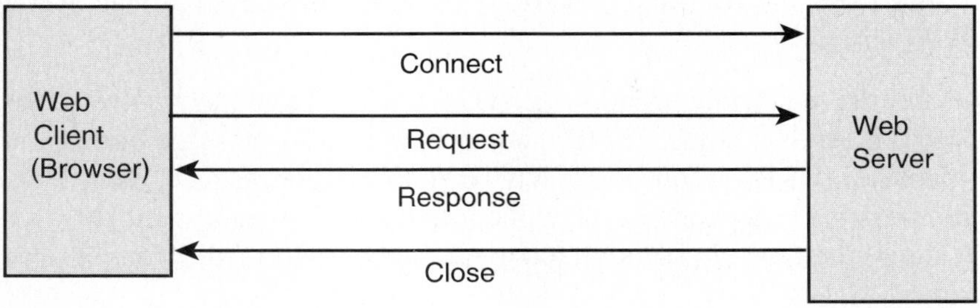

This protocol implements a single interaction consisting of a single request-and-response pair in a session with a WWW-server. For example, if you need to access a Web page "http://www.sun.com/overview.html," then **connec**t will establish a connection with the Sun Web site "www.sun.com," **request** will ask for the Web page "overview.html," **response** will transfer the page to your client, and **close** will terminate the connection.

HTTP is a stateless protocol, i.e., each connection is handled as a self-contained *session* (connection, request, response, close is treated as one session). Thus, if you access three different Web documents over the Internet, HTTP treats this as three independent, self-contained sessions. No information is maintained between these three sessions. This causes some discomforts in developing database applications over the Web, because many database applications involve conversational, ongoing interactions that require some state information between sessions.

Currently, version 1.0 of HTTP is being used most frequently. HTTP version 1.1 is currently being worked on within the Internet Engineering Task Force (IETF). Let us go through some details (if you are not interested, you can skip the following discussion).

Universal Resource Identifiers (URIs). The name URL, discussed earlier, is just one that is used to designate objects in WWW. The whole family is technically known as universal resource identifiers (URIs), of which URLs name the physical location of objects in WWW. Other main object identifiers in the URI family are universal resource names (URNs), which identify the resource name without regard to location, and universal resource citations (URCs), which describe properties of objects. Owing to the generality of URI, it is used frequently in the WWW technical documents such as HTTP specifications.

Connection. HTTP is currently implemented on top of TCP/IP, but it can be implemented on other network stacks. When using TCP/IP, port 80 is the default port for connection, but nonreserved ports may be specified in the URL. In many cases, you find W names such as www.ibm.com, www.bellcore.com, www.transarc.com, ww These are not the actual machine names but are convenient aliases (doma translate these aliases to physical machine addresses). This allows the companies to designate a general alias name for the outside world and change the physical machines that actually serve as Web servers.

Request. After the requesting program (client) establishes a connection with a receiving program (server), it sends a request to the server. The request message contains the universal resource identifier (URI), a request method, protocol version, request modifiers, client information, and possible body contents. The method is the most important part of this message because it shows the type of operation that needs to be performed. Examples of the common methods are:

- GET—This is most commonly used and indicates that a document needs to be retrieved from the server. This method retrieves either the document specified or a default document. Web servers return a default page if you do not specify a document. For example, if you type a URL (http://www.bellcore.com), then it returns Bellcore's default page. See the sidebar "Simple HTTP 1.0 GET Request."

- HEAD—This is used just to get meta information (headers) without transferring the entire document. This method is typically used to test hypertext links for validity, recent modifications, and accessibility.

- POST—This method is used for sending messages that can be posted on a bulletin board, newsgroup, or mailing list.

- PUT—This method requests that the enclosed entity be stored on the specified URI. This method is used to transfer documents to the Web server.

- DELETE—This method is used to delete the resources identified in the URI.

Simple HTTP 1.0 GET Request

```
GET project.html HTTP/1.0
```

Response. The server responds, after interpreting the request, with an HTTP response message. The response message consists of a status line (e.g., status codes), server information, meta information, and possible body contents. The server sends the requested information back to the browser in an Internet standard called ***MIME*** (multipurpose Internet mail extension). MIME defines how information other than straight ASCII text is sent between Internet machines. MIME supports exchange of text/HTML, images, video, audio, and application code. The server precedes the returned data with a MIME header containing bits of information, including the content type. The clients (Web browsers) use these headers to interpret the type of information being sent and to display it to the user.

Close. In many cases, the client establishes the connection prior to each request and the server 'loses the connection after sending the response. However, HTTP does not require this (either client or server can initiate and/or close the connection). HTTP clients and servers must be capable of handling premature connection closing from either side due to timeouts, program failures, or user actions. The closing of the connection by either party always terminates the current request, regardless of its status.

Some Comments. Basically, HTTP is a generic, stateless, and object-oriented protocol which can be used for many different tasks. An important feature of HTTP is the typing and negotiation of data representation at time of connection (i.e., MIME type requests/response), thus allowing applications to be built independently of the data being transferred. Its statelessness and the lightness are major advantages of HTTP for retrieving documents. But they create serious problems for several applications that require state information. Example of such applications are database applications, applications that maintain a "virtual shopping cart" for a particular visitor, shopping via on-line catalogs, and keeping track of customers who utilize certain Web sites. Different approaches to maintain state have been used, such as hidden fields in HTML forms and Netscape "HTTP cookies" [Schulzrinne 1996]. In addition to statelessness, HTTP has a few other problems. For example, HTTP is inefficient when you are browsing through a large number of hyperlinks (each time you click on a hyperlink, a separate HTTP session is established). HTTP 1.1 is recommending that a single TCP connection stay open for several HTTP transfers in certain situations. A short, crisp analysis of HTTP limitations can be found in Schulzrinne [1996].

As stated previously, HTTP is currently implemented on TCP/IP Sockets because Internet is based on the TCP/IP protocol. The default port is TCP 80, but other ports can be used. However, HTTP can be implemented on top of other protocols on the Internet and other networks. Proposals for making HTTP more generally available have been discussed (e.g., support for HTTP on top of the DCE RPC). In addition, work has been initiated to support different types of applications over WWW. For example, Oracle has announced a Cooperative Application suite that supports workflow management over the Internet through email and remote database access. We will discuss this topic later (Sections 4.8 and 4.10).

Information about HTTP is readily available over the Internet. The Hypertext Transfer Protocol is defined in the Web document ***http://info.cern.ch/hypertext/WWW/Protocols/HTTP/ HTTP2.html***. An HTTP Working Group is establishing future directions for HTTP and publishes Internet Drafts to indicate work in progress. The HTTP Working Group receives comments and questions at ***http-wg@cuckoo.hp1.hp.com***. Discussions of the working group are archived at URL ***http://www.ics.uci.edu/pub/ietf/http/***.

4.6   Web Browsers

Web browsers are the end-user interface to the Web servers. These browsers, also known as Web clients, typically reside on PCs, Macs, and UNIX workstations. From an end user's point of view, the browsers give a GUI and an easy-to-use view of the Internet and provide pull-down/pop-up menus and buttons for accessing remote servers, scrolling through documents, printing results, downloading code, saving retrieved documents on your local disk, performing searches, and surfing the Net. Many browsers have been introduced since 1990 and are currently in use. Examples are the NCSA X-Mosaic, NCSA Mosaic for Windows, Netscape Navigator, Spyglass, Air Mosaic, Win-Tapestry, and Web-Explorer.

Many popular browsers, such as the Netscape Navigator and the NCSA Mosaic, run on most platforms (PCs, Macs, UNIX). This is one of the many reasons for the popularity of WWW in the corporate world. While in the past a library system or a customer-information system could have been developed by using a specially designed user interface, it seems much more natural for organizations today to use Web browsers for user interfaces. Users residing on different machines can then use the same browser to interact with the corporate systems. The same browser can also allow the users to use the Web for document searches. Thus Web browsers have the potential of becoming the only user interface for all information [Bickell 1996]. This makes WWW unique, in that it makes hypermedia a key enabler of business as well as nonbusiness information that is becoming available through the Internet and Intranets.

Web browsers are designed to display information in HTML format and communicate with the Web servers through HTTP. As a matter of fact, you can develop your own browser if you provide the following two capabilities:

- HTML compliance, i.e., display information on the screen as specified by HTML tags.
- HTTP compliance, i.e., generate HTTP commands to connect to the Web server, initiate needed operations whenever a user clicks on a hyperlink, and receive/interpret the responses.

Web browsers can access resources located in Web servers, FTP servers, Telnet servers, Gopher servers, News server servers, etc. (see Figure 4.6).

Let us look at browsers as Web clients. The two basic functions of a Web client are:

- **Navigation** to facilitate the travel through cyberspace from one resource to another
- **Browsing** to facilitate the perusal of information located by the navigator

At present, these two functions have been tightly integrated and are commonly referred to as browsers or navigators. Well-designed browsers make Web browsing an enjoyable experience, but ill-conceived browsers can result in irritation and frustration. We will refer to Web browsers to include browsing as well as navigation capabilities. Commercially available browsers provide a wide range of features. An extensive analysis of the existing Web browsers has been given by Berghel [1996] in terms of the following issues:

- Compliance
- Performance
- Reconfigurability
- Integration
- Navigation aids

Figure 4.6 Web Browser Interfaces

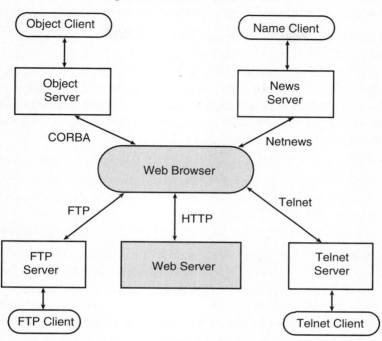

Compliance is related to the degree to which the operational characteristics of the client match the expectations of the connecting server. Basically this reduces to compliance with HTTP and HTML. HTTP compliance is absolutely essential. Most HTTP protocols at present work over TCP/IP. HTTP connectivity may also be needed over other networks, in addition to TCP/IP. It is also becoming important to support secure HTTP communications for security reasons. This can be achieved by using Secure HTTP protocol or Secure Socket Layer (you should browse the Internet for extensive information on S-HTTP and SSL). HTML compliance is needed because different versions of HTML exist (HTML 0, 1, 2, and 3) and extensions to HTML from Netscape exist in the industry. Many developers at present are using HTML version 3. In addition to HTTP and HTML, the browsers should be able to connect to popular environments such as Gopher, WAIS, FTP, and email. ***Proxy client*** support may also be needed to enable a client to behave as an intermediate server to gain passage through security firewalls.

Performance is an extremely important aspect of navigators/browsers. The limited bandwidth of many Internet communications and the lengthy load times for multimedia resources make client performance crucial. Many Web products use caching to boost performance. Caching retains visited documents or pages at the local host to reduce slow reloads over the Internet. Caching can exist for the session duration (called soft caching) or can be transferred to hard disk (hard caching). Clients may use multithreading to keep multiple, concurrent Web sessions to improve performance. Web browsers also include special features for document loading (e.g., load abort, enhanced transfer modes, incremental graphics loading).

Reconfigurability is the ability to change the look and feel of the Web client to satisfy client-site and/or user needs. For example, you can include user-defined default home pages so that your own home pages appear instead of the vendor home page (e.g., Netscape home page is shown by default whenever you use the Netscape browser but this can be reconfigured). Other configurability options may include font and color changes. Different reconfigurability options are provided by different browsers/navigators. Most of the client software is reconfigured by using menu-driven options.

Integration of the Web client software with the host desktop (i.e., the machine where the Web client resides) may become an important area of future development. For example, you should be able to seamlessly integrate graphics viewers such as GIF (Graphical Interchange Format), multimedia, and audio formats with the search capabilities. In addition, external search engines such as spiders and worms should be integrated with the browsers.

Navigation aids help to reduce the processing time of navigation. The basic problem is that the hyperlinks do not scale well (i.e., if you have to access hundreds of resources over the Internet, then it is difficult to keep track of this information). To aid navigation, "cyberlogs" are used by the Web clients to keep track of recently accessed resources. Cyberlogs keep information by document names instead of URLs and are created during navigation for subsequent displays. Cyberlog entries can be reloaded by pointing and clicking. In addition to cyberlogs, navigators/browsers provide hotlists and bookmarks that are generated by the users when needed. For example, if you access a resource frequently, then you can add it to your hotlist/bookmark for future reference. However, hotlists/bookmarks and cyberlogs do not scale well either (they become awkward after about 100 entries). The scalability problem can be solved by providing multiply nested folders or multiple hotlists.

There are navigators/browsers that provide many of the features discussed above. For example, Netscape Navigator 2.0 brings Web exploring, secure email, newsgroups, chat, and FTP capabilities together in an integrated package. It provides a platform for live on-line applications, supporting Live Objects and other interactive multimedia content such as Java applets, frames, and Netscape in-line plug-ins. Netscape Navigator 2.0 includes features such as client-side image mapping, improved bookmark features and interface, OLE support, GIF animation, FTP upload, Progressive JPEG support, and support for multiple simultaneous streaming of video, audio, and other data formats. Netscape 2.0 is available on most platforms and in many different languages. Additional information about Navigator 2.0 can be obtained from the Netscape home page *(http://www.netscape.com)*. Similar features are also available in other browsers (e.g., Microsoft Internet Explorer browsers).

Additional Web Protocols

- **Internet Protocol version 6 (IPv6)** is expected to accommodate Internet's growth, boost the real-time multimedia capabilities over the Internet, and provide added security. IPv6 is designed to run well on high-bandwidth networks such as ATM. It is also expected to run efficiently on low-bandwidth networks such as wireless.

- **Virtual-Reality Modeling Language (VRML)** is used by newer multimedia applications over the Internet.

- **Internet Relay Chat (IRC)** and **Multiuser Object-Oriented (MOO)** systems are popular for socializing and gaming.

4.7   Java and Java Applets

4.7.1   What Is Java and Why Is It So Hot?

Java is an object-oriented programming language that is playing a unique role in WWW. Technically speaking, programming languages are not considered as part of middleware. However, Java has gained a unique status for supporting a very diverse array of Web applications and is also being prepared for distributed applications across the Internet (see the sidebar "Distributed Applications with Java"). For this reason we include a discussion of Java in this chapter.

The Java programming language and environment was introduced by Sun Microsystems to develop advanced software for consumer electronics. Initially, Sun intended to use C++ for these devices, which are small, reliable, portable, distributed, real-time embedded systems. It was found that the problems were best solved by introducing a new language that was similar to C++ but drew heavily from other object-oriented languages such as Eiffel and Smalltalk. The language, initially known as Oak, is now known as Java.

Why is Java so hot? The key is in supporting user interactions with Web pages that use Java. Simply stated, small Java programs, called *Java applets*, can be embedded in Web pages (these are called *Java-powered pages*). Java-powered Web pages can be downloaded to the Web client side and make the Web browsers a powerful user tool. Web browsers at present are relatively dumb (i.e., most functionality lies in Web servers, not in Web browsers). Java is changing this because Java applets can run on Java-enabled browsers. When users access these pages, these pages along with the Java applets are downloaded to the Web browser. The Java applets run on the Web client side, thus making the browser an intelligent component. Basically, when the user clicks on the Java-powered pages, the Java applets are downloaded to the Web browser site, where they run doing whatever they were programmed to do. There are several implications of this:

- Java applets exemplify "mobile code" that is developed at one site and is migrated to another site on demand[5]. This introduces several security issues but also creates many interesting research opportunities.

- Java applets make Web applications really client/server, because the Java code can run business logic on the Web client site (i.e., the Web browser houses the first tier).

- The Web screen layout can be changed dynamically, based on the user type. A Java program can determine the user type and modify the screen layout.

- Different advertisements can be shown and highlighted to the user, depending on the user characteristics (e.g., age, job type, education level, credit history, salary level).

- Access to databases can be invoked directly from the browser, instead of by invoking a gateway program that resides on the Web server site. The Java program can ask the user to compose a request and then send this request to a remote database. A standard called JDBC (Java Database Connectivity) is being developed to allow Java programs to issue calls to relational databases.

- You can produce graphs and charts dynamically at your browser instead of fetching predefined graphs and images from the Web server (transferring images takes a very long time over the Internet).[6]

- You can run animations, invoke business transactions, and run spreadsheets at your browser site.

4.7.2   What Is HotJava?

HotJava is a browser that can run Java-powered pages; i.e., it is Java enabled. You need a special Java-enabled browser that can run Java applets. HotJava is such a browser. At the time of this writing, HotJava is available for Windows 95, Windows NT, and Solaris 2.x platforms. Owing to the popularity of Java, many other browsers are also becoming Java compatible. For example, Netscape Navigator 2.0 is Java compatible. It is expected that most commonly used browsers will be Java compatible in the near future.

If you download a Java-powered page to a browser that is not Java enabled, then nothing happens—you cannot run any Java applications (this is not terribly entertaining). You can download HotJava from *http://www.javasoft.com* and the Netscape Navigator 2.0 from *http://www.netscape.com/*.

---

5. In fact, Java applets are downloadable classes (i.e., they are transferred from one site and executed at another) and not fully mobile. A fully mobile application, such as needed for agent-oriented systems, moves from site to site on an as needed basis and carries all necessary information about its state and processes.

6. I once tried to access a home page from Germany. The home page had some image files that were somewhat complicated. I simply could not get the page even after hours of trying (the session timed out repeatedly).

Distributed Applications with Java

Java support for distributed applications at the time of this writing comes in different flavors. In other words, if you need to write a Java application where a Java applet on your Web browser invokes another Java applet on another machine, then you have the following choices:

- Write your own low-level code to invoke the remote Java applet.
- Utilize, if possible, distributed-object middleware such as CORBA or OLE/ActiveX.

The first choice is not very attractive (you are writing your own middleware). The second choice is becoming available, albeit slowly. For example, Sun has announced an ORB, written in Java, called Joe. This ORB works with the ORBs that operate in Sun's Neo environment.

Sun has developed a new feature of Java that allows Java applets to talk to each other across machines without needing any middleware such as ORBs. This feature, known as Remote Method Invocation (RMI), allows Java applets to communicate with each other over the Internet. In addition, Sun is planning to add a capability that will allow Java applets to work across a firewall.

4.7.3   What Is a Java Applet?

As stated previously, a Java applet is a small Java program. What is the difference between a Java application and a Java applet? Basically, a Java application is a complete, standalone application that uses text input and output. Java applets, on the other hand, are not standalone applications, and they run as part of a Java-enabled browser.[7] A Java applet contains methods (subroutines) to initialize itself, draw itself, respond to clicks, etc. These methods are invoked by the Java-enabled browser. How does a browser know to download Java applets. It is quite simple. A Java-powered HTML page contains a tag (the APPLET tag) that indicates the location of a Java applet. When the browser encounters this tag, it downloads it and runs it. See the sidebar "Downloading and Running Java Applets."

The Java applets are small enough to be embedded in Web pages but large enough to do something useful. The Java applets are transferred to the Web browser along with everything else embedded in the Web page (e.g., text, images, video clips). Once transferred to the Web client, they execute on the client side and thus do not suffer from the issues of network traffic between the Web client and Web server. Because these applications run on your client

---

7. PROGRAMMING NOTE: From a programming point of view, a Java application is Java code ("Java Class") that has the main () method. The Java interpreter looks for main () and executes it. Java applets do not contain main (). Instead, Java applets contain methods that are invoked by the Java-enabled browsers.

machine, you see a much more natural and efficient execution (imagine running a multimedia application on a remote Web site versus running it on your own desktop).

Downloading and Running Java Applets

The Java browser load process consists of the following steps:

- User selects an HTML page.
- Browser locates the page and starts loading it.
- While loading, it starts to format text.
- It loads graphics if indicated by IMG or FIG tags in HTML.
- Java applets are indicated by an APPLET tag. For example, the following tag indicates a Java applet called "Myapplet.class" that is run in a window size of 110 by 100:

  ```
  <APPLET CODE=myapplet.class WIDTH =110 HEIGHT=100>
  </APPLET>
  ```
- The applet code is assumed to be on the same site where the HTML page is.
- Browser loads the indicated class and other needed classes.
- Java-"enabled" browsers also keep local classes that may be used by the applets.
- After the applet has been loaded, the browser asks it to initialize itself (init() method) and draw a display area that is used for input/output.

Owing to the popularity of Java applets, many plug-and-play Java applets are already available. Once built, the Java applets can run on many different machines. The Java code is first compiled into byte-codes (byte-codes are machine instructions that are machine independent). The byte-code of the applet is loaded into the browser, where it runs efficiently on different machines by using a run-time interpreter. Owing to the appeal of Java applet style programming, other programming languages such as C++ and COBOL are beginning to produce byte code that can be invoked by Web browsers (the browsers do not know how the code was created).

Java applets have access to a wide range of libraries that allow Java applets to perform many operations such as graphics, image downloading, playing audio files, and user interface creation (i.e., buttons, scrollbars, windows, etc.). These libraries are included as part of the Java Applet API. This API is supported by all Java-compatible browsers. It is expected that these libraries will grow with time, thus making Java applets even more powerful and diversified.

4.7.4 Java Details

Java has emerged, almost suddenly, as a very popular language for developing Web applications. If you need to develop Java applets, then you need to look into Java in more detail. This discussion is intended for programmers.

According to Sun, "Java is a simple, object-oriented, distributed, interpreted, robust, secure, architecture-neutral, portable, high-performance, multithreaded, and dynamic language." The following paragraphs discuss these features of Java. The discussion is an abbreviated version of the Java white paper that can be obtained from Sun's home page (http://www.su.com).

Although Java is very popular at present, it is presenting some security concerns (see the sidebar "Java Security Concerns"). Other issues about Java's maturity for enterprisewide applications are being raised (see the *Software Magazine*, May 1996 issue).

Simplicity. Java was designed to be similar to C++ in order to make the system more comprehensible to current practitioners. Java omits many features of C++ such as operator overloading (although the Java language does have method overloading), multiple inheritance, and extensive automatic coercions. The automatic garbage collection was added, thereby simplifying the task of Java programming but making the system somewhat more complicated. A good example of a common source of complexity in many C and C++ applications is storage management: the allocation and freeing of memory. By virtue of having automatic garbage collection the Java language makes the programming task easier and also cuts down on bugs. Java is designed so that it can run standalone in small machines. The size of the basic interpreter and class support is about 40K bytes; the basic standard libraries and thread support add an additional 175K.

Object Orientation. The object-oriented facilities of Java are essentially those of C++, with extensions from Objective C for more dynamic method resolution.

Distributed. The main power of Java is that Java applications can open and access objects over the Internet via URLs in a manner similar to accessing a local file system. Java has an extensive library of routines for coping easily with TCP/IP protocols like HTTP and FTP.

Robust. Java puts a lot of emphasis on early checking for possible problems, later dynamic (run-time) checking, and elimination of error-prone situations. Java requires declarations and does not support C-style implicit declarations. The single biggest difference between Java and C/C++ is that Java does not allow pointer arithmetic. Java has arrays that allow subscript checking to be performed. In addition, Java does not allow an arbitrary integer to be converted into a pointer.

Java Security Concerns

Java designers have taken reasonable precautions about Java security by introducing a Java verifier to make sure that the byte code was generated by a valid Java compiler before running it (Java compilers restrict pointers and typecodes to minimize security risks). However, several security flaws in Java are currently being discovered and addressed. The basic premise of the security concerns is that Java applets are essentially foreign applications that are brought into your environment and executed on your browser site. This opens the floodgate to unscrupulous code being brought in from other sites and do strange things. A quick remedy to this problem is to make sure that you download Java applets from trusted sites only (e.g., corporate Web servers within your firewalls).

The examples of how Java programs can contaminate your environment abound. For example, David Hopwood at Oxford University found that Java applets can load malicious class files and libraries onto a user's system. Many "hostile applets," such as the following, have been documented and are listed on the "Hostile Applet Home Page":

- A noisy bear who refuses to be quiet.

- A barking browser

- Popping up of an untrusted applet window

- Forging email

- Obtaining a user ID

A great deal of work is needed to resolve the Java security issues. A research group at Princeton University, headed by Edward Felton, is investigating Java security problems. A paper by this group (Dean, D., Felton, E., and Wallach, D., "Java security: From HotJava to Netscape and Beyond," Proceedings of 1996 IEEE Symposium on Security and Privacy, May 1996), lists a compendium of hostile actions that a Java applet can perform.

The issues of Java security are far from settled. Many approaches are being pursued at the time of this writing (e.g., "sandboxing", applet signing). Many groups, including Sun and Netscape, are busily working on addressing Java security problems. Stay tuned.

Architecture Neutral. Java was designed to support applications on networks. Java compiler generates an architecture-neutral object file format that is executable on many processors, given the presence of the Java run-time system. The Java compiler generates byte-code instructions that are independent of computer architecture. Byte-codes are designed to be easy to interpret on any machine and can be easily translated into native machine code on the fly.

Portable. Java specifies the sizes of the primitive data types and the behavior of arithmetic on them. For example, "int" always means a signed two's-complement 32-bit integer, and "float" always means a 32-bit IEEE 754 floating-point number. The libraries that are a part of the system define portable interfaces. The Java system itself is also portable. The new compiler is written in Java and the run-time is written in ANSI C with a clean portability boundary. The portability boundary is essentially POSIX.

Interpreted. The Java interpreter can execute Java byte-codes directly on any machine to which the interpreter has been ported. And, since linking is a more incremental and lightweight process, the development process can be much more rapid and exploratory.

High Performance. In some cases, the performance of interpreted byte-codes is not adequate. Java byte-codes can be translated on the fly (at run-time) into machine code for the particular CPU the application is running on. The byte-code format was designed with generating machine codes in mind, so the actual process of generating machine code is generally simple. According to Sun, the performance of byte-codes converted to machine code is almost indistinguishable from native C or C++.

Multithreaded. Multithreading is important for performance, but writing multi-threaded programs is more difficult than writing in the conventional single-threaded programs. Java has a set of synchronization primitives that are based on the widely used monitor and condition-variable paradigm.

Dynamic. Java was designed to adapt to an evolving environment. It makes the interconnections between modules later. Java understands interfaces—a concept that is used heavily in distributed systems through Interface Definition Languages (IDLs). An interface is simply a specification of a set of methods that an object responds to. Interfaces make it possible to use objects in a dynamic distributed environment (we will talk about this when we discuss CORBA).

The best source for additional information about Java is the Sun home page *(http://www.sun.cm)*. From this home page, you can find a Java white paper that gives justification of Java, an 80-page technical document on Java and HotJava, Java applets, and additional detailed documentation.The book *Hooked on Java* [Hoff 1996] gave one of the earliest introductions to Java. An interesting analysis of Java can be found in Philips [1996]. At present, a dozen or so books are available on different aspects of Java.

4.8   Web Sites and Web Servers

A *Web site* provides the content of the World Wide Web. Having the Web without the Web sites is like having a TV without any TV stations. The growing number of Web sites containing a wide range of information (known as *resources*) that can be accessed transparently by Web users is the main strength of WWW. Examples of the Web sites at present are corporate Web sites, university Web sites, publishing/advertising Web sites, travel-agency Web sites, and small-business Web sites. Web sites can be large (e.g., large corporations may dedicate several machines as Web sites) or small (smaller companies may rent or lease portions of a Web site). Although conceptually, a Web site is a catalog of information for each content provider over the Web, in reality a Web site consists of three types of components (see Figure 4.7):

- Content files such as the HTML documents
- A Web server (a program) that receives browser calls and accesses contents, and/or
- Gateways that can generate Web content (e.g., generate HTML pages) and provide access to non-Web content (e.g., relational databases).

Figure 4.7 A Web Site

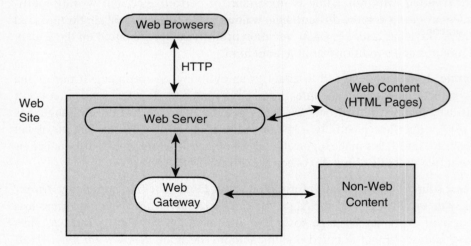

A *Web server* is essentially a scheduler of Web client requests. Specifically, the server software includes schedulers that handle the HTTP calls (libraries and directories for Web gateways, server configuration files, icons, error and access log files, utility programs, etc.). An early, and still popular, server software package, known as the *httpd (HTTP Daemon) server,* was developed by NCSA (National Center for Supercomputing Applications). Initially developed for UNIX, the NCSA HTTPD server has been ported to other platforms and extended/

modified for different environments. A closely related server software is the Windows HTTPD server. Several other servers are also available from vendors such as Netscape and Microsoft. These off-the-shelf servers make it easy to install Web sites.

Many practitioners do not differentiate between Web servers and Web sites. We will attempt to separate them by using the following equation:

Web site = Web server + contents + Web gateways

Setting up a Web site involves a large number of issues, such as the following:

- Deciding who will develop the Web site, i.e., your own organization or an outside service provider.

- Determining rent-versus-own issue; i.e., will the site be owned by your organization or will you rent/lease space on an existing Web site (this is called "virtual hosting").

- Choosing a Web site platform; i.e., will the Web server and contents reside on a UNIX or Windows NT platform.

- Choosing a sharing level; i.e., will a machine be dedicated as a Web site or will the Web site software coexist with other software (e.g., LAN software).

- Providing and controlling access to the site, i.e, determine the networking configurations and the security firewalls to be set up.

- Designing the site, i.e., designing home pages, assigning defaults, and deciding server configurations.

- Management and support considerations, such as backup/recovery, site security, site administration, hotline support, etc.

Details about setting up and running a Web site can be found in Chandler [1995]. Web servers to satisfy different classes of Web users are becoming state-of-the-market. An example is the Netscape release of a set of Web servers such as FastTrack to support Java and Java Script, SuiteSpot for enterprise Intranets, and LiveWire Pro to support Java development (see the Netscape home page "http://www.netscape.com" for more details). The choice of a server depends on factors such as ease of installation, performance, security, manageability, and user friendliness. An analysis of three Web servers (Netscape Commerce Server, Microsoft IIS, and Process Software Purveyor) based on these factors is given by Varhol [1996].

4.9   Web Gateways: Accessing Non-Web Information

4.9.1   Web Gateway Overview

Web gateways bridge the gap between Web browsers and the corporate applications and databases. These gateways are important because many Web applications at the time of this writing are document-browsing applications. There is an urgent need for integration of traditional corporate applications into the World Wide Web. Why? Mainly because most of the corporate data resides in the corporate applications, many of which are legacy applications. (The old saying: "Why do you rob banks?" The answer: "That is where the money is.") For World Wide Web to truly succeed in the corporate world as the primary user interface to *all i*nformation, it must provide access to corporate databases and applications.

Web access to corporate databases and applications is a challenging task. A major challenge is that many of the existing applications are ***stateful*** (i.e., they keep an ongoing interaction with the user where the answer to one query may depend on how far you are in your conversation). These systems are implemented by using ***stateful protocols*** where the meaning of a message depends on previous messages. Unfortunately, Web browsers do not support states (recall that HTTP is a stateless protocol, i.e., it treats each interaction independent of the previous ones). The Web gateways attempt to handle the differences between stateful and stateless protocols by using techniques such as hidden fields in HTML forms that can be used to keep track of states [Schulzrinne 1996]. In addition to handling state translations, Web gateways also generate HTML pages for display at the browsers. For example, if you issue a database query, the Web gateway will format the results of the query to HTML before sending it to the browser.Web gateways can also perform other functions such as accessing and integrating information from heterogeneous data sources.

In general, Web gateways can be used to handle almost anything that is not already adapted to browsers or HTML. At present, the following approaches are used to develop Web gateways [Perrochon 1995]:

- Common gateway interface (CGI)
- Server-side includes (SSI)
- Gateway as a standalone server
- Mobile code systems (Java gateways)

4.9.2   Common Gateway Interface (CGI)

CGI gateways are very popular at present. A CGI gateway is a program that resides on the Web server. This program can be a script (e.g., a UNIX shell script or a Perl script) or an executable program (e.g., C or C++ programs). After this program has been written, it is readied for execution by the Web server (this step typically involves placing of the gateway program in the /cgi.bin/ directory or other designated library of the server). Hyperlinks to this program can then be included in HTML documents in the same way as hyperlinks to any other resource. For example, if the gateway program is called testgate.pl, the URL for this program is

```
http://www.myserver.com/cgi.bin/testgate.pl
```

This URL is included in the HTML page at an appropriate place. For example, we can write the following HTML statement to invoke *testgate.pl* (Href is used to indicate a hypertext link):

```
<A Href="http://www.myserver.com/cgi.bin/testgate.pl">
```

When the user clicks on this hyperlink, the gateway URL is passed to the Web server. The Web server locates the gateway program in the /cgi.bin/ directory and executes it. The output produced by the gateway program is sent back to the Web browser.

The fundamental difference between accessing a regular HTML file and accessing a CGI gateway is that the CGI gateway program is executed on the server to perform some specialized functions (including creation of HTML pages, if needed) instead of just fetching and displaying an existing HTML page (see Figure 4.8).

What type of CGI gateways can be developed? Virtually anything. Examples range from simple time and date retrievals to sophisticated database applications. In general, CGI gateways fall into two categories (see Figure 4.8):

- *Single-step CGI gateway*—An application program is executed as a CGI executable itself, thereby forking the application process for every request. In this case, the CGI executable contains the application logic invoked by the Web client.

- *Two-step CGI gateway*—An application program runs as a daemon process. A CGI executable just dispatches the request rather than performing any application functions. In this case, the CGI gateway has no business logic and is just used as a dispatcher.

Figure 4.8 CGI Gateways

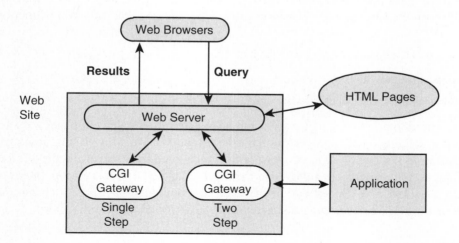

Single-step CGI gateways are typically used for quick and relatively simple functions. The two-step CGI gateways are more useful for large, in many cases, legacy applications. Often, two-step CGI gateways are used for connecting existing applications with the Web (it is easier to invoke existing programs from CGI scripts than to rewrite them completely as CGI scripts). You may also use a combination, i.e., perform some functions in the CGI executable and then dispatch existing applications where needed.

4.9.3   Server-Side Includes (SSI)

Although CGI gateways are very popular, server-side includes (SSIs) are a reasonable choice in some cases. A *server-side include (SSI)* consists of a special sequence of characters (tags) inside an HTML page. These tags are processed by the *server* when it sends the document to the Web client. For example, suppose you use a tag telling the server to insert the last date and time the current file was modified. When the server sends the file, it replaces this tag with the date and time. Basically, the server scans the HTML page for the SSI tags before sending it to the client. When a tag is found, the server interprets the instructions in the tag and performs an appropriate action.

As we stated earlier, HTML is interpreted by the Web browsers. However, the SSI tags are processed by the server as it delivers the HTML document to the Web browsers. This means that the HTML documents must be parsed by the server. Hence the documents that include SSI tags are not standard HTML, they are parsed HTML. Parsed HTML poses performance problems because of the parsing overhead at the server side. It is not a good idea to use SSI in large number of HTML pages.

You should keep in mind that not all Web servers support SSI. On the other hand, several vendors have introduced extensions to SSI. For example, an extension of SSI, called *SSI+*, is currently supported by Questar Microsystems. SSI+ supports the following functions (see Figure 4.9):

- Relational database access through ODBC (Open Database Connectivity)[8]
- Email based on the SMTP protocol
- Conditionals and flow-control statements

SSI can be used to build simple gateways, but SSI+ can be used to develop gateways for database access, sending email, and performing other functions. *Warning:* Using SSI can be very dangerous from a security point of view. If SSI is enabled by a server, then essentially any program or system call may be invoked as the result of an SSI. For this reason, most commercial sites disallow SSI. Specification of SSI+ can be found in *http://www.questar.com/ssi.html*. A tutorial on developing SSI gateways can be found in Nesbitt [1996].

---

8. We will discuss ODBC in the next Chapter.

Figure 4.9 Server-Side Includes

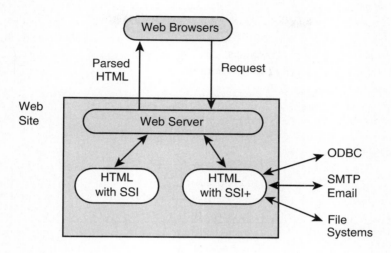

4.9.4 Gateway as a Standalone Server

A specialized standalone server can be developed to behave as a gateway (see Figure 4.10). The CGI and SSI gateways are built on top of a Web server that performs many functions (e.g., fetch and display HTML documents). The standalone servers are dedicated to gateway functionality thus they perform much better than the CGI and SSI gateways. Basically, every call received by this server is assumed to perform gateway functions. For example, a dedicated database gateway would receive SQL calls from a Web browser, send the SQL statements to the target databases, receive the results of the SQL query, build HTML pages from the results, and send the results back to the Web browsers.

Many commercially available relational database gateways fall into this category. Many of these gateways are proprietary. In addition, these gateways may use proprietary APIs. The NSAPI (NetScape API) is an example.

4.9.5 Mobile Code Systems (Java Gateways)

The gateways discussed so far operate on the server side. Java applets are changing this. The basic idea is to distribute code of the target application and send it to the Web client, where it executes. This approach suits the Java model very well. Java applets, as indicated above, can be embedded in HTML pages and sent to the Web browsers, where they execute.

By using this approach, access to remote applications and databases can be invoked directly from the browser. The Java applet can ask the user to issue a query and then send this query

Figure 4.10 A Dedicated Relational Database Gateway

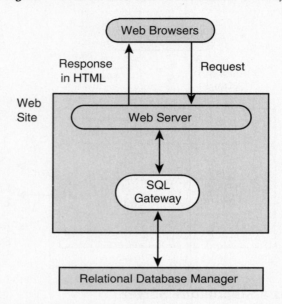

to a remote application or database (Figure 4.11). This is especially interesting for database gateways, where the database gateway functionality runs on the client side. A standard called JDBC (Java Database Connectivity) is being developed to allow Java programs to issue calls to relational databases.

We should keep in mind that an entire legacy application is difficult to convert into Java applets. However, some aspects of legacy application, perhaps the legacy user-interface processing, can be recoded as Java applets and thus used to integrate the legacy applications with WWW.

4.10   State of the Practice: Web Middleware for Enterprise Use

4.10.1 Overview

Use of the Web is growing at a phenomenal rate. At present, it is difficult to ascertain exactly the percentage of Internet traffic that is generated by Web users. Informally, it is estimated that this percentage is more than 50% [Schulzrinne 1996]. So what are people doing with the Web? Here is an incomplete sampling:

- Checking weather before travelling
- Bargain hunting for hotels and travel tips
- Advertising products and services

Figure 4.11 A Java-Based Gateway

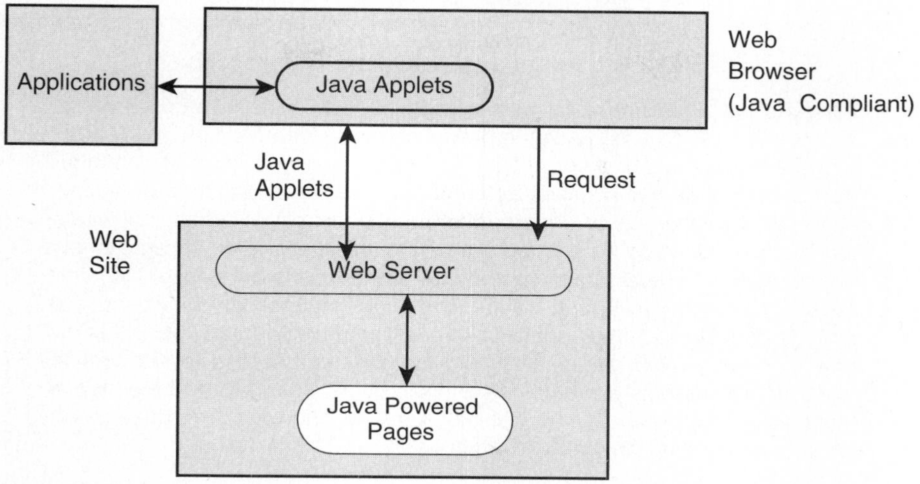

- Job hunting

- Researching and conducting literature surveys

- Collecting case-study information [Chadwick 1996]

This is all very interesting but what about use of the Web to support enterprises? For enterprisewide use, Web users must be able to easily access *corporate information* and support business applications. The corporate information is stored in data stores such as flat files (e.g., text files, graphic data), indexed files (e.g., VSAM), relational databases (e.g., Informix, Oracle, Sybase, DB2), IMS databases, and the like. Web browsers are designed for displaying HTML files. However, a large proportion of corporate information does not exist in HTML files. For example, corporations typically keep customer information, product information, inventory information, and many other critical pieces of information in relational databases.

The current state of the practice for Web usage in enterprise settings is evolving. In particular, a great deal of press is being devoted to Intranets (see the sidebar "What Are Intranets and Why Are They So Hot?") Many short excerpts about Web usage in different types of organizations for different types of applications appear regularly in trade magazines such as *Web Week* and *Information Week.* However, the Web middleware for enterprise applications is too low level [Perrochon 1995]. For example, the "middleware" for the World Wide Web at the time of this writing consists of many low-level components such as Web browsers, HTTP, HTML, and home-grown CGI gateways. In addition, Java applets are loosely thought of as part of the Web middleware. For growth, Web middleware must include off-the-shelf powerful gateways for access to relational databases and legacy information. We briefly describe these two growing areas.

What Are Intranets and Why Are They So Hot?

Intranets have become a favorite term in 1996 (just as favorite as client/server was in 1993). As we stated previously, an **Intranet** is a private TCP/IP network that is used by a corporation for its own business. In particular, Intranets employ Web technologies for corporate use. For example, the employees use Web browsers to perform their routine tasks plus access corporate information. Intranets have been called the Internet's killer application for business. Why? The reasons are that they are inexpensive (most of the infrastructure is already in place), they require minimum training (many users are already Web literate), they are easy to use and develop (many people know how to develop Web pages), they provide a natural access to the outside world (most Intranets are connected to the public Internet), and they move technology away from IS and into the hands of end users (end users can develop and deploy their own applications).

The main idea behind the Intranets is that organizations can standardize on Web browsers for the end-user access to all applications (e.g., finance, marketing, human resources, or engineering). In addition, the same Web interface can be used for applications that cross different organizational units of the company. Owing to the prevalence of Web technologies, the same user interface can be used to access information that may cross the company, industry, and country boundaries. In addition, the users can employ the same user interface when they are accessing information from home (many user interfaces developed for traditional client/server applications at present do not work over dial-up lines). The power of mobile code applications by using Java applets also creates very interesting possibilities for corporate applications (for example, each user interface can be reconfigured dynamically based on user profiles and preferences).

Intranets are initiated by first deploying one or more internal Web sites, providing some Web gateways, and encouraging/requiring use of Web browsers. There are several implications of this:

- Web browsers provide a common user interface for all employees, including telecommuters, who use different desktops.

- Web is used for groupware , i.e., for email, document exchange, workflows, and collaborative work (we will discuss groupware in a later chapter).

- Java applets can be used to perform a variety of operations on the user desktops.

Many companies, such as AT&T, Federal Express, Ely Lilly, MCI, and Sun, have successfully implemented Intranets (AT&T's Intranet has more than 100 internal Web sites that are accessed by more than 69,000 users).

4.10.2 Relational Gateways for the Web

A large proportion of corporate information is stored in relational databases. This proportion is expected to increase, owing to the widespread and continued availability of SQL servers on PCs. For example, Microsoft has announced a "300 million SQL server strategy" [Semich 1994]. This estimate is based on the following logic: there are roughly 10 million businesses in the United States and Microsoft expects to sell 30 SQL servers per business, because these servers will be so inexpensive that they could be used in copying machines. Naturally, Web access to relational databases is a crucial requirement.

Technically, Web access to relational databases is provided through a ***relational gateway*** that translates the browser requests to SQL calls and then translates the query response to HTML pages. A large number of relational gateways are being announced over the Internet. Many of these gateways are freeware—with an increasing number becoming available from vendors. Each gateway has its own promises and pitfalls. Basically, a relational gateway should support all functions typically provided by a relational database management system (RDBMS) (e.g., support simple queries, embedded SQL, ad hoc browsing, etc.). Many relational gateways at present focus on retrieval of data using simple query statements, while more sophisticated relational gateways have started to appear.

Access from Web clients to relational databases is currently available from more than 20 vendors under the relational gateway umbrella. Most of the existing relational gateways use CGI to access relational databases (see Figure 4.12). However, there is a considerable interest in Java-based relational gateways at present. From a practical standpoint, relational gateways are typical SQL gateways that have a Web front end. For this reason, we will present a technical discussion of relational gateways in the next chapter, because that chapter is devoted to distributed data access and SQL middleware.

Figure 4.12 CGI Gateway for Relational Database Access

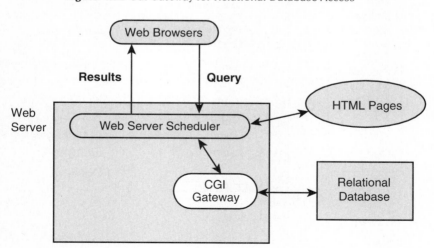

4.10.3 Web Access to Legacy Information

Before considering Web access to legacy information, let us briefly review how any new application accesses legacy information. After this, we will add the Web access considerations.

Middleware for legacy data access, also known as ***surround technologies*** and ***mediators***, is commercially available from a diverse array of vendors, with different capabilities and price ranges. At the highest level, this middleware can be categorized as (see Figure 4.13):

- Data gateways that directly access the legacy data (e.g., issue SQL calls)
- Procedure (function) gateways that invoke a procedure (function) of the legacy application (e.g., invoke an IMS procedure)
- Screen scrapers that access the legacy presentation services (e.g., 3270 terminal emulation)

Surround technologies/mediators can provide different level of support for access to one or more legacy applications. We will discuss these surround technologies and mediators technologies in Chapter 8.

Figure 4.13 Legacy Data Access from Web

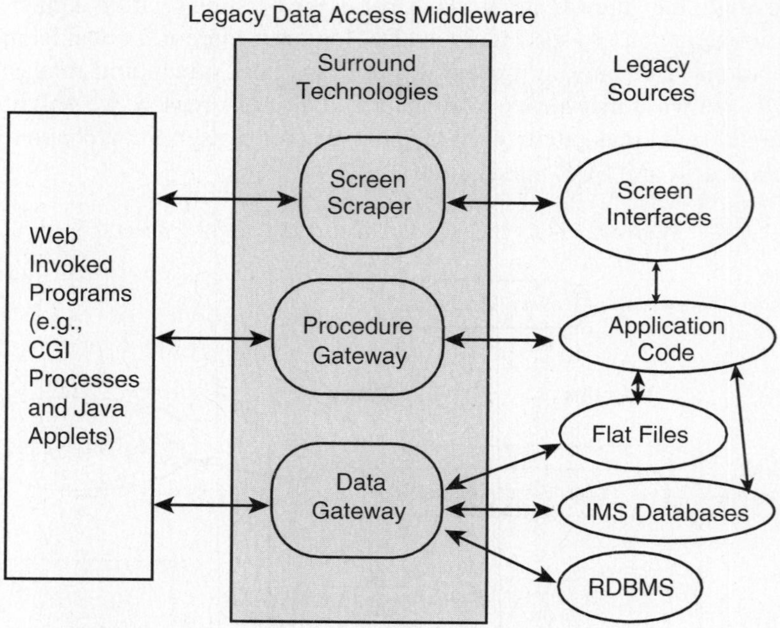

Legacy Data Access Middleware

Now, let us look at Web access to legacy information. Simply stated, Web browsers can invoke, through appropriate Web gateways, the mediators that access legacy information. For example, a CGI gateway program can invoke a screen scraper, data gateway, or procedure gateway.

Conceptually, Web browser can be used to integrate the corporate information that contains HTML documents, relational databases, and legacy information sources. A common technique is to use an object wrapper that can be invoked from a CGI gateway (see Figure 4.14). In addition to access from Web server CGI gateways, the object wrapper can also be invoked from Java applets residing in the Web browser (see Figure 4.14). In this case, the object wrapper is called from the CGI gateway as well as the Web browsers. The object wrapper is invoked from different programs by using a single OO API. It accesses the appropriate surround technologies. We will discuss object wrappers in more detail in Chapter 8.

Figure 4.14 Integrated Access through Web

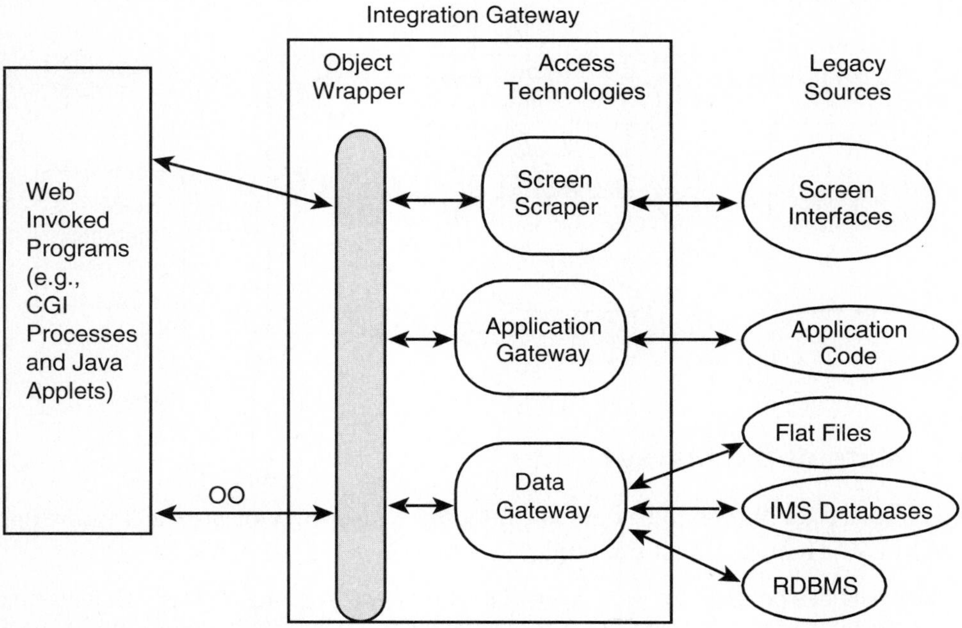

Most of the work in providing Web-based integrated access through object wrappers is not state-of-the-market at the time of this writing. However, some products are beginning to appear. An example is WebObjects from NeXT Corporation. WebObjects provides an application-development environment on the Web server side by allowing application developers to define new objects that can be accessed by Web browsers. An interesting feature of WebObjects is that it includes a set of adapters that can be used to access a variety of databases and legacy systems (see Figure 4.15). Additional information about WebObjects can be found in *http://www.next.com*.

Figure 4.15 NeXT's WebObjects

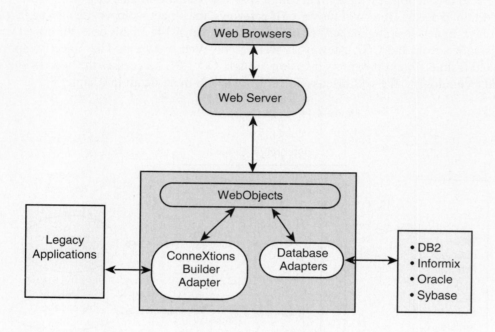

4.11   State of the Market

The marketplace for Web middleware is exploding with a bevy of products from suppliers large and small. Here is a small sampling.

- Netscape has developed a wide range of Web products (e.g., the Netscape Commerce server for electronic commerce, FastTrack to support Java and Java Script, SuiteSpot for enterprise Intranets, and LiveWire Pro to support Java development. See the Netscape home page for more information.

- Microsoft has unveiled the Microsoft Internet Strategy, which includes an Internet Information Server (an HTTP server in Windows NT environment), an Internet Explorer (a Web browser), an Internet Assistant for MS Word Windows96 (an HTML editor for MS Word), a Media server (video and audio server with support for HTTP), a Merchant Server (an Internet server for electronic commerce), and many others (e.g., ActiveX for merging Web with distributed objects).

- Sun has announced several products around Java (this includes support for distributed Java that could go across firewalls). In addition, Java-compliant Web browsers are becoming available.

- A large number of gateways are becoming available to provide Web access to relational databases. For a sampling of products, just search the Internet by using "relational gateway" as a search parameter on a search engine of your choice (e.g., Alta Vista or Yahoo).

Many Web gateways at present are intended for database-centric applications. Two major challenges exist. First, the document-centric applications (e.g., browsing through large number of documents stored in different formats) need to be addressed. For example, you should not have to convert the documents to HTML before you can access them over the Internet. The Bellcore Adapt/X Harness provides this capability (see the sidebar "Bellcore's Adapt/X Harness Software"). Second, the document-centric applications need to be integrated with the database-centric applications. This is a current area of work in Adapt/X Harness.

Integrating Documents with Databases:
Bellcore Adapt/X Harness Software

The Bellcore Adapt/X Harness software information-integration platform allows the users to encapsulate existing documents of various types (e.g., MS-Word, Framemaker, HTML, C code, text, spreadsheets) and provides access through a single consistent interface based on Web browsers. The users do not need to convert the documents to HTML format. In addition, Adapt/X Harness supports standard indexing tools (e.g., WAIS and Glimpse) for improved search capabilities. Adapt/X Harness is aimed at providing rapid access to huge amounts of heterogeneous information without any relocation, restructuring, or reformatting of data.

The Adapt/X Harness information-integration platform offers largely automatic generation of Adapt/X Harness repositories that, in turn, provide a unified view and access to large-scale distributed information. This is achieved by encapsulating information sources (documents, database tables, spreadsheets, messages, source code, etc.) with object-oriented encapsulators. These "Harness encapsulator objects" also store meta information (i.e., information about information encapsulated) and necessary indexing information for rapid query processing. Both meta information and index information are automatically extracted using information type-specific extractor programs. The Adapt/X Harness tool suite provides access to the original information sources from Mosaic and other Hypertext Transfer Protocol (HTTP)-compliant browsers through an HTTP gateway. These tools provide advanced search and browsing capabilities without imposing constraints on information suppliers or creators.

The current area of work in Adapt/X Harness includes integration of corporate databases (relational, nonrelational) and legacy applications with document-centric applications.

4.12   State of the Art: Integrating Web with Objects and AI

Many interesting areas of Web-related research are emerging such as integrating the Web with distributed objects, seamless integration of Web with corporate information, and the use of intelligent agents in Internet.

Integration of the Web with distributed objects is an area of particular interest. Although we will discuss distributed objects and CORBA[9] in a later chapter (Chapter 7), we can discuss the principal ideas here. The basic idea is to use Web interfaces to invoke objects that may be located anywhere in the network. This effort is intended to significantly improve the capabilities of middleware for Web applications. The following two prototypes at ANSA (http://www.ansa.co.uk) are attempting to address this important area:

- ANSAWEB integrates CORBA with Web by providing HTML interfaces to CORBA objects—HTML forms to invoke operations, and HTML pages to view results.

- JADE allows Java applets to issue CORBA calls. The Java applets behave as CORBA clients that interact with remote objects over the ORB.

An important landmark in this area was the combined Object Management Group (OMG) and World Wide Web Consortium Conference held in June 1996.

Seamless integration of corporate information (e.g., relational databases, IMS databases, indexed files, Cobol subroutines, 3270 terminal sessions, or a combination thereof) through the Web is a challenging task. This requires translation of requests and data between host applications, synchronization of updates between the host applications, and support of intelligent features such as distributed query processing and distributed transaction processing. The core issues in developing such technologies are not Web dependent. In fact, research in developing integration gateways for legacy applications was reported before the Web became popular [Weiderhold 1992, Brodie 1993]. We will discuss legacy integration gateways in detail in Chapter 8 and revisit this issue at that time. However, the Web has pressed the issue of integrating documents (HTML as well as non-HTML) with the traditional corporate information sources such as relational databases, IMS databases, and indexed files. More research is needed in this area.

Intelligent agents (IAs) provide an interesting area of research to use artificial intelligence in Internet and WWW. Intelligent agents, also known as Virtual Agents and Knowbots, are intelligent software entities that simulate the behavior of "capable" human agents such as an experienced travel agent or an insurance agent. In particular, IAs are capable of autonomous goal-oriented behavior in a heterogeneous computing environment. An example of an IA is a software entity that extracts, organizes and presents information on a given topic (e.g.,

---

9. CORBA, discussed in Chapter 7, is a specification developed by the Object Management Group (OMG) for distributed objects.

Intranets). Another example is an intelligent agent that makes travel arrangements (e.g., make reservations, purchase tickets) for a trip within time and money constraints.

IAs have many potential applications in Internet because of the large volume of information that needs to be organized and presented in a wide variety of ways. Many research prototypes at present are directed toward making the Internet intelligent by using IAs. Examples of the research projects are the Internet Softbot at the University of Washington that roams around Internet collecting information, Infosleuth at MCC that combines Web with OO and AI, and enabling electronic commerce between a large number of DOD participants. A good source of information for IAs in Internet is the *IEEE Expert,* August 1995 Special Issue on Intelligent Internet Services (this issue also contains a large number of references on this topic).

4.13   Summary

The "middleware" for the World Wide Web at the time of this writing consists of many low-level components such as Web browsers, HTTP, HTML, and home-grown CGI gateways. With time it is expected that many off-the shelf gateways will become commercially available. In particular, the Web gateways for relational database access are already becoming available. The key challenge is to develop middleware that can provide seamless and integrated access to structured (i.e., databases) as well as semistructured (e.g., documents) data for decision support as well as operational support applications.

4.14   Case Study: Intranet and Web for XYZCorp

The company is planning to develop a corporate "Intranet" that will serve the Web users within this organization. In particular, a "Web site subnet" is planned that will house the Web sites for internal and external use. For this Intranet effort, you need to:

- Show a "Web site subnet" that will house all the Web sites (the main server(s), backups, etc.).
- Show the Web sites. You can assume that two sites will be enough initially. ✓
- Show the rough outline of the home page (an HTML layout will be great).
- Show how you will provide access to the Web sites from the outside partners. List the alternatives and make a choice based on trade-offs. ✓

Hints about the Case Study

A possible XYZCorp Intranet with a "Web site subnet" that houses the two Web servers is shown in Figure 4.16. Access to the Web sites from the outside partners is accomplished by using the public Internet (at present, Web browsers do not run over SNA).

Figure 4.16 Proposed Intranet

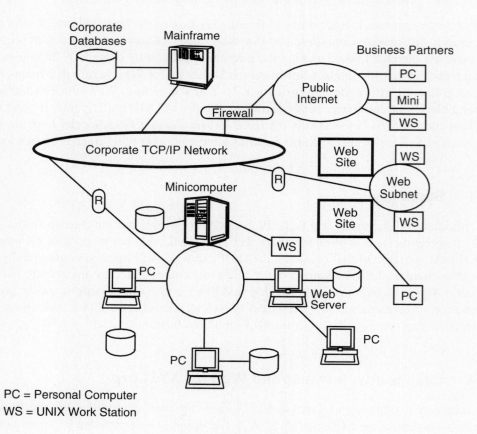

PC = Personal Computer
WS = UNIX Work Station

Figure 4.17 shows a more detailed view of the Web site subnet with the protocol stack at the client site and the various servers.

4.15 Problems and Exercises

1. Choose an industrial Web site and analyze it in detail in terms of its Web site, unique features, ease of use, etc.

2. Compare and contrast HTTP with RPC. Can HTTP be used instead of RPC?

3. What are the rewards and risks of using Java in the Internet?

4. Choose and analyze one Web gateway in detail.

5. Compare and contrast Java-based gateways to CGI-based gateways.

Figure 4.17 Web Site Subnet

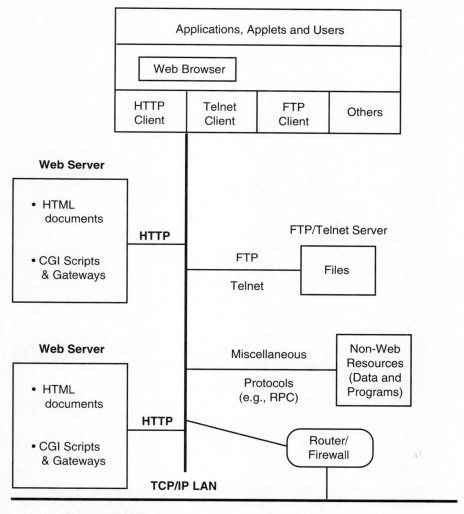

4.16   Additional Information

The best source for additional information about the Web is the Web itself. You can easily access a great deal of information by using Web surfing tools such as Yahoo. Many of these tools are currently integrated with browsers (for example, Netscape browser has a search button that automatically invokes Yahoo). For people who only like to read paper documents, many good books on the Internet and World Wide Web are available from bookstores such as Barnes & Noble and Dalton (you can find many racks of books devoted to these topics). Examples of books are Hahn [1996], Hoff [1996], Graham [1996], Chandler [1995], and December [1995]. In addition, trade magazines such as *Web Week* and *Internet Advisor* are good sources of information.

A Few Useful Home Pages

http://info.cern.ch/hypertext/WWW/Protocols/HTTP/HTTP2.html - T. Berners-Lee (1994), "HTTP: A Protocol for Networked Information" CERN, IEFT Internet Draft, original version 1991.

http://info.cern.ch/hypertext/WWW/MarkUp/HTML.html - T. Berners-Lee (1994), "Hypertext Markup Language (HTML)," version 1.2, IEFT Internet Draft.

http://hoohoo.ncsa.uiuc.edu/cgi/ - R. McCool (1993) "The Common Gateway Interface," NCSA, University of Illinois at Urbana-Champaign, updated 1994.

http://www.elsevier.nl/cgi-bin/WWW94link/01/overview - D. Eichmann, T. McGregor, D. Danley (1994), "Integrating Structured Databases into the Web: The MORE System," *Proc. of the First International Conference on the World Wide Web, CERN, Geneva, Switzerland.*

htttp://www1.cern.ch/PapersWWW94/cvarel.ps - C. Varela, C. Hayes (1994), "Zelig: Schema-Based Generation of Soft WWW Database Applications," *Proc. of the First International Conference on the World Wide Web, CERN, Geneva, Switzerland.*

http://www.ncsa.uiuc.edu:80/SDG/People/jason/pub/gsql/starthere.html - J. Ng (1993), "GSQL: A Mosaic-SQL Gateway," NCSA, University of Illinois at Urbana-Champaign.

http://dozer.us.oracle.com:8080/ - Home Page for the Oracle World Wide Web Interface Kit.

http://info.cern.ch/hypertext/WWW/Addressing/URL/Overview.html - T. Berners-Lee (1994), "Uniform Resource Locators," IEFT Internet Draft.

http://home.netscape.com/home/welcome.html - Home Page for Netscape Communications Corp.

4.17   References

Barron, B., Ellsworth, J., and Savetz, K., eds., *Internet Unleashed,* 2d ed., Sams Net Book, 1995.

Berghel, H., "The Client's Side of the World Wide Web," *Communications of the ACM,* January 1996, pp. 30–40.

Berners-Lee, T., and Cailliau, R., "World Wide Web," *Computing in High Energy Physics 92,* Anney, France, 1992.

Berners-Lee, T., Cailliau, R., Pellow, N., and Secret, A. "The World Wide Web Initiative," *Proc. INET '93,* Internet Society, San Francisco, 1993.

Berners-Lee, T., and Connolly, D., "Hypertext Markup Language 2.0," RFC 1866, IETF, November 1995.

Bickell, R., "Building Intranets," *Internet World,* pp. 72–75.

Bjorn, M., "A WWW Gateway for Interactive Relational Database Management," Doctoral Program of Socio-Economic Planning, 1-1-1 Tennodai, Tsukuba, Ibaraki 305, Japan, 1995.

Brodie, M. L., and Stonebroker, M., "DARWIN: On the Incremental Migration of Legacy Information Systems," Technical Memorandum, Electronics Research Laboratory, College of Engineering, University of California, Berkeley, March 1993.

Cassidy, P., "Wholesale Success on the Web,' *Datamation,* June 15, 1995, pp. 47–60.

Chadwick, D., "A Method for Collecting Case Study Information via the Internet," *IEEE Network,* March/April 1996, pp. 36–38.

Chandler, D., *Running a Perfect Web,* Que Books, 1995.

Comer, D., *Internetworking with TCP/IP: Principles, Protocols, Architectures,* Prentice Hall, 1988.

Comer, D., *Internetworking with TCP/IP,* 2 vols., Prentice Hall, 1991.

December, J., and Randall, N., *The World Wide Web Unleashed,* Sams Net Book, 2d ed., 1995.

Gibson, W., *Neuromancer,* Ace Books, New York, 1984.

Graham, I., *HTML Source Book,* 2d ed., Wiley, 1996.

Hahn, H., *Internet: Complete Reference,* 2d ed., 1996.

Halasz, F. and Schwarz, M., "The Dexter Hypertext Reference Model," *Communications of the ACM,* Vol. 37, No. 2, (1994).

Hoff, A., et al., *Hooked on Java; Creating Hot Web Sites with Java Applets,* Addison-Wesley, 1996.

Kador, J., "The Ultimate Middleware," *Byte Magazine,* April 1996, pp. 79–84.

Nesbitt, K., "Simplify Web Database Access withh SI," *Internet Advisor,* Premiere Issue, January 1996, pp. 18–21.

Perrochon, L., "W3 Middleware: Notions and Concepts," Institut für Informationssysteme, ETH Zurich, Switzerland, 1995.

Philips, P., "Brewing Up Applications with Java," *Internet Advisor,* Premiere Issue, January 1996, pp. 14–17.

Schulzrinne, H., "World Wide Web: Whence, Whither, What Next?" *IEEE Network,* March/April 1996, pp. 10–18.

Semich, W., "The Long View from Microsoft: Component DBMSs," *Datamation,* August 1, 1994, pp. 40–45.

Stevens, R., *UNIX Network Programming,* Prentice Hall, 1990.

Tittel, E., and James, S., *HTML for Dummies,* IDG Books, 1995.

Varhol, P., and McCarthy, V., "Who Wins the Web Server Shootout," *Datamation,* April 1, 1996, pp. 48–53.

Webref: http://info.cern.ch/hypertext/WWW/Protocols/HTTP/HTTP2.html - T. Berners-Lee (1994), "HTTP: A Protocol for Networked Information," CERN, IEFT Internet Draft, original version 1991.

Wiederhold, G., "Mediators in the Architecture of Future Information Systems," *IEEE Computer,* 25:38–49, 1992.

5

Distributed-Data Managers and SQL Middleware

197

5.1   Introduction

Enterprise data of contemporary organizations resides on a variety of platforms (PCs, UNIX, MVS) in a variety of formats (relational databases, IMS databases, object-oriented databases, indexed files, text files, spreadsheets, or CAD diagrams). In addition, this data is inherently distributed (exists at more than one computer) in the following two manners:

- Distribution without replication (e.g., price information in Chicago, customer information in New York)

- Distribution with replication (e.g., price information in Chicago as well as in New York)

Access to distributed data, in whatever format it exists, wherever it exists, and in whatever number of copies it exists, is the focus of this chapter. In particular, we concentrate on the C/S technologies that *retrieve* mission-critical distributed data (with and without replication). The complex issue of transaction processing (TP) for updating distributed/replicated/ interrelated data will be addressed in the next chapter. In other words, this chapter scrutinizes the "TP-less" aspects of distributed data in client/server environments. Data updates, if any, are assumed to be simple enough to be manageable by a database manager (i.e., no TP monitor is needed).

Middleware that manages the access to distributed and replicated data adds another layer on top of the basic C/S protocols (e.g., RPCs, RDAs, and MOMs). A highly desirable goal of this middleware is data-location transparency (access and manipulation of remotely located data without knowing the location of the data in the network). We term this C/S middleware as ***distributed-data management system (DDMS)***: a collection of software modules which manage access to all distributed data (files plus databases).

A wide range of technical and administrative challenges span data distribution and replication. A great deal of research literature has been published to address these challenges since the mid 1970s. We will primarily attempt to answer the following questions in this chapter:

- What are the main concepts, issues, and approaches in data distribution and replication (Section 5.2)?

- What are the characteristics of distributed file processing (Section 5.3)?

- How can remote databases be accessed, and how does the plethora of SQL middleware address these issues (Section 5.4)?

- What is distributed-query processing (e.g., distributed joins) and how does it relate to heterogeneous and federated databases (Section 5.5)?

- What is the role of the emerging standards such as ODBC, DRDA, and ISO RDA in accessing distributed data (Section 5.6)?

- How can the relational databases be accessed from the Web (Section 5.7)?

- What are the examples of SQL middleware and what is the role of SQL gateways (Section 5.8)?

This chapter assumes that the reader has some understanding of database concepts and SQL. The reader not familiar with database concepts should review a suitable book on database technologies (e.g., the latest edition of *An Introduction to Database Systems,* Chris Date, Addison Wesley) before proceeding. The sidebar "Relational Databases and SQL: The World's Shortest Tutorial" can be used for a very quick overview.

Key Points

- The simple SQL middleware is very commonly used to provide access to a single SQL server.

- Distributed-query processing middleware is used to join tables located on different sites.

- Heterogeneous and federated databases in network environments is an area of considerable academic research.

- The Open Database Connectivity (ODBC) API from Microsoft has become a de facto API standard for accessing remotely located heterogeneous databases.

- Distributed Relational Database Architecture (DRDA) from IBM has become a de facto exchange protocol standard for accessing DB2 data.

- The ISO RDA is still evolving.

- Many SQL gateways are commercially available from database vendors such as Oracle, Sybase, and Informix.

- A great deal of recent research is currently focusing on object-oriented multi-database systems, where multiple, autonomous and, possibly, heterogeneous databases are accessed through an OO "view integrator."

Relational Databases and SQL: The World's Shortest Tutorial

The relational database technology views all data as tables; all database operations are on tables; and all outputs produced are also tables. A relational database is a collection of tables. Each table has rows and columns. For example, an EMPLOYEE table may have columns such as employee-name, employee-address, and employee-salary; and each employee is represented as a row in the relational table.

Structured Query Language (SQL) is the standard query language for relational databases. SQL provides interactive ad hoc queries as well as program interfaces in C, Cobol, Fortran, ADA, PL1, and many other programming languages. The SQL language consists of a set of facilities for defining, manipulating, and controlling data in a relational database.

The following two SQL statements illustrate how you create a parts and a customers table:

```
CREATE TABLE parts (part_no char(4), part_name char(5)), price
numeric(5));
CREATE TABLE customers (cust_name char(30) , address char(30), cust_id
char(12), part_no char(4)).;
```

The main power of SQL lies in its data-manipulation facilities. There are four basic SQL operations: SELECT, UPDATE, INSERT, and DELETE. All data retrievals are invoked by a SELECT command, which has the following general syntax:

```
SELECT <a1,a2,a3,...,an> FROM <t1,t2,...,tm> WHERE <conditions>;
```

where a1, a2, ..., an are the attributes; t1, t2, ..., tm, are the tables; and the conditions, if specified, indicate the retrieval criteria. For example, "SELECT part_no, part_name FROM parts WHERE price > 100" would display the part_no and part_name from the parts table for prices more than 100. The joins are also performed by the select statement. The statement "SELECT part_no, part-price, cust_name FROM parts, customers WHERE customer.part_no = parts_no" lists the customer names who have ordered certain parts (the two tables, parts and customer, are "joined" on a common field).

SQL data-modification statements allow insertion, deletion, and update of data in tables through the INSERT, DELETE, and UPDATE statements. Here are some (hopefully) self-explanatory examples:

```
INSERT INTO parts(part_no, part_name, price) (xy22, rods, 100);
DELETE FROM parts where part_no = xy20;
UPDATE PARTS set price=120 where part_no=xy22;
```

5.2   Concepts and Definitions

5.2.1   Review of Basic Concepts

Figure 5.1 shows a typical centralized computing environment with interrelationships between the following components:

- A **query** is a sequence of operations (data access and manipulation commands) which display information but do not transform the state of a system. In essence, queries are read-only. Queries can be simple (e.g., display all customers living in Michigan) or complex (e.g., queries involving joins between 10 or more relational tables).

- A **data file**, also called a "flat file," consists of a collection of records such as text statements, C program statements, or graphic data. A *file manager* coordinates the access to files from the applications.

- Conceptually, a **database** is a collection of logical data items in which the granularity of a logical data item may be a file, a record, or an arbitrary collection of data fields.

- A **database management system (DBMS),** or a **database manager,** is a software package which manages the access and manipulation of a database by multiple users. Specifically, a DBMS (1) manages logical representations of data, (2) manages concurrent access to data by multiple users, and (3) enforces security and integrity controls of a database. Relational database technologies and SQL, a common database access language, are very popular at present. The sidebar "Relational Databases and SQL: The World's Shortest Tutorial" gives a very brief overview.

- The terms **node, computing site,** or **site** refer to a computer in an enterprise that participates in enterprise data management (e.g., to store data, to serve as an end-user access point).

We will refer to the shaded components collectively as a local data management system (LDMS), or a local data manager, that is responsible for access, manipulation, and modification of all data in response to application requests.

Figure 5.1 Local Data Management System

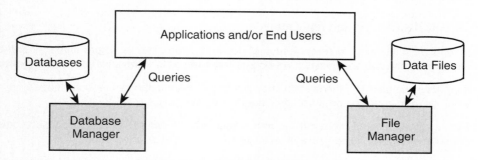

Legend: Shaded boxes are components of a Local Data Manager.

5.2.2   Distributed-Data Access Management: What and Why

Distributed data is data, in whatever format it exists, that resides on more than one computer. For example, in a medium-sized organization, customer information may be stored in an MVS DB2 database, price information may exist in a UNIX Sybase database, inventory information may reside on a Novell LAN SQL server, and sales information may be dispersed among many desktop spreadsheets. Basically, data can be distributed in the following two manners:

- *Distribution without replication (unique data distribution).* In this case only one copy of data D exists in an enterprise. For example, customer information exists only on MVS-DB2, and price information exists only on a UNIX Sybase database server.

- *Distribution with replication (duplicate distribution).* In this case, more than one copy of data D exists in an enterprise. For example, customer information may exist on MVS-DB2 as well as on a regional UNIX Sybase database server.

Figure 5.2 shows a conceptual view of distributed data in an enterprise where the customer information is uniquely assigned while the parts information is partially replicated.

Data distribution and replication offers many advantages, but at the same time it introduces several unique technical as well as management challenges. For example, data distribution and replication:

- Allows users to exercise control over their own data while allowing others to share some of the data from other sites

- Saves communication costs by providing data at the sites where it is most frequently accessed

- Improves the reliability and availability of a system by providing alternate sites from which the information can be accessed

- Increases the capacity of a system by increasing the number of sites where the data can be located

- Improves the performance of a system by allowing local access to frequently used data

However, data distribution and replication:

- Introduces challenging technical issues of update synchronization, failure handling, and distributed transaction management (we will discuss these issues in more detail later in the next chapter)

- Increases complexity of the system and introduces several management challenges, especially when geographical and organizational boundaries are crossed

- Makes central control more difficult and raises several security issues, because a data item stored at a remote site can always be accessed by the users at the remote site

- Makes performance evaluation difficult, because a process running at one node may impact the entire network

- May deteriorate the overall performance of older, private wide-area networks (WANs) which suffer from the "SUE" factor (slow, unreliable, expensive), as pointed out by Gray [1987]. Conceptually, this problem should not exist in the emerging broadband wide-area networks that operate at 100 Mbps or higher (however, these networks could get congested, too).

Figure 5.2 Example of Distributed Data

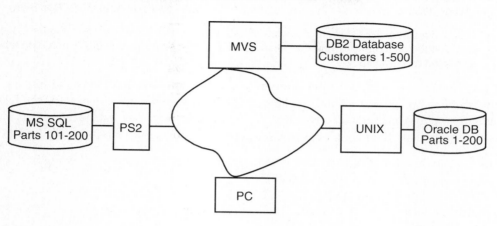

Owing to these advantages and disadvantages, data distribution and replication trade-offs must be evaluated carefully. These trade-offs are discussed in the chapter "Data Architectures" in Umar [1997]. Ideally, ***distributed-data management middleware*** should be available that maximizes the benefits of distributed data and hides the underlying complexities from the end users.

5.2.3   Distributed-Data Model [1]

We introduce the notion of a *distributed-data management system (DDMS)* that is responsible for managing all data (files plus databases) and the operations on the data in a distributed computing environment. A DDMS can be viewed as a C/S middleware which attempts to provide transparent access and manipulation of distributed data. To provide these functionalities, several other services are also needed—security services, directory/naming services, etc. Figure 5.3 shows a conceptual view of DDMS and depicts how a DDMS interacts with and interrelates to the following components:

- Applications which generate the queries (e.g., SQL statements)

- Local-data management systems (LDMSs) which perform the functions described in Section 5.2.1

- Remote communication interfaces (RCIs) for sending/receiving messages across a network. RCI may use the basic C/S protocols such as remote-procedure call (RPC), remote-data access, and message-oriented middleware (MOM); or network-dependent protocols such as LU6.2, TCP/IP Sockets, NetBIOS, etc.

---

1. The terms "data manager" and "data management system" are synonyms.

- Network services, which transport the messages between sites. The network services may include, if needed, network gateways to convert network protocols (e.g., TCP/IP to SNA).

- Global directories that show the location of data in the network. For example, Figure 5.3 shows two global directories showing that data table d1 is located on computer C1 and data table d2 is located on computer C2.

Although not shown in Figure 5.3, the modules can be configured as clients and servers. The client modules can exist at locations where an application generates a query and the DDMS plans and monitors its execution. The server modules exist where the data resides. This model does not imply that all computers must have both client and server modules of a DDMS.

Let us explain this conceptual model through an example. Consider the following SQL query issued by a user application at computer C1:

```
SELECT name, address FROM Employees
```

Figure 5.3 A Conceptual Model of Distributed-Data Management

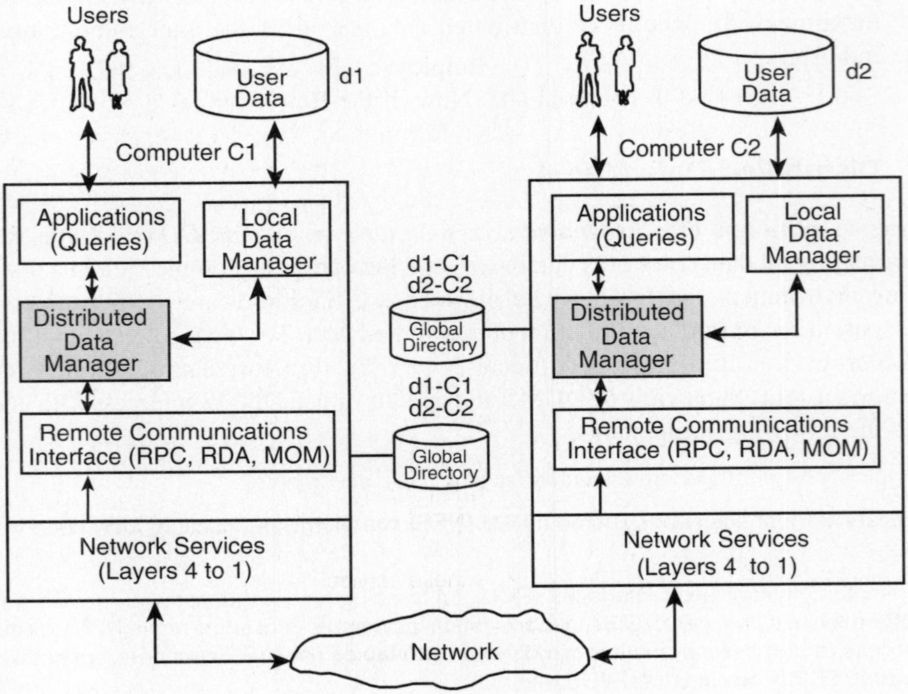

Let us assume that the Employees table is located on computer C1. In this case, DDMS will parse this query, determine that the data is at C1, and pass the query to the LDMS at C1. However, if the Employees table is at computer C2, then the following steps will take place:

- DDMS will determine, through a global directory, that the Employees table is on C2.

- DDMS will issue requests for read locks on the Employee names and addresses at C2 (this step is bypassed if locking is not supported).

- The RCI module will prepare and send the SELECT statement over to C2 by using whatever C/S protocols are used between C1 and C2.

- The RCI at C2 will receive the message and send it to the DDMS modules at C2 (DDMS operates as a server scheduler in this case).

- DDMS will pass this request to the LDMS at C2 for actual execution of the request.

- DDMS will receive the results of the SELECT statement and pass them to RCI for sending back to C1.

- RCI will send the results of the SELECT statement back to C1.

- RCI at C1 will receive the results and pass them back to DDMS.

- DDMS will free locks held, if any, and send the response back to the application to display the results to the user.

Let us now consider a few variations. If the Employee table exists at more than one computer, then the DDMS must find the optimal site. Now, if the Employee table exists at more than one computer but it needs to be updated (say through an SQL Update statement), then the DDMS module will invoke a commit protocol (we will discuss this in next chapter) to guarantee the integrity of the database. Next, if the databases at C1 and C2 are from two different vendors (e.g., Sybase on C1 and IBM DB2 on C2), then the DDMS modules at the two nodes may perform the functions of a "database gateway" by translating the data-exchange protocols between the two vendors (this gateway may reside on a separate machine; Sybase Omni Server Gateway is such an example).

It can be seen that a DDMS may perform a diverse array of functions. Conceptually, a DDMS supports the following major functionalities:

- ***Distributed-file processing (DFP)*** is responsible for providing transparent access, manipulation, and administration (e.g., security) of data files that are located at different computers in the network. The SUN Network File System (NFS) can be viewed as a distributed-file processor. Owing to their focus on flat files, these services are relatively restricted (they cannot be used to handle databases). Section 5.3 describes these services in more detail.

- ***Single-site remote-database access (SRDA)*** provides access to a single remote database per query. Thus if a join is needed between two tables at two different sites, then the user will have to issue two queries, bring the results back to the local site, and then perform the join at himself/herself. We will describe SRDA in Section 5.4.

- **Distributed-query processing (DQP)** provides transparent read-access, manipulation, and administration of remotely located databases in a network. This is an extension of SRDA, where a user issues one query that can join tables located at multiple sites. For example, an Oracle Distributed Database Manager allows a user to query relational databases located at many computers as if they were at one computer. These services cannot be used to update databases. We will describe this topic in more detail in Section 5.4.

These three functionalities, described in more detail in the next three sections, form a good foundation to categorize and study the wide range of functionalities needed to manage distributed and replicated data in modern enterprises. For example, a sophisticated DDMS may provide all three types of functionalities, while a limited DDMS may only support SRDA. In addition, some DDMS may provide facilities for distributed-transaction processing (see next chapter). We will use these functionalities to develop a DDMS evaluation model in the next chapter. It should be emphasized that DDMS is a vendor-independent conceptual model for discussing the issues and approaches in data distribution, replication, and transaction management. Different vendor products can fit in this framework depending on the services provided by them.

It is important to distinguish between a distributed database and a distributed-database manager. A *distributed database* contains information (data), usually business aware, that is physically distributed to several computers, and a *distributed-database manager* is a software package (or a collection of software modules) which manages distributed databases. An example of a distributed database is a customer database which may be partitioned and distributed to several regional customer sites for quick access. The same customer information may appear at more than one site (duplicated). An example of a distributed-database manager would be an Oracle DDBM which gives an end user a single-database view of the customer database.

5.3   Distributed-File Processing

Distributed-file processing (DFP) allows transparent access and manipulation of remotely located files. DFP supports open, read, write, and close of remotely located files from application programs and/or human users. It may provide access to a complete file or to a portion of a file across a network.Typically, DFP services include

- Selection and deselection of a remotely located file for access
- Creation and deletion of remote files
- Read and modification of remote-file data and attributes (e.g., change a file's name)
- Control of the concurrency functions through locking/unlocking
- Security from unauthorized access

These services are provided by *distributed-file managers*. Most of the distributed-file managers are currently implemented as client/server systems in which each requester of a remote-file service acts as a client which routes the file-access commands to appropriate file servers in the network. File servers allow several users to share the same files, provide backup/recovery of shared files, allow users and the files to move around the network without retraining, and support diskless workstations. Available distributed-file managers support the above stated functionalities in varying degrees. Examples of the distributed-file managers are the Open Software Foundation's Distributed File Server, IBM's Distributed Data Manager, the Andrews File System developed at Carnegie-Mellon, and SUN's NFS (Network File System). An extensive discussion of file-server issues can be found in Svobodova [1984].

5.4 Single-Site Remote-Database Access: The Simple SQL Middleware

5.4.1 Overview

Figure 5.4 illustrates the single-site remote-database access (SRDA) capability of a DDMS. As stated previously, this capability allows clients to access remote databases that are dispersed among several sites of an enterprise. However, each client call, typically an SQL query, can refer to database tables at only one site.[2] This capability provides several benefits to the end users—the databases can be moved around but the users can still access them remotely. For example, a corporate data warehouse can be housed on an Oracle server and be accessed by a variety of SQL-based decision-support clients throughout an organization.

Figure 5.4 Single-Site Remote-Data Access

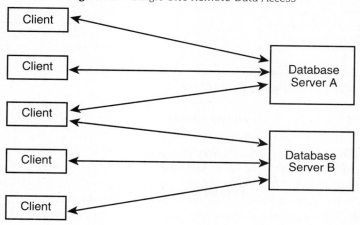

Note: Each arrow represents a single SQL statement

---

2. We should note that there may be multiple DBMSs on each site. To keep our focus on distributed systems, we will concentrate on one DBMS per site .

The SRDA capability is currently available as "simple SQL middleware" from a wide range of DBMS vendors (see Figure 5.5). SQL requests are sent to the remotely located SQL servers, and the results are sent back to the clients. A large number of vendors (e.g., IBM, Informix, Sybase, Oracle, Microsoft, Gupta) are developing SQL database servers which basically handle SQL calls from clients (e.g., applications and/or off-the-shelf end-user tools) and respond with results. SQL-based C/S environments are naturally biased toward the remote-data access (RDA) paradigm discussed in the previous chapter. Let us go through the key components of this environment.

Figure 5.5 A Typical SQL-Based C/S Environment

CLI = Command Level Interface

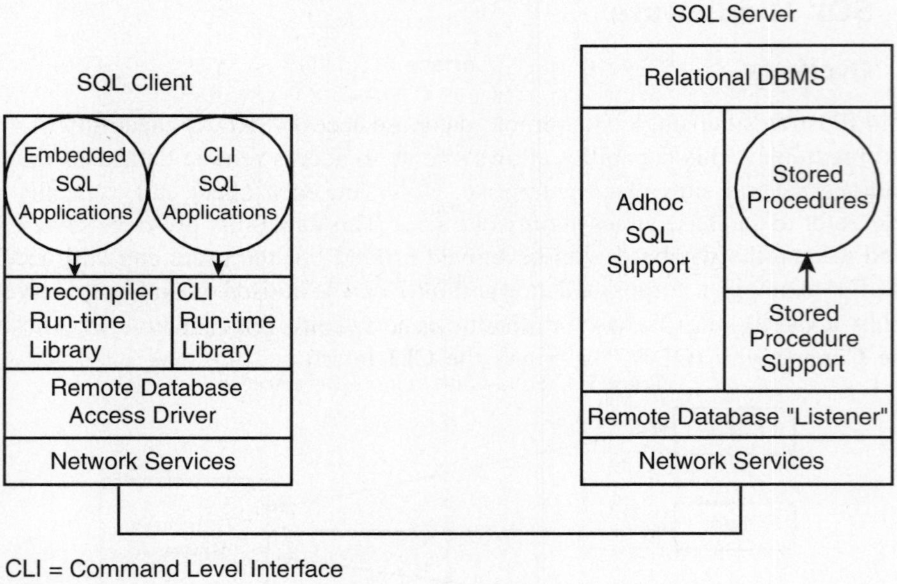

5.4.2 SQL Clients

SQL clients issue SQL calls to remote databases from applications, or end-user tools. SQL, with variations, is the standard query language for relational databases and is also being used to access nonrelational databases. The client does not need to know the data types, lengths, and location. It just sends requests to retrieve the data by issuing an SQL query. For example, a client may issue the following SQL queries:

```
SELECT NAME FROM EMPLOYEE;
SELECT NAME, ADDRESS, SALARY, AGE FROM EMPLOYEE WHERE AGE > 30;
SELECT NAME, SALARY, AGE FROM EMPLOYEE WHERE AGE > 30 AND SALARY
  < 30000;
```

The first SQL query lists names of all employees; the second query lists names, addresses, salaries, and ages of all employees older than 30; the third query is similar to the second query with an additional condition (salary < 30000). Note that the client request does not specify where the employee data table is located. This information is supplied by the remote-database access middleware. Each client machine loads the middleware "data drivers" that accept the SQL calls from users or application programs and converts these calls into network messages that are sent to the server. This middleware also receives, interprets, and converts the responses from the server.

The SQL client has many choices, such as the following:

- **Dynamic versus static SQL**. Dynamic SQL allows an application to generate and execute SQL statements at run time while static SQL is precompiled.

- **Embedded versus command-level interface SQL.** Embedded SQL allows programmers to place SQL statements into programs written in a standard programming language such as C or Cobol (these languages are known as *host languages)*. Call-level interface (CLI) for SQL consists of a library of function calls that support SQL. To submit an SQL request, the SQL statement is placed in a text buffer and the buffer is passed as a parameter in a function call. The error information is indicated by status codes.

- **Single statement versus stored procedures.** A client can send individual SQL statements or invoke a stored procedure (a set of SQL statements) at the server.

SQL middleware may support one or more of these options. For example, Microsoft's Open Database Connectivity (ODBC) supports the CLI interface, Informix supports embedded SQL, and most support stored procedures.

5.4.3   SQL Servers

The SQL servers, also known as SQL engines, provide secured access to shared relational databases. These servers provide varying degrees of SQL support (the SQL extensions for stored procedures, triggers, rules, etc.). Many SQL servers behave as front ends to nonrelational databases (i.e., they receive SQL calls and convert them to whatever form is needed by using database drivers). Examples are the Information Builder's EDA/SQL and Ingres SQL-object server. The SQL servers have the following architectures:

- Process-per-client, i.e., each database client has its own process address space.This architecture is used by Informix and DB2/2.

- Multithreaded architecture; i.e., all clients share the same address space. This architecture is used by Sybase and Microsoft SQL Server.

- Hybrids, i.e., clients are given separate processes in the beginning but are multithreaded after execution starts. This approach is used in Oracle Server 7.

Most of the SQL servers have been developed since the late 1980s. Initially developed for LANs, this technology has now moved to MVS mainframes, especially with the availability of MVS-DB2 servers from IBM, Sybase, Oracle, Ingres, and Gupta [Ricciuti 1994]. Although most SQL servers are designed around the standard bare-bone SQL, each vendor adds extensions to SQL to enhance performance. It is the responsibility of the user to choose extensions judiciously. An SQL server maintains a dictionary which describes the format and relationships of data (data schema). Some servers provide dictionary facilities for valid data ranges and display formats (YYMMDD or YY/MM/DD). Owing to their origin, many SQL servers have been installed on LAN server machines. For example, Novell Netware allows servers to be installed as network-loadable modules (NLMs) on Netware servers. NLMs run as independent tasks under Netware core operating system. This has allowed several third-party vendors to develop SQL servers as Netware NLMs.

Different vendors support SQL servers on different computing systems, which use different communication protocols with different performance and dictionary options. At present, most SQL servers run on PS/2s, UNIX workstations, minicomputers, and mainframes inter-connected over Token Ring, Ethernet, and packet-switching networks operating under TCP/IP, SNA, and Novell Netware. They also provide different levels of scalability (i.e., as an application grows, a user can migrate from a small server to a large server). Examples of some of the available SQL servers are Sybase SQL Servers, Information Builder's EDA/SQL Servers, IBM OS/2 Extended Edition Database Manager, Oracle Server for OS/2, Microsoft SQL Server, Gupta Technologies' SQLBase Server, and Novell Netware SQL. Of special industrial interest is the Microsoft "Component SQL Servers" strategy for selling 300 million SQL Servers for NT at very cheap prices [Semich 1994]. The implication of this strategy, if successful, is that inexpensive SQL servers could be used to run copying machines, cash registers, and office phones (the 300-million-server strategy is based on the assumption that the 11 million places of business in the United States will each buy about 30 inexpensive SQL servers. For a detailed discussion and analysis of these servers, the reader is referred to Semich [1994], Ricciuti [1991], and Vinzant [1990].

Many database servers may cooperate with each other to manage distributed databases. These servers, called distributed-database servers, coordinate the client access to individual database servers, where each database server manages its own database. We will discuss this topic in more detail in Section 5.5.2.

5.5   Distributed-Query Processing and Distributed-Database Servers

5.5.1   Overview

Distributed-query processing (DQP) is concerned with providing transparent and simultaneous read access to several databases that are located on, perhaps, dissimilar computer systems. For example, an end user can issue a single SQL query that joins three different tables (customer table, inventory table, and price table) located on three different computers (see Figure 5.6). The specific functions provided by a distributed-query processor are as follows (these functions can be used as a checklist to compare, evaluate, and select different DQP products):

- ***Schema integration.*** A global schema is created which represents an enterprisewide view of data and is the basis for providing transparent access to data located at different sites, perhaps in different formats. A schema shows a view of data. In a DDBM, the data may be viewed at different levels, leading to the following levels of schema (see Figure 5.7):
    - The local internal schema represents the physical data organization at each machine.
    - The local conceptual schema shows the data model at each site. This schema shows a logical view of data and is also referred to as the logical data model.
    - The external schema shows the user view of the data.
    - The global conceptual schema shows an enterprisewide view of the data. This schema is also referred to as the corporate logical data model.

Figure 5.6 Distributed-Query Processing

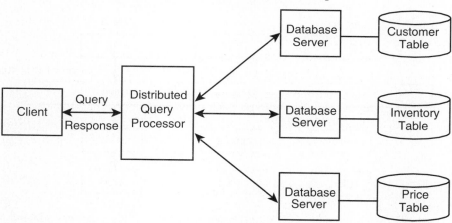

- ***Location transparency.*** This provides transparency of data access and manipulation. The database queries do not have to indicate where the databases are located. The queries are decomposed and routed to appropriate locations. If more than one copy of data exists, then an appropriate copy is accessed. This allows the databases to be allocated at different sites and moved around if needed.

- ***Table fragmentation.*** A relational table can be fragmented (partitioned) and dispersed over the network without any changes to the end-user queries. For example, a customer table T can be partitioned into fragments t1, t2, t3, say, by customer numbers (e.g., t1 has customer 1 to 100, t2 has customers 101 to 200, etc.). Let us assume that t1 was allocated to computer c1, t2 to c2, and t3 to c3. To retrieve information about customer number 135, the end user would issue the following SQL query:

```
SELECT * FROM T WHERE cust_number = 135;
```

Note that the SQL query is against table T and not the fragment t2.

- **Multiple-vendor support.** Distributed-query processing should allow a user to transparently access information from multiple vendor DBMSs (i.e., a user should be able to join tables supported by Informix, Oracle, Sybase, and DB2). This capability is currently available from some vendors (e.g., Sybase Omni Server allows joins between Sybase, DB2, and other non-Sybase tables; Oracle provides similar capabilities).

- **Multiple-data format support.** Distributed-query processing should allow users to perform SQL joins between relational as well as nonrelational data sources. Many products such as IBM's InfoHub and Information Builder's EDA/SQL provide these capabilities.

- **Multiple-site support.** Of course, distributed-query processing should allow queries to data at different sites (this is the whole idea!).

- **Administration facilities.** These facilities are needed to enforce global security and provide audit trails.

Figure 5.7 Views (Schemas) in a Distributed Database

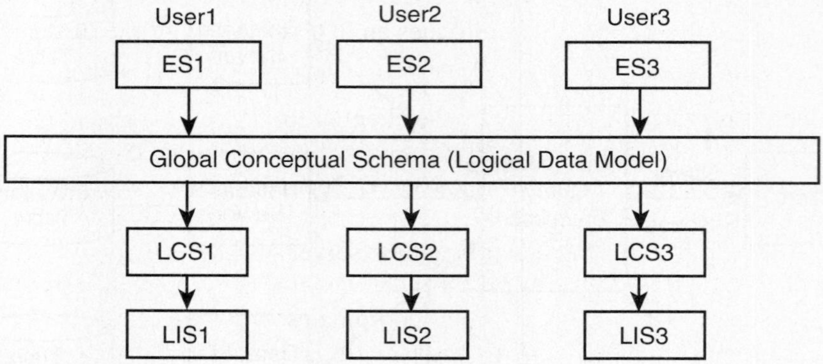

Legend:
LIS = local internal schema, LCS = local conceptual schema, ES = external schema

Distributed-query processing support for all these functions is a nontrivial task. It is not easy to provide schema integration and perform efficient joins between data stored in multiple formats, at multiple sites, under the control of multiple vendor products. We are postponing the technical discussion of these issues, along with other knotty issues of distributed-transaction processing, to the next chapter, where we will consolidate all the issues of distributed-data retrieval and update into a single framework. A brief overview of supporting heterogeneous databases, called multidatabases, is given in the next section.

5.5.2   Distributed-Database Servers

The reader should recall that distributed-query processing is a functional component of a distributed-data manager and not a standalone product. Owing to the popularity of SQL database servers, **distributed-database servers** are becoming available to provide distributed-query processing, among other functionalities. A distributed-database server coordinates the client access to individual database servers, where each SQL database server manages its own database over a LAN or WAN. Consider an example where three databases d1, d2, and d3 reside on three different computers under the control of three database servers (see Figure 5.8[3]). Let us assume that a client needs to access information from the three databases. The client can issue the following three queries (D1, D2, D3 are data tables in databases d1, d2, d3, respectively):

```
SELECT a1, a2 FROM D1
SELECT a3, a4 FROM D2
SELECT a5, a6 FROM D3
```

Each query will be sent to the appropriate server. After these queries have been executed, the client application may need to combine the responses for further analysis. Let us assume that the client application needs to join (combine) the attributes a1, a2, ..., a6 from the three databases based on a given criteria. The client issues an SQL statement of the form:

```
SELECT a1, a2,..., a6 FROM D1, D2, D3 where [condition]
```

In this case, who is responsible for the join: the client or the servers? If one of the three database servers is responsible for coordinating the join between databases residing under the control of several database servers, then this server becomes a distributed-database server. The responsibilities of a distributed-database server become more complex if some data is duplicated across servers. The distributed-database server must essentially address all of the aforementioned distributed-query processing functions. It is possible to designate one server to be the distributed-database server, which coordinates the interactions between several "local" database servers (see Figure 5.8). In this case, a three-tiered client-server system is used. The user-application client issues the database calls, which are received by the distributed-database server. This server now acts as a client and issues requests to the standalone database servers.

How are distributed-database servers different from distributed-file servers such as NFS? Basically a database server has all the capabilities of a database manager, while a file server has the capabilities of a file manager. Specifically, NFS cannot be used for accessing databases, and NFS does not include any capabilities to manage duplicate data. Database servers are more complex than file servers because they include typical DBMS capabilities, such as maintaining the integrity of a database under security and consistency constraints, different views of data, record level locking, automatic logging, failure handling, and data dictionary.

---

3. The diagrams of a distributed-query processor and a distributed-database server are similar for the purpose of illustration.

Figure 5.8 Distributed-Database Server

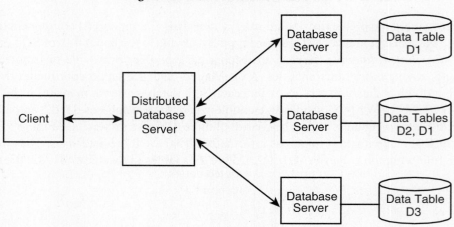

5.5.3 Heterogeneous and Federated Databases in Network Environments

Heterogeneous databases are of great practical significance because many real-life distributed databases are from different vendors, using different data models, and are accessed through a combination of LAN database servers and WAN database servers. For example, a general problem for a DDBM is to provide transparent access to the business, engineering, and manufacturing databases that may be stored on UNIX workstations, MVS mainframes, or PCs and that are interconnected through LANs, TCP/IP and SNA networks. Database heterogeneity in a network can take several forms [Thomas 1990]:

- Databases may support heterogeneous data models (hierarchical, network, relational, or object oriented).

- Different query languages may be used in different databases (for example, different languages are used to access different object-oriented databases).

- Database management systems may be provided by different vendors.

- Computing platforms may be heterogeneous (microcomputer databases, minicomputer databases, and mainframe databases) operating under heterogeneous operating systems (UNIX, MVS, OS/2).

- Networks may be heterogeneous (LANs, WANs, TCP/IP, SNA, DECNET, OSI).

Several terms are used to refer to heterogeneous database systems. For example, heterogeneous databases are also known as *multidatabase systems (MDBS)*. An MDBS is an integrated distributed-database system consisting of autonomous DBMS's which existed before integration [Soparkar 1991]. Yet another term used in this context is *federated data-*

base system. An FDBS is a collection of cooperating but autonomous component databases which are controlled and coordinated by a federated database management system (FDBMS) [Sheth 1990]. A significant aspect of FDBMS is that the component databases may operate independently as heterogeneous systems but still participate in a federation. We will use the terms heterogeneous, multidatabase and federated database synonymously, although some differences exist (see Litwin [1990] for discussion).

The basic feature that distinguishes these databases from the distributed databases discussed in the previous section is the notion of transparency. It is almost impossible to provide complete transparency in heterogeneous databases, because a complete global data schema is difficult to create. In fact, the lack of global data schema is the main distinguishing feature between heterogeneous and integrated distributed databases. Figure 5.9 shows three different levels of heterogeneity from a global-schema point of view.

In the integrated distributed-database approach shown in Figure 5.9(a), a single global schema is created which is used by all users and application programs. The local internal schema represents the physical data organization at each machine, the local conceptual schema shows the logical view of data at each site, and the external schema shows the user view of the data. As discussed previously, the global conceptual schema (GCS) shows an enterprisewide view of the data. A global schema is created from the local schemas of the local databases. In practice, global conceptual schemas in large organizations are rarely achieved, owing to social and organizational factors.

In a heterogeneous distributed DBMS, a partial global schema may exist or it may not exist at all. Figure 5.9(b) shows the partial-global-schema approach in which only portions of the local conceptual schemas are used to build the GCS. The GCS may contain, for example, the most frequently accessed corporate data. The users can issue queries either through their own external schema or through the GCS. This approach is used in the "tightly coupled" federated databases [Sheth 1990]. The FDBMS may provide an integrated view of the data included in the GCS, where the user issues a query in a "global" query language against the partial GCS. An extensive discussion about the FDBMSs has been given by Sheth [1990]. Requirements and objectives of FDBMSs are discussed by Kamel [1992].

Figure 5.9(c) represents the approach in which no global conceptual schema exists. This approach is used in some multidatabase systems with very diverse schema (the "loosely coupled" FDBMS). One approach to accessing such databases is a special multidatabase language which allows users to define and manipulate autonomous databases. This language has special capabilities, such as logical database names for queries, same definitions in different schema, etc. [Litwin 1990]. A DDBM may loosely couple the component DBMSs by providing a user interface which presents the various databases in a menu created directly from the local schemas (GCS is not used). The user may have to know the name, the local schema, and the query language of the individual databases.

Figure 5.9 Different Models of Distributed Databases

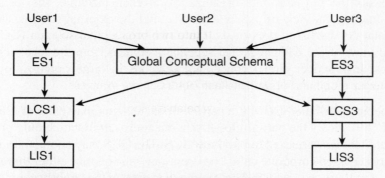

(a) Integrated Distributed-Database Management

(b) Heterogeneous DDBMS (Partial Global Schema)

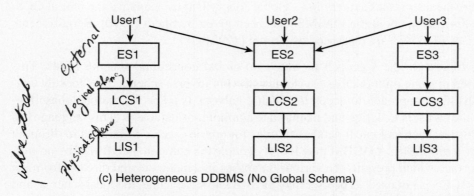

(c) Heterogeneous DDBMS (No Global Schema)

LIS = local internal schema, LCS = local conceptual schema, ES = external schema

Most DBMS vendors at present provide some heterogeneous DDBMS capabilities. For example, Sybase as well as Oracle allow remote joins between DB2 and Sybase and Oracle, respectively. Most of the research at present is focusing on object orientation in multidatabase systems (see Section 5.10).Early examples of heterogeneous DBMS products are reviewed in detail by Gomer Thomas [1990]. Many survey and research papers describe the heterogeneous distributed databases. Perhaps the most detailed material can be found in *ACM Computing Surveys,* Special Issues on Heterogeneous Distributed Databases, June 1995 and September 1990; and the *IEEE Computer,* Special Issue on Heterogeneous Distributed Databases, December 1991. Detailed state-of-the-market analysis can be found in, for example, the Forrestor Research reports, "Weaving the Data Web" (October 1994) and "Living with Fractured Data" (February 1994). Additional information can be found in Bukhres [1996], Pitoura [1995], Quinlan [1993], and Olson [1993].

5.6 Remote-Data Standards: ODBC, DRDA, and ISO RDA

The standards for distributed-data access fall into two broad categories:

- API standards, which allow client applications to be portable from one vendor environment to another vendor environment as long as the same API is used. Microsoft ODBC, and SQL Access Group's Command Level Interface (SAG CLI) are examples.

- Exchange protocol standards, which allow database servers from vendor X to interoperate with clients from vendor Y. ISO Remote Database Access (RDA) and IBM's DRDA are examples.

We will first review the ODBC API because of its current popularity. However, other emerging APIs are also discussed. We then focus our attention on two main exchange protocols: IBM's DRDA and ISO's RDA.

5.6.1 Open Database Connectivity (ODBC) API

Open Database Connectivity (ODBC) is an application-programming interface (API) introduced by Microsoft that allows applications to access databases by using SQL. The ODBC API is a call level interface (CLI). By using this API, a single application on a desktop can access remote databases under different DBMSs (e.g., Informix, Oracle, Sybase). The same ODBC calls are used by application programmers to access relational databases of different vendors. ODBC relies on data drivers to convert the ODBC calls to different database formats. For example, Informix data drivers are needed to access Informix databases; Oracle data drivers are needed to access Oracle databases, etc.

The Role of Standards: An Example

Some time ago, I was involved in a client/server project that required installation of a server on an IBM mainframe from a vendor (let us call it vendor X). The server was to allow access to DB2 and other databases from different clients. After a great deal of effort, we had the server installed and were happy to notice that we could support client programs, from the same vendor, on several workstations around the enterprise.

During the pilot project, we found that another group had purchased a C/S application from a vendor (let us call it vendor Y) that also needed access to the same DB2 database. It seemed simple enough: let us allow the vendor Y application to access the DB2 database through our server from vendor X.

The answer was a disappointing "No way."

The reason was that the vendor X server did not understand the client calls from vendor Y. Both of these vendors supported proprietary exchange protocols.

Our choice was to install yet another server on the mainframe from server Y (you can end up with 10 servers for 10 types of clients).

Ideally, open exchange protocols could allow server X to be called from clients from vendors Y, Z, or others. This could happen if, for example, all vendors used ISO RDA, or something similar.

What about open APIs? They would allow a client to use the same call to access different databases. For example, a client program that retrieves data from vendor X server could also retrieve data from vendor Y server without any reprogramming. Microsoft's ODBC has become a default open API standard.

A programmer can create an ODBC application without knowing the target DBMS. Users can add drivers to the application after it has been compiled and shipped. At development time, the application developer only needs to know the ODBC calls to connect to a database, execute SQL statements, and retrieve results.

Figure 5.10 shows a sample ODBC environment in which an ODBC application accesses an Oracle and an Informix database. The main components of ODBC are:

- **Application**. Performs business-aware logic and calls ODBC functions to submit SQL statements and retrieve results. Specifically, it performs the following tasks:
  - Requests a connection with a target database. It specifies the target-database name and any additional information needed to make the connection.
  - Passes one or more SQL statements by placing the SQL text string in a buffer.
  - Processes the produced result set or error conditions.
  - Ends each transaction with a commit or rollback.
  - Terminates the connection after the target database is not needed.

Figure 5.10 A Sample ODBC C/S Environment

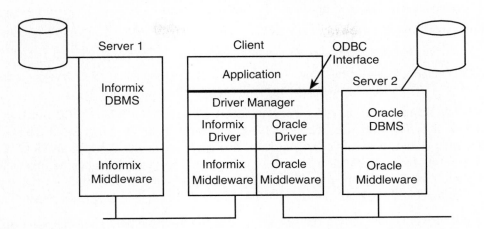

- **Driver manager.** Loads drivers on an as-needed basis for the applications. The driver manager, provided by Microsoft, is a dynamically linked library (DLL). In addition to loading drivers dynamically, the driver manager also performs the following:
  - Maps a target-database name to a specific Driver DLL
  - Processes several ODBC initialization calls
  - Validates the parameters and sequences of ODBC calls

- **Driver.** Processes the ODBC function calls, modifies them to the target-database format (if needed), submits the SQL statements to the target database, receives the results, and presents the results to the application. Drivers are DLLs that implement the ODBC function calls. If an application needs to access three target databases from three vendors, then three drivers will be needed. Different vendors, such as Q&E, have developed ODBC drivers for different target databases. In many cases, "ODBC driver suites" are available for accessing dozens of target databases.

- **Target-database middleware.** Includes the database needed by the applications and the associated middleware. This database may be located on the same machine as the application or may be located on a remote machine connected through a network. Depending on the availability of drivers, ODBC can support a very wide range of target databases from different DBMS suppliers. Examples of the supported drivers are for Oracle, Informix, and Sybase databases.

ODBC uses the SQL syntax based on the X/Open and SQL Access Group (SAG) SQL CAE specification. The ODBC API provides the following:

- A library of ODBC function calls that allow an application to connect to a target database, execute SQL statements, and retrieve results.

- Facilities to explicitly include strings containing SQL statements in source code or to construct strings at run time.

- A standard set of error codes.

- A standard way to connect and log on to a target database.

- A standard representation for data types.

- Use of same object code to access different DBMSs.

- Conformance levels for the ODBC API and ODBC SQL to assure that driver developers do support the same ODBC function calls and SQL statements.

To send an SQL statement, the statement is included as an argument in an ODBC function call. This statement is independent of the target DBMS (the drivers do the conversion). The ODBC function calls include a set of "core" functions that are based on the X/Open and SAG Command Level Interface specification. Extended functions are provided to support additional functionality such as asynchronous processing and scrollable cursors. Examples of the typical ODBC function calls are SQLConnect, SQLExecute, SQLFetch, and SQLDisconnect.

The ODBC drivers come in two flavors: single tier and multiple tier. The single-tier drivers include ODBC processing plus the data-access software, while the multiple-tiered drivers separate the data-access code from ODBC processing (see Figure 5.11). In essence, the multitiered drivers facilitate the use of a data-access gateway and are more suitable for large-scale implementations (all data-access code is localized in a data-access gateway). For example, the ODBC-to-DB2 gateway shown in Figure 5.11 uses a multitiered driver.

Figure 5.11 ODBC in Enterprise Networks

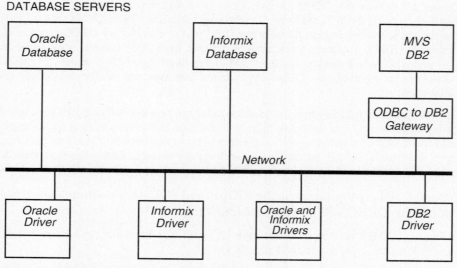

5.6.2   Other SQL API Standards

SQL APIs fall into two general categories: embedded SQL and command-level interface (CLI). Embedded SQL is an ISO SQL-92 defined standard for embedding SQL statements "as is" in programming languages such as COBOL, C, FORTRAN, PL/1, and Pascal. Embedded SQL has many benefits (e.g., the developers can test SQL interactively and then embed it in a program) but has limitations in C/S environments. For example, it is tough to target a client program to a database at run time (embedded SQL requires that the target databases be known and available at program-development time), and embedded SQL precompilers are commonly tied to vendor database products.

Most of the SQL middleware at present is oriented toward CLI APIs. The "mother" of all CLIs is the SQL Access Group's CLI (SAG CLI). Microsoft's ODBC is the best-known child of SAG CLI (ODBC uses 24 SAG CLI calls) and is becoming a de facto CLI API. However, many other CLI APIs are also "trying to find themselves." Here is a brief overview of a few:

- **IDAPI (Integrated Database Application Programming Interface) CLI.** This CLI was introduced in 1993 by Borland, IBM, Novell, and Word Perfect. IDAPI uses SAG CLI but also adds a record-at-a-time navigational CLI initiated by Borland. IDAPI is expected to interoperate with ODBC and is claimed to be more efficient than ODBC. However, IDAPI drivers are virtually nonexistent at the time of this writing.

- **X/Open CLI.** This CLI is the initial SAG CLI and is intended to differentiate SAG CLI from the ODBC and IDAPI.

- **Oracle Glue.** Oracle intends to use this glue for applications to work with everything —ODBC, IDAPI, Sybase DB LIB, Apple's DAL, dBase, Paradox, and email. Oracle has made the specification of Oracle Glue public and is planning to make this Glue available on Windows, Windows NT, OS/2, and UNIX (Glue will also access mainframe databases through the Oracle DRDA Gateway).

5.6.3   Distributed Relational Database Architecture (DRDA): An Exchange Protocol

Distributed Relational Database Architecture (DRDA) is IBM's long-term strategy for distributed relational databases in an enterprise. Introduced as part of the IBM System Application Architecture (SAA), it specifies the *exchange protocols and conventions* that govern the interactions between database clients and a database server. DRDA protocols and conventions support the following four levels of database transactions:

- *Remote request:* one SQL command to one remote database
- *Remote unit of work:* many SQL commands to one remote database (this represents a remote transaction)
- *Distributed unit of work:* many SQL commands to many databases but each command accesses one database (i.e., no joins across databases)
- *Distributed request:* many SQL commands to many databases but each command can access multiple databases (i.e., joins across databases and sites are allowed)

DRDA supports dynamic as well as static SQL. In addition, later versions of DRDA have included support for stored procedures. It requires APPC (APPC can run over SNA or TCP/IP networks by using the IBM AnyNet feature). DRDA supports two-phase commit (see the next chapter), provides common diagnostic return codes (based on SQL-92 standard), and recommends the use of SAA SQL (a subset of SQL-92).

Initially positioned as the standard for all relational databases, DRDA has become a de facto standard for access to DB2 databases. By using DRDA, clients from different DBMS vendors can access DB2 data. For example, applications and tools that operate on Informix, Oracle, and Sybase databases can access DB2 data. The access to DB2 is provided through a DRDA gateway that translates the different DBMS protocols to the DRDA exchange protocol (see Figure 5.12). DRDA gateways are commercially available from a multitude of vendors such as Informix, Oracle, and Sybase-Microdecisions. The main advantage of DRDA is that it does not require any server on the mainframe to access DB2 data (DRDA support is included as part of DB2). This saves money (most vendor-provided gateways for MVS DB2 cost from $100K to $399K) and staff effort to install multiple gateways.

Figure 5.12 Conceptual View of a DRDA Gateway

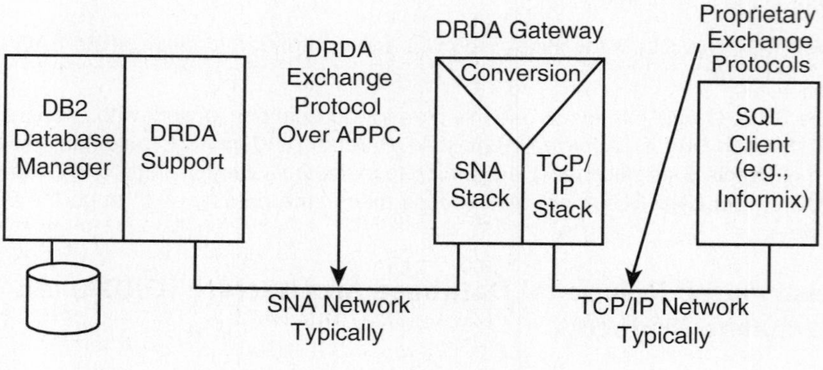

A more general use of DRDA in an enterprise is shown in Figure 5.13. This configuration can be used as follows:

- The Informix clients can access Informix databases or DB2 databases. The access to DB2 is provided by an Informix-DRDA gateway developed by Informix. The Informix-DRDA gateway resides on a standalone computer (typically a UNIX machine). As shown in Figure 5.13, the Informix DRDA gateway is installed on a TCP/IP LAN and is connected to the mainframe through an SNA WAN.

- The Oracle clients can access Oracle databases or DB2 databases. The access to DB2 is provided by an Oracle-DRDA gateway developed by Oracle. The Oracle-DRDA gateway resides on a standalone computer (PS2 or a UNIX machine). As shown in Figure 5.13, the Oracle DRDA gateway is installed on a TCP/IP WAN and is connected to the mainframe through a Token Ring LAN.

Figure 5.13 Example of DRDA

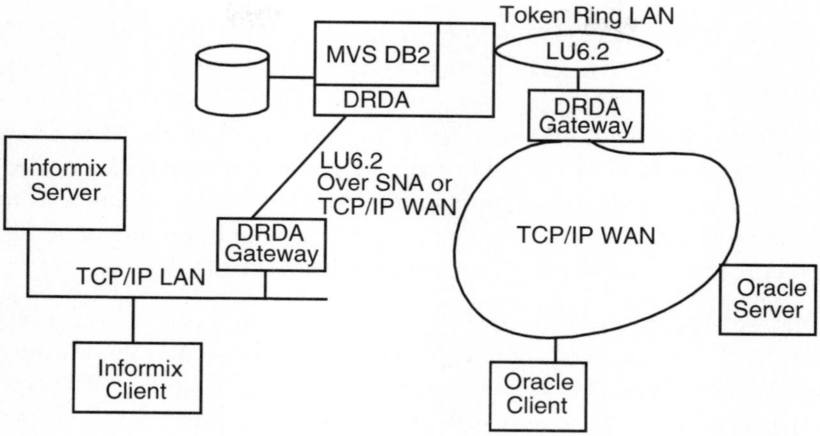

The Informix, Oracle, or other DRDA gateways provide many more interconnectivity choices than can be discussed here.

DRDA consists of the following building blocks:

- Distributed Data Management (describes the commands for passing requests and replies across systems)

- SNA LU6.2 communication protocol between data clients and servers

- Character Data Representation (describes how characters are recognized across systems)

- Formatted Data Object Content Architecture (specifies the way to describe transmitted data)

- SNA Management Services Architecture (MSA)

It is beyond the scope of this book to discuss these building blocks in detail. Details about DRDA can be found in IBM manuals such as *DRDA Connectivity Guide* (SC26-4783-00) and *DRDA Planning Guide* (SC26-4650).

5.6.4   ISO RDA

ISO Remote Database Access (RDA) is an ISO standard for "universally" accessing and manipulating remotely located databases. RDA provides capabilities for remotely

- Reading, inserting, updating, and deleting database records

- Searching or listing data located in databases

ISO RDA is developed on top of the ISO Reference Model stack. The SQL Access Group (SAG), in cooperation with X/Open, is trying to port ISO RDA over TCP/IP stack. At present, RDA functionality is equivalent to the SQL-92 (entry) standard. However, RDA is restricted to dynamic SQL, and no two-phase-commit support (these restrictions are expected to disappear in the future). RDA supports common error codes based on the SQL-92 return codes.

Not surprisingly, RDA supports a client/server model in which the application behaves as a client which issues requests to access remotely located databases. The database servers receive, parse, and execute the query (e.g., an SQL query), and send the results back to the client. Although the client and server can reside in the same machine, RDA was specifically defined to allow applications running in one vendor environment to access databases located in other vendor environments. It is important to note that the RDA standard is not intended to support distributed databases; thus, update synchronization is not supported. In the client's view, the server is just a centralized database located at a remote site.

The server may be implemented as a distributed database, but this is of no concern to the client. However, RDA does work in conjunction with ISO Transaction Processing (TP) which allows synchronization. The ISO TP standard is discussed in Chapter 6. The significance of RDA is that a user will be able to access RDA conformant remotely located databases from different vendors on different platforms. In this sense, RDA provides open access to databases located anywhere in the network. The RDA standard is divided into two parts: a Generic RDA standard which specifies the aspects common to all data models, and a set of Specialized standards for individual data models and languages. Currently, only SQL Specialization has been standardized. Thus the standard can be used for relational systems or systems which provide a relational interface. ASN.1 is used to specify the format of RDA data units. The client-server communication is established through the ISO Association Control Service Element (ACSE).

Should you use DRDA or RDA? Well, if your target databases are DB2, then DRDA seems to be the clear choice. However, if target databases are from other vendors, then DRDA does not help. Fortunately, many vendors have issued "statements of intent" to support RDA (most DBMS vendors are pledging to support DRDA and RDA). In practice, there are many DRDA gateways already in production use. When RDA becomes available, we will probably see the DRDA-to-RDA gateways (we are so lucky!). A comparison of ISO RDA, X/Open/SAG RDA, and DRDA can be found in Zimowski [1994].

5.7   Web Access to Relational Databases[4]

5.7.1   Overview

Web access to relational databases is provided through a *relational gateway* that translates the browser requests to SQL calls and then translates the query response to HTML pages.

---

4. This discussion assumes some knowledge of Web technology and Web gateways at the level presented in the previous chapter.

Since the first relational gateway was developed for Oracle databases at CERN in 1992, a large number have been announced from a variety of vendors. In essence, a relational gateway should support all functions typically provided by an RDBMS plus access from the Web. Specifically, the functional requirements should include the following:

- Ability to develop Web applications which access new or existing relational databases. This means that the application developers need support for:
    - Simple queries, repeated queries (intermediate results), nested queries
    - Automatic temporary saving of intermediate query results
    - Embedded SQL support
    - Stored-procedure invocation
    - Remote-procedure calls
- Ability for users to do ad hoc browsing and reporting (includes ad hoc, form-based SQL access)
- User-interface capability (i.e., display results in forms, produce pie charts and forms such as produced by report writers)
- Support for access and integration of results from multiple databases

Different approaches have been used to satisfy these requirements. The first gateway allowed a user to enter an SQL expression as a search text to a WWW-server. It formatted the results of the query and sent them back as plain text. Since then, considerable commercial activity has occurred in this field and many relational gateways have been configured and deployed on the WWW. Many gateways focus on retrieval of data using simple SELECT statements, while more sophisticated relational gateways have started to appear.

5.7.2   Technical and Architectural Considerations[5]

The key technical problem in designing relational gateways is that the interaction protocols in HTTP and in SQL are quite different (two other technical problems, repeated queries and timeouts, are discussed in sidebars). SQL is not limited to a single transaction when accessing a database. In a typical session with a DBMS, the user performs many SQL transactions. A typical SQL transaction allows for SQL statements a number of times before an eventual COMMIT statement is issued and the transaction is finished.

The most general role of the relational gateway program is to establish a connection between the client and the DBMS, so that information can be passed in both directions. When there is a mismatch between the HTTP interaction protocol and the SQL interaction

---

5. The technical discussion in this section is based on the analysis by Bjorn [1995].

protocol, the gateway also has to mediate between the protocols, so that consistency is maintained on both sides. In practice, the main purpose of relational gateways is to mediate between the two protocols.

Simple database gateway implementations use the single HTTP interaction (i.e., connection, request, response, close) for database access. This somewhat limits the exchanges with the DBMS. For example, no exchange with the user is allowed to continue a query based on intermediate results. A sophisticated relational gateway program, such as discussed by Bjorn [1995], can accept multiple users at the same time and maintain user integrity by managing a session number for each user. The session number is provided by the DBMS and is unique for each user. The connection between the server and the browser is broken several times, but each time it is reestablished. The session number, which is simply appended to the URL (along with the current page), allows the relational gateway to verify the user. Neither user name nor password is passed, so no additional security risk is involved. From a database point of view, sessions are not the same as transactions. For example, multiple transactions with the DBMS can occur in one session.

The relational gateways can be architected by using any of the Web gateway configurations mentioned in the previous chapter. In particular, relational gateway architectures can be categorized in terms of CGI gateways, server-side includes, dedicated gateways, and client-side (i.e. Java) gateways.

Technical Issue: Support for Repeated and Nested Queries

In a nested query, one (or more) SELECT statement(s) occur within another SELECT statement. It is not an easy task to build a GUI which handles nesting of SELECT statements. Many relational gateways do not support this approach. They allow the user to repeatedly query the database using intermediate results or combinations of intermediate results with other parts of the database. This is possible because all results of a SELECT statement produce a new table, which in turn can be queried, and so on. The use of repeated queries is an attempt to somewhat capture the power of nested queries while at the same time maintaining a simple and clean graphical user interface.

Nested versus repeated queries have performance trade-offs. Repeated queries introduce extra work to explicitly save the results of each SELECT statement into a view (or a new table if the DBMS does not support views). Most systems avoid this, because of the overhead involved. However, the intermediate saving is needed to ensure that results do not get lost when timeout errors occur. In other words, by providing necessary timeout error handling, you get a mechanism for providing repeated queries at no extra cost.

Technical Issue: Handling Timeouts

The timeout issues for each protocol must be dealt with. The HTTP timeout problem stems from limitations inherent to the HTTP protocol, whereas the SQL server timeout is a "garbage-cleaning" feature we must provide, since the user may not be online any longer to terminate his connection with the DBMS.

HTTP Timeout. The timeout period for the HTTP protocol depends on the settings for the WWW browser, but a timeout much longer than 1 minute destroys the illusion of interactivity which is very important to the Web users. This means that the relational gateway should contact the database and receive a reply which it can pass on to the server within that minute, or else there is no guarantee that a connection to the browser is still maintained between the browser and the WWW server. For simple queries, one minute is certainly sufficient, but as the complexity of the commands sent to the DBMS increases, as well as the number of simultaneous users, the likelihood that some tasks will not be accomplished within one minute increases drastically.

At the time when the query completes, two scenarios are possible:

- The connection to the browser has not timed out. In this case the result is passed back through the gateway to the user's Web browser screen.

- The connection to the browser has timed out. In this case the result may be made available in a temporary table, and all the user has to do is to go back to the previous screen of the browser and SELECT all columns of the temp table. If the user does not reconnect, the gateway may automatically finish the session with the DBMS.

To make sure that data can be returned in all circumstances, even when loads are very high, some relational gateways also offer the option of returning results by mail instead of on-screen.

SQL Server Connection Timeout. A relational gateway program, such as the one reported by Bjorn [1995], establishes and keeps a session with the DBMS independent of whether a user is currently connected to the WWW server or not. However, the gateway must have an ability to end the session, even if the user does not connect again. The relational gateway may allow the system administrator to set a connection timeout period. When the timeout occurs, the gateway ends the session with the DBMS. If, at that time, there is a temp table corresponding to the session, it will be erased. Eventual results may be emailed to the user before the session is terminated.

CGI gateways, the most popular relational gateway implementation choice, invoke relational database functionalities on the Web server. In many cases, these gateways present an HTML FORM to the user, the user fills the FORM, and this FORM invokes a CGI script which generates SQL and interfaces with the DBMS. The response from the DBMS is converted to HTML and returned to the Web browser. Basically a FORM contains some fields where the user enters data in a structured way, a button to submit the FORM (which simulates submitting a form to an office or similar in the real world), and a button to erase the user's input so that the FORM can be used again. The CGI gateways can be configured as:

- *CGI Executable:* A database application program is executed as a CGI executable itself, thereby forking the application process for every request.
- *Application Server:* A database application program runs as a daemon process. A CGI executable just dispatches the request rather than accessing the DBMS engine.

SSI gateways for relational databases are very rare at present. If the SSI security problems get solved and if SSI+ becomes more popular, then we may see the SSI gateways that use ODBC drivers. Recall that ODBC is one of the features of SSI+.

Proprietary servers are standalone servers that are dedicated to relational gateway functionality. These servers are dedicated to receiving SQL calls from a Web browser and sending the results back to the Web browsers. Many commercial relational gateways from database vendors fall into this category.

Client-side (Java) gateways allow access to SQL databases directly from the browser. The Java applet receives the user query and sends it to a remote database. In this case, the database gateway functionality runs on the client side. A standard called JDBC (Java Database Connectivity) is being developed to allow Java programs to issue calls to relational databases (see the sidebar "Java Database Connectivity (JDBC)."

5.7.3   Observations and Comments

It is possible to build very simple relational gateways by using HTML and HTTP. HTML is a powerful language for building platform-independent database interfaces, using mainly the FORM construct. However, the single-interaction nature of the HTTP protocol (i.e., each click on a hyperlink is treated as a standalone interaction) allows only for very simple database queries.

The fundamental problem with supporting SQL access from programs over the Web is that SQL is conversational (i.e., an SQL statement from a program returns a cursor that is used by programs to "fetch" different rows of the table that has been returned to the programs). Thus if a program requires multiple interactions within a transaction, then the Web gateways have to maintain cursor positions.

Many relational gateways use CGI to establish their own sessions with the database server and mediate between the single-interaction HTTP protocol and the protocol of the database server, which inherently support sequences of interactions.

Relational gateways should support insertion and deletion of tables and columns, addition and deletion of data, and simple as well as repeated queries. Furthermore, to ensure delivery of query results, temporary tables as well as a mail-reply option should be implemented. The gateway also should automatically log out users after a time period which can be specified by the system administrator. The user's password should be passed through the gateway only once, when the user logs in. However, since the password at that time is passed openly, some form of secure HTTP must be used; otherwise a security risk is incurred. Once the first connection has been established, only session numbers can be passed back and forth, and no additional security risk is incurred.

Java Database Connectivity (JDBC)

The Java Database Connectivity (JDBC) API was created by JavaSoft, a Sun Microsystems operating company, in an effort to develop Java applications for use with remote DBMSs. JDBC is based on the same Call Level Interface (CLI) that is used in ODBC. Thus if you know ODBC, learning JDBC should be a snap. JDBC implementations are native Java code, while ODBC implementations are C coded programs. Although a Java program can call C code which in turn can invoke ODBC API, a pure Java database driver promises improved performance and flexibility to the Java developer.

JDBC has been adopted by most major DBMS vendors, including Oracle, Informix, IBM, Imaginary, and Borland. JDBC drivers for some of these vendors' products are beginning to appear at the time of this writing. However, it will be a while before the number of JDBC drivers will match the ODBC drivers. Some vendors, such as Intersolv, are trying to bridge the initial gap between the existing ODBC drivers and the new JDBC specifications by introducing JDBC-ODBC bridges. Java applications can be written using the JDBC API, but the API calls are handled by the JDBC-ODBC bridge and converted into ODBC calls. The remote DBMS receives these calls through the readily available ODBC drivers and executes them accordingly. This approach, while acceptable as a transition vehicle, introduces additional layers with concomitant performance problems.

The JDBC API was officially released in June 1996 as version 1.0. To ensure that applications are portable between JDBC drivers, JavaSoft and Intersolv have jointly developed a JDBC compliance suite. Additional information about JDBC can be found through JavaSoft homepage (www.javasoft.com).

Relational gateways should allow the user to repeatedly query the database using intermediate results. This approach does not, however, capture the full expressional power of nested queries in SQL. More research should be devoted to developing more powerful HTML-pages for nested queries.

In addition, more work needs to be done on integration between HTML and various database call level interfaces. Performance measurements should be conducted in this area.

The relational gateways at present only allow for management of simple data types. A potential problem with HTML in its current incarnation is its one-way limitations in handling multimedia—the user can receive various forms of data, but the only user inputs allowed except for specifications of links are text based. If HTML is expected to be used as the sole interface for a multimedia database, it will need to be extended for the input of pictures, sound, etc., or retrieval of multimedia links specified as inputs through WWW browsers.

5.8   State of the Practice: Examples

A very large number of examples and case studies can be quoted that illustrate different aspects of distributed-data management and SQL middleware. Let us go through a few.

Figure 5.14 shows an example of Web access to heterogeneous relational databases through a CGI gateway. The CGI gateway invokes ODBC drivers to access Informix, Oracle, and Sybase databases. The main advantage of using ODBC in this case is that you can use one gateway to access these three types of databases. Otherwise, you will need one gateway for Oracle, one for Informix, and one for Sybase.

Figure 5.14 Web Access to Heterogeneous Relational Databases

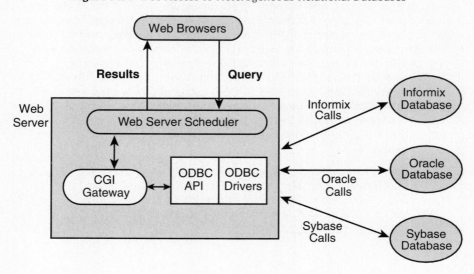

Figure 5.15 shows a general heterogeneous environment in which DB2, Oracle, and Informix databases exist. The Informix clients in the TCP/IP LAN can access Informix databases or DB2 databases (the access to DB2 is provided by an Informix-DRDA gateway developed by Informix). The Informix DRDA gateway is installed on a TCP/IP LAN and is connected to the mainframe through an SNA WAN. The ODBC client can also access the Informix and DB2 databases by using the ODBC drivers. What are the trade-offs between ODBC and "native" Informix clients in this configuration? Basically, ODBC adds overhead (ODBC drivers degrade performance) but it allows non-Informix (but ODBC-compliant) clients from any vendor to access Informix and DB2 databases. The ODBC clients in the TCP/IP WAN can access Oracle databases, Informix databases or DB2 databases (DB2 is accessed through a DRDA gateway). We can add Web-access considerations to this diagram by simply having a CGI gateway or a Java gateway that invokes any of the clients shown in the diagram.

Figure 5.15 Example of Heterogeneous Database Access

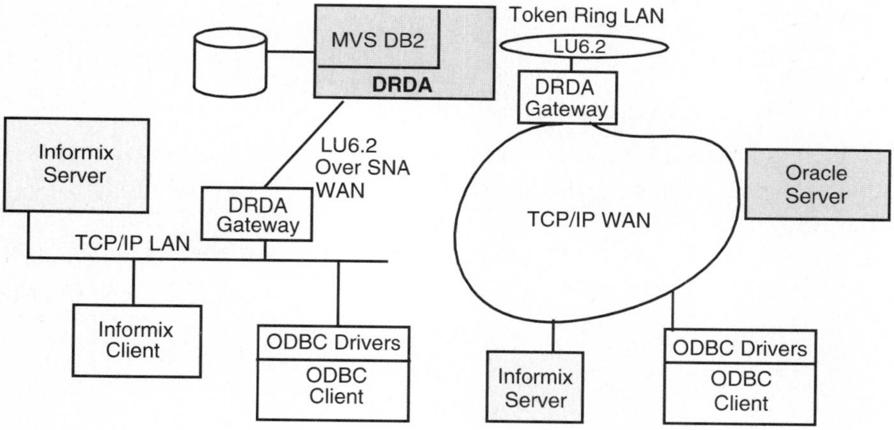

In many real-life systems, clients need to access mainframe IMS and DB2 databases. Figure 5.16 shows a typical example with some details. Let us work through the details from the client side. First, SQL clients can access DB2 databases through DRDA as discussed previously, or through proprietary gateways such as EDA/SQL. The IMS databases can be accessed from the SQL clients primarily through proprietary gateways, such as EDA/SQL or Ingres IMS. The OSF DCE clients can access IMS or DB2 databases through the OSF DCE application server that resides on MVS. The LU6.2 clients can access the IMS and DB2 databases through the IMS transaction manager or the MVS-resident APPC applications. Once again, we can add Web-access considerations to this diagram by simply having a CGI gateway or a Java gateway that invokes any of the clients shown in the diagram.

Figure 5.16 Access to Mainframe IMS and DB2 Databases

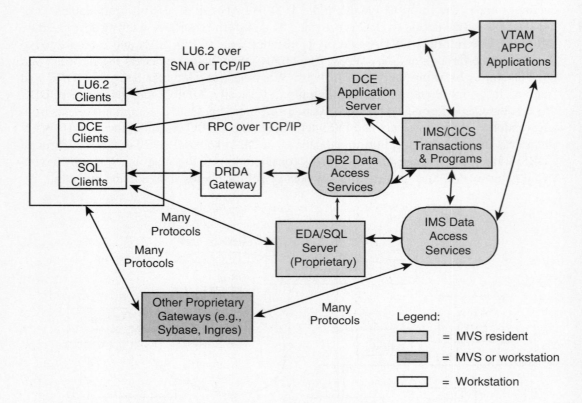

5.9   State of the Market: SQL Middleware and Gateways

A plethora of off-the-shelf products provide the distributed-data management functions discussed in this chapter. These products appear as SQL middleware for distributed-data access and SQL gateways to translate protocols between different databases.

5.9.1   SQL Middleware for Distributed-Data Access

SQL middleware to access distributed data can be categorized in terms of two factors: the SQL API used and the protocols exchanged between client and server middleware. Table 5.1 shows the four categories and Figure 5.17 illustrates these categories by showing typical configurations. Let us review these categories of SQL middleware (this discussion is a specialization of the discussion in Chapter 2 about general C/S middleware).

TABLE 5.1 CATEGORIES OF SQL MIDDLEWARE

SQL Middleware Categories	API	Exchange Protocols
Completely open middleware	Open	Open
Open API middleware	Open	Proprietary
Open exchange protocol middleware	Proprietary	Open
Proprietary middleware	Proprietary	Proprietary

The **completely open middleware** is most desirable because a common API is used by all client middleware vendors and a common exchange protocol is also used between the client and server middleware—see Figure 5.17(a). In this case, client applications are *portable* across vendors (e.g., the same client application can be used to access Informix or Oracle databases) and also *interoperable* (e.g., an Oracle database can be accessed from Informix and Sybase clients *without* translation). Basically, this middleware, if available, would allow any-client-to-any-server communication without any gateways to translate exchange protocols. We are not so lucky at present. This situation could be achieved if, for example, all SQL vendors supported SAG/Xopen CLI API and the ISO RDA exchange protocol. However, at present, the closest we can get is ODBC API and DRDA exchange protocol.

The **open API middleware** configuration, shown in Figure 5.17(b), allows clients from vendor A to be portable to vendor B because the same API is used; however, different drivers are needed to access different servers because the exchange protocols are not common. This situation is often encountered, at the time of this writing, owing to the widespread availability of the ODBC drivers. Thus the ODBC API based SQL middleware to access multiple databases is becoming a de facto standard (see Section 5.6.1 for a discussion of ODBC).

The **open exchange protocol middleware** configuration, shown in Figure 5.17(c), allows clients from different vendors to use a common exchange protocol (e.g., DRDA) to access database servers. However, the clients use proprietary APIs. This situation is currently being achieved by using the DRDA gateways, which translate the proprietary protocols to IBM's DRDA to access DB2 data. For example, Informix and Oracle clients use their own proprietary APIs and drivers but use the DRDA gateways to convert the proprietary exchange protocol to a DB2-accepted exchange protocol (see Section 5.6.3 for a discussion of DRDA).

Figure 5.17 Configurations for SQL Middleware

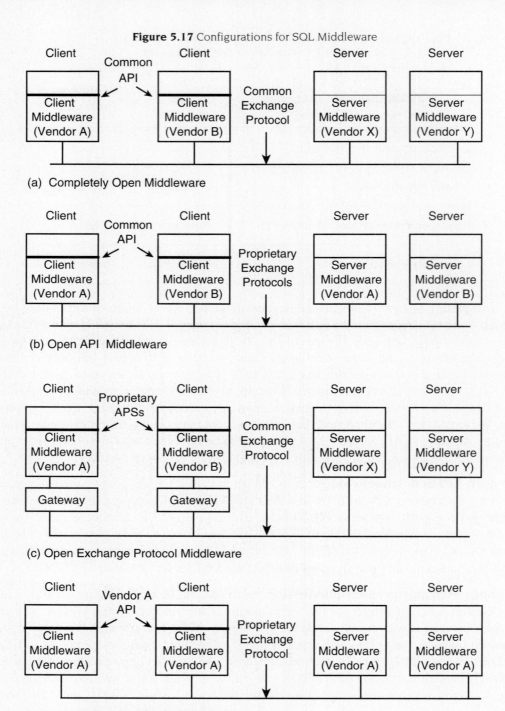

(a) Completely Open Middleware

(b) Open API Middleware

(c) Open Exchange Protocol Middleware

(d) Completely Proprietary Middleware

The **completely proprietary middleware**, shown in Figure 5.17(d), shows the most common SQL middleware at present. In this case, the APIs as well as exchange protocols are proprietary. Clients are portable among the same vendor environments (one hopes!) and can operate only with database servers supplied by the same vendor. SQL middleware from Informix, Oracle, Sybase, Gupta, and MDI is an example.

5.9.2   SQL Gateways

SQL gateways exist for two reasons. First, to allow SQL clients from vendor X to interoperate with the SQL servers from vendor Y (for example, Sybase Omni Server allows Sybase clients to access Informix, Oracle, and DB2 databases). Thus these gateways are used in the proprietary API and completely proprietary middleware categories discussed in the previous section. Second, to allow SQL clients to access non-SQL databases (e.g., the EDA/SQL from Information Builders, Inc.). Figure 5.18 shows a conceptual view of a typical SQL Gateway.

Many vendors, such as Gupta, Informix, Information Builders, Oracle, and Sybase, currently support SQL gateways. The gateway software makes a remote database look like a local database to the client applications and tools. The SQL request can be submitted as ad hoc, through a command-level interface, or embedded in a programming language such as C. Typically, these gateways are suitable for ad hoc SQL queries only, with little or no support for remote stored procedures and procedure calls. To provide access to legacy data that is stored in non-relational databases such as IMS, some database gateways provide "SQL-to-IMS" converters which cast SQL calls to IMS database access calls. This data translation is usually accomplished at the target-database server machine through data translators (for example, IBI's EDA/SQL provides many translators at the target machines that convert SQL calls to IMS and other nonrelational data sources). However, the quality of these gateways must be examined thoroughly before enterprisewide heavy usage (there are many intricate performance issues in translating SQL to non-SQL formats).

Figure 5.18 Conceptual View of SQL Gateways

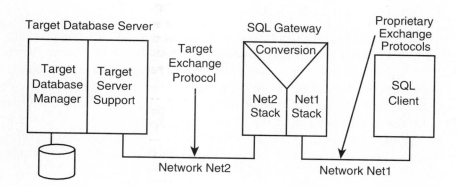

The main advantage of SQL database gateways is their flexibility and end-user control. However, these gateways assume that:

- The database schema is known and can be understood by the end users.
- The target databases are based on relational database technologies (using SQL to nonrelational formats has some performance and functionality limitations).

The database gateways raise many network and system performance issues (e.g., size of SQL results sent over the network is unpredictable, gateways can be security as well as performance bottlenecks). In addition, the database gateways can be expensive (in the range of $200K for mainframe-based systems). Most of the existing database gateways provide read

as well as update to single hosts. The capabilities for distributed-query processing among the same vendor databases are also available. However, distributed-query processing among multiple vendors and distributed-transaction processing support is sparse.

Many SQL gateways have been announced from different vendors (see sidebar "SQL Gateway Examples").

5.10   State of the Art: Object-Oriented Multidatabase Systems

Access to databases dispersed around a network has been an area of active research since the 1970s. We briefly reviewed the extant work in this area under the heading of "federated and multidatabase systems" (Section 5.5.3). Basically, the idea is to provide integrated view and use of preexisting, autonomous, and typically heterogeneous databases. Recent research in multidatabase system is employing object-oriented techniques to facilitate building of multidatabase systems [Bukhres 1996, Pitoura 1995]. Figure 5.19 shows a conceptual view of OO multidatabase systems. The global layer provides the basic mapping between OO users and the underlying multidatabase systems that may include IMS, RDBMS, OODBMS, or any other data stores. The complexity of the global layer varies from a simple data-access gateway to a sophisticated distributed transaction manager.

Object-oriented (OO) technology can influence the design of multidatabase systems at several levels (you may want to review the tutorial on OO technologies in Chapter 10 before proceeding). First, OO technology can be used to model the resources, at a very gross level, as objects. For example, each database can be modeled as an object, and the database commands can be modeled as methods. Second, a common data model based on OO technologies can be constructed for the participating databases. This approach gives a finer level of granularity for OO access to multidatabases. Third, OO technology can be used to provide heterogeneous transaction management, so that updates of data at one site are propagated to interrelated data at other sites.

Figure 5.19 Object-Oriented Multidatabase Systems

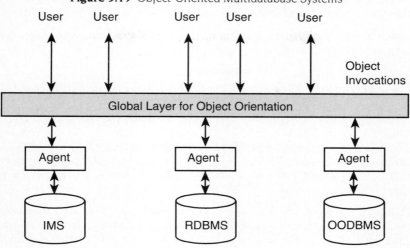

A number of prototype and research projects have been built to illustrate different aspects of OO multidatabases. Examples are the Interbase system developed at Purdue University, OMNIBASE developed at the University of Houston, the Carnot prototype developed at MCC, and HKBMS developed at University of Florida. Detailed discussion of OO multidatabase technology with analysis of aforementioned prototypes and research literature can be found in the book by Bukhres [1996]. Market analysis can be found in the Forrestor Research reports "Weaving the Data Web" (October 1994) and "Living with Fractured Data" (February 1994).

The following trends in DDMS development are worth noting:

- SQL will continue as a standard for data access across all data sources such as files and databases, but SQL conversion to nonrelational DBMS, especially to OODBMS, is not trivial.

- More DDMSs will continue to include heterogeneous data located at heterogeneous computers, interconnected through heterogeneous networks.

- Standards will play an important role in the operability and portability of DDMS. Standards are needed at two levels: APIs for portability, and exchange protocols for interoperability. ODBC is an example of a de facto standard for SQL API, and IBM's DRDA and ISO Remote Database Access (RDA) are examples of exchange protocol standards. We should note that Microsoft is planning to introduce a new data-access technology under the name "OLE DB" that will be included in all Windows environments. Since OLE DB is not compatible with ODBC, we will have to see the impact of this new technology.

- Database gateways will continue to exist for conversion of different exchange protocols and APIs as long as we do not achieve completely open C/S environments (open APIs and open exchange protocols).

- Use of OO technologies for accessing heterogeneous distributed data is an interesting and promising area of future research.

- The notion of "Universal databases" that combine multimedia data with legacy data is another area of potential industrial products [Foley 1996].

SQL Gateway Examples

DRDA (Distributed Relational Database Architecture) Gateways. These gateways convert client calls to DRDA. As stated previously in this chapter, DRDA is becoming a de facto standard for DB2 access. More than 20 vendors have announced DRDA support. Informix, Oracle, XDB, and Micro Decision DRDA gateways are commercially available; others are beginning to appear (slowly but surely).

EDA/SQL Gateway. This gateway from Information Builders, Inc., translates the SQL to access more than 30 data sources in relational as well as nonrelational formats. EDA/SQL uses a proprietary SQL API and client/server middleware (called the API/SQL and EDA/Link, respectively) to access IMS, DB2, Informix, Oracle, Sybase, Focus, Adabas, and many other data sources stored on MVS, UNIX, and Windows NT platforms. The EDA/SQL gateways provide numerous translators that convert EDA SQL to other SQL variants and non-SQL formats. A review of EDA/SQL can be found in Bland [1993]. More information can be obtained from Information Builders, Inc.

Sybase Omni Server. This gateway converts the Sybase DB-LIB calls (this is the name of Sybase SQL API) to access Oracle, Sybase, DB2, and Informix databases (others are expected in the future). Sybase Omni Server allows joins between heterogeneous data sources (e.g., joins between Sybase databases and DB2 are performed transparently for the users). More information about the Sybase Omni Server can be obtained from Sybase.

Oracle Open Gateway. This gateway converts the Oracle database calls to other data sources such as Sybase, DB2, and Informix. This gateway is very similar to the Sybase Omni Server in functionality. More information about this gateway can be obtained from Oracle.

OSI RDA (Remote Data Access) Gateways. These gateways convert proprietary exchange protocols to OSI RDA. As mentioned previously in this chapter, OSI RDA is an open standard that has not been implemented by many vendors at the time of this writing. However, we all live in hope.

5.11   Summary

Access to distributed data, with or without replication, involves a wide range of technical as well as management issues. We have primarily focussed on "TP-less" issues of data retrieval and simple updates (no transactions). Toward this goal, we have introduced the notion of distributed-data management systems (DDMSs) as a C/S middleware concerned with the access and management of distributed data (files plus databases with a certain degree of replication). DDMSs provide the following capabilities:

- Distributed-file management
- Single-site remote-data access
- Distributed-query processing

We have reviewed these capabilities and have paid particular attention to the SQL middleware, because at present most of the distributed data is accessed through SQL middleware.

5.12 Case Study: XYZCorp Provides Web Access to Corporate Data

XYZCorp wants to establish an approach to access the corporate databases (Oracle, DB2, IMS, Informix) from the Web. At present, most of the requirements point to a single remote-data access (SRDA) paradigm. Distributed-query processing is a future issue. It is also desirable to develop selection criteria for selecting appropriate SQL middleware to enable this access.

Hints about the Case Study

Figure 5.20 shows a conceptual view of a Web gateway that could provide access to XYZ-Corp corporate information. This gateway is currently shown as a CGI gateway that invokes ODBC drivers to access Informix and Oracle databases. The DB2 and IMS databases are accessed by using appropriate intermediary gateways.This CGI-ODBC gateway could be replaced with a Java-JDBC (Java Database Connectivity) gateway.

The selection criteria for such a gateway could include performance, cost, platform support, vendor support, and many other issues discussed in Section 5.7.

5.13 Problems and Exercises

1. Describe a distributed file system other than NFS.
2. List the factors which can be used to evaluate different DDBM.
3. What are the advantages of using a client-server paradigm to deliver a DDBM?
4. What are the main issues and approaches in heterogeneous database systems?
5. Define the following standards and describe their role in DDMS:
   (a) ISO RDA   (b) ODBC   (c) DRDA

Figure 5.20 XYZCorp Web Gateway For Corporate Information

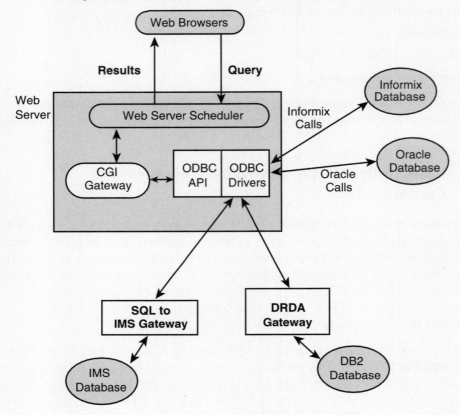

6. Suggest a framework that you can use to evaluate different SQL middleware products and gateways.

7. Choose a database gateway and analyze its capabilities by using the framework identified above.

5.14 Additional Information

We have attempted to give an overview of an area which continues to grow. The following books are recommended for additional details:

- Hackathorn, R., *Enterprise Database Connectivity,* Wiley, 1993.

- Bukhres, O., and Elmagarmid, A., *Object-Oriented Multidatabase Systems: A Solution for Advanced Applications,* Prentice Hall, 1996.

- Ozsu, M., and Valduriez, P., *Principles of Distributed Database Systems,* Prentice Hall, 1991.
- Bernstein, P. A., Hadzilacos, V., and Goodman, N., *Concurrency Control and Recovery in Database Systems,* Addison Wesley, 1987.
- Ceri, S., and Pellagitti, G., *Distributed Databases: Principles and Systems,* McGraw-Hill, 1984.

The interested reader can find additional information in a number of journals and proceedings of conference, such as:

- *ACM Transactions on Database Systems*
- ACM SIGMOD International Conferences
- IEEE International Conferences on Data Engineering
- International Conferences on Very Large Databases
- International Conferences on Distributed Computing
- *IEEE Transactions on Knowledge and Data Engineering*
- *Database Programming and Design*
- *Data Management Review*

State-of-the-market analysis can be found in, for example, the Forrestor Research reports "Weaving the Data Web" (October 1994) and "Living with Fractured Data" (February 1994).

5.15   References

Ace, E., "Replication for SQL Server NT–Today," *Database Design and Programming,* January 1995, pp. 47–52.

Adiba, Lindsay, "Database Snapshot," IBM Research Report, RJ2772, March 1980.

Barghouti, N. S., and Kaiser, G. E., "Concurrency Control in Advanced Database Applications," *ACM Computing Surveys,* September 1991, pp. 269–318.

Bernstein, P. A. and Goodman, N., "Concurrency Control in Distributed Database Systems," *ACM Computing Surveys,* Vol. 13, No. 2 (June 1981) pp. 185–222.

Bernstein, P. A. and Chiu, D. W., "Using Semi-Joins to Solve Relational Queries," *JACM,* January 1981.

Bernstein, P. A., Hadzilacos, V., and Goodman, N., *Concurrency Control and Recovery in Database Systems,* Addison Wesley, 1987.

Bjorn, M., *A WWW Gateway for Interactive Relational Database Management,* Doctoral Program of Socio-Economic Planning, 1-1-1 Tennodai, Tsukuba, Ibaraki 305, JAPAN, 1995.

Bland, D., "A Look at Information Builder's EDA/SQL," *Enterprise Systems Journal,* January 1993, pp. 87–92.

Bodarik, P., et al., "Deciding to Correct Distributed Query Processing," *IEEE Transactions on Knowledge and Data Engineering,* June 1992, pp. 253–265.

Bukhres, O., and Elmagarmid, A., *Object-Oriented Multidatabase Systems: A Solution for Advanced Applications,* Prentice Hall, 1996.

Bukhres, O., et al., "InterBase: An Execution Environment for Heterogeneous Software Systems," *IEEE Computer,* August 1993, pp. 57–65.

Bukhres, O., et al., "InterBase: A Multidatabase Prototype System," *SIGMOD,* May 1993.

Cardenas, A. F., "Heterogeneous Distributed Database Management: The HD-DBMS," *Proceedings of the IEEE,* May 1987, pp. 588–600.

Ceri, S., and G. Pellagitti, *Distributed Databases: Principles and Systems,* McGraw-Hill, 1984.

Ceri, S., Pernici, B., and Wiederhold, G., "Distributed Database Design Methodolgies," *Proceedings of the IEEE,* May 1987, pp. 533–546.

Ceri, S., and Widom, J., "Managing Semantic Heterogeneity with Production Rules and Persistent Queues," *Proceedings of 19th International Conference on Very Large Data Bases,* Dublin, Ireland, August 1993.

Chu, W. W., "Performance of File Directory Systems for Data Bases in Star and Distributed Networks," *1976 NCC,* Vol. 45 (1976).

Chu, W. W., "Distributed Data Bases," *Handbook of Software Engineering,* ed. C. R. Vick and C. V. Ramamoorthy, Van Nostrand Reinhold, 1984

CICS, *Customer Information System: Concepts and Facilities,* IBM manual, 1995 (ask for latest release).

Date, C. J., *An Introduction to Database Systems,* 5th ed., Vols.1 and 2, Addison Wesley, 1990.

Date, C. J., "Twelve Rules for a Distributed Database," *InfoDB,* Vol. 2, Nos. 2 and 3 (Summer/ Fall 1987).

Date, C. J., *A Guide to DB2,* Addison Wesley, 1984.

Elmagarmid, A., Chen, J., and Bukhres, O., "Remote System Interfaces: An Approach to Overcoming Heterogeneity Barrier and Retaining Local Autonomy in the Integration of Heterogeneous Systems," *International Journal of Intelligent and Cooperative Information Systems,* 1995.

Elmagarmid, A., *Database Transaction Models for Advanced Applications,* Morgan Kaufmann Publishers, 1992.

ENCINA, *Encina for Open OLTP,* Transarc Corporation publication, 1995 (ask for latest edition).

Epstein, R., Stonebraker, M., and Wong, E., "Distributed Query Processing in a Relational Database System," *ACM SIGMOD,* Austin, TX, 1978.

Epstein, R., "Query Optimization: A Game of Time and Statistics," *UNIX Review,* May 1987, pp. 28–29.

Eswaran, K. P; Gray, J.N, et al., "Notions of Consistency and Predicate Locks in a Database System," *CACM,* Vol. 19, No. 11 (November 1976).

Foley, J., "Open the Gates to Objects," *Information Week,* May 13, 1996, pp. 44–51.

Garcia-Molina, H., "Performance of Update Synchronization Algorithms for Replicated Data in a Distributed Database," Ph.D. Dissertation, Stanford University, June 1979.

Garcia-Molina, H., and Abbot, R. K., "Reliable Distributed Database Management," *Proceedings of the IEEE,* Vol. 75, No. 5 (May 1987) pp. 601–620.

Graham, G., "Real-World Distributed Databases," *UNIX Review*, May 1987.

Gray, J., "Notes on Database Operating Systems," in *Operating Systems: An Advanced Course,* Springer-Verlag, New York, 1979, pp. 393–481.

Gray, J., "The Transaction Concept: Virtues and Limitations," *Proceedings of Conference on Very Large Databases,* September 1981, pp. 144–154.

Gray, J., "Transparency in Its Place," *UNIX Review,* May 1987.

Gray, J.N., and Anderson, M., "Distributed Computer Systems: Four Cases," *Proceedings of the IEEE,* May 1987, pp. 719–729.

Hackathorn, R., *Enterprise Database Connectivity,* Wiley, 1993.

Hammer, J., et al., "The Stanford Data Warehousing Project," *IEEE Data Engineering,* June 1995, pp. 41–47.

Hevner, A. R., and Yao, S. B., "Query Processing in Distributed Database Systems," *IEEE Transactions on Software Engineering,* Vol. SE-5, No. 3 (May 1979).

Hevner, A. R., "A Survey of Data Allocation and Retrieval Methods for Distributed Systems", School of Business and Management Working Paper # 81-036, University of Maryland, October 1981.

Hevner, A. R., and Yao, S. B., "Querying Distributed Databases on Local Area Networks," *Proceedings of the IEEE,* May 1987, pp. 563–572.

Rauch-Hinden, W., "True Distributed DBMSes Presage Big Dividends," *Mini-Micro Systems,* May and June 1987.

Jarke, M., and Koch, J., "Query Optimization in Database Systems," *ACM Computing Surveys,* June 1984, pp. 111–152.

Kamel, M. N., and Kamel, N. N., "The Federated Database Management Systems," *Computer Communications,* Vol. 15, No. 4 (May 1992), pp. 270–278.

Kohler, W. H., "A Survey of Techniques for Synchronization and Recovery in Decentralized Computer Systems," *ACM Computing Surveys,* Vol.13, No.2 (June 1981), pp. 149–184.

Korzeniowski, P., "Replication Gains in Distributed Databases," *Software Magazine,* April 1993, pp. 93–96.

Krasowski, M., "Integrating Distributed Databases into the Information Architecture," *Journal of Information Systems Management,* Spring 1991, pp. 38–46.

Larson, J. A., "A Flexible Reference Architecture for Distributed Database Management," *Proceedings of ACM 13th Annual Computer Science Conference, March, 1985, New Orleans,* pp. 58–72.

Larson, B., "A Retrospective of R*: A Distributed Database Management System," *Proceedings of the IEEE,* May 1987, pp. 668–673.

Lef, A., and Pu, C., "A Classification of Transaction Processing Systems," *IEEE Computer,* June 1991, pp. 63–76.

Leinfuss, E., "Replication Synchronizes Distributed Databases over Time," *Software Magazine,* July 1993, pp. 31–35.

Litwin, W., Mark, L., and Roussopoulos, N., "Interoperability of Multiple Autonomous Databases," *ACM Computing Surveys,* September 1990, pp. 267–293

Mack, S., "Sybase to Address Update Problems," *Infoworld,* November 16, 1992.

McCord, R., and Hanner, M., "Connecting Islands of Information," *UNIX Review,* May 1987.

McGovern, D., "Two-Phased Commit or Replication?" Database Programming and Design, May 1993, pp. 35–44.

Olson, J., "From Centralized to Distributed," *Database Programming and Design,* December 1993, pp. 50–57.

Ozsu, M., and Valduriez, P., *Principles of Distributed Database Systems,* Prentice Hall, 1991.

Ozsu, M., and Valduriez, P., "Distributed Database Systems: Where Are We Now?" *IEEE Computer,* August 1991, pp. 68–78.

Papakonstantinou, Y., Garcia-Molina, H., and Widom, J., "Object Exchange across Heterogeneous Information Sources," *Proceedings of the 11th International Conference on Data Engineering, Taipei, Taiwan,* March 1995.

Pitoura, E., Bukhres, O., and Elmagarmid, A., "Object-Orientation in Multidatabase Systems," *ACM Computing Surveys,* June 1995, pp. 142–165.

Pu, C., Leff, A., and Chen, S., "Heterogeneous and Autonomous Transaction Processing," *IEEE Computer,* December 1991, pp. 64–72.

Quinlan, T., "Heterogeneous Distributed Databases," *Database Programming and Design,* October 1993, pp. 29–33.

Ricciuti, M., "The Mainframe as Server: Is IBM Totally Bonkers—or Brilliant?" *Datamation,* May 15, 1994, pp. 61–64.

Ricciuti, M., "Universal Database Access," *Datamation,* November 1, 1991.

Richter, J., "Distributing Data," *Byte Magazine,* June 1994, pp. 139–182

Sacco, G. V., and Yao, S. B., "Query Optimization in Distributed Databases," Working Paper MS/S #81-029, College of Business Administration, University of Maryland, 1981.

Semich, W., "The Long View from Microsoft: Component DBMSs," *Datamation,* August 1, 1994.

Semich, J., and McMullen, J., "Sybase's Big Blue Connection," *Datamation,* April 1, 1991.

Schlack, M., "Key to Client/Server OLTP," *Datamation,* April 1, 1995, pp. 53–56.

Schussel, G., "Database Replication: Playing Both Ends with the Middleware," *Client/Server Today,* November 1994, pp. 57–67.

Sheth, A. P., and Larson, J. A., "Federated Database Systems for Managing Distributed, Heterogeneous, and Autonomous Databases," *ACM Computing Surveys,* September 1990, pp. 183–236.

Soparkar, N., Korth, H., and Silberschatz, A., "Failure-Resilient Transaction Management in Multi-Databases," *IEEE Computer,* December 1991, pp. 28–37.

Stacey, D., "Replication: DB2, Oracle, or Sybase?" Database Programming and Design, December 1994, pp. 42–51.

Stone, H., "Parallel Querying of Large Databases: A Case Study," *IEEE Computer,* October, 1987, pp. 11–21.

Svobodova, L., "File Servers for Network-Based Distributed Systems," *ACM Computing Surveys,* December 1984, pp. 353–398.

Teorey, T.J., and Fry, J.P., *Design of Database Structures,* Prentice Hall, 1982.

Thomas, G., et al., "Heterogeneous Distributed Database Systems for Production Use," *ACM Computing Surveys,* September 1990, pp. 237–266.

Triantafillo, P., and Taylor, D., "The Location-Based Paradigm for Replication: Achieving Efficiency and Availability in Distributed Systems," *IEEE Transactions on Software Engineering,* January 1995.

Tuxedo, *Transaction Processing with Tuxedo,* UNIX Systems Laboratories Publication.

Umar, A., *Distributed Computing and Client/Server Systems,* Prentice Hall, rev. ed. 1993.

Umar, A., *Application (Re)Engineering in Object-Oriented Client/Server Internet Environments,* Prentice Hall, 1997.

Vinzant, D., "SQL Database Servers," *Data Communications,* January 1990, pp. 72–88.

Walpole, J. et al., "Transaction Mechanisms for Distributed Programming Environments," *Software Engineering Journal,* September 1987, pp. 169–171.

White, C., "Data Replication Techniques, Tools, and Case Studies," *DB/EXPO,* New York, December 6–8, 1994.

Wiederhold, "Mediators in the Architectures of Future Information Systems," *IEEE Computer,* March 1992.

Wiederhold, G., "Intelligent Integration of Information," *Proceedings of the ACM SIGMOD International Conference on Management of Data, Washington, DC, May 1993,* pp. 434–437.

Wilbur, S., and Bacarisse, J., "Building Distributed Systems with Remote Procedure Call," *Software Engineering Journal,* September 1987, pp. 148–159.

Wolfson, O., "The Overhead of Locking (and Commit) Protocols in Distributed Databases," *ACM Transactions on Database Systems,* Vol. 12, No. 3 (September 1987), pp. 453-471.

Yu, C., and Chang, C., "Distributed Query Processing," *ACM Computing Surveys,* Vol. 16, No. 4 (December 1984), pp. 399–433.

Zimowski, M., "DRDA, ISO RDA, X/Open RDA: A Comparison," *Database Programming and Design,* June 1994, pp. 54–61.

Zhou, G., et al., "Supporting Data Integration and Warehousing Using H2O," *IEEE Data Engineering,* June 1995, pp. 29–40.

6

Client/Server Transaction Processing

6.1   Introduction

Simply stated, a transaction is a group of statements that must be executed as a unit. For example, a transaction may be a group of SQL statements that transfer funds from one bank account to another (these statements must be executed as a unit, because if the funds have been debited from one account, then they must be credited to the other). Transaction processing, in the form of on-line transaction processing (OLTP), has been a backbone of commercial data processing since the early 1970s. Mainframe-based transaction managers (TMs), such as CICS and IMS-DC/IMS-TM have matured over the years to provide high performance and reliable service. The main question is how to process transactions in client/sever environments. A popular example is electronic commerce over the Internet (i.e., users purchase goods, and funds are transferred between business entities, over the Internet).

Most of the work in C/S computing so far has focused on data access by using SQL middleware described in the previous chapter. This middleware allows you to retrieve data that is distributed, with or without replication, to many sites. This middleware is also at present allowing users to access distributed data in different formats, on different machines, and under the control of different DBMS vendors (see the discussion in the previous chapter). However, how do you update related data that may be stored on different machines?

Currently, the approaches to C/S transaction processing fall into the following categories:

- **TP-less**, i.e., do not use any transaction-management considerations (we discussed this approach in the previous chapter)
- **TP-lite**, i.e., use database procedures to handle updates
- **TP-heavy**, i.e., use a distributed-transaction manager to handle updates

Why the difference in opinion? Why can we not use the same OLTP philosophy and approaches that have worked for a number of years? To answer these and other related questions, we will first introduce the key transaction concepts and definitions (Section 6.2), and then discuss the special issues and emerging standards of distributed-transaction processing (Sections 6.3 and 3.4). This discussion will give you an idea of the complexities of TP-heavy and why everyone is not jumping on this bandwagon. We will then discuss, in Section 6.5, the currently popular data-replication servers that provide periodic data synchronization for TP-Lite instead of the instantaneous synchronization used by the distributed-transaction processors (TP-heavy). Section 6.6 discusses the trade-offs between using data-replication servers versus the instant-update synchronization protocol (known as two-phase commit) used in TP-heavy solutions. Eventually, Section 6.7 discusses the trade-offs between TP-less, TP-lite, and TP-heavy for C/S transaction processing. Our own feeling is that while TP-lite may serve many C/S applications needs, TP-heavy must be considered for large mission-critical applications. Keeping this in mind, we consolidate the distributed-data access (discussed in the previous chapter) and distributed-transaction management into a single framework to highlight the wide range of technical issues and approaches involved (Sections 6.8 and 6.9). We conclude this chapter by reviewing Encina as an example of an open DTP (distributed-transaction processing) system that can be used for TP-heavy solutions.

After reading this chapter, you should be able to answer the following questions:

- What are the main concepts, issues, and approaches in C/S transaction processing?
- What are the main characteristics of distributed-transaction processing and why is it considered "TP-heavy"?
- What are data-replication servers and why are they becoming so popular?
- What are the key failure-handling techniques in distributed systems (e.g., two-phase commit and replication servers), and what are the trade-offs between these approaches?
- What are the trade-offs between the various C/S transaction-processing approaches?
- What are the key technical challenges, accepted solution approaches, and standards in distributed-data and transaction management?
- Can a framework be developed which allows IS staff to systematically approach data-distribution and replication management and develop acceptable strategies?

Key Points

● The approaches to C/S transaction processing fall into the following categories: TP-less, TP-lite, and TP-heavy.

● Data-replication servers are used in conjunction with TP-lite and thus play a vital role in managing replicated data, owing to their flexibility and owing to the limitations of two-phase commit.

● Message-oriented middleware (MOM) can also provide a lightweight mechanism for distributed-transaction processing.

● A distributed-data and transaction management system (DDTMS) is a C/S middleware that is concerned with the management of distributed data (files plus databases with certain degree of replication) and distributed transactions.

● DDTMSs attempt to include heterogeneous data located at heterogeneous computers, interconnected through heterogeneous networks.

● Standards play an important role in the operability and portability of DDTMS. For example, ODBC, DRDA, and ISO Remote Database Access (RDA) standards for database access, and the ISO Transaction Processing (TP) and the X/Open Distributed Transaction Processing (DTP) standards are worth noting.

● Future work will focus on object-oriented distributed transactions, where an object invocation will enforce the ACID properties.

6.2   Review of Transaction Concepts

The concept of a transaction originates from the field of contract law [Gray 1981, Walpole 1987] in which each contract between two parties (a transaction) is carried out unless either party is willing to break the law. From a business and end-user point of view, transactions occur at two levels: customer to business and business to business (see Figure 6.1). In computer science, a **transaction** is defined as a sequence of data *operations* (read, write and manipulation commands) that transform one consistent state of the system into a new consistent state [Eswaran 1976]. Examples of business transactions are: electronic transfer of money from one account to another, update of an inventory database, and purchase of a ticket electronically. To accomplish these business transactions, computer transactions are executed. Examples of the computer transactions are a group of database operations (e.g., SQL statements) that need to be executed as a single unit, a program with embedded SQL statements that updates one or more relational tables, and a Cobol program that modifies indexed files [Ozsu 1991 (book), p. 259].

Figure 6.1 Transaction Example: Customer to Business and Business to Business

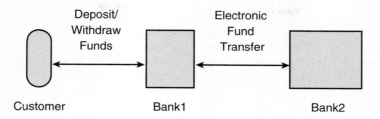

6.2.1   The ACID Properties

A transaction has four properties, known as the ACID properties:

Atomicity: A transaction is treated as a single unit of operation; either all the transaction's actions are completed, or none of them are. This is also known as the "all-or-nothing property." If a transaction completes all of its actions successfully, then it is said to be ***committed***.

Consistency: A transaction maps one consistent (correct) state of the database to another. Informally, consistency is concerned with correctly reflecting the reality in the database. For example, if a company has 500 employees, then a database consistent with this reality should also show 500 employees. The notion of a consistent state is highly dependent on the semantics of the database. A set of constraints, called semantic integrity constraints, is used to verify database consistency.

Isolation: A transaction cannot reveal its results to other concurrent transactions before commitment. Isolation assures that transactions do not access data that is being updated (temporarily inconsistent and incomplete during the execution of a transaction).

Durability: Once completed successfully (committed), the results of a transaction are permanent and cannot be erased from the database. The DBMS ensures that the results of a transaction are not altered due to system failures (transactions endure failures).

Detailed discussion of the ACID properties for transactions can be found in Gray [1993], and Ozsu [1991, pp. 266–269]. The implications of the ACID properties for transaction management are as follows:

Serializability (concurrency control): This allows transactions to execute concurrently while achieving the same logical result as if they had executed serially. Concurrency control allows multiple transactions to read and update data simultaneously, and includes transaction scheduling and management of the resources needed by transactions during execution. Transactions can be scheduled serially ("single-threaded") to minimize conflicts or in parallel ("multithreaded") to maximize concurrency.

Commit processing: This allows commitment of transaction changes if the transaction executes properly and removal of the changes if the transaction fails. The transactions usually
"bracket" their operations by using "begin-transaction" and "end-transaction" statements.
The transaction manager permanently enters the changes made by a transaction when it
encounters the "end-transaction" statement; otherwise, it removes the changes. Transaction
managers also log the results of transactions on a separate medium, so that the effects of
transactions can be recovered even in the event of a crash which destroys the database.

Although the ACID properties as well as the serializability and commit processing implications are important, it has been argued that all these properties amount to atomicity and serializability [Triantafillou 1995]. This is a pragmatic view that greatly simplifies the discussion
of transaction processing.

6.2.2   Transaction Models

Transactions may be classified into the following broad models:

- **Single-site versus multiple-site (distributed) transactions.** The transaction may be
  restricted to a single site (e.g., one database server) or it may span many sites. We will discuss
  distributed transactions in the next section.

- **Queued or conversational transactions.** In queued-transaction processing, such as found in
  IMS-DC, arriving transactions are first queued and then scheduled for execution. Once execution begins, the transaction does not interact with the user. In conversational-transaction processing, such as found in CICS, the transactions interact with the outside world during
  execution.

- **Short (flat) or long (workflow) transactions.** Short, also known as flat, transactions start with
  a "begin-transaction" instruction and end with a "commit-transaction" or "abort-transaction"
  instruction. Flat transactions are all-or-nothing-at-all activities (you cannot commit a portion of a
  flat transaction). Long-duration transactions (also known as workflows, sagas, and flexible
  transactions), consist of a sequence of distributed or queued transactions to perform a multitude
  of activities that may span several business units of an organization [Elmagarmid 1992]. Long
  transactions may be constructed by chaining or nesting individual transactions. These transactions cannot be typically satisfied by a single transaction (distributed or queued). A special case
  of long transactions is massive batch updates. These transactions are typically handled by providing a series of "synch points" at which all the changes made are committed (e.g., a synch
  point after every 100 updates).

6.2.3   Transaction Managers

A *transaction manager (TM)*, also known as a transaction-processing monitor (TP monitor),
specializes in managing transactions from their point of origin to their termination (planned
or unplanned). The TM facilities are traditionally integrated with the DBMS facilities, as
shown in Figure 6.2. This allows database queries from different transactions to access/
update one or several data items. However, some products specialize only in TM with special
focus on handling thousands of OLTP users. These TMs provide a variety of monitoring,
dynamic load-balancing, process-restarts, and priority-scheduling capabilities. Under the

control of a sophisticated TM, a transaction may be decomposed into subtransactions to optimize I/O and/or response time (see Jarke [1984] for a comprehensive discussion). Examples of commercially available TMs are IBM's CICS [CICS 1995], Transarc's Encina [Encina 1995] and BEA's Tuxedo [Tuxedo 1995]. It is not always possible to find separate TMs in commercial products. In some systems, TM facilities are embedded in communication managers, operating systems, and/or database managers. In particular, most RDBMS vendors at present provide some TP facilities, known as TP-lite (see Section 6.7).

Figure 6.2 Conceptual View of a Transaction Manager

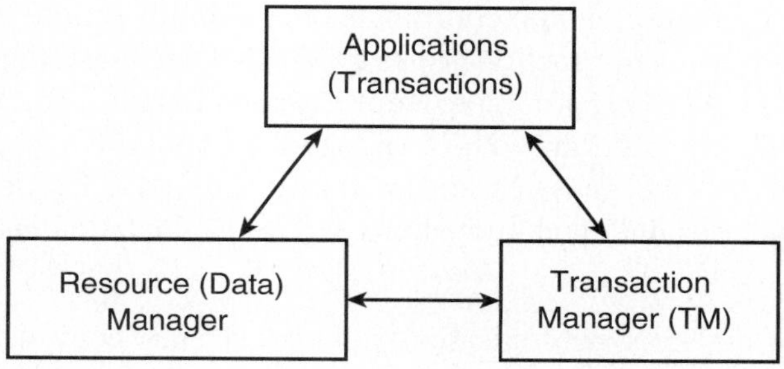

The book by Jim Gray and Audreas Reuter [Gray 1993] is the classic reference on transaction processing. An introduction to TMS facilities is given in Ozsu [1991 (book), chap. 10]. A detailed classification of transaction-processing systems can be found in Leff [1991]. For additional discussion of transaction management, see Elmagarmid [1992], Walpole [1987], and Gray [1981].

6.3 Distributed-Transaction Processing Concepts

Distributed-transaction processing (DTP) allows multiple computers to coordinate the execution of a single transaction. This occurs when the data needed by a transaction resides at many computers. Atomicity of a transaction is of key importance—all the activities performed on different computers by a transaction must be completed properly or else entirely withdrawn in the event of a failure in the network, application code, and/or computing hardware. A distributed-transaction manager (DTM), a collection of software modules, is responsible for managing *distributed (also known as multi-site) transactions,* which access data at several different sites. A distributed transaction consists of several *local (also known as single-site) transactions,* which access data at one site.

6.3.1   Distributed ACID

Each distributed transaction is treated as a single recoverable unit and must pass the "ACID" (atomicity, consistency, isolation, and durability) test. Consequently, the main responsibilities of a DTM are as follows:

- Atomicity of transactions through commit processing for failure handling and recovery
- Serializability of transactions through update synchronization and concurrency control

It is important for different sites to reach commit agreement while processing subtransactions of a global transaction. The most widely used solution to this problem is the two-phase-commit (2PC) protocol, which coordinates the commit actions needed to run a distributed transaction. When a transaction issues a COMMIT request, then the commit action is performed in two phases: prepare for commit and then commit. If a failure occurs in the prepare phase, then the transaction can be terminated without difficulty; otherwise all subtransactions are undone. Two-phase commit will be discussed in Section 6.6.1. Two-phase commit has been implemented in many systems and is also included in the ISO Transaction Processing (TP) standard.

Many algorithms for update synchronization and concurrency control have been proposed and implemented since the mid-1970s. Most algorithms used in practice are variants of two-phase locking (2PL), which allows a transaction to lock the resources in first phase and unlock in the second phase after performing reads/writes. Algorithms are also used to resolve distributed deadlocks, which occur when transactions wait on each other. A review of these algorithms can be found in Umar [1993, chap. 6].

6.3.2   Distributed-Transaction Models

Figure 6.3 shows a few basic models of distributed transactions. In case of remote transactions, the client submits (ships) the request to execute the transaction on a remote system. The remote transaction either commits or aborts, independent of the requesting system. In case of commit coordination, the requesting site manages the execution of the transaction across multiple sites. The protocol used in this case is two-phase commit. Serial execution moves the coordination from one site to next to complete a multisite transaction.

These three basic models can be combined to produce many other DTP models for long-running distributed transactions. In addition, the activities performed on different systems can be coordinated as queued or conversational transactions. In queued DTP, the transaction managers at different sites queue the incoming transactions and then execute them later, thus allowing for organizational boundaries and control between systems. In conversational DTP, the transaction managers interact with each other directly through the communication network. Note that queued DTP is not suitable for commit coordination—Figure 6.3(b)—because the sending site can communicate with other sites only through queues. The queued model does work quite well for remote and serial transactions.

Figure 6.3 Models of Distributed Transactions

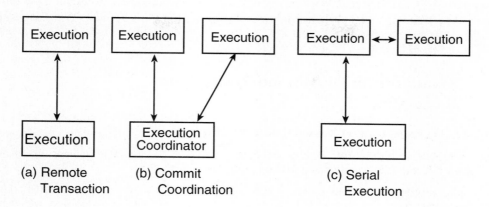

(a) Remote
    Transaction

(b) Commit
    Coordination

(c) Serial
    Execution

It is important to briefly discuss read-only distributed transactions: This happens for the following reasons:

- Updates issued by transactions did not modify any records (e.g., telephone number was changed to what it originally was).

- Updates were issued but did not occur, owing to violations of integrity constraints or programmed triggers.

Read-only distributed transactions process more quickly and incur minimal overhead.

6.3.3 Distributed-Transaction Managers: The TP-Heavy Approach

A distributed-transaction manager (DTM) is responsible for the execution of a distributed transaction from its beginning to its end and is in charge of ACID in a distributed environment. Thus a DTM must address numerous technically challenging issues such as concurrency control in distributed environments, update synchronization, and data integrity after failures in the C/S environment. Owing to the complexity of DTMs, they are referred to as "TP-heavy." Research in distributed-transaction management has actively pursued heterogeneous databases [Pu 1991, Soparkar 1991]. Although detailed technical discussion of these topics is beyond the scope of this book, we will review the key technical challenges and approaches in Section 6.8 and suggest additional sources of information.

Examples of DTM products are NCR's Top-End, BEA's Tuxedo, and Transarc's Encina. Encina is of particular importance to us because it is based on open protocols. We will describe Encina at the end of this chapter. Many DTM products at present operate in UNIX environments. It is expected that in the future more products will become available and products will operate across PC, UNIX, and MVS environments. In addition, these products will conform to the ISO and X/Open standards for distributed-transaction management. We discuss these standards next.

6.4   Standards for Distributed-Transaction Processing[1]

Standards are needed for DTP for the following reasons:

- Interoperability of two TMs from two different vendors to provide DTP services. For example, allow Tuxedo, CICS, and Encina to interoperate with each other.
- Interoperability of TMs with database managers, so that a TM from vendor X can interoperate with database managers from vendors Y and Z. For example, allow CICS to work with Informix, Oracle, and Sybase databases.

To respond to these requirements, two open standards for distributed-transaction processing are under active development:

- The X/Open Distributed Transaction Processing (DTP) Model
- The ISO Transaction Processing (OSI TP) standard.

Figure 6.4 and Figure 6.5 show two different views of the relationships between these two standards. Conceptually, each computer system has a transaction-processing environment consisting of four components: the applications (APs), the resource (database) managers (RMs), the transaction managers (TMs), and the communication resource managers (CRMs) X/Open defines the interfaces among the four components at each computer. The OSI TP protocol is used between two distributed-transation managers (possibly from two different ven-

Figure 6.4 Standards for Distributed-Transaction Processing (Single-System View)

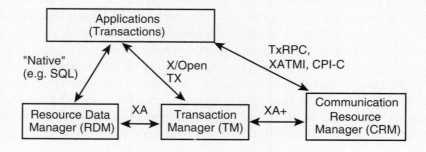

---

1. This section uses the jargon introduced by the Standards. It may be bitter medicine for some.

dors) to communicate with each other via the communication-resource managers. Let us briefly review these interfaces (the standard APIs).

The X/Open DTP defines the following application-program interfaces:

- XA is the API between the transaction manager and database (resource) managers. For example, a TM issues an *xa_prepare, xa_commit,* and *xa_rollback* to perform a two-phase commit.
- TX is the API between application programs and the transaction manager. For example, an application program issues a *tx_begin* command to start a transaction.
- "Native" calls, e.g., SQL, are issued from the transaction to the resource managers.
- XA+ is the API between a transaction manager and a communication-resource manager. This API is used by a TM to communicate with a TM on another computer through the CRM.
- Many applications to CRM APIs are being developed. Examples are the TxRPC (transactional RPC, based on DEC's Remote Task Invocation technology), CPI-C (a peer-to-peer API used in the IBM APPC environments), and XATMI (a Tuxedo Application/Transaction Management Interface).

OSI TP is primarily used between CRMs at different sites to provide global transaction control. OSI TP is a layer-7 application service element (ASE) designed to work with other layer-7 OSI ASEs such as:

- Commitment, Concurrency and Recovery (CCR), a two-phase commit protocol
- Association Control Service Element (ACSE), an association/release protocol
- User-ASE(s), a user-defined ASE which performs functions such as data transfer

Figure 6.5 Standards for Distributed-Transaction Processing (Multiple-System View)

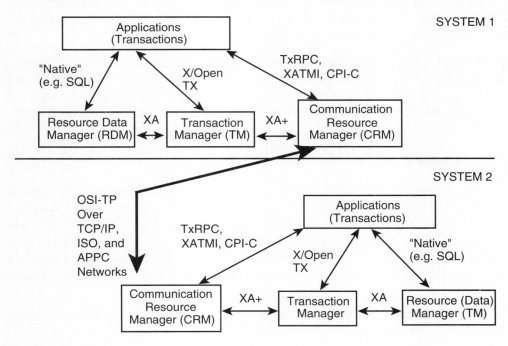

OSI-TP is a synchronization protocol between transaction managers (TMs). It does not provide data transfer and relies on the User-ASE(s) for data transfer. The protocol allows different levels of coordination between TMs; examples are "none" and "commitment." The coordination level "commitment" provides two-phase commit functionality through the CCR. The coordination level "none" bypasses this functionality and can be used as a starting point in distributed-transaction management.

The X/Open DTP is evolving and other standards are being considered (for example, the standards for queued distributed transactions are under consideration). X/Open DTP has been widely accepted by the DBMS as well TM vendors. With standardization of XA, XA+ and other aforementioned APIs, multi-vendor DBMS products that support X/Open DTP can participate in global transaction coordination.

6.5   Data-Replication Servers

A great deal of attention is being paid at present to "data-replication servers" that are responsible for managing replicated data. The work ranges from development of new algorithms (see, for example, Triantafillou [1995]) to discussion and analysis of commercially available replication servers from a wide range of vendors [Ace 1995, Leinfuss 1993, White 1994, Korzeniowski 1993, Stacey 1994, McGovern 1993]. This section presents an overview of the main concepts, defines the main terms, outlines the key technical considerations, suggests a generic architecture of replication servers, and presents a framework that can be used to analyze and evaluate various vendor offerings.

It is being argued that the data-replication servers are an alternative to distributed-transaction processing (see, for example, Schlack [1995], and McGovern [1993]). The basic argument is that instead of being updated in real time (the DTP approach), the replicated data can be updated periodically (e.g., once an hour) by using a replication server. We will examine this issue in Section 6.6.

6.5.1   Overview

Data replication is concerned with copying data, completely or partially, to multiple sites. The main advantage of replication is that the data is stored where it is used most often. In addition, replicated data can be accessed from alternate sites. Replication improves the read performance and data availability but can degrade the update performance, owing to the need to synchronize replicated copies. Depending on the business needs, data may be replicated to support operational processing or informational processing. Here are some examples of data replication:

- Price information is replicated at all stores to speed up the checkout-counter processing. The price information may be completely or partially replicated.

- Skeleton customer information (e.g., customer name, account number, credit limit) is kept at all stores to speed up the order processing. Complete customer information is kept at a central site.

- Data warehouses containing portions of data from operational systems are constructed by many enterprises to support decisions in marketing and business planning.

- Detachable computers (e.g., mobile computers) are not always connected to the data source and therefore typically keep redundant data. Detachable computers usually extract needed data and store it on their local disk for access while operating in a detached mode.

Data may be replicated for the following reasons [White 1994, Triantafillou 1995]:

- Data may be distributed to where it is used to improve performance, e.g., the price file.

- Data may be replicated to improve its availability.

- Data may be copied to detachable computers for off-line processing.

- Data from different decentralized servers or detachable clients may be integrated into one copy.

- Data is extracted from multiple operational databases and loaded/replicated into a data warehouse.

- The database on some platforms may have better tools for application development and/or administration. Thus it may be quicker and cheaper to develop and maintain new applications around the replicated data on new platforms.

- Some platforms may provide better and easier data-access and manipulation tools.

- Data may be replicated during a gradual migration period.

However, data replication can be an expensive and time-consuming activity that must be carefully coordinated. In particular, the issue of keeping the replicated data synchronized with master/primary data is of key importance.

6.5.2   Definitions and Technical Considerations

6.5.2.1   Data-Replication Servers

Data-replication servers, or just *replication servers,* manage replicated data and attempt to maximize the benefits of data replication by minimizing the costs and risks associated with replication. In essence, a replication server provides software components that replicate the changes being made at one site to other sites. The three main logical components of a replication server are (see Section 6.5.3 for more details):

- Data extractor that captures the data being changed

- Replication manager that knows the sites where the replicated copies are and sends the changes to the appropriate sites

- Data synchronizer that actually applies the changes to the replicated copies

6.5.2.2 Read-Only versus Updatable Data

Data replication is based largely on the notion of primary versus secondary copies of data:

> *Primary (Updatable) Copy.* This copy can be read as well as updated by the end users. In many practical cases, there is only one primary copy of a given data object (a data object can be a relational table, a set of data records, or a set of data fields) that is assigned to a particular site (*primary site*). However, the primary copy of data object d1 may reside on site s1, while the primary copy of data object d2 may reside on site s2 (e.g., the primary copy of prices may be in Chicago but the primary copy of customers may be in New York).

> *Secondary (Read-Only) Copies.* Each primary copy may have one or more secondary copies at other sites (*secondary sites*) that are read-only. The users of the secondary copies perform updates by submitting a special update transaction that updates the primary data. The changes in the primary data are propagated to the secondary copies periodically (asynchronously) or in real time (synchronously).

This division of data into read-only and updatable data objects provides many benefits. In some cases, the read-only copies are referred to as "snapshots." The notion of snapshots was first proposed by Adiba and Lindsay [Adiba 1980]:

> The point of the snapshot concept is that many applications—probably a majority— can tolerate or may even require data as of some particular earlier point in time.

Read-only copies are particularly useful for decision-support applications, however, they introduce serious performance problems for applications that require on-line updates. If only one primary updatable copy is maintained then all updates must be directed to this primary site. However, if multiple updatable copies are kept, then the multiple copies must be synchronized through locking mechanisms to avoid update conflicts (see the discussion on two-phase commit versus replication in Section 6.6).

6.5.2.3 Initial Replication

The data is initially replicated by using one of the following methods:

> *Full Copy.* The source data tables are copied completely (dumped) to target locations. An example is price files.

> *Subset Copy.* Segments of a table are copied to different sites. For example, the customer information may be partitioned by regions and sent to regional offices for their use.

> *Merged Copy.* Data from different tables (or table fragments) is copied to populate one or more target tables. For example, a data warehouse may be populated by extracting and merging information from different operational databases.

> *Enhanced Copy.* The target data is extracted, cleaned up, consolidated, and summarized before being loaded into a target database. This type of copying is typically used to establish data warehouses.

6.5.2.4   Update Synchronization (Transaction versus Periodic)

Update synchronization, also known as *update propagation,* refers to making all copies of data reflect the same values (i.e., if one copy is updated, then the others must be also updated). The main challenge in data replication is to keep the replicated data consistent with each other. A significant body of technical literature has been published to propose solutions that minimize the performance degradation due to data synchronization [Barghouti 1991, Bernstein 1981, Bernstein 1987, Ceri 1984, Garcia-Molina 1979, Gray 1993, Triantafillou 1995]. At the highest level, the solutions fall into two categories:

- *Transaction-level synchronization (synchronous) schemes.* These schemes are based on the assumption that if one copy of data is updated, then all other copies must be updated before the transaction terminates. If this cannot be accomplished, then the transaction must be aborted. These schemes are used by the contemporary distributed-transaction managers. The synchronization is transparent to the end users. The core technique used in these schemes is two-phase commit (see Section 6.6.1).

- *Periodic synchronization (asynchronous) schemes.* The transaction updates the primary copy and then terminates. Other copies are updated through replication servers (an off-line process) periodically (based on time and/or events).

Since the late 1980s, a great deal of industrial attention has been paid to periodic data-replication techniques and tools. This is in sharp contrast to the extensive theoretical work accumulated in transaction-level update-synchronization algorithms since the early 1970s. The trade-offs between the two approaches are discussed by McGovern [1993]. We will review these trade-offs in detail in Section 6.6. At this point let us use a simple example of detachable computers to illustrate the key points. Detachable computers (e.g., mobile laptop/notebook computers) are not always connected to the data source and therefore typically keep redundant data for quick local data access. For such systems data synchronization has to be asynchronous because the detachable computers, because of their very nature, do not know when other copies of data are being updated. In these cases, the typical periodic data synchronization technique used is:[2]

- The detachable computer calls a data server to access the latest copy of data

- The data server receives the request and then disconnects the detachable computer (this is done to save connection time while the server goes out and tries to find the needed data).

- The data server finds the needed data and calls the detachable computer.

- The data server downloads the data and then disconnects the detachable computer.

---

2. In some systems such as Lotus Notes, no callback is required. The exchange takes place immediately.

6.5.2.5 Data Refreshing versus Incremental Updating

Data refresh means that the data is recreated from scratch every time it is synchronized. In essence, this is similar to initial load discussed above (i.e., the target databases are scratched and reloaded with new data). This method is very simple but is not suitable for large databases that may require several hours to reload.

Incremental updates means that the changes (*deltas*) to one data copy are applied to other copies of data. In other words, only the changed data values are sent to the secondary copies. Incremental updates should be considered for large databases that require frequent synchronizations. This method is also known as *update propagation*. Incremental updating is more complicated than data refresh because it requires:

- A change-capture program that only extracts data that has changed.

- An incremental updater that updates only those data records that have changed.

6.5.3   General Architecture of Replication Servers

Figure 6.6 shows a set of logical components of a generalized data-replication server. In essence, a data-replication server provides software components that replicate the changes being made at a primary site to one or more secondary sites. These logical components are customized and specialized by different vendors depending on how the data is initially loaded, how it is synchronized (refreshed or incrementally updated), whether the replicated data is read-only or updatable, how the data changes are captured, and how frequently the data is synchronized.

6.5.3.1   Data Extractor

The data-extractor component is responsible for selection (capture) of needed data from the primary databases. The entire database may be selected for refresh or only deltas (i.e., data changes) may be captured. Data capture for refresh is straightforward, but considerable effort is required for delta captures. The delta captures can be achieved through a variety of techniques such as the following:

- Capture the data changes from the logs. The capture program continuously monitors the logs and extracts the needed changes. This technique is commonly known as "log scraping."

- Use database triggers, commonly available in RDBMSs, to capture the changes. The triggers can be set for times (e.g., 6 PM every day) or other events such as whenever a new order arrives.

- Employ programmatic captures from the database. A capture program scans the source databases and selects data based on predefined business rules. The capture logic is application dependent and not part of the replication server. An example of a business rule is: "Extract all data since yesterday 5 PM on highest sales in the southwestern region of the company."

Figure 6.6 Data-Replication Server Architecture

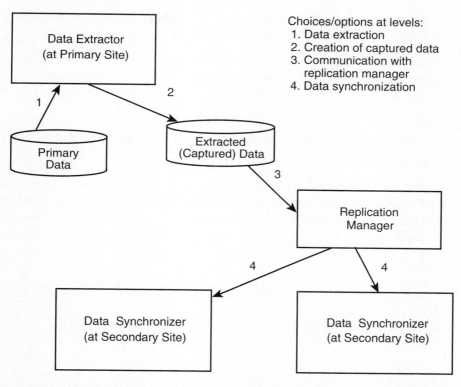

There are many trade-offs between these approaches. Basically, the log scrapers are off-line processes and do not interfere with the operation of the system. The triggers provide more flexibility but require extra programming effort. The specialized data-capture programming gives maximum flexibility to the end users but can be an expensive undertaking.

The data-extractor component may also transform the primary data into the secondary data formats, if needed. This includes conversions of data formats and data models (e.g., IMS to RDBMS). Many data replicators convert data to ASCII format and/or transform it into a target data load format. For most of the data replications, the need for extensive data conversion may not exist, because the same data in same format may be replicated at several sites (e.g., customer information at multiple sites). However, some applications such as data warehousing, require considerable transformation, such as data consolidation (unification of different values), summarization, and derivation (generation of new fields).

6.5.3.2 Replication Manager

This component is the heart of the data-replication server. It receives the data from the primary site(s) and transmits it to the appropriate secondary site(s). The replication manager may itself reside on the primary site(s), on a separate "replication server machine," on secondary site(s), or on a combination. Associated with the replication manager is a directory which shows what data is to be extracted, where it is to be sent (i.e., the secondary site(s)), how frequently it is to be sent, and whether the sent data is to be applied immediately or delayed.

The replication manager usually includes an administrative module that enables users to define, generate, initialize, and customize the various replication-server components. Examples of the administrative functionalities are:

- Generation of data-extraction and conversion programs
- Specification of the primary and secondary sites for the replicated data items
- Specification of the parameters to govern the operation of various components

The administrative functionality can be provided through a GUI operating from a desktop. The generated programs can run on a desktop or on the primary data site. The administrative facilities may also include scripting languages to ease the burden of operating and administering a data-replication server.

6.5.3.3 Data Synchronizer

This component is responsible for transmission of captured data from the primary site to the secondary site(s) and resultant data load/update at the secondary site(s). The secondary data may be replaced entirely with the new data (*refreshed*) or it may be updated selectively to reflect changes *(deltas)*. In many data-replication servers, a staging area is created on the primary sites to store the captured data. Data synchronizers employ remote data-transfer service, such as bulk data transfer or interactive data exchanges, depending on how quickly the secondary data is to be synchronized. Depending on the amount of data to be transmitted and loaded, special techniques may be used to speed up the transmission/load process (e.g., bulk database load). Typical options for this component are:

- Establish client/server sessions between the primary and secondary sites to apply the updates in real time as they become available, or employ bulk data transfer for batch update processing (e.g., end-of-day processing).

- Resolve conflicts, if applicable. Many older replicators allowed updates of primary copy only, thus no conflict resolution was needed. Newer replication servers (e.g., the latest Oracle Replicator) are beginning to add "advanced" features that allow multiple copies to be updated based on a conflict-resolution scheme. Typical conflict-resolution schemes are based on time stamps (i.e., if copy A is being updated but copy B has more recent changes, then A is not updated and the request is sent to copy B).

- Broadcast the data to all secondary sites simultaneously, or serialize the updates one secondary site at a time.

- Lock all secondary sites when they are being updated to assure that all secondary sites have the same copy of data, or ignore this locking.

- Apply updates immediately when they are received at the secondary sites, or perform bulk updates periodically.

- Use bulk load utilities and/or SQL load for RDBMSs.

6.5.4 Framework for Analyzing/Selecting Data-Replication Servers

A number of data-replication servers are becoming commercially available from a diverse array of vendors. Here is a partial list of data-replication servers, listed alphabetically:

- IBM Data Replication Toolset (Data Refresher, Data Hub, Data Propagator)
- Oracle Replicator
- Prism Warehouse Manager
- Sybase Replication Server
- Trinzic Infopump and InfoHub
- Praxis Omni Replicator

Some of these servers are oriented toward data warehousing; the others are intended for distributed-transaction processing. Analysis of these state-of-the-market servers can be found in a number of sources [Amaru 1995, Hansen 1995, Korzeniowski 1993, Leinfuss 1993, Stacey 1994, White 1994]. It is beyond the scope of this book to discuss these and other data-replication products. However, the generic architecture presented in the previous section can be used as a basis to analyze, evaluate, and select the most appropriate data-replication tools. For example, the generic architecture can be used to analyze the data-replication servers based on the following factors:

Type of primary data sources

Type of secondary sites (read-only or update)

Mechanism to capture data changes (e.g., log scrapers versus triggers)

Data-refresh and/or delta-update capabilities

Real-time versus periodic-batch update synchronization

Conflict-resolution options

Table 6.1 shows the factors that can be used to analyze/evaluate data-replication servers. These factors are presented in terms of the logical architectural components presented in the previous section. Table 6.1 can be used as a basis for generating questions that can be included in a request for proposal (RFP).

TABLE 6.1 ANALYSIS MATRIX FOR DATA-REPLICATION SERVERS

Evaluation Factors	Product 1	Product 2	Product 3
Extraction capabilities • Primary data supported (e.g., IMS, DB2, Oracle, Sybase) • Ability to select records/fields from primary databases • Method of data extraction (log scraping, triggers, programs) • Any data conversions performed			
Server management/administration capabilities • Automatic extraction/conversion of code-generation capability • Quality of code generated • Completeness of code generated • Efficiency of generated code • Ease of use (user GUI interface, training requirements) • Data-dictionary capability (ties to data dictionaries) • Productivity aids (e.g., generation of scripts, JCL created)			
Update-synchronization capabilities • Client/server sessions between the primary and secondary sites or bulk data transfers • Broadcast the data to all secondary sites, or serialize • Lock all secondary tables (or rows) when they are being updated, or ignore this locking • Apply updates immediately when they are received at the secondary sites, or perform bulk updates periodically • Use bulk load utilities and/or SQL load for RDBMSs			
Operability (environment needed for tool operation, e.g., PCs, UNIX workstations)			
Vendor maturity (strength of company, market position, etc.)			

Evaluation Factors	Product 1	Product 2	Product 3
Replication-server maturity (product reliability, product direction)			
Product support (based on other client feedback and customer-service contracts, technical support, help-desk support)			

6.6 Two-Phase Commit versus Data-Replication Servers

Implementation of algorithms for failure handling of distributed transactions is an expensive undertaking. Two-phase commit (2PC) and data-replication servers are two different approaches to guarantee integrity of distributed data under failures. Two-phase commit as well as replication servers have some trade-offs. Owing to the academic and industrial activity in two-phase commit and the widespread availability of replication servers, a careful analysis of the trade-offs is essential for several practical situations.

The reader should keep in mind that both issues are transparent to the end users. The discussion in this section is intended for a general understanding of the issues and approaches that should lead to improved strategies for the overall architecture.

6.6.1 Two-Phase Commit

Two-phase commit is the principal method of ensuring atomicity of distributed transactions. For a single-site transaction, updates are made permanent when a transaction commits, and updates are rolled back if a transaction aborts. However, a distributed transaction may commit at one node and abort at another. For example, update completes at node n1 and fails at n2. A transaction, distributed or not, may terminate abnormally for two reasons: "suicide," indicating that a transaction terminates due to an internal error like a program error, or "murder," indicating an external-error-like system crash [Gray 1979]. It is the responsibility of two-phase commit software to remove all changes made by a failing transaction from all nodes so that the transaction can be reinitiated. Basically, for atomic actions to be recoverable, the following two conditions must be met:

- Updated objects are not released until the action is completed.
- The initial states of all objects modified by the action can be reconstructed through the use of a log.

The two-phase-commit protocol adheres to these conditions and coordinates the commit actions needed to run a transaction. When a transaction issues a COMMIT request, then a series of actions are initiated. These actions are divided into two distinct phases:

Phase 1 (Prepare). This phase is preparatory; the commit is not actually carried out in this phase. The participating sites record enough information in the logs so that a transaction can be rolled back or committed, if needed. The specific steps in this phase are:

1. The "commit global coordinator" (the initiating node) sends a PREPARE message to all cohorts (commit coordinators running on nodes participating in the execution of this transaction).

2. Each cohort logs enough information so that it can roll back or commit the transaction.

3. Each cohort sends one of the following responses to the global coordinator:

    "prepared"—the modified data has been prepared for commit or rollback

    "read-only"—no data on the node has been modified, so no prepare is needed

    "abort"—the node cannot successfully prepare

4. The global coordinator waits for a reply from all cohorts.

5. If all cohorts indicate "prepared," then the next phase is initiated; if any cohort indicates "abort," then the entire transaction is rolled back at all sites; if a cohort indicates "read-only," then that cohort is bypassed from commit processing (this expedites the two-phase-commit processing).

Phase 2 (Commit). If all cohorts respond "prepared" and/or "read-only," then the initiating site (global coordinator):

1. Writes a COMMIT entry into the log

2. Sends a COMMIT message to each cohort

3. Waits for positive response from each cohort; if no response, then writes abort message and terminates the transaction

4. Writes a complete entry in the log and terminates

The key problem in two-phase commit is failure of the global coordinator (i.e., the originating node fails during commit processing). In addition, two-phase commit causes tremendous delays and "discomfort" in an unreliable environment (it is tough to succeed in two-phase commit if any cohort fails for one reason or another!).

The protocol described here shows the basic two-phase-commit processing. A great deal of intricate processing takes place at the originating node and cohorts (see Gray [1993] for details). Two-phase commit (2PC) has been implemented in several systems with some variations to deal with different failure conditions. In general, two-phase commit is offered by DBMS vendors as automatic (i.e., totally done on behalf of application developers) or programmatic (i.e., 2PC subroutines are provided to application developers for customized usage). An extensive discussion of the reliability issues for no data replication, data replication, full replication, and network partitioning is given by Garcia-Molina [1987].

6.6.2   Trade-offs between Two-Phase Commit and Replication Servers

Two-phase commit (2PC) and data-replication servers are two different approaches to guarantee integrity of distributed and replicated data under failures. The fundamental difference between them is the transaction-level versus periodic propagation of updates (update synchronization).

Transaction-level update synchronization, as discussed in Section 6.5.2.4, is the basis of 2PC. In this synchronization scheme, a distributed transaction is treated as an atomic action, and thus all updates must be synchronized during a distributed transaction or the entire transaction must be rolled back. This is the basic reason for the somewhat complicated steps of 2PC. Periodic update synchronization, on the other hand, synchronizes updates after completion of a transaction. This approach, used in the commonly available data-replication servers, does not respect the boundaries of distributed transactions (i.e., data is synchronized after a transaction has completed).

Both approaches have certain advantages and disadvantages. 2PC has the following major pluses and minuses:

+ All updates are simultaneously available to end users.
+ Guarantees atomicity of a distributed transaction.
+ Is fully transparent to end users.
+ Many improvements have been introduced to increase robustness, flexibility, and efficiency.
− Chances of failures are high in unreliable systems (transactions abort too many times).
− Takes too long if many copies of data exist (too many cohorts).
− Creates difficult situations if the global commit coordinator (the originating site) fails during 2PC.
− Does not allow many customizations and complicated application rules (e.g., retry prepare if cohort responds with "abort," apply an update after certain time).

Owing to these limitations of 2PC, replication servers are becoming a viable alternative for many organizations. However, the periodic update-synchronization scheme used in many replication servers also has some pluses and minuses:

+ Very flexible (can be configured for different situations such as events, time, triggers, etc.).
+ Can offer additional capabilities (i.e., conversion and transformation of data).

+ Can be used for large and occasionally unreliable networks.

– Requires a primary/secondary copy (this paradigm may not fit some applications). This restriction is being removed in modern replication servers by introducing conflict resolutions that are based on rules or manual intervention.

– Some notion of global time must be maintained to assure that updates are synchronized at certain times.

Owing to these trade-offs, some systems provide transaction as well as periodic update synchronization. For example, several replication servers allow transactional update synchronization that employs 2PC.

The following guidelines are suggested to the users of 2PC and replication servers [McGovern 1993]:

• Keep data replication as minimal as possible. Large number of replicates can cause serious problems in 2PC as well as replication servers.

• If data must be synchronized as a transaction, then keep the number of copies small and use 2PC.

• If concurrency requirements outweigh "subsecond" data-integrity requirements (i.e., data can be synchronized periodically), then use replication servers.

• If the network and nodes are unreliable, then use replication servers

A detailed discussion of the trade-offs with examples from Oracle and Sybase is given by McGovern [1993]. Extensive discussion of this topic can be found in Schussel [1994], Gray [1993], and Garcia-Molina [1987].

6.7 C/S Transaction Processing: TP-Less, TP-Lite, TP-Heavy

In C/S environments, approaches to handle transactions (data update) vary widely, owing to the wide range of C/S configurations (small PC LAN-based systems versus large systems involving multiple mainframes), query versus update traffic (ad hoc SQL queries versus massive updates), vendor offerings (database vendors versus TP vendors), and user/developer background (PC users/developers versus mainframe users/developers). The approaches now being used fall into the following categories:

• TP-less, i.e., do not use any transaction-management considerations.

• TP-lite, i.e., use database procedures to handle updates.

• TP-heavy, i.e., use a transaction manager to handle updates.

Another approach, somewhere between TP-lite and TP-heavy (perhaps TP-medium), is becoming increasingly popular, owing to the growth in message-oriented middleware (MOM). See the sidebar "Running to MOM for Distributed-Transaction Processing."

6.7.1 TP-Less

In this case, the database and file-management capabilities for retrieving and updating data are used. For example, some relational-database vendors treat each SQL statement as a transaction. Thus each SQL select, update, insert, and delete is treated as a unit of consistency. However, a group of SQL statements are not combined into a transaction that must be committed or aborted. Similarly, in file systems, each file read and update is treated by the users as a transaction (there is a potentially serious problem here, because many file systems do not provide the capabilities to treat each file I/O as a transaction).

TP-less is currently being used heavily in small C/S environments with PCs and UNIX machines. In particular, this approach is favored heavily when all data needed by the users is on one SQL server. TP-less has the advantage of being efficient and inexpensive (no additional overhead and software is needed). However, it has several limitations. First, it cannot be used when some data is in flat files (the ability of file managers to provide ACID properties should be examined carefully). Second, related updates cannot be grouped together as a transaction. Finally, all data must reside on one site (TP-less may use a data-replication server to handle duplicate data on multiple sites).

6.7.2 TP-Lite

TP-lite goes a step beyond TP-less by implementing each transaction as a stored procedure. Recall that a stored procedure is a collection of SQL statements that are performed as a unit. A user can define, for example, a set of SQL statements that update a customer account and store them in a database-management system as a stored procedure that is invoked from different programs that need to update customer-account information. Any updates that need to be performed together and any retrievals that are dependent on these updates can be embedded in a stored procedure. In addition, stored procedures can enforce any additional integrity and security restrictions. TP-lite capabilities are provided by most RDBMS vendors, such as Informix, Oracle, and Sybase (basically, any vendor that supports stored procedures is in the TP-lite business).

TP-lite works well with replication servers, i.e., update the primary copy by using stored procedures and replicate the secondary copies by using a replication server.

TP-lite is mainly the invention of database vendors to provide *some* transaction-management capabilities. This approach, when combined with data replication servers to synchronize replicated-data, appeals to many C/S application developers. TP-lite is being widely used to manage transactions in C/S environments where the data resides on a single SQL server. TP-lite is better than TP-less (it supports a group of SQL statements as a transaction), but it does not provide any global transaction control. In addition, TP-lite cannot be used to handle transactions that need access to data stored in flat files (stored procedures are the domain of database vendors).

Running to MOM for Distributed-Transaction Processing

Message-oriented middleware (MOM) is gaining popularity for many applications, including lightweight implementations of distributed-transaction processing (DTP).

MOM, discussed in detail in Chapter 3, allows an application A to put a message on a queue that is later picked up by application B (or C and D) to process asynchronously. A queue can be a print stream or any intermediate file. This simple approach can be used to link existing applications very easily without modifying any code at either side (i.e., redirect the output of application A to a disk queue and redirect the input of system B to the same disk queue). This approach does not require the additional software development on either side (you do not need a client that issues an RPC and a server that receives, parses and dispatches processes). This also eliminates the need for staff training on both sides.

The main appeal of MOM for DTP is that the queue messaging can be transactional (i.e., MOM can make sure that only one message is transferred and that automated roll/back recovery is available). This is a very familiar territory for mainframe-based transaction managers such as IMS (IMS has been using queued messages since the 1970s).

For example, message queues can be used to perform distributed-transaction processing (TP-heavy) without having to implement the two-phase commit. The basic idea is to divide the transaction into three units of work [Dolgicer 1996]:

- The first unit of work writes the messages on the client machine queue, reads any responses from this queue, and processes them.

- The second unit of work transfers the messages between the client machine queue and the server machine queue, and vice versa.

- The third unit of work picks the messages from the server queue, processes them and stores the responses on the server queue.

These three units of work can be committed individually by using the MOM facilities and can collectively support reliable distributed transactions.

MOM providers such as IBM, DEC, Peer Logic and Covia Technologies are actively pursuing this opportunity. A state-of-the-market analysis of this topic can be found in Brett [1996].

6.7.3   TP-Heavy

TP-heavy uses a separate TM to manage transactions in C/S environments. As discussed previously in this chapter, these TMs maintain the ACID properties of transactions that may span many database servers (i.e., they support DTP). For example, they allow PCs to initiate complex multiserver transactions from the desktop. TP-heavy systems support the DTP functions discussed earlier in this chapter (i.e., global concurrency control, distributed two-phase commit, failure handling). More importantly, TP-heavy systems are not restricted to database transactions—they manage all data (flat files, databases, and queues). Examples of TP-heavy products for C/S environments include CICS, Encina, Tuxedo, and Top End.

TP-heavy has the obvious appeal that it takes transaction management seriously. TP-heavy is essential when transactions involve data stored in multiple formats on multiple sites. However, TP-heavy may be too "heavy" for small C/S applications that need access to data stored on a single SQL server.

6.7.4   Trade-offs between TP-Lite and TP-Heavy

It appears that TP-lite and TP-heavy have certain pluses and minuses in C/S environments (TP-less is too restricted for most serious business applications). The following questions should be asked by an application developer before deciding on TP-lite versus TP-heavy:

- In what format is the data stored (databases, flat files)? If the data is stored in multiple databases and flat files, then TP-lite is not suitable (database procedures work only in RDBMS environments).

- How many SQL servers does the data reside on? If the application needs to update and commit data that is stored on multiple servers, then TP-heavy should be used (database procedures cannot participate with other database procedures in a distributed transaction).

- What is the requirement for data synchronization? If the data-synchronization interval is periodic, then a TP-lite solution combined with a data-replication server may be useful to handle updates against replicated data.

- What are the requirements for performance and load balancing? TP-lite solutions with database procedures are much faster, on the surface, than the TP-heavy solutions that require synchronization between sites. But TP-heavy solutions provide many sophisticated procedures for dynamic load balancing, priority scheduling, process restarts, and prestarted servers that are especially useful for large-scale production environment. These features are the main strength of TP-heavy products, because many of these products have been used over the years to handle thousands of transactions in production OLTP (on-line transaction processing) environments.

While the debate between the TP-lite and TP-heavy proponents continues (see, for example, Peterson [1995], and Schlack [1995]), small C/S applications are being deployed by using TP-lite, while large mission-critical C/S applications, especially the ones that were "downsized" from mainframe OLTP environments, are using TP-heavy. In the meantime, many PC LAN-based applications are quite happy with TP-less.

6.8 Distributed-Data and Transaction Management: A Consolidation

So far, we have considered several aspects of C/S transaction processing. Let us now consolidate this material with the distributed-data access approaches discussed in the previous chapter. Our objective is to develop a consistent framework to deal with the access as well as update of distributed and replicated data in distributed environments.

Let us introduce the notion of a *distributed-data and transaction management system (DDTMS)* that is responsible for managing all data (files plus databases) and the operations on the data (queries, updates) in a distributed computing environment. A DDTMS can be viewed as middleware that extends the functionality of the distributed-data manager (described in the previous chapter) to include the C/S transaction-processing capabilities discussed in this chapter. Figure 6.7 shows a conceptual view of DDTMS and depicts how DDTMS interacts with and interrelates to the following components (note the similarity between this model and the distributed-data management model described in the previous chapter):

- Applications (transactions) which generate the queries/transactions (e.g., SQL statements).

- Local data and transaction management systems (LDTMSs) which manage access and update of local data.

- Remote communication interfaces (RCIs) for sending/receiving messages across a network. RCI may use the typical C/S protocols such as remote-procedure call (RPC), remote-data access, and message-oriented middleware (MOM).

- Network services which transport the messages between sites. The network services may include, if needed, network gateways to convert network protocols (e.g., TCP/IP to SNA).

- Global directories that show the location of data and other servers in the network. For example, Figure 6.7 shows two global directories showing that data table d1 is located on computer C1 and data table d2 is located on computer C2.

A DDTMS performs a diverse array of functions. A DDTMS designer encounters the following main challenges:

- Global data definition and translation, i.e., how to provide view integration.

- Global directory allocation, i.e., where to place the global directories.

- Distributed-file processing (DFP), i.e., how to provide transparent access, manipulation, and administration (e.g., security) of data files that are located at different computers in the network (we covered this topic in the previous chapter).

- Single-site remote-data access and distributed query processing (DQP), i.e., how to provide transparent read-access and query processing of remotely located databases in a network (we covered this topic in the previous chapter).

- Distributed-transaction processing (DTP), i.e., how to coordinate the execution of a single transaction across multiple systems and how to assure concurrency (i.e., simultaneous access) and data integrity (i.e., the transaction must be completed properly or entirely withdrawn in the event of a failure). We have discussed DTP earlier in this chapter.

Figure 6.7 A Conceptual Model of DDTMS

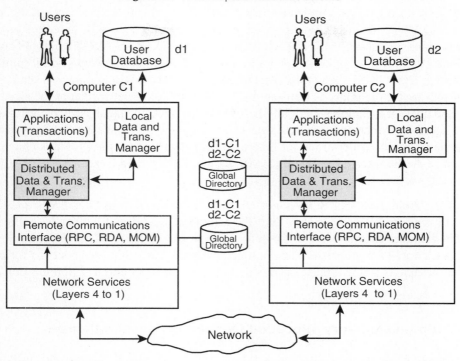

These challenges are briefly reviewed and the key approaches to meet these challenges are outlined. A more detailed technical discussion of these topics can be found in Umar [1993, chap. 6].

6.8.1   Global Data Definition and Translation Challenges

The target data may be stored in homogeneous (e.g., all relational) or heterogeneous data sources (e.g., IMS, DB2, indexed files, OODBMS). A common global schema is needed to parse the queries against these data sources. The global schema shows all the data in the network and shows where the data is located. The problem of global schema design is straightforward if all the data sources are homogeneous but is nontrivial in a network with heterogeneous databases. In such cases, the key challenges are:

- How to define data
- Where the query is translated (originating node or target node)

At present, most DDTMS (distributed data and transaction management systems) use SQL for schema definition and manipulation [Richter 1994, Ozsu 1991 (book), Rauch-Hinden

1987, Thomas 1990, Ricciuti 1991]. This is primarily due to the popularity of SQL. In most cases, SQL is used to issue queries against nonrelational databases and even flat files. For example, EDA/SQL from Information Builders Incorporated uses SQL to access more than 35 data sources, including IMS, DB2, Sybase, Oracle, ADABAS, VSAM files, Focus files, etc. [Bland 1993]. Similarly, IBM's Data Joiner uses SQL to define views and join information stored in DB2, IMS, VSAM, Sybase, Oracle, and other ODBC-compliant data sources. In almost all cases, the query is translated from SQL to the target format at the target computers. The query translation is typically accomplished through "database drivers" that translate SQL to other formats (e.g., SQL to IMS Data Language calls). We have already discussed the schema design considerations for heterogeneous databases in the previous chapter. The interested reader is referred to Sheth [1990], Litwin [1990], and Cardenas [1987] for more details on this topic.

The reader should note that SQL is not adequate to represent the OODBMS queries (the OODBMS data model is far richer than the relational model and cannot be expressed in SQL). On the other extreme, it is difficult to use SQL for the legacy databases and file structures that are not in common use. For example, although many SQL drivers exist for popular file systems such as VSAM, these drivers do not exist for older and less popular flat files.

6.8.2   Global Directory Allocation (Name Services) Challenges

It is customary to show the [data, node assigned] pair in the global schema and store the global schema in a *global directory*. Owing to the number of global directory accesses, it is crucial to allocate the global directory carefully. The directory-allocation problem can be treated as a file-allocation problem (FAP), where a file F is allocated to N nodes to minimize a given objective function. For example, Chu [1976, 1984] has studied the directory-allocation problem as an FAP. The following trade-offs can be observed:

- If the directory is at a central site, then the communication cost is high, because every transaction will need to access the central site to locate data.

- If the directory is at every site, then the update cost will increase, owing to duplicate directory updates.

A common approach used in small networks is to store the directory at a central node with the following processing rules:

- Search the local directory at the arriving node.

- If not found, then search the directory at the central site.

Many other approaches for directory allocation are conceivable. For example, instead of one centralized directory, many "regional" directories may be established where each directory shows the location of data within a subnet (see Ozsu [1991 (book)], and Bernstein [1987] for details).

6.8.3   Distributed-File Processing Challenges

The DDTMS challenge is to integrate the access and manipulation of remotely located flat files with databases. In other words, the end user should not know if the target data being accessed is in a flat file or a relational database. As mentioned previously, SQL has become a de facto standard to provide this end-user transparency. This capability is currently included in many commercially available products (e.g., IBM's Data Joiner and IBI's EDA/SQL). The reader should once again note that integration of older file systems into DDTMS is a nontrivial task, because off-the-shelf products for remote processing of such file systems are not readily available. Most commercially available products are targeted toward heavily used file systems such as IBM's VSAM (Virtual Sequential Access Method).

6.8.4   Distributed-Query Processing Challenges

The technical challenge is to develop an access strategy to minimize communication cost (or response time). In practice, the most important pragmatic issue is how to do the joins between remotely located tables. Joins between remote sites can cause a considerable amount of communication traffic. For example, a remote join between an N-row table and an M-row table can theoretically cause $N \times M$ network messages (imagine remote joins between tables with millions of rows!). A technique known as *semijoin* has been proposed to optimize remote joins by sending only the necessary data between computers to perform a join [Bernstein 1981 *(JACM)*]. Simply stated, semijoin consists of the following steps for joining R1 and R2 on attribute A:

- Relation R1 is projected on attribute A, giving R1'. In other words, R1' is the column A of R1.

- R1' is transmitted to R2 and joined with R2, giving R2'. In other words, only one column of R1 is transmitted to R2 site. The join is performed at the destination site and not over the network. This significantly reduces the network traffic.

- R2' is transmitted to R1 and joined with R1, giving the final join. In other words, only a small fraction of R2 is transmitted, once again reducing the network traffic.

In addition to remote joins, the following distributed-query optimization algorithms issues need to be considered:

- Where to access the data if duplicate copies of data exist. In most cases, the nearest copy of data is accessed.

- What paradigm to use to access the remotely located data. A query may send ad hoc SQL or invoke remotely located procedures to access the remote databases. We have discussed this issue under the remote-data-access (RDA) and remote-procedure-call (RPC) paradigms.

- How to utilize the trade-offs between slow networks (e.g., WANs) or slow computers (e.g., congested systems). Many query-optimization algorithms have been published in the literature for slow networks (these algorithms minimize communication and maximize use of CPU) and for fast networks (these algorithms maximize communication traffic and avoid CPU utilization).

- How to do joins between heterogeneous data sources (e.g., joins between RDBMSs from two different vendors, join between RDBMS and a flat file). The current state-of-the-market solution for this problem is to use ANSI SQL for joins.

More details about these topics are available [Umar 1993, Ozsu 1991 (book), Ozsu 1991, Ceri 1984, Hevner 1979].

6.8.5   Distributed-Transaction Processing Challenges

Database consistency/concurrency and data integrity to handle failures of distributed transactions are the two key challenges.

6.8.5.1   Database Consistency/Concurrency

Concurrency control coordinates simultaneous access to shared data. The problem of concurrency control in centralized DBMSs is well understood, and one approach, called *two-phase locking*, has been accepted as a standard solution for a long time [Eswaran 1976]. However, concurrency control in distributed systems is an area of considerable activity with few accepted solutions. This is due to three main complicating factors.

- Data may be duplicated in a DDTMS, consequently, the DDTMS is responsible for updating the duplicate data.

- If some sites fail or if some communication links fail while an update is being executed, the DDTMS must make sure that the effects will be reflected on the failing node after recovery.

- Synchronization of transactions on multiple sites is very difficult, because each site cannot obtain immediate information on the actions currently being carried out on other sites.

Owing to these difficulties, over 50 concurrency-control algorithms have been proposed in the past, and others continue to appear. Literature surveys have shown that most algorithms are variants of two-phase locking and time-stamped algorithms [Bernstein 1987, Bernstein 1981 *(ACM)*]. However, several algorithms do not fall into any category. A review of these algorithms can be found in Umar [1993]. For a very detailed discussion of concurrency-control algorithms, refer to Bernstein [1981 *(ACM)*], Kohler [1981], Bernstein [1987], and Elmagarmid [1992].

The reader should note that most of these algorithms assume a transaction-level update-synchronization interval (i.e., updates to one database must be synchronized with all other copies before a transaction terminates). As we saw in the discussion of replication servers, many organizations have found that a periodic (e.g., once an hour or once a day) synchronization interval is an adequate pragmatic solution instead of the expensive and complicated concurrency-control algorithms.

6.8.5.2   Failure Detection and Transaction Recovery

As stated previously, when a transaction commits, all transaction updates are permanent, but if a transaction aborts, updates are rolled back. In DDTMS, transaction may commit at one site and abort at another, owing to failures in the network and/or the computing sites. For example, an update at node n1 completes but fails at n2 because of system failure at n2. The common approach used is two-phase commit (2PC) discussed in Section 6.6.

An extensive recovery system for distributed-database management systems was first proposed by Gray [1979] and implemented in System R. The approach used in System R has been used widely as a generic solution. This system consists of four protocols:

- *Consistency locks:* This means that each transaction must be well formed and two phase. A transaction is well formed if it locks an object before accessing it, does not lock an already locked item, and unlocks each locked item before termination. A transaction exhibits two-phase behavior if no objects are unlocked before all objects are locked. Transactions using 2PL are automatically well formed and two phase.

- *DO-UNDO-REDO log:* This is an incremental log of changes to the databases which records the before/after images of each update during the transaction processing (DO operation). This log also allows removal (UNDO) of a failed transaction's updates and reapplication (REDO) of the successful transaction's updates in the event of a database crash.

- *Write-ahead log:* This protocol consists of writing an update to a log before applying it to the database.

- *Two-phase commit:* This protocol coordinates the commit actions needed to run a transaction. When the transaction issues a COMMIT request, then a "commit coordinator" initiates the two-phase commit process we have discussed previously.

For comprehensive failure handling in distributed environments, the concurrency-control techniques are combined with consistency control for failure handling and timeout for deadlock resolution into a single algorithm of distributed-transaction management. For example, the two-phase-locking, two-phase-commit, and timeout algorithms are combined into a single concurrency- and consistency-control algorithm of a potential DDTMS.

Implementation of sophisticated algorithms for failure handling is an expensive and time-consuming undertaking. Replication servers are becoming a viable alternative for many organizations, because two-phase commit does not behave very well when data is updated at many sites and when the network is unreliable (see the discussion in Section 6.6). Owing to the widespread availability of replication servers, and the many additional features (e.g., conversion) offered by these servers, a careful analysis of the trade-offs between using two-phase-commit-based algorithms versus using replication servers is needed (see Section 6.6).

6.9   Evaluation Framework

A DDTMS can be configured and implemented by using a variety of approaches discussed in the previous section. At a high level, we can categorize DDTMS in terms of the following major capabilities discussed in the previous section:

- Global data-definition and translation capabilities
- Global directory-allocation capabilities
- Distributed-file processing capabilities
- Distributed-query processing capabilities
- Distributed-transaction processing capabilities

These capabilities depend on the choices of appropriate techniques and algorithms to address the challenges discussed in the previous section. For example, one DDTMS may not include any distributed-file processing capabilities, another may only provide distributed-query processing, while a third may provide distributed-transaction processing capabilities only through periodic update synchronizations.

Another dimension to evaluating DDTMS products is the type of environment in which the distributed and replicated data needs to be managed (we can add other dimensions also, such as the business drivers, etc.). Let us use the following variables as a starting point to represent the target operating environment:

- *Homogeneous versus heterogeneous data sources.* The data sources may all be RDBMSs from the same vendor or may be widely heterogeneous.
- *Network control (central, distributed).* One node may be designated to coordinate all DDTMS interactions, or the interactions may be peer-to-peer.
- *Number of copies allowed in a network.* There may be a single, two (one at central site, one at local site), and more than two replicated copies.

Table 6.2 shows a simple two-dimensional framework to categorize the complexity of data distribution and replication-management decisions and to help the managers to evaluate appropriate products. The rows of Table 6.2 reflect the various capabilities (e.g., global database definition, global directory allocation, distributed-transaction processing). The columns of Table 6.2 show five environment configurations based on the environment variables (e.g., data sources, network control, level of replication). The configurations in Table 6.2 show the complexity range of a user environment. The simplest implementation of a DDTMS is for configuration 1 (homogeneous, centrally controlled, unique data allocation). It is most difficult for configuration 5, when the data sources are widely heterogeneous, there is no central control, and the data can be replicated at several sites. This is why many products support configurations 1 and 2, and very few support configuration 5. Let us review the entries in Table 6.2.

The first configuration is straightforward to support for the following reasons:

- Database definition and translation are not difficult, because all data sources are relational (SQL can be used everywhere).

- Directory allocation is not difficult, because the central site can be used to house the global data directory.

- Distributed-file processing capability is not required, because all data is housed in relational databases.

- Distributed-query optimization is simple, because data is at unique sites and the algorithms do not need to find the "nearest" data site for optimal results.

- Distributed-transaction processing capability is also not difficult. Specifically, database consistency/concurrency control is relatively simple, because data is not duplicated and update synchronization is not needed. Failure handling is also simple, because there is no need to synchronize updates after failures.

In summary, configuration 1 is quite simple to implement and can be supported easily by a DDTMS product. Consequently, several commercially available DDTMS from vendors such as IBM, Oracle, Informix, and Sybase support this configuration. For example, most systems support relational DBMS, assume some level of centralized control, and allow limited or no data distribution. Remote-procedure call (RPC) and remote-data access (RDA) paradigms are supported by many C/S middleware products to directly access the data where it resides. This approach allows a single application to access many databases (i.e., program P can access table T1 on node n1 and T2 on node n2).

Configuration 2 is somewhat more difficult to implement because the database consistency/concurrency, distributed-query optimization, and failure handling have to deal with limited data duplication. This configuration is also supported by many vendor products (the key database vendors such as IBM, Oracle, Informix, and Sybase support this option).

Configuration 3 becomes more difficult to implement, because the number of options in database consistency/concurrency, query optimization, and failure handling increase, owing to many copies of data in the system. In this case, two-phase commit may not be suitable, especially if large numbers of duplicated copies are allowed. Data-replication servers may be more suitable for this configuration (and also for the later configurations).

Configuration 4 becomes even harder to implement; the directory allocation is complicated, because there are many sites where the data can exist. Configuration 5 is the most difficult configuration to support, because many choices and trade-offs exist at all levels; consequently, it is not supported by many vendor products.

The main point is that organizations should strive to stay with configurations 1 and 2, if possible, by controlling the level of data replication and data heterogeneity.

TABLE 6.2 A FRAMEWORK FOR EVALUATION OF DDTMS FACILITIES

	Global data definition	Global directory allocation	Distributed-file processing	Distributed-query processing	Distributed-transaction processing
Config. 1 • Homogeneous data sources • No data duplication • Centrally controlled network	Not difficult (use SQL)	Allocate directory to central site	Not applicable	Not difficult (use remote joins)	Not difficult (no need for update synchronization)
Config. 2 • Same as config. 1 • One copy can exist at central site	Not difficult (use SQL)	Allocate directory to central site	Not applicable	Moderate difficulty (use of an alternate copy)	Moderate difficulty (need for synchronizing two copies). Can use 2PC.
Config. 3 • Same as config. 2 • Several copies can exist at other sites	Not difficult (use SQL)	Allocate directory to central site	Not applicable	Optimization difficult (choice between many alternate copies)	Very difficult (need for synchronizing many copies). 2PC may not be adequate.
Config. 4 • Same as config. 3 • No central control	Not difficult (use SQL)	Directory cannot be allocated to central site	Not applicable	Optimization difficult (choice between many alternate copies)	Very difficult (need for synchronizing many copies). 2PC may not be adequate.
Config. 5 • Same as config. 4 • Heterogeneous data sources (e.g., heterogeneity with OODBMS, old flat files)	Many difficulties (cannot use SQL for OODBMS)	Directory cannot be allocated to central site	Many difficulties with older files	Optimization difficult (choice between many alternate copies)	Very difficult (need for synchronizing many copies). 2PC may not be adequate.

DDTMSs have moved from research to commercial products. However, the differences between the research results and commercial availability need to be understood. Evaluation of commercial DDTMS is difficult, owing to the discrepancies between promised versus available facilities. In general, the complexity of the DDTMS to be developed depends on the options supported (requirements to be satisfied). It is easier to develop DDTMS which support single-copy and homogeneous-data sources. The difficulties encountered in implementing DDTMS must be carefully weighed against the advantages of DDTMS over centralized systems. For several applications, it may still be better to provide a centralized database or use a single copy DDTMS after all of the costs for query processing, concurrency control, and failure management have been taken into account.

It is beyond the scope of this book to discuss various DDTMS products. Some analysis can be found in Graham [1987], Rauch-Hinden [1987], Ricciuti [1991], Semich [1991], and McCord [1987]. Some of the oldest implementations of DDTMS, e.g., the Tandem Encompass, are described in detail by Gray [1987]. In addition to the commercially available DDTMS, several research-and-development DDTMS are being developed in different parts of the world. The book by Ozsu and Valduriez [Ozsu 1991] describes many such efforts.

6.10   Example of an Open Distributed-Transaction Processor: Encina

6.10.1   Overview

Encina is a distributed-transaction processor developed by Transarc, a spin-off from Carnegie Mellon University.[3] Encina, currently available on many UNIX platforms, is built over DCE—OSF DCE is used as a transport for Encina (see Figure 6.8). Encina makes extensive use of DCE facilities such as DCE RPCs, threads, security, directory services, and Interface Definition Language. In addition, Encina provides database support over DCE (e.g., Informix and Oracle support over DCE RPCs) and it follows X/Open standards (e.g., TX and XA). It thus provides DDTMS capabilities. Basically:

Encina = DCE + transactional RPC + application recovery
      + monitor functions + database support

As shown in Figure 6.8, Encina functionality can be described in terms of the following layers over OSF DCE:

- *Encina Toolkit Executive:* programming interfaces for defining transactional clients and servers and for two-phase-commit support

---

3. At the time of this writing, Transarc is owned by IBM.

- *Encina Toolkit Server Core:* extensions of Toolkit Executive to support recoverable data
- *Encina Extended Transaction-Processing Services:* additional services needed for transaction monitoring, file systems, and peer-to-peer communications gateways for mainframe access

Figure 6.8 Encina Services

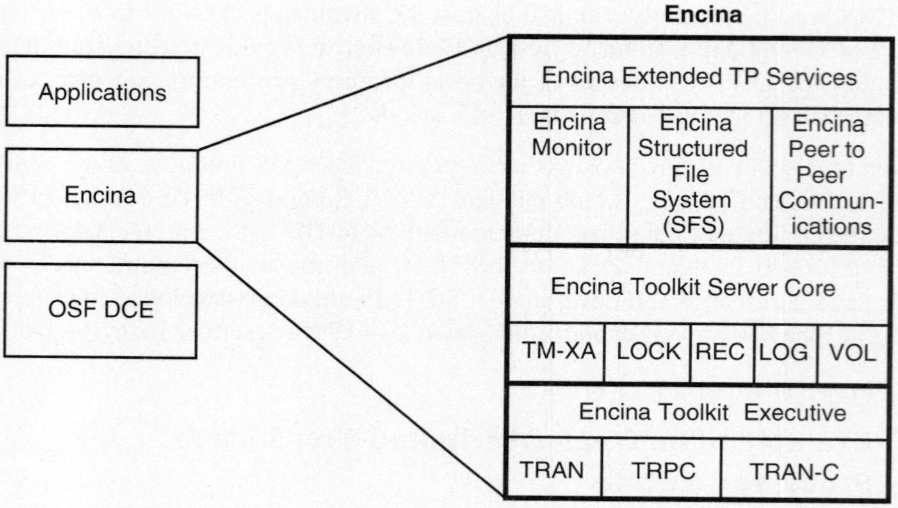

The next sections briefly review the Encina layers. Owing to the dependence of Encina on OSF DCE, the reader should review OSF DCE in chapter 3 before proceeding.

6.10.2 Encina Toolkit Executive

The purpose of Encina Toolkit Executive is to provide programming interfaces for defining transactional clients and servers and to perform two-phase-commit processing. The components of the Toolkit Executive are:

Transactional Services (TRAN): TRAN provides the basic services needed by a transaction. Examples of the transactional services provided by Encina are transaction demarcation verbs that programs can use (e.g., begin, prepare, commit, abort), support for nested transactions (i.e., one transaction can invoke other transactions), and distributed two-phase commit

Transactional RPC (TRPC): TRPCs extend DCE RPC to support transaction processing. For example, if an RPC fails, then DCE does not guarantee that any of the changes made by the RPC will be rolled out. In contrast, each TRPC is treated as a unit of consistency. In particular, a TRPC supports ACID properties and provides additional guarantees (e.g., 0-1 semantics) to handle transaction failures. Transaction Interface Definition Language (TIDL) is introduced to define the TRPC parameters being exchanged between clients and servers. TIDL essentially extends DCE IDL for transactions. TRPC also utilizes DCE name services, DCE security, DCE RPC transport, and DCE threads. A TRPC may involve one or more servers. For example, you can issue TRPCs from one client to multiple servers within scope of a single transaction.

Transactional-C (TRAN-C): TRAN-C is a programming language that provides a C interface to simplify coding of concurrent transactional programs. TRAN-C consists of macros and libraries that can be invoked by application developers, thus reducing the number of calls needed to code transactional programs. TRAN-C supports threading through a Threads Transactional Identification (TID).

6.10.3   Encina Toolkit Server Core

The purpose of the Toolkit Server Core is to extend the Toolkit Executive to support recoverable data. The Toolkit Server Core components are:

TRAN-XA Interface (TM-XA): This interface supports the X/Open standard for database transactions. Recall that XA is an XA standard for transaction managers to interact with database managers. By using XA, a transaction manager from vendor Y can interoperate with a database manager from vendor Z, and vice versa. TM-XA works in conjunction with TRAN to provide the database interactions.

Lock Service (LOCK): The LOCK service is responsible for locking/unlocking mechanisms between transactions and resources (e.g., databases). In particular, it supports read/write locks, shared/exclusive locks, and intention locks for hierarchical data (e.g., indicate that datum in this hierarchy could be updated).

Recovery Service (REC): This service provides rollback after abort and rollforward for restart after system crashes.

Log Service (LOG): This service provides a variety of logging capabilities such as write-ahead logs and archivals to support recovery services. The logging facility is common and can be shared by many participants. However, each application sees only its own data.

Volume Service (VOL): This service supports multiple physical disks as one virtual file and provides mirroring of data for reliability.

6.10.4   Encina Extended TP Services

The Encina Extended Transaction Processing Services provide monitoring, interconnectivity, and file services. In particular, these services include the following components:

Encina Monitor: The Encina Monitor provides an environment for creating and administering distributed TP applications. The Monitor provides traditional transaction-monitoring features such as scalability and performance for increased number of users, availability for on-line access to data, data integrity for concurrent updates and system failures, security, authentication (verify who you are), and authorization (allow access to specified resources). The additional features of the Encina Monitor are portability through standard APIs (e.g., Tran-C and X/Open standards) and hardware/OS independence (this is achieved through relying on DCE to support lower-level services), and Interoperability through DCE, TRPC, LU6.2, and XA. The Monitor uses the Encina LOG and Structured File Services (SFS) for internal processing.

Encina PPC (Peer-to-Peer Communications): Encina PPC offers services for interconnecting Encina applications to non-Encina applications. In particular, Encina PPC supports LU6.2 protocol to access mainframe data. Encina uses the term "peer-to-peer" for this service because LU6.2 is essentially a peer-to-peer protocol. In peer-to-peer communications, either participant can initiate message exchange (in contrast, C/S communication restricts the initiation to clients). PPC allows mainframe updates to participate in Encina transactions (rollback and commit). Encina PPC consists of two components: PPC Executive that provides LU6.2 over TCP/IP, and PPC Gateway for LU6.2 over SNA. The primary difference between these two components is that LU6.2 is currently available on TCP/IP as well as SNA networks. (See Chapter 11 for a review of LU6.2.)

Encina SFS (Structured File System): SFS supports record-oriented files (entry sequence, ISAM, B-tree) for Encina transactions. Recall that Encina provides database access through X/Open XA interface (TM-XA component of Encina). SFS utilizes DCE security to protect files from unauthorized access and provides restarts and recovery by using Toolkit logging and recovery services.

6.10.5 Encina Summary and Trends

Encina supports DTP in an open environment and is available on many platforms (heavily UNIX at the time of this writing). Owing to its tight coupling with OSF/DCE, Encina is used for DTP where a large embedded base for OSF/DCE exists. Encina provides interfaces with mainframe systems through LU6.2, (this implies that if a legacy host application does not use LU6.2 then Encina cannot interface with it). The database access needed by Encina is provided through XA. The Encina administrative facilities for DTP include logging and locking, load balancing, parallelism through multithreading, and transaction monitoring.

Encina, like DCE, needs better GUI front-end tool support. A major challenge is integration of Encina with non-Encina environments, especially legacy applications. DTP issues can be handled if all activities are under the Encina umbrella. However, if DTP in a given enterprise crosses many umbrellas (e.g., PC-based applications on Novell LANs, UNIX applications under Encina, and mainframe applications under MVS), then many difficult challenges in security and failure handling emerge.

Additional information about Encina can be obtained from the Transarc home page (*http://www.transarc.com*).

6.11   State of the Practice: Examples and Case Studies

C/S transaction processing is not completely state-of-the-practice, but examples are beginning to appear. The following examples and case studies illustrate different aspects of C/S transaction processing.

Encina Example. Figure 6.9 shows an example of an Encina environment. In an Encina environment, computing nodes fall into three broad categories:

- Encina secure nodes, where the Encina application servers run. An application server receives Encina client requests and processes them, typically after interacting with resource managers (DBMSs). The secure nodes are basically "trusted computers" (typically restricted access, operating in physically secure area) that require a high level of reliability, security, and performance. The secure nodes house DCE as well as Encina Toolkit.

- Encina public nodes, where the Encina clients reside. The public nodes can be desktop computers that do not require a high level of reliability, performance, or security. The public nodes house DCE and Encina client libraries (the libraries that are used to develop DCE and Encina clients).

- Non-Encina nodes are typically mainframes or other systems that are not running Encina and DCE. These systems are accessed by Encina applications through the Encina PPC component.

Figure 6.9 Encina Example

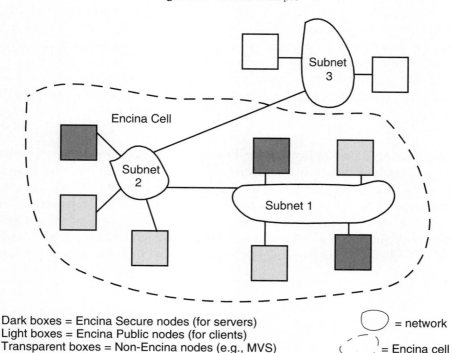

Dark boxes = Encina Secure nodes (for servers)
Light boxes = Encina Public nodes (for clients)
Transparent boxes = Non-Encina nodes (e.g., MVS)

= network

= Encina cell

Figure 6.9 shows three subnets that are interconnected to each other. The first two are contained in an "Encina Monitor Cell" that is under the control of Encina Monitor. The Encina Monitor Cell consists of a collection of Encina public and secure nodes (Figure 6.9 shows three secure nodes and four public nodes). Different application servers and resource managers (e.g., database managers) can be allocated to the three secure nodes and accessed from the four public nodes. To provide monitoring of a cell, each cell consists of one cell manager. In addition, each node (secure plus public) is assigned a node manager.

Case Study—An Object-Transaction Service. Most distributed-transaction management systems at present are not based on object-oriented technologies. A distributed-transaction management service over CORBA has been reported by Chang [1996]. Each transaction in this system is treated as an object; thus object invocations need to adhere to ACID properties. At the time of this writing, CORBA (discussed in the next chapter), is finalizing the object-transaction management services over CORBA. It is expected that we will see many similar efforts in the future.

Case Study—CICS Transaction Processing with Teradata. The Abbey National Share Registration System represents an interesting, albeit somewhat dated, example of processing CICS transactions against a separate database computer housing Teradata databases (*source:* "Spectrum Open Transaction Management Report," August 1993). This project required addressing the lack of two-phase-commit procedure within the Teradata environment when working with the CICS transaction management (TM) environment. It should be noted that CICS TM environments support two-phase commit between different MVS machines. However, what can be done if one partner, in this case Teradata, does not support two-phase commit? To address this, the Abbey National Share Registration System was designed so that it needs to commit as infrequently as possible to ensure that an entire transaction is a complete unit of work (i.e., no intermediate checkpoints). In addition, most data was kept in the Teradata machine, thus minimizing the need for distributed-data management (and reducing the need for two-phase commit).

Case Study—Using Data Replication for Transaction Processing. Data replication needs to be planned to support distributed-transaction processing. An example of the planning process used at CIGNA, a large health insurance company, is reported by Meador [1995]. The replication planning includes building a replication architecture (how data moves between applications and replicated databases), network architecture (physical layout and data rates), information requirements (e.g., response-time requirements), scheduling (e.g., when replicated data will be synchronized), and change management (e.g., changes in the underlying technologies).

6.12 State of the Market

C/S transaction management solutions are roughly clustered into two families of products: the TP-heavy products and the TP-lite products.

In the TP-heavy family, products such as Transarc's Encina, AT&T's Tuxedo, and IBM's CICS are worth noting. We have discussed Encina in the previous section. IBM is adopting the strategy of "CICS on everything." CICS is currently available on many platforms, such as MVS, AIX, OS/2, OS/400, Windows NT, and HP-UX. Tuxedo is also being ported to almost all UNIX platforms.

Standards are playing an important role in the C/S TP products. Basically, most of these products support the XA and XA+ interface, so that a given TP monitor can interoperate with many database managers and communication managers (see Section 6.4 for a discussion of XA and XA+). However, the following three application-to-communication-resource-manager APIs are being developed:

- *TxRPC (transactional RPC)*. This API is based on DEC's Remote Task Invocation technology,
- *CPI-C*. This is a peer-to-peer API used in the IBM APPC environments.
- *XATMI*. This is a Tuxedo Application/Transaction Management Interface.

With the major C/S transaction processing products becoming available on almost all platforms, you have to decide whether to standardize on a product or to standardize on standards. It might be appropriate for small environments to stay within the offerings of a single product. But for large-scale organizations that need C/S transaction processing across many platforms, it is best to stay within standards.

For TP-lite, several data-replication servers are becoming commercially available from a diverse array of vendors. Examples are IBM Data Replication Toolset (Data Refresher, Data Hub, Data Propagator), Oracle Snapshot, Prism Warehouse Manager, Sybase Replication Server, Trinzic Infopump and InfoHub, and Praxis Omini Replicator. Some of these replicators are used for data warehousing; the others are intended for distributed-transaction processing. Analysis of these state of the market tools can be found in a number of sources [Amaru 1995, Hansen 1995, Korzeniowski 1993, Leinfuss 1993, Richman 1996, Stacey 1994, White 1994].

6.13 State of the Art: Object Orientation in Transaction Management

Object orientation in transaction management has been an area of considerable academic and industrial investigation. The *Spectrum Reports on Open Transaction Management,* August 1993 and May 1994, are early examples (consult the Spectrum home page at *http://*

www.aladdin.co.uk for information about more recent reports). Broadly speaking, object orientation in transaction management exists at the following levels:

- Object-oriented transaction programming
- Transaction processing with distributed objects
- Transaction processing with object-oriented databases

Object-oriented transaction programming simply accounts for programs written in an object-oriented programming language (e.g., C++, Smalltalk) to perform the transaction operations (i.e., commit, rollback). This approach is in principle the same as any other transaction programming and is currently state-of-the-practice and state-of-the-market. After all, C++ programs can be used in Encina and Tuxedo environments. From a transaction-processing point of view, no complications are introduced.

Transaction processing with distributed objects is concerned with performing ACID operations between objects across machines. This introduces many complex issues. In particular, messages exchanged between objects can carry transaction semantics. For example, if an object sends a message to a remote object, then operations such as concurrency control and recovery may be needed between the distributed objects. The traditional object models do not use this type of processing. Specialized middleware is needed for transaction processing with distributed objects. The Object Management Group (OMG) has been considering transaction processing with distributed objects as a service for its Common Object Broker Architecture (CORBA). CORBA 2.0, the latest version of CORBA at the time of this writing, has specified an Object Transaction Management service and a Concurrency Control service as part of CORBA Object Services (see the next chapter for a discussion of CORBA 2.0). These two services are expected to boost industrial products to support transaction management with distributed objects. In addition, Microsoft ActiveX is supposed to support distributed transactions—we will discuss CORBA and ActiveX in the next chapter.

Transaction processing with object-oriented databases is concerned with introducing TP-heavy type of operations on top of OODBMSs. Most of the TP-heavy type of operations are currently available on relational and hierarchical databases. The fundamental difference is that, unlike older DBMSs that provide read and write operations, the OODBMSs support methods that are rich in semantics. Most of the research in OODBMS has concentrated on query and modeling aspects. In particular, transaction management in object-oriented multidatabase systems has received serious attention only recently [Agrawal 1996]. Many old research prototypes that support transaction management in OO multidatabase have been reported in the literature. Examples are the O2 system [Bancilhon 1992] and the ORION system [Garza 1988]. A great deal of research is needed in this area [Bukhres 1996].

The following general trends in C/S transaction processing are worth noting:

- More future work will focus on object-oriented distributed transactions where an object invocation will enforce the ACID properties. This work is the intended direction for CORBA, discussed in next chapter.

- SQL will continue as a standard for data access across all data sources such as files and databases, but SQL conversion to nonrelational DBMS, especially to OODBMS, is not trivial.

- More DDTMSs will attempt to include heterogeneous data located at heterogeneous computers, interconnected through heterogeneous networks.

- Standards will play an important role in the operability and portability of DDTMS. For example, ODBC, DRDA, and ISO Remote Database Access (RDA) standards for database access, and the ISO Transaction Processing (TP) and the X/Open Distributed Transaction Processing (DTP) standards are worth noting.

- Data-replication servers will continue to play a vital role in managing replicated data, owing to their flexibility and to the limitations of two-phase commit. However, improvements in two-phase commit will also continue.

6.14 Summary

The approaches to C/S transaction processing fall into the following categories:

- TP-less
- TP-lite
- TP-heavy

We have introduced the key transaction concepts and definitions and discussed the special issues and emerging standards of distributed transaction processing (TP-heavy). The currently popular data-replication servers are used in conjunction with TP-lite. We have discussed the trade-offs between TP-less, TP-lite, and TP-heavy for C/S transaction processing. We have reviewed Encina as an example of an open DTP system that can be used for TP-heavy solutions.

We have introduced the notion of a distributed-data and transaction management system (DDTMS) as middleware that is concerned with the management of:

- Distributed data (files plus databases with a certain degree of replication)
- Distributed transactions.

A DDTMS provides location transparency of read activity, store/update activity, transaction execution and failures for data stored in files and databases in a network. Design and implementation of DDTMS involves many challenges and choices, such as global data definition and translation, global directory allocation, distributed file processing (e.g., transparent access to remote files), distributed-query processing (e.g., joins between remotely located databases), and distributed-transaction processing (e.g., database consistency/concurrency, failure detection and transaction recovery, replication services).

6.15   Case Study: XYZCorp Uses Client/Server Transaction Processing

The financial information systems department is interested in a strategy for transaction processing for XYZCorp. A corporate-data management group has gotten into action and has identified the following key questions:

- Which of the financial data should be considered as corporate data? Why?

- What data will be duplicated, if any?

- Should we choose TP-lite or TP-heavy for financial data (which DDTMS model should we choose as our solution approach)?

- What factors are to be considered in choosing distributed-data and transaction management middleware?

Hints about the Case Study

- Most of the financial data can be considered as corporate data (it is shared by multiple people for business use).

- Only a very small portion of financial data should be duplicated.

- The DDTMS evaluation model discussed in Section 6.9 can be used to evaluate the various trade-offs. Basically, TP-lite should be used where possible. This represents Case 2 or 3 of the DDTMS evaluation model (these two cases are quite suitable for many real-life situations).

- The following table can be used to evaluate DDTMS middleware.

Evaluating Factors	Application 1	Application 2	Application 3
General Considerations • Distributed-file services • Distributed-database support • Distributed-transaction proc. • Replication servers			
Detailed Considerations (see Section 6.8) • Data translation • Directory design • Update synchronization (TP-lite, TP-heavy) • Distributed-query optimization • Failure handling			

Evaluating Factors	Application 1	Application 2	Application 3
Network Support • Network architectures needed (TCP/IP, SNA, Novell IPX/SPX, OSI, NetBIOS)			
Operating Systems Support • PC DOS, Windows, Windows NT • Macintosh • UNIX • MVS			
Vendor Information • Company size • Staying power • Current installed base • Cost range • Level of support			

6.16   Problems and Exercises

1. What are the key challenges in C/S transaction processing, and why is there no agreement on a common approach?

2. What are the main functions provided by a DTP (TP-heavy)? How do these functions differ from those of a local transaction manager?

3. Define the following standards and describe their role in DTP.

    (a) ISO TP   (b) X/Open DTP   (c) XA+   (d) XA

4. In your own words, when is it better to use a replication server versus two-phase commit?

5. Use the framework introduced to analyze a replication server. What changes/ extensions would you recommend to the framework?

6. Develop a decision table that shows the trade-offs between TP-lite, TP-less, and TP-heavy.

7. List the architectural components of the DDTMS architecture in which the following problems are addressed: concurrency control, commit processing, global schema generation, deadlock detection, distributed-query processing, RPCs.

6.17   Additional Information

We have attempted to give an overview of an area which continues to grow. A more theoretical coverage of DDTMS can be found in Umar [1993, chap. 6]. The following books are recommended for additional details:

- Elmagarmid, A., *Database Transaction Models for Advanced Applications,* Morgan Kaufmann Publishers, 1992.

- Bernstein, P. A., Hadzilacos, V., and Goodman, N., *Concurrency Control and Recovery in Database Systems,* Addison Wesley, 1987.

- Gray, J., and Reuter, A., *Transaction Processing: Concepts and Techniques,* Morgan Kaufmann Publishers, 1993.

The interested reader can find additional information in a number of journals and proceedings of conferences, such as:

- *ACM Transactions on Database Systems*
- ACM SIGMOD International Conferences
- IEEE International Conferences on Data Engineering
- International Conferences on Very Large Databases
- International Conferences on Distributed Computing
- *IEEE Transactions on Knowledge and Data Engineering*
- *Spectrum Reports (http://www.aladdin.co.uk)*
- *Standish Consulting Group Reports*
- *Database Programming and Design*
- *Data Management Review*

6.18   References

Ace, E., "Replication for SQL Server NT—Today," Database Design and Programming, January 1995, pp. 47–52.

Adiba, Lindsay, "Database Snapshot," IBM Research Report, RJ2772, March 1980.

Agrawal, D., and El Abbadi, A., "Transaction Management in OODBMS," in Bukhres, O., and Elmagarmid, A. eds., *Object-Oriented Multidatabase Systems,* Prentice Hall, 1996.

Amaru, C., "SQL Server Bundles Replication," *Datamation*, June 15, 1995, pp. 61–75.

Bancilhon, F., et al., eds., *Building an Object-Oriented Database System: The Story of O2,* Morgan Kaufmann, 1992.

Barghouti, N. S., and Kaiser, G. E., "Concurrency Control in Advanced Database Applications," *ACM Computing Surveys,* September 1991, pp. 269–318.

Bernstein, P. A., and Goodman, N., "Concurrency Control in Distributed Database Systems," *ACM Computing Surveys,* Vol. 13, No. 2 (June 1981), pp. 185–222.

Bernstein, P. A., and Chiu, D. W., "Using Semi-Joins to Solve Relational Queries," *JACM,* January 1981.

Bernstein, P. A., Hadzilacos, V., and Goodman, N., *Concurrency Control and Recovery in Database Systems,* Addison Wesley, 1987.

Bland, D., "A Look at Information Builder's EDA/SQL," *Enterprise Systems Journal,* January 1993, pp. 87–92.

Bodarik, P., et al., "Deciding to Correct Distributed Query Processing," *IEEE Transactions on Knowledge and Data Engineering,* June 1992, pp. 253–265.

Brett, C., "The Rise of Messaging Middleware: The Decline of DOLTP," *Spectrum Report on Open Transaction Management,* last updated: January 1996 *(http://www.aladdin.co.uk).*

Bukhres, O., and Elmagarmid, A., *Object-Oriented Multidatabase Systems,* Prentice Hall, 1996.

Cardenas, A. F., "Heterogeneous Distributed Database Management: The HD-DBMS," *Proceedings of the IEEE,* May 1987, pp. 588–600.

Ceri, S., and G. Pellagitti, *Distributed Databases: Principles and Systems,* McGraw-Hill, 1984.

Ceri, S., Pernici, B., and Wiederhold, "Distributed Database Design Methodolgies," *Proceedings of the IEEE,* May 1987, pp. 533–546.

Chang, Y. S., Kao, Y. M., Yuan, S. M., and Liang, D., "An Object Transaction Service Based on the CORBA Architecture," International Conference in Distributed Platforms, February-March, Dresden, 1996.

Chu, W. W., "Performance of File Directory Systems for Data Bases in Star and Distributed Networks," *1976 NCC,* Vol. 45 (1976).

Chu, W. W., "Distributed Data Bases," *Handbook of Software Engineering,* ed. by C. R. Vick and C. V. Ramamoorthy, Van Nostrand Reinhold, 1984.

CICS, "Customer Information System: Concepts and Facilities," IBM Manual, 1995 (ask for latest release)

Date, C. J., *An Introduction to Database Systems,* 5th ed., Vols. 1 and 2, Addison Wesley, 1990.

Date, C. J., "Twelve Rules for a Distributed Database," *InfoDB,* Vol. 2, Nos. 2 and 3, Summer/ Fall 1987.

Date, C. J., *A Guide to DB2,* Addison Wesley, 1984.

Dolgicer, M., "Unmasking the Mysteries of Message Queuing," *Application Development Trends,* June 1996, pp. 57–67.

Elmagarmid, A., *Database Transaction Models for Advanced Applications,* Morgan Kaufmann Publishers, 1992.

ENCINA, "Encina for Open OLTP," Transarc Corporation publication, 1995 (ask for the latest edition).

Epstein, R., Stonebraker, M., and Wong, E., "Distributed Query Processing in a Relational Database System," *ACM SIGMOD,* Austin, TX, 1978.

Epstein, R., "Query Optimization: A Game of Time and Statistics," *UNIX Review,* May 1987, pp. 28–29.

Eswaran, K. P., Gray, J. N, et al., "Notions of Consistency and Predicate Locks in a Database System," *CACM,* Vol. 19, No. 11 (November 1976).

Garcia-Molina, H., "Performance of Update Synchronization Algorithms for Replicated Data in a Distributed Database," Ph.D. Dissertation, Stanford University, June 1979.

Garcia-Molina, H., and Abbot, R. K., "Reliable Distributed Database Management," *Proceedings of the IEEE,* Vol. 75, No. 5 (May 1987), pp. 601–620.

Graham, G., "Real-World Distributed Databases," *UNIX Review,* May 1987.

Gray, J., "Notes on Database Operating Systems," in *Operating Systems: An Advanced Course,* Springer-Verlag, New York 1979, pp. 393–481.

Gray, J., "The Transaction Concept: Virtues and Limitations," *Proceedings of Conference on Very Large Databases,* September 1981, pp. 144–154.

Gray, J., "Transparency in Its Place," *UNIX Review,* May 1987.

Gray, J. N., and Anderson, M., "Distributed Computer Systems: Four Cases," *Proceedings of the IEEE,* May 1987, pp. 719–729.

Gray, J. , and Reuter, A., *Transaction Processing: Concepts and Techniques,* Morgan Kaufman Publishers, 1993.

Garza, J., and Kim, W., "Transaction Management in an Object-Oriented Data Model," *Proceeding of ACM SIGMOD International Conference on Management of Data,* June 1988, pp. 37–55.

Hansen, M., and Follette, J., "Getting in Front of Lotus Notes Replication," *Business Communications Review,* May 1995.

Hevner, A. R., and Yao, S. B., "Query Processing in Distributed Database Systems," *IEEE Transactions on Software Engineering,* Vol. SE-5, No. 3 (May 1979).

Hevner, A. R., "A Survey of Data Allocation and Retrieval Methods for Distributed Systems," School of Business and Management Working Paper # 81-036, University of Maryland, October 1981.

Hevner, A. R., and Yao, S. B., "Querying Distributed Databases on Local Area Networks," *Proceedings of the IEEE,* May 1987, pp. 563–572.

Jarke, M., and Koch, J., "Query Optimization in Database Systems," *ACM Computing Surveys,* June 1984, pp. 111–152.

Kamel, M. N., and Kamel, N. N., "The Federated Database Management Systems," *Computer Communications,* Vol. 15, No. 4 (May 1992), pp. 270–278.

Kohler, W. H., "A Survey of Techniques for Synchronization and Recovery in Decentralized Computer Systems," *ACM Computing Surveys,* Vol. 13, No. 2 (June 1981), pp. 149–184.

Korzeniowski, P., "Replication Gains in Distributed Databases," *Software Magazine,* April 1993, pp. 93–96.

Krasowski, M., "Integrating Distributed Databases into the Information Architecture," *Journal of Information Systems Management,* Spring 1991, pp. 38–46.

Larson, J. A., "A Flexible Reference Architecture for Distributed Database Management," *Proceedings of ACM 13th Annual Computer Science Conference,* March 1985, New Orleans, pp. 58–72.

Larson, B., "A Retrospective of R*: A Distributed Database Management System," *Proceedings of the IEEE,* May 1987, pp. 668–673.

Leff, A., and Pu, C., "A Classification of Transaction Processing Systems," *IEEE Computer,* June 1991, pp. 63–76.

Leinfuss, E., "Replication Synchronizes Distributed Databases over Time," *Software Magazine,* July 1993, pp. 31–35.

Litwin, W., Mark, L., and Roussopoulos, N., "Interoperability of Multiple Autonomous Databases," *ACM Computing Surveys,* September 1990, pp. 267–293.

Mack, S., "Sybase to Address Update Problems," *Infoworld,* November 16, 1992.

McCord, R., and Hanner, M., "Connecting Islands of Information," *UNIX Review,* May 1987.

McGovern, D., "Two-Phased Commit or Replication?" *Database Programming and Design,* May 1993, pp. 35–44.

Meador, C., "Planning for Data Replication," *Information Week,* December 18, 1995, pp. 90–96.

Olson, J., "From Centralized to Distributed," *Database Programming and Design,* December 1993, pp. 50-57.

Ozsu, M., and Valduriez, P., *Principles of Distributed Database Systems,* Prentice Hall, 1991.

Ozsu, M., and Valduriez, P., "Distributed Database Systems: Where Are We Now?" *IEEE Computer,* August 1991, pp. 68–78.

Peterson, D., "The Great Debate: OLTP vs. RDBMS," *Business Communications Review,* May 1995.

Pu, C., Leff, A., and Chen, S., "Heterogeneous and Autonomous Transaction Processing," *IEEE Computer,* December 1991, pp. 64–72.

Quinlan, T., "Heterogeneous Distributed Databases," *Database Programming and Design,* October 1993, pp. 29–33.

Rauch-Hinden, W., "True Distributed DBMSes Presage Big Dividends," *Mini-Micro Systems,* May and June 1987.

Ricciuti, M., "Universal Database Access," *Datamation,* November 1, 1991.

Richman, D., "Replication Heats Up," *Computerworld,* July 15, 1996, pp. 51–55.

Richter, J., "Distributing Data," *Byte Magazine,* June 1994, pp. 139–182.

Sacco, G. V., and Yao, S. B., "Query Optimization in Distributed Databases," Working Paper MS/S #81-029, College of Business Administration, University of Maryland, 1981.

Semich, J., and McMullen, J., "Sybase's Big Blue Connection," *Datamation,* April 1, 1991.

Schlack, M., "Key to Client/Server OLTP," *Datamation,* April 1, 1995, pp. 53–56.

Schussel, G., "Database Replication: Playing Both Ends with the Middleware," *Client/Server Today,* November 1994, pp. 57–67.

Sheth, A. P., and Larson, J. A., "Federated Database Systems for Managing Distributed, Heterogeneous, and Autonomous Databases," *ACM Computing Surveys,* September 1990, pp. 183–236.

Soparkar, N., Korth, H., and Silberschatz, A., "Failure-Resilient Transaction Management in Multi-Databases," *IEEE Computer,* December 1991, pp. 28–37.

Spectrum Report, "The Changing Shape of Open Transaction Management," Vol. 7, report 3, August 1993.

Stacey, D., "Replication: DB2, Oracle, or Sybase?" *Database Programming and Design,* December 1994, pp. 42–51.

Stone, H., "Parallel Querying of Large Databases: A Case Study," *IEEE Computer,* October, 1987, pp. 11–21.

Svobodova, L., "File Servers for Network-Based Distributed Systems," *ACM Computing Surveys,* December 1984, pp. 353–398.

Teorey, T. J., and Fry, J. P., *Design of Database Structures,* Prentice Hall, 1982.

Thomas, G., et al., "Heterogeneous Distributed Database Systems for Production Use," *ACM Computing Surveys,* September 1990, pp. 237–266.

Triantafillou, P., and Taylor, D., "The Location-Based Paradigm for Replication: Achieving Efficiency and Availability in Distributed Systems," *IEEE Transactions on Software Engineering,* January 1995.

Tuxedo, "Transaction Processing with Tuxedo," UNIX Systems Laboratories Publication.

Umar, A., *Distributed Computing and Client/Server Systems,* Prentice Hall, rev. ed. 1993.

Vinzant, D., "SQL Database Servers," *Data Communications,* January 1990, pp. 72–88.

White, C., "Data Replication Techniques, Tools, and Case Studies," DB/EXPO, New York, December 6–8, 1994.

Wilbur, S., and Bacarisse, J., "Building Distributed Systems with Remote Procedure Call," *Software Engineering Journal,* September 1987, pp.148–159.

Walpole, J., et al., "Transaction Mechanisms for Distributed Programming Environments," *Software Engineering Journal,* September 1987, pp. 169–171.

Wolfson, O., "The Overhead of Locking (and Commit) Protocols in Distributed Databases," *ACM Transactions on Database Systems,* Vol. 12, No. 3 (September 1987), pp. 453–471.

Yu, C., and Chang, C., "Distributed Query Processing," *ACM Computing Surveys,* Vol. 16, No. 4 (December 1984), pp. 399–433.

Zimowski, M., "DRDA, ISO RDA, X/Open RDA: A Comparison," *Database Programming and Design,* June 1994, pp. 54–61.

7

Distributed Objects (CORBA and OLE/ActiveX)

7.1   Introduction

Most of the new applications being developed at present are based on the OO concepts. However, these objects are increasingly dispersed on multiple machines. Consequently, many new applications are being based on distributed-object concepts. These applications combine two very powerful concepts to deliver business value: object orientation and distributed systems. The users of these applications interact with objects that may be located locally or on remote machines. There are many interesting examples of distributed-object applications. A common example is the compound documents that serve as containers for objects such as text paragraphs, spreadsheets, graphs, and sound bites from different sites. Other examples exist in marketing, retail, entertainment, telecommunications, health, and many other areas.

The purpose of this chapter is to review the distributed-object concepts and examine the middleware that enables distributed-object applications. In particular, we will attempt to answer the following questions (this chapter assumes that the reader has a basic understanding of object-oriented concepts as discussed in the tutorial in Chapter 10):

- What are the key concepts of distributed objects? (Section 7.2)
- What are the emerging standards in distributed objects and what exactly is CORBA? (Section 7.3)

- What are the standards in compound documents such as OLE and OpenDoc? (Section 7.3.2)
- How is ActiveX being positioned as middleware for distributed objects? (Section 7.5)
- What is the state of the practice, state of the market and state of the art in distributed objects? (Sections 7.6, 7.7 and 7.8)
- What is the current state of the art, state of the market, and state of the practice in middleware for distributed objects?

Key Points

- Enterprisewide applications can be decomposed and viewed as objects that can reside on different machines. An object on one machine can send messages to objects on other machines, thus viewing the entire network as a collection of objects.
- Emerging object technologies, such as Object Frameworks, Business Objects, and Component Software and "Applets," when combined with distributed objects, provide a very promising technology for enterprisewide applications.
- Interfaces and IDLs (Interface Definition Languages) provide the basic glue for distributed-object computing.
- IDL is used not only to define new services provided by objects, but also to "wrap" existing and legacy systems so that they behave externally as objects.
- Object Management Group (OMG) was formed to define a suite of standard languages, interfaces, protocols, and services for interoperability of applications in heterogeneous distributed-object environments.
- CORBA (Common Object Request Broker Architecture) is an OMG specification for middleware needed to enable distributed-object applications. CORBA 2.0, the latest CORBA specification at the time of this writing, includes an extensive array of capabilities and APIs for developing interoperability bridges.
- Microsoft's OLE (Object Linking and Embedding) and Component Integration Labs' OpenDoc are intended to support compound documents. OLE and Open-Doc share the same goals and provide the same basic functionalities, but there are some "plumbing" differences.
- Microsoft is positioning ActiveX as a complete environment for components and distributed objects. Almost everything coming out of Microsoft is being based on ActiveX. OLE has been superseded by ActiveX.

7.2   Objects in Distributed Systems

7.2.1   Concepts

A distributed application can be viewed as a collection of objects (user interfaces, databases, application modules, customers). Each object has its own attributes and has some methods which define the behavior of the object (e.g., an order can be viewed in terms of its data and the methods which create, delete, and update the order object). Interactions between the components of an application can be modeled through "messages" which invoke appropriate methods. In particular, classes and inheritance are extremely useful in modeling applications because these concepts lead to reuse and encapsulation—critical to managing the complexity of distributed systems. For example:

- A customer can be defined as a class from which other business classes that define different types of customers can inherit properties.
- An inventory can be defined as a class from which other properties of specific inventory items can be inherited.
- A database server can be defined as a class from which other vendor-specific database servers can inherit properties.
- A network can be defined as a class from which other networks inherit properties (e.g., a generic network from which TCP/IP, SNA, and OSI networks can inherit properties).

Before getting involved with details about objects in distributed systems, let us quickly review some of the key concepts. Figure 7.1 shows a conceptual view that will be expanded and refined later:

- **Objects** are data surrounded by code with properties such as inheritance, polymorphism, encapsulation, etc. Objects can be clients, servers, or both (see sidebar "Key Object-Oriented Concepts" for definitions).
- **Object brokers** allow objects to dynamically find each other in a distributed environment and interact with each other over a network. Object brokers are the backbone of distributed object-oriented systems.
- **Object services** allow the users to create, name, move, copy, store, delete, restore, and manage objects.

It should be kept in mind that modeling in terms of object-oriented (OO) concepts does not necessarily imply use of object-oriented programming languages such as C++ or object-oriented database managers. In fact, it is possible to *view* systems in terms of GUI objects and then implement them in whatever technology makes sense.

Most of the applications so far have used OO technologies at the client side to implement GUIs. However, there is no reason why this technology should not be equally valuable to servers also. In fact, the reuse and encapsulation features of OO technologies should be of value to manage the complexity of server implementations. It appears that the OO technologies will be increasingly used at the client as well as server sides of applications (see, for example, Shan [1995] and Rymer [1993]).

Owing to the interest in object-oriented systems, the elegance with which complex distributed systems can be modeled by using OO concepts, and the appeal of OO technologies in developing new applications ranging from inventory control to network management, many attempts have focused on standardized middleware to support object-oriented distributed systems [Rymer 1995, Rymer 1993, Harmon 1993, Wayner 1994]. The Common Object Request Broker Architecture (CORBA) from the Object Management Group is a prime example of such a standard.

Figure 7.1 The Basic Distributed-Objects Model

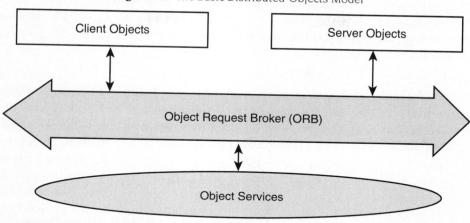

Shaded area indicates middleware

7.2.2 Object Frameworks, Business Objects, and Components

A very wide range of OO products are commercially available from a diverse array of suppliers. These products include user-interface development aids such as Galaxy; compilers for OO programming languages such as C++, Smalltalk, Simula, and Eiffel; OODBMSs such as ObjectStore and Gemstone; and complete OO development environments such as Expersoft to support code reuse. In addition, class libraries such as Tools.h++ are becoming widely available. Instead of reviewing these products, let us briefly review the following three emerging areas:

- Object Frameworks
- Business Objects
- Component Software

Object Frameworks. Object frameworks are essentially descendants of object-oriented class libraries. Class libraries are collections of predefined object classes that define commonly used presentation, business processing logic, and data-management structures and methods. A framework simply defines how given sets of classes are related and arranged for different applications. It is possible to think of frameworks at three levels: foundation classes, middleware frameworks, and application frameworks (or high-level frameworks). The *foundation classes* provide fine-grained data and control statements, I/O functions, GUI structures, memory-management functions, and database-access functions. The *middleware framework* covers an extensive set of C/S middleware services such as transaction processing, database access, directory services, telephony, authentication, and systems management. The *application frameworks,* also known as desktop frameworks, provide programmer productivity tools for compound documents, multimedia, groupware, mail, 3D graphics, and decision-support applications. An example of commercial object frameworks is the IBM object-frameworks strategy that is beginning to materialize as products. The objective of this strategy is to create "seas of objects" with object frameworks as the glue to tie these objects into applications. Examples of other players in this market are ParcPlace Systems, Rogue Wave, ILOG, Next, Sun Microsystems, and Easel.

Business Objects. The basic idea of business objects is that the users can construct objects that represent the real-world concepts of the business world. Examples of business objects are customer, order, products, and regional office. If software could be structured around such objects and other business concepts, then organizations would be able to build software that simulated current business strategy. Moreover, businesses could reuse these objects to build new applications by using the OO paradigm. Business objects started appearing in the marketplace around 1994 when OLE 2.0, OpenDoc, and CORBA-based products started emerging. Since then, OO tools designed to support creation of business objects have appeared from vendors such as Easel and applications that employ business objects have appeared from vendors such as IMRS. The Object Management Group (OMG) has founded the Business Object Management Special Interest Group (BOMSIG) to help the industry understand and utilize this technology effectively. System integrators such as Anderson Consulting are also committing to deliver software environments that can be used to build custom applications based on business objects. Additional information about business objects can be found in Sims [1995], and Rymer [1995].

Component Software and "Applets." Components are high-level "plug and play" software modules that perform a limited set of tasks within an application. Components are essentially small applications, also known as *applets*, that are *recognizable* by the users (i.e., they do not perform internal programming tasks such as initialize internal memory locations). For example, Microsoft Draw is an applet within Microsoft applications. This particular component is high-level enough to perform end-user type functions (it draws boxes, arrows, circles, etc.). However, it is not a standalone application; it only works with other applications components. At present, Microsoft appears to lead in component software by producing applets for Windows environments that draw, produce charts, perform calculations, etc. Java applets are another popular example. Depending on the size of the application, the components may be small or large. Components are very much like objects; however, the emphasis is on recognition by users (many objects are oriented toward programming tasks). Thus component software can be used as plug and play to build complete applications. Many desktop tools are currently becoming available as components. Examples of typical desktop components are spell-checkers, SQL query builders, and print managers (conceptually, each icon on your toolbar can be a separate component).

These and other emerging technologies and market segments are leading toward reusable software that can be assembled to quickly build new applications. However, these technologies are introducing new terms and jargon. Owing to an ever growing list of object-oriented "things," many groups are trying to figure out what to do. An example is the Object Management Group (OMG) that has been formed as a nonprofit consortium of more than 500 software and systems manufacturers and technology information providers. OMG is specifying a set of standard terms and interfaces for interoperable software by using the object-oriented concepts.

Object-Oriented Databases

Object-oriented databases allow storage and retrieval of objects to/from persistent storage (i.e., disks). Object-oriented databases, also known as ***object databases***, allow you to store and retrieve nontraditional data types such as bitmaps, icons, text, polygons, sets, arrays, and lists. The stored objects can be simple or complex, can be related to each other through complex relationships, and can inherit properties from other objects. ***Object-oriented database management systems (OODBMS)***, which can store, retrieve, and manipulate objects, have been an area of active research and exploration since the mid 1980s.

Relational databases are suitable for many applications, and SQL use is widespread. However, it is not easy to represent complex information in terms of relational tables. For example, a car design, a computing-network layout, and software design of an airline reservation system cannot be represented easily in terms of tables. For these cases, we need to represent complex interrelationships between data elements, retrieve several versions of design, represent the semantics (meaning) of relationships, and utilize the concepts of similarities to reduce redundancies.

OODBMSs and RDBMSs both have their strengths and weaknesses. For example, RDBMSs are very mature and heavily used but cannot handle complex objects well. OODBMSs, on the other hand, lack the maturity and ease of use offered by the RDBMSs. A compromise, known as ***object-relational databases,*** provides a hybrid solution where relational and object-oriented technologies are combined into a single product. Different vendors use different approaches to object-relational databases. For example, Odaptor from HP uses an underlying relational database with OO front ends, while UniSQL from UniSQL is an OO database that subsumes the relational model. See Chapter 10 for more details.

7.2.3 Distributed Objects for Enterprisewide Applications

The trend at present is to extend the OO concepts to enterprisewide distributed applications. Simply stated, ***distributed objects*** are objects that can be dispersed across the network and can be accessed by users across the network. Conceptually, we are talking about decomposing enterprisewide applications into objects that can be dispersed around different machines on a network. An object on one machine can send messages to objects on other machines, thus viewing the entire network as a collection of objects. This concept naturally extends the notions of object frameworks, business objects, and component software to distributed systems. When, and if, fully realized, distributed objects present a very powerful technology that has the potential of addressing many problems facing the IT community today (i.e., reuse, portability, and interoperability). This is because applications can be constructed by using reusable components that encapsulate many internal details and can interoperate across multiple networks and platforms.

Support of distributed-object-based applications requires special-purpose middleware that will allow remotely located objects to communicate with each other. A common mechanism used by such middleware is an object-request broker (ORB) that receives an object invocation and delivers the message to an appropriate object. Examples of middleware for distributed objects include OMG's CORBA (Common Object Request Broker Architecture), Microsoft's OLE (Object Linking and Embedding), and Component Integration Laboratories' OpenDoc.

7.2.4   Interfaces and Interface Definition Language

Interfaces and interface definition languages (IDLs) are at the core of distributed-object applications. Simply stated, an **interface** specifies the API that the clients can use to invoke operations on objects. In particular, an interface describes:

- The set of operations that can be performed on an object
- The parameters needed to perform the operations

For distributed-object applications, interface definitions are used to advertise the set of operations that an object can provide to prospective clients. Thus the object's data is accessible only through the interface. Consequently, any server that is encapsulated by its interface can be viewed as an object [Mowbray 1995, Nicol 1993].[1] Figure 7.2 shows an interface of a simple inventory object that supports two operations: query inventory and update price (a definition of this interface is given in Table 7.1). These operations can be invoked by client programs.

Figure 7.2 Example of an Interface

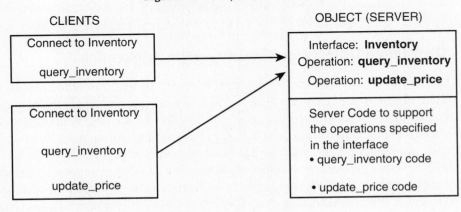

---

1. Some OO purists contend that CORBA does not directly support inheritance and polymorphism. This is a good student assignment.

One or more interfaces may be defined for an object. For example, given an object such as inventory, you may need to define three different interfaces: one for the manager of inventory (i.e., to create, monitor, and replenish the inventory), one for the order-processing system (i.e., to retrieve and update the inventory), and one for the authorized customers (i.e., to browse through the available products). It is a good practice to design interfaces for different classes of users and to group-related operations together. An interface definition includes some or all of the following:

- The interface header that shows an interface name and interface header attributes that uniquely identify the interface. Examples of such attributes are UUIDs (universal unique identifiers) and version numbers of the interfaces.
- Constant and data type definitions that are used to specify data properties (e.g., size) so that clients and servers can exchange data conveniently between different machines.
- A set of operations (methods) and the signatures for each operation. A *signature* specifies the operation's name, its arguments, and argument types.

The interfaces are defined by using an **interface definition language (IDL)**. Different middleware products provide IDL compilers that parse the IDL and produce header files and code segments that are used by the client and server programs (we will discuss this in more detail later). For example, OSF DCE, CORBA, and OLE all provide IDL compilers. In addition, middleware products support utilities and commands to store and retrieve IDLs from *interface repositories*. Client application developers can browse through these interface repositories to learn about the available server objects and determine the type of operations that can be invoked on an object.

IDLs are basically declarative languages—they do not specify any executable code. IDL declarations (e.g., syntax, character types allowed, argument coding, etc.) must conform to the vendor-provided IDL compilers. After you create the interface definition using IDL, you compile the IDL file to create header files and "stubs" that are used in building clients and servers. Table 7.1 shows the IDL of a simple inventory system that supports query-inventory and update-price operations. The syntax used in this example is abstract. We have seen the DCE IDL in a previous chapter and will see actual IDL specifications for CORBA.

TABLE 7.1   A SAMPLE ABSTRACT IDL

```
uuid 008B3C84-11c7-8580), version (1.0) /* Header */
interface inventory /* interface name is inventory */
   query_inventory (/*The operation to query inventory */
     in char item_id; /* input is item id */
     out integer on_hand; /output is on hand */
     out integer status ) /* output status */
   update_price ( /*The operation is to update price */
     in char item_id; /* input parameter is item -id */
     in integer new_price; /* input: new price */
     out integer status ) /*output parameter */
```

Types of Interfaces

Interfaces and interface definitions are of two kinds: **operational interfaces** which contain a set of named operations (i.e., procedures or methods); and **stream interfaces**, in which communication is organized as a set of linked directional flows. This chapter focuses primarily on operational interfaces. *Stream interfaces are used to support distributed-multimedia systems.* Basically, stream interfaces are used to describe unstructured communications such as voice and video streams in multimedia systems. Stream interfaces can also be used for electronic mail. The basic characteristic of stream interfaces is that they must support *continuous data transfers* over relatively long periods of time, e.g., real-time playout of video from a remote surveillance camera. In addition, the timeliness of such transmissions must be maintained for the duration of the media presentation. We will pick up the discussion of stream interfaces in a later chapter when we discuss distributed-multimedia applications.

Interfaces significantly impact the design of distributed-object applications. First, the server object is required to implement at least the operations specified in the IDL, and the client is required to accept at least the set of results generated by the IDL operations. This implies that the server will never respond with a "method/procedure not supported" message to a prospective client. Second, the clients may not use some of the operations provided by the interface. This implies that the server interfaces can be extended to include more operations without requiring any change to the client. Finally, and most importantly, the "size" of the interface needs to be carefully examined. For example, it is not a good idea to specify an interface that supports 100 operations. In such a case, if one operation needs to be changed, then a new IDL will have to be compiled and *all* client programs will have to be recompiled (this could be quite irritating). It is best to design a separate interface for each group of users (e.g., one interface for end users, one for the system administrators, etc.).

Interfaces and IDL provide the basic glue for distributed-object computing. IDL is used not only to define new services provided by objects, but also to "wrap" existing and legacy systems so that they behave externally as objects. For example, a legacy application written in COBOL could behave as a server object as long as it has an IDL and it provides the operations defined by the IDL. Thus the "IDL-ized" programs run on top of an ORB without revealing their internal details (see Figure 7.3).

7.3   Common Object-Request-Broker Architecture (CORBA)

7.3.1   Object-Management Architecture

Common Object Request Broker Architecture (CORBA) is a specification proposed by the Object Management Group (OMG)—a nonprofit industry consortium formed in 1989 with the following goals [Soley 1994]:

Figure 7.3 Interface Definition Language in Action

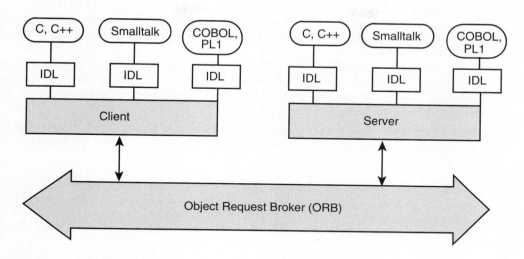

- Solve problems of interoperability in distributed systems by using object technology.
- Use de facto standards in object technology and commercial availability of technology.
- Create a suite of standard languages, interfaces and protocols for interoperability of applications in heterogeneous distributed environments.
- Build upon, not replace, existing interfaces.

DEC, HP, IBM, and Sun were among the original members of OMG, which has exceeded more than 500 members ranging from hardware vendors to end users. Interestingly, OMG was formed *before* any major products were introduced. (Most standards bodies are formed to develop standards *after* products are already in use. For example, ISO/OSI Reference Model for networks was introduced in 1977, almost five to seven years after the introduction of SNA, Decnet, and TCP/IP.) OMG's first attempt at meeting its goals resulted in an Object Management Architecture (OMA), released in 1990; it was revised in 1992. OMA specified the overall object model for distributed-object computing environments, including how objects are defined and created, how client applications invoke objects, and how objects can be shared and reused. The four components of this management architecture are (see Figure 7.4):[2]

- **Application Objects**: These are business-aware objects specific to end-user applications. These objects can be pieces of data, software, or user artifacts that can reside on one or many machines. The application objects may be created by an OO language or encapsulated by using

---

2. OMG is refining this model. For example, platform versus domain components are being introduced. Browse through the OMG site (http://www.omg.org) for developments.

a "wrapper" around old systems. Applications are typically built from a large number of basic object classes.

- **Object Request Broker (ORB)**: ORB is responsible for communication between objects. ORB finds an object on the network, delivers requests to the object, activates the object (if not already active), and returns any messages back to the sender. ORB is the backbone of OMA. We will discuss ORB in more detail later.

- **Object Services**: This component supports the request broker by providing services such as object naming, event notification, persistence, and object-life-cycle management (e.g., creation, modification, deletion). Extensions to these services may include object-oriented transaction management, security, and change management.

- **Common Facilities**: These are commonly used facilities in OO applications. Examples include email, database access, and compound documents. These facilities will be developed for classes of applications.

Figure 7.4 Object-Management Architecture

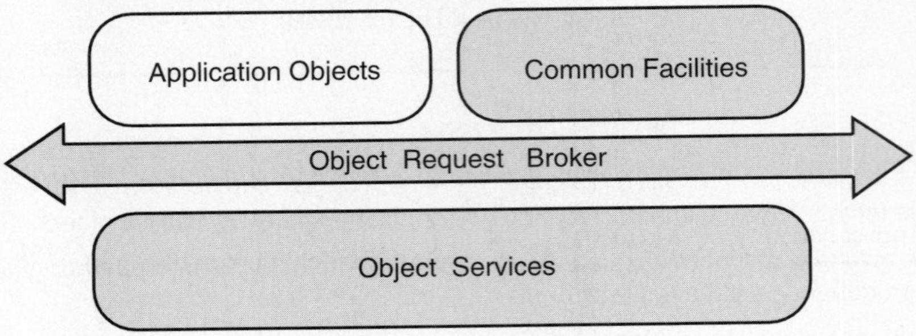

Note: Shaded area represents middleware

It is important to note that the Application Objects, Common Facilities, and Object Services are simply *categories* of objects. Every piece of software in the OMA model is represented as an object that communicates with other objects via the object-request broker. These objects were grouped into three broad categories to ease the standardization process.

7.3.2 Basic CORBA Concepts

CORBA was introduced in 1991 by OMG to go a step beyond OMA to specify the technology for interoperable distributed OO systems. CORBA specifications represent the ORB technology adopted by OMG and are published as OMG documents. The key concepts of CORBA are (see Figure 7.5):

- CORBA essentially specifies the middleware services that will be used by the application objects.

- Any object (application) can be a client, server or both. For purposes of description, CORBA uses the C/S model where clients issue requests to objects (service providers).

- Any interaction between objects is through requests. The information associated with a request is an operation to be performed, a target object, zero or more parameters, etc.

- CORBA supports **static** as well as **dynamic binding**. Dynamic binding between objects uses run-time identification of objects and parameters. See the discussion in next section for trade-offs between static and dynamic binding.[3]

- An **interface** represents contracts between client and server applications. A typical interface definition shows the parameters being passed and a unique interface identifier. The concept of interface in CORBA is the same as in OSF DCE. An **Interface Definition Language (IDL)** has been defined specifically for CORBA. Program stubs and skeletons are produced as part of the IDL compiling.

- CORBA objects do not know the underlying implementation details—an **object adapter** maps a generic model to implementation and is the primary way that an object implementation accesses services provided by the ORB.

Let us now go through the main components of Figure 7.5 and show how they interrelate with each other. Let us start from the left.

Figure 7.5 CORBA Components and Interfaces

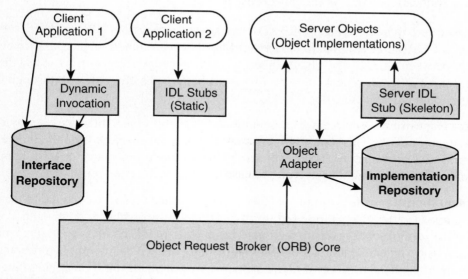

Note: Shaded areas represent middleware

---

3. For people familiar with SQL processing, CORBA static and dynamic binding is similar to the SQL static and dynamic binding (i.e., static binding is done at compile time while dynamic binding happens at run time).

Dynamic Invocation Interface. This interface allows dynamic construction of object invocation. The interface details are filled in by consulting with the interface repository and or other run-time sources. By using the dynamic invocation, client application 1 can interact with server objects (provided descriptions of these server objects could be found in the interface repository).

Client IDL Stubs. The client stubs make calls to the ORB core. These precompiled stubs make it easier for the clients to issue static requests to objects across a network (see the sidebar "What Are Stubs?") Client application 2 uses this option.

Object Adapters. An object adapter allows an object implementation to access the ORB services. Services provided by the ORB through an adapter often include security interaction, method invocation, and generation of object IDs (*object references*). CORBA specifies that each ORB must support a standard adapter called the *basic object adapter (BOA).* Server objects use object adapters. CORBA supports different kinds of object adapters.

Server IDL Stub. These stubs, also known as server skeletons, provide the code that invokes specific server methods. These stubs are generated as part of the IDL compilation and are very similar to the client IDL stubs. They provide the interface between object adapters and the server application code. Server Objects use this stub.

Object-Request Broker (ORB). ORB is obviously at the heart of CORBA. ORB acts as a switch in a CORBA environment—it sets up links between remote objects and routes the messages between objects. Any client object can make a request from a server object through the ORB and any server object can send responses back to the client objects through ORB. We will discuss ORB in more detail in the next section.

Interface Repository. A dynamic representation of available object interfaces is provided in an interface repository. This repository represents the interfaces (or classes) of all objects in the distributed environment. The clients access the interface repository to learn about the server objects and determine what type of operations can be invoked on an object.

Implementation Repository. Implementation details of each interface, including the operating-system-specific information used for invocation, the attributes used for method selection, and the methods that make up the implementation, are loaded into the implementation repository. The implementation repository can be implemented differently by different vendors. Some implementations of CORBA support IML (implementation mapping language) to describe the implementation details.

7.3.3   Object-Request Broker Structure

As defined by the OMG, the ORB provides mechanisms by which objects transparently interact with each other. It enables the objects to establish connections, communicate with one another, make requests, and receive responses. To achieve this, ORB sets up communications

links and routes information between objects as needed. It literally provides brokerage services between clients and servers by determining the most efficient way for a client to receive
a service and for a server to provide the service. The interfaces to the ORB and the interfaces
to the objects built using the ORB are well defined. The underlying implementation of the
ORB is not important to the developers building distributed-object-oriented applications.
Different interfaces can be defined for an object, and multiple ORBs can exist in a system.
Thus different client applications can refer to the same object residing on a server, but each
client application can be given its own interface.

Figure 7.6 shows a few more details about the structure of an object-request broker (ORB)
and the interfaces to the ORB. The arrows indicate whether the ORB is called or performs an
up-call across the interface. The client can use the dynamic invocation interface or an IDL
stub (determined at compile time). The client can also directly interact with the ORB for operations. The object implementation (the server) receives a request from the ORB through the
IDL-generated skeleton. The object implementation may need to call the object adapter and
the ORB while processing a request.

Figure 7.6 The Structure of Object-Request Broker Interfaces

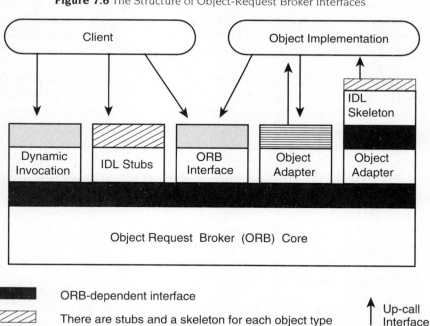

We have already reviewed most of the ORB interfaces shown in Figure 7.6. However, we have not yet described the ***ORB interface***. Basically, this interface goes directly to the ORB for operations that are common across all objects. It consists of a few APIs to local services that may be of interest to some applications. The interface is commonly used by a server object to tell the ORB that it is running and ready to accept calls.

Static versus Dynamic Binding. CORBA ORBs allow static as well as dynamic binding between objects. From a developer's point of view, each serves the same purpose (i.e., establishes a link between a client and server object for invoking an operation). However, a developer chooses between these two options, depending on how much information is available at compile time. The static binding between objects is based on compile-time specification of objects and parameters. Static binding, initially proposed by HP and Sun, is more efficient at run time because all needed libraries are included at compile time. It is also quite simple (a C call with parameters which specify the object to be invoked, the environment of the object, and any other values needed by the server object). On the other hand, dynamic binding between objects uses run-time identification of objects and parameters. Dynamic binding, initially proposed by DEC, incurs more overhead at run time but is very flexible (it can be used when some of the information needed to complete an operation is not available at compile time). Dynamic binding needs extensive run-time support (i.e., a repository that can be accessed at run time to locate objects). It is particularly useful for applications that are undergoing rapid changes or for a tool to support interactive browsing.

Interface Definition Language. CORBA includes a single object model embodied in IDL and uses a single specification language, the OMG Interface Definition Language (IDL), to specify the services provided by an object. The CORBA IDL is similar in principle to the OSF DCE IDL, especially when static binding is used. The parameters needed for each task are specified for static as well as dynamic binding. OMG IDL syntax resembles C++. IDL compilers are being provided by vendors. CORBA API is also defined in IDL. The IDL itself does not say anything about implementation of an interface; however, all CORBA products generate bindings in languages such as C, C++, and Smalltalk. IDL definitions are stored in a public interface directory. Access to this repository can be controlled through access control lists (ACLs). CORBA also specifies language bindings, i.e., mapping of IDL constructs to programming languages.

7.3.4 Object Adapters

Object adapters provide the primary mechanism for an object server to access the ORB services. Specifically, object adaptors provide services such as registering server classes with the implementation repository; creating object instances to handle incoming client calls; assigning unique IDs, known as object references, to the newly created objects; broadcasting the availability of object servers; and handles the incoming client calls by passing them along to the server stub (skeleton).

A variety of object adapters can be envisioned to support different types of requests (see Figure 7.7). To avoid proliferation of too many object adapters, OMG has specified a **basic object adapter (BOA)** that can be used for most ORB object servers. A BOA is required by CORBA in every ORB, so that an object server based on BOA can be used by any ORB. A BOA provides functions such as support of an implementation repository, facilities for generating and interpreting object references, identification (authentication) of the client (or principal) who submitted the request, activation and deactivation of server objects, and method invocation through the server stubs. BOA supports many scheduling policies to support different types of object servers. Examples of the scheduling policies are shared server (i.e., one server handles multiple clients calls), unshared server (i.e., new server is started when a request is made for an object that is not yet active), server per method (i.e, new server is started each time a request is made), and persistent server (servers are activated by means outside BOA).

Some object adapters are being developed for specialized CORBA situations. For example, an adaptor for accessing objects in OODBMs is being considered. In addition, a "streams adaptor" has been proposed to OMG to handle distributed-multimedia applications over CORBA (see next chapter for additional information).

Figure 7.7 Object Adapter in CORBA

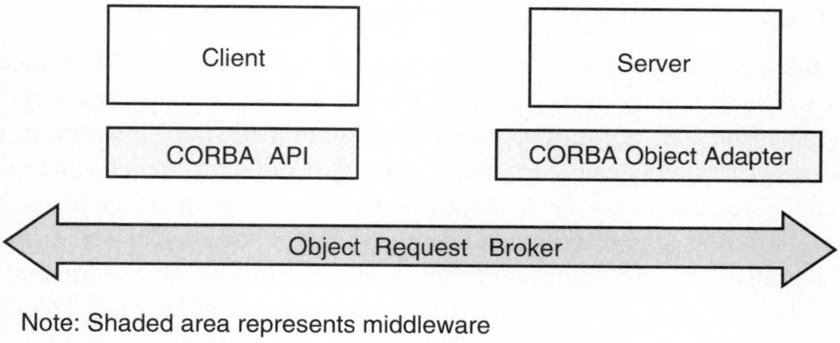

Note: Shaded area represents middleware

7.3.5   Using CORBA

Let us quickly review the overall process used in building CORBA applications to illustrate the key concepts. (A more detailed example with code samples is given in Section 7.15.) The activities involved in developing OO applications in CORBA environments involve the following major activities (see Figure 7.8):

- Create CORBA definitions by using OMG IDL.
- Build the server.
- Build the client(s).
- Deploy the application.

Figure 7.8 CORBA Application Development

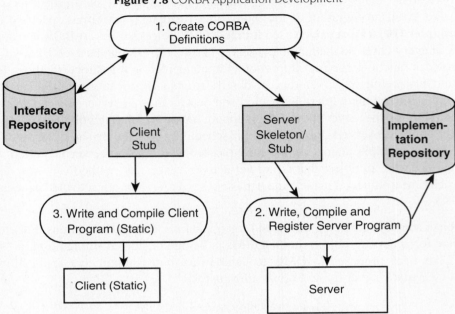

Create CORBA Definitions. The main activity in this step is creation of interface definitions in the CORBA IDL format by using a text editor. The IDL statements are compiled by using an IDL compiler. The IDL definitions can be kept in text files or be stored in an interface repository, so that the clients can learn about the server objects and determine what type of operations can be invoked on an object. As stated previously, the interface of an object is used to declare the operations supported by an object. It consists of a collection of the operations and their signatures, i.e., the operation's name, its arguments, and argument types.[4] For example, the following statements specify the interface for a bank-account object in CORBA IDL (we have simplified it somewhat for illustrative purposes):

```
interface bank_account_interf /* interface name is
bank_account_interf */
make_deposit (/*The operation is make_deposit */
    in integer amount_deposited; /* input is
    amount_deposited represented as an integer */
    in integer account_no; /* input is account_no */
    out integer current_balance ) /* output parameter
    is current_balance */
```

---

4. Some programming languages such as Java explicitly support interfaces (there is a Java construct "interface" that you can use for interface specification).

```
make-withdrawal ( /*Operation is make-withdrawal */
    in integer amount_withdrawn; /* input is
    amount_withdrawn */
    in integer account_no; /* input is account_no */
    out integer current_balance ) /* output parameter
    is current_balance */
```

The interface statement shows what operations can be performed on the order object. Each interface statement defines an interface and contains the descriptions of the operations (operation signatures).

In addition to IDL, the implementation details of each interface are created. You can use CORBA commands to generate a default implementation description from the interface definition. These implementations are loaded into the implementation repository.

After you create the interface definition using IDL, you compile the IDL file to create two very important components for building your application: the client stub and the server skeleton. The client stub and server skeleton are the code templates for building CORBA client and server programs (see Figure 7.8). The client stub is used only to build client programs that use static binding, i.e., the client code is linked with the client stub to form the client application. The client stub is not used to build client programs that use dynamic invocation. The server skeleton is always used as the framework for building the server application, regardless of the invocation type used by the client.

Build the Server. CORBA servers can be quite complex and diverse. Building of program servers requires the following steps:

- *Generate server skeletons.* The IDL statements are compiled to generate a server skeleton . The server skeleton contains method templates that show entry points for all of the implementation methods. The server skeleton also contains the server dispatcher code that makes the implementations and the methods known to the ORB (the dispatcher is called by the **basic object adapter**).[5] A registration routine is also generated as part of the server code (this routine is called at server start-up).

- *Develop server initialization code.* Each server initialization needs code to register the implementation, activate the server's implementation, enter a main loop to receive requests, and exit after unregistering and releasing resources. In addition, the server needs routines for creating objects and managing references to these objects. The server skeleton is used to develop this code.

- *Develop the methods.* The major activity in building a CORBA server is to write the code for the methods that execute the operations. For each method template, you must create the code for the methods. Methods can be implemented as executable code, calls to legacy applications, or scripts to integrate command-line interfaces with existing applications.

---

5. Basic object adapter (BOA) can be used for most ORB objects with conventional implementations. CORBA requires that a BOA be available in every ORB.

Build Clients (Static and Dynamic). After a server has been built and registered, clients can be built to invoke the servers. As stated previously, CORBA clients can use static invocations (i.e., clients know at compile time the objects and the operations on these objects) or dynamic invocation (i.e., the clients determine at run time the objects and the operations on these objects). Static invocation has several advantages over dynamic invocations. First, it is easier to program—you call the remote method by simply invoking it by name and passing it the parameters. Second, it provides more robust type checking, because the compiler enforces type checking at build time. Finally, it performs well and is self-documenting. The main steps involved in building a static invocation CORBA client are (a) generate client stub from IDL or from the interface repository (b) build the client code, and (c) compile and link the client. Building a client for dynamic invocation involves the following steps: (a) obtain the method description from the interface repository (b) create the argument list (c) create the request, and d) invoke the request. CORBA specifies a set of API calls for locating and obtaining objects from the repository.

Deploy and Run the Application. CORBA applications can be packaged and shipped as server only, client only, or a collection of clients and servers. To accomplish this, you need to send your IDL implementation specifications, in addition to the executables. The application is installed and used in a CORBA run-time environment (see Figure 7.9). The IDLs and IML (implementation mapping language) are loaded into the interface and implementation repositories first. Then the server is installed. At server start-up, it registers itself so that the invoking clients can locate it. The dynamic invocation interface allows dynamic construction of object invocation. The interface details are filled in by consulting with the interface repository and or other run-time sources. The client IDL stubs make calls to the ORB, using interfaces, and make it easier for the clients to issue static requests to objects across a network. Object adapters allow an object implementation to access the ORB services. CORBA specifies that each ORB must support a standard adapter called the basic object adapter (BOA). Server skeletons (server IDL stubs) provide the static interfaces to each service supported by the server.

Script Servers

Some vendors support script servers that use operating-system commands in a script (e.g., Bourne shell in UNIX), or command procedures. Building of script servers requires somewhat different steps. First, the implementation must indicate "activation_type (script)" parameter. In addition, special techniques for handling input-output are needed, because scripts are not interactive. Passing information from clients to the scripts also requires calls to special routines. Script servers also have several limitations, such as data types, performance restrictions, and object creation. Nonetheless, script servers are handy tools for quickly developing CORBA applications.

Figure 7.9 CORBA Run-Time Environment

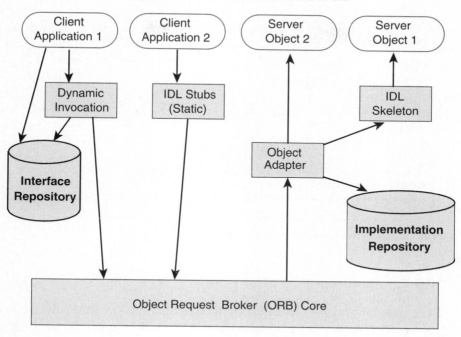

7.3.6   CORBA 2.0 Overview

Initial specifications of CORBA (i.e., CORBA 1.1 and 1.2) did not specify many important services, such as security, concurrency, and transaction processing. This had two major consequences.   First, the CORBA-based applications were limited in scope (e.g., they provided no security). Second, different vendors chose to plug different services (many built ORBs on top of OSF DCE, thus using the DCE facilities of security, etc.). This has led to CORBA implementations by vendors that do not interoperate with each other (recall that interoperability is the main goal of CORBA!). ORBs from different vendors interoperate with each other only through deliberate efforts and joint agreements between vendors.

CORBA 2.0, introduced in December 1994, addressed these problems by adding many new services. Examples of CORBA 2.0 services are shown in Figure 7.10 (CORBA 2.0 is a superset of CORBA 1.2). Basically, the ORB 2.0 has added some capabilities. However, most of the new capabilities have been added in the distributed-object services of CORBA. These capabilities are discussed in Sections 7.3.7 through 7.3.9.

CORBA 2.0 addresses the problem of ORB interoperability by defining *inter-ORB protocols (IOPs)* for interoperability of object-request brokers. Although the IOPs do not impact application software development (IOPs are too low level for applications), they play a key role in an overall middleware architecture. We briefly review IOPs in Section 7.3.10.

Figure 7.10 CORBA 2.0 Facilities (The Object-Management Architecture

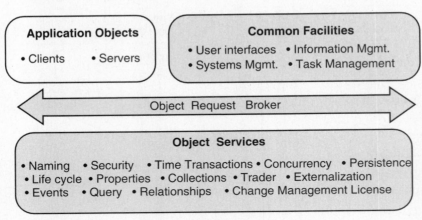

Note: Shaded area represents middleware

7.3.7   ORB 2.0 Features

ORB 2.0 has extended the features of earlier ORBs (see Figure 7.11). Basically, the interface repository has been expanded and a new interface (dynamic skeleton interface) for servers has been added.

ORB 2.0 Interface Repository. CORBA provides an interface repository that keeps track of all registered interfaces, the methods provided by each interface, and the parameters required for each method (these are the method signatures). A set of APIs are provided so that application programs can retrieve, and if authorized, modify the interface definitions. With CORBA 2.0, the interface repositories provide global identifiers to uniquely and globally identify a component and its interface across multivendor ORBs. This is accomplished through *repository IDs*. A repository ID is a unique, system-generated, string that is used across interface repositories. You can generate repository IDs by using the DCE Universal Unique Identifiers (UUIDs) or via a user-supplied unique prefix that is appended to IDL generated names.

Dynamic Skeleton Interface (DSI). The DSI provides a run-time binding for servers that do not have IDL generated stubs. These dynamic skeletons can be very useful for scripting languages to dynamically generate server objects. When invoked, the DSI determines the server object to be invoked and the method to be invoked (the selection is based on parameters values supplied by an incoming message). In contrast, the server skeletons generated through IDL compiles are defined for a certain object class and expect a method implementation for each method specified in the IDL. The DSI can receive calls from static or dynamic client invocations.

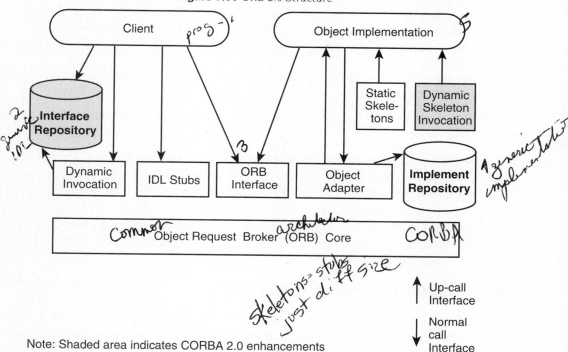

Figure 7.11 ORB 2.0 Structure

Note: Shaded area indicates CORBA 2.0 enhancements

7.3.8   CORBA 2.0 Object Services[6]

The (distributed) object services are packaged as components with IDL-specified interfaces. These services augment the ORB functionality by providing easy mechanisms for creating,

naming, and including new components into the CORBA environment. CORBA 2.0 specifies standards for the following object services:

- **Object Naming Service** to allow different components to locate each other in a CORBA environment.
- **Event Service** to support notification to objects for different events.
- **Persistence Service** for storing components in data stores such as object databases, relational databases and flat files.
- **Object Life Cycle Service** for creation, modification, and deletion of objects.
- **Transaction Management Service** to support object-oriented transactions in distributed environments.
- **Concurrency Control Service** for obtaining and freeing locks.
- **Security Service** to protect components from unauthorized users.
- **Time Service** to provide universal timing service.

---

6. Strictly speaking, the services are independent of CORBA revisions—some date back to CORBA 1.1.

- **Licensing Service** to meter the use of components.
- **Query Service** to provide SQL and OQL (Object Query Language).
- **Properties Service** to associate properties (e.g., time and date) to components.
- **Relationship Service** to establish dynamic associations (e.g., referential integrity) between components.
- **Externalization Service** to get data in and out of a component in streams (this can be used in multimedia applications).

Other object services such as change management, trader, and collections are being defined at the time of this writing.

You may be thinking that not all applications need all these services. In fact, only needed services can be included at system-configuration time. These object services provide a powerful set of capabilities for creating customized middleware. For example, a CORBA "heavy" middleware can be built for transaction management with high security and con-currency requirements by including the CORBA transaction, security, and concurrency-control services. On the other hand, a CORBA "light" middleware can be created by ignoring many object services.

7.3.9 CORBA 2.0 Common Facilities

The CORBA common facilities are IDL-defined components that are common to different classes of applications. The line between common facilities and object services is somewhat fuzzy. Basically, OMG is defining vertical as well as horizontal facilities. For example, vertical facilities will provide IDL-defined interfaces for vertical markets such as finance, tele-communications, and health. Examples of horizontal facilities are user interfaces, information-management services such as compound documents, systems management facilities for managing distributed systems, and task management such as workflow. The vertical as well as horizontal facilities are being developed gradually.

7.3.10 CORBA 2.0 Inter-ORB Architecture

As specified previously, initial specifications of CORBA (i.e., CORBA 1.1 and 1.2) did not specify many implementation details such as security. This has led to CORBA implementations by vendors that do not interoperate with each other. In particular, ORBs based on CORBA 1.1 and 1.2 from different vendors interoperate with each other only through joint agreements and partnerships between vendors. CORBA 2.0 addressed this problem by defining *inter-ORB protocols (IOPs)* for interoperability of object-request brokers. For existing ORBs that do not interoperate, OMG is specifying an API for adding bridges between ORBs.

The IOP specifications are significant feature of CORBA 2.0 because they allow ORBs, potentially from different suppliers, to interoperate with each other. These specifications do not impact application developers (application programmers will typically not write code at

CORBA Versus DCE

At a high level, DCE RPC and CORBA ORB provide somewhat similar functionality. They both support the development and integration of client/server applications in heterogeneous distributed environments. Both are open and are supported by multiple suppliers. In addition, they both use IDLs (Interface Definition Languages) and hide platform differences and the details of where the clients and servers are located on the network.

But there are several key differences. The basic difference between DCE and CORBA is that DCE is an *implementation* (OSF sends the DCE code to vendors so that they can customize it) while CORBA is a *specification* that is used by vendors for implementation. Thus OSF DCE from different vendors is by and large identical (a big plus for DCE) while CORBA implementations between vendors can vary widely (whoever heard of bridges between OSF DCE from different vendors?).

Another fundamental difference is that DCE was designed from a procedural point of view while CORBA was designed for object-orientation. This has many implications such as: (a) CORBA IDL supports inheritance while DCE IDL does not, and (b) CORBA passes object references that allow applications to support dynamic binding to objects.

The efficiency of ORB versus that of DCE RPC is debatable. The basic issue is that DCE RPC includes many functions (e.g., directory and security) that add processing overhead. However, ORBs bypass this functionality (if needed) and can be implemented efficiently on "native" protocols such as TCP/IP sockets. Thus ORBs can be lightweight and more efficient. But ORBs are being implemented on top of DCE RPCs in some CORBA implementations. In such cases, ORBs add another layer of complexity. So you decide between added layers (of complexity) versus functionality.

Will CORBA replace DCE, will CORBA coexist with DCE, or will CORBA be an "also ran?" Nobody knows. It does seem that the popularity of OSF DCE is suffering a setback while the popularity of CORBA is on the rise. It was initially thought that CORBA will be required to operate on top of DCE. However, CORBA 2.0 has not included DCE as a required feature (the DCE-ORB interoperability feature, DCE/ESIOP, is optional in CORBA 2.0). Instead, CORBA 2.0 includes a required feature for ORBs to interoperate over TCP/IP (the IIOP). This bypasses DCE.

Source for detailed discussion: Brando, T., "Comparing CORBA and DCE", *Object Magazine*, March 1996, pp. 52–57.

this level), but they do play an important role in how an application developed on one ORB can interoperate with an application developed on another ORB. Figure 7.12 shows the principal IOPs and depicts how they interrelate with each other.

Figure 7.12 CORBA 2.0 Inter-ORB Architecture

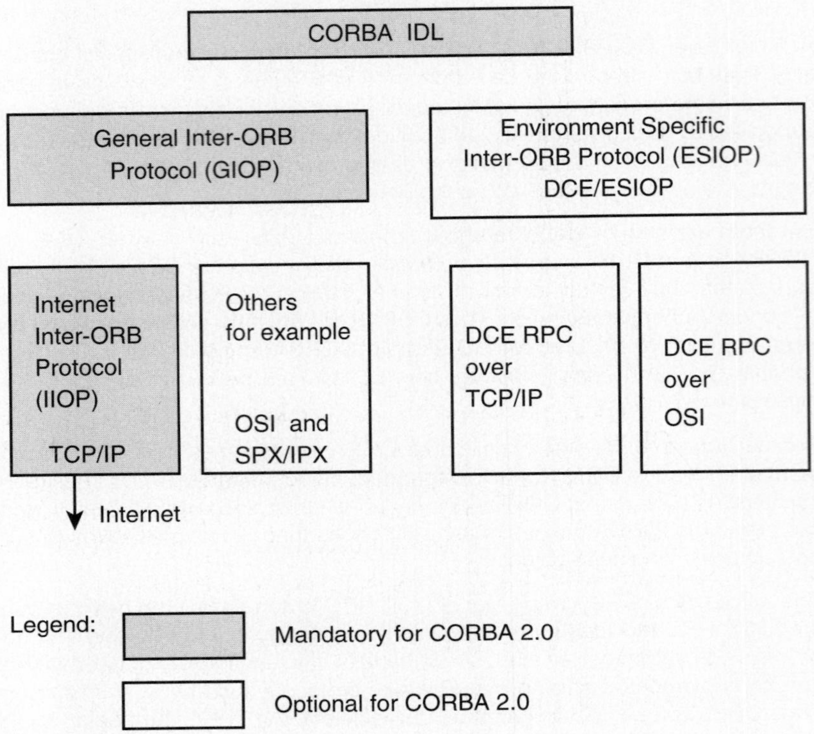

Source: Orfali [1996].

General Inter-ORB Protocol (GIOP). This IOP specifies a set of message formats and common data representations for interactions between ORBs. The GIOP is especially designed for ORB-to-ORB communications. It is intended to operate over any connection-oriented transport protocol. The common data representation (CDR) is used to map OMG IDL data types (pointers and linked lists) into a "flattened" network message that can be transported over the network. GIOP also specifies a format for interoperable object references so that a given object can be accessed from different ORBs.

Internet Inter-ORB Protocol (IIOP). This IOP specifies how GIOP messages are exchanged over a TCP/IP network. IIOP allows a lightweight implementation of CORBA so that CORBA can operate directly on top of TCP/IP and not on top of DCE. IIOP is a *required* feature of CORBA 2.0. In other words, an ORB must support IIOP to be CORBA 2.0 compliant. In the future, GIOP specifications on top of IPX/SPX and OSI may be developed.

Environment-Specific Inter-ORB Protocols (ESIOPs). These IOPs are an alternative to GIOP and are specified for specific environments. CORBA 2.0 has specified DCE as the first of many optional ESIOPs. DCE/ESIOP does not require DCE IDL (OMG IDL does the job). The DCE/ESIOP includes many features that are important for mission-critical applications. Examples of these features are the DCE security, cell and global directories, authenticated RPCs, and distributed time services (all these features are part of OSF DCE). However, this makes CORBA 2.0 applications heavyweight ("CORBA Heavy"). In the future, ESIOPs may be specified for other environments.

7.3.11 Bridges between ORBs (Half and Full Bridges)

CORBA 2.0 provides facilities for developing generic ORB-to-ORB bridges. These bridges come in two flavors: half bridges and full bridges. Figure 7.13 shows these bridges.

ORB Half Bridges. An ORB half bridge relies on a common ORB (the "backbone" ORB) to interconnect different ORBs. For example, Figure 7.13(a) shows how an IIOP backbone can be used to interconnect different proprietary ORBs. The key point is that your ORB needs to communicate with an IIOP through a half bridge that translates your ORB to IIOP. After this, the IIOP can be used as a "global ORB" bus. Keep in mind that IIOP runs on top of the Internet. The ORB half bridges are similar to the gateways used in networks that convert different network protocols (e.g., SNA, SPX/IPX, OSI) to a backbone network protocol (e.g., TCP/IP). Half bridges allow a federation of different ORBs around an IIOP backbone.

Figure 7.13 ORB-to-ORB Bridges

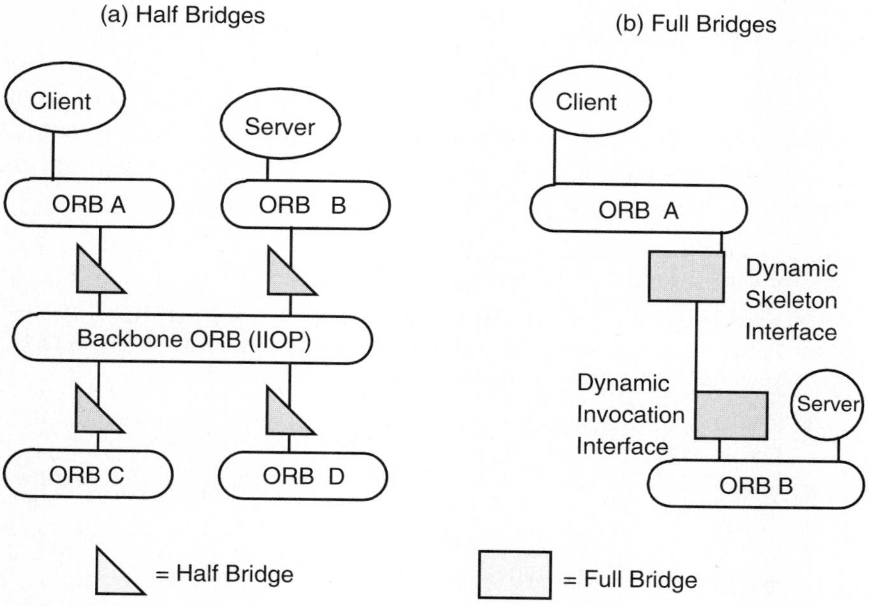

Source: Orfali [1996].

ORB Full Bridges. The full bridges directly convert one ORB to another without requiring a common backbone ORB. The CORBA 2.0 Dynamic Skeleton Interface (DSI) is used to receive outgoing messages and the Dynamic Invocation Interface (DII) is used to receive inputs and invoke destination objects—see Figure 7.13(b). Thus an ORB from one vendor can communicate with an ORB from another vendor directly. This approach is used in some bridges such as CORBA/OLE bridges [Orfali 1996].

7.3.12 CORBA Summary

Object-oriented technologies and techniques have natural applications in distributed systems. Entities in distributed systems can be viewed as objects exchanging messages. OMG was formed to create a suite of standard languages, interfaces, and protocols for interoperability of applications in heterogeneous distributed environments. CORBA is an OMG specification for invoking objects in a distributed environment.

Initial specifications of CORBA did not specify many implementation details such as security and transaction processing protocol. This has led to CORBA implementations by vendors that do not interoperate with each other. CORBA 2.0 has added many additional capabilities and has specified APIs for adding bridges between ORBs. For example, CORBA 2.0 specifies several important areas such as security, concurrency, transactions, and replication. There are different opinions about how CORBBA 2.0 will actually succeed (see Orfali [1996] and Shelton [1994] for an analysis of CORBA 2.0).

Many vendors are announcing CORBA-compliant software. Examples are the Distributed Systems Object Model (DSOM) from IBM, Distributed Objects Everywhere (DOE) from SUN, ObjectBroker from Digital, and Object Request Broker (Orbix) from Iona Corporation. In addition, as we will see in the next section, CORBA plays an important role in the composite document standards, because these standards are based on object-oriented concepts. An area of considerable activity is combining CORBA with the Web (see the sidebar "CORBA and the Web").

CORBA and the Web

Many efforts are underway at present in combining/integrating CORBA with the Web. Perhaps the oldest and the best-known method is to invoke CORBA calls from a CGI gateway. Other approaches becoming available are:

- Invoke CORBA directly from the Web browser. Netscape has announced that the Netscape browsers will issue the CORBA IIOP calls.
- Use HTTP as a transport protocol underneath ORBs. A few small companies have implemented this option.
- Use CORBA to interact between Java applets across machines. This option is currently supported by a few vendors (especially Sun).

The main idea is to integrate CORBA with the Web so that Web browsers can directly work with CORBA objects.

Additional details about CORBA can be found in the books [Siegel 1996, Orfali 1996, Mowbray 1995, Otte 1996]. The OMG home page *(http://www.omg.org)* is an excellent source of the recent activities in CORBA.

Although we have concentrated on the object-request brokers so far, the concept of brokers is general and is currently exploited in the message broker architectures (see sidebar "Message Broker: Another Kind of Broker").

7.4 Compound Document Middleware: OLE and OpenDoc

7.4.1 Overview

A *compound document* is essentially a container for data that comes from a variety of sources such as text editors, spreadsheets, graphics, multimedia information and other applications. The software tools that create different components of a compound document are referred to as *applications*. For example, consider a compound document that consists of Microsoft Word text, Lotus spreadsheets, and Powerpoint graphics. In this compound document, Microsoft Word, Lotus, and Powerpoint are all considered as applications. The objective of the compound-document standards and associated middleware is to provide seamless integration of a wide variety of objects to form a document. We will review two promising middleware products for compound documents: Object Linking and Embedding (OLE) from Microsoft and OpenDoc from Components Integration Laboratories (CI Labs).

7.4.2 Microsoft's Object Linking and Embedding (OLE)

Microsoft introduced Object Linking and Embedding (OLE) technology in 1990 as its basic strategy for integrating multimedia data types with multiple applications for compound documents. Basically, OLE allows objects from one application to be included in another application. The objects can be graphs, drawings, pictures, tables, spreadsheets, text, selected cells of a spreadsheet, sound bites, video segments, and anything else that can be controlled or displayed by an application. Instead of access to the structured data stored in databases, OLE is suited for access to the unstructured data located in documents or other "flat" files. For example, OLE can be used to access a segment of a video application from a Visual Basic application, and then display the video segment based on the Visual Basic application.

OLE allows access to objects from other applications in two manners:

- *Object linking*. A placeholder (link) of the needed object is placed in the container application. The actual object is not copied. The linked object is accessed at run time, thus the latest value of the object is retrieved. An object can be linked into many applications simultaneously. For example, let us assume that a greeting sound object is linked into several Visual Basic applications that play the greeting message whenever a user logs on to any of these applications. The greeting message is modified for holidays and/or emergencies. The appropriate greeting message will be played whenever any of these applications run.

Message Broker: Another Kind of Broker

A broker mediates between clients and servers (i.e., instead of a client directly connecting to a server, it first connects to a broker that in turn finds a suitable server). The concept of a broker is independent of the implementation of the broker. For example, the best-known implementation of the broker architecture is the object-request broker (ORB) as presented in OMG CORBA specification. In CORBA, the ORB mediates the interactions between remote objects. Another type of broker, called a message broker, is being presented as a viable implementation of the broker architecture.

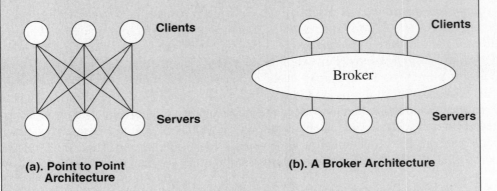

(a). Point to Point Architecture

(b). A Broker Architecture

A message broker is not restricted to objects. Instead, it delivers messages between disparate applications, including legacy applications. The underlying technologies used by the message broker may consist of RPCs or MOMs, although MOM does appear to fit this model quite well. The basic idea of a message broker is that it can provide brokerage services asynchronously and, if needed, support a "publish/subscribe" model. The message broker can also be rule-based, i.e., you specify the rules to be used by the middleware to perform certain actions. See, for example, NeoNET (http//www.neonsoft.com). Message brokers can be very effective in a wide range of distributed applications including group communications, integration of existing applications, and large scale workflow.

The Gartner Group is advocating message brokers as key to the future success of distributed computing. The Gartner Group predicts that by 1998, message brokers will be as widespread as database gateways and data warehouses (Source: Bort, J., "Can Message Brokers Deliver?" *Applications Software Magazine,* June 1996, pp.70–76).

- **Embedding**. The data of the needed object is copied into the container application. Naturally, once embedded, the container application only accesses the embedded object. For a new copy of the needed object, the object has to be reembedded. For example, the greeting message will have to be reembedded into all container applications whenever the greetings change.

The trade-offs between these two options are obvious. Linking allows maximum flexibility in accessing the latest data of an object and also minimizes storage requirements, because only one copy of the object exists. However, linked objects suffer in performance, owing to dynamic linking. A potential risk in object linking is that the link may be lost if the linked object is moved or if the container application is run on another computer. With object embedding, you never have to worry about losing the data, and the performance is improved. However, some objects can take too much space (10 seconds of sampled sound can run over 100 KB). The actual process of linking and embedding objects by using OLE depends on the applications being used. The process is based on pointing and clicking on the OLE icon and then following intuitive steps.

OLE has evolved and continues to evolve. OLE 1 was based on a protocol built on top of DDE (Dynamic Data Exchange) and was somewhat limited in its capabilities. OLE 2.0, introduced in 1993, provides many new features and is based on a new object-encapsulation technology known as the Component Object Model (COM). The main architectural components of OLE 2.0 are (see Figure 7.14):

- *Component Object Model (COM)*. COM specifies the interfaces between component objects of a compound document. Conceptually, COM is similar to CORBA in the sense that it separates the interfaces from the implementations. COM is now known as **DCOM (Distributed Common Object Model)**, owing to the emphases of OLE on distributed environments. DCOM, in addition to its role in OLE, is the foundation of the ActiveX technology that is expected to be used in Microsoft's next-generation operating system (see Section 7.6 for a discussion of ActiveX).

- *Structured Storage System*. This component provides an internal directory for organizing the contents of a compound document.

Figure 7.14 OLE 2.0 Components

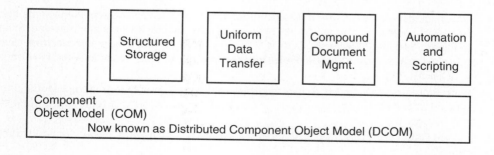

- *Uniform Data Transfer Model.* This component allows users to transfer data uniformly through copy and paste, drag and drop, or API calls.

- *Compound -Document Management.* This component seamlessly integrates data of different formats (e.g., sound clips, spreadsheet cells, bit maps) within a compound document.

- *Automation and Scripting.* This component allows applications to expose their COM interfaces so that other applications and scripting languages can use OLE objects.

In summary, OLE provides an architecture for compound documents. It includes facilities for defining object interfaces independent of the implementation and includes method invocation and object encapsulation (some of these capabilities are primitive because OLE does not support inheritance and polymorphism). Microsoft is including OLE in its enterprisewide distributed-object computing strategy known as ActiveX (see Section 7.5 for ActiveX details). Programming details of OLE are beyond the scope of this book and can be found in *Object Linking and Embedding: Programmer's Reference,* Microsoft Corporation. The book by Brockschmidt [1995] contains a great deal of technical information about OLE.

7.4.3   OpenDoc

OpenDoc is a set of APIs and software for compound documents. OpenDoc, originated by Apple, is similar in scope and function to OLE 2.0 and is considered as an alternative to OLE 2.0 (see, for example, Orfali [1994]). At present, OpenDoc is managed and promoted by Components Integration Laboratories (CI Labs)—established in September 1993 jointly by Apple, IBM, Oracle, Novell, Taligent,[7] Sunsoft, Word Perfect, and Xerox.

The CI Labs technology includes:
- Apple's OpenDoc software for Windows, OS/2, UNIX, and Macintosh.
- IBM's System Model (SOM), a CORBA-compliant architecture, for dynamic object linking.
- Apple's Bento technology for handling multimedia information
- Apple's Open Scripting Architecture (OSA) for the coexistence of scripting systems from multiple suppliers.

Figure 7.15 shows the components of OpenDoc. Let us briefly review these components:
- System Object Model (SOM) provides interoperability of OpenDoc objects in the same address space (local objects), across address spaces (remote objects) on the same machine, or across machines. As stated previously, SOM is CORBA compliant, so it allows object communications across machines and supports static as well as dynamic method invocation (see the discussion on CORBA).
- Bento Storage, named after Japanese plates with compartments for different foods, provides containers for different objects. Bento containers allow applications to retrieve and store collections of objects.
- Uniform Data Transfer Model provides transfer of data via copy and paste, drag and drop, and linking.

---

7. Taligent is reportedly ceasing operations.

- Compound-Document Management supports OpenDoc "parts" which are the basic building blocks of OpenDoc. OpenDoc compound documents are composed of parts—each document has a top-level part in which other parts are embedded, each part contains data (e.g., video parts contain video clips) and parts can contain other parts.
- Open Scripting Architecture is based on the Mac AppleScript. It defines about a dozen polymorphic commands for parts (e.g., "delete" could mean delete a word or a video image depending on the type of part that receives the command.

Figure 7.15 OpenDoc Components

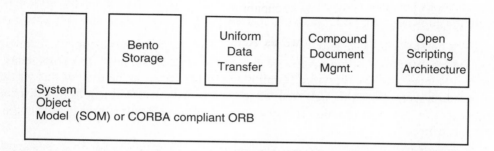

CI Labs intends to make source code for the OpenDoc technologies available to the industry. CI Labs also plans to make OpenDoc compatible with OLE, i.e., an OpenDoc container would see an OLE object as an OpenDoc part, and vice versa. OpenDoc is targeted for deployment on Microsoft Windows, OS/2, Macintosh, and UNIX. Information about Open-Doc can be found in Orfali [May 1995, March 1995].

7.4.4   Compound-Document Middleware Summary and Trends

OLE and OpenDoc share the same goals and provide the same basic functionalities. However, at present, OLE and OpenDoc have several differences. Some differences are at the core (e.g., OLE does not support inheritance, polymorphism, and multiple machine documents while OpenDoc does), while others are behavioral (double clicks to select an object versus moving the cursor to the right spot for object selection). In addition, there are differences in suppliers (OLE is provided by Microsoft while OpenDoc is vendor independent). OLE is much more used than OpenDoc for obvious reasons (Microsoft's presence on the desktops may have something to do with it!). However, it is expected, and hoped, that these two technologies will interoperate with each other. In either case, use of CORBA for object invocation appears to be imminent (OpenDoc uses CORBA-compliant middleware, and bridges between COM/DCOM to CORBA are commercially available). In addition, OMG's Common Facilities are expected to provide compound-document objects.

7.5   ActiveX: Going Beyond OLE

7.5.1   Overview

In March 1996, Microsoft announced its "ActiveX" strategy which goes far beyond OLE by combining the desktop services with the World Wide Web. In other words, ActiveX combines Web browsers and Java applets with the desktop services such as Word documents, spreadsheets, transaction support, scripting, and many other (still evolving) capabilities. Like OLE, DCOM (Distributed Component Object Model) serves as a core technology for remote communications between ActiveX components. Figure 7.16 shows a conceptual view of the interrelationships between OLE, ActiveX, and DCOM.

Microsoft is making it clear that ActiveX is not just a compound-document technology. Instead, Microsoft is positioning ActiveX as a complete environment for components and distributed objects. Almost everything coming out of Microsoft at the time of this writing is being based on ActiveX. Although ActiveX provides many capabilities, from a distributed objects point of view, the following features are significant (we will see the details in the following subsections):

- All ActiveX components communicate with each other by using DCOM. So a Java applet (an ActiveX component) can call a remotely located Microsoft Word document (another ActiveX component) over DCOM. See Section 7.5.2.

Figure 7.16 OLE, ActiveX and DCOM

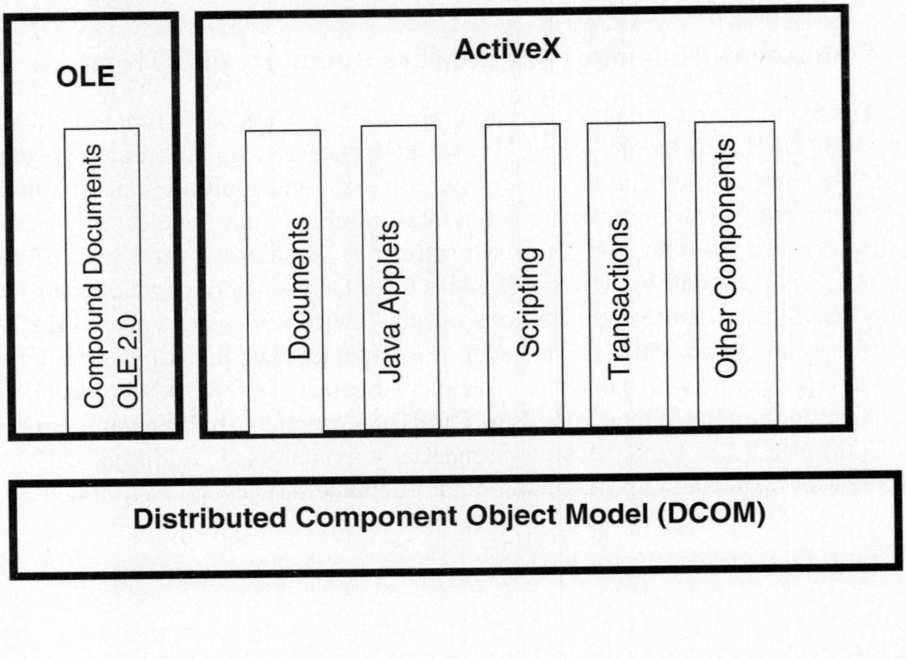

- The Web browser can behave as a container. For example, the Microsoft Internet Explorer can contain components such as Word documents, Java applets, C code, and Excell spreadsheets. See Section 7.5.3.
- Web technologies (browsers, HTML pages Java applets) can be intermixed with desktop tools (spreadsheets, word processors) for distributed applications. See Section 7.5.4.
- Serve facilities such as SQL servers and legacy access gateways can be invoked from ActiveX clients. See Section 7.5.5.

7.5.2   DCOM (Distributed Component Object Model) as an ORB

As discussed previously, ActiveX uses DCOM (the distributed version of COM) to provide communications between remote ActiveX components. In this sense, DCOM is the ORB for ActiveX. The basic scenario is that Windows will be a huge collection of ActiveX components and interfaces, with DCOM serving as the ORB. It is expected that all system services will be written as DCOM objects. These, and other services, can be provided by Microsoft or any third-party vendors.

DCOM provides the basic brokerage services for ActiveX. It supports APIs for static as well as dynamic invocation of objects. DCOM uses DCE RPC for interactions between DCOM objects. DCOM's object model is somewhat limited because DCOM does not support multiple inheritance. In other words, DCOM supports inheritance through pointers that link different interfaces together. Figure 7.17 shows the role of DCOM in ActiveX.

Figure 7.17 Communications Between ActiveX Components

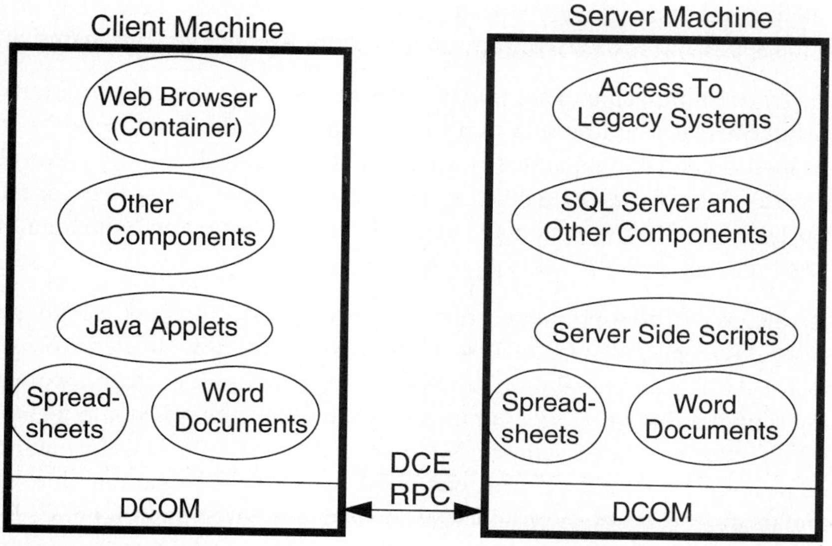

The following facilities of DCOM should be noted (see the sidebar "DCOM versus CORBA" for additional discussion):

- **Interface Definition Language (IDL).** DCOM uses interfaces that are very similar, in concept, to the CORBA interfaces. Basically, an interface defines a set of related functions. The DCOM IDL is used to define an interface, the method it supports, and the parameters used by each method. DCOM IDL can be used to define your own interfaces, in addition to the Microsoft provided interfaces. For example, at the time of this writing, OLE/ActiveX consists of more than 100 interfaces, each supporting about six functions. In addition, more than 100 Win32-style APIs are supported.
- **Object Definition Language (ODL) and Type Libraries.** DCOM supports an Object Definition Language (ODL) that is used to describe metadata. The interface specifications and metadata are stored in a repository, known as *Type Library*. Type Libraries are equivalent to the CORBA Interface Repositories.
- **Object Services.** DCOM provides very rudimentary object services at the time of this writing. Examples of the services provided are a basic licensing mechanism, a local directory service based on the Windows Registry, a basic life cycle facility, persistence services for file systems, and a very simple event service called connectable objects. This is in addition to the naming services provided by the Type Libraries. However, the overall ActiveX Platform is expected to support other services such as X.500 directories.

7.5.3 Web Browsers as Containers of ActiveX Components

An ActiveX component is the basic unit of ActiveX applications. Different components can be combined to develop and deploy new applications. These components may be specifically written for this application or reused from some other project or even purchased off the shelf.

Components by definition cannot survive on their own—they require *containers* in which to execute. Visual Basic is a common example of a container in the desktop world. Visual Basic applications load needed components from a machine's local disk or a file server. In the Internet World, the Web browsers are a common example of a container—they load Java applets (Java applets are basically components) and provide an environment to run them (i.e., contain them). Let us focus on Web browsers as containers.

Before ActiveX, Web browsers were primarily serving as containers for Java applets. We have discussed Java applets in Chapter 4. These applets are downloaded from Web servers (embedded in HTML pages) and then the Web browser is used as a container. ActiveX has extended the scope of browsers as a container by allowing ActiveX components to be "contained" by Web browsers. At present, the Microsoft Internet Explorer is the main browser that can be used as ActiveX container. This can be very useful. For example, the Web browser can now contain spreadsheets, Word documents, and code written in C++, C, Java, or other programming languages. You can build powerful applications that may, for example, supply

DCOM versus CORBA: Similarities and Differences

We will start with the typical disclaimer about technology comparisons, i.e., both technologies are evolving at the time of this writing and consequently the similarities/dissimilarities will also change with time. Our objective is to present, what appears to be, the philosophical and fundamental approaches being used by the two technologies.

At a high level, there are several similarities between CORBA and DCOM. However, several differences appear when you look closely.

Similarities:

- Both are based on the object model.
- Both utilize the interface concept and utilize an Interface Definition Language (IDL).
- Both use static and dynamic calls from clients to servers.
- Both use a repository to locate objects and invoke them (CORBA calls it the Interface Repository and DCOM calls it a Type Library).

Dissimilarities:

- DCOM uses, in addition to IDL, Object Definition Language (ODL), for defining metadata. CORBA uses a single IDL for everything.
- DCOM uses the universal unique ID (UUID), based on OSF DCE, to locate and invoke objects. CORBA does not use UUIDs. It uses object references and repository to locate and invoke objects.
- DCOM uses the OSF DCE RPC as the basic transport mechanism between remote objects. CORBA uses several options such as IIOP (Internet Inter-ORB Protocol) that uses TCP/IP sockets and ESIOP (Environment Specific Inter-ORB Protocol) that runs on top of DCE.
- CORBA only uses connection-based (i.e, TCP) services while DCOM favors connectionless (i.e., UDP) services. DCOM does support TCP connections but it favors UDP for purpose of scaling (do not have to keep track of large number of open sessions).
- CORBA 2.0 has specified a very extensive set of services that include transaction management, security, concurrency control, life cycle, query, etc. In comparison, DCOM services at present are somewhat limited (these are being added through the ActiveX Platform).

Additional discussion about differences between DCOM and CORBA can be found in Orfali [1996], and Foody [1996]. The WWW Consortium held an excellent technical seminar on November 18, 1996, on trade-offs between DCOM and CORBA. Public information discussed in this seminar can be obtained from the Web site (http://www.w3.org).

specialized viewers with the data to be viewed (the viewer and the data is loaded as needed from the network and runs inside the Web browser as a container).

7.5.4   ActiveX Controls—Building Downloadable Web-based Components

Microsoft's ActiveX Controls (formerly called either OLE controls or OCXs) are the special brand of ActiveX components that perform common tasks in standard ways and have been optimized for Internet use. ActiveX controls are, in principle, very similar to Java applets. For example, ActiveX controls, like Java applets, are self-contained pieces of functionality that run inside some kind of container (e.g., a Web browser). Thus ActiveX controls can be embedded in Web pages and downloaded on demand. However, unlike Java applets, ActiveX controls can be written in various languages such as C, C++, in addition to Java. Unlike Java applets, which are downloaded in a machine-independent format and usually interpreted within the browser, ActiveX controls are binaries. Another difference is that Java applets today are supported primarily by only one kind of container—the Web browsers. ActiveX controls, on the other hand, are supported by different kinds of containers (e.g., Visual Basic applications).

Developers of downloadable Web-based application developers have two basic choices: Java applets or ActiveX Controls. See the sidebar "Java versus ActiveX Controls" for discussion.

A plethora of different ActiveX controls already exist in the marketplace. Examples are the controls that implement spreadsheets, data viewing, mainframe connectivity, voice recognition, and the like. Many of these existing controls can be downloaded and executed within an ActiveX-capable browser. Thus there is an instant supply of available ActiveX components for Web-based applications.

7.5.5   ActiveX Server

The ActiveX Server is based on the Microsoft Information Server (IIS) that is integrated with the Windows NT network operating system. The ActiveX Server includes the Microsoft BackOffice family which includes the Microsoft SQL Server and the Microsoft Systems Management Server. ActiveX Server provides scripting and control facilities to tie into legacy systems or to perform other specialized functions on the server side. The scripting capabilities support PERL, JavaScript and Visual Basic Script.

7.5.6   General Observations and Comments

The facilities of ActiveX will evolve with time. However, competitors to ActiveX such as CORBA are expected to mature considerably while ActiveX for distributed objects is still in its very initial stages at the time of this writing. Depending on the market shifts, ActiveX may be combined and "bridged" to CORBA and other technologies. For example, before ActiveX,

---

Java versus ActiveX Controls

Java applets and ActiveX Controls are two valid choices for building download-able Web applications. The leading browsers, Netscape Navigator and Microsoft's Internet Explorer, support both options. Let us discuss the choice between these two options.

Java applets should be chosen if a component must run on heterogeneous cli-ent systems, if the Java security exposures are manageable, and if you are not concerned with the performance limitations of the Java interpretive model (interpreters can be slower than binary code).

ActiveX Controls should be chosen if the component is targeted at Microsoft systems, is needed in a wider range of containers than just Web browsers, and must run as efficiently as possible (ActiveX Controls download binary code).

As expected, both of these models will evolve. For example, "just-in-time" com-pilers for Java will improve the performance by compiling an applet byte code on arrival. The platform independence issue may disappear becuase Microsoft is planning to port ActiveX on multiple platforms. Keep in mind that ActiveX Controls also support Java applets (Java environment is modified so that it uses DCOM).

Source: Chappell, D., "Component Software Meets the Web: Java Applets vs. ActiveX Controls," *Network World,* May 1996.

---

proposals for uniting OLE and CORBA had been discussed actively in the industrial press (see, for example, Hayes [1994]). At present, DCOM to CORBA bridges are available from companies such as Iona. For example, the Iona COM/CORBA bridge provides two way map-ping: it allows DCOM objects to be treated as CORBA and vice versa.

Literature on ActiveX is growing rapidly. The Microsoft Web site (http://www.micro-soft.com) provides access to latest announcements, white papers, and frequently asked ques-tions (FAQs). The book by David Chappell, *Understanding ActiveX and OLE*, Microsoft Press, 1996, is a good overview of the subject matter.

7.6   State of the Practice: Examples

At the time of this writing, CORBA, OLE, ActiveX, and OpenDoc are not widely state of the practice. The case studies published in literature mostly discuss small prototypes and exper-iments, although some real examples are beginning to appear. Here is a small sample of case studies:

- Hubert [1996] describes how CORBA is being used in ABB corporation to build new applications and to integrate legacy applications. The lessons learned include advantages of distributed object technologies over conventional techniques.

- Mowbray [1995] gives an in-depth example of how CORBA is used to build a U.S. government application, called DISCUS (Data Interchange and Synergistic Collateral Usage Study). A great deal of details including the OMG IDL and code fragments are discussed.
- Koschel and Leibfried [1996] describe experiences of using IBM's DSOM in implementing distributed-object applications. Experiences include observations about writing and configuring applications, using metaclasses, stability and debugging issues, and documentation.
- An example of integrating OLE and CORBA for Boeing Aerospace is described by Horn [1996]. This example, described in a presentation, showed how Boeing used OLE at client side and CORBA at the back end.
- Konstantas [1996] describes a case study of how a legacy system is being migrated to CORBA. The objective of this project is to provide an interoperability layer between several heterogeneous legacy systems that include CAD-CAM and very large Fortran programs.

To gain some insights, a detailed CORBA development example of a simple inventory system is discussed at the end of this chapter (see Appendix 7A: Section 7.14).

7.7   State of the Market: Commercial Products

Current middleware products in the market to support distributed objects fall into two broad categories:

- Individual products for CORBA, OLE, OpenDoc, and ActiveX
- Interoperability products between CORBA, OLE, OpenDoc, and ActiveX

CORBA-based products are available from many vendors. Examples are the Distributed Systems Object Model (DSOM) from IBM, Distributed Objects Everywhere (DOE) from SUN.[8] ObjectBroker from Digital, and ORBIX from Iona Corporation. CORBA support is available on Windows, Mac, OS/2, various UNIX versions, Tandem, IBM OS/400, and MVS. OLE products are, understandably, becoming available from Microsoft on Windows and Mac. OpenDoc products are still very sparse. Microsoft has gone beyond OLE and is posing ActiveX as *the* platform for distributed-object computing that combines Web technologies, desktop services, and distributed computing into an integrated environment.

Interoperability between OLE/ActiveX, OpenDoc and CORBA will be primarily achieved through gateways. An example of such a gateway is the Novell ComponentGlue that makes OLE look like OpenDoc, and vice versa. In addition, Digital's ObjectBroker, Iona's Orbix/OLE, and IBM's SOMobjects for Windows provide two-way gateways between CORBA and OLE (these gateways, in fact go between CORBA and COM/DCOM—the underlying infrastructure shared by OLE and ActiveX). These gateways are proprietary at present, but could become open because OMG, with Microsoft's concurrence, has issued an RFP for a two-way CORBA/COM gateway. Details of interoperability issues between different distributed-object technologies can be found in Orfali [1996], and Rymer [1995].

---

8. DOE has been renamed NEO by SUN

7.8   State of the Art: ANSA and ISO ODP

Distributed objects is an area of active research and development. For example, [Adler April 1995, March 1995] examines various coordination models needed to support distributed objects and analyzes emerging standards for component software (OLE, CORBA, Open-Doc). Issues include service request management, process planning, server groupings, and server reliability. In recent years, research initiatives and standards organizations have focused on several issues that are based on the distributed object model. The two key players, described below, are the ANSA Consortium and the International Standards Organization.

7.8.1   ANSA Consortium

The ANSA Consortium is a Cambridge, England-based collaborative-industry laboratory to advance distributed-systems technology. In its initial phase (1985–1988), the ANSA project focused on developing a basic understanding of distributed architectures. In this phase, the ANSA team built a prototype DCE-like platform (called ANSAWARE) over MSDOS, VMS, and UNIX. During the second phase (1988–1993), ANSA shifted its focus to distributed objects and developed ANSAWARE as a full function ORB. Many ANSAWARE ideas were used in OMG CORBA. During this phase, ANSA gained several sponsors in Europe and U.S., coordinated by APM Ltd., the parent company founded to coordinate ANSA. Sponsors included companies such as Bellcore,[9] Bell Northern Research (BNR) Europe, British Telecom, DEC, France Telecom, and HP. In the third phase (since 1993), ANSA has been conducting a jointly agreed program of research and development between sponsors with focus on international standards (e.g., ISO ODP) for architectural framework and strong ties with industry standards (OMG, OSF, X/Open) for technology. ANSA is paying special attention to telecommunications by providing strong architectural input into a TINA (Telecommunications Intelligent Network Architecture) Consortium and by participating in TINA auxiliary projects.

ANSA recommends a set of components, rules, recipes, and guidelines to help designers make design decisions. The key ANSA principles are shown in the sidebar "ANSA Principles." At present, the focus of ANSA is on:

- Architecture for distributed applications
- Vendor neutrality
- Contribution to standards
- Advanced technology prototypes
- Technical resource (services)
- Concentration on computer and telecommunications services integration

In particular, ANSA is concentrating on developing advanced prototypes which utilize the emerging distributed-object technologies. Examples of the recent prototypes include

---

9. At the time of this writing, Dr. Gomer Thomas and I represent Bellcore on ANSA's Technical Committee.

ANSAWEB (use of CORBA to develop Web applications), JADE (Java applets issuing CORBA calls), DIMMA (distributed-multimedia applications over CORBA), and QUARTZ (running workflow over Web). In addition to the prototypes developed at ANSA, many university research projects currently use the ANSAWARE platform to investigate distributed systems because the ANSAWARE platform is available at nominal cost to the academic institutions. Examples are extensions to ANSAWARE for advanced mobile applications [Friday 1996], translation of LOTUS specifications to ANSAWARE implementations [Rosa 1996], and implementation of models for evolution of distributed systems on ANSAWARE [Senivongse 1996].

We will review some of the ANSA work in the next chapters where appropriate. An overview of ANSA is given by Herbert [1994]. Additional information about ANSA can be found from the ANSA home page (*http://www.ansa.co.uk*).

ANSA Principles

- Specify systems using application concepts (i.e., good abstractions)
- Define a high level model for distributed programming (use objects)
- Use tools to automatically generate the engineering detail (generalization of stub generator)
- Define structures for integration
  - Object management and monitoring
  - Trading (directory and selection)
  - Transparency

7.8.2   ISO ODP (Open Distributed Processing)

International Standards Organization (ISO) and International Telecommunications Union (ITU), previously known as CCITT, initiated a joint effort known as *Open Distributed Processing (ODP)*. ODP was approved as a New Work Item by ISO in 1987. The goal of ODP has been the creation of a Reference Model, known as *ODP-RM*, that will integrate a wide range of future distributed-systems standards and maintain consistency across such systems. The scope of the ISO ODP is quite different from the scope of the ISO OSI reference model. The focus of OSI is on *interconnection* that spans all seven layers while ODP primarily concentrates on the application issues (layers five to seven). An ODP system is intended to supply the mechanisms which mask the underlying component heterogeneity from users and applications. In particular, these mechanisms are intended to address a set of fundamental transparency properties. Examples of the key transparency properties include:

- Location transparency, which masks the differences between local and remote invocations.

- Migration transparency, which is an extension of location transparency masking dynamic relocation of objects, typically for load balancing.

- Access transparency, which masks differences in access mechanisms.
- Federation transparency, which makes boundaries between federated administration domains (see sidebar "Traders—The Matchmakers in Distributed Environments").
- Failure transparency, which masks the failure and possible recovery of objects.
- Transaction transparency, which masks coordination of transactional operations.

To achieve these, and other transparency goals, ODP-RM includes descriptive as well as prescriptive elements. The ***descriptive elements*** provide a common vocabulary while the ***prescriptive elements*** constrain what can be built as required by an open distributed system. In particular, the prescriptive elements are based on the following models shown in Figure 7.18 (known as viewpoints):

- Enterprise viewpoint for system boundaries, policies, and purpose.
- Information viewpoint to represent distributed information
- Computational viewpoint for decomposition of system into distributable units
- Engineering viewpoint for description of components needed
- Technology viewpoint for describing the implementation details of components

Figure 7.18 ISO ODP Viewpoints

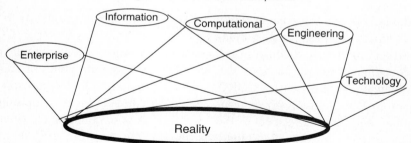

The prescriptive elements are subdivided into two parts: (a) a set of viewpoint languages that are used to specify the elements, and (b) and the definition of architectural components to populate the computational and engineering viewpoints. The architecture is based on object-oriented concepts. The ODP-RM includes concepts such as trading and federation.

How does ODP-RM interrelate with OMG CORBA and ANSA? Work has been initiated to coordinate the activities of OMG and ODP. In particular, a liaison has been established between ODP and OMG to avoid duplication of work. ANSA continues to provide input to ISO ODP (in fact, the five viewpoints that are at the heart of ODP-RM originated from ANSA and ANSA has input to OMG and tracks OMG status in this area).

The ODP-RM is documented in four parts. Part 1 contains an overview and guide to use ODP-RM, Part 2 (foundations) contains the descriptive model, Part 3 (architecture) specifies

---

Traders—The Matchmakers in Distributed Environments

A trader locates instances of a service in a network. It basically provides a selection mechanism, through directories, to find matching partners. Trading services are a core component of the ISO ODP Model. A service provider (exporter) nominates a trader service and describes the service it is offering in terms of a service specification and a reference to the interface that provides it. A service consumer (importer) makes a request to a trader, describing the service required, and the trader selects a matching partner.

Traders are being specified by OMG as part of the CORBA specifications. Visit the OMG site (http://www.omg.org) for developments.

---

the prescriptive model, and Part 4 contains architectural semantics (i.e., formal descriptions of ODP concepts). These four documents are available from ISO as documents ISO/IEC 10748-1 through ISO/IEC 10748-4, respectively. Overviews of ISO ODP can be found in Schurmann [1996, and Farooqi [1995].

7.9 Summary

Object-orientation (OO) has a great deal of promise in reducing the complexity of C/S applications. The primary standard for distributed OO systems is OMG's CORBA. CORBA is a very powerful and important specification for distributed-object-oriented applications. The compound-document standards such as OLE and OpenDoc are being built on top of object-oriented middleware (OpenDoc uses CORBA and OLE uses DCOM). Microsoft shifted its attention from OLE to ActiveX for enterprisewide distributed-object computing over the Internet/Intranet. An important aspect of the current work is to combine distributed objects with the Web (see the sidebar "Combining Distributed Objects with the Web" for different options).

7.10 Case Study: XYZCorp Investigates Distributed-Object Technologies

XYZCorp has initiated a technology-assessment effort that focuses on distributed-object technologies. The advanced-technology group in the corporation believes that the distributed-object model should be used as the ONLY model throughout the corporation. You have been asked to:

- Investigate the use of distributed-object technologies for XYZCorp. What type of applications is this technology most suitable for? Can distributed-object middleware do everything needed for this corporation? What can it not handle and why not?

Combining Distributed Objects with the Web
Let Me Count the Ways

There are several ways to combine distributed objects with the Web. Here are the principal ones that use CORBA, OLE/ActiveX and others.

The CORBA route:

- Invoke CORBA calls from a CGI procedure (a script or a subroutine written in C or in any other language) that resides on the Web server. In this case, the CGI procedure is the CORBA client. This is the oldest and the best-known method.

- Invoke CORBA directly from the Web browser. Netscape browsers are beginning to support the CORBA IIOP calls directly. Thus, the Web browser sites behave as CORBA clients.

- Use CORBA to interact between Java applets across machines. This option is currently supported by a few vendors (especially SUN).

The OLE/ActiveX route:

- Invoke DCOM calls from a CGI procedure (a script or a subroutine written in C or in any other language) that resides on the Web server.

- Invoke DCOM calls directly from the components contained in the Web browser (e.g., the Microsoft Internet Explorer). These components may be written in C, C++, Visual Basic, Java or other programming languages behaving as ActiveX Controls and contained inside the browser.

- Invoke DCOM calls from the ActiveX components such as spreadsheets that may invoke Java applets or other components residing on Web servers.

Other routes:

- Use the SUN Remote Method Invocation (RMI) between remotely located Java applets. This technology is very well supported by SunSoft tools but is restricted, at the time of this writing, to interactions between Java applets only.

- Use HTTP to invoke remote objects. A few small companies have implemented this option. This option should be used rarely, if at all. We are mentioning it for completeness.

- Is distributed-object technology as reflected by CORBA and OLE much better than OSF/DCE? Compare and contrast these middleware technologies in terms of their promises, pitfalls, and application fit (i.e., what type of applications are best supported by these middleware types?).

- Select the appropriate middleware product to support this strategy. In particular, should the company consider CORBA or ActiveX?

- Show how the Web will interoperate with distributed objects.

Hints about the Case Study:

- For a high-tech company like XYZCorp, use of distributed objects is almost natural.

- At the time of this writing, distributed-object technologies have many promises but they cannot easily handle decision-support applications very well (these applications require extensive remote-SQL access). In addition, client/server transaction processing cannot be supported by CORBA or ActiveX (CORBA specifications for transaction processing are still evolving).

- The following table can be used to compare and contrast distributed-object technologies with OSF DCE. Completion of this table is left as an exercise.

Middleware	Strengths	Weaknesses	Sample Applications
CORBA			
ActiveX			
OSF DCE			

- The main issue for several organizations at present is to determine whether CORBA or ActiveX should be chosen as a middleware for distributed objects at a high level, CORBA is more suitable for heterogeneous computing environments consisting of PCs, Macs, UNIX, and mainframes. ActiveX is designed for Windows and Windows NT environments. Obviously ActiveX is developed and supported by Microsoft. CORBA products are supported by many vendors—such as Iona, IBM, HP, DEC and Sun. Comparison of these products is beyond the scope of this book.

- Different approaches can be used to integrate distributed objects, especially CORBA, with the Web. Examples are invoking CORBA calls from a CGI gateway, invoking CORBA directly from the Web browser, using HTTP as a transport protocol underneath ORBs, and using CORBA to interact between Java applets across machines. The following diagram can be used to establish a strategy for integrating Web with OO. Perhaps the most natural way will be to use the Web browsers that invoke CORBA objects directly (this technology is currently just becoming state of the market as we go to press). You can add ActiveX considerations to this diagram or to a separate diagram.

7.11   Problems and Exercises

1. Compare and contrast CORBA with DCE. Can you identify classes of applications for which you would choose one versus the other?

2. Does CORBA directly support inheritance and polymorphism? Justify your answer with examples.

3. Suppose you have been given the responsibility of managing compound documents in a medium-sized (about 3000 employees) organization. Will you choose OLE or OpenDoc? Justify your answer.

4. Review the OMG home page, the Microsoft home page, and the OpenDoc home page on the Internet. Note the most recent activities in the last two months.

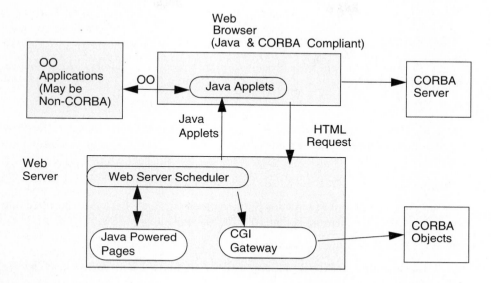

7.12   Additional Information

The book by Orfali [1996] is an excellent reference for distributed objects and covers CORBA, OLE, and OpenDoc in great detail. The books by Mowbray [1995], Otte [1996] and Siegel [1996] describe CORBA in great detail. OMG also publishes on different aspects of CORBA. For example, *CORBA: Architecture and Specification, CORBA Services,* and *CORBA Facilities* are all OMG-published books. Examples of additional books on CORBA are Otte [1996], Orfali [1996], and Mowbray [1995]. For the most recent information about CORBA, consult the OMG home page *(http://www.omg.org)*.

For OLE technical details, the book by Brockschmidt [1995] should be consulted. Most books on Visual C++ at present include discussion of OLE. For additional information on ActiveX, the book by Chapell [1996] should be reviewed. For additional information, consult the Microsoft home page *(http://www.microsoft.com)*. Information about OpenDoc can be obtained from the CI Labs home page *(http://www.cilabs.org)*.

State-of-the-art information about distributed objects appears in *IEEE Software, IEEE Computer,* and *Communications of ACM* (see, for example, the May 1995 issue of *IEEE Computer*). State-of-the-market and state-of-the-practice information appears in trade magazines such as *Client/Server Today, Datamation,* and *Object Magazine.* Detailed analysis of industrial trends can be found in Gartner Group reports and Seybold Group reports (see, for example, *Seybold Distributed Computing Monitor,* March 1995).

7.13   References

Adler, R., "Distributed Coordination Models for Client/Server Computing," *IEEE Computer,* April 1995, pp. 14–22.

Adler, R., "Emerging Standards for Component Software," *IEEE Computer,* pp. 68–77.

Benantar, M., Blakely, B., and Nadalin, A. "Use of DSOM Before/After Metaclass for Enabling Object Access Control," International Conference on Distributed Platforms, Dresden, February 1996.

Brockschmidt, K., "Inside OLE 2," 2d ed., Microsoft Press, 1995.

Chang, Y., et al., "An Object Transaction Service Based on the CORBA Architecture," International Conference on Distributed Platforms, Dresden, February 1996.

Chappell, D., "Understanding ActiveX and OLE," Microsoft Press, 1996.

Eldred, E., and Sylvester, T., "To Build a Hype-Free Case for OLE and OpenDoc," *Client/Server Today,* August 1994, pp. 73–80.

Farooqi, K., Loggripo, L., and Demeere, J., "The ISO Reference Model for Open Distributed Processing: An Introduction," *Computer Networks and ISDN Networks,* July 1995, pp. 1215–29.

Foody, M., "OLE and COM Versus CORBA," *UNIX Review,* April 1996, pp. 43–45.

Friday, A., Blair, G. S., Cheverst, K., and Davies, N., "Extensions to ANSAware for Advanced Mobile Applications," International Conference on Distributed Platforms, Dresden, February 1996.

Harmon, P., "Object-Oriented Client-Server Systems," *Object-Oriented Strategies,* Vol. III, No. 5 (San Francisco, 1993).

Harmon, P., "Object-Oriented Client-Server Systems," *Object-Oriented Strategies,* Vol. III, No. 9 (San Francisco, 1993).

Hayes, F., and Faden, M., "A Move to Unite OLE and CORBA," *Open Systems Today,* September 5, 1994, p. 1.

Herbert, A., "An ANSA Overview," *IEEE Network,* January-February 1994, pp. 18–23.

Horn, C., and O'Toole, A., "Distributed Object Oriented Approach," International Conference on Distributed Platforms, Dresden, February 1996.

Hubert, R., "Distributed Object Technology in EDS," International Conference on Distributed Platforms, Dresden, February 1996.

Konstantas, D., "Migration of Legacy Applications to a CORBA Platform: A Case Study," International Conference on Distributed Platforms, Dresden, February 1996.

Koschel, A. and Leibfriend, "Experiences in using the CORBA implementation DSOM," International Conference on Distributed Platforms, Dresden, February 1996.

Minton, G., "Programming with CORBA," *UNIX Review,* April 1996, pp. 29–39.

Millikin, M., "DCE: Building the Distributed Future," *Byte Magazine,* June 1994, pp. 125–134.

Mowbray, T., and Zahavi, R., *The Essential CORBA,* Wiley, 1995.

Nicol, J., et al., "Object Orientation in Heterogeneous Distributed Computing Systems," *IEEE Computer,* June 1993. pp. 57–67.

Orfali, R., Harkey, D., and Edwards, J., *The Essential Distributed Objects Survival Guide,* Wiley, 1996.

Orfali, R., Harkey, D., and Edwards, J., *Client/Server Survival Guide,* Wiley, 1994.

Orfali, R., Harkey, D., and Edwards, J., "OLE vs OpenDoc: Are All Parts JUST Parts?" *Datamation,* September 1994, pp. 38–46.

Orfali, R., Harkey, D., and Edwards, J., "Client/Server Components: CORBA Meets OpenDoc," *Object Magazine,* May 1995, pp. 55–59.

Orfali, R., and Harkey, D., "Building a SOM OpenDoc Part," *Dr. Dobbs Journal,* March 1995.

Otte, R., Patrick, P., and Roy, M., *Understanding CORBA,* Prentice Hall, 1996.

Rosenberry, W., Kenney, D., and Fisher, G., *Understanding DCE,* O'Reilly & Associates, 1993.

Riccuit, M., "The Mainframe as Server: Is IBM Totally Bonkers—or Brilliant?" *Datamation,* May 15, 1994, pp. 61–64.

Rosa, N.S., Cunha, P. R. F., Sadok, D. F. H., "A Methodology for Realization of LOTOS Specifications in the ANSAware," International Conference on Distributed Platforms, Dresden, February 1996.

Rymer, J., "Modeling Network Behavior Using Objects," *Distributed Computing Monitor,* Seybold Group, Vol. 7, No. 9 (Boston, 1992).

Rymer, J., "Distributed Object Computing," *Distributed Computing Monitor,* Seybold Group, Vol. 8, No. 8 (Boston, 1993).

Rymer, J., "Distributed Object Interoperability," *Distributed Computing Monitor,* Seybold Group, Vol. 10, No. 3 (Boston, March 1995).

Rymer, J., "Business Objects," *Distributed Computing Monitor,* Patricia Seybold Group, January 1995.

Schurmann, G., "The Evolution from Open Systems Interconnection (OSI) to Open Distributed Processing (ODP)," *Computer Standards and Interfaces,* Vol. 17 (1995), pp. 107–113.

Semich, W., "What's the Next Step After Client/Server?" *Datamation,* March 15, 1994, pp. 26–34.

Senivongse, T., and Utting, I.A., "A Model for Evolution of Services in Distributed Systems," International Conference on Distributed Platforms, Dresden, February 1996.

Shan, Y., Earle, R., and McGaughey, S., "Objects on the Server," *Object Magazine,* May 1995, pp. 49–54.

Shelton, R., "OMG's CORBA 2.0," *Distributed Computing Monitor,* Vol. 8, No. 5 (San Francisco, 1994).

Sheton, R., "Enterprise Reuse," *Distributed Computing Monitor,* Patricia Seybold Group, August 1995.

Siegel, J., *CORBA Fundamentals and Programming,* Wiley, 1996.

Simpon, D., "Objects May Appear Closer Than They Are," *Client/Server Today,* August 1995, pp. 59–69.

Sims, O., *Business Objects,* McGraw-Hill, 1994.

Soley, R., "Role of Object Technology in Distributed Systems," *Distributed Computing,* ed. by R. Khanna, Prentice Hall, 1994.

Soley, R., "Standards for Distributed Platforms," International Conference on Distributed Platforms, Dresden, February 1996.

Steinder, M., Uszok, A., and Zielinski, K., "A Framework for Inter-ORB Request Level Bridge Construction," International Conference on Distributed Platforms, Dresden, February 1996.

Tibbits, F., "CORBA: A Common Touch for Distributed Applications," *Data Communications Magazine,* May 21, 1995, pp. 71–75.

Wayner, P., "Object on the March," *BYTE,* McGraw-Hill, January 1994.

Williams, T., "Principles of OLE 2.0: An Exposition of Microsoft's Object-Oriented Systems Architecture," University Video Communications, 1994.

7.14   Appendix 7A: A Detailed CORBA Example

7.14.1   Overview

Let us go through an example of developing a simple inventory system by using CORBA. The inventory system consists of a relational table that contains product information (e.g., product ID, product name, price, and quantity on hand). This table is managed by a "product object" that responds to requests from clients to add, view, update, and delete a product. For example, a client invokes a product-view operation by passing a product ID. The product object receives the request and invokes a method that reads the product information and sends it back to the client. Table 7.2 shows the object model for the customer object. In the sections that follow, we will use this model as a starting point for defining the interface, building a server, and building clients in CORBA.

This example is intended to give an overview of the process needed for CORBA application development. Additional details can be found in books and articles [Otte 1996, Minton 1996, Orfali 1996, Mowbray 1995].

TABLE 7.2 THE PRODUCT OBJECT

Object	Operations	Inputs	Outputs
Product	1. Add a product	Product information	Status
	2. View a product information	Product ID	Product information
	3. Update a product information	Product ID, new information	Status
	4. Delete a product	Product ID	Status

Figure 7.19 shows the activities involved in developing OO applications in CORBA (this figure is repeated from an earlier discussion):

- Create CORBA definitions by using OMG IDL.
- Build the server.
- Build the client.

7.14.2 Create CORBA Definitions

The following CORBA definitions are created as the first step in CORBA application development:

- Define the interface.
- Define the implementation.
- Define the method map.

As stated previously, the interface of an object is used to declare the behavior of an object. For example, the following statements specify the interface for the product object in CORBA IDL. This interface supports only two operations (we have simplified it somewhat for illustrative purposes):

Figure 7.19 CORBA Application Development

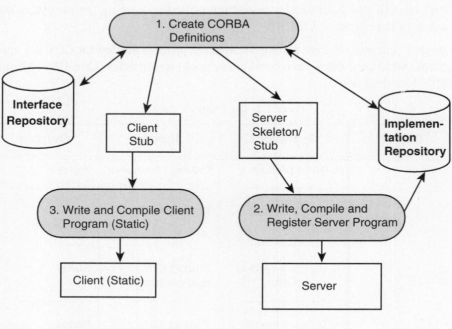

```
module PRODUCT_PACKAGE {
      interface product_interf /* interface name is product */
      insert_product (/*Operation is insert_product */
         in char product_obj; /* input is product object */
         out integer status ) /* output parameter */
      view_product ( /*Operation is view_product */
         in char product_id; /* input parameter is product-id */
         out object product_obj; /* output: product object */
         out integer status ) /*output parameter 2 */
}
```

The module statement is used to name a group of interfaces that relate to each other and can be used to represent a **package** (i.e., a group of objects). The module name becomes part of the name that the client and server use to reference an interface. The interface statement shows what operations can be performed on the customer object (we have shown only two operations; others can be filled in by the reader). Each interface statement defines an interface and contains the descriptions of the operations (operation signatures). The complete name of an operation includes the module and the interface name. For example, "PRODUCT_ PACK-AGE::product_interf::create_product" is the fully qualified name of the operation that creates a new product.

The IDL file is compiled to create the client stub and the server skeleton. The client stub and server skeleton are the code templates for building CORBA client and server programs (see

Figure 7.19). The client stub is used only to build client programs that use static binding (see Section 7.14.4). The server skeleton is always used as the framework for building the server application, regardless of the invocation type used by the client (see Section 7.14.3).

Operations on objects are implemented by executable code called **methods.** For example, the product object must contain the code ("add-product-method") that will be executed to actually create a new product when an operation "add-product" is invoked by a client. The collection of methods that accomplishes the set of operations required for an object is called an **implementation**. Some CORBA implementations offer a mapping language for describing implementations called the **Implementation Mapping Language (IML).** The implementation descriptions can be stored in an **implementation repository**. which can be displayed by CORBA compliant commands or the **repository manager**. The following statements show the implementation of product methods (once again, we have simplified this somewhat):

```
implementation productImpl
    (
    activation_type (program);
    implementation _identifier ("676873.0c.03.00.00.00.00");
    add_product_method ()
        implements
        (PRODUCT_PACKAGE::product_interf::add_product);
        invoke_builtin ("add_p_function)
        ;
        );
```

The `implementation` statement is used to specify the name of the implementation. The first few, in our case the first two, statements in an implementation specification are used at start-up time. The `activation_type()` statement specifies the manner in which the implementation is started once it is selected. For example, (program) indicates that a program will be started; other options indicate dynamic load and script executions. The `implementation _identifier()` clause is used to assign a unique identifier to an implementation. The unique identifier is automatically generated in response to the CORBA command "orbgen." For each method in the implementation, you define the method name, the operation it supports, and how to run it. In our example, we have defined only one method (add_product_method) that implements the add_product operation defined in the IDL and invokes a built-in module. Method specifications allow invocation options for dynamic and script executions.

In addition to IML, you may need to define **method maps.** These maps are used by the ORB to locate the best server method for the object operation requested when there is more than one active implementation of an interface. For example, when a client invokes the "add_product" operation, then the ORB looks at the method maps to determine the most appropriate method to invoke. The method map can be stored in the interface repository along with the interface definitions. You can use CORBA commands to generate a default method map from the interface definitions.

7.14.3   Build the Server

Building of program servers requires the following steps:

- Generate the server skeleton.
- Develop server initialization code.
- Develop code for each method.
- Compile, link, and test the server components.
- Register the server.

The first step is to specify the IDL statements and then compile these statements to generate a server skeleton. This compilation also uses the information contained in the IML files. The server skeleton contains method templates that show entry points for all of the implementation methods, the server dispatcher code that makes the implementations, and the methods known to the ORB; a registration routine is also generated as part of the server code. The skeleton code simplifies the task of building a server.

Each server initialization needs code to register the implementation (e.g., make itself available for use), activate the server's implementation, enter a main loop to receive requests, and exit after unregistering and releasing resources. In addition, the server needs routines for creating objects and managing references to these objects. The server skeleton is used to develop this code. The initialization code uses CORBA run-time routines (these routines are identified as CORBA_ or ORB_). An example of the server C-type pseudocode for the product example is listed below (we have simplified this code by ignoring the error checking and by using a generic "parameter" for the CORBA-provided functions):

```
   #include <stdio.h>

   #include <orb.h>

   #include product.h  /* the IDL generated header */
main ()
{
printf ("product server starting \n");

/* Register the implementation */
status = RegisterImpls (parameters);

/* Create object and its reference */
status = CreateObjRefs(parameters);

/*Make server ready */
CORBA_BOA_impl_is_ready (parameters); /* indicate server ready */

/* main loop to listen to client messages */
ORB_BOA_main_loop (parameters); /* enter the main loop */

/* exit code */
CORBA_BOA_dispose(parameters); /* Frees object references */
```

```
ORB_BOA_imp_unregister (parameters); /* Unregister */

/* Methods code templates */
        void add_product (product_obj, status);
        /* .... insert code for add_product method ...*/
        void view_product ( product-id, product_info, status);
        /* .... insert code for view_product method ...*/
}
```

The major activity in building a CORBA server is to write the code for the methods that execute the operations. For each method template, you must develop the code for the methods. Methods can be implemented as executable code, calls to legacy applications, or scripts to integrate command-line interfaces with existing applications. Methods can be written to invoke OLE (Object Linking and Embedding), DDE (Dynamic Data Exchange), and SQL database accesses. For example, the following pseudocode to access the product relational table can be added to the add_product and view_product methods:

```
        void add_product (product_obj, status);
        /* code for converting product_obj object into
        SQL table attributes such as pid, pname, price, on_hand */
        exec sql;
        insert pid, pname, price, on_hand into product_table;
        end sql;
        /* .. include other code */

        void view_product (product-id, product_obj, status);
        exec sql;
        select pid, pname, price, on_hand from product_table where
        pid=:product_id;
        end sql;
        /* code for storing pid, pname, price, on_hand into an object */
}
```

The final step in building a server is to compile and link the methods, server initialization code, the generated server dispatcher, and the generated registration routine. The server code can be tested and debugged by using CORBA tracing facilities.

7.14.4 Build Client (Static Invocation)

After a server has been built and registered, clients can be built to invoke the servers. As stated previously, CORBA clients can use static invocations (i.e., clients know at compile time the objects and the operations on these objects) or dynamic invocation (i.e., the clients determine at run time the objects and the operations on these objects). We will focus on static invocation in this section and review dynamic invocation in the next. The steps involved in building a static-invocation CORBA client are:

- Generate client stub.
- Define the context object.
- Build the client code.
- Compile and link the client.

The client stub can be generated from IDL, IML, and MML source files or from the interface repository. The generated stub consists of a header file that contains definitions, and the C language stub routines.

A **context object** shows a set of properties providing information about the client, the environment, or characteristics of the request. The context object is used by ORB during method resolution to identify user preferences for server selection. Basically, it provides a means of maintaining information between requests for conversational applications. The context information is difficult to pass as parameters in a distributed application. The IDL is used to specify whether the ORB should also retrieve information regarding the request from the context object (the "context" clause in IDL). If no context object is specified, the ORB uses the default context object definition. Context objects can be specified at user level (e.g., user preferences), group level (e.g., data restricted to a group of users), or system level (e.g., display types for an application).

The client code includes header file generated by IDL, "local" client code (e.g., communicate with the user), invoke object operations defined in IDL, and handle errors/exceptions.

To invoke the object operations, a client needs to first get an object reference (object references can be stored by the server at start-up in an external file or registry) and then invoke a method on the object. The following client pseudocode illustrates the key points of a client that invokes the add_product and view_product methods:

```
 #include <stdio.h>
 #include product.h  /. the IDL generated header ./
/* define variables, etc. */
 main ()
{
 /* code to obtain object reference. This code depends on where the server
stored the reference. If object reference is in a file, then use fget, for
example, to read the object reference */

  product_interf *pptr;  /* *pptr is the object reference */

/* Now invoke the add_product and view_product methods */

         /* put information in product_obj */
         pptr->add_product (product_obj, status); /* invoke the object
         method */
```

```
printf ("product added");
product_id = "1111";
pptr->view_product ( product-id, product_obj, status); /* invoke
the object method */
printf ("product information", product_info);
```
/* Other client code, e.g., free resources, error processing, etc. */

After coding, the client is compiled, linked and debugged by using the CORBA environment compilers and tracing facilities?

7.14.5 Building a Client (Dynamic Invocation)

CORBA's Dynamic Invocation APIs allow a client program to build and invoke requests on objects at run time. These APIs provide maximum flexibility by allowing new objects to be added at run time. The client specifies, at run time, the object to be invoked, the method to be performed, and the set of parameters through a call or a sequence of calls. The client code typically obtains this information from the interface repository. To invoke a dynamic method on an object, the client must perform the following steps:

- Obtain the method description from the interface repository.
- Create the argument list.
- Create the request.
- Invoke the request.

CORBA specifies about ten API calls for locating and obtaining objects from the repository. An example of such an API call is *lookup_name()*. A *describe* call is issued, after an object is located, to obtain its full IDL definition. To create an argument list, CORBA specifies a *NameValue list* as a self-defining data structure for passing parameters. The list is created by using the *create_list operation*. After this, the request is created using the CORBA *create_request* call. Eventually, the client can invoke the request by using either an *invoke* call (send the request and obtain the results, i.e., a synchronous call), or a *send* call (an asynchronous call). The following pseudocode shows a sample dynamic invocation:

```
/* Create method description */
lookup_name()
describe ()
/* Create argument list */
create_list ()
add_arg(),,, add_arg(),,,, add_arg()
/* create the request */
create_request(Object Reference, Methods, Argument List)
/* Invoke the remote method synchronously - as an RPC */
invoke ()
/* Now process the results */
```

8

Mobile Computing, Multimedia, Groupware, and Legacy Access Middleware

8.1   Introduction

Many emerging technologies are being utilized in developing new applications, and the need to integrate legacy systems with new applications is growing. For example, the mobile computing applications that utilize wireless network are growing to meet the demands of "people on the move." Many multimedia applications are also being developed for business and entertainment. In addition, groupware products such as Lotus Notes are being used to allow people in different parts of an organization, in many cases at remote sites, to work together by collecting and sharing information such as documents, graphs, spreadsheets, and email. Workflow software is also becoming popular to support automation of business processes. On the other side of the spectrum, the legacy systems that have been used to serve corporations for decades cannot be ignored and need to be integrated with the new breed of object-oriented, client/server, Internet-based applications.

These emerging trends are creating new requirements for middleware. The purpose of this chapter is to examine the current state of the art, state of the market, and state of the practice in these emerging areas and attempt to answer the following questions:

- What are the key characteristics of mobile computing applications and what type of middleware is needed for them?

- Why are distributed multimedia applications being developed and what type of middleware is needed for them?

- What are the special middleware products being developed for groupware (e.g., Lotus Notes) and workflows?

- What type of middleware is needed to access and integrate legacy applications?

The topics discussed in this chapter are evolving at the time of this writing. Our purpose is to scan the field by pointing out the key principles and suggesting sources for additional and continued education.

8.2   Mobile Computing Applications

Use of wireless networks to access corporate information is increasing rapidly, owing to the growth of mobile computers (typically laptop computers and personal digital assistants). However, many of these laptop users cannot access many corporate distributed applications such as database queries and remote LAN access. This is because wireless networks pose

---

Key Points

- Many mobile computing applications need middleware that will smooth over the mobile computing issues, as much as possible, so that the same applications can run on wired as well as wireless networks.

- Advanced mobile computing applications require middleware that exploits the network quality of service, cost, and location information for optimum performance.

- Distributed multimedia applications require middleware that provides high compression rates, minimum processing delays, multipeer communication support, and continuous support for streams of data.

- Groupware requires middleware that enables groups at different locations to collaborate with each other.

- Workflow requires middleware that routes work between tasks, tracks work as it flows through an organization, and provides access to the documents and data needed by the individual workers.

- Legacy access middleware must be able to hide the intricacies of the legacy systems and provide a uniform user interface to the legacy system resources.

---

many unique problems that most commonly available applications do not have to worry about. For example, wireless networks are typically slower, get congested frequently, and are more error prone and susceptible to outages. Middleware for applications that operate on mobile computers, called mobile computing middleware or wireless middleware, is urgently needed to address the growing demand for wireless applications.

Before presenting the middleware for mobile computing, we review the characteristics of mobile computing environments that are unique and then discuss the categories of applications that place different demands on the underlying network and middleware.

8.2.1   Overview of Mobile Computing Environments

Mobile computing applications, residing fully or partially on laptop computers, use cellular networks to transmit information. It is well known that cellular telephones and residential cordless telephones (wireless systems) are enjoying widespread public approval with a rapidly increasing demand.

Figure 8.1 shows a conceptual view of a cellular communication network. The basic cellular technology consists of many "cells," typically 1 to 25 miles in area. The mobile units in each cell communicate with a base transceiver station (BTS) by using wireless communications; i.e., the users communicate within a cell through cordless devices. One BTS is assigned to each cell. The BTSs are connected to the mobile telephone switching office (MTSO) through regular cable communication channels. MTSO is the control center for cellular communications—it determines the destination of the call received from a BTS and routes it to a proper destination by sending it either to another BTS or to a regular telephone network. Keep in mind that the communications is wireless within a cell only. The bulk of cell-to-cell communication is carried through regular telephone lines (see Chapter 11 for discussion of the cellular technologies and wireless LANs and WANs).

Figure 8.1 A Cellular Communication Network

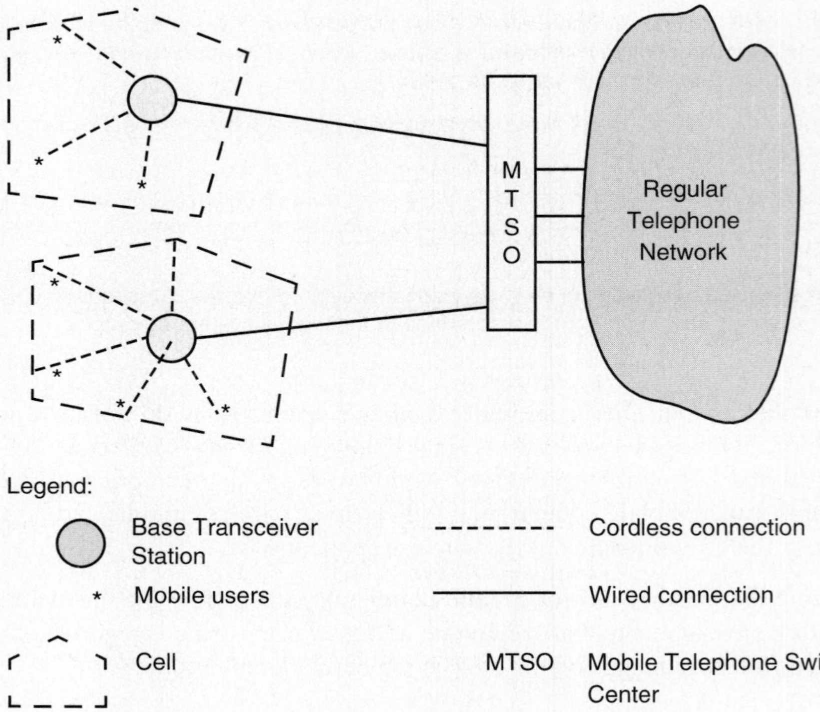

Mobile communications have been developed primarily for voice users. Consequently, cellular networks are predominantly analog. However, the use of cellular networks to support mobile computing applications is increasing rapidly. In particular, as the use of laptop computers increases, the need to communicate from these "mobile" computers to access remote databases is also increasing. Standards are emerging to provide digital services over cellular networks to support mobile applications. Two well-known examples are:

- CDPD (Cellular Digital Packet Data)
- GSM (Global System for Mobile Communications)

CDPD (Cellular Digital Packet Data) technology is being developed to carry digital data for TCP/IP networks over analog cellular networks. CDPD is very popular at present in the United States. A CDPD Consortium of large telecommunications providers and an ATM Forum is promoting the commercialization of CDPD networks. Basically, a CDPD-compliant modem segments, encrypts, and formats transmitting data into 138-byte frames. These frames are sent over the cellular networks by using a protocol that is similar to the Ethernet protocol. CDPD gives voice priority over data. CDPD protocol is intelligent enough to look for clear cells on the cellular networks. This can be a limitation of CDPD, because CDPD users may have difficulty in finding empty cells in congested areas or at peak times. The main strength of CDPD is that it supports TCP/IP networks at 19.2 Kbps and thus plugs into corporate information processing [Gareiss 1995]. Details about CDPD can be found in the book on CDPD [Sreetharan 1996].

While CDPD is popular in the United States, *GSM (Global System for Mobile Communications)* is very popular in Europe. GSM operators set up radio antennas throughout their coverage areas. Each antenna constitutes a coverage cell. A GSM user makes a call by using a GSM phone. This call is picked up by the closest antenna and passed from cell to cell as the user crosses coverage areas. At present, GSM is limited to voice-only services. However, GSM operators are expanding their services to include data services. In particular, some GSM operators are adding packet assembler/disassemblers (PADs) to access X.25 services, and others are providing access to ISDN networks. GSM networks are based on international standards defined by the European Telecommunications Standards Institute (ETSI). More than 100 GSM operators are providing GSM services, with many extending their services to cross borders, especially in Europe [Gronert 1995]. Details about GSM can be found in the book on GSM by Redl [1995].

Technologies needed to support digital applications over analog networks designed for human users are only one aspect of mobile computing. Several other issues arise in supporting applications over cellular networks. Examples of these issues are [Davies 1996, Friday 1996]:

- Network quality of service (QoS)
- Cost of service
- Location of users
- Characteristics of end systems

Network QoS for cellular networks is much lower than for the traditional fixed networks. While wired LANs are providing data rates around 100 Mbps (million bits per second), the wireless LANs are struggling with data rates in the range of 10 Kbps to 2 Mbps. In wireless WANs, the data rates can range from 0 Kbps to 9.6 Kbps (both GSM and CDPD support 9.6-Kbps data rates over cellular WANs). The data rate of 0 Kbps indicates that, in a wireless WAN, a complete disconnect can happen frequently. Another serious QoS issue is the error rate and the loss of packets in cellular networks. It has been shown that TCP performance degrades significantly owing to loss of packets in cellular networks [Caceres 1994].

The costs of network access are very different for mobile users as than for fixed-network users. Users of a cellular network are charged based on time of day, the tariffs, connection time, the user location (city versus rural areas), etc. Thus, casual browsing through databases and documents can be very expensive for cellular users. This fact should be taken into account while designing an application for mobile computing.

The location of mobile computing users can change during an application session, thus impacting QoS and cost. It may be necessary for applications to check the location of users and the variations in QoS (for example, moving from a wireless LAN to wireless WAN range) continually during an application session. This is unheard of in wired networks.

The end systems in mobile computing are portable computers. These computers, although improving rapidly, still differ dramatically from desktop computers in screen sizes and I/O devices that can operate with batteries. Thus, screen design that may look quite impressive on a large screen may be terribly busy and difficult to operate in mobile applications. This consideration must also be taken into account when designing mobile applications.

8.2.2 Mobile Computing Application Issues

Applications for mobile users face many unique challenges, because wireless networks pose many unique problems that most commonly available fixed networks do not have. As stated previously, wireless networks are typically slower, get congested frequently, and are more error prone and susceptible to outages. Thus mobile computing application designers should have some knowledge of the underlying communication network. For example, database queries over wireless networks should not attempt to send thousands of rows, because the network may not be available that long. This somewhat contradicts the commonly used practice in distributed applications, where the underlying communication network details are hidden from the application designers by middleware such as OSF DCE and CORBA.

Design of mobile computing applications depends on how extensively the applications use the underlying network. From this point of view, applications in mobile computing fall into the following three broad categories [Davies 1996]:

- Standalone applications
- Simple client/server applications
- Advanced mobile applications

Standalone applications run entirely on mobile computers in disconnect (detached) mode. Some of the data needed by these applications is located remotely. This data is accessed through wireless networks and typically transferred to local disk. This approach works very well if most remote data accesses are retrievals and currency of data is not a big concern.

These applications do not require extensive use of wireless networks and typically need simple middleware (e.g., file transfer over wireless networks).

Simple C/S applications are distributed between mobile computers as well as remote computers. Typically, client software runs on mobile computers, and the database services are provided by remote sites. In these applications, there is a need to access remote "live" data interactively (as compared to the batch-extract method used by the standalone applications). Moreover, the amount of remote data accessed is small and must be current. Thus the connection time for C/S interactions is short. These applications do not need extensive cellular network and wireless middleware support.

Advanced mobile applications involve a combination of groupware and distributed multimedia over the wireless networks. These applications typically require peer-to-peer group interactions that may use multimedia information. The information exchanged is time critical (i.e., real time), and the exchanged sessions may last for a long time. These applications demand extensive of network and middleware services.

8.2.3   Middleware for Mobile Computing Applications

Middleware for mobile computing applications appears to follow two approaches:

- Information hiding
- Information providing

The *"information-hiding" wireless middleware* attempts to smooth over the mobile computing issues, as much as possible, so that the same applications can run on wired as well as wireless networks. This is a conceptually desirable goal because application developers should not have to know the underlying network characteristics. This goal is met by the wireless middleware typically through specialized APIs that provide functionalities such as the following:

- Monitoring to determine whether a mobile device is powered on and within the range of wireless WAN coverage. The middleware provides this information to the applications as a status indicator and/or end users as a screen icon.

- Optimization techniques to improve throughput by using a combination of data compression, intelligent restarts (i.e., restart at the point of disconnection and not from the beginning of session), prefetching, and data-caching (keep data at local sites in case it needs to be accessed again) techniques. This middleware may also provide bundling of smaller packets to larger packets to save communication costs (most wireless systems charge by number of packets sent, thus this reduces end-user costs).

- Monitor and limit the number of simultaneous wireless to be maintained by the applications.

- Provide agents that reside on the wireless servers. Agents can perform a variety of services such as optimizing bandwidth, notifying the clients asynchronously if a special situation arises (e.g., a new customer arrives), automatically setting up sessions, contacting "dormant" users, and handling ad hoc queries.

This type of middleware is suitable for standalone and simple C/S applications. An example of "information-hiding" wireless middleware is IBM's ARTour C/S middleware that allows TCP/IP applications to run, unchanged, over wireless networks [Wexler 1995]. ARTour runs on top of CDPD and several other services. While it is theoretically possible to run TCP/IP applications directly over CDPD, you do need CDPD running everywhere to support such applications (CDPD may not be provided by several cellular operators). The advantage of using packages such as ARTour is that they can run on top of CDPD and non-CDPD networks. Middleware packages like ARTour also use compression and reduce the IP header information (IP headers are 40 characters long) to maximize throughput.

The *"information-providing" wireless middleware* provides as much information about the underlying environment to the application as possible. In fact, this class of middleware exploits the network quality of service, cost, and location information for optimum performance. In particular [Davies 1996]:

- Network QoS can be used to modify application behavior. For example, the MOST project at Lancaster University uses a database application that determines the response to be sent to the user based on number of matches and the network QoS. Thus, if the application has many matches (i.e., long response to a query) but the network is slow, then the application dynamically sends only a few selected matches. Similarly, different compression techniques can be used for different network QoSs (i.e., use more compression for slower networks). Another example is the system described by Friday [1996] that uses different color schemes on the screen to interact with different classes of users (i.e., red for slow).

- Cost information can be used by the middleware to modify application behavior. For example, if a user is being charged per second, then messages can be batched up before transmission.

- Location information can be used by the middleware to direct application behavior. For example, location information can be used to route information to the nearest printers or computers.

- End-system characteristics can also be exploited by the middleware. For example, specialized user interfaces can be displayed for mobile users, and the laptop can be put in a "doze" mode to conserve batteries while it is waiting for chunks of data from remote sites.

The basic philosophy of this class of middleware is to detect changes in the mobile environments and supply the change information to the applications so that they can modify their behavior changes in the mobile environments. This type of middleware, currently not state-of-the-market, is essential for advanced mobile applications.

Table 8.1 shows the middleware characteristics needed for different classes of mobile applications.

8.2.4   State of the Practice, Market, and Art

At present, the vendors are providing wireless middleware with proprietary APIs. This creates application portability problems if a user changes middleware vendors. Work on standardizing wireless APIs has been initiated. An example of the current efforts is the Winsock

TABLE 8.1 WIRELESS MIDDLEWARE SUMMARY

Application Types	Application Characteristics	Middleware Characteristics
Standalone Applications	1. Mobile computers run applications entirely on mobile computers in disconnect (standalone) mode. 2. Need to access remote files through wireless networks 3. Most data accesses are reads and currency of data is not a big concern	Requirements are modest. Information-hiding middleware can do the job Typical operation: 1. Cache copies of files at mobile computers over fixed networks and then disconnect 2. Use the cached files in disconnect mode 3. Reconnect to integrate the cached changes with master files
Simple Client/ Server Applications	1. Client software runs on mobile computers 2. Need to access remote data interactively 3. Amount of data transferred is small and not time critical 4. Connection time is short	Require modest middleware. Information hiding is desirable Typical functions needed are: 1. Establish connection over wireless 2. Support client/server interactions for a short duration 3. Disconnect
Advanced Mobile Applications	1. Peer-to-peer group interactions 2. Information is time critical (i.e., real time) 3. May use multimedia information 4. Sessions may last for a long time	Requires extensive middleware support. Information-providing middleware is essential

2 Forum that is developing a vendor-independent API for Microsoft-Windows applications to use wireless middleware by using Windows Sockets 2 API. In addition, the Portable Computer and Communications Association (PCCA) is working on a standard API between wireless middleware and network layer protocols.

At the time of this writing, about a dozen wireless middleware products are being marketed. Examples of products are Oracle in Motion by Oracle, Wireless Mobile Enabler by IBM, and Airmobile from Motorola. In addition, IBM has introduced the ARTour C/S middleware that allows TCP/IP applications to run, unchanged, over wireless networks. An example of another wireless middleware is the Virtual Office from Ericsson (*http://www.ericson.com*) that supports mobile computing for Microsoft environments [Bruno 1996].

A state of the market review of mobile computing middleware can be found in Johnson [1995] and Gary [1995]. Technical discussions about middleware issues such as authentication of mobile users, protocols for improved throughput, multimedia nomadic services, and maps for describing the locations and characteristics of objects as they change over time in regions can be found in Molva [1994], Pollini [1994], Schmandt [1994], and Schlit [1994], respectively.

State of the art in mobile computing is evolving rapidly. Standards in cellular networks and in mobile computing APIs are also emerging. In addition the data rates of cellular networks are expected to improve. Many wireless data networks are slow at present (9.6 Kbps is typical, 19.2 Kbps is being popularized by CDPD, 56 Kbps is promised at the time of this writing). Many vendors are beginning to provide wireless LANs and WANs (Motorola, MCI, NCR are examples). Cost for wireless depends on per minute ($1 is typical), per month flat ($30), per packet (10 cents).

Literature on mobile computing is also becoming available. For detailed trade-offs among the different types of mobile data networks, the underlying technologies, potential applications, and the research trends, see Davies [1996], Diehl [1996], Friday [1996], Han [1996], and Johnson [1995]. *Data Communications Magazine* is a good source of information for evolutions in state of the market in this very interesting area.

8.3   Distributed-Multimedia Applications

8.3.1   Overview

The term multimedia is used by different people differently. The following discussion illustrates different views [Rodrigues 1995]:

> Some people see multimedia as the effort to combine text, graphics, images, video, and audio in computers to convey enriched information to users. Others see multimedia simply as a marriage between computer and TV. Still others view it as a new generation of computer applications featuring video but demanding new computer software and hardware architectures. . . . One central ingredient of multimedia computing and processing, however, is real-time execution to enable delivery of and presentation of continuous synchronous media.

We will view multimedia as a combination of text, graphics, video, and audio that is executed in real time and presented as continuous streams. Although multimedia defies rigorous definition, it is best illustrated through examples. Here are a few:

- **Real-estate search applications** which allow users to search for a house by using a combination of text, voice, pictures, and video. A user first browses through descriptions and pictures of the houses on his or her workstation. A "visit" to the house can be requested, which plays a movie about the house on a window of the workstation.

- **Multimedia MedNet,** a medical collaboration and consultation system, combines neurophysiological, audio, and video data in a remote diagnostic and monitoring system [Simon 1995]. This system, with enhancements from earlier systems, has been in use on a daily basis in seven hospitals at the University of Pittsburgh Medical Center since 1985.

- **Desktop videoconferencing,** discussed frequently in trade magazines (see, for example, McCarthy [1995]), promises to provide videoconferencing on your desktops. Although these services are not fully state-of-the-market, several products such as AT&T's Vistium Personal Video System, Intel's ProShare, and Picture Tel's Live PCS 100 are commercially available.

- **Digital news systems** that integrate interactive computing, newspapers, televisions, and high-speed networks into one news package. These systems combine the best aspects of newspapers (user control in browsing, selecting, and reading), television (dynamics and power of moving images and sound) and personal computers (interactive commands and displays). The users of this system can "drive" the news by directly going to the items of interest or can browse through news items. An early example of a digital news system is described by Hoffert [1991].

- **Multimedia learning environments,** known as pedagogues, allow students to participate in educational processes through intelligent simulation, dynamic links, and multimedia composition and creation. Case studies of multimedia educational systems are presented by Woolf [1995].

- **The MediaView digital publication system,** which was designed to take maximum advantage of the media-rich hardware and software capabilities of computer systems such as NeXT [Phillips 1991]. MediaView extends the what-you-see-is-what-you-get (WYSIWYG) word-processing metaphor to multimedia components such as graphics, audio, video, and object- and image-based animations. These components are subject to the select/cut/copy/paste paradigm just like text, thus giving the user powerful editing capabilities. In addition, anything Mediaview displays on the screen can be printed on a printer or stored as a PostScript or TIFF file for processing by other applications.

Distributed multimedia applications support business functions by exploiting the multimedia technologies among different machines. Many of the multimedia applications discussed above, in fact, are distributed. Many new applications in office automation and factory automation could use distributed multimedia owing to the tight integration of voice, video, and data among processes that reside on different machines. Specific examples are innovative applications in document storage and retrieval systems which intermix voice, data, and images; multimedia electronic mail which can allow the correspondents to exchange formatted text, pictures, animations, audio, and video; applications in teleconferencing which establish a group rapport through a feeling of "presence" and body language; the voice annotation of text and graphics, and "videotex videos" with synchronized animation and music; and audio and visual two-way communications on broadcast and cable TV.

8.3.2   Middleware for Distributed-Multimedia Applications

Middleware for distributed multimedia has to deal with applications fundamentally different from the traditional C/S applications based on the request/response model (e.g., query a customer-account information). Middleware for distributed multimedia applications must provide:

- High communication bandwidth (i.e, data rates) support for real-time interactions

- High compression rates for efficiently transferring large volumes of information

- Minimum processing delays at participating nodes to assure that the end systems do not become the bottleneck

- Multipeer communication support for collaborative work

- Synchronization and flow control of related information (i.e., synchronizing of lip movement with sound)

- Continuous and real-time support for streams of data instead of discrete request/response

Let us illustrate some of these requirements through the following example presented by McQuillan [1990]. A color workstation screen requiring 1024 x 1024 bit resolution with 24 bits of color would require 24 million bits of data storage. For moving video, each frame (screen) needs to be transmitted several times per second. At 30 frames per second, 720 million bits would need to be transmitted per second. In other words, the communication channel would need a 720-Mbps data rate. This is much higher than the FDDI and many other technologies of 100 Mbps. At present, cards are becoming available for workstations for 30:1 data compression. Even with 50:1 compression, this still requires 15 Mbps to support one multimedia application. Keep in mind that we have not included sound transmission in this example. In many cases, additional trade-offs are needed to reduce network requirements for these applications. For example, you can reduce the number of color bits, cut down on screen sizes, and minimize the number of screen refreshes per second. After extensive compression, smaller screen sizes, fewer color bits, and reduced screen refreshes, many multimedia applications require between 1 to 1.5 Mbps.

Owing to the high bandwidth requirements, most of the work in distributed multimedia has focused on computer networks. Particular attention is paid to high-bandwidth transmission networks and to managing network resources such as switch capacity so that the stated quality of service (QoS) requirements (e.g., throughput, delay, jitter, and loss rate) are met. Only recently, attention is being paid to higher-level issues. Let us briefly review these issues.

Multipeer communication support for distributed multimedia applications is an especially challenging task in distributed-multimedia applications. Specifically, discrete as well as continuous media data has to be exchanged between a group of users located in different geographical locations. This information also has to be synchronized properly (e.g., lip movement has to be synchronized with sound). Each user's capabilities to process multimedia data depend on the capability of his/her computing machine and the characteristics of the

Streaming Multimedia Over the Web

It has always been possible to download audio or video files (in various formats) and then play them. This is usually an extremely slow and boring process. For example, if you are connected to the Internet over a modem, it may take you 20 minutes to download a 20-second video clip. You basically sit and stare at an indicator that tells you how long you have to wait.

This is changing with streaming media over the Web. On your Web browser, you install a "helper application" that plays the audio/video clips as they are being downloaded to your Web site. Some of these helper applications are server-based so they can "scale" the amount of information being downloaded based on the data rate of your connection. These helper applications use a variety of compression techniques. Many helper applications, also known as "plug-ins," are commercially available from many vendors such as Real Audio from Progressive Networks, MovieStar from Intelligence at Large, and Xing Streamworks from Xing. In the future, some of these "applications" may be built into your browser.

interconnecting network. For example, in desktop videoconferencing systems, streams of voice and video between participating sites have to flow at an acceptable quality-of-service (Qos) level and the flows have to be synchronized properly. Additional details about this topic can be found in Garcia [1996].

The end-system resources need to be managed according to QoS guidelines. The end systems include presentation points such as PCs, workstations, and home terminals as well as servers for storage of multimedia information. In particular, the storage servers need to be designed carefully for recording and retrieval of high volumes of continuous streams of data. For example, the server must (a) continuously supply the stream buffers with enough data so that the display of media is not jittery, (b) process several streams simultaneously, (c) provide disk scheduling that conforms to QoS deadlines, and (d) exercise admission-control algorithms to determine whether a new stream can be serviced without affecting the streams that are already being serviced. A detailed discussion of these and many other issues can be found in a tutorial on multimedia storage servers by Gemmell [1995].

Database support is also an important aspect of distributed-multimedia applications. First, storage and retrieval of multimedia information needs object-oriented databases that can store the complex multimedia objects. Second, some services such as video on demand require enormous centralized multimedia databases that must be accessed quickly. Third, distributed-transaction processing across broadband networks is needed for real-time high-volume transaction processing and high-speed data access. Detailed discussion of database issues for multimedia applications can be found in Rao [1995].

The key point is that middleware for distributed multimedia has to deal with applications that are fundamentally different from traditional C/S applications that are based on the request/response model.

8.3.3   State of the Practice, Market, and Art

Most of the work in developing middleware for multimedia applications is in its infancy. However, some general trends are emerging. It seems that the approaches fall into two broad categories;

- **Communication approach** such as used in video on demand, where the multimedia applications are "hardwired" over high-performance networks such as ATM

- **Computing approach** where the multimedia applications are viewed as a special breed of distributed applications

There is a need to combine these two approaches. Development of stream interfaces to support distributed-multimedia applications is one possible avenue of progress. For example, support of streams over CORBA is being pursued (see the sidebar "Multimedia over CORBA"). Distributed objects for multimedia is an area of considerable research and standardization activity (including the ISO standards for Open Data Processing for distributed multimedia). Examples of research issues include distributed object-based approaches for sharing multimedia information [Pinto 1996], multipeer communication support for distributed-multimedia applications [Garcia 1996], formal specification and verification of multimedia systems [Blair 1995], and QoS management for distributed-multimedia applications [Sreenan 1996].

Most of the work in distributed multimedia is still in prototyping stages at different universities (several projects at Lancaster University in England and Edinburgh University in Scotland are concentrating in this area). Desktop videoconferencing is probably the closest to state of the market. For example, videoconferencing platforms are being announced by IBM, AT&T, and several other vendors. A state-of-the-market survey of desktop videoconferencing can be found in McCarthy [1995].

It remains to be seen whether video communications emerge as a separate networking application or as an integrated component of data communications. In the latter case, a videoconference may appear as another window on a workstation.

The literature on multimedia systems is growing quickly. The book *Distributed Multimedia* by Agnew [1996] provides a rich source of information for users and providers of distributed multimedia. In addition, the book *A Guided Tour of Multimedia Systems and Applications,* by Borko Furht and Milan Milenkovic (IEEE Computer Society, 1995) has many good articles on this topic. The *IEEE Computer* magazine's May 1995 issue is devoted to multimedia systems. For ongoing state-of-the-art information, the *IEEE Multimedia* magazine contains many articles on technical and research aspects of multimedia systems. State-of-the-market and state-of-the-practice articles appear in *Data Communications* magazine, *Business Communications Review,* and *Datamation.*

Multimedia over CORBA

Support of multimedia applications over CORBA is an interesting area of research and development. The main idea is to support stream interfaces over CORBA.

Stream interfaces are used to support distributed-multimedia applications. The basic characteristic of stream interfaces is that they support *continuous data transfers* over relatively long periods of time, e.g., real-time playout of video from a remote surveillance camera. In addition, the timeliness of such transmissions must be maintained for the duration of the media presentation.

To support stream interfaces over CORBA, several extensions to CORBA are needed. For example, a stream adapter will be needed to serve streams. Recall that CORBA has several adapters for different types of services (e.g., a basic object adapter for common services and other specialized adapters for special services). In addition a stream IDL may be needed for stream interactions. See Kinane [1996] for details.

This work is currently under consideration by the OMG in cooperation with ANSA.

8.4 Middleware for Collaboration: Groupware and Workflows

8.4.1 Overview

Computer-supported cooperative work (CSCW) is intended to allow people and processes in different parts of an organization to work together. Under this somewhat broad and vague umbrella, many application areas ranging from computer assisted learning to business-process automation have emerged. Two areas, groupware and workflows, have especially gained momentum and are briefly discussed in this section.

8.4.2 Groupware and Lotus Notes

Groupware is the middleware that allows people in different parts of an organization, in many cases at remote sites, to work together by collecting and sharing information, such as documents, graphs, spreadsheets, and email. The workgroup members can be across the hall connected over an office LAN or across the country connected over a WAN. For example, groupware users from different parts of an organization can work together to prepare proposals, comment on each other's work, track projects, create documents, and exchange email. According to Lotus Corporation, a leading groupware vendor currently owned by IBM, groupware "is software that uniquely enables organizations to communicate, collaborate and coordinate key business processes." Groupware relies on the following foundation technologies:

- Multimedia document management
- Email
- Flow of work and associated information
- Conferencing
- Scheduling

Lotus Notes is a very popular middleware for workgroups. Lotus Notes provides:

- Group communications for creation and access of document-oriented information over LANs, WANs, and dial-up lines
- Application development tool for combining documents, email, and conferencing capabilities.

Lotus Notes consists of one or more Notes servers that are connected to the Notes clients over an enterprise network (see Figure 8.2). The Notes Server houses the Notes building blocks: databases (collection of Notes documents), documents (text and graphics files), views (list of documents), forms (description of document structure), and fields (predefined fields in a form). The Notes server manages the repository of information for the workgroup members.

The Notes users (the clients) see a Microsoft Windows type GUI screen to send email, perform spreadsheet analysis, and work on documents (create, compose, navigate, print, search, etc.). The users perform most of their operations by using the typical pointing and clicking.

In addition to document database server, email, and GUI client environment, Lotus Notes provides a variety of tools for application developers to combine these building blocks quickly to develop new applications. The tools include a GUI forms generator, ODBC sup-

Figure 8.2 Conceptual View of Lotus Notes

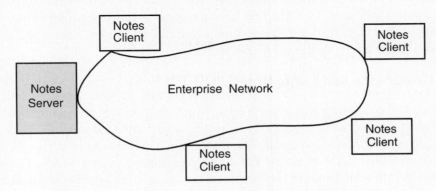

port, tools for creating databases, a scripting language, and a Lotus Notes API. This C programming API can be used to create or delete databases, read, write, and modify documents, write custom tasks that can be added to the Notes server, issue mail gateway calls, etc. These development tools are quite powerful and allow the users to quickly develop Lotus Notes applications.

Lotus Notes provides a set of services such as database replication (the replication mechanism synchronizes copies of the database located on multiple server or client machines), security and access-control lists, database administration services, and an X.500-based global namespace.

Information about Lotus Notes can be found in the Lotus Notes documents, the popular books [Kerwien 1994, Londergan 1994, Reber 1994], and end user experiences (see Gallagher [1996], and Baum [1994]). In addition to Lotus Notes, other workgroup products such as LinkWorks from DEC are being used (see Schiper [1996], and Eldrid [1994] for a comparison between Lotus Notes and LinkWorks). General information about groupware technology is given by Cristian [1996], Powell [1996], and Simpson [1994].

8.4.3 Workflow

Simply stated, *workflow* is concerned with automatically routing the work from one process to the next—it defines the operations that must be performed between the origin of work and its completion. The term workflow is often used to refer to various aspects of describing, reengineering, and automating business and information processes [Georgakopoulos 1996]. In particular, it focuses on the sequence of tasks, the information flow to support the tasks, and the tracking and reporting mechanisms needed for monitoring and control [Silver 1995]. Figure 8.3 shows a simplified view of workflow.

Workflow is a core component of business-process automation. For example, workflow technology could reduce the time involved in processing a mortgage loan application to a few hours. In a business environment, each business process involves many tasks that are performed in a certain sequence; these tasks are performed by different people, the information between certain tasks flows in a certain order, and the tasks are tracked for appropriate monitoring and control. At a high level, similar activities take place between business processes. For example, you can find out the intricacies of the processes in your business if you need to move your office while keeping the same phone number and the same computing equipment.

Workflow middleware is the software that enables improvements in business processes through automated workflow. Specifically, the workflow middleware performs the following tasks:

- It routes work in the proper sequence.
- It provides access to the data and documents required by the individual work performers.
- It tracks all aspects of process execution.

Figure 8.3 A Simplified View of Workflow for Loan Processing

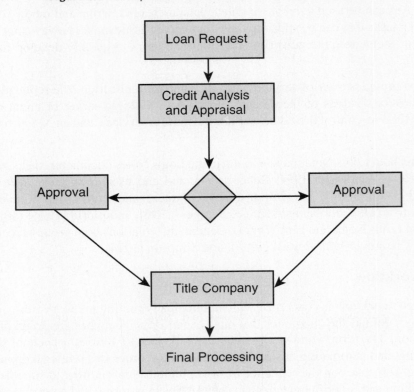

This middleware must provide the capabilities to control the sequence of activities, arrange for the delivery of work to the appropriate resources, track the status of the activities, coordinate the flow of information among activities, and utilize data to decide among alternative execution paths.

Different types of workflow middleware are being developed for a wide range of applications. Initial versions of workflow middleware focused on document imaging. Some of the early products were extensions of document-imaging and management software. For example, many "office automation" systems of the 1980s have matured into the workflow systems of the 1990s. Workflow middleware has also been greatly influenced by computer-integrated manufacturing (CIM). Many new concepts and technologies are gradually being included in workflows, and predictions of a rapidly expanding market have drawn significant interest of software companies and spawned a host of new middleware for workflow.

Commercially available workflow middleware is using C/S technology to effectively support office automation tasks involving document management, imaging, application launching,

EDI—Middleware for Electronic Commerce

Electronic commerce, the activity of conducting business over a network, has gained prominence due to the popularity of Web technologies and public/private Internets. The main focus of electronic commerce is buying and selling products over the Internet. At present, U.S. companies buy $500 billion worth of goods electronically [Verity 1996]. This is a small fraction (reportedly about 10%) of their total purchases. This is why it is widely believed that business-to-business electronic commerce is a critical application for the Internet.

Electronic Data Interchange (EDI) is the core midddleware for electronic commerce. EDI middleware is based on the EDI standard that specifies the encoding of messages to be used for transactions (e.g., purchasing, order processing, shipping/receiving, and accounts payable) between business partners. EDI standards have evolved into two families:

- EDIFACT standards that are newer and specify more complex encoding syntax. These standards are accepted internationally.

- ANSI X12 standards that are older and specify simpler encoding syntax. These standards, accepted throughout North America, are expected to migrate to EDIFACT.

EDI applications in the past ran on mainframes and communicated via point-to-point network protocols on proprietary networks (e.g., SNA). The current trend is toward PC or workstation EDI applications communicating via public/private Internet (see the figure below). A typical business interaction may involve a sequence of EDI messages flowing back and forth between the business partners, with the role of client and server reversing from time to time (clients encode the messages and send them over the network and the servers receive and decode the messages). .

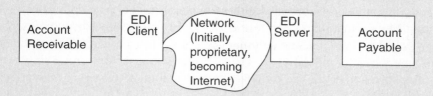

EDI does not provide any mechanisms for control of the entire process flow. That depends on appropriate mechanisms operating internally within the domain of each of the business partners. Research and development work is proceeding to tie work flows with EDI for end-to-end automaton [Lehman 1996].

- Verity, J., "Invoice? What's an Invoice?" *Business Week,* June 10, 1996, pp. 110–112.

- Lehman, F., "Machine-Negotiated, Ontology-Based EDI," *Electronic Commerce,* Springer, 1996, ed.: N. Adams and Y. Yesha.

and/or human coordination, collaboration, and codecision. In addition to email, faxes, telephones, and document images, the new breed of middleware for workflows is beginning to include:

- **Administrative/ad hoc facilities** to support structured as well as unstructured business automation needs. This includes electronic forms, groupware, and other facilities needed for administrative support.

- **Integration with other applications** by sending messages through email, by using common databases, or by using other C/S messaging services such as RPCs, MOM, and more recently CORBA [Duschinger 1996, Costa 1996, Powell 1996].

- **Production capabilities** to support the collaborative transaction workflow in an organization. In many cases, these transactions are "long" transactions that are fundamentally different from the C/S transactions we discussed in an earlier chapter (see Schiper [1996] for more details).

- **Collaborative technologies** to support document management, collaborative process management, and tracking work-in-progress and other related activities.

- **Improved visual programming aids and APIs** to aid in the development, customization and integration of workflow applications.

- **Improved user capabilities** to view, monitor, and control the work. This includes help panels for the users that tell them how to complete an action.

Many middleware products are being introduced with varying degrees of capabilities. Examples of the products are FlowMark from IBM, Inconcert from Xerox, and Sigma from Xerox. Although the capabilities of middleware for workflows are improving, many available workflow middleware packages do not address key aspects of interoperability and integration between heterogeneous, autonomous, and/or distributed systems. Specifically, the lack of standards is a serious issue. In other words, if part of your organization uses a workflow middleware package from vendor X and another part uses the workflow package from vendor Y, then there is no smooth workflow between these two parts of the same organization. A Workflow Coalition Management has been formed to address the standardization issue. In addition, current workflow systems do not ensure correct and reliable workflow execution in the presence of concurrency and failures. The distributed-transaction-processing technology needs to be extended and employed for workflows (this is an active area of research [Schiper 1996, Mittasch 1996]).

The discussion of middleware for workflows here is admittedly brief. An extensive discussion of workflow middleware can be found in the *BIS Guide to Workflow Software* [Silver 1995]. Additional information can be found in Frye [1995], Frye [1996], and Georgakopoulos [1996].

8.4.4   State of the Practice, Market, and Art

Groupware and workflows are generally being discussed under the umbrella of computer-supported cooperative work (CSCW). In groupware, Lotus Notes is a very heavily used product, while other groupware products from Microsoft, Netscape, Novell and Hewlett-

---

Intranet versus Groupware

Groupware products, such as Lotus Notes, have gained an established stature for collaborative computing. However, the arrival of World Wide Web technologies has raised questions about the need for groupware products. For example, if users can collaborate with each other by using Web technologies over a company Internet (i.e., Intranet), then why would they need yet another middleware for collaborative work? The key question is: can the Intranet provide the same or better services at a lower cost than the popular groupware products such as Lotus Notes?

Lotus Notes, and other groupware products, provide services such as a graphical user interface, email, synchronized replication, server security, customizable templates for common business applications, support for multiple platforms, and third-party utilities.

Intranets use the Internet technologies within organizations and can perform many of the groupware functions. For example, Web browsers provide GUI user interactions, email is very easy to use on the Intranets, server security can be maintained through secure HTTP and secure socket layer (SSL) programming, a plethora of Web tools are becoming available for common business applications on different platforms, and CGI gateways and Java applets can be used to interface Web applications with legacy applications. It seems that, other than synchronized replication, Intranet can provide more services than Lotus Notes.

The main difference is in cost and openness. Intranet solutions are much cheaper than Lotus Notes (Lotus Notes requires expensive middleware and highly skilled staff). In addition, Intranets are open, as compared to the proprietary nature of Lotus Notes.

The main question is user acceptance. While Web is very popular, Lotus Notes is also used very heavily and has a very loyal following. It is hoped, and expected, that the two technologies will merge. For example, the latest versions of Lotus Notes are becoming very Web aware.

Packard are also gaining momentum (see the *Information Week* March 4, 1996, issue). Several workflow products from IBM, Hewlett-Packard, Wang, Action Technologies, and others are being marketed.

The current work in CSCW is proceeding in the following directions:

- **Increased use and collaboration of WWW** in groupware, workflows, and other related products. As a matter of fact, the Intranet is being thought of as an alternative and a threat to Lotus Notes. For example, if users can collaborate with each other by using Web browsers, then why would they need yet another middleware for collaborative work (see the sidebar "Intranet versus Groupware")?

- **Increased use of multimedia** for collaborative work. For example, the teaching/tutoring collaborative systems are increasingly utilizing multimedia technologies.

- **Increased coordination and integration between different sets of technologies** for collaborative work. For example, many systems are moving toward integrating email, telephone, workflow, imaging, multimedia, distributed objects, and transaction processing technologies under the same umbrella.

Several interesting research areas in CSCW are being pursued. For example, current research thinking in group communications can be found in the articles published in the *Communications of the ACM* April 1996 issue. Examples of the articles include an overview of research issues in group communications [Powell 1996]; discussion of Totem—a fault-tolerant multicast group-communication system being developed at the University of California, Santa Barbara [Moser 1996], fault tolerance and high availability in group communications [Dolev 1996]; distribution of trust among a group of nodes in a distributed system [Reiter 1996], flexible protocol stacks for group communications [Van Renesse 1996], transaction processing in group communications [Schiper 1996], and integration of synchronous and asynchronous communications for collaborative tasks [Cristian 1996]. Other relevant research areas are design of multimedia global picture archiving and communication systems [Martinez 1996], design of object-group models over CORBA [Costa 1996], and use of traders to distributed office applications [Mittasch 1996]. Research articles on different aspects of computer-supported cooperative work appear regularly in the *Computer Supported Cooperative Work Journal* published by Kluwer Academic Publications.

8.5   Legacy Access/Integration Middleware

8.5.1   Overview

Our discussion has focused on middleware needed for developing a new breed of applications, which utilize object-orientation, client/server and Internet technologies. However, these new applications need to coexist with the existing legacy applications. Middleware is needed for this coexistence. Let us discuss this important middleware.

Simply stated, a legacy application is an *application of value* that has been passed on to the next generation. Many of these are old applications (many were developed in late 1960s and early 1970s) that are showing signs of age and years of patching and fixing. These systems are vital to the survival of some organizations; however, they are becoming increasingly expensive to maintain and operate (some systems take several months for a simple enhancement such as a new calculation). As the business pressures to provide flexible and timely information for management decisions and operational support grow, the inadequacy of legacy applications is highlighted. In addition, off-the-shelf software and flexible C/S architectures are showing the weaknesses of legacy applications. However, legacy applications are the workhorses for most organizations and cannot be thrown away (it is difficult to throw away applications that support critical services such as billing, inventory control, payables/

receivables, and purchasing). This presents a serious dilemma: you cannot live with them or without them.

Approaches to deal with legacy applications include rewrite from scratch, gradual migration, data warehousing, and access/integration in place. The access/integration in place has the benefit that it allows legacy applications to coexist with new applications. A wide range of middleware products, also known as **surround technologies** and **mediators**, are becoming available to enable legacy information access and integration. This type of middleware can be purchased from a diverse array of vendors, with different capabilities and price ranges. At the highest level, this middleware provides (see Figure 8.4):

- Screen scraping for legacy presentation access
- Database gateways for legacy data access
- Application gateways for legacy function access
- Object wrappers
- Integration gateways

These technologies can provide different levels of support for access to a single application, multiple applications on the same machine, applications across machines, read or update capabilities, distributed-query processing support, and distributed-transaction processing support.

Figure 8.4 Legacy Acccess Mediators

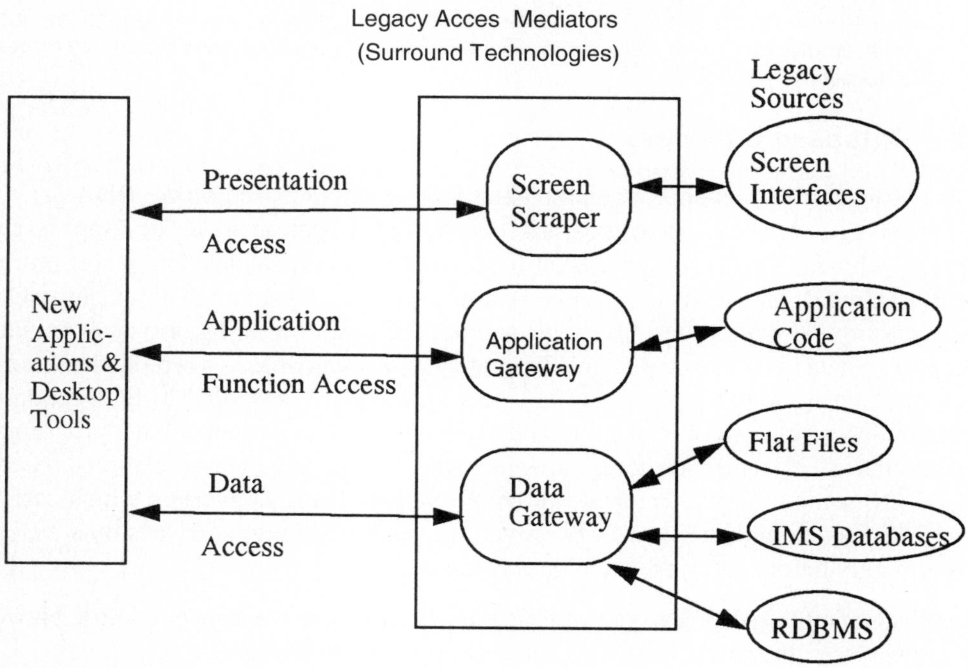

8.5.2   Screen Scrapers

Screen scraping is an extension of the well-known terminal emulation technology. Terminal emulators basically allow end users to remotely access application presentation services. *Screen scrapers* allow client applications to simulate the terminal keyboard/display features and thus act as programmable terminal emulators. Screen scrapers provide APIs that can be used by application programs to build screen images, send the screens to the host applications, simulate keyboard strokes, receive screen images from the host, and retrieve the new fields from the screen image by "scraping" the screen images (i.e., removing all screen formatting tags). Screen scrapers also provide programmer productivity aids, such as facilities for automatically capturing and storing screens from a running terminal-emulation session.

Screen scrapers are inexpensive and are frequently used to access legacy applications that are not well structured (monolithic). In many old systems, terminal emulation and screen scraping is the only way to access legacy data. As a matter of fact, screen scrapers work even when nothing else can be done to access legacy information. The major disadvantage of screen scraping is that the user must explicitly log on to each application to access the needed information. Other limitations are:

- Screen scraping is a slow and tedious process which can cause performance problems.

- Each user must be assigned a host user ID (an administrative issue).

- The mainframe workload increases as more users log on to it.

- Many end-user tools such as Lotus spreadsheets do not provide screen-scraping interfaces to access remote data. Most tools, as mentioned previously, issue ad hoc SQL calls for remote-data access.

8.5.3   Database Gateways

Many vendors currently support database gateways which are based on the RDA paradigm. To use these gateways, the client program (e.g., a spreadsheet on a user desktop) issues an SQL query which is sent to an SQL server (e.g., MVS-DB2 or Oracle). The server processes the SQL statements and sends the results back to the client. The main distinguishing feature of these gateways is that the end-user tools and/or applications running on a desktop interactively retrieve data in an ad hoc manner. The gateway software makes a remote database look like a local database to the applications and tools running on a desktop. The SQL request can be submitted as ad hoc, through a command-level interface, or embedded in a programming language such as C. To provide access to legacy data that is stored in nonrelational databases such as IMS, some database gateways provide "SQL-to-IMS" converters which cast SQL calls to IMS data manipulation calls. However, the quality of these gateways must be examined thoroughly before enterprisewide heavy usage.

The main advantage of database gateways is their flexibility and end-user control. However, these gateways are primarily suitable for legacy applications that are:

- Decomposable (e.g., the database schema is known and can be understood by the end users)
- Based on relational database technologies (SQL to nonrelational formats has some performance and functionality limitations)

The database gateways raise many network and system performance issues (e.g., size of SQL results sent over the network is unpredictable). In addition, the database gateways can be expensive (in the range of $200K and up for mainframe-based systems).

Many database vendors (e.g., Sybase, Oracle, Ingres, Informix, Gupta) provide proprietary gateways (clients from one vendor do not interoperate with other vendor servers). OSI RDA (Remote Data Access) is an open standard that has not been implemented by many vendors at the time of this writing. IBM's DRDA (Distributed Relational Database Architecture) is becoming a de facto standard for DB2 access. More than 20 vendors have announced DRDA support. Informix, Oracle, XDB, and Micro Decision DRDA gateways are commercially available; others are expected to appear before too long. Microsoft ODBC (Open Database Connectivity) API is also of great interest in developing database gateways.

Most of the existing database gateways provide read as well as update to single hosts. The capabilities for distributed query processing among the same vendor databases are also available. However, distributed-query processing between multiple vendors and distributed-transaction processing support is sparse. We have discussed the database gateways in detail in Chapter 5.

8.5.4 Application Gateways

These gateways allow invocation of remote functionality to access legacy information and typically include some host-application-related information. The application gateway client program issues a call to a remote function. The remote function can be a simple COBOL or PL1 routine, or it may contain precompiled SQL statements or a complete transaction. An application-gateway may incorporate screen scraping in addition to remote-function access. The main characteristics of application gateways are:

- Hide the host-application environment information from the client applications (i.e., act as the surround technology). The application gateway essentially serves as a translator between application calls. For example, it would translate an RPC call from an OSF-DCE-based client application to an IMS transaction on an MVS-based application.

- An API and additional software for remote calls are needed by the client applications. The client applications specify client code and interface definition. No additional software is needed on the host site.

- Several operational features such as security are important, because the application gateway may have to act as trusted partners.

Off-the-shelf application gateways are not widely available. Most application gateways are "homegrown" at present.

8.5.5   Object Wrappers—A Step Toward Integration

The integration technologies provide a layer on top of the access technologies to consolidate and synthesize the interactions between the legacy applications and the new applications and tools. Object wrappers and integration gateways are the most promising integration technologies.

An *object wrapper* is essentially a software layer between an OO system and a non-OO system—it receives object invocations and issues appropriate calls (e.g., 3270 data streams, remote procedure calls, SQL statements, IMS messages) to one or more non-OO applications servers). Object wrappers can be used as surround technologies for integrating legacy applications into the new world (see Figure 8.5). How do object wrappers differ from the access technologies discussed in the previous section? Well, the object wrappers sit on top of the access technologies and encapsulate the access technologies as objects. For example, a databases gateway allows your program to issue remote SQL calls to legacy databases. But SQL is not OO. So if your program invokes an operation on an object "customer," then an object wrapper would provide a layer above the database gateway and would translate the object invocation to the database gateway-specific call. An object wrapper is developed as a class with methods which construct and issue SQL or any other "non-OO" interactions. The client application code invokes methods provided by the object wrapper (the wrapper basically creates an object view of the legacy system). An object wrapper may be thin (e.g., just issue SQL calls) or thick (integrate information from different legacy systems residing on different computing platforms of different vintages). We will discuss the thick object wrappers later as "integration gateways."

Object wrappers provide a fundamentally powerful technique for integrating diverse legacy applications. For example, a new sales application may need to look at customer information and salesperson information located in two different systems: one in IMS the other in DB2. Two different object wrappers can wrap these two pieces of information and present an OO view to the sales application. The sales application just invokes operations on customers and sales personnel without knowing the underlying access technologies being employed by the two object wrappers (the IMS wrapper may use an EDA/SQL gateway while the DB2 wrapper may use a DRDA gateway). The underlying access technologies and the target legacy applications can be transitioned without impacting the sales application calls.

Object Management Group's Common Object Request Broker Architecture (OMG CORBA), discussed in great detail in Chapter 7 of this book, is a promising technology for object wrapping. The following basic steps are used in building CORBA object wrappers:

- Identify the components (functions, databases, user interfaces) of the legacy application that need to be accessed/integrated. In some cases, you are not wrapping a legacy system but a surround technology that access the legacy application (e.g., screen scraper, database gateway).

Figure 8.5 Object Wrappers

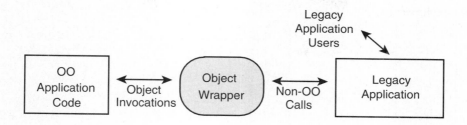

- Analyze whether the components are separable (i.e., does the component have well-specified interfaces? For legacy applications, this analysis leads to identifying an appropriate access/integration approach (i.e., legacy data access, legacy function access, or legacy presentation access).

- Map the functions performed by the components to CORBA Interface Definition Language (IDL). CORBA IDL specifies the objects, the operations performed on the objects, and the signature (the parameters) of the operations.

- Build a CORBA object server that receives the object invocations specified by IDL and then invokes the appropriate legacy component. This code is at the heart of an object wrapper and implements all the mapping needed between CORBA objects to the legacy components. For thick object wrappers, the object server may invoke an intermediate layer for mapping between legacy and CORBA views.

- Register the IDL in the CORBA interface repository so that clients can access the new objects statically or dynamically.

- Build the clients that invoke IDL-specified operations.

Let us briefly discuss some examples of object wrappers for legacy systems.

Wrapping Legacy Data. Object wrapping of legacy data encapsulates the IMS, relational database, and flat-file entities as objects. Although an OO program written in languages such as C++ can issue SQL, IMS, and flat-file calls, it becomes cumbersome to translate an object view in C++ to a non-OO data model for queries (the "impedance" mismatch between programming code and data-manipulation languages). Object wrapping of legacy data is a non-trivial task, owing to the complexity (mapping of different data models into OO classes) and magnitude of effort (legacy applications are typically large-database applications). The sophistication of the object wrapper can range from a simple API, to a limited query interpreter, to a database gateway that has been "objectified." In many practical cases, object wrappers provide an extra layer on top of legacy data access technologies (see Figure 8.6). Some object wrappers for relational databases are commercially available from vendors such as Rogue Wave (Dbtools.h++) and Persistence Software Inc.

Figure 8.6 Object Wrappers for Legacy Data Integration

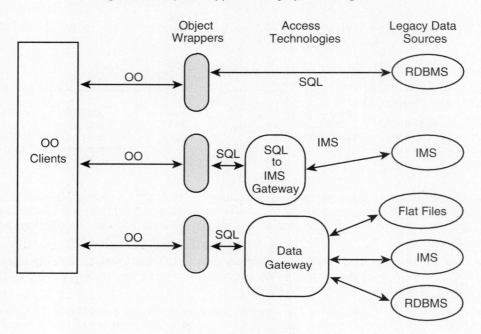

Wrapping Legacy Code (Functions). Object wrapping of legacy code is a feasible approach if the target legacy code can be invoked from another program such as a CORBA object-server. For example, a COBOL subroutine written in 1972 can be invoked by a CORBA object server written in 1995 (isn't technology just wonderful!). To accomplish this, you need to map the COBOL subroutine function (let us say a net sales subroutine) into a CORBA IDL definition (let us say an object called *sales* with an operation called *net_sales*), create the CORBA IDL definitions, build the object server that responds to the OO invocation *net_sales.sales* and issues the call to the COBOL subroutine, and store the IDL into CORBA interface repository so that clients can issue the OO calls. An important aspect of object wrappers is that they can also enhance the legacy code. For example, the object server could provide additional code that uses net sales to compute, say, projected sales, provided additional information is available to the object server.

Wrapping Legacy Presentation. Object wrapping of legacy presentation may be the only option available to integrate legacy applications that are very old and unstructured. Basically, the object wrapper in this case is a layer on top of the screen scraper. For example, let us assume that an old legacy system uses six 3270 screens to query order status: one screen for logging on, one greeting screen, one screen for menu options, one screen to enter the order status, one screen for response, and one for logging off (do not be surprised, it is common to go through 10 to 20 screens for one piece of information). An object wrapper can be built which receives an operation (*status*) on an object (*order*) and then works with a screen scraper to send the six screens and scrape the screens to return a response back. Note that the object invocation must include all information that the user actually types during this session (logon ID, password, keystrokes, order number, etc.).

We have discussed different object-wrapping implementation issues previously (e.g., wrappers for OSF DCE and Encina). The book by Mowbray and Zahavi [Mowbray 1995, chap. 8] contains many detailed implementation examples about developing CORBA object wrappers for remote-procedure calls, files, sockets, C API, Common Lisp, Smalltalk, Scripts, events, shared memory, dynamic queries, interprocess communications, macros, and headers. Off-the-shelf object wrappers are becoming commercially available (see Winsberg [1995] for a state-of-the-market review).

8.5.6 Integration Gateways—The Super Wrappers

Integration gateways integrate and synthesize object wrappers with various access technologies (screen scrapers, file-transfer packages, database gateways, and application gateways) into a single framework (see Figure 8.7). These "super object wrappers" provide an OO view to the clients, even though the needed information may be imbedded in IMS databases, indexed files, COBOL subroutines, 3270 terminal sessions, or a combination thereof. These integration gateways, henceforth referred to as *legacy integration gateways* to highlight the focus on legacy application integration, can:

- Provide standard OO APIs for client applications to invoke screen scraping, file transfer, database queries, and RPC function calls.

- Insulate the applications and end-user tools from any changes being made to the legacy applications. For example, the same user interface may be invoking new modules and databases. On the other hand, new GUIs may be accessing legacy data. Users do not know if the legacy, the new system, or a combination is supporting a given function.

- Serve as network gateways also between the legacy networks and the emerging new networks. For example, an integration gateway can reside on a UNIX machine that is connected to a fast FDDI or ATM network operating under TCP/IP on the client side and an old SNA network operating over an X.25 packet-switching network on the legacy application side.

- Translate the requests and data between more than one host application. For example, one client application call may result in accessing two different host applications on two different computers. The results from the two host applications are synthesized by the gateway and are translated to the client application.

- Synchronize updates between the host applications. The synchronization may be needed during a migration period between an old legacy application and a new "target" application which provides the same functionality. The synchronization may be done by using two-phase commit or replication algorithms.

- Support intelligent features such as distributed-query processing and distributed transaction processing.

Figure 8.7 Integration Gateway

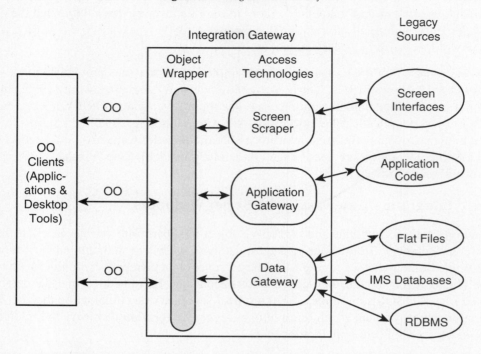

- Provide a global schema which is an integration of individual schemas for global query processing between federated, heterogeneous, and autonomous databases (see Sheth [1990] for details).

- Support automated selection of best paradigm (RPC, RDA, queuing) for accessing data.

- Provide security, logging and other administrative features. The host integration gateways can be used for enterprise data access or for migration of legacy applications.

As expected, these gateways are complex and can be quite expensive to build. However, their main benefit is that they can provide a single point of contact for a very diverse array of applications that are expanding and transitioning continuously. These gateways implement a three-tiered computing architecture where the gateway resides on the middle tier. A legacy integration gateway can reside on a midrange computer that is connected to legacy networks (e.g., X.25) on one side and the new networks (e.g., frame relay, ATM, and wireless) on the other. These gateways can become performance and security bottlenecks if not designed properly.

Few, if any, legacy integration gateways with the aforementioned characteristics are available commercially. It is difficult to build general-purpose legacy integration gateways, owing to the wide number of choices in client environments (e.g., CORBA, DCE, Encina, Novell LANs, Tuxedo) and host environments (terminal emulators, IMS or DB2 databases, X.25 or

SNA networks). The best approach appears to be to build these gateways for specific purposes and then expand them gradually for additional capabilities/environments.

Some research in developing the legacy integration gateways has been reported [Wiederhold 1992]. For example, the TSIMMIS Project at Stanford is aimed at rapid integration of heterogeneous information sources that may be structured or unstructured [Chawathe 1994]. The DARWIN Project describes concepts of a legacy integration gateway for incremental migration of legacy systems [Brodie 1993]. Adapt/X TraxWay, developed at Bellcore, is another example of legacy integration gateways.

8.6   Summary

The emerging applications in mobile computing, distributed multimedia, and groupware are creating new requirements for middleware. In addition, middleware is needed to access and integrate legacy applications with the new and emerging applications. We have briefly reviewed the main characteristics of these special-purpose middleware packages. The specialized middleware will continue to evolve as new application areas are discovered.

8.7   Case Study: XYZCorp Investigates Emerging Technologies

XYZCorp is planning to support a variety of services for its employees and customers in the next few years. The services include groupware, mobile computing applications, multimedia applications, and access to legacy applications. You need to develop an IT infrastructure architecture for the corporation that will support these services. You have been asked to outline a strategy that indicates the various servers and the protocol "stack" at each client that will be needed to use these services.

Hints about the Case Study:

Figure 8.8 shows a conceptual view of the IT infrastructure architecture needed to support the aforementioned services (we are not showing the TCP/IP stack for simplicity).

8.8   Problems and Exercises

1. List the factors you will use to analyze and evaluate the middleware products to support mobile computing applications.

2. Suppose you need to support video conferencing on your desktops. What short range and long-range considerations do you need to take into account to support these applications?

Figure 8.8 XYZCorp Environment

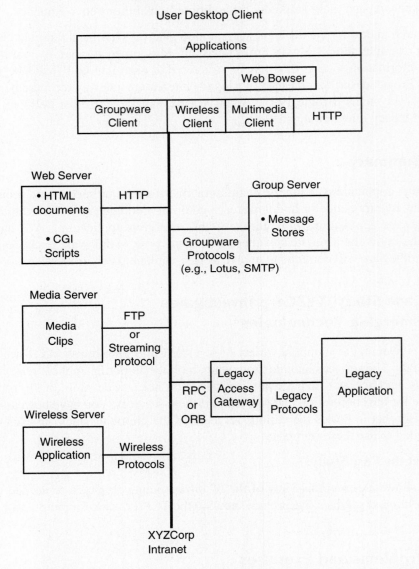

User Desktop Client

3. How do EDI and electronic mail integrate with groupware and collaborative computing services to support electronic commerce over the Internet? Give examples.

4. Survey and evaluate a few legacy access gateways that provide screen scraping, data, and application gateways.

8.9   Additional Information

Information about specialized middleware is scattered around different trade journals and magazines. We have pointed to these sources in each section. A particularly good source of additional information is the ICDP96 (International Conference on Distributed Platforms), held in Dresden, Germany, February 27–March 1, 1996. The conference proceedings are published as *Distributed Platforms,* edited by Schill, et al., Chapman and Hall, 1996. Other sources are the books by [Agnew 1996, Walters 1995, Silver 1995].

8.10   References

Agnew, P., and Kellerman, A., *Distributed Multimedia,* ACM Publications, ACM Order No. 704961, 1996.

Baum, D., "Developing Serious Applications with Notes," *Datamation,* April 15, 1994, pp. 28–32.

Berger, M., "CoNus–A CSCW System Supporting Synchronous, Asynchronous and Autonomous Collaborative Work," *ICDP96 Proceedings,* Dresden, February 1996.

Blair, L. et al., "Formal Specification and Verification of Multimedia Systems in Open Distributed Processing," *Computer Standards and Interfaces,* Vol. 17 (1995), pp. 413–436.

Brodie, M. L., and Stonebroker, M., "DARWIN: On the Incremental Migration of Legacy Information Systems," Technical Memorandum, Electronics Research Laboratory, College of Engineering, University of California, Berkeley, March 1993.

Bruno, L., "Middleware Makes Wireless Apps a Snap," *Data Communications,* May 1996, pp. 44–45.

Caceres, R,. and Ifrode, L., "The Effects of Mobility on Reliable Transport Protocols," *Proc. of 14th International Conference on Distributed Computer Systems,* Poznan, Poland, June 22–24, 1994, pp. 12–20.

Chawathe, S., et al., "The TSIMMIS Project: Integration of Heterogeneous Information Sources", Department of Computer Science, Stanford University, 1994.

Cole, B., "Oracle Adding Workflow and Net Access to Applications," *Network World,* July 3, 1995, p. 1.

Costa, F. M., and Madeira, E. R. M., "An Object Group Model and Its Implementation to Support Cooperative Applications on CORBA," *ICDP96 Proceedings,* Dresden, February 1996.

Cristian, F., "Synchronous and Asynchronous Group Communications," *Communications of ACM,* April 1996, pp. 88–97.

Davies, N., "The Impact of Mobility on Distributed System Platforms," Invited paper, *ICDP96 Proceedings,* Dresden, February 1996.

Diehl, N., Grill, D., Held, A., Kroh, R., Reigber, T., and Ziegert,Th., "System-Integration for Mobile Computing and Service Mobility," *ICDP96 Proceedings,* Dresden, February 1996.

Dolev, D., and Malki, D., "The Trans Approach to High Availability Cluster Communication," *Communications of ACM,* April 1996, pp. 64–70.

Duschinger, H., and Schuster, H., "An Architecture for Distributed Workflow Management Systems using OSF DCE," *ICDP96 Proceedings,* Dresden, February 1996.

Eldred, E., and Sylvester, T., "A Groupware Duet with Gusto," *Client/Server Today,* July 1994, pp. 69–79.

Friday, A., Blair, G.S., Cheverst, K., and Davies, N., "Extensions to ANSAware for Advanced Mobile Applications," *ICDP96 Proceedings,* Dresden, February 1996.

Frye, C., "A Forest to be Reckoned With," *Applications Software Magazine,* April 1996, pp. 80–87.

Frye, C., "Workflow Joins with Document Management, Imaging, Faxing and More," *Client/ Server Computing,* December 1995, pp. 57–63.

Furht, B., and Milenkovic, M., ed., "A Guided Tour of Multimedia Systems and Applications," IEEE Computer Society Tutorial, March 1995.

Gallagher, S., "High Marks For Notes 4.0," *Information Week,* Jan. 22, 1996, pp. 75–76.

Garcia, F., et al., "QoS Support for Distributed Multimedia Communications," *IICDP96 Proceedings,* February 1996.

Gareiss, R., "Wireless Data: More Than Wishful Thinking," *Data Communications,* March 21, 1995, pp. 52–64.

Gary, G., "Client/Server Hits the Road," *Datamation,* August 1, 1995, pp. 43–45.

Gemmell, A., et al., "Multimedia Storage Servers: A Tutorial," *IEEE Computer,* May 1995, pp. 40–51.

Georgakapoulos, D. and Elmargarmid, A., "Realizing the Workflow Paradigm in Products, Methodologies, and Infrastructure Technologies," *Data Base Management,* Fall 1996.

Gronert, E., and Heywood, P., "GSM: A Wireless Cure for Cross-Border Data Chaos," *Data Communications,* March 21, 1995, pp. 88–94. .

Han, K., and Ghosh, S., "A Comparative Analysis of Virtual Versus Physical Process-Migration," *ICDP96 Proceedings,* Dresden, February 1996.

Harmon, P., "Object-Oriented Client-Server Systems," *Object-Oriented Strategies,* Vol. III, No. 5 (San Francisco, 1993).

Harmon, P., "Object-Oriented Client-Server Systems," Object-Oriented Strategies, Vol. III, No. 9 (San Francisco, 1993).

Heuser, L., Schill, A., and Boehmak,W., "Mobile Database Access," *ICDP96 Proceedings,* Dresden, February 1996

Hoffert, E., and Gretson, G., "The Digital News System at EDUCOM: A Convergence of Interactive Computing, Newspapers, Television and High-Speed Networks," *Communications of the ACM,* April 1991, pp. 113–116.

Johnson, J., "Middleware Makes Wireless WAN Magic," *Data Communications,* March 21, 1995, pp. 67–74.

Kerwien, E., *Lotus Notes Application Development Handbook,* IDS Books, 1996, 2d ed..

Kinane, B., and Muldowney, D., "Distributing Multimedia Systems using CORBA," *Computer Communications,* Vol. 19 (Issue 1, 1996), pp. 13–21.

Londergan, S., *Lotus Notes for Dummies,* IDS Books Worldwide, 1994.

Martinez, R., and Hsieh, S. L., "Design of Multimedia Global PACS CORBA Environment," *ICDP96 Proceedings,* Dresden, February 1996.

McCarthy, V., "Desktop Videoconferencing: Still a Rough Cut," *Datamation,* March 15, 1995, pp. 51–55.

McQuillan, J., "Broadband Networks," *Data Communications,* June 1990, pp. 76–86.

Millikin, M., "DCE: Building the Distributed Future," *Byte Magazine,* June 1994, pp. 125–134.

Mittasch, Ch., Koenig, W., and Funke, R., "Trader Supported Distributed Office Applications," *ICDP96 Proceedings,* Dresden, February 1996.

Molva, R., Somfot, D., and Tsudik, G., "Authentication of Mobile Users," *IEEE Network,* March/April, 1994, pp. 26–35.

Moser, L., et al., "Totem: A Fault-Tolerant Multicast Group Communication System," *Communication of ACM,* April 1996, pp. 54–63.

Mowbray, T., and Aahavi, R., *The Essential CORBA,* Wiley, 1995.

Nicol, J., et al., "Object Orientation in Heterogeneous Distributed Computing Systems," *IEEE Computer,* June 1993, pp. 57–67.

Orfali, R., Harkey, D., and Edwards, J., *Client/Server Survival Guide* Van Nostrand Reinholt, 1994.

Perrochon, L., *W3 Middleware: Notions and Concepts,* Institut für Informationssysteme, ETH Zurich, Switzerland, 1995.

Phillips, R., "MediaView: A General Multimedia Digital Publication System," *Communications of the ACM,* July 1991, pp. 75–83.

Pinto, P., "Distributed Objects: An Approach to Sharing Multimedia Information," *ICDP96 Proceedings,* February 1996.

Pollini, G., and Haas, Z., "E-RAMA and RAMA," *IEEE Network,* March/April 1994, pp. 18–25.

Powell, D., "Introduction to Group Communication," *Communication of ACM,* April 1996, pp. 50–53.

Rao, R., "Distributed Applications? Don't Forget the Database," *Data Communications,* October 1995, pp. 113–120.

Reber, S., *Database Development in Lotus Notes,* Ziff-Davis Books, 1994.

Redl, S., Weber, M., and Oliphant, M., *An Introduction to GSM,* ARTech House, 1995.

Reiter, M., "Distributing Trust with the Ramport Toolkit," *Communications of ACM,* April 1996, pp. 71–75.

Richter, K., Rudolf, St., and Irmscher, K., "Mediator Services for Mobile Clients," *ICDP96 Proceedings,* Dresden, February 1996.

Riccuit, M., "The Mainframe as Server: Is IBM Totally Bonkers—or Brilliant?" *Datamation,* May 15, 1994, pp. 61–64.

Rodriguez, A., and Rowe, L., "Guest Editor's Introduction: Multimedia Systems and Applications," *IEEE Computer,* May 1995, pp. 20–24.

Rymer, J., "Modeling Network Behavior Using Objects," *Distributed Computing Monitor,* Vol. 7, No. 9 (Boston, 1992).

Rymer, J., "Distributed Object Computing," *Distributed Computing Monitor,* Vol. 8, No. 8 (Boston, 1993).

Schlit, B., and Theimer, M., "Disseminating Active Map Information to Mobile Hosts," *IEEE Network,* September/October 1994, pp. 22–31.

Schiper, A., and Raynal, M., "From Group Communications to Transactions in Distributed Systems," *Communications of ACM,* April 1996, pp. 84-87.

Schmandt, C., "Multimedia Nomadic Services on Today's Hardware," *IEEE Network,* September/October 1994, pp. 12–21.

Shan, Y., Earle, R., and McGaughey, S., "Objects on the Server," *Object Magazine,* May 1995, pp. 49–54.

Sheth, A. P., and Larson, J. A., "Federated Database Systems for Managing Distributed, Heterogeneous, and Autonomous Databases," *ACM Computing Surveys,* September 1990, pp. 183–236.

Silver, B., ed., *The BIS Guide to Workflow Software,* BIS Strategic Decisions, Norwell, MA, 1995.

Simon, R., et al., "Multimedia MedNet: A Medical Collaboration and Consultation System," *IEEE Computer,* May 1995, pp. 65–73. .

Simpson, D., "Variations on a Theme: Groupware," *Client/Server Today,* July 1994, pp. 45–55.

Sreenan, C., and Mishra, P., "Equus: A QoS Manager for Distributed Applications," *ICDP96 Proceedings,* February 1996.

Sreetharan, M., and Kumar, R., *Cellular Digital Packet Data,* ARTech House, 1996.

Van Renesse, R., et al., "Horus: A Flexible Group Communication System," *Communications of ACM,* April 1996, pp.76–83.

Walters, B., *Computer-Mediated Communications: Multimedia Applications,* ARTech House, 1995.

Wexler, J., "IBM Insulates Apps from Wireless," *Network World,* June 15, 1995, p. 1.

Wiederhold, G., "Mediators in the Architecture of Future Information Systems," *IEEE Computer,* No. 25, pp.38–49, 1992.

Winsberg, P., "Legacy Code: Don't Bag It, Wrap It," *Datamation,* May 15, 1995, pp. 36–41.

Woolf, B. P., and Hall, W., "Multimedia Pedagogues: Interactive Systems for Teaching and Learning," *IEEE Computer,* May 1995, pp. 74–80.

9

Putting The Pieces Together—A Synthesis

9.1   Introduction

Owing to the popularity of object-oriented, client/server, Internet-based applications, a plethora of middleware products have become state-of-the-market since 1990. In the 1980s, and before, it was possible to develop C/S applications by using the APIs (application programming interfaces) available on network services (e.g., TCP/IP Sockets and LU6.2). However, this approach had two major limitations: the programming had to be done at an intricate physical level, and the C/S applications were "hard-wired" to the underlying network. Consequently, very few business applications were developed by using the C/S paradigm before 1990. Since then, middleware products from database vendors, computer manufacturers, and consortia have made it easier to develop and deploy C/S applications.

Although the growth in middleware has accelerated the development and deployment of many interesting distributed applications, it has also introduced an almost unimaginable array of confusing and complex terms and jargon. In the 1980s, we had not heard about popular terms such as OSF DCE, RPCs, Kerberos, CORBA, OMG, OLE/ActiveX, OpenDoc, MOM, World Wide Web, Lotus Notes, Encina, DRDA, ODBC, and HTTP. We have reviewed these terms in previous chapters. The purpose of this chapter is to consolidate the middleware discussion with other services needed in an IT infrastructure. Specifically, we intend to answer the following questions:

- How can we put all these pieces together into a functioning IT infrastructure that can support the variety of business services and applications needed by modern enterprises?

- Are there any efforts to consolidate and synthesize the existing infrastructure offerings (middleware, network services, local computing services) into a single product line?

- What is the overall state of the art, market, and practice in middleware?

To answer these questions, we revisit the IT framework introduced in Chapter 1 and use it as a basis for developing a functioning IT infrastructure that consolidates the middleware services with its neighbors, such as networks, applications, and local computing services (Section 9.2). IBM's Open Distributed Computing (ODC) is discussed as example of an attempt to synthesize the variety of middleware products into a single offering. In addition, ODC can play a pivotal role in the (re)engineering of legacy applications and databases because most of the legacy applications and databases, currently reside on IBM mainframes. This chapter concludes by making general observations about middleware state of the art, state of the market, and state of the practice.

Key Points

- You need the following iterative steps to put all the middleware pieces together into a functioning IT infrastructure that can support the variety of business services and applications needed by the modern enterprises:
    - Analyze the requirements for infrastructure.
    - Architect the infrastructure services.
    - Implement, deploy, and support the infrastructure services.

- Middleware should be chosen based on business drivers, type of applications that need to be supported, APIs needed, portability and interoperability issues, and vendor-support information.

- The commercially available middleware generally falls into three broad categories:
    - Middleware components that provide only one service
    - Middleware environments that combine many services from one or more layers to provide integrated middleware services
    - Compound middleware environments that combine many middleware environments into a single framework

- MIddleware will continue to support the trend toward higher-level object-oriented, client/server, Web-based applications.

- The issue of high-level APIs will gain more importance as more middleware layers are introduced with a proliferation of APIs.

- Middleware to support the wide range of distributed applications is evolving rapidly. Consequently, it is becoming more complex and requires more training and effort to install and support.

- IBM's Open Distributed Computing (the Open Blueprint) is an example of synthesizing many middleware products and services into a single framework. Other attempts of this nature, such as DEC-sponsored Forte, will emerge.

9.2   Putting the Pieces Together—IT Infrastructure

9.2.1   Overview

We have discussed several middleware products that provide a variety of services such as remote messaging, distributed-data management, distributed-transaction management, distributed-object support, Internet support, and emerging-technologies support. Middleware should combine and integrate these services into APIs that are used by applications across a network. In other words, the users should not know what services are being provided by which middleware component. In fact, the entire IT infrastructure should appear as a tightly integrated environment which provides a range of networking, database, transaction-management, remote-messaging, naming, directory, security, and other services needed by the applications.

Figure 9.1 shows a layered view that we have used as a framework for discussion throughout this book. For the sake of simplicity, this view does not show the operating systems and local support services. The applications (client/server processes) are at the highest layer and the network services are at the lowest layers. We have discussed the various middleware layers in the previous chapters.

The key question is: how can we put all these pieces together into a functioning IT infrastructure that can support the variety of services and applications needed by modern enterprises? The following iterative steps are suggested as a starting point:

- Analyze the requirements for infrastructure.
- Architect the infrastructure services.
- Implement, deploy and support the infrastructure services.

Table 9.1 summarizes the main activities needed for the infrastructure services. The rows of this table show the three generic steps (i.e., analysis, architecture, implementation), and the columns represent the three classes of infrastructure services (i.e., middleware, network, local). We briefly discuss the entries in this table in the next three subsections.

TABLE 9.1 SUMMARY OF INFRASTRUCTURE

Stage	Middleware	Network Services	Local Computing Services
Analysis	Specification and analysis of requirements for middleware services	Specification and analysis of requirements for network services	Specification and analysis of requirements for local computing services
Architecture	Select proper middleware(e.g., Web services, distributed objects, distributed data middleware)	Select proper network products (e.g., communication technologies, interconnectivity devices)	Select proper local computing products (e.g., database managers, operating systems)
Implementation and Support	Select, acquire, install and support new vendor products and/or upgrades of existing	Select, acquire, install and support new vendor products and/or upgrades of existing	Select, acquire, install and support new vendor products and/or upgrades of existing

Figure 9.1 IT Infrastructure Layers

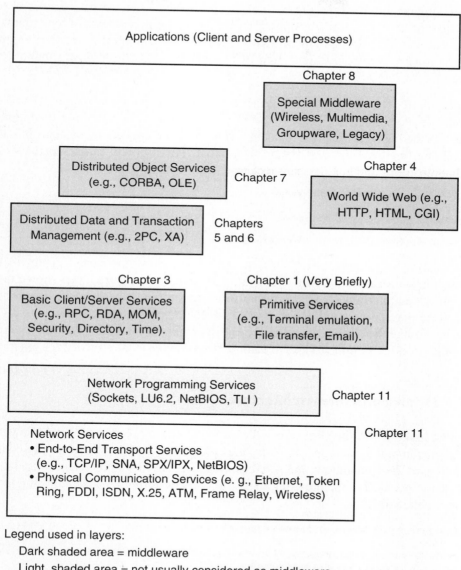

Legend used in layers:

Dark shaded area = middleware

Light shaded area = not usually considered as middleware

Unshaded area = not middleware

9.2.2   Analysis of Infrastructure Requirements

The infrastructure capabilities (middleware, network services, local computing services) needed to support applications and business services depend on a large number of factors such as the type of applications/business services being supported, size of the organization, growth areas, etc. For example, the infrastructure needed to support a small 200-employee trucking company is very different than that of a large 20,000-employee manufacturing organization.

It is important to determine clear requirements that determine the most appropriate technology. This is a crucial activity because the IT infrastructure (i.e., computer communication platforms) is the basic delivery mechanism for not only the application systems but also the manufacturing, engineering, and financial services. For different classes of existing and planned applications and business services, you need to specify and analyze :

- Requirements for middleware services
- Requirements for network services
- Requirements for local computing services

Table 9.2 shows a "planning sheet" that can help you capture the necessary details for the important applications and services. This table casts the infrastructure layers shown in Figure 9.1 into an evaluation framework. It is desirable to work through these details for every application and service for an overall understanding of the infrastructure requirements. In particular, the requirements for critical and future high-visibility applications and services must be clearly understood to minimize risks of failure. Gross analysis may suffice for others.

9.2.3   IT Infrastructure Architecture

An IT infrastructure architecture shows the various building blocks (e.g., middleware, networks, local computing services), the roles they play and their interrelationships and interactions to support the applications and services. In particular, this architecture must satisfy the requirements specified in the previous step. The two key activities in establishing the infrastructure architecture are:

- Choose the middleware and network layers/services needed.
- Show how the various middleware layers will interrelate and interact with each other, with network services, and with the applications.

Choice of layers/services depends on the application needs. A given application system should use an appropriate layer of middleware. For example, consider an application object hat needs to send a message to a remote object for synchronizing a database. The application developer has the following choices shown in Figure 9.2:

TABLE 9.2 PLANNING SHEET FOR INFRASTRUCTURE

Infrastructure Services Needed	Application	Application	Business Service (e.g., Financial Service)
Middleware Services Needed • Web support • Distributed-object support • Wireless applications support • Groupware support • Distributed-file services • Distributed-database support • Distributed-transaction processing • Replication servers • Basic C/S protocol support (RDA, RPC, MOM) • Other support (Email, bulk data transfer, etc.)			
Management and Support Services • Security • Directory and naming services • Time services • Management services			
Network Support • Network architectures needed (TCP/IP, SNA, Novell IPX/SPX, OSI, NetBIOS) • Network interconnectivity support (routers, bridges, gateways) • Communication technologies needed (ATM, Frame Relay, FDDI, etc.)			
Local Computing Support Needed • Operating-systems support (e.g., PC DOS, Windows, Windows NT, Macintosh, UNIX, MVS). • Database support (DB2, Oracle, Informix, Sybase) • Other local services needed			

1. Use an object-oriented interface such as CORBA which directly supports interactions between remote objects. CORBA implementation may activate lower layers to actually perform the database synchronization.

2. Use the distributed-data management services to access and synchronize the remotely located data. In this case, the developer may have to develop his/her own "wrapper," say in C++, which receives the method invocation and issues the call needed by the distributed-data management services.

3. Use the basic services such as RPCs and do update synchronization yourself, in addition to a wrapper that receives an object message and invokes the needed RPCs.

Figure 9.2 Using Middleware Layers

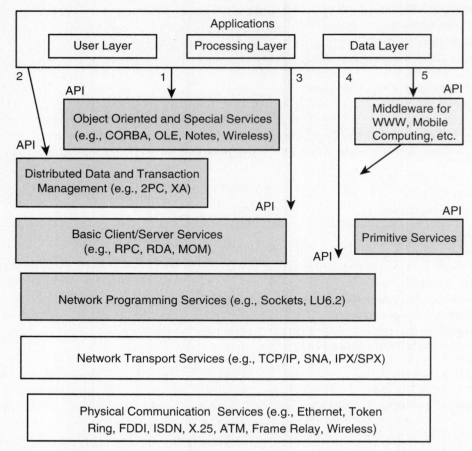

Note: Shaded area = C/S middleware
C/S middleware is shown at 4 layers

4. Use the network programming services (e.g., Sockets) and do whatever programming needs to be done to wrap, access, and update duplicated data.
5. Use a Web browser that uses a CGI or other Web gateway in conjunction with other middleware layers to synchronize the database.

Naturally, it is desirable to use high-level middleware layers to reduce application development costs (the higher the layer, the less code application developers have to write).

The chosen middleware layers can be arranged in a variety of ways. Figure 9.3 shows a sample middleware architecture that shows how a user desktop can communicate, over a TCP/IP network, with a variety of servers (e.g., Web servers, CORBA servers, database servers, and transaction servers). The client site shows the protocol stack that needs to exist at the client desktops. Of course, this configuration can be adjusted to meet different users' needs. For example, if a client does not need to invoke CORBA applications, then the CORBA stack does not need to exist at that client's desktop. Similarly, one physical machine can house a database server and a transaction server (we showed these servers separately for conceptual simplicity).

Application and platform architects must be aware of the interplays between middleware and applications. In particular, it must be kept in mind that middleware stacks (layers) impact the performance as well as cost of an application. Higher level middleware makes it easier and cheaper to develop complex applications, but too many stacks can impede the performance of an application and introduce the administrative overhead of installing, interfacing, maintaining, and supporting the middleware software from different suppliers. In addition, too many layers of middleware may impede the enterprisewide deployment of an application. For example, if an inventory-control application requires CORBA, then *all* sites of the enterprise that use this inventory-control application must house CORBA middleware.

The issues of portability and interoperability also play a key role. Application programming interfaces (APIs) provided by the middleware impact the portability of applications. For example, a client program that uses an RDA API cannot be ported to an RPC environment without some reengineering. Exchange protocols used between the C/S middleware impact the interoperability of C/S applications. For example, if a server uses RPCs, then the clients must adhere to the specific RPC implementation used by the server.

The requirements for middleware should be reexamined carefully while establishing an infrastructure architecture. Not surprisingly, a very large number of Web-based applications are being developed to operate on the Internet ranging from entertainment to electronic commerce. In addition, many applications being developed at present are based on distributed-object concepts. Compound documents, for example, are an interesting application of distributed objects, because a compound document essentially serves as a container for objects such as text paragraphs, spreadsheets, graphs, and sound bites. Moreover, groupware products such as Lotus Notes are being used to allow people in different parts of an organization to

Figure 9.3 A Middleware Architecture

User Desktop (Client)

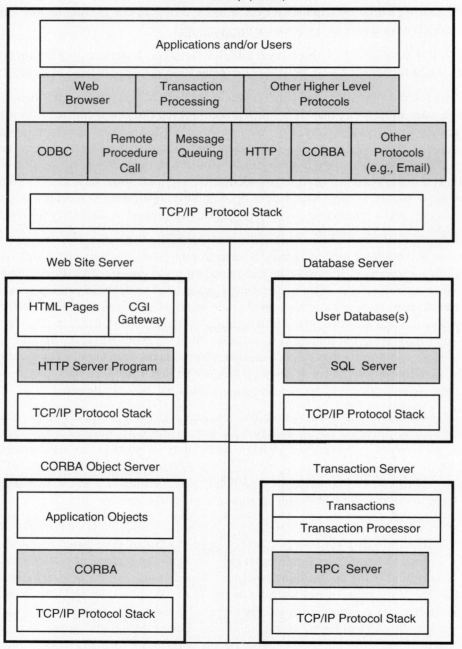

Web Site Server

Database Server

CORBA Object Server

Transaction Server

work together by collecting and sharing information, such as documents, graphs, spread-sheets, and email. More applications are also using wireless communications and utilizing distributed multimedia technologies.

These emerging applications require specialized middleware. The architects of these applications must ask the following questions:

- Does the middleware support CORBA at an enterprisewide level?
- Are the standards in compound documents (OLE and OpenDoc) supported?
- Is the middleware for Internet application development adequate?
- Are the special middleware products available for groupware (e.g., Lotus Notes), wireless applications, and distributed-multimedia applications?

9.2.4 Implementation Considerations

Implementation entails selection, acquisition, and installation of the middleware, network, and local computing support components. Network and local computing support components are widely available as commercial-off-the-shelf technologies. The commercially available middleware generally falls into three broad categories:

- **Middleware components** that provide only one service. For example, ODBC drivers allow access to remote databases, Netwise RPC supports only RPC, and IBM's MQSeries supports only MOM.

- **Middleware environments** that combine many services from one or more layers to provide integrated middleware services. For example, OSF DCE integrates RPC, security, directory, time, and file services into a single package. Similarly, Encina provides distributed-transaction processing over DCE, and CORBA 2.0 is defining many services over ORB.

- **Compound middleware environments** that combine many middleware environments into a single framework. For example, IBM's Open Distributed Computing (ODC) Blueprint combines OSF DCE, MQSeries, CORBA, distributed-data management, and distributed-transaction management into a single framework.

We have discussed various middleware components and middleware environments in previous chapters. We will discuss the IBM Open Distributed Computing to illustrate the concepts of compound middleware in Section 9.4.

What vendor products should be chosen? The key idea is to choose those products that best satisfy current and future business (i.e., enterprise application) needs in a robust and cost-effective manner. In addition, we need to consider the application developers and system architects. Application developers are, and should be, mainly concerned with APIs and proper CASE tools to get their job done. But systems architects must supply the middleware that, in addition to the APIs, must support interoperability, facilitate different interaction paradigms, enable system management (e.g., security, naming/directory, failure handling, performance management), and ensure needed network services for connectivity between remotely located client and server processes.

Table 9.3 shows a checklist of the issues that should be considered to analyze/select vendor products. This table essentially extends the planning sheet presented in Table 9.2 to include development considerations and vendor information. This evaluation framework also can be used to illustrate the capabilities of middleware strategies such as the IBM Open Distributed Computing Blueprint that attempt to synthesize several infrastructure products into a single environment.

9.3   IBM's Open Distributed Computing Blueprint

9.3.1   Overview

IBM's *Open Distributed Computing (ODC) Blueprint* is a good example of an attempt to synthesize the various middleware services, network services, and local computing services into a single IT infrastructure offering. In addition to studying ODC as an illustration of middleware synthesis, it is also important to pay some attention to IBM's strategies for middleware owing primarily to the large embedded base of mission-critical applications and databases that reside on IBM MVS mainframes (according to a 1993 survey conducted by Forrester Research, more than 80 percent of mission-critical databases and applications reside on MVS mainframes).

IBM's distributed computing and client/server strategies have evolved since the mid 1980s. The IBM System Application Architecture (SAA), announced in 1987, was one of the first industrial efforts toward application distribution, portability, and interoperability, albeit within IBM environments. In February 1990, IBM announced AIX (IBM's version of UNIX) on its RISC processors (RS6000). This announcement included UNIX in IBM's strategy and stated that SAA and AIX will coexist. In 1993, IBM announced its Open Distributed Computing (ODC) strategy, which attempts to integrate non-IBM and non-SAA products into a single framework. ODC, also known as *IBM's Open Blueprint for Distributed Computing,* attempts to integrate several existing and evolving platform technologies, such as the following, into a single framework:

- IBM's SAA/AIX
- Open Software Foundation's DCE
- IBM's MQSeries for queued messages
- Common network services (SNA, TCP/IP, OSI, NetBIOS and Novell IPX), system services (remote-procedure calls, directory, security, time)
- Distributed-database services (e.g., DRDA) and transaction managers (e.g., CICS).
- Application-development and management services
- IBM's DSOM for CORBA-style distributed-object support.

TABLE 9.3 A Checklist for Evaluating Vendor Products

Services Needed	Product 1	Product 2	Product 3
Development Environment Issues • CASE Tools • APIs supported • Interoperability and portability			
Middleware Services Needed • Web support • Distributed-object support • Wireless applications support • Groupware support • Legacy mediation support • Distributed-file services • Distributed-database support • Distributed-transaction processing • Replication servers • Basic C/S protocol support (RDA, RPC, MOM) • Other support (e.g., email)			
Management and Support Services • Security • Directory and naming services • Time services • Management services			
Network Support • Network architectures needed (TCP/IP, SNA, Novell IPX/SPX, OSI, NetBIOS) • Network interconnectivity support (routers, bridges, gateways) • Communication technologies needed (ATM, Frame Relay, FDDI)			
Local Computing Support Needed • Operating systems support (e.g., PC DOS, Windows, Windows NT, Macintosh, UNIX, MVS) • Database support (DB2, Oracle, Informix, Sybase) • Other local services needed			
Vendor Information • Cost ranges, licensing options • Company size and staying power • Installed base and type of support			

The goal of ODC, shown in Figure 9.4, is to establish MVS mainframe as an enterprisewide server for corporate databases and applications. Middleware (shaded areas in Figure 9.4) consists of system support services (e.g., RPCs, message queues, directory, and security) and distributed resource management (database and transaction support, distributed-object support). This middleware is of primary interest to us and is discussed in Sections 9.3.2 and 9.3.3. The other components of ODC are briefly reviewed in Section 9.3.4.

9.3.2   The Distributed System Services

The Distributed System Services provide the core middleware support for distributed C/S applications in IBM environments. These services include the following.

OSF/DCE remote procedure call (RPC) is used to support RPCs between client and server processes located on MVS, UNIX, and PCs. Although other RPCs (e.g., SUN RPC) are technically supported, OSF/DCE has become a core component of IBM's MVS strategy. In particular, OSF/DCE Security, Directory, and Time Recovery Services are key components of the IBM Open Distributed Computing (see Figure 9.4). We have described OSF/DCE in a previous chapter. The OSF/DCE on MVS provides access to mainframe databases such as IMS and DB2. The OSF/DCE applications on MVS interoperate with OSF/DCE applications developed on other platforms (e.g., UNIX and PCs). For example, a DCE client developed on a UNIX machine by using the OSF/DCE provided by Hewlett-Packard can issue an RPC to an MVS-based server developed by using the IBM implementation of DCE. The MVS DCE server can access IMS or DB2 databases as part of the processing and send a response back to the DCE client. The DCE Security and Directory Services will be used in this heterogeneous environment to locate the server and to authenticate/authorize the RPC.

Figure 9.4 IBM's Open Distributed Computing

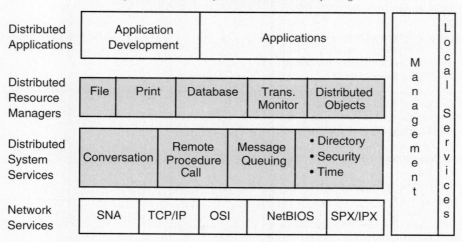

Legend: Shaded area shows the middleware

Conversational paradigm between clients and servers is supported through the Advanced Program-to-Program Communications (APPC). In conversational paradigm, client and server processes establish a dialog in which the context is maintained by both processes. APPC, a central offering in IBM's System Application Architecture (SAA), provides the application programming interfaces (APIs) for applications to use the LU6.2 protocol for distributed applications. Most of the literature does not differentiate between LU6.2 and APPC. We will use the term APPC/LU6.2 when there is no need to differentiate between the two. Examples of APPC support in IBM environments are APPC/SNA, APPC/PC, and APPC/MVS. Other vendors have also implemented APPC/LU6.2 as part of their network offering. Examples are DEC/APPC on DECNet, APPC/SUN for SUN Microsystems TCP/IP networks, Novell's Netware APPC for Novell LANs, and MAC/APPC for Apple networks. The SNA AnyNet feature allows APPC/LU6.2 to be transported over TCP/IP networks. APPC/LU6.2 is also used in DRDA. Thus to install a DRDA gateway, an LU6.2 connection is needed. See Chapter 11 for a brief review of APPC/LU6.2.

Message-queuing paradigm is supported through the IBM Message Queuing product line (i.e., MQSeries). Message queuing has been used in IBM mainframe environments for a long time for IMS and CICS transaction managers. For distributed environments, a Message Queuing Interface (MQI) has been developed to support client processes on one platform (e.g., a PS2) to submit requests for a server process on another processor (e.g., MVS). The client requests are stored in a queue and picked by the server processes for processing. We discussed the message-queuing paradigm and middleware in Chapter 3.

Security services provide the authentication and authorization services needed in a distributed environment. IBM's ODC intends to integrate and support the IBM RACF (Resource Access Control Facility) with the DCE Security. The overall objective is to provide a single signon for enterprisewide computing and an enterprise view of security administration and enforcement.

Directory and naming services are provided so that client processes can locate and establish connections with server processes located anywhere in an enterprise. IBM's ODC supports the DCE directory and naming services (i.e., X.500 Global Directory and Cell Directory).

Time services of IBM ODC are based on the OSF/DCE time services.

9.3.3 Distributed Resource Management

The Distributed Resource Management Services support services for distributed files, printers, databases, and transactions.

File Services provide access to data files in an IBM environment. ODC includes OSF DCE Distributed File System (Andrews), Sun Network File Services (NFS), and IBM's Distributed Data Management (DDM).

Print Services provide support for printing in a multivendor heterogeneous environment. ODC includes postscript printing (e.g., the ADOBE postscript interpreter) and Remote Print Manager for DOS. It is assumed that more printing in distributed environments will be done at LANs.

Database Services provide support for databases anywhere in an IBM environment. These services are of vital importance in providing access to IBM mainframe databases. The key components of these services are:

- **Distributed Relational Database Architecture (DRDA)** that specifies the protocols and conventions that govern the interactions between database clients and a database server. DRDA has become a de facto standard for access to DB2 databases. By using DRDA, clients from different DBMS vendors can access DB2 data. The access to DB2 is provided through a DRDA gateway that translates the different DBMS protocols to the DRDA protocol. DRDA gateways have become commercially available from a multitude of vendors to provide access to DB2 data. We have described DRDA in Chapter 5.

- **Information warehouse** support for accessing nonrelational databases through SQL. A variety of gateways are supported for translating SQL queries to target database formats. An example of such a gateway is Enterprise Data Access/SQL (EDA/SQL) from Information Builders, Inc. EDA/SQL allows a variety of desktop tools and applications to issue SQL calls against more than 35 relational as well as nonrelational databases that reside on LANs, UNIX machines and MVS. The translation of SQL to target databases is provided through "database drivers" that are installed at the database server machines. However, EDA/SQL uses proprietary APIs and exchange protocols—EDA/SQL clients interoperate only with EDA/SQL servers, and vice versa, unless the exchange protocols are shared through business partnerships. We discussed EDA/SQL in Chapter 5.

- **FTP/SQL (File Transfer Protocol/SQL)** for TCP/IP users on MVS. The standard FTP protocol on TCP/IP is restricted to transferring flat files only. Thus, if customer records from a relational database are to be downloaded to a PC, then an SQL extract program must be written to extract the records and store them into a flat file before using FTP to transfer the file. By using FTP/SQL, the SQL statements are issued at MVS, and the results are transferred by using FTP.

Transaction-Processing Services provide management of transactions in IBM environments. At present, MVS supports two very popular transaction processors: CICS (Customer Information Control System) and IMS/TM (Information Management System/Transaction Manager). These transaction processors have provided on-line transaction processing (OLTP) against IMS, DB2, and other MVS databases for a number of years. For IBM ODC, the key components of the Transaction Processing Services are:

- **IMS/Client Server (IMS/CS)** strategy was announced in 1993. The purpose of this strategy is to make IMS an "enterprise transaction server" for clients located at different sites in an organization. In particular, this strategy allows clients on PCs and UNIX machines to access IMS databases and transactions. The business significance of this strategy is to transition the large embedded base of corporate legacy databases to client/server environments. This strategy includes access to IMS transactions from:

- LU2 (IBM 3270 terminals). This is the original terminal host model supported by IMS since the early 1970s. Many client applications use "screen scrapers" that emulate 3270 terminal sessions from client applications.

- APPC clients residing typically on OS2, AIX, and MVS machines establish LU6.2 sessions with IMS transactions on MVS. Recall that APPC is an API for the LU6.2 protocol. APPC/LU6.2 provides a rich set of verbs for developing distributed applications.

- Clients that use TCP/IP Sockets for C/S interactions. For example, a UNIX client can use the TCP/IP Socket commands (e.g., send data, receive data) to exchange information from IMS transactions.

- DCE clients that issue DCE RPC calls. These calls are received by the DCE/RPC server on MVS that invokes IMS transactions.

- Object oriented clients that may issue OO calls (e.g., CORBA) to invoke IMS transactions. For example, IBM's CORBA compliant offering DSOM (Distributed System Object Model) is expected to interoperate with IMS transactions.

- **CICS** is also expected to follow a similar strategy as IMS/CS. Unlike IMS that has primarily been used on MVS mainframes, CICS is currently on UNIX as well as PC platforms. The considerations for making CICS into a a transaction manager are somewhat similar to IMS/CS and are not repeated here.

- **Encina** for distributed transaction processing. IBM has acquired Transarc, the company that develops and markets the Encina distributed transaction processing system. Due to this acquisition, Encina, described in Chapter 6, is expected to play a key role in IBM's distributed transaction processing strategy.

Distributed-Object Services are an important part of ODC and are expected to be part of ODC as it evolves. In particular, DSOM (Distributed Systems Object Management), IBM's CORBA-compliant product is targeted for ODC. We have discussed CORBA in Chapter 7.

9.3.4 Other Open Distributed Computing Services

So far, we have focussed on the middleware of IBM's ODC. Let us briefly review the other ODC Services shown in Figure 9.4.

Local Services provide the operating system and other local programming interfaces.The services include standard programming languages such as C, COBOL, Fortran, ADA and SQL. More importantly, these services include standard interface specifications such as the IEEE Portable Operating System Interface (POSIX) and the X/Open Portability Guides (XPGs). In particular, MVS OpenEdition is IBM's direction to conform to these standard interfaces. Conceptually, OpenEdition allows MVS to appear as a "UNIX-like" machine.

Management Services include network management and distributed-application management tools (e.g., Netview/6000). In particular, a framework "SystemView" has been introduced for providing management services in heterogeneous multivendor environments.

Network Services provide transport and interconnectivity services over a wide range of communications networks. These services include SNA, TCP/IP, OSI, NetBIOS LANs and Novell SPX/IPX LANs. In particular, the network services include the SNA Anynet feature that allows LU6.2/APPC to be transported over TCP/IP networks and supports TCP/IP Sockets over SNA networks. This has several benefits. First, the mainframe applications can be accessed on TCP/IP networks. Second, this provides a migration path from SNA to TCP/IP networks. Finally, applications written for TCP/IP Sockets can be used over SNA networks. The tutorial in Chapter 11 describes network technologies and architectures and reviews many of these topics. Interested readers should review Chapter 11.

Distributed applications are the business-aware databases, programs, and presentations that are developed by using ODC. These applications use APIs provided by the Distributed System Services and Distributed Resource Management described in Sections 9.3.2 and 9.3.3, respectively. The Distributed Application Development Services enable development of distributed applications. ODC includes IBM's AD/Cycle for distributed application development.

ODC is evolving and will include new services that fit the overall framework.

9.3.5   Summary of IBM's Open Distributed Computing (ODC)

In summary, ODC integrates OSF/DCE with earlier IBM architectures such as SAA. Specifically, it includes support for DCE RPCs, DRDA, IMS/CS, distributed transaction processing through Encina, and CORBA. ODC also includes support for non-SNA networks such as TCP/IP and Novell SPX/IPX. MVS OpenEdition makes MVS look like a UNIX machine and the emphasis on OSF/DCE hides many lower level details (the developers and users are concerned with DCE clients and servers that are running on PCs, UNIX and MVS machines).

Recall that the main goal of ODC is to establish MVS mainframe as an enterprisewide server for corporate databases and applications. The emphasis is on coexistence and interoperability with non-IBM computing environments while positioning MVS as an enterprisewide server [Kramer 1995, Ricciuti 1994]. There are several potential reasons why MVS mainframes are good candidates for corporate servers. Some of the main reasons are:

- Most of the corporate data resides on MVS at the time of this writing. Since data and application migration/reengineering are expensive undertakings, it would be better to keep the data where it is by making MVS applications behave as servers.

- Administrative support (monitoring, tracing, debugging, backup/recovery) for MVS-based systems has matured over several years and is currently quite good (much better than for PC-based LANs).

- There is a tremendous reservoir of mainframe knowledge and experience that can be used effectively for developing and managing server applications for mainframe.

Opinions in the industry about the suitability of MVS as a server differ widely owing to the organizational politics, ease-of-use, and cost issues (see, for example, Ricciuti [1994],

Kramer [1995], Colosimo [1995], and Gartner Group Briefing: "Enterprise Client/Server: Can We Get There from Here?" July/August 1994).

Additional information about IBM's ODC can be obtained from IBM documents such as "An Introduction to the Open Blueprint" (GC326-0395) and "Open Blueprint Technical Overview" (GC23-3808). Documents are also available through the Internet (*http://www. torlab.com*).

9.4   Middleware State of the Practice

Different types of middleware are being used at present to support distributed applications in modern enterprises. Which type of middleware is used more frequently? Figure 9.5 attempts to answer this question by displaying the state of the practice in terms of a 0-to-10 scale (0 means not used at all, 10 means used heavily). We can make the following observations from this figure.

First, commonly used middleware includes primitive middleware such as terminal emulation, email, and file transfer; basic client/server middleware for remote-procedure call (RPC), queued messages, and remote-data access (RDA); and distributed-data management middleware such as database gateways for remote joins. In many cases, organizations pick and choose between these individual packages and "assemble" their own middleware environments to best suit their needs. For example, many organizations use terminal emulation, bulk data transfer, email, and remote SQL middleware (e.g., ODBC drivers).

Second, middleware environments such as OSF DCE, distributed-transaction processors (DTPs) such as Encina, and distributed-object environments such as CORBA are not widely state-of-the-practice at the time of this writing. The reasons for this vary. Basically, DCE and DTP may be too heavy for several organizations (recall that DCE and Encina are integrated environments that cannot be purchased/installed in pieces). Distributed object middleware such as CORBA and Microsoft ActiveX are relatively new at present and are not widely deployed/practiced.

Third, midddleware for emerging applications is becoming very popular. For example, Web middleware is gaining popularity dramatically for corporate information systems. Middleware for mobile computing, groupware, distributed multimedia, and legacy system integration is also evolving.

Finally, compound middleware environments that integrate diverse middleware packages into a single framework are gaining popularity somewhat slowly. For example, IBM's Open Distributed Computing (ODC) and Digital's Forte are used very rarely at present. Recall that IBM's ODC combines DCE, DDM, DTP, CORBA, and many other middleware environments and services. It seems that most companies at present pick and choose different middleware packages from different vendors for different applications instead of buying into a single-vendor compound middleware environment.

We should note that Figure 9.5 is not based on any formal analysis. Instead, it uses our general knowledge of the industry and numerous literature surveys. This picture will change with time.

9.5   Middleware State of the Market

Off-the-shelf middleware software is currently available from a very large number of providers. According to an International Data Corp. report, total 1995 revenues due to middleware

Figure 9.5 Middleware Current State of Practice

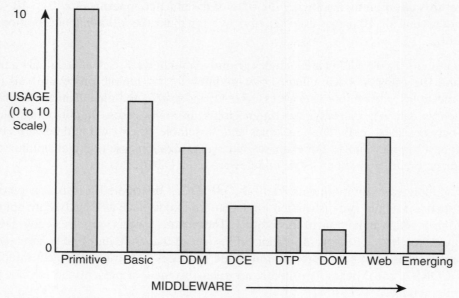

Legend:
  • Primitive middleware (e.g., terminal emulation, file transfer, email)
  • Basic C/S middleware (e.g., RPCs, MOM, RDA)
  • DCE (Open Software Foundation's DCE)
  • DDM (Distributed data management middleware)
  • DTP (Distributed transaction processing middleware)
  • DOM (Distributed object middleware such as CORBA, ActiveX)
  • Web (Web middleware for "serious" business applications)
  • Emerging middleware (e.g., mobile computing, distributed multimedia, groupware, and legacy system integration)

were $1 billion. For example, the distributed-data management middleware such as remote SQL gateways is available from database vendors such as Oracle, Sybase, Informix, and IBM. Distributed-transaction processing middleware is available from companies such as IBM, Transarc, and AT&T. Open Software Foundation's DCE is currently supported by vendors such as IBM, HP, and Sun. A large number of vendors at present are beginning to provide distributed-object middleware such as CORBA, and Microsoft is marketing its ActiveX. Middleware for Web is being provided by relatively new companies such as Netscape, many large organizations such as Microsoft and IBM, and almost innumerable small enterprising firms.

Figure 9.6 displays the interrelationships among the commercially available middleware environments. Table 9.4 shows the type of middleware that is available and being used for different classes of applications. This picture may change with time. We can make the following observations about the current state of the market for middleware:

- OSF DCE provides the core capabilities that are currently being used in many other higher-level middleware products. For example, Encina is built on top of DCE, and implementation of CORBA over DCE is being considered by many CORBA vendors.

- OSF DCE does not directly support databases (no RDA support). However, database support over DCE is available through distributed-transaction managers such as Encina. In addition, some standalone products such as the Open Horizon DCE/Connect are commercially available for database support through ODBC over DCE RPC.

Figure 9.6 Interrelationships among Middleware

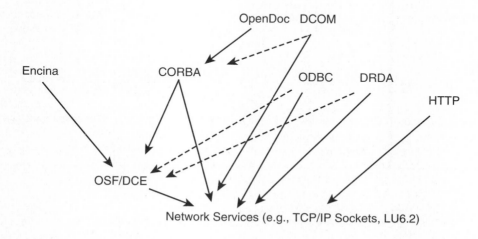

- CORBA is a very powerful and important specification for distributed-object-oriented applications. However, CORBA 1.2 did not specify all services needed (e.g., security) and thus faces interoperability problems. CORBA 2.0 is attempting to address this problem by defining inter-ORB protocols (IOPs) for interoperability of object request brokers. Two IOPs are currently being specified—one for interoperability of ORBS using the TCP/IP Sockets and the other for interoperability of ORBs using DCE RPCs. Some vendors will build CORBA on top of DCE, some will choose TCP/IP Sockets, and some will use both.

- The compound-document standards such as OLE and OpenDoc are being built on top of object-oriented middleware (OpenDoc uses CORBA and OLE uses COM). OLE is being positioned by Microsoft for distributed-object computing.

- IBM's Open Distributed Computing (ODC) strategy includes most of the emerging technologies (e.g., OSF DCE, CORBA, DRDA).

TABLE 9.4 USAGE OF MIDDLEWARE—A SUMMARY

TYPE / SIZE	Operational Support/ OLTP	Decision Support/ Retrieval	Real Time
Group/departmental	• C/S transaction processing is still evolving	Basic C/S middleware (RPC, RDA) very mature • OO is emerging • Groupware is mature	Multimedia technology is maturing
Enterprisewide	C/S not mature at present	C/S is possible, but not mature • Groupware is maturing • Web over Intranets is becoming popular	Middleware not commercially available
Inter-enterprise	C/S not mature • Web technology maturing	• Web technology for document-centric work	Middleware not available

9.6   State of the Art: General Trends

As businesses continue to face the pressures of flexibility, quick turnarounds, and efficiency, the need to provide flexible and portable applications for inter- as well as intraenterprise work will grow. The need for middleware to quickly enable such applications will also grow accordingly. The following general trends in client/server middleware are worth noting [Bernstein 1996, Lewis 1995, Elliot 1995]:

- Middleware will continue to become more sophisticated by extending the scope of local services to distributed environments so that users and applications can perform the same actions across networks that are typically performed on local machines. For example, the current research in distributed operating systems is attempting to provide an operating system across networks.

- Middleware for new application areas will emerge on an as needed basis. For example, as "intelligent agents (IAs)" become more popular, the need for middleware for IAs will grow. See the sidebar "Middleware for Intelligent Agents."

- Standards will play an important role, because without standards each new middleware component will add more complexity. Consortia such as X/Open and Object Management Group that are attempting to introduce standards into industrial products will play a significant role.

- As middleware becomes more popular, some middleware services will shift down to database managers, network services and operating systems. This will reduce the number of separate middleware products.

- More off-the-shelf compound middleware environments such as IBM's ODC will emerge.

- The notion of client/server paradigm could be outdated, owing to the emergence of many new situations in which processes cooperate with each other as peers without any clients or servers. The object-oriented systems, especially CORBA, are moving in this direction.

- The trend toward higher-level object-oriented services and protocols which are independent of the underlying network architectures will continue. The notion of object-oriented message systems will continue to be increasingly popular. In these systems, all clients and servers will be treated as objects which exchange messages. The format of the messages will be independent of the location of the objects.

- More off-the-shelf software will become available for "zero-programming" client/server applications. At present, many decision-support applications which access remotely located SQL databases without any programming are state-of-the-market and practice. Other off-the-shelf client/server applications in manufacturing, finance, and human-resource management are also becoming available from database vendors. This trend will continue.

- The issue of high-level APIs will gain more importance as more middleware layers are introduced with a proliferation of APIs. High-level APIs should give a programmer a uniform object invocation for accessing objects. The invocation method should internally issue an RPC, RDA or any other call.

- The middleware will continue an effort to provide transparency at the following levels (the first two levels are already achievable):
  - End-user transparency; i.e. the end user does not know what parts of an application are running where
  - Developer transparency; i.e., the developers do not have to know where their code will run (e.g., code portability)
  - Manager transparency; i.e., the managers do not have to know if one system or many systems need to be managed

Middleware for Intelligent Agents

Intelligent agents (IAs), also known as Virtual Agents and Knowbots, are intelligent software entities that simulate the behavior of "capable" human agents such as an experienced travel agent or an insurance agent. IAs have many potential applications in Internet because of the large volume of information available through Internet that needs to be organized and presented in an organized manner. An example of an IA is a software entity that searches the Internet for a particular topic (e.g., pottery in ancient Egypt) and extracts, organizes and presents it in a suitable format. Another example is an intelligent agent that makes travel arrangements (e.g., make reservations, purchase tickets) for a trip within time and money constraints. Many research prototypes at present are directed toward making the Internet intelligent by using IAs.

The key characteristics of Intelligent Agents are:

- Knowledge representation (rules, semantic networks)

- Learning capabilities (acquire new knowledge)

- Goal specification and reasoning (backward/forward reasoning)

- Interaction with environment (e.g., network, databases)

- Interact with other agents (human or software)

- Object orientation (each IA is an object)

- Deal with unexpected situations

- Use mobile code where needed (e.g., Java)

Middleware for IAs, not commercially available as we go to press, must provide a comprehensive set of services such as collaboration services between agents, domain knowledge, intelligent discovery engines, and pattern recognition algorithms. An example of such a middleware is the InfloSleuth Project at MCC [Woelk 1995]. The middleware itself can be rule-based, i.e., you specify the rules to be used by the middleware to perform certain actions. For example, NEONet (http://www.neonsoft.com) reads the incoming message and uses rules to determine what to do with the message (e.g., find the most appropriate destination, return it back to the sender, etc.).

Sources:

- Woelk, et al., "Uncovering the Next Generation of Active Objects," *Object Magazine*, July./August 1995, pp. 33–40

- *IEEE Expert,* August 1995 Special Issue on Intelligent Internet Services (this issue also contains a large number of references on this topic).

- *Communications of the ACM,* 37(7), 1994, is a Special Issue on Intelligent Agents

- *Object Magazine,* July./August 1995, has a special section on Intelligent Agents.

A potential future scenario is the three-tiered architecture shown in Figure 9.7. In this scenario, the Web browsers are used as the primary entry point for users to access all resources. Web middleware is used as a front end to access Web resources over the public Internet or private Internet (Intranet). The middle tier will house Web resources, i.e. the databases and the programs that can be directly accessed/invoked from Web clients (e.g., HTML pages, Java applets). It appears that Web browsers are increasing their capabilities to directly access more and more resources (e.g., invoking CORBA calls from Web browsers). The middle tier will consequently grow, as more databases and applications can be directly accessed from the Web browsers.

Figure 9.7 A Potential Future Scenario—High-Level View

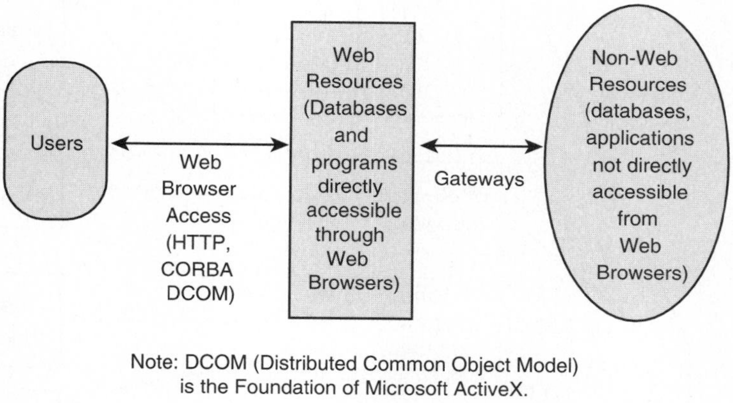

Note: DCOM (Distributed Common Object Model)
is the Foundation of Microsoft ActiveX.

The middle tier will also serve as a gateway to the back-end non-Web (mostly legacy) resources. The back-end non-Web resources are accessed from the middle tier by using the traditional middleware such as remote SQL, screen scrapers, and file transfers. As the back-end resources become more OO (either through object wrappers or migration), the communication between the middle and third tier can increasingly use the distributed-object model. The middle tier can serve as a transition gateway to gradually migrate the legacy resources to employ the distributed-object middleware. This marriage of object orientation with the Web is a very promising direction that is being pursued jointly by the OMG and WWW Consortium. A more detailed view is presented in Figure 9.8.

9.7 Concluding Comments

This book has attempted to scan and synthesize the wide range of middleware products and analyze the interrelationships among the key players. Earlier chapters discussed individual middleware services such as RPC, MOM, RDA, security, directory services, etc. We later discussed "middleware environments" such as DCE, DTP, and CORBA. We also discussed emerging middleware for the World Wide Web, mobile computing, groupware, distributed multimedia, and legacy data access.

Figure 9.8 Potential Future Scenario—Detailed View

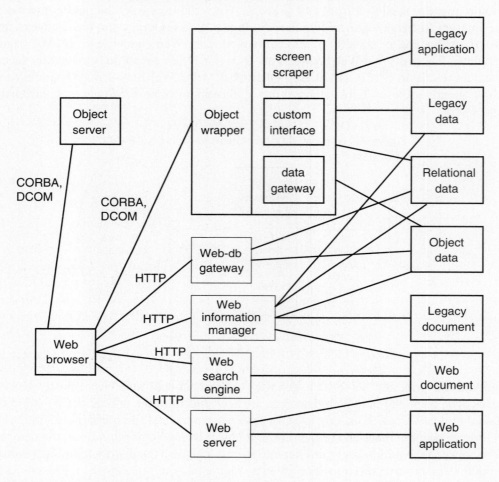

In this chapter we discussed IBM's ODC, which attempts to synthesize most of the middleware discussed in this book into a single framework. Similar attempts to synthesize several middleware products have been announced by other organizations such as Digital Equipment Corporation (DEC) and Information Builders Incorporated. DEC-initiated Forte[1] is a complete environment for distributed applications. It provides services at different levels in a fashion similar to IBM's ODC; i.e., the basic distributed computing services include DCE services, message queuing, and transaction messaging; and the enabling services include DEC's ObjectBroker, DEC's DB Integrator for distributed-data access, and distributed-trans-

---

1. Forte is actually a separate company at present with strong ties, affiliations, and strategic partnership with DEC.

action management. Information Builders Incorporated is extending its EDA/SQL middleware to include DCE, ODBC, and CORBA services. It is expected that other vendors will also start providing the distributed computing infrastructure as a single package that will typically include Web, SQL middleware, MOM, CORBA, and distributed-transaction processing capabilities.

The key idea is that middleware should be chosen based on business drivers. In particular, the type of current and future applications to be supported by the enterprise must be the key determining factor. In other words, if your applications do not need distributed-object support, then there is no reason to introduce CORBA into your IT infrastructure, even if CORBA is very popular. We have introduced a simple framework in this chapter to help you analyze and select appropriate middleware.

9.8   Case Study: XYZCorp Synthesis of IT Infrastructure Architecture

XYZCorp wants to synthesize the results of the various projects into a cohesive IT infrastructure architecture. This architecture should serve as the platform for all the services and applications to be provided by XYZCorp. In particular, it should show how the networking services, the middleware components, and other services will support the growing number of Web-based OO applications that will also utilize mobile computing and groupware. You have been asked to:

- Analyze the various requirements and give a final assessment of different middleware technologies for XYZCorp. Specifically, you should assess the middleware technologies that have been studied by the earlier projects (e.g., DCE, CORBA, Web, SQL middleware, C/S transaction processing) in terms of their promises, pitfalls, and application fit (i.e., what type of applications are best supported by these middleware types). You should present this information as a table.

- Show an overall architecture that ties the chosen middleware together.

- Show the sites where the servers (Web servers, Group servers, database servers, etc.) will be housed and the protocols to be used by each of these servers.

- Show the protocol "stack" at each client that will be needed to use these services.

- Describe an approach to select vendor products to support this architecture.

Hints about the Case Study:

The discussion in Section 9.2 is relevant to this case study and should be reviewed before proceeding.

Table 9.2 can be used to analyze the various requirements, and Table 9.5 can be used to evaluate the various middleware technologies we have studied so far. It is important to identify the specific applications and services for which the middleware will be used. Without a clear need, middleware adds unnecessary cost and performance overhead.

Figure 9.9 shows the overall IT infrastructure architecture that ties in the chosen middleware with network services. We have shown a few components for the purpose of illustration. The sites where the servers (Web servers, group servers, database servers, etc.) will be housed and the protocols to be used by each of these servers are also suggested. The protocol "stack" at each client is also shown.

After the overall architecture has been established, the next step is to select the specific vendor products that will support this architecture. Table 9.3 can be used for this purpose.

9.9　　Problems and Exercises

1. Use the framework suggested in this chapter to compare and contrast at least two vendor middleware products.

2. Do you think that the framework needs to be extended? How?

3. Read the article by Ted Lewis [1995] and discuss how his analysis differs from the one presented in this chapter.

4. Read the article by Ricciuti [1994] and discuss whether you agree or disagree with his analysis of IBM's ODC.

TABLE 9.5 MIDDLEWARE SELECTION

Middleware	Strengths	Weaknesses	XYZCorp Applications and Services	Final Decision (Include/ Exclude)
OSF DCE				
SQL middleware (e.g., ODBC)				
Web middleware				
C/S transaction-processing middleware				
Groupware (email, EDI workflows ...)				
CORBA				
OLE				
Mobile computing middleware				
Distributed-multi-media middleware				
Legacy access middleware				

Figure 9.9 XYZCorp IT Infrastructure Architecture

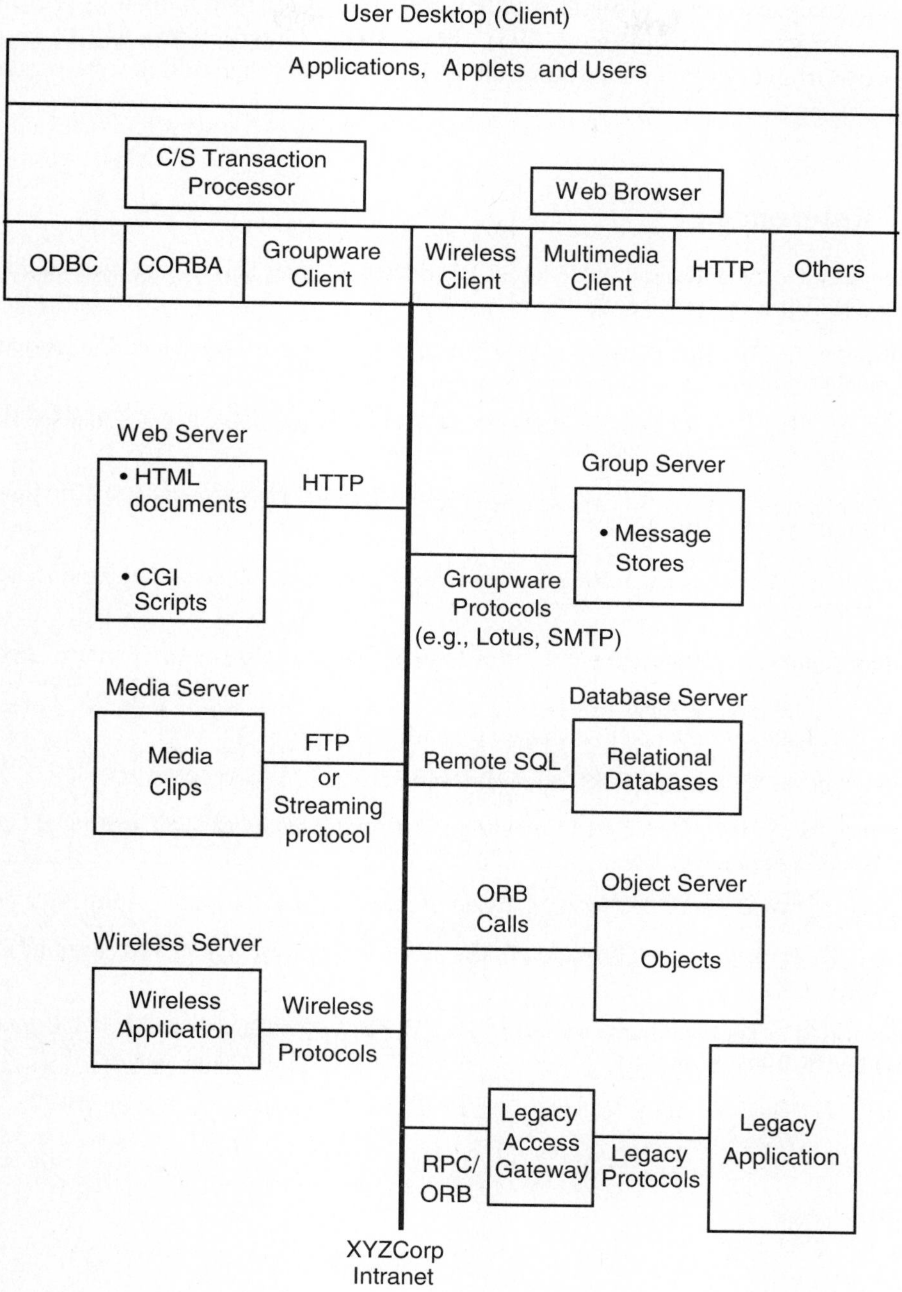

User Desktop (Client)

9.10   Additional Information

Attempts to analyze the ever-growing middleware products are beginning to appear in the literature (see for example, Colosimo [1995], Elliot [1995], Guteri [1995], and Lewis [1995]. The book by Orfali [1994] contains many analysis of the individual middleware products discussed in this book.

9.11   References

Bernstein, P., "Middleware: A Model for Distributed Systems Services," *Communications of ACM,* February 1996, pp. 86–98.

Colosimo, J., "The Role of IBM's Open Blueprint Approach in Distributed Computing," Technical Forum, *IBM System Journal,* Vol. 34, No. 1 (1995), pp. 138–141.

Elliot, B., "Battle of the Desktop APIs," *Business Communications Review,* January 1995, pp. 35–39.

Gartner Group Briefing: "Enterprise Client/Server: Can We Get There from Here?" July/August 1994.

Guteri, F., "Mainframes Are Breaking out of the Glasshouse," *Datamation,* June 15, 1995, pp. 34–37.

IBM Programming Announcement, "IBM System Open and Distributed Strategy," February 9, 1993.

IBM Manual, "Introduction to the Open Blueprint," GC326-0395, 1994.

IBM Manual, "Open Blueprint Technical Overview," GC23-3808, 1994.

Kramer, M., "IBM's Distributed Computing Strategy," *Seybold Group Distributed Computing Monitor,* September 1995.

Lewis, T., "Where Is Client/Server Software Headed?" *IEEE Computer,* April 1995, pp. 41–48.

Orfali, R., Harkey, D., and Edwards, J., *Client/Server Survival Guide,* Van Nostrand Reinholt, 1994.

Riccuiti, M., "The Mainframe as Server: Is IBM Totally Bonkers–or Brilliant?" *Datamation,* May 15, 1994, pp. 61–64.

Snell, N., "The New MVS: Tuned to Serve?" *Datamation,* July 15, 1992, pp.76–77.

PART

TUTORIALS ON SPECIAL TOPICS

III

Chapter 10: Object-Oriented Concepts and Technologies—A Tutorial
Chapter 11: Network Technologies and Architectures—A Tutorial

10

Object-Oriented Concepts and Technologies— A Tutorial

429

10.1   Introduction

At present, we are in the midst of object orientation (OO), with names like OO programming, OO design, OO databases, OO user interfaces, and so on. Most new software being developed at present and in the future will use some level of OO (at least in the user interface displays). The purpose of this short tutorial is to give you the basic OO concepts and introduce you to the core OO technologies that are of relevance to object-oriented client/server Internet environments. In particular, our objective is to answer questions such as the following:

- What are the underlying object concepts? (Section 10.2)
- What exactly is object orientation and how does it differ from object-based systems? (Section 10.3)
- How are OO concepts used in designing user interfaces? (Section 10.4)
- What is object-oriented design, and what type of OO programming languages are available to implement these designs? (Section 10.5)
- What are object-oriented databases, and how do they differ from the current genre of relational databases? (Section 10.6)

10.2   Basic Object Concepts

The basic object concepts comprise of object, message, class, and inheritance (see the sidebar "Key Object-Oriented Concepts"). Let us use an example of cars to quickly illustrate these concepts (programming-type details can wait).

- A Buick car is an **object**. The attributes of this object are model, year, color, etc. The behavior of a car is given by start, stop, go-left, go-right, forward, reverse, etc. These are the **methods** of the object.
- Turning the ignition key and putting the car in reverse gear represent the **messages** which invoke the methods of start and reverse, respectively.
- All cars have similar properties. For example, Buicks, Toyotas, and Hondas have similar properties. Car can be used to represent the common properties of automobiles. Car is a **class**. Buicks, Toyotas, Hondas, and so on are *instances* of class car.
- Classes can *inherit* common properties from other classes. For example, a vehicle class can be used to represent the common properties of classes such as cars, trucks, buses, and taxis. Vehicle is the *superclass* from which *subclasses* such as cars, taxis, trucks, and buses inherit common attributes (model, year, color) and methods (start, stop, go-left, go-right, forward, reverse). However, some properties are unique to each subclass and are not inherited (e.g., taxis have meters).

These key concepts can be of great value in developing reusable and flexible software systems. Let us describe these concepts in more detail.

Key Object-Oriented Concepts

What Are the Basic Object Concepts?

Object: A software object is a piece of data surrounded by code (i.e., the data can only be accessed through code). This code is known as *methods* of an object. The data has certain *attributes* (e.g., name, address, age), and the methods are used to operate on these attributes.

Messages. Objects communicate with each other through messages. A message invokes a method of the target object (the object internals are known to the method and not to the object).

Classes: A collection of like objects makes up a class. A class acts as a template for similar objects (e.g., a class representing all Chevrolets). An object is an instance of a class.

Inheritance: Objects can inherit properties from other objects. Technically, inheritance allows you to create subclasses from parent classes. Subclasses inherit properties from parent classes. Subclasses can inherit multiple properties from multiple parent classes.

What Is Object Orientation?

The following classic definition of object orientation is given by Wegner [1987]:

Object oriented = objects + classes + inheritance

A more generalized definition, more suitable for distributed systems, is given by Nicol [1993]:

Object oriented = encapsulation + abstraction + polymorphism

Encapsulation: The restriction of access to the object state via a well-defined interface (the operations). This involves a combination of two aspects: the grouping of object state and operation, and data hiding.

Abstraction: The ability to group associated entities according to common properties; for example, the set of instances belonging to a class.

Polymorphism: The ability of abstractions to overlap and intersect. A popular form of polymorphism is inclusion polymorphism, in which operations on a given type are also applicable to its subtype (for example, start a printer will start all types of printers). Inclusion polymorphism is often implemented via an inheritance mechanism.

Wegner, P., "Dimensions of Object-Based Language Design," *SIGPlan Notices,* Vol. 22, No. 12 (December 1987), pp. 168–182.

Nicol, J., et al., "Object Orientation in Heterogeneous Distributed Computing Systems," *IEEE Computer,* June 1993, pp. 57–67.

10.2.1   Object: The Basic Building Block

An object, according to Webster's dictionary, is something mental or physical toward which thought, feeling, or action is directed. In computing, an object is something that can be represented in computer memory. Examples of objects are a program variable, a robot, a car, an employee, a factory, and a company. Different objects can be defined in different problem areas. In distributed computing, for example, each file, printer, spreadsheet, program, user, communication line, workstation, and device can be viewed as an object.

Specifically, ***software objects*** *are data guarded by a protective layer of code.* Figure 10.1 shows the conceptual view of a customer object that is the key to understanding object concepts. Basically, an object is represented by at least two properties:

- Attributes
- Methods

The data represents the ***attributes*** of the object, and the code that surrounds the data represents the ***methods*** of the object. Methods are the only way any outsider can interact with the object (you cannot directly view or update customer balance without invoking the "Get-Balance-Due" or "Update-Customer" methods). Thus the outside world does not know how the customer data is internally stored (this leads to information hiding).

Figure 10.1 Conceptual View of a Customer Object

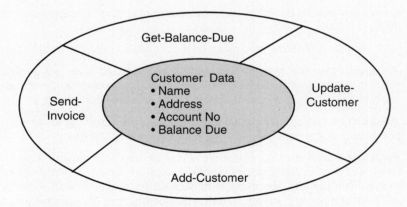

Customer object is customer data surrounded by code (methods)
- The attributes of the customer object are name, address, account no, balance due
- The methods associated with the customer object are Add-Customer,
  Update-Customer, Get-Balance-Due, and Send-Invoice.

Attributes uniquely identify an object. For example, attributes of an employee object are name, social security number, etc. A method shows the object behavior (what it can do or what can be done to it) and contains the code (a list of detailed instructions) that define how the method will respond when invoked. A method hides the implementation details from the users of an object. A method typically receives a message, performs some operations, and sends the response back. An object essentially is a collection of attributes and the valid methods that manipulate the data elements.

Objects can represent small entities such as an icon on a display terminal, or large business entities, such as customers. For example, consider the following object definitions:

1. Object Name = invoice
   Attributes = customer name, items purchased, price per item, total invoice, etc.
   Methods = prepare, send, review status, update status

2. Object Name = employee
   Attributes = employee name, employee address, employee pay
   Methods = add employee, retrieve employee, update employee

3. Object Name = workstation
   Attributes = workstation type, vendor name, OS used, assigned to, etc.
   Methods = view, reassign, change operating system

4. Object Name = supplier
   Attributes = supplier name, address, items supplied, cost per item
   Methods = view, update items supplied, update item cost

An object can be defined in a program or in a database stored on a permanent (persistent) medium such as disks. The objects in a database are referred to as *persistent* and the ones in a program storage are referred to as *nonpersistent*. The data access is the same whether the objects are nonpersistent or persistent.

10.2.2 Messages: Activating Objects

Objects interact with each other through *messages*. These messages invoke particular methods. A message is simply the name of an object followed by the name of an appropriate method. In addition, the message may contain a set of parameters that the invoked method needs. Figure 10.2 illustrates two messages sent to the customer object—one with parameters, the other without. The "send sales material to customer Sam" message does not have a parameter. However, the "get balance due for customer Joe" does have a parameter (date of 02/02/96). We are at present not following any programming-language syntax to describe these messages (if you have not guessed, different programming languages use different syntaxes).

Figure 10.2 Messages to Customer Object

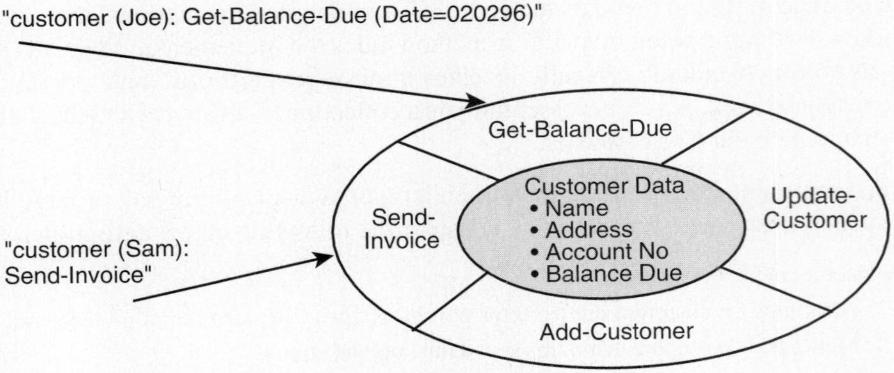

"customer (Joe): Get-Balance-Due (Date=020296)"

"customer (Sam):
Send-Invoice"

Each method of an object knows the list of messages it can respond to and how it will respond to each. The object that receives the message is responsible for providing the code that is needed for the invoked object. The receiver should also advertise its methods and the parameters to be invoked for each method so that the outside world can take full advantage of objects. In distributed systems, the advertised methods are known as interfaces and are typically defined by using *interface definition languages (IDLs).* The sender of the message is responsible for sending the appropriate message and processing the response, including error codes, status codes, etc. In particular, the sender should know that the way a receiver object responds to a message may be affected by the value of its attributes.

10.2.3   Classes

A *class* is a template which represents the properties that are common among similar objects. The basic purpose of class is to define a particular type of object. For example, the class employee can be used to represent the common properties of all company employees. The common properties include attributes such as name, address, employee ID, grade, pay scale, etc. and methods such as view, update, terminate, etc. So, if in a programming system you have identified object types such as employees, customers, and products, then you will define three classes to correspond to these object types. Each class will define the properties of each object type.

The objects belonging to a particular class are known as *instances* of that class. For example, the objects Joe Smith, Harry Kline, and Pat Hemsath are instances of the class employee. Once you have created a class, you can create any number of instances of each class (object-oriented programming languages provide statements to create instances). The instances contain the information that makes them unique. For example, the object instance of Joe Smith will have information unique to Joe Smith.

From a programming point of view, a class is similar to a structure that shows the layout of, say, an employee. Objects are instantiations or initializations of the structure to represent different employees.

10.2.4 Inheritance

Classes can be defined independently of each other. For example, the employee, customer, and product classes can be defined independently of each other. However, classes can *inherit* common properties from other classes. The properties to be inherited can be attributes as well as methods. A class hierarchy can be constructed where lower-level classes (*subclasses*) inherit the properties from higher-level classes (*superclass*). Figure 10.3 illustrates a class hierarchy. We can set up a class hierarchy for our employee class with subclasses such as managers, technical support, administrative support, consultants, visiting residents, and part-time staff.

A subclass can possess unique (specialized) properties which are not inherited from any class. For example, the resident visitor object has a predefined termination date (some others may also have a predefined termination date but they never know!). Inheritance comes in two flavors: single inheritance, in which an object can only inherit from one class, and multiple inheritance, in which an object can inherit from many classes. Multiple inheritance allows creation of new objects from existing objects. Inheritance is based on the "is-a" relationship in artificial intelligence (see Figure 10.3).

10.3 Object Based versus Object Orientation

The basic object concepts can be used to represent powerful programming systems. An object-based system is defined as follows [Taylor 1994]:

> *Object based* = objects + classes

For example, an object-based programming language supports objects and classes as a language feature but does not support the concept of inheritance. ADA and Modula-2 are examples. Object-based concepts are quite general and can be found in application programs that existed before object technologies became fashionable. For example, many good structured programs developed in the 1970s decomposed each application into modules (i.e., objects), where each module hid the internal information and had well-defined procedures that could be invoked from other modules. In addition, many such programs used templates of data definitions which were stored in libraries and used by different programs (this is somewhat similar to classes). Thus many programs could claim to be object based.

Our interest is in *object-oriented* systems that go beyond object-based systems. The following widely accepted definition of object orientation is given by Wegner [1987]:

> *Object oriented* = objects + classes + inheritance

Figure 10.3 Class Hierarchies

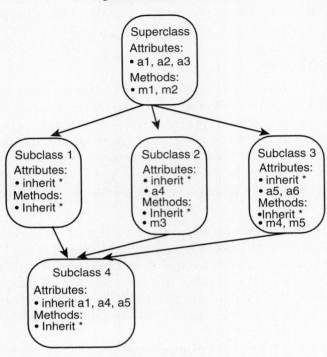

Notes:
1. The superclass defines the attributes a1, a2, a3 and the methods m1, m2 which are inherited by all immediate subclasses (and objects) in this system. "Inherit *" means that all properties of a superclass are inherited. If these properties are changed in the super-class, then all other classes inherit these changes.
2. The subclass 1 inherits all properties (methods and attributes) from the superclass. It does not define any of its own properties.
3. The subclass 2 inherits all properties (methods and attributes) from the superclass. In addition, it defines its own properties (attribute a4 and method m3).
4. The subclass 3 inherits all properties (methods and attributes) from the superclass. In addition, it defines its own properties (attributes a5, a6 and methods m4, m5).
5. The subclass 4 inherits attributes and methods from different subclasses. This is an example of multiple inheritance.

Source: Umar [1993].

Thus the object-oriented programming languages (OOPLs) support inheritance. OOPLs support classes, objects, methods, messages, and inheritance (note that methods and messages are implicit in this definition). This definition works very well for programming-language design. However, it is not well suited to distributed systems, where objects could be stored on different machines in different formats. A more generalized definition, more suitable for distributed systems, is given by Nicol [1993]:

Object oriented = encapsulation + abstraction + polymorphism

Let us review the three ingredients of this definition of OO. As we will see, it is quite similar to the Wegner's definition, albeit more general.

10.3.1 Abstraction

Abstraction focuses on the outside view of an object, i.e., how it will appear to the outside world. The following definition of abstraction has been given by Booch [1994]:

> An abstraction denotes the essential characteristics of an object that distinguish it from all other kinds of objects and thus provide crisply defined conceptual boundaries, relative to the perspective of the viewer.

For example, in an inventory-control system of a grocery store, you may abstract different categories of food items into different objects (e.g., eggs, fruits, frozen foods, and juices are identified as different objects). This abstraction is based on the observation that these food items have different characteristics that distinguish them from one another. For each object, you can assign the necessary attributes and methods that outsiders (e.g., the store manager) need to know. This is one abstraction. Another abstraction may decompose the frozen foods and fruits to smaller objects.

Thus, abstraction allows us to group associated entities according to common properties—for example, the set of instances belonging to a class. Abstraction represents the object properties without attention to implementation details. Methods as well as messages support abstraction by focusing on the outside view of an object.

10.3.2 Encapsulation (Information Hiding)

Encapsulation, also known as information hiding, prevents the clients from seeing the internals of an object. Encapsulation complements abstraction—encapsulation focuses on hiding the internals while abstraction focuses on presenting an external view. Encapsulation has been defined by Booch [1994] as follows:

> Encapsulation is the process of hiding all of the details of an object that do not contribute to its essential characteristics.

Encapsulation as well as abstraction are important to the design of an OO system, especially when the objects can be at different sites. In particular, each object must have two parts: an interface and an implementation. The *interface* of an object only captures its external view (i.e., the object name, the method to be invoked, the parameters to be passed). The *implementation* of an object contains the mechanisms that achieve the desired behavior (i.e., the code for each method). The interface is also known as the *public part* of an object, and the implementation is known as the *private part*.

Interfaces are becoming a popular construct in modern programming languages. For example, Java supports an interface statement. The following segment shows an example of Java interface specification code:

```
interface customer { /* interface name is customer */
Operation create_cust (/*The operation is create_cust */
    char customer_info; /* input parameter */
    integer status ) /* output parameter */
Operation view_cust ( /*The operation is view_cust */
    char cust-id; /* input parameter is cust-id */
    char customer_info; /* output parameter 1*/
    integer status ) /* output parameter 2 */
}
```

In distributed systems, interfaces and implementations play an important role, because the interface definitions of an object are created by using an *interface definition language* (IDL) and stored in directories. These directories are accessed by remote objects to send messages to each other. Different type of IDLs are provided by different middleware packages, such as Open Software Foundation's Distributed Computing Environment (OSF DCE) and Object Management Group's Common Object Request Broker Architecture (OMG's CORBA). For example, the following IDL statements could be used to specify the interface for a customer object that supports three operations: create_customer, view_customer, and delete_customer (this IDL is a simplified version of actual IDLs):

```
interface customer /* interface name is customer */
Operation create_cust (/*The operation is create_cust */
    [in] char customer_info; /* input parameter */
    [out] integer status ) /* output parameter */
Operation view_cust ( /*The operation is view_cust */
    [in] char cust_id; /* input parameter is cust-id */
    [out] char customer_info; /* output parameter 1*/
    [out] integer status ) /* output parameter 2 */
Operation delete_cust (/*The operation is delete_cust */
    [in] char customer_info; /* input parameter */
    [out] integer status ) /* output parameter */
```

This interface definition is the result of an abstraction and shows the three operations (methods) and the parameters for each method. This interface restricts access to the customer object state via a well-defined interface that does not reveal any internal details about the customer object (i.e., information hiding). Encapsulation and abstraction lead to distinct borders, well-defined interfaces, and a protected internal representation.

10.3.3 Polymorphism

Polymorphism is a Greek term meaning "many forms." Polymorphism allows you to hide alternative procedures behind a common interface. Basically, you can use the same method name in more than one class. A popular form of polymorphism is inclusion polymorphism, in which operations on a given type are also applicable to its subtype (for example, start a printer will start all types of printers). Inclusion polymorphism is often implemented via an inheritance mechanism.

Polymorphism is defined as the quality or state of being able to assume different forms [Taylor 1994]. Polymorphism can be displayed in messages and/or objects. An example is send the same message, "delete," to different objects which respond to it differently. For example, some objects may completely erase the information, while the others may just flag it for erasure at a later stage.

Polymorphism is considered as one of the defining characteristics of object-oriented technology. It distinguishes object-oriented programming languages from more traditional programming. By allowing the same method name in different classes, you can use the same message (e.g., delete, print, draw) to get different results by simply pointing to a different class at run time. Thus polymorphism takes advantage of inheritance and "dynamic binding" (i.e., deciding at run time what object do you want to communicate with).

10.4   Object-Oriented User Interfaces

The user interfaces provide the "look and feel" for the services provided by an application. The user interfaces have been by far most influenced by object orientation. At present, almost all new applications provide user interfaces that are either *GUI* (graphical user interface) or *OOUI* (object-oriented user interface).

GUI provides graphic dialogues, menu bars, color, scroll boxes, pull-down and pop-up windows. GUI dialogs use the object/action model where users can select objects and then choose the actions to be performed on the selected objects. Most GUI dialogs at present are serial in nature (i.e., perform one operation at a time). GUIs are currently very popular and are used in Microsoft Windows 3.X and OSF Motif applications. In addition, the Web browsers use the GUI user interfaces.

OOUIs are highly iconic, object-oriented user interfaces to support multiple, variable tasks whose sequence cannot be predicted. Examples include multimedia-based training systems, executive and decision-support systems, and stockbroker workstations. OOUIs are supported by commercial products such as NextStep, OS/2 Workplace Shell, and Macintosh.

Although GUIs and OOUIs are very fashionable at present, we should not forget the non-GUI/OOUI clients that generate server requests with a minimal amount of human interaction. Examples of such clients are daemon programs, barcode readers, robots, automatic teller machines, cellular phones, fax machines, intelligent metering equipment, and automated testers.

Discussion of GUIs/OOUIs with numerous examples can be found in Orfali [1994].

10.5   Object-Oriented Design and Programming

Object-oriented systems are intended to maximize information hiding (through methods) and reusability (through inheritance). The following steps are used to design a system by using an object-oriented paradigm [Booch 1994, Booch 1986]:

- Decompose a given system in terms of objects and not the operations (functions) performed.

- For each object, identify the attributes and the methods. Make sure that the methods hide internal information.

- Develop an initial hierarchy of classes.

- Enforce reusability by inheriting attributes and methods from existing systems. Attempt to maximize inheritance.

- List the messages which invoke methods. These messages establish relationships between objects.

- Develop a prototype solution approach which maps each object into a module. Some of these modules may be implemented as program modules or as database objects (see Section 10.6 for a discussion of object-oriented databases).

- Evaluate and refine the design iteratively.

The object-oriented design produced by these steps is translated into code by using object-oriented or object-based programming languages. Object-based programming languages such as ADA and Modula support objects as a language feature but do not support the concept of inheritance. Our interest here is in the object-oriented programming languages (OOPLs) which support inheritance. OOPLs support classes, objects, methods, messages, and inheritance. Other properties supported by OOPL include abstraction, encapsulation, and polymorphism.

Several object-oriented programming languages have been introduced over the years. The first object-oriented language, Simula, was introduced in the 1960s. Since then, OOPLs have evolved as follows:

- Extensions of procedural languages to support inheritance and other features of OOP. Examples are C++ [Stroustrup 1986], Objective C [Pinsen 1991], and Object Pascal [Pascal 1989].

- Extensions of AI languages to include object-oriented concepts. Examples are Lisp extensions such as Loops and the Common Lisp Object System [Alpert 1990].

- Languages which are fundamentally based on object-oriented concepts and provide basic building blocks for object oriented systems. Eiffel [Meyer 1988], Smalltalk-80 [Goldberg 1995, 1989], and Java [Hoff 1996] are examples.

An early review of some of these and many other OOPLs can be found in the OOPL survey by Saunders [1989]. More recent reviews can be found in Meade [1995], and Pancake [1995]. For continued developments in OOPL, the *Journal of Object Oriented Programming Languages* should be consulted.

The main advantages of object-oriented programming and design are:

- Most changes in software systems are related to objects in real life. Thus object-oriented systems are easier to maintain.

- New objects can be created from existing objects by using inheritance, thus allowing clustering of similar objects and reducing the complexity of the system.

- The modules can encapsulate (i.e., hide internal details) by allowing external objects to invoke appropriate methods (the external objects invoke methods but do not know how the methods are implemented).

The combined effect is that OOPL can improve code reusability and maintainability.

10.6   Object-Oriented Databases

Simply stated, *object-oriented databases* allow storage and retrieval of objects to/from persistent storage (i.e., disks). Object-oriented databases, also known as *object databases*, allow you to store and retrieve nontraditional data types such as bitmaps, icons, text, polygons, sets, arrays, and lists. The stored objects can be simple or complex, can be related to each other through complex relationships, and can inherit properties from other objects. *Object-oriented database-management systems (OODBMS)*, which can store, retrieve, and manipulate objects, have been an area of active research and exploration since the mid-1980s. The initial work in OODBMSs was driven by the computer-aided design and computer-aided manufacturing (CAD/CAM) applications [Spooner 1986].

Relational database management systems (RDBMSs) are suitable for many applications, and SQL use is widespread. However, it is not easy to represent complex information in terms of relational tables. For example, a car design, a computing network layout, and software design of large-scale systems cannot be represented easily in terms of tables. For these cases, we need to represent complex interrelationships between data elements, retrieve several versions of design, represent the semantics (meaning) of relationships, and utilize the concepts of similarities to reduce redundancies.

The commonly known object-oriented database-management systems (OODBMSs) have been developed to support applications in computer-aided design and computer-aided manufacturing (CAD/CAM), expert systems, computer-aided software engineering (CASE), and office automation. Simply stated, OODBMSs combine and extend the features of database-management systems, artificial intelligence, and "object-oriented programming" for these and other applications.

OODBMSs and RDBMSs both have their strengths and weaknesses. For example, RDBMSs are very mature and heavily used but cannot handle complex objects. OODBMSs, on the other hand, lack the maturity and ease of use offered by the RDBMSs. A compromise, known as *object-relational databases,* provides a hybrid solution where relational and object-oriented technologies are combined into a single product. Different vendors use different approaches to object-relational databases. For example, Odaptor from HP uses an underlying relational database with OO front ends, while UniSQL from UniSQL is an OO database that subsumes the relational model. Detailed discussion of object-relational database managers can be found in Davis [1995].

Not everybody has always agreed on exactly what an OODBMS is. The debate over defining an OODBMS has continued since the mid-1980s. In 1989, a group of computer scientists got together and established "The Object Oriented Database Manifesto" [Atkinson 1989]. This manifesto, displayed in the sidebar "The Object Oriented Database Manifesto," establishes the basic properties of OODBMS by combining conventional database functionalities with object-oriented functionalities. Let us highlight the most significant properties of OODBMSs in terms of the following features mentioned in the Manifesto.

The Object Oriented Database Manifesto [Atkinson 1989]

Object-Oriented Features

- Complex objects
- Object identity
- Encapsulation
- Types and classes
- Inheritance
- Overriding, overloading, and late binding
- Computational completeness
- Extensibility

Database-Management Features

- Persistence
- Secondary storage management
- Concurrency
- Recovery
- Ad hoc queries

Complex Objects. Data may be stored, retrieved, and manipulated as complex objects, which consist of sets, lists, arrays, or relational rows. For example, a relational table represents a simple object while a composite of many tables represents a complex object. A complex object may represent a factory, which consists of simple objects such as personnel, buildings, and equipment. In addition, many factory objects can be combined to form a manufacturing-corporation object, and so on. OODBMSs provide data definition and manipulation facilities for complex objects.

Inheritance. OODBMSs allow creation of objects from existing objects by using inheritance of properties. This greatly simplifies the description of complex data. A DDL, for example, would allow creation of a new object which inherits its properties from existing objects in the database. Single or multiple inheritances may be used.

Procedural Encapsulation (Passive and Active Databases). Procedures can be stored as objects in the database. These procedures can be used as methods to encapsulate object semantics. Two types of object-oriented databases are commonly discussed: *passive databases,* which only store the data attributes, and *active databases,* which store the data plus the methods associated with the object. Passive databases represent a more conventional view of the database, where the data is stored in the databases and the procedures are embedded in the programs. Procedural encapsulation implies active databases, where the code associated with the object is stored in the database. Active databases have the attractive feature that entire systems can be stored and retrieved as objects [Loomis 1995, Kroha 1993]. Gemstone, Starburst, and POSTGRES are examples of active OODBMSs.

Links. The relationships between objects can be complex, many-to-many relationships. In OODBMS, objects are related to other objects through relationships which carry semantic information. The syntax of relationships is much more convenient than the relational joins. For example, relationships between objects can be assigned names such as SUBPART_OF, CREATED_BY, COMPONENTS_ARE, DOCUMENTATION_IS, etc. The DDL allows definition of such relationships, and the DML allows retrieval and manipulation of objects by using these relationships. For example, an OODBMS query could say: RETRIEVE SUBPARTS_OF CAR.

Multimedia Data. Objects can contain very large values to store pictures, voice, or text. Most OODBMS provide facilities to store and retrieve multimedia data. In some relational DBMS, multimedia data is referred to as BLOB (Binary Large Objects). A BLOB appears as any other object in the database and can be retrieved and displayed. This allows integration of multimedia applications around a database.

Versions. Most OODBMSs provide facilities to track multiple versions of an object. Many versions can be linked with one object. A user can issue queries such as "retrieve all versions of design" and "retrieve the documentation associated with version 3.1 of the design."

Integration with programming languages. In many OODBMS, the data-manipulation language is closely related to the programming language. In some object-oriented systems, it is difficult to say if a system is a database or a programming system. This leads to powerful DML (data manipulation language) capabilities such as use of AI and pattern matching for data manipulation. In addition, same operations can be used to operate on persistent or nonpersistent data. For example, let us assume that we need to evaluate the expression C=A+B. In conventional programming systems, we would use a statement such as "C:=A+B;" in a program if A, B, and C were all in main memory (nonpersistent). But if these three variables were on persistent storage, say a relational table, then different statements (e.g., SQL Select) would be needed before the addition. Thus the language syntax depends on where the data is. OODBMS programming languages attempt to eliminate this difference by providing a common syntax independent of where the data is: nonpersistent, persistent, or remotely located.

The OODBMS systems generally fall into two categories:

- Extensions of the object-oriented programming languages (OOPL) to include the features of DBMS. Examples are O2 and Gemstone systems.

- Extensions of the relational DBMS to include the features of OOPL. Examples are Starburst and POSTGRES.

Different databases are used for different applications in a distributed computing environment. As stated previously, relational database technology is state-of-the-market and state-of- the-practice. SQL, the query language for relational DBMS has become a de facto standard for enterprisewide data access, even for nonrelational data sources. However, relational DBMSs are not suitable for many engineering and other emerging applications discussed in the previous section. Object-oriented DBMSs are state-of-the-market but not state-of-the-practice at the time of this writing.

Additional information about object-oriented databases can be found in Davis [1995], Kim [1990], Kramer [1995], Kroha [1993], Loomis [1995].

10.7   State of the Practice: General Observations

Although OO technology has come into the limelight in the 1990s, it has been with us since the late 1960s, when the Simula programming language was introduced. OO technologies are at present becoming a de facto practice for developing new applications. Case studies and examples of using OO technologies are frequently discussed in the literature. For example, the October 1995 *Communications of the ACM* is a special issue on OO experiences and trends. This issue contains many insightful articles on topics such as lessons learned from the OS/400 OO Project, developing reusable object-oriented communications software, developing an object-oriented software testing and maintenance environment, and object-oriented parallel computation. Similarly, a "virtual roundtable" on object technology [El-Rewini 1995] has many short assessments on vast aspects of OO technologies such as distributed objects, parallelism and objects, object databases, software quality and object orientation, and theoretical foundations. In addition, trade journals such as *Object Magazine* regularly publish case studies and experiences in OO technologies.

Let us make some general observations about the current state of the practice in OO technologies. First, almost all new applications are using OO technologies in user interfaces. Second, OO programming is steadily gaining ground, especially owing to the availability of off-the-shelf class libraries. In particular, OO programming in C++ is quite popular, and the relatively new OO language Java has gained tremendous popularity for Web applications. Finally, OO databases still have a long way to go. Although OODBMSs have been commercially available since the mid 1980s, only 3 percent to 5 percent of corporate data is currently being stored in OODBMS.

10.8 Summary

The object-orientation (OO) revolution appears to be well entrenched at present in state of the practice as well as state of the market. The emphasis on business objects [Sims 1994, Rymer 1995] and distributed objects [Orfali 1996] is a very promising area of current and future developments. This very short tutorial has attempted to give you the basic OO concepts and introduced you to the core OO technologies that are of relevance to this book.

10.9 Case Study: XYZCorp Investigates OO

XYZCorp management needs to investigate and select the specific OO technologies to be used in the corporation.

Hints about the Case Study:

Use of OO technologies in high-technology firms such as XYZCorp is almost a zero-risk undertaking. Naturally all user interfaces should be OO, and a programming language like C++ seems appropriate (Java is a natural candidate for Web-based development). OODBMSs should be used cautiously.

10.10 Additional Information

Many books give more details about the topics discussed in this short tutorial. The books by Grady Booch [1994] and Rumbaugh [1994] present a good overview for programmers/analysts. The book by David Taylor [1994] is an effective management tutorial. Other material about OO concepts can be found in books such as Sims [1994], and Kroha [1993]. Many books on object-oriented databases have been published. Examples are Davis [1995], Kim [1990], Kramer [1995], Kroha [1993], and Loomis [1995]. In addition, state-of-the-art and state-of-the-market information about OO technologies appears in magazines such as *Object Magazine* and *Datamation*. In addition, special magazine issues on OO technologies should be consulted for continued developments (see, for example, *Communications of the ACM*, October 1995; *IEEE Computer,* October 1995; and *Open Systems Today,* April 1, 1994). An interesting discussion of alternative perspectives on object technology can be found in Powell [1995].

10.11 References

Alpert, S., et al., "Guest Editor's Introduction: Object Oriented Programming in AI," *IEEE Expert,* December 1990, special issue on Object-Oriented Programming.

Atkinson, M., et al., "The Object Oriented Database Manifesto," *Proceedings of the International Conference on Deductive and Object-Oriented Databases,* Kyoto, Japan, December 1989.

Bic, L., and Gilbert, J., "Learning from AI: New Trends in Database Technology," *IEEE Computer,* March, 1986

Booch, G., "Object Oriented Design," *IEEE Transactions on Software Engineering,* February 1986.

Booch, G., *Object Oriented Design with Applications,* Benjamin Cummings, 2d ed., 1994.

Bray, O., *CIM: The Data Management Strategy,* Digital Press, 1988.

Bretl, B., et al., *The Gemstone Data Management System: Object Oriented Concepts, Applications, and Databases,* Addison-Wesley, 1989.

Butterworth, P., et al, "The Gemstone Object Database Management System," *Communications of the ACM,* October 1991, pp. 64–77.

Catteli, R. G. G, "Introduction to the Next Generation Database Systems," *Communications of the ACM,* October 1991, pp. 33–38.

Davis, J., "Object-Relational Databases," *Distributed Computing Monitor,* Patricia Seybold Group, February 1995.

Deux, G., et al., "The O2 System," *Communications of the ACM,* October 1991, pp. 34–49.

Deux, G., et al., "The Story of O2," *IEEE Transactions on Knowledge and Data Engineering,* March 1990.

El-Rewini, H., and Hamilton, S., "Object Technology: A Virtual Roundtable," *IEEE Computer,* October 1995, pp. 58–72.

Fayad, M. et al., "Introduction (Object Oriented Experiences)," *Communications of the ACM,* October 1995, pp. 50–53.

Goldberg, A., "Why Smalltalk?" *Communications of the ACM,* October 1995, pp. 105–107.

Goldberg, A., and Robson, D., *Smalltalk-80: The Language,* Addison-Wesley, 1989.

Hardwick, M., and D. L. Spooner, "Comparison of Some Data Models for Engineering Objects," *IEEE CG&A,* March 1987.

Haas, L., et al., "Starburst Mid-Flight: As the Dust Clears," *IEEE Transactions on Knowledge and Data Engineering,* March 1990.

Hoff, A., et al., *Hooked on Java; Creating Hot Web Sites with Java Applets,* Addison-Wesley, 1996.

Ketabchi, M., and Berzins, V., "Modeling and Managing CAD Databases," *IEEE Computer,* February 1987, pp. 93–102.

Kemnitz, G., and Stonebraker, M., "The POSTGRES Tutorial," Electronics Research Laboratory, Memo M91/82, UC Berkeley, February 1991.

Kim, W., *Introduction to Object Databases,* MIT Press, 1990.

Kramer, M., "Object Databases," *Distributed Computing Monitor,* Patricia Seybold Group, April 1995.

Kroha, P., *Objects and Databases,* McGraw-Hill, 1993.

Lohman, G. M. et al., "Extensions to Starburst: Objects, Types, Functions, and Rules," *Communications of the ACM,* October 1991, pp. 94–109.

Loomis, M., *Object Databases: The Essentials,* Addison Wesley, 1995.

Martin, D., *Advanced Database Techniques,* MIT Press, 1986.

Meade, D., "Object Lessons," *Beyond Computing,* July/August 1995, pp. 41–42.

Meyer, Bertrand, *Object Oriented Software Construction,* Prentice Hall, 1988.

Nicol, J., et al., "Object Orientation in Heterogeneous Distributed Computing Systems," *IEEE Computer,* June 1993, pp. 57–67.

Orfali, R., Harkey, D., and Edwards, J., *Essential Client/Server Survival Guide,* Wiley, 1994.

Orfali, R., Harkey, D., and Edwards, J., *Distributed Objects Survival Guide,* Wiley, 1996.

Pancake, C., "The Promise and the Cost of Object Technology: A Five-Year Forecast," *Communications of the ACM,* October 1995, pp. 32–49.

Pascal, "Macintosh Programmer's Workshop Pascal 3.0 Reference," Apple Computer, 1989.

Pinsen, L.J., and Weiner, R.S., *Objective-C,* Addison-Wesley, 1991.

Powell, M., "Alternative Perspectives on Object Technology," Software; Practice and Experience, Vol. 25, Issue 4, 1995, pp. 131-141.

Rasdorf, M., "Extending DBMSs for Engineering Applications," *Computers in Mechanical Engineering,* March 1987, pp. 62–69.

Rentsh, T., *Sigplan Notices,* Vol. 17, No. 9 (1982).

Ricciuti, M., "Object Databases Find Their Niche," *Datamation,* September 15, 1993, pp. 56–60.

Rumbaugh, J., et al., *Object-Oriented Modeling and Design,* Prentice Hall, 2d ed., 1994.

Rymer, J., "Business Objects," *Distributed Computing Monitor,* Patricia Seybold Group, January 1995.

Saunders, J., "A Survey of Object Oriented Programming Languages," *Journal of Object Oriented Programming Languages,* March/April 1989.

Semich, W., "What's the Next Step after Client/Server?" *Datamation,* March 15, 1994, pp. 26–34.

Shan, Y., "Introduction (Smalltalk on the Rise)," *Communications of the ACM,* October 1995, pp. 102–105.

Sheton, R., "Enterprise Reuse," *Distributed Computing Monitor,* Patricia Seybold Group, August 1995.

Silberschatz, A., et al., "Database Systems: Achievements and Opportunities," *Comm. of ACM,* October 1991, pp. 110–120.

Simpson, D., "Objects May Appear Closer Than They Are," *Client/Server Today,* August 1995, pp. 59–69.

Sims, O., *Business Objects,* McGraw-Hill, 1994.

Spooner, D., "An Object Oriented Data Management System for Mechanical CAD," *IEEE,* 1986 Conference on Graphics.

Stroustrup, B., *The C++ Programming Language,* Addison-Wesley, 1986.

Stonebraker, M., and Kemnitz, G., "The POSTGRES Next Generation Database System," *Communications of the ACM*, October 1991, pp. 78–93.

Sudama, R., "Get Ready for Distributed Objects," *Datamation,* October 1, 1995, pp. 67–72.

Taylor, D., *Object-Oriented Technology: A Manager's Guide,* Addison-Wesley, 1994.

Ullman, J., *Principles of Database Systems,* Wiley, 1982.

Ullman, J., *"Principles of Database and Knowledge-Base Systems,"* Computer Science Press, 1988.

Umar, A., *Distributed Computing and Client/Server Systems,* Prentice Hall, 1993, rev. ed.

Wegner, P., "Dimensions of Object-Based Language Design," *SIGPlan Notices,* Vol. 22, No. 12 (December 1987), pp. 168–182.

Wirfs-Brock, R., Wilkerson, B., and Wiener, L., *Designing Object-Oriented Software,* Prentice Hall, 1990.

11

Network Technologies and Architectures—A Tutorial

11.1   Introduction

Networks are an important building block of IT infrastructure—they play a key role in enabling/disabling the enterprisewide applications. This tutorial gives an overview of the networking issues that are of importance from an IT infrastructure point of view. Specifically, we will attempt to answer the following questions:

- What are the basic concepts needed to understand enterprise networks? (Section 11.2)

- What are the properties and components of typical wide-area networks, local-area networks, and metropolitan-area networks used in enterprise networks? (Section 11.3)

- What are network architectures, and how does the OSI Model help in defining these architectures? (Section 11.4)

- What are the basic concepts of emerging communication technologies, such as fast digital communication networks that operate at 100 million bits per second, or higher, and mobile communication technologies? (Section 11.5)

- How do all the hardware and software products fit together to form a network architecture, and what are the key properties of network "stacks" such as TCP/IP and SNA? (Section 11.6)

- How does one network interconnect with other networks, and what are the network interconnectivity devices such as routers, bridges, and gateways? (Section 11.7)

- What is the state of the practice, market, and art in enterprise networks? (Sections 11.8, 11.9, and 11.10)

This tutorial is an updated abbreviation of networking issues discussed in several chapters in Umar [1993].

Key Points

- Enterprise networks consist of LANs, MANs, and WANs that are glued together through network interconnectivity devices.

- Emerging network technologies include fast packet-switching systems (e.g., ATM, Frame Relay), fast LANs (e.g., Fast Ethernet), and improved wireless networks.

- *Network architecture* describes the components, the functions performed by the components, and the interfaces/interactions between the components of a network.

- The OSI (Open System Interconnection) Reference Model is a good framework for discussing network architectures.

- TCP/IP "stack" is a very popular network architecture (it is used in the Internet).

- Network Interconnectiveity is essential between different segments of an enterprise network for end-to-end services.

- *Bridging, routing, and protocol conversions ("gatewaying") are functions and not devices.* These functions may be consolidated, packaged, and marketed in a variety of manners.

11.2   Enterprise Network Concepts

A *communication network* is a collection of equipment and physical media (e.g., telephone lines, cables, wireless systems), viewed as one autonomous whole, that interconnects two or more stations. A *station* is an end point (source/sink) in a communication network and can be a terminal, computer, sensor, or TV. Stations are connected to the network through *interfaces* (also known as user-to-network interfaces) that convert the signals and data between the stations and the communication network equipment (see Figure 11.1). Communication networks, also referred to as *networks*, provide the information-exchange services in distributed computing. Specifically, they are responsible for three types of services:

- Delivery,
- Understanding, and
- Agreement.

Delivery is the physical transport of data between stations. Data, in this context, is anything that conveys meaning to a user (e.g., customer names, bank balances, voice, and images). Delivery involves finding a path for the data and sending the data correctly over the selected path. *Understanding* assures that the data sent is in a format which can be understood by the receiver. Data may need to be translated between senders and receivers. *Agreement* assures

Figure 11.1 Conceptual View of a Communication Network

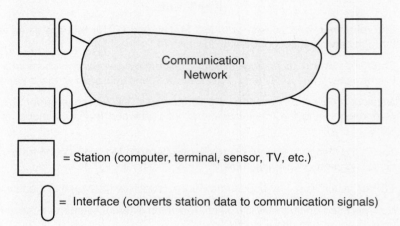

= Station (computer, terminal, sensor, TV, etc.)

= Interface (converts station data to communication signals)

that the data is sent when the receiver is ready to receive it. This means that the rules of exchange (***protocol***) must be established between a sender and a receiver.

From a management point of view, *networks are the transport mechanisms that transfer data between stations at a given data rate*. ***Data rates***, represented in kilo or million bits per second (Kbps or Mbps), are especially important for C/S applications, because a C/S application architecture in a fast network may work very well but in a slow network may be a miserable failure.

Networks are generally classified into three categories based on the geographical area covered (see Sections 11.3, 11.3.2, and 11.3.3 for additional details):

- ***Local-Area Networks (LANs),*** which do not use common carrier facilities over short distances. The LAN data rates are around 10 Mbps and higher (up to 100 Mbps).

- ***Metropolitan-Area Networks (MANs),*** which are essentially large LANs that may cover an entire city, perhaps by using cable television facilities.

- ***Wide-Area Networks (WANs),*** which use common-carrier facilities over long distances with speeds up to a few million bits per second (Mbps).

The major growth in networking is interconnection and integration of LANs, MANs and WANs into large and high-speed supernetworks (see Figure 11.2). In these networks, many computers in a building are connected to a LAN, many LANs are interconnected through a

Figure 11.2 Combining LANs, MANs, and WANs

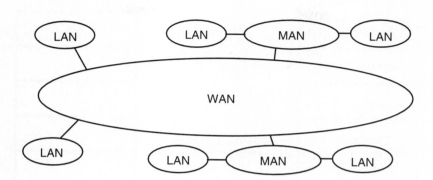

MAN, and many MANs are interconnected through WANs at very high speeds. The primary business pressure behind these networks is the large number of LANs which need to exchange information with each other, and the expected growth of Internet and C/S applications. It is desirable to operate the backbone WAN at 100 million bits per second (Mbps) or higher in order to interconnect the MANs and LANs, which are also operating at these speeds. This provides "wall-to-wall" 100-Mbps and higher networks. Section 11.5 reviews this important and interesting development area in networks.

Standards are needed to interconnect different networks from different vendors with different capabilities. For example, Internet users regularly communicate with each other spanning multiple physical networks. A *network architecture* describes the physical components, the functions performed by the components, and the interfaces between the components of a network. Network architectures are the foundation of network interconnectivity. The *Open System Interconnection (OSI) Reference Model* specifies standards for networks from different vendors to exchange information freely. The OSI Model casts the functions needed to exchange information between interconnected computers in terms of seven layers (see Figure 11.3). The lower four layers are related with networking issues (transporting messages between end systems) and the higher three layers are concerned with application issues (e.g., encryption, compression). Many network architectures have evolved in the last 20 years. Examples of the state-of-the-market/practice network architectures are the *Transmission Control Protocol/Internet Protocol (called TCP/IP)* stack, IBM's *System Network Architecture (SNA)*, Novell's *NetWare LAN*, and the Open System Interconnection (OSI) Model. We will discuss these network architectures later in this chapter.

Figure 11.3 The OSI Reference Model

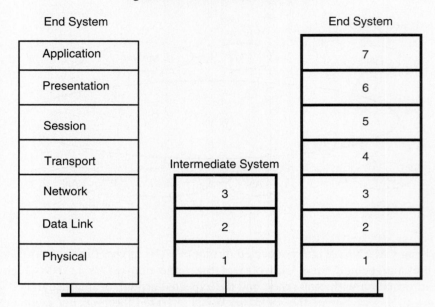

11.3   Typical Existing Networks

Existing networks combine LANs and WANs, in some cases also MANs, to provide enter-prisewide network services. Such a network is shown in Figure 11.4 (we use this network-configuration in the main body of this book). Let us discuss various components of this network.

11.3.1   Local-Area Networks

Simply stated, a local-area network (LAN) is a network of data-communication devices within a small area (typically less than 10 kilometers). The main characteristics of local area networks, also called local networks, are:

- **Private ownership.** The LAN equipment, including the communication media, is privately owned.

- **High data rates**. The data rates of LANs are much higher than those of the common wide area networks. Most wide-area networks use data rates ranging from 1200 bps (bits per second) to 1.54 Mbps, while most local-area networks use data rates from 1 to 100 Mbps.

Figure 11.4 A Sample Enterprise Network

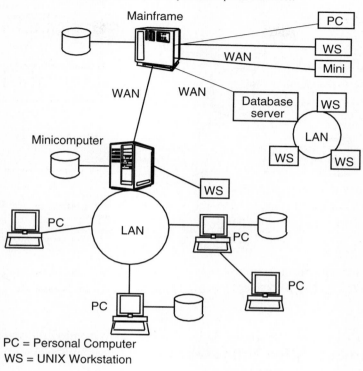

PC = Personal Computer
WS = UNIX Workstation

- **Low error rates**. The error rates in LANs are much lower than in the typical wide-area networks. This is mainly because of the short distances and the use of simple communication devices in LANs.

- **Broadcast services**. LANs typically broadcast the messages to receivers, whereas WANs usually select a receiver before sending a message. Broadcasts, if misused and disregarded, can cause many administrative problems.

Figure 11.5 shows two LANs that may serve two different user communities. The devices on the LAN may be personal computers, workstations, terminals, printers, and/or sensors. A LAN "server" is a computer on the LAN which allows the users to share common resources. A server may be a personal computer, a workstation, a specialized computer, or a minicomputer. LAN servers are used for one or more of the following services:

- Printer sharing
- Disk sharing
- File/database services
- Application services

Figure 11.5 Local-Area Networks

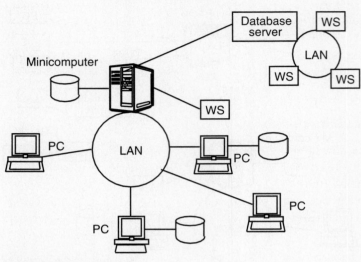

PC = Personal Computer
WS = UNIX Workstation

The IEEE 802 Committee was formed in February 1980 to develop the standards for local-area networks (802 is a code for 1980, second month). The committee has organized its major work into the following subcommittees:

- 802.1: High Level Interface
- 802.2: Logical Link Control
- 802.3: CSMA/CD Networks
- 802.4: Token Bus Networks
- 802.5: Token Ring Networks
- 802.6: Metropolitan Area Networks
- 802.7: Broadband Technical Advisory Group
- 802.8: Fiber Optic Technical Advisory Group
- 802.9: Integrated Data and Voice Networks

IEEE 802 has especially focused on link-control protocols that are used to describe the format and the rules used in exchanging messages between LAN devices. The following two link protocols, adopted by the IEEE 802 LAN Standardization Committee, are used most frequently in commercially available LANs:

- CSMA/CD (Carrier Sense Multiple Access/Collision Detect) is very close to the heavily used *Ethernet protocol.* For most practical purposes, IEEE 802.3 and Ethernet are the same. Ethernet LANs are used very extensively at present. The conventional Ethernet LANs operate at 10 Mbps; newer Ethernet LANs operate at 100 Mbps (this is known as Fast Ethernet).[1]

- *Token Ring Protocol* (IEEE 802.5 Standard) is used in the IBM Token Ring LAN. A token is a packet that moves around a ring to which the LAN devices are attached. The token is used to pick up and deliver messages on the LAN. Older versions of Token Ring LANs operate at 4 Mbps; newer versions operate at 16 Mbps.

11.3.2 Metropolitan-Area Networks—The Large LANs

The metropolitan-area networks (MANs) extend the scope of local-area networks beyond the customer premises to cover a geographical area (e.g., a city or a county). A common definition (there are many slightly varying definitions) is that a MAN is a large LAN under the control of one authority and using a shared transmission medium. A MAN typically covers 50 km diameter and operates at data rates above 50 Mbps. Three approaches are being developed for MANs:

- The FDDI standard, discussed in Section 2.5.2, is popular for MANs because it operates at 100 Mbps over 100 km. However, FDDI is aimed at the data-communications users; voice communication is of little concern in this standard.

- The DQDB standard, discussed in Section 2.5.3, has been adopted by the IEEE 802.6 Committee as the primary MAN standard. This standard offers up to 155 Mbps data rates.

- The SMDS (Switched Multimegabit Data Service) is being developed by the telephone companies as a MAN as well as WAN offering. Initially targeted at the low-cost T1 (1.54 Mbps) and T3 (45 Mbps) transmission services, SMDS will provide access to a very high speed and reliable public packet-switching network.

Owing to its size and data rate, a MAN can be used as a backbone which transports messages between various LANs and PBXs. Figure 11.6 shows FDDI being used as a backbone to interconnect several LANs and several hosts (workstations, midrange computers, and mainframes).

11.3.3 Typical Wide-Area Networks

Wide-area networks (WANs) are the oldest form of communication networks. WANs use the telecommunication facilities of common carriers (telephone companies) to exchange data between computing devices. Figure 11.7 shows a typical wide-area network configuration. In this wide-area network the mainframe is connected to many devices over a dial-up network. In addition, many terminals, computers and local-area networks are connected to the mainframe through a packet-switching system. Existing WANs use one or more of the following networking facilities:

- Dial-up/leased networks
- Packet-switching systems

---

1. Technically speaking, Fast Ethernet uses a different physical-layer protocol.

Figure 11.6 An FDDI MAN as a Backbone

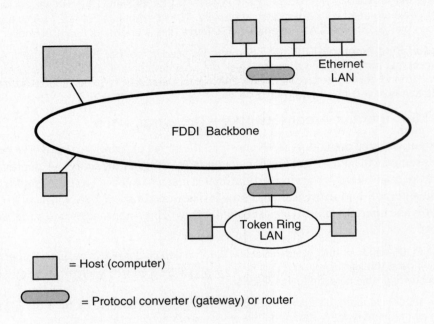

Figure 11.7 A Typical WAN

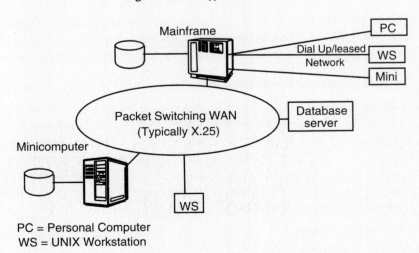

The dial-up networks use modems that operate at data rates of 14.4 Kbps or 28.8 Kbps over voice-grade lines. Higher data rates over the dial-up lines are possible. The leased lines may use 56-Kbps digital data services lines. However, many of the existing leased WANs use the T1 carrier lines that operate at 1.54 Mbps (million bits per second) data rate. T3 carrier lines at data rates of 44.76 Mbps are also used when high data rates over WAN are needed. As we will see in our discussion of high-speed (broadband) networks, the data rate of evolving WANs easily exceeds 100 Mbps.

Packet switching systems are currently the most popular systems for wide-area data communications. In these systems, a message is broken into "packets," which are sent out to the network. The packet switches select the path for each packet and then assemble the packets into the original message at the receiving end. The principle of packet switching can be illustrated by using a military example. If a caravan of 20 trucks has to pass through a city, it is better to break this big caravan into smaller "packets" of trucks (say four per packet) and then let each packet find its way to the destination. This technique can reduce total transmission time. For example, if a message is broken into five packets and the five packets are transmitted simultaneously, then theoretically the message can be transmitted in one-fifth of the time needed to transmit the complete message. However, we need to keep the following things in mind:

- Enough paths must be available for the packets to travel in parallel.

- The processing required to break up the message into packets and then to reassemble them on the other side adds overhead and delays.

- Additional logic and intelligence is required to detect out-of-sequence packets and lost packets.

X.25 packet switching is used in traditional packet-switching networks. X.25 is a standard which defines the formats and message-exchange rules between switches. Packet-switching networks are becoming more economical with evolving technologies. In practice, packet switches are expected to be the main delivery mechanisms for wide-area networks of the future. In particular, digitized data, voice, and images need to use one path independent of data type, and packet switching seems to be the prime candidate. We will consider the fast packet switches being developed for future networks in Section 11.5.5.

Integrated Services Digital Network (ISDN) is becoming popular at present for WANs. ISDN provides end-to-end digital connectivity to support a wide range of services, including voice and nonvoice services. ISDN combines digital lines with standard interfaces to provide integrated services in voice, data, graphics, text, and video over the same physical lines. It attempts to provide a set of international standards and interfaces to allow computers, telephones, and terminals to communicate freely with each other without any vendor-imposed limitations. ISDN provides two 64-Kbps channels (called the B channels) and one 16 Kbps channel (called the D channel). These "2B + D services" are supported on the same wire pair that provides voice-grade telephone service.

Although ISDN has been around since the mid 1980s, it has not gained popularity with end users despite the support of the key telecommunications organizations. What has occurred recently is an increase in telecommuting and the home use of Internet. The telecommuters find ISDN attractive because it offers a 64-Kbps data rate from home as compared to the 28.8-Kbps modems (these modems have some performance problems). The home users of Internet also like the ISDN data rate as compared to the 14.4 or 28.8 Kbps modems.

11.4   Network Architectures and the OSI Reference Model

11.4.1   Overview

Simply stated, a ***network architecture*** describes the components, the functions performed by the components, and the interfaces/interactions among the components of a network. Network architectures help designers of enterprise networks to answer two fundamental questions:

- How do all the hardware and software products fit together to form a functioning ("operable") network?

- How does one network interconnect with other networks?

The Open System Interconnection (OSI) Reference Model is intended to provide a network architecture standard for different networks from different suppliers. The OSI Reference Model, commonly referred to as the OSI Model, was proposed by the International Standards Organizations (ISO) Committee 97 in March 1977. This model consists of 7 layers, shown in Figure 11.8. The objective of the ISO subcommittee was to describe a layered set of generic functions that every network must fulfill. Such a generic definition makes it easier to develop interfaces between different networks.

The ISO subcommittee precisely defined the set of layers and the functions/services performed by each layer. According to the conceptual framework shown in Figure 11.8, the first four layers (Physical, Data Link, Network, and Transport) are lower level layers which are responsible for the delivery of data between applications. These layers perform the following functions:

- The Physical Layer is concerned with transmission of bit streams over a physical medium and deals with the mechanical, electrical, functional, and procedural characteristics to access the physical medium. For example, the physical interfaces such as RS232 are handled by this layer.

- The Data Link Layer provides for the transfer of information across the physical link by sending blocks of data (frames) with necessary synchronization, error-control, and flow-control functions. For example, this layer handles the reception, recognition, and transmission of tokens and Ethernet messages.

Figure 11.8 The ISO OSI Model

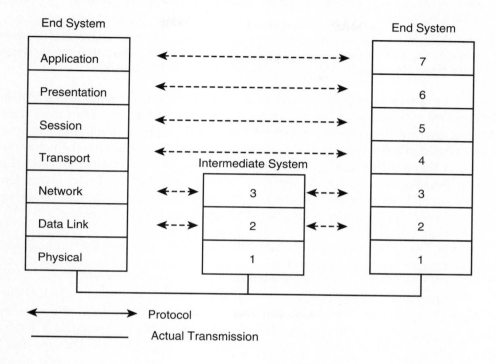

- The Network Layer provides upper layers with independence from the data-transmission, switching, and routing technologies needed when the end devices have to cross many networks. For example, the packet-switching activities of breaking up and reassembling the messages are performed by this layer.

- The Transport Layer provides transparent transfer of data between end systems and is responsible for end-to-end error recovery and flow control. The Transport Layer resides only in end systems (see Figure 11.8). For example, in a large network with many interconnected LANs and WANs, the transport layer at the end systems will make sure that the messages exchanged between end systems of this network are not lost while fighting their way through various LANs and WANs. A message may be exchanged correctly between two stations of a LAN in a building, but it may not be sent properly to a remote computer located in another city.

Whereas the lower four layers are responsible for transport of information between applications, the upper layers support applications (Figure 11.8). Specifically

- The Session Layer controls the communication between applications by establishing, managing, and terminating connections (sessions) between cooperating applications. For example, this layer establishes the full- versus half-duplex interactions between applications.

- The Presentation Layer provides independence to the application processes from differences in data representation (syntax). The encryption/decryption for security purposes is usually performed in this layer.

- The Application Layer supports the application and user processes which need network services. Examples of the services provided by this layer are terminal emulation, file transfer, electronic mail, client/server middleware, distributed-database managers, etc.

Figure 11.8 illustrates the concept of end systems and intermediate systems in OSI. An ***intermediate system*** only performs functions related to the lowest three layers of the Reference Model (e.g., routing, flow control, and bit transmission). Functions of intermediate systems are implemented in ***relay systems***. An example of a relay system is a router which connects many LANs together. An ***end system*** provides the functions above the Network Layer (Transport, Session, Presentation, Application), in addition to the lowest three layers. Examples of end systems are computers on which applications reside. End system is a synonym of "host," a term commonly used to refer to computers where applications reside.

The OSI model has provided a consistent set of terms and vocabulary. For our purpose, the protocol and connection/connectionless services are of vital importance.

Protocols. A protocol is a set of precisely defined rules and conventions for behavior between two parties. For example, diplomatic protocols define the conventions and rules to be observed by diplomats. According to the OSI Model, a communication protocol is defined as rules of exchange between entities at the same layers of the OSI Model. Thus the data link protocols define the rules of exchange between the layer-2 entities, the transport protocols define the rules of exchange between the layer-4 entities, and the application protocols define the rules of exchange between the application-layer entities of two systems. Higher-level protocols (e.g., business processing protocols) can also be defined by using this framework.

Protocols, especially at higher layers, guarantee correct exchange of information. A protocol basically consists of two basic elements:

- Format of message, which shows precisely how the data, the commands/flags, the sender/receiver identification, and the response will be sent and received (recognized) by the two entities.

- Rules of message exchange, which specify what to do if a message is received incorrectly, not received, received out of sequence, or distorted.

For example, the X.25 protocol defines the format of the packets exchanged and the rules to handle out-of-sequence packets. Similarly, X.400 protocol defines the format of the messages exchanged and the rules to handle out-of-sequence messages in electronic mail.

Figure 11.9 shows the protocols used in different layers of the OSI Model.

Figure 11.9 The OSI Protocol Stack

Layer 7—Application Layer
Function: User-level formats and procedures, programs, operators, devices
Examples: Virtual terminal, FTAM, X.400 email
CMISE (Common Management Information Service Element)
EDI (Electronic Data Interchange)
ODA (Office Document Architecture)
X.409 (Message-Handling Systems)
X.500 (Directory Services)
TP (Transaction Processing).

Layer 6—Presentation Layer
Function: Management of entry, exchange, display, and control of data; interface transformation
Example: ISO 8822 (Connection Oriented Presentation)
ASN.1 (Abstract Syntax Notation 1).

Layer 5—Session Layer
Function: Session administration services, control of data exchange; delineating/synchronizing
Examples: X.215 and X.225 (Session Service and
Protocol Definition), accepted as ISO 8326 and 8327

Layer 4—Transport Layer
Function: Transparent transfer of data between sessions; optimize use of available communications services
Examples: X.214 (Transport Service Definition) and X.224 (Transport Service
Definition) equivalent to ISO8072 and ISO8073

Layer 3—Network Layer
Function: Form and route packets across networks of networks
Examples: X.25, X.75, ISDN interfaces (I.450/I.451), subnetworks (ISO 8473)

Layer 2—Link Layer
Function: Data-flow initialization, control, termination, recovery
Examples: HDLC, IEEE 802.3, IEEE 802.4, IEEE 802.5, IEEE 802.6
FDDI frames, ISDN frames (I.441)

Layer 1—Physical Layer
Function: Electrical/mechanical interfaces to communication media
Examples: RS232, RS449, X.21, ISDN interfaces
(I.430, I.431), FDDI physical interface

Connection-Based and Connectionless Communications. The OSI Model supports connectionless as well as connection-based communications. The basic idea of a connection-based service, also called a reliable service, is that before any communication between two entities at layer N takes place, a connection between end systems at $N - 1$ must be established. Connection-based communications involves three phases: connection establishment, data transfer, and connection release. Owing to the overhead of connection establishment and connection release, several systems use a "connectionless" service. The notion of connectionless service is almost oximoronic: How can you provide a service when you are not even connected? Basically, a connectionless service means that the communicating parties send and receive self-contained data packets without a priori connection (i.e., there is no separate connection establishment and connection release).

An analogy will explain the difference between connectionless and connection-based services. Connection-based services are similar to telephone communication, while the connectionless services are similar to the postal system. If you use a telephone, then you first dial the number (connection establishment), talk (data transfer), and hang up (connection release). In this case, you establish a connection before data transfer. In contrast, you do not establish a connection before you send a message in a letter, and there is no assurance that the receiver has received the message. However, you can design your own protocol to make sure that the mail was delivered (e.g., put a note in your letter indicating that the receiver must call you immediately to claim one million dollars he has won in a lottery). Owing to this analogy, the connection-based service is referred to as a *virtual call* and the connectionless service is referred to as a *datagram service*.

11.4.2   Network Interconnectivity

As stated previously, a communication network is a collection of equipment and physical media, viewed as one autonomous whole, that interconnects two or more end systems. In most real-life situations, many networks are interconnected to form large networks. Each constituent network of large networks is called a "subnetwork." The OSI Model can be used to classify the interconnectivity issues at three levels:

- **Physical-device interconnectivity:** This defines how the stations will be connected through physical cables and adapter cards. The layer 1 and 2 issues of voltage levels, analog versus digital interfaces, and link-control message formats and flow control are important for this type of interconnectivity.

- **Network interconnectivity:** This defines how a station S1 connected to a network NET1 can communicate with a station S2 connected to a network NET2. The layers 3 and 4 issues of routing and transport between end systems are important for this type of interconnectivity.

- **Application interconnectivity**: This defines how the data between an application A1 on station S1 is shared/exchanged by an application A2 on station S2. The higher-level issues of using terminal emulation, file transfer, client-server interactions, and remote-data access are important for this type of interconnectivity.

Protocols play an important role in all these levels of interconnectivity. Lower-level protocols are used for physical-device interconnectity and higher-level protocols are used to interconnect applications. For example, to connect two computers on a physical cable, the two computers must use the same link protocol (e.g., Ethernet, token ring, X.25). Protocol converters may be needed to convert one type of link protocol to another (many Ethernet-to-token-ring protocol converters are commercially available). Similarly, the same application protocols are needed to connect higher-level applications. Since most higher-level protocols are embedded in software, software protocol converters or gateways may be needed to convert higher-level protocols. We will discuss the interconnectivity devices in Section 11.7.

11.5 Emerging Communication Technologies

11.5.1 Overview

The network communication technologies are advancing at a very rapid pace. In particular, we are witnessing growth of high speed, also known as **broadband**, networks that exceed 100-Mbps data rates (see the sidebar "Main Characteristics of Emerging Networks"). In addition, we are also seeing an increased availability of mobile communications systems. This section presents an overview of the main emerging communication technologies and their role in the enterprise networks of the future. In particular, we will review technologies such as frame relay, ATM (asynchronous transfer mode), Sonet, SMDS (Switched Multimegabit Data Service), BISDN (Broadband ISDN), and mobile communication systems such as cellular networks and wireless LANs. We will focus on the interrelationships and key concepts instead of detailed technical discussions.

Major emphasis of the emerging communications technologies is to provide reliable high-data-rate networks at LAN, WAN, and MAN level. Why? Here are some reasons:

LAN Interconnectivity: Basically, LANs are fast but WANs are not. The demand for high speed LAN-to-LAN interconnection is driving high-speed requirements (it is silly to connect high-speed 100-Mbps LANs through a 56-Kbps WAN).

Client/Server Applications. Clients and servers exchange messages in real time. Many such applications have been developed for group/departmental use over fast LANs. The push toward enterprisewide client/server applications is a major driver for high WAN data rates. It is very difficult to support enterprisewide C/S applications over slow WANs.

Growth in Internet Usage. The growth in the number of Internet users as well as the type of applications is unprecedented. In particular, the growth of World Wide Web applications is straining the existing slow WANs.

Multimedia Applications. These applications require more than 100 Mbps. Steady growth of applications in imaging and high-definition TV require high-speed services (see sidebar "Bandwidth Consumers").

Growth in Data-Communications Traffic. The expected growth in data communications over voice communications is another driver. Currently data traffic in typical organizations is 30%, the rest is voice. This ratio is expected to reverse, with data traffic to comprise 70% of the network traffic in organizations.

11.5.2 Interrelationships between Emerging Technologies

Figure 11.10 and Figure 11.11 present two different views which may help to put some of the emerging technologies in perspective. These two figures also include some important emerged technologies for sake of completeness. Figure 11.10 shows an end-user view and

Figure 11.10 Emerging Technologies in Terms of Distance and Data Rate (Mbps)

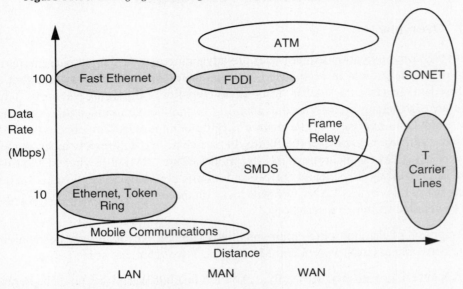

Legend: Shaded areas indicate emerged technologies

attempts to answer the question: which technologies can be used at different distances at what data rates? This is a crucial question in corporate networks. Figure 11.11 looks at these technologies in terms of the technology layers. Keep in mind that most of these technologies are concerned with the first two layers of the ISO Reference Model. Let us go through this in more detail.

Main Characteristics of Emerging Networks

- Fiber optic transmission media
- Data rates at 100 Mbps or higher over wide areas
- Ability to handle millions of packets per second as compared to the thousands per second of today's networks
- Designed to handle data, voice, and video
- Extremely low error rate of bits transmitted
- More error control at end points than intermediate "hops"
- Network propagation delay is significant compared to transmission delay
- Low switching delays (2 to 5 milliseconds versus 50 to 100 milliseconds)
- Active development of standards before widespread deployment of products

Figure 11.11 Emerging Technologies in Terms of Distance and ISO Layers

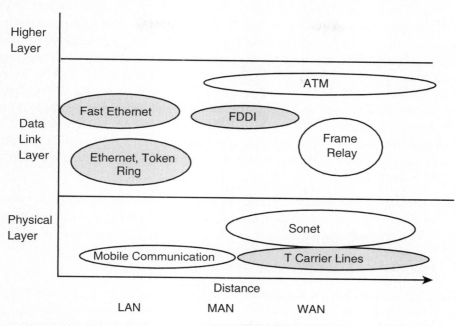

Legend: Shaded areas indicate emerged technologies

In the first layer in Figure 11.11 are the fiber optic digital technologies. SONET (Synchronous Optical Network), discussed in Section 11.5.4, uses fiber optic to provide data rates which are much higher than the currently popular T1 and T3 lines. Growth in the use of fiber optics for local-, wide-, and metropolitan-area networks is unprecedented.

Bandwidth Consumers (Source: [Umar 1993])

Example: How much is 150 Mbps?

- 3,000,000 typists at 50 words/minute
- 30,000 FAX terminals
- 16,000 high-speed asynchronous terminals
- 2400 high-quality voice channels
- 100 high-quality stereo audio channels
- 100 video teleconferences
- 15 high-speed local-area networks (Ethernets)
- 6 high-resolution color images/second
- 3 studio-quality TV channels
- 1 high-definition TV channel

At the next level in Figure 11.11, standardization efforts are laying the foundation for wide-spread deployment of high-speed technology over fiber networks. Examples of MAN standards, already discussed, are FDDI and DQDB. In wide-area networks, fast packet-switching systems such as frame relay (variable-sized packets) and cell relay (fixed-sized packets) are becoming state-of-the-practice. Fast packet-switching system principles, frame relay, and ATM are discussed in Sections 11.5.5, 11.5.6, and 11.5.7, respectively. SMDS, discussed in Section 11.5.8, is a standard for broadband MANs as well as WANs. Broadband ISDN (BISDN) is expected to consolidate many of the technologies shown in Figure 11.11 through a limited number of interfaces. This role of BISDN is discussed in Section 11.5.9. Mobile communication systems such as cellular networks and wireless LANs provide low data rates and cover small geographic areas but have many interesting applications. We discuss these technologies in Section 11.5.10.

We are not discussing other extant technologies that are of no direct importance to enterprise networks for client/server applications. Examples of such technologies are telephone over TV cable, and TV over telephone lines.

11.5.3   Foundations of Emerging Technologies

The emerging communication technologies are improving the data rates by exploiting a combination of basic and systematic principles. Examples of these common principles are (see Black [1994] for detailed discussion):

- Use of fiber optic versus copper facilities
- Less error checking
- Consolidation of redundant functions
- More functions moving to hardware
- Faster computer chips
- Use of bandwidth on demand

Fiber optic is a core technology for most of the emerging communication systems. A series of breakthroughs since the late 1970s have increased the capacity (i.e., more bandwidth) and lowered the cost of fiber optic. Fiber optic systems at present can carry between 2.5 to 10 Gbits/s with constantly decreasing costs owing to mass production and maturing technology.

The emerging networks use far less error checking than the older systems such as X.25. These networks assume that the transmission facility is reliable. In addition, there is an increased use of "connectionless" services instead of the "leased-line" connection-oriented services which require a connection to be established before data exchange. In *connectionless services*, no connection is established between the end points, which saves considerable time in large networks. Instead, each party sends a "datagram" which contains the data being sent plus the destination address and the routing information. This datagram fights its way to the destination, finding alternate paths in case of failures and congestions in the network. Datagrams were used initially in LANs, where the message was "broadcasted" to all stations and picked up by the addressed station. The main implication of the connectionless service is that the senders and receivers must do their own error checking to handle missing and out-of-sequence datagrams.

Consolidation of redundant functions is a common practice in emerging networks. In the earlier systems, many functions at different levels in systems were duplicated. For example, error checking, flow control, and sequencing are redundant in the first three layers of many existing networks.

More functions are also moving gradually to hardware to improve the network performance. For example, many hardware cards at present handle layers 1–3.

We should not forget the impact of faster computer chips on network performance. Fast computer chips are employed frequently to perform many network functions such as error checking, switching, and routing.

Use of bandwidth on demand is also a common feature of many new networks. Basically, users are given a committed information rate (CIR). If needed, the users can get more than CIR. However, this involves tricky charging.

11.5.4   SONET (Synchronous Optical Network)

Synchronous Optical Networks (SONET) is one of the basic high-speed transmission technologies. SONET, known as SDH (Synchronous Digital Hierarchy) in Europe, was proposed by Bellcore based on the requirements from the Bell Operating Companies (BOCs) to interconnect high-speed fiber networks. SONET specifies optical-based carrier services at layer 1 (Physical Layer of the OSI Model) and has higher quality and reliability than the older T-carrier lines. For these reasons, SONET is used heavily in the emerging fast packet-switching WANs such as ATM and frame relays.

SONET is a fiber-optic-based standard which provides a hierarchy of services ranging from 51.84 Mbps to 2488 Mbps. Higher rates will be possibly included into SONET services as the technology for higher data rates becomes available. These services represented as OC-1 through OC-48, are hierarchies of line speeds that can carry data at much higher speeds than the existing T-carrier technology. Table 11.1 shows the SONET OC (optical-carrier) level characteristics and the existing T-carrier services. It can be seen that SONET can carry data almost 50 times faster than the popular T3 rates (OC-48 can carry up to 2488 Mbps). More information about SONET can be found [Black 1994, Violino 1991, Babcock 1990].

11.5.5 Fast Packet-Switching Networks ("Fast Relays")

The high-speed WANs use fast packet-switching systems which move millions of packets per second over fiber networks. Fast packet-switching systems, also known as fast relays, are much more reliable than older packet-switching systems. In addition, these networks have intelligent end points which can deal with errors in transmission. These systems use the following techniques:

- Move the error processing and flow control from the network to the end points. Frame relays, discussed later, support such technologies.

- Simplify the switch processing to route the message through the network. Several fast switches have been developed for this purpose [Taylor 1994].

- Employ new multiplexing techniques to multiplex different traffic patterns into SONET frames. Asynchronous Transfer Mode (ATM) is such a technique.

- Use connectionless instead of connection-based services to eliminate the call-setup time.

Fast packet-switching systems basically used either variable-sized or fixed-sized packets (see Figure 11.12). Variable-sized packets are currently being used in commercially available frame relay systems, and the fixed-sized packets are used in ATM and SMDS networks. We will discuss these networks in the next few sections.

TABLE 11.1 SONET AND T-CARRIER SERVICES

(a) The SONET Hierarchy of Services	
Level	Line Data Rate (Mbps)
OC-1	51.84
OC-3	155.52
OC-9	466.56
OC-12	622.08
OC-18	933.12
OC-24	1244.16
OC-36	1866.24
OC-48	2488.32

(b) T-Carrier Services			
Service Type	Carrier Type	Million Bits per Second (Mbps)	No. of Voice Channels
DS-1	T1	1.544	24
DS-1c	T1C	3.152	48
DS-2	T2	6.312	96
DS-3	T3	44.736	672
DS-4	T4M	274.176	4032

Figure 11.12 Fast Packet-Switching Taxonomy [Davidson 1991]

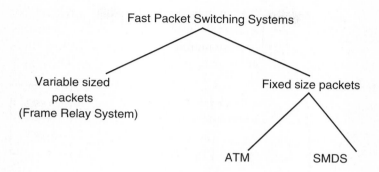

11.5.6   Frame Relay

Frame relay is essentially a stripped-down version of X.25 packet-switching systems. It removes much of the X.25 tables and processing overhead, thus providing a giant step toward fast packet-switching systems. Frame relay allows dynamic bandwidth allocation and provides error control and flow control at the network end points. Frame relay uses variable-length packets, called *frames*. The frame sizes are typically of the same length generated by LANS (token ring and Ethernet LANs generate variable-length frames). This eliminates the overhead to break LAN messages into fixed-size packets. Thus frame relays are especially well suited for LAN interconnect.

Frame relay was initially intended to give WAN speeds at T3 level (45 Mbps), which is not possible through older technologies. For this reason, frame relay has become the next generation of X.25 systems. At present, many frame-relay networks are commercially available over T-lines (T1 and T3) as well as SONET/SDH where possible.

A typical frame-relay configuration is shown in Figure 11.13. Routers are connected to frame-relay switches by using the user-to-network interface (UNI). UNI can be implemented also in end-user devices. Frame-relay WAN consists of a collection of frame-relay switches. These switches implement network-to-network interfaces (NNI) to interconnect with each other. Standards for frame-relay UNI, NNI, and other interfaces (e.g., ISDN) are defined by ITU (International Telecommunications Union) and ANSI. A Frame Relay Forum consisting of networking vendors and users has been formed to promote and participate in different aspects of frame-relay developments. An issue of particular importance is to develop NNI standards so that frame-relay switches from different vendors can be used in a frame-relay network. About 2000 corporate networks were using frame relay in 1995 [Gareiss 1995], and the number is going up steadily.

Figure 11.13 A Typical Frame-Relay Configuration

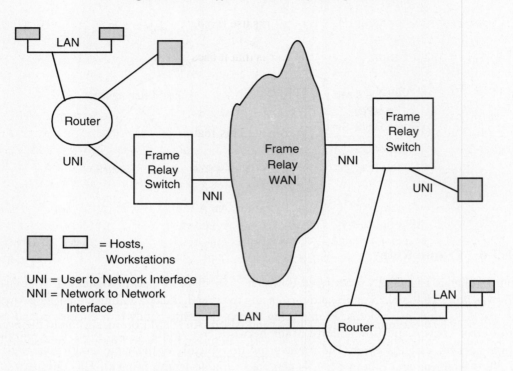

Technically, frame relay is designed to reduce and/or eliminate many operations residing in layers 3 and 2 of the conventional 7-layer model. Figure 11.14 depicts this graphically. Basically, frame relay assumes very reliable and fast fiber networks. Thus many error checking and retransmission functions are eliminated. The main limitation of frame-relay service is its poor flow control (it drops packets) and lack of error control. It is not a good idea to run frame relay on noisy and unreliable communication facilities . Details about frame relay can be found in Black [1994], Gareiss [1995], Gasparro [1993], and Nolle [1992].

Figure 11.14 Frame-Relay Layers

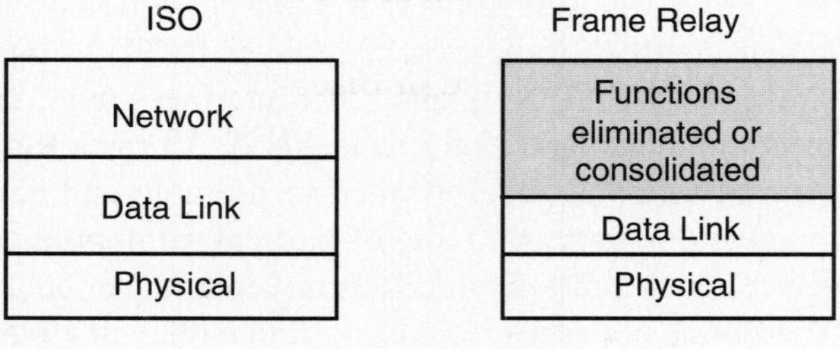

ISO	Frame Relay
Network	Functions eliminated or consolidated
Data Link	Data Link
Physical	Physical

11.5.7 ATM (Asynchronous Transfer Mode)

Asynchronous transfer mode (ATM) networks use fixed packet ("cell") sizes. The frame size in ATM, a cell-relay system, is 48 bytes of data plus a five-byte header. The main advantage of ATM over other multiplexing techniques is that it uses small, fixed-sized packets and simple protocols, which are essential for fast packet-switching. ATM, like frame relay, is also a stripped-down version of X.25 networks.

ATM is intended for any type of traffic (voice, data, video), because as long as this traffic can be broken into ATM cells, ATM can carry it. This feature distinguishes ATM from frame relay (recall that frame relay is more suitable for LAN interconnection owing to its variable packet sizes). Packets (cells) are multiplexed/routed over fast switches. ATM provides limited error detection (no retransmissions occur); thus, it should not be used on unreliable lines.

Figure 11.15 shows a typical ATM configuration. An ATM WAN consists of a collection of ATM switches. Although these switches can be connected in a variety of topologies, many ATM switches are usually connected point-to-point at present. ATM switches can be used as hubs, or backbone, for local-area networks and as a switch for WAN access. ATM switches implement network-to-network interfaces (NNIs) to connect to other switches and user-to-network interfaces (UNIs) for connecting switches to end-user devices such as computers, LANs, PBXs, TVs, and so on. Standards for ATM interfaces (e.g., ISDN) are defined by ITU (International Telecommunications Union) and ANSI. An ATM Forum, similar to the Frame Relay Forum, consisting of networking vendors and users has been formed to oversee ATM developments. ATM Forum is considering proprietary NNI (PNNI) standards to allow heterogeneous ATM networks consisting of switches from numerous vendors [Swallow 1994].

Figure 11.16 shows a conceptual view of ATM layers. ATM processing is mainly performed in the second (Data Link) layer. The ATM-specific processing (i.e., shuffling the fixed-sized cells around) is performed in the lower half of the Data Link layer. The ATM Adaptive Layer (AAL) handles the differences for connections with LANs, video, and voice. ATM is commercially available over T-lines (T1 and T3) as well as SONET/SDH where available. Thus ATM is available at 1.54 Mbps (T1), 44.7 Mbps (T3), 5184 Mbps (OC1), and 155.2 Mbps (OC3) data rates. This wide range data rate and the capability to handle voice, video, and data are the main strengths of ATM [Nolle 1995]. At present, ATM is very popular with users as well as vendors. Even computer vendors such as IBM are actively involved in ATM [Birenbaum 1994]. However, frame relay over gigabit Ethernet is a good competitor to ATM. Additional information about ATM can be found in Black [1994], Nolle [1995], Hindin [1994], and Marks [1994].

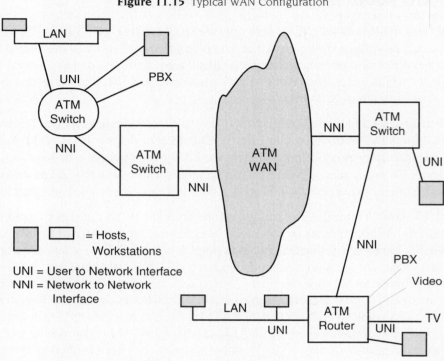

Figure 11.15 Typical WAN Configuration

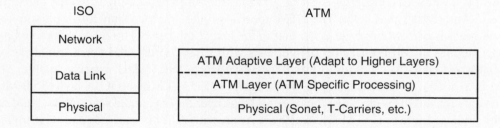

Figure 11.16 ATM Layers

11.5.8   Switched Multimegabit Data Service (SMDS)

SMDS, introduced by Bellcore, is a public packet-switched data service that provides LAN-like performance and features over wide- or metropolitan-area networks. SMDS currently allows several remotely located LANs to communicate with each other at data rates up to 45 Mbps (T3 speeds). The objectives of SMDS are to

- Provide customers with the ability to interconnect LANs, computer systems, and workstations across a MAN and WAN.

- Provide a public (24 hours a day, 7 days a week) MAN/WAN solution at high speeds which may eventually support faster services than the private FDDI, DQDB, and frame-relay networks. In addition, SMDS is expected to provide MAN as well as WAN services.

- Provide high-throughput and low-delay performance (20 milliseconds for 95% of the packets at T3 speed).

- Support extremely low error rate (about 5 undetected errors in 10 trillion) and high packet delivery rate (about 1 packet loss for every 1000 delivered).

- Allow integration into existing communication architectures, that is, evolve the SMDS service as the underlying technologies (e.g., SONET) evolve without changing user access points.

Initial deployments of SMDS provide T1 and T3 speeds, with higher speeds expected in the future. Figure 11.17 shows a typical SMDS configuration. The users would access the SMDS public network through SMDS access points. Many equipment vendors such as SUN Microsystems have developed SMDS cards for SMDS access. SMDS is based on the IEEE 802.6 switching standard and currently uses T1/T3 speeds. More details about SMDS technology can be found from Bellcore and in articles by Dix [1990], Piscitello [1990], and Lang [1990].

Figure 11.17 Typical SMDS Network

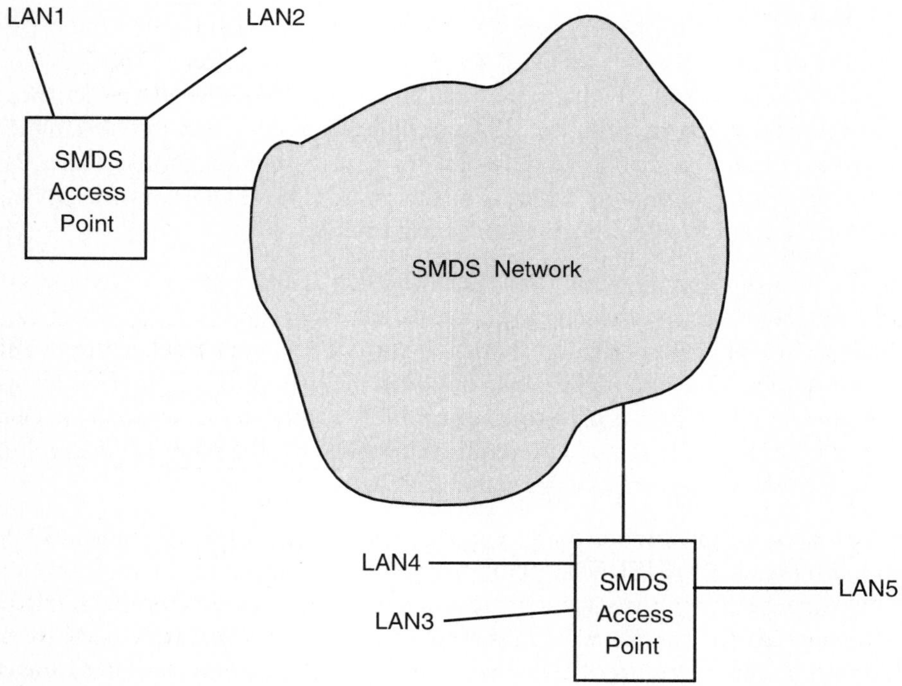

11.5.9 Broadband ISDN (BISDN)

Each emerging technology is introducing its own interfaces (UNIs) at the customer site. It would be very nice if a single interface, or at least a minimal number, would allow the customers to access different communication technologies such as frame relay, ATM, SMDS, and others. This is exactly the purpose of BISDN. Broadband ISDN (BISDN) is intended for end-to-end digital communications using high-speed fiber optics all the way to the subscriber. BISDN is expected to offer the individual high-speed services of several evolving transmission technologies as options so that the users can choose from many broadband services.

BISDN is an all-fiber-optic ISDN operating at more than 100 Mbps slated for the early twenty-first century. BISDN is expected to allow the subscriber (home, business) to access a variety of technologies from a single service access point. A typical application of BISDN would be to allow SMDS, frame relays, ATM, FDDI MANs, or any other services as options to a BISDN user (Figure 11.18). For example, if two remotely located LANs need to be connected, BISDN will give the user the choices between various technologies based on the speed and cost requirements. The LANs may need high-speed interconnections owing to, say, image-processing applications which require rapid exchange of large data files. In other cases, the two sites may be using video conferencing, which requires integration of voice, data, and images at high speed.

Let us consider the use of Broadband ISDN (BISDN) in interconnecting FDDI MANs to form very fast wide-area networks. Owing to the 100-Mbps speed of FDDI MANs and the BISDN wide-area networks which interconnect, it is possible to envision end-to-end 100-Mbps networks. However, FDDI is primarily designed for data communications, while BISDN is expected to carry voice communications. For this reason, the FDDI and BISDN standards need to be harmonized. For details, refer to Verma [1990].

BISDN is a significant improvement over ISDN (BISDN is much faster). Owing to the difficulties and costs involved in replacing the current subscriber loops with fiber optics, BISDN is not expected to be commercially available until the twenty-first century. BISDN is expected to usher in a new era of communications in the twenty-first century with audio and visual communications of high quality and large variety available to home and business users. Although narrowband ISDN is not a prerequisite for BISDN, the latter is a natural technical successor to the former and shares many common features.

Owing to its distant application, many details about BISDN are not currently available. Generic requirements for BISDN are being developed at the time of this writing. These requirements are prompting early interactions between equipment vendors and potential users. Many sources for additional information are available. The ISDN book by Stallings [1989, chap. 9] has an overview of BISDN. Handel [1989] describes the evolution of ISDN into BISDN and gives details of early BISDN standardization efforts. An architectural and technical overview of BISDN is given by Byrne [1989]. Additional details about BISDN can be found in Reingold [1992], and White [1991].

Figure 11.18 Conceptual View of BISDN Network

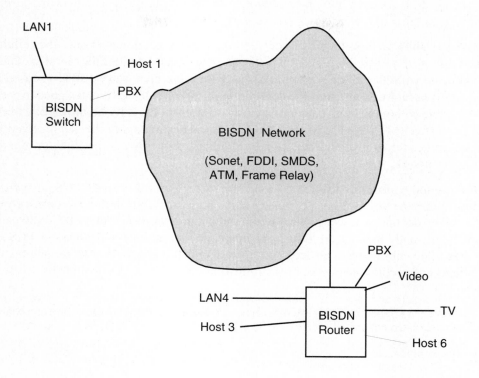

11.5.10 Mobile Communications (Cellular Networks and Wireless LANs/WANs)

While the fiber-optic-based communication-network technologies are achieving higher data rates for enterprisewide networks, the flexibility and power of mobile communication systems are also increasing dramatically. This subsection gives an overview of the two main players in this exciting area: cellular networks and mobile data services (i.e., wireless LANs and WANs).

11.5.10.1 Cellular Networks

Cellular telephones and residential cordless telephones (wireless systems) were introduced in the mid-1980s. These technologies are enjoying widespread public approval with a rapidly increasing demand. For example, AT&T predicted in the mid-1980s that there would be about 1 million cellular telephone users by year 2000 [Ziegler 1993]. However, the number of cellular telephone users exceeded 12 million in 1994. To meet this demand, mobile communications technologies are emerging with digital speech transmission and the ability to integrate cordless systems into other networks. In the meantime, researchers are developing the next generation of technologies for the next century.

Figure 11.19 shows a high-level view of a cellular communication network. The cellular network is comprised of many "cells," which typically cover 1 to 25 miles in area. The users communicate within a cell through cordless. A base transceiver station (BTS) is used by the mobile units in each cell by using wireless communications. One BTS is assigned to each cell. Regular cable communication channels are used to connect the BTSs to the mobile telephone switching office (MTSO). The MTSO determines the destination of the call received from a BTS and routes it to a proper destination by sending it either to another BTS or to a regular telephone network.

PCS (Personal communication services) is for "people on the move." PCS, also known as cordless communications, basically has the same principle as the cellular systems. However, PCS systems operate at lower power (suitable for light telephone devices), so the cell sizes are smaller (usually within a building as compared to several miles). Basically, a PCS system has many more cells that can be accessed by weaker cellular devices. The unique features of the cellular and cordless networks are as follows:

- The senders and receivers of information are not physically connected to a network. Thus the location of a sender/receiver is unknown prior to the start of communication and can change during the conversation.

- The communication channel between senders/receivers is often impaired by noise, interference, and weather fluctuations.

- The bandwidths, and consequently data rates, of communication channels are restricted by government regulations. The government policies allow only a few frequency ranges for wireless communications.

The current wireless systems use many different, incompatible standards which rely on analog frequency-modulation techniques. Each cordless telephone, for example, comes with its own base station and needs to be compatible only with that base station. The focus of the next-generation systems is on a single network which will combine a variety of wireless services.

Many groups are at present working on the architectures, standards, and underlying technologies related to cordless and cellular services. Examples are researchers at Bell Communications Research (Bellcore) and Rutgers University Wireless Information Network Laboratory (WINLAB). A technical overview of the trends and research in cellular and wireless services can be found in Black [1994], and Goodman [1991]. The *Encyclopedia of Telecommunications,* Vol. 2 [Froehlich 1991] has four chapters devoted to cellular technology, systems design, regulatory matters, and subscriber products.

Figure 11.19 A Cellular Communication Network

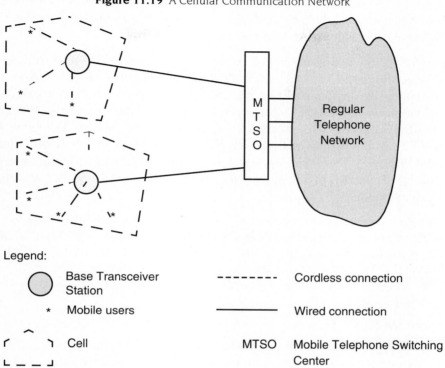

Legend:

⬤	Base Transceiver Station	- - - - - - - -	Cordless connection
*	Mobile users	───────────	Wired connection
Cell		MTSO	Mobile Telephone Switching Center

11.5.10.2 Mobile Data Services (Wireless LANs and WANs)

Mobile communications have been developed primarily for voice users. Consequently, cellular networks are predominantly analog. However, the use of cellular networks to support mobile computing applications is of great interest. In particular, as the use of laptop computers increases, the need to communicate from these "mobile" computers to access remote databases is also increasing. We can categorize these developments in terms of wireless WANs and wireless LANs. Then we will briefly review the emerging standards in this area.

Wireless WANs use the cellular networks to establish a connection to remote corporate databases and applications. Basically, you connect your laptop to a cellular modem that uses special cellular protocols for digital data transmission over the analog cellular network. Different techniques are used by the modems. An example is the "switched cellular technology" that allows digital data to switch among the various connections on the analog cellular voice network [Gasparo 1994]. Another option is to carry data over packet radio technology in data packets of size 1 to 512 bytes. This technology is used, for example, in the Ram Mobile Data systems. Another technology is the CDPD (Cellular Digital Packet Data) based systems that carry Ethernet type packets for TCP/IP networks (see the discussion of CDPD later in this section). An interesting example of wireless LANs is the MCI's Xstream Air service that carries X.25 packets over cellular networks [Gareiss 1994].

Wireless LANs allow workstations in a building to communicate with each other without having to be connected to physical cables. This is a major benefit, because LAN wiring can be the most expensive component of a LAN. At the time of this writing, wireless LANs have several limitations, such as short distances, lack of wireless adapter cards for PCs and workstations, limited connectivity to other LANs, and relatively low speeds. However, this technology is still in its infancy. In addition, the popularity of portable computers is fueling the demand for wireless LANs. Wireless technology can also be used to interconnect LANs across buildings. Examples of wireless are the Motorola Altair Plus, NCR's WaveLAN, and Altair Vistapoint modules.

Wireless LANs allow LAN workstations to communicate with the server without cables by using special cards (transmitters/receivers). Currently available wireless LANs use one of three signal types to transmit data:

- infrared,
- spread spectrum, and
- narrowband microwave.

Infrared signals behave like ordinary light (they cannot penetrate solid objects). Thus infrared wireless LANs are limited to data transmission on line of sight. Infrared technology is simple and well proven (it is used commonly in remote controls for VCRs and TVs). In addition, infrared signals are not regulated by the Federal Communications Commission (FCC). Spread spectrum is most widely used in wireless LANs. These LANs transmit in the industrial, scientific, and medical bands designated by the FCC. These bands are not licensed but are regulated by the FCC to prevent interference. This technology was developed for military and intelligence operations (the message is "spread" over a range of frequencies to make it jam-resistant). Wireless LANs based on narrowband microwave technology use the 18.82-to-18.87 GHz and 19.6-to-19.21 GHz frequency ranges. These frequency ranges are licensed by the FCC, which means that a vendor must be approved by the agency to use these frequency ranges. Many wireless LAN vendors consider this to be a restriction.

Standards for Digital Services over Cellular Networks. Cellular networks, as mentioned previously, are predominantly analog. However, the use of cellular networks to support mobile computing applications is increasing. The following two standards are emerging to provide digital services over cellular networks:

- **CDPD (Cellular Digital Packet Data).** CDPD is being developed to carry digital data for TCP/IP networks over analog cellular networks.

- **GSM (Global System for Mobile Communications).** GSM operators are providing access to X.25 services and to ISDN networks.

At present, CDPD is popular in the United States and GSM is more popular in Europe. These two standards are especially important for middleware needed to develop mobile computing applications. We discuss these two standards briefly in Chapter 8 (section on Middleware for Mobile Computing).

Summary. Many wireless data networks are slow (9.6 Kbps is typical, 19.2 Kbps is being popularized by CDPD, 56 Kbps is promised at the time of this writing). Many vendors are beginning to provide wireless LANs and WANs (Motorola, MCI, NCR are examples). Costs for wireless depend on per minute ($1 is typical), per month flat ($30), per packet (10 cents). For detailed trade-offs among the different types of mobile data networks, the underlying technologies, potential applications, and the market trends, see Gasparro [1994], Layland [1994] (1), Johnson [1995], Hills [1995], Mathias [1992], Axner [1992], Arnum and [1992]. *Data Communications Magazine* is a good source of information on evolutions in state-of-the-market in this very interesting area.

11.5.11 Summary of Emerging Technologies

It can be seen from the preceding discussion that the networks are moving toward fiber optic-based enterprisewide networks with interconnected LANs, MANs, and WANs, operating at 100 Mbps or more. In addition, mobile communication technologies, although very slow at present, are evolving rapidly and beginning to find their way into corporate networks. Many new networking technologies are emerging and compete with each other for certain segment of users. Figure 11.20 shows these technologies in terms of distance and data rate (we showed this figure earlier also). BISDN will try to consolidate many of these technologies, so that the end user can access most of these technologies from a single access point. The main point is to provide wall-to-wall 100-Mbps data rates to end users. The following statements summarize current and future high-speed trends:

- New applications are expected to drive the demand for high-speed networks.
- ISDN and T1 and T3 networks are widely available.
- For LANs, FDDI and Fast Ethernet (100 Mbps) are quite popular.
- For MANs, FDDI is common, and SMDS (around 50 Mbps) is evolving.
- For WANs, ATM (up to 155 Mbps) and frame relay (at about 50 Mbps) are emerging as corporate WAN technologies.
- Cellular networks and wireless LANS/ WANs are evolving toward TCP/IP networks owing to developments in CDPD.
- BISDN will become available toward the end of this century to provide a common access.

Basically, enterprise networks with "wall-to-wall" data rates of about 100 Mbps offer many interesting scenarios, because the transfer rate between a CPU and a local disk is at about 100 Mbps. Thus a user could potentially access a file on a local disk, on a LAN server in the same building, or on a computer in another city with roughly the same speed. This raises the question of remote versus local processing: What is remote and what is local? For this reason, the high-speed networks essentially eliminate the notion of distance in communications.

11.6 Sample Network Architectures (TCP/IP, SNA, LAN NOSs)

11.6.1 Overview

The Open System Interconnection (OSI) Reference Model is intended to provide a single network architecture standard for enterprise networks. The principles and the layers of the OSI Reference Model were introduced in Section 11.2. Although the OSI Model itself has not materialized into a widely used commercial technology, it provides an excellent framework for understanding and analyzing the state-of-the-art as well as state-of-the-market developments in networking.

Network architectures have been an area of considerable commercial activity since the 1970s. In particular, different network protocol stacks have been developed by different industry segments and vendors. We give an overview of the main network stacks and use the OSI Model as a framework for comparing/contrasting network stacks such as Transmission Control Protocol/Internet Protocol (TCP/IP), IBM's System Network Architecture (SNA), and LAN network architectures.

Figure 11.20 Emerging Communications Technologies

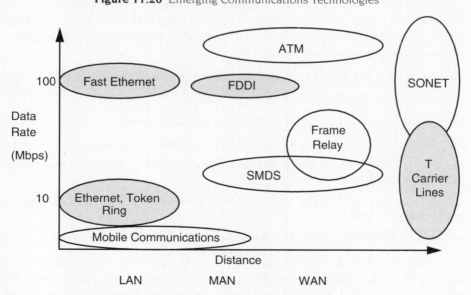

Legend: Shaded areas indicate emerged technologies

Cable Modems

A "Cable Modem" is a device that allows high speed data access via a cable TV (CATV) network. Cable modems are appealing to the "domestic" Internet users because they will enable data connections of much higher data rates than ISDN. ISDN transmits and receives at data rate of 64 Kbps and 128 Kbps. Cable modems will be able to receive data at up to 10 Mbps and send data at data rates up to 2 Mbps (some up to 10 Mbps). Naturally, the most popular application of cable modems will be high speed Internet access. This will enable the Internet services at data rates of 100 to 1000 times faster than the telephone modem. Other services may include access to streaming audio and video servers, local content (community information and services), access to CD-ROM servers, and a wide variety of other service offerings still being explored.

A cable modem typically has two connections: one to the cable network (wall outlet) and the other to a computer (e.g., PC). In the downstream direction (from the network to the computer), data rate can be anywhere up to 36 Mbps (a few computers will be capable of connecting at this data rate, so a more realistic number is 4–10 Mbps). In the upstream direction (from computer to network), data rates can be up to 10 Mbps. This "asymmetric setup" where the downstream channel has a much faster data rate than the upstream channel works well for World Wide Web applications because Web browsers receive much more data than they send.

Here are additional pieces of information about cable modems:

- In addition to modem functions (e.g., MOdulate and DEModulate signals), the cable modems can perform other functions such as encryption/decryption, bridging/routing and network management.

- Cable modems send and receive data in two slightly different fashions and employ several modulation schemes.

- It appears that Ethernet 10BaseT is emerging as the most predominant method for computer connection.

- Producing the cable modem as an internal card for the computer would require different printed-circuit cards for different kinds of computers, and additionally would make the demarcation between cable network and the subscriber's computer too fuzzy. Do not wait for this to happen quickly.

Many companies are working on producing cable modem products. Examples are: 3COM, AT&T, General Instrument, HP, IBM, Intel, LANCity, Motorola, Nortel, Panasonic, Terayon, Toshiba, and Zenith..

11.6.2 Transmission Control Program/Internet Protocol (TCP/IP) Stack

In the late 1960s and early 1970s, the Defense Advanced Research Projects Agency (DARPA) defined a set of network standards and protocols for interconnecting many computers in the ARPANET (Advanced Research Projects Agency Network). Initially referred to as the DOD (Department of Defense) or ARPANET Protocol Suite, these protocols were intended for military networks. For example, the original DOD protocols were issued as military standards. These protocols have dramatically grown in popularity and have become the de facto standards for heterogeneous enterprise networks. At present, TCP/IP is the underlying network architecture used by the Internet.

Although many new protocols have been added to the DOD Suite, Transmission Control Protocol (TCP) and Internet Protocol (IP) are the best-known DOD protocols. At present, the entire DOD/ARPANET Protocol Suite is commonly referred to as the **TCP/IP Protocol Stack**. Figure 11.21 shows the architectural layers of TCP/IP. The TCP/IP Suite, as shown in Figure 11.21, addresses the layer 3 and above issues. Let us discuss these components briefly.

Figure 11.21 TCP/IP Protocol Suite

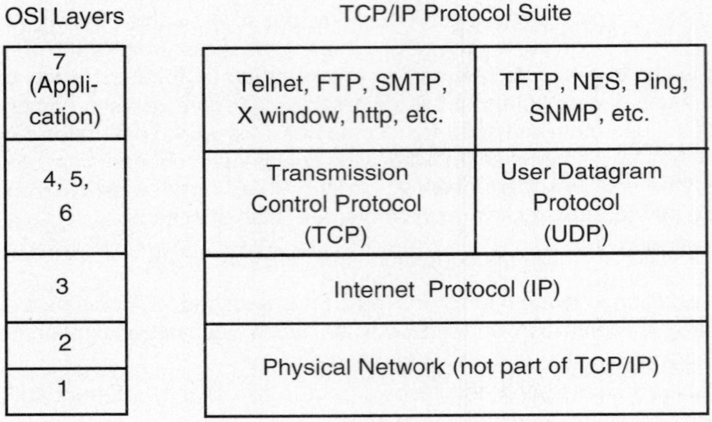

OSI Layers	TCP/IP Protocol Suite	
7 (Application)	Telnet, FTP, SMTP, X window, http, etc.	TFTP, NFS, Ping, SNMP, etc.
4, 5, 6	Transmission Control Protocol (TCP)	User Datagram Protocol (UDP)
3	Internet Protocol (IP)	
2	Physical Network (not part of TCP/IP)	
1		

Internet Protocol (IP) is roughly at layer 3 and can reside on a very large number of physical networks such as Ethernets, token rings, FDDI, ISDN, and X.25. In addition, IP also currently supports several emerging technologies such as cellular networks, ATM, frame relay and SMDS. In fact, the diversity of physical networks supported by IP is a major strength of TCP/IP. IP connects hosts across multiple networks and provides a way of moving a block of data from one host machine to another through the network. This block of data is known as a datagram. The delivery of datagrams is made possible by assigning an IP address to every host in the Internet. These addresses are 32 bits in length and are commonly denoted as four decimal numbers separated by periods (e.g., 21.152.214.2). The first part of the address shows which network the host resides on, and the rest of the address shows where within that network the host can be found. IP is an unreliable (connectionless) protocol. This means that datagrams sent from one host to another may not be delivered in the order in which they were sent, may be delivered more than once, or may not be delivered at all. Higher-layer protocols are expected to correct this deficiency.

Transmission Control Protocol (TCP) resides on top of IP and is responsible for reliable transport between end systems. TCP connects the application-layer processes to IP and provides the functions that are roughly equivalent to layers 4, 5, and 6 of the OSI Model. TCP provides a reliable, ordered connection between processes on different hosts. One host may run many processes, so a process-to-process connection is needed. This means that application processes can establish a TCP connection and expect that data will arrive successfully and in order. A TCP connection is essentially an error-free pipe from one host process to another. This generality allows a variety of higher-layer protocols to run on top of TCP.

User Datagram Protocol (UDP) also runs on top of IP and is an alternative to using TCP. Like IP, UDP is an unreliable protocol. In fact, the major function that UDP adds to IP is a way to differentiate more than one stream of data going to or from a host (IP addresses identify only the hosts and not the processes within a host). Owing to the unreliability of UDP, it is up to higher-layer protocols running on top of UDP to provide reliability if it is needed.

Higher (Application) Layer Protocols run on top of TCP and UDP. The application layer of TCP/IP provides a rich set of file-transfer, terminal-emulation, network file-access, and electronic-mail services. New protocols and services for emerging technologies such as the World Wide Web are also being continually added to the TCP/IP application layer. It is also possible to define private application protocols, as long as both hosts agree on the protocol. The following protocols (the first three belong to the original DOD Suite) are among the best-known application protocols defined in the TCP/IP Suite.

- **Telnet:** This protocol is used to provide terminal access to hosts and runs on top of TCP.

- **File Transfer Protocol (FTP):** This TCP-based protocol provides a way to transfer files between hosts on the Internet.

- **Simple Mail Transfer Protocol (SMTP):** This TCP-based protocol is the Internet electronic mail exchange mechanism.

- **Trivial File Transfer Protocol (TFTP):** This UDP-based protocol also transfers files between hosts, but with less functionality (e.g., no authorization mechanism). This protocol is used typically for "booting" over the network.

- **Network File System (NFS) Protocol:** This UDP-based protocol has become a de facto standard for use in building distributed-file systems through transparent access.

- **Xwindow:** This is a windowing system that provides uniform user views of several executing programs and processes on bit-mapped displays. Although Xwindow is supposedly network independent, it has been implemented widely on top of TCP.

- **SUN Remote Procedure Call (RPC):** This protocol allows programs to execute subroutines that are actually at remote sites. RPCs, like Xwindow, are supposedly network independent but have been implemented widely on top of TCP. SUN RPC is one of the oldest RPCs. Examples of other RPCs are OSF DCE RPC and Netwise RPC.

- **Domain Naming Services:** This protocol defines hierarchical naming structures, which are much easier to remember than the IP addresses. The naming structures define the organization type, organization name, etc.

- **SNMP (Simple Network Management Protocol):** This is a protocol defined for managing (monitoring and controlling) networks.

- **Kerberos**: This is a security authentication protocol developed at MIT.

- **Time and Daytime Protocol**: This provides machine-readable time and day information.

We should mention here the protocols and services being developed for the Internet **World Wide Web (WWW).** For example, the Web browsers, the Web servers, and the HTTP protocol used in WWW reside in the TCP/IP application layer. As the use of Internet grows, more services and protocols for TCP/IP application layer will emerge. See Chapter 4 for more details on WWW.

Other frequently used services in TCP/IP are Ping (an echo command), Netstat (command to display the network status of the local host, e.g., active TCP connection and IP routing tables), and Finger (displays information about users of a remote host, e.g., list of all users logged on to the remote host). In addition, the OSI upper layers can be implemented on TCP/IP as specified in the RFC1006.

TCP/IP Berkeley Sockets. TCP/IP Berkeley Sockets, simply called sockets, allow new applications and protocols to be developed on top of TCP/IP. For example, the application-layer protocols developed above use sockets. Sockets are application programming interfaces (APIs) that can be used by C programs residing on two IP hosts to communicate with each other. Let us briefly review TCP/IP sockets.

A socket is an addressed end point of communication which conceptually resides above TCP. The addresses associated with the sockets are commonly the IP physical addresses (32-bit host number, 16-bit port number). There are several types of sockets, grouped according to the services they provide. The services include *stream sockets*, which provide duplex, sequenced flow of data, with no record boundaries; *datagram sockets,* which transfer messages of different sizes in both directions and which are not promised to be reliable and sequenced; and *sequenced packet sockets,* which are similar to stream sockets, with the difference that record boundaries are preserved. Applications in UNIX environments are written by using stream (reliable connection) or datagram mode; by using forking which allows several processes to be initiated by one process; and/or by using mailboxes, which allow an intermediate file for message transmission.

Table 11.2 shows a summary of the socket commands for stream or datagram services. The commands, available as UNIX system calls, are shown generically, because different versions of UNIX support different command verbs for the same activity through different facilities. It can be seen that sockets support relatively few commands. The first five commands are initialization commands. SOCKET creates a socket; BIND is used by the servers to register their well-known address to the system so that the clients can connect and transfer information; CONNECT is used by the client to establish a connection with the server after the server has issued a BIND; and LISTEN and ACCEPT are issued by the server to indicate that it is willing to accept connections from the clients and then to queue the connections for later processing. Commands 6 and 7 are the main information-transfer commands for connection-based (TCP) client-server systems, and commands 8 and 9 are the main information-transfer commands for connectionless (UDP) client-server systems.

A detailed description of Berkeley Sockets with numerous C examples is given in Chapter 5 of Stevens' book, *UNIX Network Programming* [Stevens 1990].

TABLE 11.2 BERKELEY SOCKET COMMAND SUMMARY

```
1. SOCKET = creates a socket and specifies socket type
   (TCP,UDP)
2. BIND = assigns a name to an unnamed socket (handle)
3. CONNECT = establishes a connection between local and remote
   server
4. LISTEN = server is willing to accept connections
5. ACCEPT = accept a connection and put it on queue
6. WRITE = send data on TCP socket
7. READ = read data from TCP socket
8. SENDTO = send data on UDP socket
9. RECVFRROM = read data from UDP socket
```

A Typical TCP/IP Network. Figure 11.22 shows a simplified view of a TCP/IP network. The network consists of an Ethernet TCP/IP LAN and a frame relay TCP/IP WAN, interconnected through a router (we will discuss routers later). A Mac and a PC are connected to the LAN, and a UNIX machine is connected to the WAN (there may be several other devices, but we are showing these three just to highlight key points). Each computer ("host") on this network has an IP address and also has been assigned a domain name (e.g., Gruber, Warner, Gomer). This TCP/IP network is very heterogeneous (different computers, different physical networks). However, to the users of this network, it provides a set of uniform TCP/IP services (TCP/IP hides many details). Let us illustrate the use of this network.

Let us assume that the Mac user needs to transfer a file from the PC ("Warner"). The user would use the following steps (the steps are explained through comments in /* */):

```
> ftp warner               /* invoke FTP. Could have typed " ftp 112.52.10."*/
warner> enter logon: umar  /* prompt from warner for logon ID. umar is ID */
warner> password: xxxx     /* prompt from warner for password */
warner> get file1 file2    /* FTP file transfer command */
warner> quit               /* quit FTP */
```

Figure 11.22 A Typical TCP/IP Network

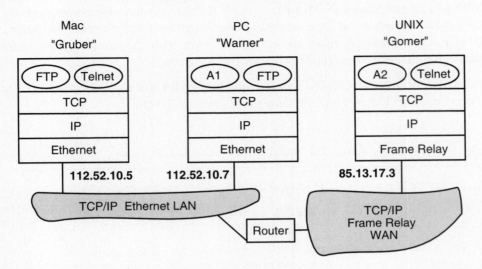

Now let us assume that the Mac user needs to remotely log on to the UNIX machine "Gomer" to run a program "account." The user would use the following steps (the steps are explained through comments in /* */):

```
> telnet gomer              /* invoke Telnet.Could have typed " telnet
                                85.13.17.3".*/
gomer> enter logon: umar    /* prompt from gomer for logon ID. umar is ID */
gomer> password: xxxx       /* prompt from gomer for password */
gomer> account             /* run the program "account" */
gomer> quit                /* quit telnet */
```

A client/server application runs between the PC and UNIX machine (A1 is client and A2 is the server). A1 and A2 use TCP/IP sockets to exchange information over the TCP/IP network. To use this application, the following steps would be needed:

```
start A2 on gomer
start A1 on warner
use A1 (this usage will automatically send the
requests to A2)
```

Notice that the user does not know anything about the underlying network technologies to remotely log on, transfer files and invoke client/server applications. The user needs to know only the address of the host to perform interactions.

Why Is TCP/IP So Popular? TCP/IP Protocol Suite is by far the most popular network architecture at present. For example, TCP/IP can be, and is, used for WANs (TCP/IP operates on top of X.25, frame-relay, and ATM communication technologies) as well as LANs (TCP/IP operates on top of Ethernet, Token Ring, and FDDI communication technologies). Thus TCP/IP can be used to support the entire enterprise network. Many organizations are running enterprisewide networks that are entirely based on TCP/IP. Many others are transitioning to TCP/IP. Why is TCP/IP so popular? Here are some reasons:

- The TCP/IP Suite is available on almost all computing systems today, including microcomputers, minicomputers, and mainframes (it is estimated that there are more than 300 TCP/IP vendors at present). For example, TCP/IP can be used to transfer files between IBM, DEC, SUN, PRIME, Macintosh, and several other machines. In addition, TCP/IP is closely associated with the UNIX operating system, and most UNIX vendors support TCP/IP. For example, the SUN Microsystems UNIX and the Hewlett-Packard HP-UX systems include TCP/IP as part of the basic software package. In addition, Microsoft is shipping TCP/IP free [Layland 1995].

- The TCP/IP Suite is based on the experience gained in the ARPANET project which resulted in the Internet supernetwork—one of the largest heterogeneous networks in the world. ARPANET itself was discontinued in 1990, but it supported the evolution of different types and numbers of computers over a long time (ARPANET evolution is illustrated in the "ARPANET Maps: 1969–1990," *Computer Communications Reviews,* October 1990, pp. 81–110).

- TCP/IP is currently the underlying network architecture for the Internet. The popularity of Internet is giving a tremendous boost to TCP/IP. In particular, World Wide Web applications are making TCP/IP indispensable.

- IP, the lowest protocol in this Suite, can reside on a very wide variety of physical networks such as Ethernets, FDDI-based fiber optic LANs, dial-up lines, X.25-based packet-switching networks or ISDN digital networks. In addition, IP support exists for almost all emerging communications technologies such as cellular networks, ATM, frame relay, and SMDS. The internet technology used by IP allows many computers to communicate across many networks.

- TCP, the layer above IP, supports a very wide variety of higher-level (application) protocols which allow users to emulate terminals, transfer files, and send/receive mail between different computers.

- The TCP/IP Suite provides a framework and the tools for :hp1.interoperability:ehp1., where interoperability refers to the ability of diverse computing systems to cooperate in solving computational problems.

- Simplified Network Management Protocol (SNMP), a recently developed TCP/IP-based network-management protocol, has become widely accepted by vendors and users for network management in heterogeneous networks. Owing to the growing importance of network management, SNMP has furthered the popularity of TCP/IP Suite as the glue between disparate networks and devices.

For these reasons, TCP/IP has become the de facto standard for interconnecting heterogeneous computer systems. Owing to its popularity, the TCP/IP Protocol Suite continues to evolve. However, TCP/IP is beginning to show its age (remember, TCP/IP was introduced around 1969). In particular, IP is running out of addresses. To address this and other related problems, IPng (IP next generation) is being developed. However, there is some controversy about the impact of IPng (see, for example, Johnson [1994]).

The Internet Activities Board (IAB) provides a framework and focus for most of the research and development of these protocols. IAB was originally organized by DARPA to promote R&D. At present, IAB has evolved into an autonomous organization consisting of many task forces with various charters. A series of technical reports, called Internet Request for Comments (RFC), describe the protocol proposals and standards. An RFC is a formal document which can become a standard. For example, almost all of the current TCP/IP protocols are specified as RFCs.

Additional information about TCP/IP can be found in TCP/IP books by Comer and Stevens.

11.6.3 IBM's System Network Architecture (SNA)

System Network Architecture (SNA) was introduced by IBM in 1973 as a single network architecture for all computer communication products in IBM environments. SNA is IBM's strategic solution and long-range direction for computer communication networks. Despite the growth in TCP/IP, SNA is still the most heavily used proprietary network architecture. In particular, a majority of insurance and financial institutions rely on SNA. Because of this, many vendors have developed interfaces between different network architectures and SNA.

SNA was originally released for centrally controlled, single-mainframe, hierarchical networks. It has evolved over the years with facilities for networking between mainframes, peer-to-peer communications, and extensive network management. For example, SNA has added support for large networks, dynamic routing, multiple mainframes, packet-switching and LAN systems, voice/image processing, network management operations, peer-to-peer networking, distributed cooperative processing, and interconnectivity to other networks. SNA has also included support for emerging fast packet-switching systems such as frame relay and ATM.

SNA is arranged in 7 layers, although the 7 layers of SNA do not exactly correspond to the 7 layers of the OSI Model (see Figure 11.23). Synchronous Data Link Control (SDLC) is used in the first two layers of IBM's wide-area networks and token ring protocol is used in IBM LANs. The Network Control Program (NCP) roughly performs the layer 3 and 4 functions and resides in a front-end communications processor (e.g., IBM's 3725). Layers 5 and 6 of SNA are handled by the Virtual Telecommunications Access Method (VTAM) which resides in IBM mainframes. The main application-layer protocol offered by IBM is the Advanced Program to Program Communications (APPC) protocol, which supports distributed cooperative processing for business applications.

Figure 11.23 SNA Layers and Components

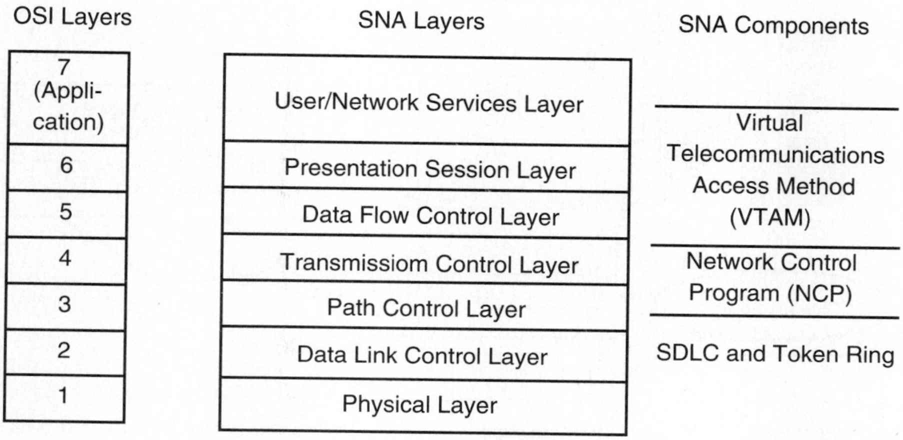

OSI Layers	SNA Layers	SNA Components
7 (Application)	User/Network Services Layer	Virtual Telecommunications Access Method (VTAM)
6	Presentation Session Layer	
5	Data Flow Control Layer	
4	Transmissiom Control Layer	Network Control Program (NCP)
3	Path Control Layer	
2	Data Link Control Layer	SDLC and Token Ring
1	Physical Layer	

Typical SNA Networks. Figure 11.24 shows a typical SNA network. The network consists of a mainframe, a minicomputer, a "communications controller" (a device that controls communications lines in SNA), and several PCs and terminals. The PCs are connected to the minicomputer through a Token Ring LAN. The minicomputer and the terminals are connected to the communications controller through SDLC lines. A Network Control Program (NCP) resides in the communications controller. The main "brain" of SNA (VTAM) resides in the mainframe.

Every SNA network user is assigned a **logical unit (LU)** in SNA. A network user is an end point in a network and may be a program or a terminal. For example, in Figure 11.24, each terminal and PC has certain LUs that represent the terminal users and/or the programs that reside in PCs. The LUs in the mainframe represent the mainframe applications that can be accessed over SNA lines. SNA has introduced different LU types to represent different capabilities of end points. For example, LU type 0 to 4, written as LU0 to LU4, were introduced in the 1970s to represent different terminal types. LU6 was introduced to represent programs, and LU6.2 represents a program capable of peer-to-peer communications.Table 11.3 shows the SNA LUs. A session between two end points is called an LU-LU session. Roughly speaking, an SNA LU is similar to a TCP/IP socket (in fact, the SNA-to-TCP/IP gateways map LU operations to socket operations).

Each physical device in SNA is termed a **physical unit (PU)**. Thus, the mainframe, the communications controller, the minicomputer, and each PC and terminal is defined as a PU. See Figure 11.24. SNA defines different PU types to represent different hardware-device characteristics.

Figure 11.24 A Typical SNA Network

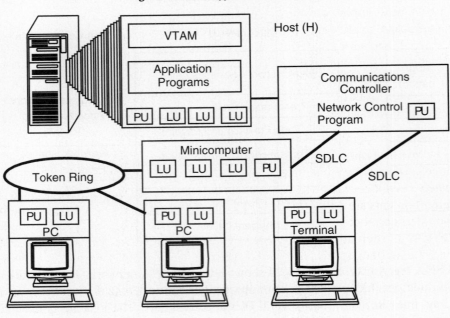

LU = Logical Unit,   PU = Physical Unit

TABLE 11.3 SNA LOGICAL UNITS

- LU Type 0 represents non-SNA devices and protocols (e.g., BSC).
- LU Type 1 represents a terminal cluster (printers, readers, CRTs) such as an IBM 8100 system.
- LU Type 2 represents a single workstation/terminal (e.g., IBM 3277).
- LU Type 3 represents a printer.
- LU Type 4 can be used to represent a word-processor (e.g., IBM 6670).
- LU Type 6 represents a program for peer-to-peer communications. Programs are subdivided into two categories:
    - LU 6.1 represents subsystem communication (e.g., IMS to CICS).
    - LU 6.2 is used for generalized, any-to-any communication between programs.
- LU Type 7 can be used between host application and a midrange system (e.g., System 36).

Advanced Program-to-Program Communications (APPC) and LU6.2. In the IBM SNA environments, most applications in the past have been based on the terminal-host model in which a mainframe application receives input from remotely located dumb terminals, processes the input, and sends responses back. IBM developed the LU6.2 protocol for any-to-any communications among remotely located applications. LU6.2 is IBM's strategic protocol for interprogram communications for its SNA networks and has been used in IBM's Customer Information Control System (CICS) to access remote data. A large number of local- and wide-area networks are already supporting or planning to support LU6.2.

APPC (Advanced Program-to-Program Communication) is an implementation of LU6.2. It provides the application-programming interfaces (APIs) for applications to use LU6.2. Most of the literature does not differentiate between LU6.2 and APPC. We will use the term APPC/ LU6.2 when it is not necessary to differentiate between the two. Examples of APPC support in IBM environments are APPC/MVS, APPC/SNA, and APPC/PC. LU6.2 is a common program-to-program protocol which encourages compatible distributed programs. It coordinates the processes on different nodes and may also involve distributed databases. LU6.2 allows both LUs to be masters, so that any LU can be responsible for error recovery. The other LU types in SNA (e.g., LU types 0 to 4) are master-slave and are not suitable for distributed cooperative applications. LU6.2 introduces the concept of conversation between two programs. A conversation is a short interaction, usually a transaction. Conversations are efficient for short data transfers.

LU6.2 has been available on SNA networks. However, a special SNA feature, called the Any-Net Feature, allows LU6.2 to be transported over TCP/IP networks. This has several benefits. First, the mainframe applications can be accessed on the TCP/IP network. This can also provide a migration path from SNA to TCP/IP networks. LU6.2 is used in the IBM Distributed Relational Database Architecture (DRDA) that allows access to DB2 databases. Thus, to install a DRDA gateway an LU6.2 connection is needed. Table 11.4 shows the main LU6.2 commands (verbs) which can be issued by the transaction programs P1 and P2.

Details about APPC characteristics and programming can be found in the book, *APPC: Introduction to LU6.2,* by Alex Berson [1990]. Additional information can be found in numerous IBM manuals.

Advanced Peer-to-Peer Networking (APPN). An SNA network is a collection of domains, where a mainframe is at the top of hierarchy in each domain. Complex networks can be built in SNA by using multiple domain networks. The initial versions of SNA allowed peer-to-peer communications only at the communications controller level; two users within a subarea could not directly communicate with each other without having to go through the host subarea. A new feature, called the Advanced Peer-to-Peer Networking (APPN), allows cluster controllers/minicomputers to communicate directly with each other. APPN is a key component of SNA's future direction [Passmore 1995].

TABLE 11.4 APPC/LU6.2 COMMANDS

- ALLOCATE: initiate a conversation
- DEALLOCATE: terminate a conversation
- SEND-DATA: send data
- RECEIVE-AND-WAIT: receive
- REQUEST-TO-SEND: program wants to send
- PREPARE-TO-RECEIVE: ready to receive
- SEND-ERROR: program error
- CONFIRM: send a confirmation request
- CONFIRMED: response to confirm
- GET-ATTRIBUTE: read conversation type

SNA Interconnectivity. SNA supports many interconnectivity options through SNA gateways. Examples are SNA-LAN gateways to connect local-area networks to hosts and gateways to connect DECNet, TCP/IP, and MAP networks to SNA. Most of these interconnectivity products have been developed by other network vendors who wish to communicate with SNA, owing to its market dominance. Examples of the SNA gateways are Microsoft's SNA Server and Novell's NetWare Gateway for SAA [Routt 1995].

SNA Evolution. The following statements summarize SNA evolution.

- Initial systems were for one mainframe (single domain). Support for many domains was added later.
- "Advanced Peer-to-Peer Communication" provides LU6.2 support for distributed programs:
    - Each LU is a program which can reside on mainframes, midranges, and PCs
    - Information is sent/received through API verbs—send data, receive, etc.
- "Advanced Peer-to-Peer Networking (APPN)" developed for LU-to-LU networking without having to go through mainframe.
- Support of many new transmission technologies (X.25, ISDN, Token Ring, Ethernet, voice).
- Interconnectivity to other networks (TCP/IP, DECNET, OSI) through gateways.
- Enhanced network management through Netview.
- Many other developments (IBM's strategic direction).
- AnyNet Feature: allows
    - LU6.2 over TCP/IP
    - TCP/IP sockets over SDLC

11.6.4 LAN Network Stacks and Network Operating Systems

The LAN standards have been developed by the IEEE 802 Committee. This committee has recognized that some local area networks (LANs) use only layers 1, 2, and 7 of the OSI Model. The IEEE 802 Committee has divided layers 1 and 2 into sublayers (see Figure 11.25). In some LANs, layers 3, 4, 5, and 6 are null. Some functions of these layers are simplified and included in the application, data link and physical layers of the LAN stack. However, many LANs support all 7 layers (a large number of LANs at present use the TCP/IP protocol Suite). We have already discussed the IEEE 802 standards in the first two layers. Let us now discuss the higher-layer issues.

Figure 11.25 LAN Layers Defined by IEEE 802

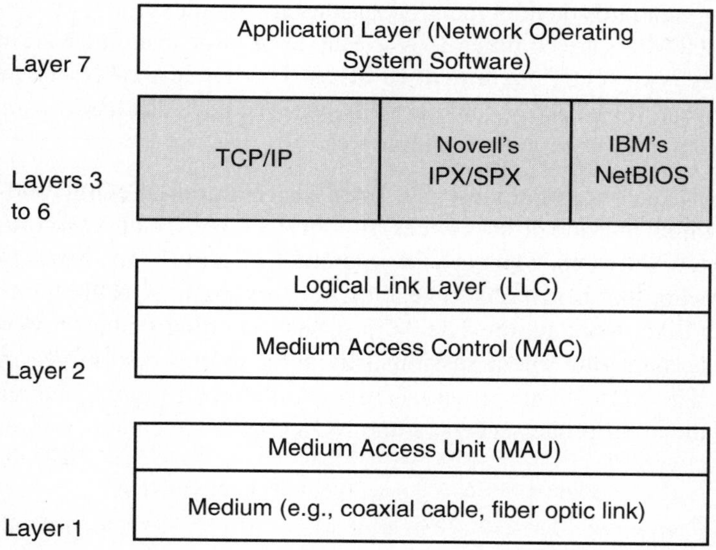

Layer 7	Application Layer (Network Operating System Software)

	TCP/IP	Novell's IPX/SPX	IBM's NetBIOS
Layers 3 to 6			

Layer 2	Logical Link Layer (LLC)
	Medium Access Control (MAC)

Layer 1	Medium Access Unit (MAU)
	Medium (e.g., coaxial cable, fiber optic link)

The application layer of LANs usually includes LAN *network operating system (NOS)* software that provides services such as print servers, file servers, and user profile managers. In addition, this layer supports the workstation software which routes the workstation requests to the server. Examples of LAN NOSs are Novell NetWare, Microsoft Windows NT, IBM LANA Manager, and Banyan Vines (we will discuss these NOSs later on in this section).

Different LANs use different layer 3 to 6 protocols (in some LANs these layers are null). The following protocols are used commonly at present:

- TCP/IP
- Novell's IPX/SPX
- IBM's NetBIOS

We have already discussed TCP/IP in a previous section (Section 11.6.2).

Internetwork Packet Exchange, (IPX) and Sequenced Packet Exchange (SPX) are used in the Novell NetWare LANs. IPX/SPX stack is available on many other LANs for connectivity and interoperability. IPX, a datagram-delivery service, operates at the OSI Network Layer level, while SPX, a connection-based service, operates at the OSI Session Layer. Technical details about IPX/SPX can be found in the Novell NetWare manuals and tutorials.

NetBIOS (Network Basic Input Output System) is a Session Layer programming interface for IBM PC LANs. NetBIOS is widely used in IBM PC LANS and is currently supported by most major LAN vendors. For example, NetBIOS stack can run in the Novell NetWare LANs. Basically, NetBIOS provides a programming interface at the OSI Session Layer level for sending/receiving data in LAN environments. Technical details about NetBIOS can be found in the IBM Technical Reference Manual SC30-3383-2.

An area of active standards development is concerned with the wireless LANs. For example, wireless LANs at 2 Mbps are commercially available. A large installed base of wired (copper or fiber optic) LANs currently operates at 10 Mbps. The wireless LANs are also being aimed at this speed, at least, for an equivalent performance. We have discussed wireless LANs previously in the section on Emerging Technologies.

Figure 11.26 shows a conceptual view of a LAN configuration. Each LAN has one or more "LAN servers" which provide print services, file services, etc. The LAN workstations operate as clients to the LAN servers. The network operating system (NOS) consists of two parts: a NOS server software that is installed on each LAN server and a NOS client software that is installed on each LAN workstation. The NOS server operating system performs a variety of functions such as managing client sessions, initiating printer operations, managing server shared disk, etc. The NOS client software is in principle much simpler and mainly directs the user requests to the appropriate servers (some NOS clients are called "redirectors").

Figure 11.26 A Conceptual LAN Configuration

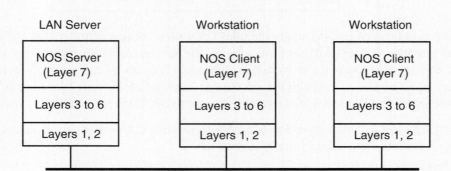

Many LAN NOSs have been developed and marketed by different software vendors since the mid 1980s. At present, the main contenders are Novell NetWare, Microsoft's Windows NT, IBM's LAN Manager, and Banyan Vines. Table 11.5 shows the main features of these NOSs. Detailed discussion of NOSs is beyond the scope of this tutorial. Many articles in the trade magazines compare and contrast these and other NOSs on a regular basis. An example of such an analysis can be found in [Johnson, J. 1995].

TABLE 11.5 MAIN CHARACTERISTICS OF COMMON NETWORK OPERATING SYSTEMS (NOSs)

LAN NOSs	Novell NetWare	Windows NT	IBM LAN	Banyan Vines
NOS Server Characteristics	• Server runs on 486 or Pentium PCs, UNIX	• Server runs on 486 or Pentium PC, DEC Alpha	• Server runs on 486 or Pentium PC, AIX, AS/400, MVS	• Server runs on 486 or Pentium PC, many UNIX machines
NOS Client Characteristics	• Clients run on DOS, Windows, Mac, OS/2, NT, UNIX	• Clients run on Mac, OS/2, Windows, Windows NT	• Clients run on DOS, Mac, OS/2, Windows, Windows NT	• Clients run on DOS, Mac, OS/2, Windows, Windows NT
Network Characteristics	• Layers 3-6: SPX/ IPX, TCP/IP, Appletalk, NetBios • Layers 1-2: Ethernet, Token Ring, X.25, ISDN, FDDI	• Layers 3-6: TCP/IP, SPX/IPX, Appletalk • Layers 1-2: Ethernet (mostly)	• Layers 3-6 TCP/IP, NetBios, Appletalk • Layers 1-2: Most supported by TCP/IP	• Layers 3-6: TCP/IP, NetBios, Appletalk • Layers 1-2: Most supported by TCP/IP

11.6.5 Analysis and Comparison of Network Stacks

Figure 11.27 shows how the functions provided by many available network stacks compare with the OSI stack. The following observations can be made from this analysis:

- Many network stacks provide 7 layers. However, there is not a one-to-one mapping between the OSI Model and older network architectures such as SNA and TCP/IP.
- The OSI layers define the relative issues addressed by most networks, even if the exact layer meanings may change. For example, layer 1 and 2 are always concerned with computer attachment to network, and layer 7 connects applications to the network.

- Vendors can provide layer-7 protocols and services without having to provide all of the lower layers. For example, APPC was originally developed on SNA but is now available on Token Ring LANs, DECnet, and TCP/IP networks.

- The advancements in communication technology are hidden from higher layers. For example, most network architectures are planning to support fiber optics and ISDN services at the first two layers without having to modify the higher-level layers. However, this is not exactly true for the applications being designed for the emerging high-speed networks. In some cases, high speed application requirements are being mapped to the lower-level capabilities (i.e., special applications are developed for special lower-level capabilities).

The main observation is that most networks at present support layered views although there is no one-to-one mapping between layers of different network architectures. In addition, most vendors are currently supporting TCP/IP. For example, Novell NetWare initially used SPX/IPX but now supports TCP/IP. Comparisons of SNA and TCP/IP can be found in Joyce [1995], and Waclawsky [1995]. For state-of-the-market information about SNA to TCP/IP connectivity products, see the TCP/IP supplements of the Enterprise Internetworking Journal.

Figure 11.27 Comparison of Network Stacks

OSI	TCP/IP	SNA	NOVELL	IBM-LAN
Application Layer (Layer 7)	Telnet, FTP, SNMP, SMTP	IMS, CICS, TSO, LU-LU LU6.2	Programs, NetWare Operating system, NetBIOS	Programs, IBM PC LAN Program
Presentation Layer (Layer 6)		VTAM		
Session Layer (Layer 5)		VTAM		
Transport Layer (Layer 4)	TCP, UDP	NCP	SPX	
Network Layer (Layer 3)	IP Many	NCP	IPX	NetBIOS
Data Link Layer (Layer 2)	Many	SDLC, X.25, ISDN, Token Ring	Ethernet, Token Ring	Token Ring
Physical Layer (Layer 1)	An extremely large family of physical media	Many physical media used in LANs and WANs	Most LAN physical media	LAN physical media (e.g., coaxial cables)

11.7   Network Interconnectivity (Routers, Bridges, Gateways)

Network interconnectivity, also known as ***internetworking***, glues together networks from different vendors, with different protocol stacks, and utilizing different communication technologies to form an enterprisewide network. The key devices used in network interconnectivity are bridges, routers, and gateways. Discussion of these internetworking devices in this section is brief. For more information, the following sources are recommended:

- *IEEE Communications Magazine,* Special Issue on Enterprise Networking, January 1996.
- Derfler, F., *PC Magazine Guide to Connectivity,* 3d ed., Ziff-Davis, 1995.
- Perlman, R., *Interconnections: Bridges and Routers,* McGraw-Hill, 1992.
- White, G., *Internetworking and Addressing,* McGraw-Hill, 1992.
- Stallings, W., *Networks and Data Communications,* latest edition, MacMillan (chapter on internetworking).

11.7.1   Bridges

A bridge connects two similar or dissimilar LANS to form a larger network at the data-link layer. Bridges are simple devices which operate only at layer 1 and 2 of the OSI Model and do not deal with any higher-level issues such as network routing and session control (see Figure 11.28). Bridges require that the networks have consistent addressing schemes and packet sizes. Common examples of using bridges are as follows:

- Interconnections of LANs with different layer-1 technologies. Bridges are used frequently to connect Ethernet LANs. For example, many bridges connect thinwire Ethernet to thickwire Ethernet. A bridge between two LANs (LAN1 and LAN2) will basically read a message from LAN1 stations, pass the messages destined for LAN2 to LAN2 in the needed layer-1 format, and pass the rest back to LAN 1.

- Bridges can be used to divide a large network into smaller subnets to control traffic. For example, consider an Ethernet LAN with 100 stations. Since all 100 stations chattering simultaneously can cause collisions, a bridge can be used to subdivide the network into two 50-station LANs. This division must be done carefully. Let us assume that S1 and S2 frequently exchange information. In this case, it is better to keep S1 and S2 on the same bridge segment, otherwise the bridge could become a bottleneck. The division of a network must subdivide the network in such a fashion so that the escape ratio of each subnet (percentage of messages leaving the subnet) is minimal. This can be achieved by grouping the devices that exchange information frequently in a subnet.

Figure 11.28 A Typical Bridge Connection

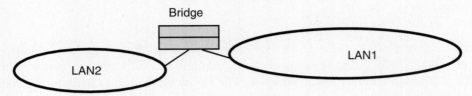

11.7.2   Routers and Firewalls

A router operates at layers 1, 2, and 3. It finds a path for a message and then sends the message on the selected path. A router may appear to be the same as a bridge, but the main distinguishing feature of a router is that it knows alternate routes for a message and uses the alternate route to send a message if the primary route is not available (Figure 11.29). Consequently, a router must know the network topology (a layer-3 issue). Owing to the routing algorithms, routers are more complex and more expensive than bridges. Some bridges, called "brouters" (like "brunch"), include some routing facilities and compete with routers [Sevcik 1992]. Over the years, the following capabilities have been added to routers:

- Multiprotocol capabilities
- Security features (i.e., firewalls)
- Value-added features such as compression and prioritization

Figure 11.29 Routers

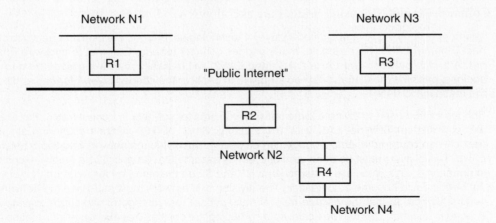

"Multiple protocol" routers are currently available to allow different network protocols to use the same "wire," i.e., the backbone network. These routers, for example, allow one corporate backbone to be shared by different protocols such as TCP/IP, OSI, SNA, DECnet, Appletalk, Novell IPX/SPX, and Token Ring. The main advantage of these routers is that different wiring is not needed for different protocols. Many multiprotocol routers are becoming available from IBM, DEC, Cisco and other vendors, and are reviewed regularly in trade journals such as Data Communications. In particular, the router manufacturers are paying special attention to carrying SNA and NetBIOS traffic over the TCP/IP internetworks. This is accomplished through development of Data Link Switching (DLSW) technology (see Tolly [1994] for details).

"Firewalls" are security features that are added to the routers. Basically, a firewall is a collection of components placed between two networks that collectively have the following properties: (a) all traffic from inside to outside, and vice versa, must pass through the firewall (b) only authorized traffic will be allowed to pass, and (c) the firewall itself is immune to penetration [Bellovin 1994]. For example, a router, acting as a firewall, can check each packet to see if it should be sent or received over the network. Let us assume, in Figure 11.29, that the routers R1, R2, and R3 serve as firewalls to their respective networks N1, N2, and N3. For example, R4 is within the firewall of R2 (it is part of the network N2) and can send information within R2 firewall. But if R1 sends information to R4, then the firewall code at R2 can check to see if this message can be passed along. Firewalls typically allow email to pass through but may restrict file transfers, remote log ons, and other types of interactions. More information about firewalls can be found in Bellovin [1994], Bhimani [1996], Ganesan [1994], and Ranum [1992].

Additional features are being added to routers by router suppliers. For example, many routers at present have included compression features. This greatly improves the efficiency of the network, because sophisticated compression can reduce network traffic by a factor of up to 50. This reduces the need to upgrade network bandwidth (high data rates over international networks are extremely expensive). More information about compression in routers can be found in Heywood [1995]. In addition, routers are including priority schemes to adjust TCP/IP and SNA traffic. For example, SNA requires a controlled connection while TCP/IP traffic battles for whatever bandwidth it can get. In this situation, SNA traffic suffers. Routers are beginning to employ bandwidth-reservation schemes to give SNA traffic an equal opportunity. This is particularly good news for SNA-based client/server applications. See Layland [1994 (2)] for more details.

Addition of multiprotocol handling, firewalls, compression, and prioritization schemes is adding overhead to routers. Routers are becoming performance bottlenecks owing to the addition of this extra logic in addition to the basic routing functions of routing algorithms. For this reason, among others, many vendors and organizations are considering switched LANs, known as "switched virtual LANS."

Switched Virtual LANS

Switched virtual LANs, also known as virtual LANs, describe software defined logical groupings of network devices that may or may not be physically linked. Thus, devices in different parts of an organization can be configured as a virtual LAN.

The idea of virtual LANs has been very controversial in the networking industry. Benefits include more flexible network moves, additions, and changes. Drawbacks include lack of standards.

Many vendors have announced virtual LAN products for desktop and enterprisewide environments. For discussion of switched virtual LANs, refer to *Data Communications,* September 1994 (special issue on switched virtual networks).

11.7.3 Network Gateways

In most large networks, protocols of some attached subnetworks need to be converted to protocols of other subnetworks for end-to-end communications. A ***network gateway*** connects two dissimilar network architectures and is essentially a protocol converter. A network gateway can convert protocols at any layer to achieve interoperability between two different networks. In practice, many gateways translate an application-layer protocol from one network architecture to a corresponding application-layer protocol of another architecture (see Figure 11.30). Keep in mind that a *network gateway is a function and not a device*. This function may be performed by a special purpose dedicated computer, a workstation with associated software (e.g., a PS2 with gateway software), or a software module which runs as a task in a general-purpose computer. Here are some examples of network gateways.

- Ethernet-to-token-ring gateways convert layer-2 protocols. Another example of a layer 2 gateway is the IBM 3708, which converts serial to SDLC (an IBM layer-2 protocol).

- OSI to TCP/IP gateways allow OSI and TCP/IP subnetworks to interoperate by converting OSI Transport Layer Class 4 (TP4) to TCP .

Figure 11.30 Conceptual View of a Network Gateway Between TCP/IP and SNA

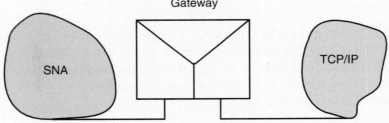

- Digital's SNA gateway allows DEC devices to communicate with IBM mainframes by converting the DEC application protocols to IBM 3270 protocol. This allows IBM mainframe applications to be accessed from DEC applications.

- LAN-Host gateways allow LAN users to access mainframe applications by converting LAN layer-7 protocols to mainframe layer-7 protocols. An example is the Token-Ring-to-SNA gateway. Such gateways can be used in situations where several stations can do local processing, interact with other stations on a LAN, and log on to a mainframe and submit/receive jobs through the LAN-Host gateway.

- TCP/IP-to-SNA gateways allow TCP/IP and SNA applications to communicate with each other interactively. An example is the Sybase Open Net Gateway, which converts TCP/IP Socket calls to SNA LU6.2 for client-server applications between MVS hosts and TCP/IP UNIX machines.

- OSI-to-OSI gateways may be needed to interconnect a connectionless OSI subnetwork to a connection-based OSI subnetwork.

Many network gateways are commercially available. Many network gateways concentrate on accessing SNA mainframes because 80% of corporate information is stored on mainframes. Two popular SNA gateways are the Novell NetWare for SAA and the Microsoft SNA Server. For detailed discussion and comparative analysis of these two gateways, see Routt [1995]. In addition, IBM is building SNA gateways that employ the Anynet Feature (i.e., run TCP/IP over SNA and vice versa). See Johnson [1994].

Our focus at present is on network gateways that convert protocols between different network protocol stacks. However, a gateway may convert *any* type of protocol. For instance, *electronic mail gateways* allow different electronic mail packages to exchange mail by converting one mail format to another. An example is the Softswitch Mail Gateway, which converts many mail protocols for mail exchange. Another category of gateways, known as *database gateways*, convert database calls from one format to another (e.g., SQL to Oracle and vice versa). Once again, keep in mind that a gateway is a function and not a device. A given gateway may consolidate many protocol conversions. For example, the Informix Distributed Relational Database Architecture (DRDA) Gateway, conceptually shown in Figure 11.31, converts Informix database calls to the IBM DB2 format. However, it also converts TCP/IP to SNA LU6.2 network protocol. This particular gateway resides on a Sun or PS/2 machine (we discuss DRDA in more detail in Chapter 5).

Figure 11.31 Informix DRDA Gateway

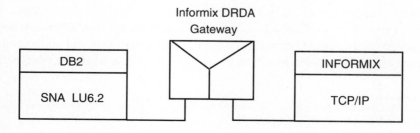

Gateways of different types are crucial building blocks of contemporary IT infrastructure. For this reason, more information about gateways will be given in the main text where appropriate.

We should observe that the aforementioned terms are not always adhered to in the commercially available products. For example, some bridges are marketed as routers and some routers are marketed as gateways. Often, too, many different interconnectivity functions are packaged into a single package. To avoid confusion, keep in mind the basic principle that *bridging, routing, and protocol conversions ("gatewaying") are functions and not devices*. These functions may be consolidated, packaged, and marketed in a variety of manners.

11.8   State of the Practice: Enterprise Network Examples

Enterprise networks consist of a potpourri of LANs and WANs interconnected through disparate routers, bridges and network gateways. Let us go through a few examples to illustrate the typical state of practice.

Figure 11.32 shows a very high-level view of an enterprise network of an organization with three types of offices: a corporate business office that uses IBM mainframes and SNA, one or more engineering sites that use UNIX and TCP/IP, and a few manufacturing plants with factory floor equipment, interconnected through MAP (Manufacturing Automation Protocol).[2] These three sites are connected through three different types of network gateways that convert protocols between SNA, TCP/IP, and MAP. This figure illustrates the role of network gateways in heterogeneous network environments. These gateways can become security, availability and performance bottlenecks. As mentioned previously, many network gateways use UNIX or PS/2 platforms. These gateways must be kept in secure environments, because a gateway user can see *everything* being transmitted through it. Alternate gateways must be available if one gateway crashes. Many network gateways have trouble sustaining more than 100 sessions; thus many gateways may be needed for improved performance and load balancing.

Ideally, network gateways should be completed eliminated by using the same network protocol stack at every site. In particular, the network should be open so that different vendors can supply the same protocol stack or different parts of the stack. Basically, an ***open network*** is a vendor-independent network which conforms to international standards. "Openness" does not imply any implementation but refers to the mutual recognition and support of the applicable standards by different vendors. The OSI Model is a framework for open networking.

---

2. MAP is an ISO-based network protocol stack that was initiated by General Motors to standardize manufacturing networks. For a tutorial on MAP, see Umar [1993, Appendix D].

Figure 11.32 Conceptual View of an Enterprise Network

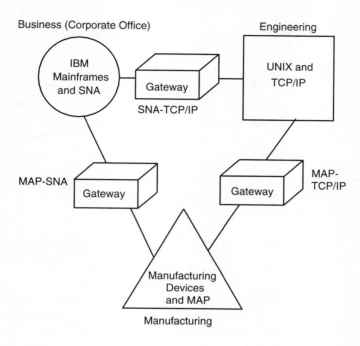

The term Open Systems Interconnection (OSI) qualifies standards for the exchange of information among systems that are "open" to one another because of their mutual use of the applicable standards. However, OSI-based open networks are not state-of-the-market or practice for reasons that are beyond the scope of this book.

The most common approach used in enterprise networks is to employ a common "backbone network protocol stack" between sites. Figure 11.33 shows a large network in which a corporate backbone is connected to many subnets through routers and gateways. The backbone uses TCP/IP (i.e., TCP/IP is the native protocol stack). The TCP/IP subnets only use routers to exchange information among each other. However, an SNA subnet will need to use a TCP/IP-to-SNA gateway, in addition to a router, to communicate with a TCP/IP subnet. The routers are important in this network because they can recognize the destination and route the messages to the destination. Most of the routers in this configuration would support multiple protocols (some corporate networks are replacing routers with switches [King 1994, Saunders 1994]). The gateways would convert different protocols (e.g., Novell SPX/IPX to TCP/IP, SNA to TCP/IP). It may be possible to purchase one "box" which provides routing as well as gateway functions, or to install router/gateway software on a PS2 or SUN workstation. The subnets may utilize FDDI, Ethernet, or Token Ring communications technologies. The corporate backbone is typically a wide-area network that may utilize frame relay, ATM, or X.25 communications technologies.

Figure 11.33 Another Look at Enterprise Networks

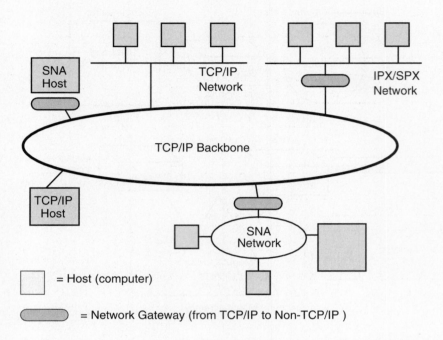

Figure 11.34 shows a real-life enterprise network which consists of an IBM SNA mainframe and many Ethernet LANs (UNIX TCP/IP LANs, a Novel LAN, and an Appleshare LAN), all interconnected through a TCP/IP corporatewide backbone. The routers are used to find the appropriate paths between various computers in this network. A gateway is used to convert the TCP/IP network protocols to Token Ring and SNA. All computers on this network can access other computer resources through terminal emulation and file transfer. The Novell and Appleshare servers are used in this network for file and print services. A small FDDI LAN is used to connect a few UNIX machines together for fast database access. We use this network to illustrate different aspects of client/server architectures in earlier chapters of this book.

These examples illustrate the device-to-network and the network-to-network interconnectivity scenarios. Application interconnectivity is handled by the higher-level layers at the end systems. Two applications at two different end systems, independent of the network interconnectivity option chosen, need to agree on the format and rules of message exchange. When this is not easily done, application gateways are introduced in the network. For example, two subnets may use different email systems. However, to exchange mail from one subnet to another, a mail gateway may be needed with security features. Application interconnectivity is the main objective of middleware and is the focus of this book.

Figure 11.34 A Real-Life Enterprise Network

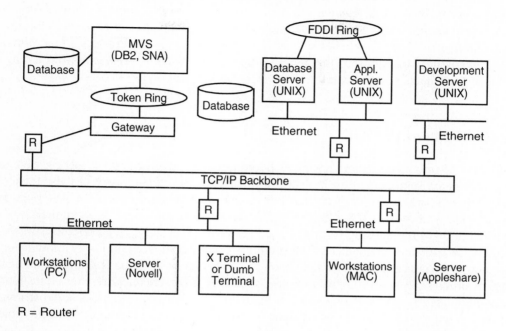

R = Router

11.9   State of the Market: General Observations

Most topics discussed in this tutorial are currently state-of-the-market. At LAN level, for example, Ethernet, Token Ring, and FDDI LANs have been around for a while (many of these LANs are being called "legacy LANs"). Fast Ethernet LANs are also state-of-the-market at present. However, wireless LANs are not widely state-of-the-market. At MAN level, FDDI and SMDS are state-of-the-market also.

The major market activity at present is in fast packet-switching systems such as frame relay and ATM. At the time of this writing, frame relay is state-of-the-market with offerings from several vendors such as AT&T, MCI, Sprint, CompuServe, Unispan, and Witel, among others. ATM is also becoming state-of-the-market with offerings from, generally, the same class of vendors. BISDN is not state-of-the-market at present. However, ISDN is gaining more market owing to the growth in Internet use and telecommuting. Network interconnectivity devices are another area of considerable market growth with routers, switches, hubs, and network gateways being offered by a multitude of vendors such as CISCO, Bay Networks, BBN, IBM, Novell, and others.

Owing to the flux in the market for network products, it is best to periodically review trade publications such as *Data Communications, Network World, Communications Week,* and *Business Communications Review* for state of the market analysis. For example, *Data Communications* periodically publishes special issues on "Hot Network Products" (e.g., the January 1995 issue). In addition, the Black Box Inc. produces a very extensive listing of networking products with short tutorials on different product lines.

11.10 State of the Art

Many new communication networking technologies are emerging and competing with each other for certain segments of users. BISDN will try to consolidate many of these technologies, so that the end user can access most of them from a single access point. The main idea is to provide wall-to-wall 100-Mbps or higher data rates to end users. New applications are expected to drive the demand for high-speed networks. Basically, enterprise networks with wall-to-wall data rates of about 100 Mbps offer many interesting scenarios by allowing users to potentially access a file on a local disk, on a LAN server in the same building, or on a computer in another city with roughly the same speed. This presents new research questions in distributed systems, because a majority of the work in distributed databases and distributed-transaction processing assumes that distance is bad (i.e., put resources as close as possible to the user). An interesting research question is: what are the new distributed system design approaches for the high-speed networks?

New network architecture standards are focusing on integrating newer technologies into existing networks. Examples are the standards being developed for cellular networks and broadband networks. The standardizing bodies are cooperating with each other. More work on network protocols is being done for newer and faster networks. The work is being pursued on protocol efficiency as well as reliability. An example is the Xpress Transfer Protocol (XTP), which is being developed for fiber optics and very fast networks. Another example is the work being done in the area of protocols for multimedia applications. The OSI standards are shifting focus toward interoperability of networks between functioning areas of organizations. An example is the development of OSI Profiles, which define subsets and/or combinations of standards for specific functions (e.g., factory automation) and conformance tests for interoperability. The ISO TR 10000 document describes a framework and taxonomy of international standardized profiles.

New architectures are being developed for the evolving high-speed broadband networks. These networks are characterized by high transmission rates and low error rates. The multi-layered network stacks discussed in this chapter (e.g., TCP/IP, ISO, SNA) were developed mostly in the 1970s for networks which suffered from the "SUE" (Slow, Unreliable, Expensive) effect. These stacks perform too much error checking and incur considerable processing delays in several layers, and consequently are not suitable for high-speed networks of the '90s and beyond. Network architectures for high-speed networks are an area of considerable research activity. See, for example, Bernstein [1996].

11.11   Summary

Enterprise networks consist of many technologies, devices, protocols, and interfaces supplied by a multitude of vendors. Network architecture standards are needed for compatibility of intervendor and intravendor network products and services. This is an important issue, because the advances in network technologies and facilities have led to an explosion of network-related hardware/software products from many computer manufacturers, common carriers, software vendors, and data-communications equipment manufacturers. These products provide similar functions differently. Standards are needed to assure that all the products fit together to form a functioning network.

The Open Systems Interconnection (OSI) Model is widely accepted as a framework for network-architecture standards. The OSI Model presents a layered view of the network, where each layer performs well-defined functions. This functional model divides the network activities into seven layers. The high-level layers (Application, Presentation, and Session) are concerned with issues related to the applications in different machines. The four lower layers (Transport, Network, Data Link, and Physical) provide the transparent data exchange between computers.

Communication protocols play an important role in integration and interconnection. The discussion of protocols and the OSI Model in this chapter lays a good foundation for comparing different network architectures, defining and classifying network products, and discussing levels of interconnectivity. We have also used the OSI Model as a framework for discussing, comparing, and contrasting various network architectures such as TCP/IP, SNA, and LAN architectures. We have also classified and defined network interconnectivity products (e.g., routers, bridges, gateways, protocol converters).

11.12   Case Study: XYZCorp Establishes a Network Architecture

XYZCorp wants to develop a network architecture that will support high-bandwidth services for future applications. The management is really interested in exploring the use of new and innovative applications in voice, data, and images for office automation, factory floors, and engineering CAD/CAM work. There is a particular interest in a paperless company. A network-architecture task force has been established to:

- Develop a physical communication layout
- Establish a network interconnectivity plan

The physical-communication layout should show how the emerging high-speed communication technologies can be used in this corporation. The overall network layout of the company for the next three years is needed to show a companywide backbone with interconnected WANs, MANs, and LANs. Specifically, where would the evolving technologies such as ATM, frame relay, ISDN, FDDI, SONET, SMDS, and BISDN may be utilized in this network.

The network interconnectivity plan should show how all sites will be interconnected in the next three years. In addition, XYZCorp has recently acquired a chain of retail stores. Each store has a Novell LAN that uses IPX/SPX (the TCP/IP version of Novell is not currently used in these stores). These stores need to be connected to the corporate network for basic terminal emulation and file transfer from other computers. There is also a need to connect the mainframe with the business partners (all business partners have SNA networks). The network interconnectivity plan should include the new stores.

The overall network architecture should show a long-range conceptual view that will satisfy the needs of the enterprise. The company is planning to use this network as a corporate "Intranet" that will serve the Web users within this organization.

Hints about the Case Study

Figure 11.35 shows a conceptual view of the network architecture. The network layout of the company in the next few years should show a companywide backbone which interconnects each LAN at an office. The evolving technologies described in Section 11.5 should be reviewed for their utilization in this network (it seems that ATM is a good candidate for corporate WAN and FDDI/Fast Ethernet is a good option for LANs in different regions).

Based on the corporate direction toward Internet, it is best to convert the stores network to TCP/IP (gateways not needed if most systems use TCP/IP). This will allow all users to employ Internet protocols such as Web browsers (HTTP), email (SMTP), file transfer (FTP), and terminal emulation (Telnet) throughout the corporation (any computer to any computer).

11.13   Additional Information

The interested reader can find additional information about network technologies, architectures, and network interconnectivity (internetworking) in books [Black 1994, Drefler 1995, Stallings 1991, Umar 1993]. The *IEEE Communications Magazine,* January 1996, is a special issue on enterprise networking and has several excellent technical articles on different aspects of enterprise networks. The following journals and magazines are recommended for continued studies: *Internetworking: Research and Experience, Computer Networks and ISDN Systems, IEEE Network Magazine, IEEE Communications Magazine, Computer Communications, Data Communications* (product highlights and regular column on internetworking), and *Business Communications Review* (case studies and market analysis).

Figure 11.35

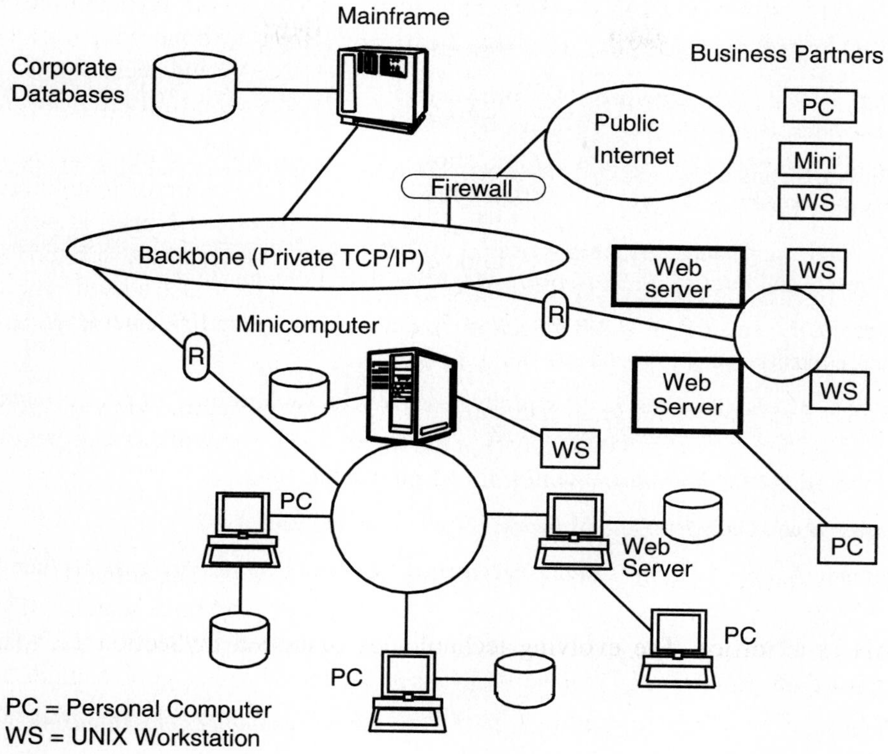

PC = Personal Computer
WS = UNIX Workstation

11.14   References

Aprille, T., "Introducing SONET into the Local Exchange Carrier Network," *IEEE Communications Magazine,* August 1990, pp. 34–38.

An ISDN Primer: Technology and Network Implications, ed. by *Business Communications Review.*

Arnum, E., "Wireless Messaging—Will the Rubber Meet the Road?" *Business Communications Review,* July 1992, pp. 48–55.

Axner, D., "Can Microwave Expand Its Horizon," *Business Communications Review,* July 1992, pp. 43–47.

Babcock, J., "SONET: A Practical Perspective," *Business Communications Review,* September 1990, pp. 59–63.

Barret, J., and Wunderlich, E., "LAN Interconnection Using X.25 Network Services," *IEEE Network,* September 1991, pp. 12–17.

Bartree, T., *Digital Communications,* Howard W. Sams, 1986

Behm, J., et al., "The Enterprise Network Manager," *Enterprise Network Event Conference Proceedings,* Baltimore, May 1988, pp. 6.27–6.37

Bellovin, S., and Cheswick, W., "Network Firewalls," *IEEE Communications Magazine,* September 1994, pp. 50–58.

Ben-Artzi, A., Chandna, A., and Warrier, U., "Network Management of TCP/IP Networks: Present and Future," *IEEE Network Magazine,* July 1990, pp. 35–43.

Bernstein, L., and Yuhas, C. M., "Network Architectures for the 21st Century," *IEEE Communications,* January 1996, pp. 24–30.

Berman, R., and Brewster, J., "Perspectives on the AIN Architecture," *IEEE Communications Magazine,* February 1992, pp. 27–33.

Berson, A., *APPC; Introduction to LU6.2*, McGraw-Hill, 1992.

Bertsekas and Gallager, *Data Networks,* 2d ed., Prentice Hall, 1992.

Bhimani, A., "Securing the Commecial Internet," *Communications of the ACM,* June 1996, pp. 25–29.

Biersack, E. W., et al., "Gigabit Networking Research at Bellcore," *IEEE Network,* March 1992, pp. 42–49.

Birenbaum, E., "IBM's Big Blueprint for ATM," *Data Communications Magazine,* August 1994, pp. 31–32.

Bisdikioan, C., "A Performance Analysis of the IEEE 802.6 (DQDB) Subnetwork with the Bandwidth Balancing Mechanism," *Computer Networks and ISDN Systems,* Vol. 24, No. 5 (1992), pp. 367–386.

Black, U., *Emerging Communications Technologies*, Prentice Hall, 1994.

Black, U. D., *Data Communications, Networks and Distributed Processing,* 2nd ed., Reston Publishing Co., 1987.

Byrne, W., et al., *Broadband ISDN Technology and Architecture, IEEE Network,* January 1989, pp. 23–28.

Chernick, M., Mills, K., Aronoff, R., and Strauch, J., "A Survey of OSI Network Management Standards Activities," Technical Report NMSIG87/16 ICST-SNA-87-01, National Bureau of Standards, 1987.

Christiansen, P., *Networking with Novell NetWare*, Computer Science Press, 1991.

Clapp, G., "LAN Interconnection Across SMDS," *IEEE Network,* September 1991, pp. 25–32.

Comer, D., *Internetworking with TCP/IP: Principles, Protocols, Architectures,* Prentice Hall, 1988.

Comer, D., *Internetworking with TCP/IP,* multiple volumes, Prentice Hall, 1995.

Davidson, J., *An Introduction to TCP/IP,* Springer-Verlag, 1988.

Davidson, R., and Muller, N., *The Guide to Sonet,* Telecom Library, Inc. 1991.

Dix, F., Kelly, M., and Klessing, R., "Access to a Public Switched Multi-Megabit Data Service Offering," *ACM SIGCOMM Computer Communication Review,* July 1990, pp. 46–61.

Drefler, F., "Maximum Modems: 14,400 bps and Rising," *PC Magazine,* March 17, 1992, pp. 285–339.

Drefler, F., *PC Magazine Guide to Connectivity,* 3rd ed., Ziff-Davis, 1995.

Duran, J., and Visser, J., "International Standards for Intelligent Networks," *IEEE Communications Magazine,* February 1992, pp. 34–43.

Froehlich, F., and Kent, A., "Encyclopedia of Telecommunications," Vols.1, 2, 3, 4, Marcel Dekkar, Inc., 1990–1991.

Ganesan, R., "BA Firewall: A Modern Design," *Proc. of the Internet Society Symposium on Networks and Distributed Systems Security,* San Diego, CA, February 3, 1994.

Gareiss, R., "The Frame Relay Explosion: How to Get the Biggest Bang From Your Carrier," *Data Communications Magazine,* February 1995, pp. 59–68.

Gareiss, R., "X.25 Packet Switching Goes Mobile," *Data Communications Magazine,* September 1994, pp. 41–42.

Gasparro, D., et al., "Case Study: Booz, Allen Buys a Frame Relay Network," *Data Communications Magazine,* July 1993, pp. 71–84.

Gasparro, D., "Wireless Data Services: What's Really There?" *Data Communications Magazine,* November 21, 1994, pp. 31–32.

Gibson, R., "IEEE 802 Standards Efforts," *Computer Networks and ISDN Systems,* 19, 1990, pp. 95–104.

Goodman, D., "Trends in Cellular and Cordless Communications," *IEEE Communications Magazine,* June 1991, pp. 31–40.

Green, J.H., *The Dow Jones-Irwin Handbook of Telecommunications,* Dow Jones-Irwin, 1986.

Halsall, F., and Modiri, N., "An Implementation of an OSI Network Management System," *IEEE Network Magazine,* July 1990, pp. 44–53.

Hoffert, E., and Gretson, G., "The Digital News System at EDUCOM: A Convergence of Interactive Computing, Newspapers, Television and High-Speed Networks," *Communications of the ACM,* April 1991, pp.113–116.

Hoss, R., *Fiber Optic Communications Design Handbook,* Prentice Hall, 1990.

Hancock, B., *Designing and Implementing Ethernet Networks,* QED Information Sciences, 1988.

Handel, R., "Evolution of ISDN Towards Broadband ISDN," *IEEE Network,* January 1989, pp.7–13.

Harris and Sweeney, "Example of a Broadband Layout," *Datamation,* March 1983

Hawley, G., "Historical Perspectives on the U.S. Telephone Loop," *IEEE Communications,* March 1991, pp. 24–30.

Heywood, P., "Compression and Routers, Together at Last," *Data Communications Magazine,* April 1995, pp. 55–56.

Hills, A., and Hovey, R., "CDPD Puts IP Networks on the Move," Business Communications Review, May 1995, pp. 58–61.

Hindin, E., "ATM Deployment: Notes From the Leading Edge," *Data Communications Magazine,* September 21, 1994, pp. 84–92.

Horwitt, E., "ISDN Passes First Real-World Test," *Computerworld,* Vol. 20, No. 47, 1986.

Johnson, T., "Doubts about IPng Could Create TCP/IP Chaos," *Data Communications Magazine,* November 1994, pp. 55–60.

Johnson, J., "A Novel Concept for Gateways; Efficiency," *Data Communications Magazine,* December 1994, pp. 43–44.

Johnson, T., "A Standards Boost for Wireless Software," *Data Communications Magazine,* April 1995, pp. 49–52.

Johnson, J., "Enterprise NOSs: Now's the Time," *Data Communications,* May 21, 1995, pp. 40–50.

Joseph, C. and Muralidhar, K., "Network Management: A Manager's Perspective," *Enterprise Network Event Conf. Proceedings,* Baltimore, May 1988, pp. 5.163–5.174.

Joyce, S., "Taming the Titans: A Comparison of SNA and TCP/IP," *Enterprise Internetworking Journal,* October 1995, pp. 40-45.

Kahl, P., "The Broadband ISDN, An Upward Compatible Evolution of the 64 Kbps ISDN," *Proc. IEEE International Conference on Communications (ICC),* Seattle, June 1987, pp. 609–613.

Kaminski, M. A. Jr., "Protocols for Communicating in the Factory," *IEEE Spectrum,* April 1986.

Kenedi, R., and C. L. Wong, "Architectures for Implementation," *IEEE Communications Magazine,* Vol. 24, No. 3 (1986).

Kessler, G., *ISDN,* McGraw-Hill, 1990

King, S., "Switched Virtual Networks," *Data Communications Magazine,* September 1994, pp. 66–84.

Kleinrock, L., *Queuing Systems—Vol. 2,* Wiley, 1976.

Kleinrock, L., "The Road to Broadband Networks," Technology Transfer Institute Seminar, January 1992.

Knight, Fred, "CCITT's Director on the Evolution of ISDN," *Business Communications Review,* January-February, 1987, pp. 27–32.

Lang, L., and Watson, J., "Connecting Remote FDDI Installations with Single-Mode Fiber, Dedicated Lines, or SMDS," *ACM SIGCOMM Computer Communication Review,* July 1990, pp. 72–82.

Layland, R., "Wireless Airlink Over Easy," *Data Communications Magazine,* November 1994, pp. 33–34. (1).

Layland, R., "Router Makers Get Their Priorities Straight," *Data Communications Magazine,* July 1994, pp. 29–30 (2).

Layland, R., "Microsoft's Free TCP/IP: The Price is Right," *Data Communications Magazine,* April 1995, pp. 29–30.

Little, T., "Multimedia as a Network Technology," *Business Communications Review,* May 1991, pp. 65–70.

Marks, D., "ATM from A to Z," *Data Communications Magazine,* December 1994, pp. 113–122.

Martin, J., *Telecommunications and the Computer,* Prentice Hall, 5th ed., 1992.

Martin, J., *Local Area Networks,* Prentice Hall, 1989.

Mathias, C. J., "Wireless LANs: The Next Wave," *Data Communications,* March 21, 1992, pp. 83–87.

Mayo, John, "Computer Communications: Today and the Decade Ahead," Keynote Address, First Pacific Conference on Computer Communications, Seoul, Korea, October 1985, pp. 2–8.

McClimans, F., "Top 10 Myths about ATM," *Data Communications Magazine,* July 1994, pp. 25–26.

McQuillan, J., "Broadband Networks," *Data Communications,* June 1990, pp.76–86.

McQuillan, J., "An Introduction to Multimedia Networking," *Business Communications Review,* November 1991, pp. 74–79.

Nolle, T., "Voice and ATM: Is Anybody Talking?" *Business Communications Review,* June 1995, pp. 43–51.

Nolle, T., "Getting Real about Frame Relay," *Business Communications Review,* May 1992, pp. 31–36.

Passmore, D., "APPN: The Once and Future SNA," *Business Communications Review,* May 1995, pp. 16–17.

Piscetello, D., and Kramer, M., "Internetworking using SMDS in TCP/IP Environments," *ACM SIGCOMM Computer Communication Review,* July 1990, pp. 62–71.

Phillips, R., "MediaView: A General Multimedia Digital Publication System," *Communications of the ACM,* July 1991, pp. 75–83.

Powers, J., and Stair, H., *Megabit Data Communications,* Prentice Hall, 1990.

Purtan, P., and Tate, P., "The ISDN Ingredient," *Datamation,* January 1, 1987, pp. 78–82.

Ramos, E., Schroeder, Al, and Simpson, L., *Data Communications and Networking Fundamentals Using Novell NetWare,* Macmillan, 1992.

Ranum, M., "A Network Firewall," *Proc. World Conference on System Administration and Security, Washington, D.C, July 1992.*

Reingold, L., and Lisowski, B., "Sprint's Evolution to Broadband ISDN," *IEEE Communications,* August 1992, pp. 28–31.

Ross, F., and Hamstra, R., "FDDI—A LAN Among MANs," *ACM SIGCOMM Computer Communication Review,* July 1990, pp. 16–31.

Routt, T., and Villanueva, D., "Microsoft's SNA Server vs. Novell's NetWare for SAA," *Business Communications Review,* June 1995.

Rudin, H. , "Trends in Computer Communications," *IEEE Computer,* Vol. 19, No. 10 (1986).

Sandesara, N., Ritchie, G., and Engel-Smith, B., "Plans and Considerations for SONET Deployment," *IEEE Communications Magazine,* August 1990, pp. 26–34.

Saunders, S., "Traffic Jam at the LAN Switch," *Data Communications Magazine,* November 1994, pp. 53–58.

Saunders, S., "Wireless LAN Users: Take a Hike," *Data Communications Magazine,* July 1993, pp. 49–50.

Sevcik, P., "Making the Right Connections: Routers, B/Routers and INPs," *Business Communications Review,* May 1992, pp. 37–46.

Schlack, M., "NetWare 's Latest Mainframe Link," *Datamation,* April 15, 1992, pp. 62–65.

Shepherd, D. and Salmony, M., "Extending OSI to Support Synchronization Required by Multimedia Applications," *Computer Communications,* September 1990, pp. 399–406.

Stallings, W., *ISDN: An Introduction,* Macmillan, 1989.

Stallings, W., *Networks and Data Communications,* 3rd ed., Macmillan, 1991.

Stallings, W., *Local Networks,* 3rd ed., Macmillan, 1990.

Stallings, W., "Handbook of Computer Communications Standards," Vol. 2, *Local Network Standards,* Macmillan, 1987

Sterling, D., *Technician's Guide to Fiber Optics,* Delmer Publishers, Inc., 1987

Stevens, R., *UNIX Network Programming,* Prentice Hall, 1990.

Swallow, G., "PNNI: Weaving a Multivendor ATM Network," *Data Communications Magazine,* December 1994, pp. 102–110.

Tannenbaum, A., *Computing Networks,* Prentice Hall, 2d ed., 1988.

Taylor, S., "Making the Switch to High-Speed WAN Services," *Data Communications Magazine,* July 1994, pp. 87–94.

Tolly, K., "Routers and SNA: Improving the State of the Art," Data Communications Magazine, October 1994, pp. 60–72.

Townsend, C., *Networking with the IBM Token-Ring,* TAB Books, 1987.

Umar, A., *Distributed Computing and Client/Server Systems,* Prentice Hall, rev. ed., 1993.

Van Norman, H., "WAN Design Tools: The New Generation," *Data Communications,* October 1990, pp. 129–138.

Violino, R., and Knight, F., "SONET Moves Down a Long and Winding Road," *Business Communications Review,* July 1991, pp. 49–52.

Waclawsky, J., "Thinking Strategically about TCP/IP and SNA," *Business Communications Review,* July 1995.

White, P., "The Role of the Broadband Integrated Services Digital Network," *IEEE Communications,* March 1991, pp. 116–121.

Verma, P., *ISDN Systems,* Prentice Hall, 1990

Ziegler, B., "Building a Wireless Future," *Business Week,* April 5, 1993, pp. 56–60.

Glossary of Acronyms

ACM	Association of Computing Machinery
ACSE	Association Control Service Elements (used in ISO OSI Model)
AI	Artificial Intelligence
API	Application Programming Interface
APPC	Advanced Program to Program Communications
ANSI	American National Standards Institute
ATM	Asynchronous Transfer Mode
BISDN	Broadband Integrated Services Digital Network
BSP	Business System Planning
CAD	Computer Aided Design
CAM	Computer Aided Manufacture
CBX	Computerized Branch Exchange
CCITT	The International Telegraph and Telephone Consultative Committee
CDPD	Cellular Digital Packet Data (a standard for wireless networks)
CGI	Common Gateway Interface (an interface for developing gateways for World Wide Web)
CICS	Customer Information Control System - an IBM mainframe transaction manager
CLI	Command Level Interface (command level API for SQL)
CORBA	Common Object Request Architecture
CPU	Central Processing Unit
CSMA/CD	Carrier Sense Multiple Access/Collision Detect
DBMS	Database Management System
DCE	Distributed Computing Environment
DCP	Distributed Computing Platform
DDBM	Distributed Database Manager
DDBMS	Distributed Database Management System
DDL	Data Definition Language
DDTMS	Distributed Data and Transaction Management System
DFM	Distributed File Manager
DIS	Draft International Standard
DML	Data Manipulation Language
DNA	Digital Network Architecture
DOD	Department of Defense
DQDB	Distributed Queue Dual Bus
DRDA	Distributed Relational Database Architecture (from IBM)
DS	Directory Services

DTM	Distributed Transaction Management
DTMS	Distributed Transaction Management System
DTP	Distributed Transaction Processing
ES-IS	End System to Intermediate System
FAP	File Allocation Program (Procedure)
FDM	Frequency Division Multiplexing
FDDI	Fiber Distributed Data Interface
FEP	Front End Processor
FMS	Flexible Manufacturing System
FTAM	File Transfer, Access, and Management
FTP	File Transfer Protocol
GSM	Global System for Mobile Communications
GUI	Graphical User Interface
HTML	Hypertext Markup Language
HTTP	Hypertext Transfer Protocol
IEEE	Institute for Electrical and Electronic Engineers
IIOP	Internet Inter-ORB Protocol
IMS	Information Management System - IBM DB/DC system on mainframes
I/O	Input/Output
IP	Internet protocol
IPC	Interprocess Communication
ISDN	Integrated Services Digital Network
ISO	International Organization for Standardization
IT	Information Technology
JDBC	Java Database Connectivity
LAN	Local Area Network
LDBMS	Local Database Management System
LLC	Logical Link Control
LU	Logical Unit - an endpoint in the IBM SNA environment
MAN	Metropolitan Area Network
MAC	Medium Access Control
Mbps	Million bits per second
MHS	Message Handling Service
MIME	Multipurpose Internet Mail Extension
MIPS	Million Instructions Per Second
MOM	Message Oriented Middleware
MMS	Manufacturing Messaging Specification
MVS	Multiple Virtual System - operating system on IBM's mainframes

NAS	Network Application Support - DEC's open architecture
NBS	National Bureau of Standards
NCP	Network Control Program - a component of IBM's SNA
NFS	Network File Services - SUN Microsystem's File System for Networks
NIST	National Institute of Standards and Technology
NLM	Network Loadable Module (A Novell Netware feature)
NM	Network Management
NMS	Network Management System
OCSI	Object Oriented Client/Server Internet
ODBC	Open Database Connectivity (a Microsoft standard for database connectivity)
ODP	Open Distributed Processing (ISO Model)
ODIF	Office Document Interchange Format
OLE	Object Linking and Embedding (a Microsoft specification for distributed objects) s
OODBMS	Object-Oriented Database Management System
OOPL	Object-Oriented Programming Language
OSF	Open Software Foundation
OSF DCE	OSF Distributed Computing Environment
OSF DME	OSF Distributed Management Environment
OSI	Open System Interconnection
PU	Physical Unit (used in IBM's SNA)
RDA	Remote Database Access
RPC	Remote Procedure Call
SAA	System Application Architecture, IBM's "Open" Environment
SDLC	Synchronous Data Link Control - Layer 2 Protocol in IBM's SNA
SQL	Structured Query Language
SMDS	Switched Multi-megabit Data Service
SNA	System Network Architecture - IBM's Network Architecture
SNMP	Simple Network Management Protocol - TCP/IP Network Management Protocol
SONET	Synchronous Optical Network
SSI	Server Side Includes (an interface used in World Wide Web) b
TCP/IP	Transmission Control Protocol/Internet Protocol
TCP	Transmission Control Protocol
UDP	User Datagram Protocol
URL	Universal Resource Locator
VT	Virtual Terminal
VTAM	Virtual Telecommunications Access Method - a component of IBM's SNA
WAN	Wide Area Network
WWW	World Wide Web

Index